KEY STUDIES IN PSYCHOLOGY

FIFTH EDITION

RICHARD GROSS

HODDER
EDUCATION
AN HACHETTE UK COMPANY

Dedication

To Freya Louise, a true ray of sunshine and constant source of delight and joy. Welcome to the world!

Orders: please contact Bookpoint Ltd, 130 Milton Park, Abingdon, Oxon OX14 4SB.
Telephone: (44) 01235 827720. Fax: (44) 01235 400454. Lines are open from 9.00–5.00,
Monday to Saturday, with a 24-hour message answering service.
You can also order through our website www.hoddereducation.co.uk.

British Library Cataloguing in Publication Data
A catalogue record for this title is available from the British Library.

ISBN: 978 0 340 947 395

First Published 2008
Impression number   10 9 8 7 6 5 4 3
Year   2012 2011 2010 2009

Copyright © 2008 Richard Gross

Typeset by Dorchester Typesetting Group Ltd, Dorset
Printed in Malta for Hodder Education, an Hachette UK Company, 338 Euston Road, London NW1 3BH

Contents

INTRODUCTION

By the time this book is published, it will be 18 years since publication of the first edition of *Key Studies*. The book has clearly changed in that time, as has the discipline of psychology itself and the way it's taught, at both pre-degree and undergraduate level. This fifth edition attempts to reflect some of the changes as well as what has stayed basically the same.

The first four editions aimed at helping students (at whatever level and whatever their particular course) make sense of and critically evaluate journal articles and research papers, which are often very lengthy, dense, technically demanding and generally 'difficult'. In addition, they may be difficult to access physically (although this is made easier through electronic means), so a secondary aim was to present sufficiently detailed summaries of original articles/research papers to make going to the library and photocopying them unnecessary.

The first aim hasn't changed – but the means of achieving it has. Since the first edition, several teachers/lecturers have commented that the summaries are too … lengthy, dense, technically demanding and generally 'difficult' for many of their students. So, always aiming to please, I've reduced the summaries now to what I hope these teachers/lecturers and their students will find much more manageable. I've also imposed a structure on every journal article/research paper: the Summary appears under the general heading of Aim and Nature, which is broken down into Hypothesis, Method/Design, Results and Conclusions. This provides a consistency that's often lacking in the original articles/papers. Where possible, I've used the headings used in the original publication, but sometimes I've had to 'invent' headings not in the original (this is the downside to trying to provide consistency). This is most likely in the case of review articles/papers, where the author(s) isn't reporting any original research but summarises, assesses and evaluates a large amount of data (reported by others and/or themselves); the headings in my structure (familiar to you from your practical work) don't occur 'naturally' in such articles.

However, everything else that appears in previous editions (with the exception of the first) remains – and hasn't been reduced. So, before the Summary, 'Context and Background' puts the study/review article in a historical and/or theoretical context, 'setting the scene'. After the Summary, the study/review article is evaluated under the headings of Methodological Issues, Theoretical Issues (including gender, culture and ethics), Subsequent Research, and Applications and Implications. While these headings are used consistently, the order is sometimes reversed and sometimes two have been combined.

As before, there are 'Exercises' at the end of each study, comprising questions that make you consider methodological and theoretical aspects of the study/review article, sometimes testing straightforward understanding (there may be a correct answer), sometimes stretching and challenging your understanding (there isn't 'a' correct answer). In all cases, 'answers' are provided at the back of the book; these sometimes include additional material and References. (Note that the Exercises no longer include questions specifically concerned with statistical aspects of the study. I'll leave it up to teachers and lecturers to add these at their discretion.)

Another new feature is an Introductory chapter on psychology as a science and research methods. The inclusion of this is also a response to feedback on earlier editions. It discusses definitions of science and how well these apply to a discipline which takes the behaviour and inner experience of human beings as its subject matter. It also considers the nature, strengths and weaknesses of different research methods commonly used in psychology in relation to the specific studies described throughout the book.

This brings me on to, arguably, the key question: how did I select the studies to be included? As with previous editions, the aim was to sample a range of methods (experiments – laboratory/true, laboratory/quasi, naturalistic, natural – correlational studies, case studies and so on) as well as research reviews. One new study uses a popular *qualitative* method (interpretative phenomenological analysis – IPA), while most of these other, more traditional, methods, are *quantitative*.

The number of studies has increased (from 35 to 40). This reflects the inclusion of some very recent studies, which deal with issues such as the effects of abortion on young women, treatment of anorexia, the development of adolescents' brains, and nurses' understanding of the concept of care. These are intended to complement the older, 'classic' studies, two of which have been brought back from earlier editions.

As with previous editions, the aim is to provide students on any course that has a psychology component with a text that enhances a basic, general textbook. These courses include A level, International Baccalaureate and undergraduate. The contextualising of research methods within specific studies is meant to make them feel much less 'dry' than they sometimes can. While the results/conclusions of any study can only be as valid as the research method(s) used, these methods can be modified and made to work more effectively in the 'right' hands; they are 'living' instruments for investigating human behaviour and experience, not 'tools' that can only be used in a particular way. (Although this is especially true of qualitative methods, it also applies to quantitative ones.)

The net result is a much shorter fifth edition (530 pages as compared with 750), which offers more studies, greater accessibility, a wider range of research methods, and, I believe, a better balance between the old and the new. Please let me know, via the publisher, whether or not you agree.

ACKNOWLEDGEMENTS

I'd like to thank Phil Banyard and Matt Jarvis for commenting on the proposal for this fifth edition, including my suggestions for new studies. Thanks to Phil also for suggesting the return of one of the 'old' studies from the first edition. I'd also like to thank Jette Hannibal for commenting on the proposal from the perspective of a senior examiner for the International Baccalaureate. It was she who originally suggested that *Key Studies* might be 'trimmed' and tailored to suit the needs of IB students. Thanks too to Nancy Kinnison and Geoff Rolls for reading early drafts of the new Introductory chapter; their constructive criticisms have been taken on board, but responsibility for any errors that remain is, of course, wholly mine.

Thanks to Alison Thomas for her thorough and efficient copy-editing, and to Kate Short at Hodder for her patient and good-natured management of the whole project. Also, I love the new cover (a variation of that of the fourth edition) – so thanks to the designer. Finally, thank you, Emma Woolf, for continuing to believe in the book – and me – and providing the perfect balance between freedom to go my own way and editorial guidance and support.

The author and publisher would like to thank the following for the use of photographs in this volume:

p.86 Pratik Mukherjee and Donna R. Roberts/University of California, San Francisco/Scientific American 293(6), 2005, p.92; p.394 Mary Evans Picture Library, p.395 Keystone/Getty Images.

1 Psychology as a science

IS PSYCHOLOGY A SCIENCE?

Throughout its history as a separate discipline/field of study, psychologists, as well as philosophers of science and other interested parties, have continued to ask this question. One feature of psychology that makes it special is that its scientific status is part of its subject matter: it's as though we need to know what kind of discipline it is before we can evaluate and apply the research findings that are published under the name of psychology.

Behind the question 'Is psychology a science?' is the fundamental assumption of *scientism*: 'the borrowing of methods and a characteristic vocabulary from the natural sciences in order to discover causal mechanisms that explain psychological phenomena' (van Langenhove, 1995). For much of its history (usually dated from 1879, when Wundt established the first psychology laboratory, in Leipzig, Germany) psychology has taken physics and chemistry as the 'model' it aspired to; this perhaps suggests that we might rephrase the original question and ask: 'How successful is psychology in identifying causal mechanisms which explain psychological phenomena?' This, in turn, begs all sorts of crucial questions about the aims or goals of psychology, how psychology has changed during its near 130-year history, and the appropriateness and viability of studying human beings using the methods of natural science.

This chapter does not allow for discussion of most of these issues (for a detailed account see Gross, 2003, 2005; Gross *et al.*, 1997). But in order to attempt an answer to the original question, we need to define both psychology and science.

WHAT IS PSYCHOLOGY?

According to Zimbardo (1992), 'Psychology is formally defined as the scientific study of the behaviour of individuals and their mental processes'. This is fairly representative of current definitions, showing that most psychologists themselves accept psychology's status as a science.

One way of illustrating this is by reference to Skinner's (1987) concept of *methodological behaviourism*. According to Skinner, '"Methodological" behaviourists often accept the existence of feelings and states of mind, but do not deal with them because they are not public and hence statements about them are not subject to confirmation by more than one person'.

Wundt's original *introspectionist* approach was an attempt to analyse the structure of conscious thought by observing it 'directly', under *controlled conditions*. It was this emphasis on measurement and control that marked the separation of the 'new psychology' from its parent discipline of philosophy. However, Watson (1913) revolutionized psychology by rejecting Wundt's *structuralism* and advocating the study of observable behaviour: only by modelling itself on the natural sciences could psychology legitimately call itself a science.

What was revolutionary when Watson delivered his 'behaviourist manifesto' in 1913 (changing psychology's subject matter from 'mind' to 'behaviour') has become almost taken for granted, 'orthodox' psychology. It could be argued that *all* psychologists are methodological behaviourists (Blackman, 1980): belief in the importance of *empirical* or scientific methods (empirical = 'through the senses'), in particular the experiment, as a way of collecting data about humans (and non-humans), which can be quantified and statistically analysed, is a major feature of *mainstream psychology*.

Quantitative versus qualitative methods

However, not all psychologists would describe themselves as methodological behaviourists, especially those who advocate the use of *qualitative* (as opposed to quantitative) methods. If 'quantitative' implies 'how much' (i.e. *measurement*), 'qualitative' implies 'what something is like' (i.e. *description*).

Again, quantitative research requires the reduction of phenomena to numerical values in order to carry out statistical analysis. Although the experiment is the quantitative 'method of choice' (for reasons explained below), it is not the only one that can provide quantitative data. For example, although much quantitative research begins with verbal data (such as answers to questionnaire items), the verbal material is then transformed into numbers so that quantitative analysis can be carried out.

By contrast, qualitative research involves collecting data in the form of naturalistic verbal reports, such as transcripts of tape-recorded interviews, or the written account of some event (as in a newspaper or magazine article). The analysis of these data is *textual* (rather than numerical/statistical): the concern is with interpreting what a piece of text *means*, rather than finding its numerical properties (Smith, 2003). (The best example in this book of this kind of study is Bassett, 2002, Chapter 37.)

EXPERIMENTS AS SCIENTIFIC SITUATIONS: IT'S ALL ABOUT CONTROL

So what is it about experiments that makes them the 'method of choice'? According to scientism, the methods of natural science claim to be the only means of establishing 'objective truth'. This can be achieved by studying phenomena removed from any particular context (*context-stripping* exposes them in their 'pure form'), and in a *value-free* way (there is no bias on the investigator's part). The most reliable way of doing this is through the laboratory experiment, the method that provides the greatest degree of *control* over relevant variables.

What are variables?

A variable is anything that can have different values (i.e. that can vary). They are two main types:

1   *participant variables* (e.g. personality, gender, age, cultural background, diet);

2   *situational variables* (e.g. the type and difficulty of an experimental task, task instructions, time of day, room temperature).

In a (true) experiment, the researcher *manipulates* (deliberately changes) one variable (the *independent variable* – IV) in order to see its effect on another (the *dependent variable* – DV). These correspond, roughly, to cause and effect. Straightforward examples include the following:

● McGinnies (1949) manipulated the kind of words (emotive or neutral) presented to participants in order to see what physiological effects they had when the participants later tried to recall them (see Chapter 2).

● Loftus and Palmer (1974) manipulated the way a question was worded about a filmed car accident shown to participants, to see how this affected participants' recall of details of the accident (see Chapter 6).

● Festinger and Carlsmith (1959) deliberately altered the size of the financial reward they offered participants for saying that a boring task was actually interesting. They wanted to see how participants would rate the task themselves, depending on the size of reward they had been offered (see Chapter 9).

● Schachter and Singer (1962) gave participants an injection of adrenaline, but provided different explanations of what it was and what effects it was likely to have. The aim was to see how different explanations affected participants' emotional responses to subsequent situations (see Chapter 18).

● Bandura *et al.* (1961) exposed young children to different kinds of adult behaviour in order to see how often they imitated the adult's behaviour (see Chapter 24).

These five examples (the first two from *cognitive* psychology, the third from *social* psychology, the fourth from *bio-/physiological* psychology and the fifth from *developmental* psychology) all took place in a psychology laboratory and all involved the IV–DV relationship in a fairly clear-cut, uncomplicated way. (Note that the word 'manipulated' was not used every time; it does not need to be, provided it is clear which variable is which.) Also, in every case, the IV was a situational variable. Note too that in every case there are at least two 'values' of the IV (e.g. emotive and non-emotive words in the McGinnies experiment). Each value corresponds to a 'condition' of the experiment.

However, not all experiments display (all) these characteristics:

1   Sometimes experiments take place outside the laboratory, in real-life situations; these are called *naturalistic* (or *field*) experiments. An IV is still manipulated, but participants will not know that an experiment is taking place: this raises methodological as well as fundamental ethical issues (see Gross, 2005). A good example of this is the New York subway experiment (Piliavin *et al.*, 1969: see Chapter 11): passengers witnessed a staged 'emergency' in which an actor collapsed.

2   In other cases, the IV that the researcher is interested in cannot be manipulated: this applies to the vast majority of participant variables. So, if we are interested in:

● the effect of culture on the perception of pictures (Deregowski, 1972: see Chapter 4);

● how split-brain patients perform on certain cognitive tasks, especially those involving language (Sperry, 1968: see Chapter 20);

● how being asked just the post-transformation question in Piaget's conservation task affects the child's ability to conserve (Samuel and Bryant, 1984: see Chapter 25);

we must *select* participants who already have these characteristics or already engage in certain activities. In other words, the IV occurs 'naturally' (without intervention by the researcher). Because of this, such studies are sometimes referred to as *quasi-experiments* (literally, 'somewhat' or 'almost' experiments).

3   Sometimes the same study may combine both these features, that is, one (or more) IV is manipulated, and another one (or more) is selected. For example, Samuel and Bryant wanted to see how children of different ages performed on the only-one-question version of the conservation task. (They were also interested in different types of conservation.) This can be thought of as a 'mixed' form of experiment.

4   Occasionally, things happen – completely beyond the researcher's control (and, indeed, without his/her knowledge until some time after the event) – which come close to what the researcher would have wanted to happen, if there were not ethical and/or practical barriers. One of the best examples is the separation of identical (monozygotic – MZ) twins at birth (or some time afterwards), or non-twin siblings being adopted. In both cases, children grow up outside their natural (biological) families and are raised in biologically unrelated families. This allows investigators to examine the relative influence of biology (nature/genetics) and environment (nurture) on the development of, say, measured intelligence (as in Bouchard and McGue's (1981) review: see Chapter 34). Twin studies are referred to as a *natural* experiment: MZ twins reared together are compared with those reared apart (the non-manipulated IV) in terms of their measured intelligence (IQ) – the DV.

5   While most experiments involve groups of participants, some very famous experiments have involved just one individual (*single-case* or *participant* experiments). Examples include Ebbinghaus's (1885) pioneering studies of forgetting, the case of Little Albert (Watson and Rayner, 1920: see Chapter 23) and Gardner and Gardner's (1969) attempt to teach sign language to Washoe, a female chimpanzee (see Chapter 3).

Note that:

● Naturally occurring events are often the focus of other kinds of studies, using *non-experimental* methods, such as *case studies* and *longitudinal/follow-up studies* (see below).

● Studies may take place in a laboratory without being experiments: these may involve the use of methods for studying brain activity, such as the electroencephalogram (EEG) or brain-imaging techniques (see Blakemore and Choudhury, 2006: Chapter 29; Raine *et al.*, 1997: Chapter 36). Such investigations are likely to be *correlational studies* (again, see below).

THE PSYCHOLOGY EXPERIMENT AS A SOCIAL SITUATION

To regard empirical research in general, and the experiment in particular, as objective involves two related assumptions:

● Researchers only influence the participant's behaviour (the outcome of the experiment) to the extent that they decide what hypothesis to test, how the variables are to be *operationalized* (defined in a way that allows them to be measured), what design to use (see below), and so on. However, the experimenter's *expectations* as to the outcome of the experiment may unwittingly affect the outcome (*experimenter bias*): rather than biased experimenters mishandling the data, the bias somehow creates a changed environment, in which participants (both humans and non-humans) *behave differently* (Valentine, 1992; see Gross, 2005).

● The only factors influencing the participant's performance are the objectively defined variables manipulated by the experimenter. However, instead of seeing the person being studied as a passive responder to whom things are done ('subject'), Orne (1962) stresses what the person *does*, implying a far more *active* role. Participants' performance in an experiment could be thought of as a form of *problem-solving behaviour*: at some level, they see their task as working out the true purpose of the experiment and responding in a way that will support the hypothesis being tested. In this context, the cues that convey the experimental hypothesis to participants represent important influences on their behaviour, and the sum total of these cues is known as the *demand characteristics* of the experimental situation. These cues include all explicit and implicit communications during the actual experiment (Orne, 1962). This tendency to identify the demand characteristics is related to the strong tendency to want to please the experimenter and not 'upset' the experiment; it is mainly in this sense that Orne sees the experiment as a *social situation*.

Experimental design: gaining control over participant variables

As we have seen, the experiment (especially the *real* kind) is the most valued tool in the methodological behaviourist's tool bag, because it affords the greatest degree of *control*: if we want to investigate the effects of a particular IV on a particular DV, we want to be confident that there are no other rogue (*extraneous*, i.e. uncontrolled) variables which are also affecting the DV (or worse, which are the real influence on the DV and not the manipulated IV at all: *confounding variables*).

There are three main ways of trying to make sure other variables do not get in the way:

1   Many (but not all) experiments include a condition in which the IV is not manipulated at all (i.e. it does not have a 'value' as such). For example, in Schachter and Singer's (1962) adrenaline experiment, some participants were given an injection of saline solution (the *placebo* condition). This acted as a *control* condition, a *baseline* against which to compare the other (experimental) conditions – and those with each other. In McGinnies' (1949) experiment, the neutral word condition was the control condition (although it was not referred to as such). Whatever form it may take, the control condition is crucial to the *logic* of an experiment – without it, we cannot be sure that the outcome (the DV) would not have happened anyway. To be sure that the IV actively influenced the DV, we need to know what happens when the IV is *not* manipulated.

2   As far as *situational* variables are concerned, these should be kept *constant*, that is, the only feature of the experimental situation which changes is the IV.

3   As far as *participant* variables are concerned, these are controlled by the use of different kinds of *experimental design*. The three main kinds are *independent groups/samples*, *repeated measures* and *matched pairs*:

●   *Independent groups/samples*: participants are *randomly* allocated to one or other experimental condition, that is, every participant has an equal chance of being allocated to one or other condition. Once allocated, participants are referred to as (for example), 'experimental group 1'/'experimental group 2'/'the control group', and so on.

●   *Repeated measures*: each participant is tested under both/all experimental conditions. It then has to be decided in what *order* the different conditions are presented: this can either be the same *random* order for all participants, or half the participants do things in one order (AB), and half in another order (BA) (hence, ABBA: *counterbalancing*). Whichever method is used, the aim is to remove/minimize *order effects* (such as fatigue and practice effects).

●   *Matched pairs*: each participant is paired with another participant who is very similar with regard to variables thought to be relevant in the particular experiment (e.g. intelligence, ethnic background, personality). Once they

Table 1.1

Advantages and disadvantages of different types of experimental design

Independent groups/samples	Repeated measures	Matched pairs
Advantages		
No problem with order effects – each participant is tested only once.	Half the number of participants is required compared with independent groups/samples.	Participant variables are controlled through the matching process.
	Participant variables are perfectly controlled – since each participant is tested under both/all conditions.	No problem with order effects – each participant is tested only once.
Disadvantages		
Twice as many participants are needed as in repeated measures.	Order effects need to be controlled (either through randomization or counterbalancing).	The matching process is time-consuming and can be expensive. It must first be decided which variables are relevant and need to be matched.

have been matched in this way, they are randomly allocated to one or other experimental condition.

Some difficulties with the notion of experimental control

If the experimental setting (and task) is seen as similar or relevant enough to everyday situations to allow us to generalize the results, we say that the study has high *external* or *ecological validity*. But what about *internal validity*? This is where control of extraneous variables comes in – but it begs the question: how do we know when all the relevant extraneous variables have been controlled?

While it is relatively easy to control the more obvious situational variables, it is more difficult with participant variables, either for practical reasons (such as the availability of particular populations) or because it is not always obvious exactly what the relevant variables are. Ultimately, it is down to the researcher's judgement and intuition: what s/he believes it is important (and possible) to control (Deese, 1972).

If judgement and intuition are involved, then control – and objectivity – is a matter of degree (whether in psychology or chemistry or physics). In the case of psychology, it is the *variability/heterogeneity* of human beings that makes them so much more difficult to study than, say, chemicals. Chemists do not usually have to worry about how two samples of a particular chemical might differ from each other, but psychologists need to allow for *individual differences* between participants.

We cannot just assume that the IV (or stimulus or input) is identical for every participant, definable in some objective way, independent of the participant and exerting a standard effect on everyone.

Complete control would mean that the IV alone was responsible for the DV, so that experimenter bias and demand characteristics were irrelevant. But even if complete control were possible (even if we could guarantee the *internal validity* of the experiment), we would still be left facing a fundamental dilemma: the greater the degree of control over the experimental situation, the more different it becomes from real-life situations (the more artificial it gets and the lower its *external* or *ecological validity*).

Note that validity – and reliability – are characteristics of *psychometric tests*, such as intelligence/IQ tests (see Chapters 34 and 35) and Bem's Sex Role Inventory – BSRI (see Chapter 41). Both reliability and validity are defined and measured in different ways, but reliability refers basically to the *consistency* of the scores produced by the test, while validity refers to whether or not the test measures what it *claims* to measure (see Coolican, 2004).

In order to discover the relationship between variables (necessary for understanding human behaviour in natural, real-life situations), psychologists must 'bring' the behaviour into a specially created environment (the laboratory), where the relevant variables can be controlled in a way that is impossible in naturally occurring situations. But in doing so, they create an artificial environment and the resulting behaviour is similarly artificial – it is no longer the behaviour they were trying to understand!

Sampling: where do participants come from in the first place?

Experimental design, as we have seen, is concerned with the control of participant variables. But before that decision can be made, we must have selected some participants to take part (a *sample*). So, how do we obtain our participant sample?

The first point that needs to be made is that the sample will (almost) always be a proportion (or subsection) of a larger group (the *target population*). Target populations are usually much smaller and more specific than the term 'population' conveys (such as 'the population of the world', 'the population of the UK' or 'the population of London'). Actual examples (which do not just apply to experiments) include:

● 12-year-old Bristol schoolboys (Tajfel, 1970: see Chapter 12);

● black and white passengers using a particular stretch of the New York subway (Piliavin *et al.*, 1969: see Chapter 11);

● split-brain patients (Sperry, 1968: see Chapter 20);

● 5- to 8-year-old children (Samuel and Bryant, 1984: see Chapter 25);

● 16-year-olds who had spent at least the first two years of their lives in institutional care (Hodges and Tizard, 1989: see Chapter 27);

● widows and widowers attending a particular health centre in Mid-Wales (Rees, 1971: see Chapter 32);

● 13- to 19-year-olds diagnosed with anorexia nervosa and attending an eating disorders unit in Barcelona, Spain (Amettler *et al.*, 2005: see Chapter 38);

● 4- to 8-year-old black and white children attending five public schools in Lincoln, Nebraska, USA (Hraba and Grant, 1970: see Chapter 40).

Exceptions to the general rule that it is only samples, and not whole populations, which are studied, typically involve *longitudinal* (follow-up) studies of birth cohorts (all children born during a particular time period in a particular place). For example, Fergusson *et al.* (2006: see Chapter 39) studied all females born in the Christchurch

Table 1.2

Advantages and disadvantages of different methods of sampling

	Description	Advantages	Disadvantages
Random sample	Every member of the target population has an equal chance of being selected (either by drawing names from a hat or using random numbers table/software).	Theoretically, this is the most likely way of producing a representative sample (but a larger sample size is required). Unaffected by experimenter bias.	In practice, very difficult to achieve, especially if sample size is (relatively) small.
Opportunity sample	Selecting (asking) the first people who come along, or using a ready-made group of people (such as fellow students or your family).	Cheap, easy, convenient and quick.	You cannot be sure it is representative – although this will depend on what your stated population is.
Quota sample	The selected sample comprises specified groups in proportion to the target population. For example, from a target population of 100 Muslims and 60 Jews, a quota sample might contain 20 Muslims and 12 Jews.	This is likely to be a representative sample, thus allowing generalization.	In itself, it is not a random sample (it does not specify *how* the sample would be drawn); this makes it more difficult to be sure of its representativeness. Can be time-consuming and costly.
Stratified sample	The researcher identifies the different groups in the target population, then, as in quota sampling, an appropriate number is selected from each group, but this is done randomly.	As a combination of random and quota sampling, it is likely to produce a representative sample, thus allowing generalization.	Can be time-consuming and costly.
Systematic sample	Every *n*th person is selected from a list.	Unaffected by experimenter bias.	May not be representative. Depending on how the list is arranged, there may be an over-representation of one or more groups relative to others.
Self-selecting (volunteer) sample	Volunteers respond to an advertisement for participation in a study.	Once the advert has been placed, it is a quick and easy way of recruiting participants.	The volunteers can only be representative of those who saw the advert in the first place (e.g. readers of a particular newspaper/ magazine). Even then, volunteers may differ from non-volunteers in important ways.

(New Zealand) urban area, who were followed up until age 25. The researchers were interested in the effects of abortion between the ages of 15 and 25. Werner (1989: see Chapter 26) began with all children born on the Hawaiian island of Kauai in 1955, then followed them up at ages 1, 2, 10, 18 and 31/32; she focused on a sample from this birth cohort.

Whenever a sample is being selected from some larger population, the aim is to choose a *representative* sample, so that the findings can be generalized to the population as a whole (in other words, what is true for the sample is also true of the population). How can this be done? Some answers are provided in Table 1.2.

The problem of representativeness

The issues raised in Table 1.2 only scratch the surface of the problem of obtaining representative samples:

- As we noted above, Orne's (1962) view of the psychology experiment as a social situation centres around the idea that the experimenter and participants are playing different but complementary roles. In order for this interaction to proceed reasonably smoothly, each must have some idea of what the other expects of him/her; these expectations are part of the culturally shared understandings of what science in general, and psychology in particular, involves, and without which the experiment could not 'happen' (Moghaddam *et al.*, 1993). So not only is the experiment a social situation, but science itself is a *culture-related phenomenon*. (This represents another respect in which science cannot claim complete objectivity.)

- Traditional, mainstream experimental psychology adopts a *nomothetic* (law-like) approach. This involves generalization from limited samples of participants to 'people in general', as part of the attempt to establish general 'laws' or principles of behaviour. In American psychology at least, the typical participant (in both experimental and non-experimental research) is a psychology undergraduate who is obliged to take part in a certain number of studies as a course requirement, and who receives 'course credits' for doing so (Krupat and Garonzik, 1994). Examples of such participants are Loftus and Palmer (1974: see Chapter 6), Festinger and Carlsmith (1959: see Chapter 9), Nisbett *et al.* (1973: see Chapter 14), Schachter and Singer (1962: see Chapter 18), and Bem (1974: see Chapter 41).

- Mainstream British and US psychology has implicitly equated 'human being' with 'member of Western culture'. Despite the fact that the vast majority of research participants are members of Western societies, the resulting findings and theories have been applied to 'human beings' as if culture makes no difference (they are 'culture-bound and culture-blind': Sinha, 1997). This Anglocentric or Eurocentric *bias* (a form of *ethnocentrism*) is matched by the *andocentric* or *masculinity bias* (a form of *sexism*): the behaviour and experience of men are taken as the standard against which women are judged (see Gross, 2005).

● According to Moghaddam (2005), most so-called 'cross-cultural' research continues to rely on undergraduates recruited in both Western and non-Western societies. Students in the modern universities of Asia are more similar to Western students than they are to people in the traditional sector of their own Asian societies. The result is that behaviour in the laboratory is often reported to be 'cross-culturally consistent', when in fact the participants are all from the same undergraduate culture. The inclusion of illiterate villagers from rural areas of Bangladesh, for example, would be a much truer test of the cross-cultural applicability of laboratory methods. Moghaddam's own attempts to do this demonstrated how limited the laboratory method is when participants are from outside Western culture and the modern sector of non-Western societies.

● Even in those cases where specific target populations are involved (such as Spanish anorexic teenagers, or 12-year-old Bristol schoolboys: see above), there is often an implicit assumption that the results can be generalized to populations beyond the target population (e.g. anorexic teenagers living in Western Europe, or 'English schoolboys'). Ultimately, the only way of being sure that the findings from one study can be generalized is to repeat (*replicate*) it using a different sample. In the case of anorexia, this could only be another sample of anorexics (although it might be a sample of late-onset anorexics, rather than teenagers). In the case of Tajfel's study of 'minimal groups', the experiment has been repeated using very different target populations (adults in many parts of the world): the nature of the behaviour being studied determines to some extent who the actual – and potential – target populations will be. However, it is often unclear how specific or broad these populations are meant to be.

(Note that 'replicate' is often used to refer to confirmation of the results of a previous study in a later study: a later study can replicate the *methods/procedures* of the earlier study (it is *repeated*), and can replicate the *findings* of the earlier study (it is *supported*).

NON-EXPERIMENTAL RESEARCH

So far, the focus of this chapter has been on experiments, although, as we have seen, they come in different forms; only when the IV is manipulated *and* participants are randomly allocated to experimental conditions can the study be described as a (true) experiment. By definition, where participants are selected for particular characteristics which constitute the IV (e.g. age, gender, cultural background), the IV is not being manipulated and participants cannot be randomly allocated – the group they are assigned to is predetermined. But such studies may still be looking for a *difference*. For example, Baron-Cohen *et al.*'s (1997: see Chapter 7) study of adults with autism or Asperger's syndrome compared them with normal adults and those with Tourette's syndrome, and Raine *et al.* (1997: see Chapter 36) compared the brains of murderers (who pleaded not guilty by reason of insanity) and matched controls (non-murderers).

Correlational research

In *correlational studies*, not only is the IV not manipulated, but there is no IV at all. Two (or more) variables are measured to see how they are *related*: neither can logically be designated as the cause of the other. For example, Dement and Kleitman (1957: see Chapter 17) investigated the relationship between sleep and dreams, and Hazan and Shaver (1987: see Chapter 15) studied the relationship between adults' memories of

---

Correlational studies may or may not use statistical measures of correlation; whether they do so or not, a correlation can mean different things:

● A *positive* correlation means that two variables *change in the same direction*: as one increases (or decreases), the other increases (or decreases). For example, the more (or less) experience a psychotherapist has had, the more (or less) effective they are in helping patients (see Eysenck, 1952: Chapter 30). A *perfect* positive correlation as a number is +1.00 (i.e. 100 per cent).

● A *negative* (or *inverse*) correlation means that two variables *change in opposite directions*: as one increases, the other decreases (or vice versa). To take the previous example, the *more* experienced the psychotherapist, the *less* effective they are in helping patients. A *perfect* negative correlation as a number is –1.00.

● In both cases, if you know the value of one variable, you can *predict* the value of the other.

● One reason for not inferring that one variable *causes* the other is that they could both be caused by a third variable. For example, both low IQ and little time spent in school among African Americans could be caused by (a history of) racial discrimination (see Gould, 1982: Chapter 35).

● A *zero* correlation (0.00) means that there is no particular relationship between the two variables (i.e. they are not actually related), so we cannot predict anything about one by knowing about the other.

● The full range of values for a correlation runs from +1.00 to –1.00. This figure is calculated by using one or other statistical test of correlation (see Coolican, 2004).

Box 1.1 The meaning of correlation

their parents' sensitivity towards them as children and their current attitudes towards romantic relationships. Although Dement and Kleitman's participants were studied in a sleep laboratory, and Hazan and Shaver's study involved the use of statistics (see Box 1.1), both are *non-experimental*.

Case studies

From mainstream experimental psychology's perspective, the case study is the least scientific of all research methods available to psychologists. It usually involves an in-depth study of a single individual (or sometimes a twin pair) who has:

● exceptional abilities of some kind (such as Kim Peek, the man with Asperger's syndrome who inspired the film *Rain Man*, studied by Treffert and Christensen, 2005: see Chapter 8);

● suffered an extreme early trauma which challenges some of our basic beliefs about human behaviour, as in the case of an identical twin whose penis was accidentally destroyed and who was raised as a girl (Diamond and Sigmundson, 1997: see Chapter 28);

● an exceptional mental disorder which brought them to the attention of psychiatrists, who report on their work with the patient (Thigpen and Cleckley, 1954: see Chapter 31).

Others are well known for other reasons, such as Little Hans, who was the only child patient of Freud (1909: see Chapter 22).

Since these individuals are unique (an *idiographic* approach), the study, by definition, cannot be replicated. This is traditionally seen as contrary to what is required by mainstream psychology's nomothetic approach, whose goal is to make statements about people in general (see above). However, these approaches are not necessarily mutually exclusive (see Gross, 2003).

The case study is more of an overall approach and can incorporate a range of more specific research methods, including psychometric testing (mental measurement) and physiological testing (such as the EEG), as well as a detailed case history and an account of the individual's psychotherapy. These produce quantitative data, but the case study is more usually associated with *qualitative data* – another reason for its rejection by mainstream psychology.

Surveys and questionnaires, interviews and observation

Surveys usually involve using *questionnaires* with large numbers of people (either by post or in a face-to-face situation). These can both generate quantitative data, but, as we saw above, qualitative research often involves transcribing tape-recorded interviews, that is, putting on paper, word for word, the content of an interview (usually with one participant at a time). This is extremely time-consuming, so the numbers involved are usually much smaller than in a survey (see below). A survey was used by Hazan and Shaver (in the form of a 'love quiz' that appeared in a local newspaper), which provided quantitative data. Rees's (1971) study of hallucinations in widows and widowers was an interview-based study (see Chapter 32) .

Observation can stand alone as a research method, in which it may be:

● *controlled* (i.e. laboratory-based): for example, Ainsworth *et al.*'s (1978) 'Strange Situation' technique for studying attachment in young children (see Hazan and Shaver, 1987: Chapter 15);

● *naturalistic*: people's behaviour is observed and recorded in its natural 'habitat', unaffected by the fact of being observed; this is very popular in student projects, but surprisingly rare in psychology, and is usually confined to children and non-human animals;

● *participant*: the observer becomes a member of the social group or institution being studied, as in Rosenhan's (1973) study of pseudo-patients being admitted to psychiatric hospitals and observing the way the wards were run (see Chapter 33).

As well as these, observation can be used as part of an alternative overall design, as in Milgram's (1963) experimental study of obedience (see Chapter 10), Haney *et al.*'s (1973) Stanford prison study (see Chapter 13), and Piliavin *et al.*'s (1969) field experiment of bystander intervention in the New York subway (see Chapter 11).

In some of these examples, observation was used to record quantitative data (e.g. how many passengers went to the aid of someone apparently drunk or ill in Piliavin *et al.*'s study); in others, it was used to record qualitative data (e.g. how 'prisoners' reacted to their increasingly harsh treatment at the hands of the 'guards' in Haney *et al.*'s simulated prison). Observation is clearly a highly versatile research method.

Hypothesis testing and statistical analysis

Even experiments can provide qualitative data (e.g. participants are asked to describe what it was like to perform the experimental task), but these are *secondary* to the quantitative data and the statistical analysis.

- In a *(true) experiment*, statistical tests are (typically) used to test a specific *hypothesis*, a prediction (often derived from a theory or explanatory model) about how two or more groups will differ (the DV).

- In a *quasi-experiment*, statistical analysis will also be used to test a hypothesis about the difference between two or more conditions.

- In a *correlational* study, the hypothesis makes a prediction about the relationship between variables.

Sometimes, hypotheses are very specific about the outcome they predict and are called *directional*; for example:

1   Adults with autism or Asperger's syndrome will be *less* successful on the eyes task than either normal adults or those with Tourette's syndrome (see Baron-Cohen *et al.*, 1997: Chapter 7).

2   There is a *significant positive correlation* between the subjective estimate of the duration of dreams and the length of eye-movement period prior to awakening (see Dement and Kleitman, 1957: Chapter 17).

Other hypotheses are less specific (more 'open-ended'), allowing for the outcome to go one way or another (*non-directional*); the non-directional versions of the two hypotheses above would be:

1   There will be a *difference* between adults with autism or Asperger's syndrome, compared with normal adults and those with Tourette's syndrome in their success on the eyes task.

2   There is a *significant correlation* between the subjective estimate of the duration of dreams and the length of eye-movement period prior to awakening.

Qualitative research

As a general rule, non-experimental research is less likely to involve hypothesis testing than experimental research; this is especially true of case studies.

Qualitative approaches are generally concerned with exploring, describing and interpreting the personal and social experience of participants (Smith, 2003). An attempt is usually made to understand a small number of participants' frame of reference (or view of the world), rather than trying to test a preconceived hypothesis on a large sample. One form of qualitative research is *interpretative phenomenological analysis* (IPA); its aim is to explore in detail how participants are making sense of their personal and social world, and its main currency is the *meanings* that particular experiences, events and states hold for participants (see Bassett, 2002: Chapter 37).

While qualitative and quantitative research usually differ considerably in terms of research question, orientation and execution, it is actually difficult to make any hard-and-fast distinction between the methods involved. For example:

● as we have seen, observation can be used in what, overall, is an experimental design to provide qualitative data;

● statistical analysis can take the form of either *descriptive statistics*, which summarize data in the form of percentages, averages (mean/median) or graphs; or *inferential statistics*, that is, the use of statistical *tests* to determine whether the outcome of a study could have occurred by chance (a fluke) or was *statistically significant* (in the case of an experiment, the IV really did affect the DV);

● the process of analysis in qualitative research often involves the researcher making judgements (implicitly or explicitly) of the strength or otherwise of a category or property being reported, and individuals are compared with each other on various dimensions (Hayes, 1997, in Smith, 2003);

● it can be argued that quantitative research always involves interpretation by the researcher, and this process is essentially a qualitative one.

As with experimental, quantitative psychology, 'qualitative psychology' refers to a number of quite different approaches, each with overlapping but different theoretical and/or methodological emphases (see Smith, 2003).

CONCLUSIONS

If psychology is a science it is a very special science. Instead of using one major research method (the laboratory experiment), psychology's methods are extremely diverse and versatile, reflecting the complex nature of its subject matter. Qualitative methods especially are constantly evolving, reflecting changing views regarding what it is about human beings that psychologists can validly and appropriately study.

2 Emotionality and perceptual defence

McGinnies, E. (1949)

Psychological Review, 56: 244–51

BACKGROUND AND CONTEXT

A commonly held view of perception is that it is an active process, influenced by motivational, emotional and cognitive processes. The opposite view is of a passive receipt of sensory information from and about the external world. Allport (1955) distinguished six types of motivational-emotional influence on perception: the value of objects, bodily needs, reward and punishment, individual values, personality, and emotional connotation.

The first (value of objects) and last (emotional connotation) of these are the most directly related to perceptual defence. The value of objects refers to the phenomenon of *perceptual accentuation* (or *sensitization*): things that are relevant or salient for us are perceived as larger/brighter/more attractive/more valuable, and so on, than those which are not (and compared with their objective characteristics).

Emotional connotation refers to the accentuation of *negative* (anxiety-/frustration-producing) stimuli. The term *perceptual defence* (Postman *et al.*, 1948; McGinnies, 1949) refers to the findings from laboratory experiments that subliminally perceived words (that is, below the threshold of consciousness) that evoke unpleasant emotions take longer to perceive consciously than neutral words.

Recognition can occur *before* perception enters conscious awareness (autonomic discrimination without awareness, or the 'subception' effect). A commonly used indicator of autonomic activity is the galvanic skin response (GSR); this measures the skin's resistance to electricity, which decreases as anxiety is raised through increased sweating. In the subception effect, enough information is somehow transmitted to the autonomic nervous system (ANS) to determine different levels of GSR; but insufficient information reaches the brain centres responsible for correct verbal identification.

AIM AND NATURE

● HYPOTHESES

McGinnies wished to explore the question: how is a raised or lowered recognition threshold for harmful stimulus objects achieved before the observer discriminates them and becomes aware of their threatening character? One way of trying to answer this question is to detect any one aspect of autonomic arousal (physiological arousal beyond the participant's conscious control) that accompanies perceptual behaviour: this should throw some light on the processes involved in perceptual defence.

Taking GSR as a measure of autonomic arousal, McGinnies predicted that:

1   There will be a significant change in GSR in reaction to visually presented stimuli (words) with emotive connotations before the participant is able to report the exact nature of the stimulus, compared with stimuli without such connotations.

2   The mean recognition threshold for the words with emotive connotations will be significantly higher than that for words without emotive connotations (i.e. it will take longer to recognize the former).

It is the reference to the higher recognition threshold which represents the concept of perceptual defence.

● METHOD/DESIGN

The study is a laboratory experiment using a repeated measures design: all 16 participants (8 male and 8 female undergraduates from an elementary psychology class) were presented with all 18 words (11 neutral, 7 emotionally toned). These two kinds of words comprise the two experimental conditions. The stimulus words represent the independent variable; the dependent variable was measured as mean GSR and mean recognition threshold.

The words were presented via a tachistoscope, which allowed controlled variation of exposure time, starting at 0.01 seconds. Each participant sat in front of the tachistoscope, with electrodes strapped to both palms for measuring GSR. Each participant's threshold was first determined for four trial words, by exposing the word once at 0.01 seconds, once at 0.02 seconds, and so on, until it was correctly identified.

The stimulus words are shown in Table 2.1.

Table 2.1

Stimulus words used in order of presentation to each participant
Critical or emotional words are shown in bold.

apple	**kotex***
dance	broom
raped	stove
child	**penis**
belly	music
glass	trade
river	**filth**
whore	clear
sleep	**bitch**

* A form of sanitary towel.

Before the experiment began, participants were told that they would be shown words which they might not be able to recognize at first. They were instructed to report whatever they saw or thought they saw on each exposure, regardless of what it was.

● RESULTS

Emotionality (hypothesis 1)

Because McGinnies was interested primarily in participants' GSR during the period *preceding correct recognition* of the stimulus words, analysis was based only on those recordings taken on exposure trials up to – but not including – the trial on which recognition finally occurred.

Emotionality was significantly greater during pre-recognition exposures of the critical than of the neutral words. The results are shown in Figure 2.1.

Thresholds (hypothesis 2)

As shown in Figure 2.2, without exception, the mean recognition thresholds were greater for the critical than for the neutral words. The difference was statistically significant.

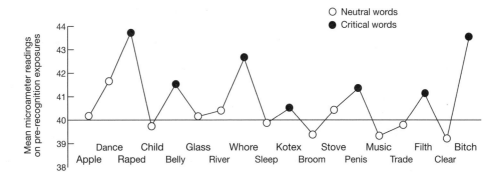

Figure 2.1. Group averages of galvanic skin response to neutral and critical words during pre-recognition exposures.

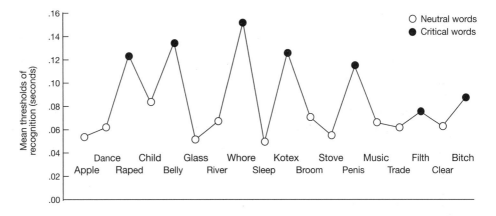

Figure 2.2. Mean thresholds of recognition of the observers to the neutral and emotionally charged words.

Content analysis

Since participants were instructed to report whatever they saw, they typically volunteered several pre-recognition 'hypotheses' before recognition occurred. Four content categories were used to code their perceptual 'guesses':

● *structurally similar* (e.g. 'trace' for 'trade'; 'whose' for 'whore');

● *structurally unlike* (e.g. 'roared' for 'belly'; 'ideal' for 'glass');

● *nonsense* (e.g. 'egtry' for 'kotex'; 'widge' for 'stove');

● *part* (e.g. these guesses were fractional or incomplete, consisting of any disconnected group of letters).

Participants made proportionately more *unlike* and *nonsense* responses to the critical words.

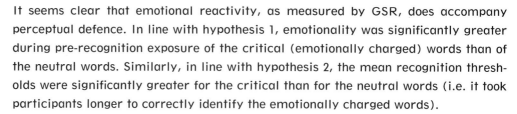

● CONCLUSIONS

It seems clear that emotional reactivity, as measured by GSR, does accompany perceptual defence. In line with hypothesis 1, emotionality was significantly greater during pre-recognition exposure of the critical (emotionally charged) words than of the neutral words. Similarly, in line with hypothesis 2, the mean recognition thresholds were significantly greater for the critical than for the neutral words (i.e. it took participants longer to correctly identify the emotionally charged words).

EVALUATION

Methodological issues

One criticism of McGinnies' study is that participants were not failing to recognize the critical words as quickly as the neutral words, but rather they may have felt too embarrassed to say them out loud (remember, the year was 1949!). Some support for this interpretation came from a study by Aronfreed *et al.* (1953), in which female participants were tested by a male experimenter. Longer recognition thresholds and greater GSRs were produced for the emotive words compared with those produced by other combinations of experimenters and participants. (Note that McGinnies found no significant gender difference either in GSRs or thresholds during the pre-recognition period.) Support also comes from a study by Bitterman and Kniffin (1953): there was no perceptual defence effect if participants were allowed to write down their answers. Also, the perceptual defence effect could be eliminated if participants were warned that emotive words would be shown (Lacy *et al.*, 1953; Postman *et al.*, 1953).

However, McGinnies asked participants after the experiment whether they had reported their perception of the words promptly and accurately. In all cases they assured the experimenters that, with the occasional exception of the first critical words, they did not withhold or modify their verbal response because of reluctance to say the word. McGinnies took this to indicate that the GSR was recording genuine pre-recognition responses to the stimulus words.

In his Discussion, McGinnies refers to Bruner's observation that critical words appear less often in print. This could mean that the greater threshold for these words is a function of their *unfamiliarity*: greater 'effort' is required to recognize them, which, in turn, causes an increase in GSR. McGinnies rejects this interpretation in the following ways:

1   The critical words are, in fact, used quite commonly in conversation, despite their infrequent appearance in print.

2   There is no reason why unfamiliarity should produce a greater number of *nonsense* and *structurally unlike* responses.

3   If GSR merely accompanies increased effort spent in recognizing words with higher thresholds, there should be a correlation between mean GSRs and mean thresholds for both the neutral and critical words. No such correlations were found.

McGinnies concludes that the results may be viewed as reflecting genuine emotional response, rather than mere autonomic reactivity that accompanies effort at recognition.

Theoretical issues

Is perceptual defence a truly *perceptual* phenomenon, or is the increased recognition threshold for emotive words due to some kind of *response bias* (Eysenck, 1984)? Hardy and Legge (1968) asked participants to detect the presence of a faint auditory stimulus while watching a screen on which emotive or neutral words were presented subliminally. Although almost all of them failed to notice that any words had been presented, the auditory threshold was *higher* when the emotive words were being presented. The visually presented words made it more difficult to detect the sound (there was a reduction in sensitivity to auditory stimulation). Because the words were presented subliminally (they were not noticed consciously), participants could not have been switching their attention away from the sound and towards the words (a shift in response bias). Hardy and Legge concluded that perceptual defence is a genuine perceptual phenomenon.

However, there remains a paradox. According to Howie (1952), when we talk about perceptual defence, we are speaking of 'perceptual processing as somehow being both a process of knowing and a process of not knowing'; that is, how is it that the perceiver can selectively defend him/herself against an emotional stimulus *unless* s/he has already perceived and identified it (Eysenck, 1984)?

The concept of subliminal perception in general, and perceptual defence in particular, becomes more acceptable if perception is thought of *not* as a unitary process, but one that involves multiple processing stages and mechanisms; consciousness might just represent the final level of processing (Dixon, 1981; Erdelyi, 1974). Put another way, consciousness may not be essential to cognition (Eysenck, 1984).

A common, everyday occurrence such as only becoming aware of music coming from the house next door *after* it has been turned off, suggests that you must have been hearing the music all the time – in some unconscious way. This challenges the simplistic (and common-sense) idea that perception implies consciousness and that 'I' must know what my own brain is perceiving (Merikle *et al.*, 2001, in Blackmore, 2003).

The concept of perceptual defence is related to Freud's concept of *repression.* According to Freud (1915): 'The essence of repression lies simply in turning something away, and keeping it at a distance, from the conscious'. Dangerous or threatening memories, ideas or feelings are made unconscious and so inaccessible to the conscious mind. Clearly, this plays a crucial defensive function, both in the developing child and the 'normal' and neurotic adult; indeed, Freud (1914) described repression as a special cornerstone 'on which the whole structure of psychoanalysis rests. It is the most essential part of it'. It is one of several *ego defence mechanisms* which Freud described.

As a theory of forgetting, Freud's *repression hypothesis* was tested experimentally by Levinger and Clark (1961) in a way that parallels McGinnies's study. Participants were asked to remember a number of negatively charged and neutral words. When they were asked to give immediate free associations to the words (to say exactly what came into their minds), it took them longer to respond to the emotional words. These words also produced higher GSRs. Immediately afterwards, participants were given the cue words again and asked to recall their associations; they had particular trouble remembering the associations to the emotionally charged words. This is exactly what the repression hypothesis would have predicted.

However, other studies have shown that, while highly arousing words may be poorly recalled when tested immediately, the effect *reverses* after a delay (Eysenck and Wilson, 1973). If the words are being repressed, this should not happen (they should *stay* repressed); this suggests that *arousal* was the crucial factor. Although others have found support for the arousal hypothesis (Bradley and Baddeley, 1990; Parkin *et al.*, 1982), the question of emotional inhibition remains open (Parkin, 1993).

Subsequent research

Dixon (1971) reviewed several studies which showed that verbal stimuli that are too quick or too dim to be consciously perceived will nonetheless affect the participant's associative processes. It was found that:

● associations following the subliminal perception of a word were linked to its meaning (Marcel and Patterson, 1978);

● participants' self-ratings of anxiety increased following the subliminal presentations of unpleasant words, such as 'cancer' (Tyrer *et al.*, 1978);

● GSRs increased following the subliminal presentation of emotive picture stimuli, such as a breast (O'Grady, 1977).

Brain scans have also been used to investigate unconscious perception. Functional magnetic resonance imaging (fMRI), which shows changes in blood flow within the brain as participants work on a task (see Chapter 29), has found that unconsciously perceived fearful faces produce greater activity in the amygdala than happy faces (Whalen *et al.*, 1998, in Blackmore, 2003). The amygdala is involved in the processing of information related to emotion. Blackmore cites another study (Morris *et al.*, 1998) which showed that angry faces activate only the right side of the amygdala. This confirms that even when information is not consciously perceived, it can affect the same parts of the brain that would be activated by consciously seen stimuli of the same kind (see Chapter 20).

Applications and implications

According to Blackmore (2003), evidence for unconscious perception challenges some ideas about consciousness that are popular among those who study consciousness, both neuroscientists and philosophers. According to one of these ideas, any stimulus is either 'in' or 'out' of consciousness. However, the evidence described above suggests that sensory information is processed in a wide variety of ways, with different consequences for different kinds of behaviour. Some of these behaviours are usually taken as indicators of consciousness, such as verbal reports or choices between clearly perceptible stimuli, while others are generally considered to be unconscious, such as fast reflexes, guesses or certain measures of brain activity. However, nothing is ever 'in' or 'out' of consciousness, and phrases such as 'available to consciousness' or 'reaching consciousness' are either meaningless or are shorthand for 'leading to verbal report' or 'available to influence behaviours taken to indicate consciousness'. We should reject any clear-cut distinction between what is conscious and what is not (Blackmore, 2003).

Arguably the most controversial application of subliminal perception is *subliminal advertising*. It originated with Jim Vicary, a US market researcher. He arranged with the owner of a New Jersey cinema to install a second special projector which, during the film, flashed on the screen phrases such as, 'Hungry? Eat popcorn', and 'Drink Coca-Cola'. These were either flashed so quickly, or printed so faintly, that they could not be consciously perceived – even after a warning that they were about to appear.

Films treated in this way were alternated with untreated films throughout the summer of 1956. Whether the tactic actually worked is not clear (LeDoux, 1998). Vicary himself believed that prospective customers had to be already intending to buy before a subliminal stimulus could produce any effect. Nevertheless, subliminal advertising caused a storm of protest in the American press, and later on in the UK too. The public was outraged over this unethical act of manipulation and invasion of privacy (Moore, 1988, in LeDoux, 1998) and it was subsequently banned.

However, advertisers use emotional cues (implicitly and explicitly) to persuade consumers to buy products all the time. As Packard noted in his famous book, *The Hidden Persuaders* (1957), persuasion is their business. Persuasion always works better when the persuadee is not aware that s/he is being influenced (Eagly and Chaiken, 1993), and implicit messages are the bread and butter of many advertising campaigns (LeDoux, 1998).

Subliminal messages reappeared in the mid 1970s, this time in an attempt to scare, rather than sell. For example, in *The Exorcist* (1974) a death mask was flashed onto the screen subliminally. More recently, in an attempt to reduce theft, several department stores in the USA began mixing barely audible and rapidly repeated whispers (such as 'I am honest', 'I will not steal') with their piped music. Many stores reported dramatic decreases in shoplifting. Also, audio cassette tapes are readily available which supposedly reduce stress with soothing sub-audible messages covered by mood music or the ambient sounds of nature (Zimbardo and Leippe, 1991). However, there is no evidence that these actually make any difference (Merikle, 2000, in Blackmore, 2003).

EXERCISES

1　Why was it important to determine each participant's GSR threshold for four trial words?

2　Why was it important to have an equal number of male and female participants?

3　Are you surprised that more critical words than neutral words were distorted when being named (i.e. there were proportionately more unlike and nonsense responses)?

4　(a)　How might the order of the words have been determined?

　　(b)　Why is this an important thing to control for in this kind of experimental design?

5　If the independent variable was the neutrality/emotionality of the words, what other word characteristics should have been controlled?

6　(a)　Why might subliminal advertising be considered unethical?

　　(b)　Try to think of some examples of advertisements/campaigns which use *implicit* emotional messages.

　　(c)　Do the same for *explicit* emotional messages.

3 Teaching sign language to a chimpanzee

Gardner, R.A. and Gardner, B.T. (1969)

Science, 165(3894): 664–72

BACKGROUND AND CONTEXT

For many psychologists, philosophers and linguists, language is the characteristic which makes human beings unique among animals: it is what makes us the intelligent species we are. Chomsky (1957, 1965), for example, believes that language is unique to humans (it is *species-specific*) and so cannot be acquired by other species; language learning can only occur in organisms possessing various innate linguistic mechanisms, and only humans possess such a *language acquisition device* (LAD).

According to Aitchison (1998), to ask if humans are the only 'articulate mammals' has a very serious purpose:

> *Some animals, such as dolphins and chimpanzees, have a high level of intelligence. If, in spite of this, we find that language is beyond their capability, then we may have found some indication that language is a genetically programmed activity which is largely separate from general intelligence.*

Early attempts to teach chimps to speak (Kellogg and Kellogg, 1933; Hayes and Hayes, 1951) were almost totally unsuccessful: their vocal apparatus is unsuited to making speech sounds. But this does not rule out the possibility that they are capable of learning language in some non-spoken form, and it was the Gardners who first attempted to do this using American Sign Language (ASL or Ameslan), as used by many deaf people in the USA.

Many subsequent studies have used ASL or some alternative method for teaching language. (See **Methodological issues** and **Subsequent research** below.) But whichever method has been used, the debate has always been about how to evaluate the findings. To be able to judge a chimp's signing as language clearly depends on how we define language in the first place. The starting point for making such a judgement is Hockett's (1960) criteria for language (or *design features*), which reflect the *discontinuity* *theory of language.* According to this view, there are *qualitative* (and not just quantitative) *differences* between human and non-human animal language.

Based on Hockett, Aitchison (1998) proposes that ten criteria/design features should be sufficient (not all identified by Hockett); by analysing human and non-human language in terms of all ten, she concludes that four are unique to humans, namely:

1   *semanticity*: the use of symbols to *mean* or refer to objects/actions;

2   *displacement*: reference to things not present in time or space;

3   *structure-dependence*: the patterned nature of language and use of 'structured chunks', such as word order;

4   *creativity*: the ability to produce and understand an infinite number of novel utterances – what Brown (1973) calls *productivity*.

Studies like the Gardners' should be evaluated in terms of these four criteria/design features.

AIM AND NATURE

● HYPOTHESIS

The aim of the study was to help answer the question (a classical problem in *comparative* psychology): to what extent might another species be able to use human language? One way to approach the problem is to try to teach a form of human language to a non-human animal.

The article describes the first phase of a training project, involving an infant female chimp called Washoe (estimated to be between 8 and 14 months when training began). It is a kind of case study of a single subject, in which detailed records were kept of Washoe's progress over an extended period of time (32 months). Unlike most case studies involving human beings (see Freud, 1909: Chapter 22), there was no problem the participant had for which she was receiving help. Instead, this was a deliberate attempt to change the subject's behaviour in a particular way, in order to test a scientific hypothesis. This raises ethical issues not faced by most case studies. (See **Applications and implications** below.)

● METHOD/DESIGN

Use of the hands is a prominent feature of chimp behaviour, and even caged, laboratory chimps develop begging and other gestures spontaneously. It was reasoned that gestures for chimps are equivalent to bar-pressing for rats, key-pecking for pigeons and babbling for humans. This makes ASL particularly suitable for teaching language to chimps.

ASL consists of a set of manual configurations and gestures which correspond to particular words or concepts. Some gestures are quite arbitrary (they bear no relation to the word or concept being signed), while others are quite representational or iconic (although all signs are arbitrary to some degree). ASL allows a great range of expression; technical terms and proper names are a problem when first introduced, but it is quite easy to get round these. For example, the Gardners signed 'think doctor' for 'psychologist' and 'think science' for 'psychology'.

Instrumental (operant) *conditioning* was used to teach Washoe as many gestures (signs) as possible. The most effective reward used was tickling. It was decided to shape an arbitrary response which Washoe could use for requesting more tickling. The Gardners noticed that, when being tickled, she tended to bring her arms together to cover the place being tickled: the result was a very crude approximation to the ASL sign for 'more' (see Table 3.1). The 'more' sign later transferred to all activities.

Clapping, smiling and repeating the gesture (just as you might repeat 'goo-goo' to a baby) were used to encourage Washoe's manual 'babbling', that is, spontaneous movements which involve touching part of the head and body that are important components of many signs. When the babbled gesture resembled an ASL sign, the companion made the correct form of the sign and tried to engage Washoe in some appropriate activity.

Imitative prompting was also used, in combination with instrumental conditioning. Chimps are natural imitators, but only of visual events/stimuli. Imitative prompting was used extensively to increase the frequency and refine the form of signs, especially new ones that were still being learned. Basically, the human companion would make the correct sign to Washoe, repeating the performance until she made the correct sign herself.

Some of her signs appeared to have been acquired originally by *delayed imitation*; a good example is the sign for 'toothbrush'. Some ten months into the project she made the toothbrush sign, in what was the first and one of the clearest examples of Washoe apparently naming an object or event for no other motive than communication. (See **Theoretical issues** below.)

Laboratory conditions

Because the Gardners wanted Washoe to develop 'conversation' (i.e. to ask for objects, answer questions and also to ask them questions), confinement was made about the same as for a human infant. Her human companions were to be friends and playmates as well as providers and protectors, and they were to introduce a great many games and activities which would maximize interaction with her.

At least one person was with her during all her waking hours. All her companions had to master ASL and used it extensively in her presence, in conjunction with interesting activities and also in a general way, as one chatters at a human infant. Occasional *finger-spelling* was allowed and, inevitably, there were lapses into spoken English, as when she was examined by medical personnel.

The basic rule was that all meaningful sounds (including laughing, expressions of pleasure and displeasure, whistles and drums, and hand-clapping) must be sounds that a chimp could imitate.

● RESULTS/FINDINGS

Vocabulary

During the 16th month, the Gardners settled on the following procedure: when a new sign appeared, they waited for it to be reported by three different observers as having occurred in an appropriate context and spontaneously (i.e. with no prompting other than a question such as 'What is it?' or 'What do you want?'). The sign was then added to a checklist. A reported frequency of at least one appropriate and spontaneous occurrence each day over a period of 15 consecutive days was taken as the criterion of acquisition. Table 3.1 shows 30 signs which met this criterion by the end of the 22nd month. Four others ('dog', 'smell', 'me', 'clean') are included, which were judged to be stable without meeting these strict criteria.

Table 3.1

Signs used reliably by chimpanzee Washoe within 22 months of the beginning of training (in order of their original appearance)

Signs	Context	Signs	Context
Come-gimme	Sign made to person or animals, also for objects out of reach. Often combined: 'come tickle', 'gimme sweet', etc.	Flower	For flowers.
More	When asking for continuation or repetition of activities such as swinging or tickling, for second helpings of food, etc.	Cover-blanket	At bedtime or naptime and on cold days when Washoe wants to be taken out.
Up	Wants a lift to reach objects such as grapes on vine, or leaves, or wants to be placed on someone's shoulders or wants to leave potty-chair.	Dog	For dogs and for barking.

AIM AND NATURE

AIM AND NATURE

Sign	Description	Sign	Description
Sweet	For dessert, used spontaneously at end of meal. Also when asking for candy.	You	Indicates successive turns in games. Also used in response to questions such as 'Who tickle?', 'Who brush?'
Open	At door of house, room, car, fridge or cupboard, or containers such as jars, and for taps.	Napkin-bib	For bib, washcloth, Kleenex.
Tickle	For tickling or chasing games.	In	Wants to go indoors or wants someone to join her indoors.
Go	While walking hand in hand or riding on someone's shoulders. Washoe usually indicates the direction desired.	Brush	For hairbrush and when asking for brushing.
Out	When passing through doorways, until recently used for both 'in' and 'out'. Also when asking to be taken outdoors.	Hat	For hats and caps.
Hurry	Often follows signs such as 'come-gimme', 'out', 'open', 'go', particularly if there is a delay before Washoe obeys. Also while her meal is being prepared.	I-me	Indicates Washoe's turn when she and companion share food, drink, etc. Also in phrases such as 'I drink', and in reply to questions such as 'Who tickle?' (Washoe: 'you'), 'Who I tickle?' (Washoe: 'me').
Hear-listen	For loud/strange sounds: bells, car horns, sonic booms, etc. Also for asking for someone to hold a watch to her ear.	Shoes	For shoes.
Tooth-brush	When Washoe has finished her meal, or at other times when shown a toothbrush.	Smell	For scented objects: tobacco, perfume, sage, etc.
Drink	For water formula, soda pop. For soda pop, often combined with 'sweet'.	Pants	For diapers, rubber pants, trousers.
Hurt	To indicate cuts and bruises on herself or on others. Can be elicited by red stains on a person's skin or by tears in clothing.	Clothes	For Washoe's jacket, nightgown, shirts, and for people's clothing.
Sorry	After biting someone, or when someone has been hurt in another way (not necessarily by Washoe), when told to apologize for mischief.	Cat	For cats.
Funny	When soliciting interaction play, and during games. Occasionally when being pursued after mischief.	Key	Used for keys and locks and to ask for a door to be unlocked.
Please	When asking for objects and activities. Often combined 'please go', 'out please', 'please drink'.	Baby	For dolls, including animals, such as toy horse and duck.
Food-eat	During meals and preparation of meals.	Clean	Used when Washoe is washing/being washed, when a companion is washing hands or some other object. Also used for 'soap'.

Differentiation

The first and third columns in Table 3.1 show the English equivalent for each of Washoe's signs. But this equivalence was only approximate for various reasons:

● Equivalence between ASL and English is only approximate.

● Washoe's usage differs from that of standard ASL.

● The definition of any given sign must always depend on Washoe's constantly changing vocabulary.

When she had very few signs for specific things, Washoe used 'more' for a wide class of requests; but as she acquired signs for specific requests this declined, until she was using it mainly to request repetition of some actions she could not name (such as a somersault). Differentiation of the signs for 'flower' and 'smell' is another illustration of usage depending on size of vocabulary. As the 'flower' sign became more frequent, it occurred in many inappropriate contexts which all seemed to involve odours. Gradually, she came to make the appropriate distinction, although 'flower' continued to be used incorrectly in 'smell' contexts.

Transfer

In general, when introducing new signs, the Gardners used a very specific referent (i.e. a particular door for 'open', a particular hat for 'hat'), but Washoe was able to transfer the signs spontaneously to new members of each class of referents. One example is her transfer of the 'dog' sign to the sound of barking of an unknown dog.

Combinations

No deliberate attempt was made to elicit combinations or strings of signs, and Washoe seemed to do this spontaneously. Almost as soon as she had eight to ten signs in her vocabulary, she began to use two or three of them at a time. As her vocabulary increased, so did this tendency to string signs together. Although the Gardners tended to use combinations of signs themselves, Washoe invented several combinations (e.g. 'gimme tickle', before they had even asked her to tickle them, and 'open food drink' when referring to the fridge, which they had always called 'cold box'). Signs learned late included 'I-me' and 'you', so that combinations resembling short sentences began to appear.

● CONCLUSIONS

It is very difficult to answer questions such as, 'Do you think that Washoe has language?' or, 'At what point will it be possible to say that Washoe has language?', because they imply that it is possible to distinguish between communication that

can be called language and communication that cannot be distinguished in this way.

The study showed clearly that sign language is an appropriate medium of two-way communication for chimps. The increasing rate of her progress, her ability to spontaneously transfer signs to new referents, and the emergence of simple combinations, all suggested that she could achieve more (such as being able to describe events and situations to an observer who has no other source of information).

EVALUATION

Methodological issues

As the Gardners point out, ASL is particularly well suited for teaching to chimps. But when discussing *differentiation* of Washoe's vocabulary, they also observe that there is only an approximate equivalence between Washoe's signs and English words. This point can be taken one step further: the very status of ASL as a language is questionable.

Eysenck (1984), for example, notes that ASL signs are defined in terms of four parameters: hand configurations, movement, orientation and location. But the Gardners consistently focused only on hand configuration. According to Brown (1986), ASL is not related to spoken English and is very unlike English in grammatical structure. Nevertheless, it has the capacity to express any meaning whatsoever: it is language in a *manual-visual* (as opposed to vocal-auditory) modality.

However, while ASL when used by humans is undoubtedly a language, we cannot simply *assume* that it is so when used by chimps. (If we did, we would be guilty of *anthropomorphizing*: see **Exercises** at the end of the chapter.) But we must also be careful not to exclude signing as language just because it is chimps rather than humans moving their hands (Brown, 1986).

Some of the major studies that followed the Gardners' work with Washoe include:

● Premack (1971): Sarah, a female chimp, was taught to use small plastic symbols of various shapes and colours, each standing for a word and arranged on a special magnetized board.

● Rumbaugh (1977) and Savage-Rumbaugh *et al.* (1980): Lana, another female chimp, was taught to use a special typewriter (controlled by a computer), with 50 keys, each displaying a geometric pattern representing a word in a specially devised language ('Yerkish'); when typed, the pattern appeared on a screen in front of her.

● Patterson (1978, 1980): Koko, a female gorilla, was taught ASL.

● Terrace (1979a): taught ASL to Nim (Neam) Chimpsky, a male chimp.

According to Rumbaugh and Savage-Rumbaugh (1994), all these studies (including their own and that of the Gardners) made one serious omission: they only taught the apes to 'speak', not to listen (*production* vs *comprehension*). This represents a fundamental error, since children understand speech *before* they can produce it, yet the apes were expected to generate language before they had a basis from which to comprehend it. It is not surprising that the studies revealed little more than sophisticated signalling. (See **Theoretical issues** below.)

Starting in the 1980s, at the Yerkes Primate Centre and Georgia State University, Savage-Rumbaugh has been working with chimps in a way that is much more like the way children acquire language. Instead of being production-based, the guiding principle is that language is first acquired through *comprehension*, from which *production* then flows. This new approach was applied on a limited scale with Austin and Sherman, two common chimps (*Pan troglodytes*). But it really got going with pygmy chimps (*Pan paniscus*), or bonobos, which are slightly smaller than common chimps, but more vocal and more communicative through facial expressions and gestures. (See **Subsequent research** below.)

Theoretical issues

It seems almost indisputable that Washoe displayed *semanticity*: after four years of intensive training (based on later reports), she had acquired 132 signs. She had no difficulty in understanding that a sign 'means' a certain object or action (Aitchison, 1998). She was also able to generalize from one situation to another (e.g. 'open', 'more'), and sometimes *overgeneralized* (e.g. 'hurt').

There is also some limited evidence of *displacement*, as when she asked for absent objects or people (e.g. 'all gone cup'/'more milk'). Once Washoe had learned eight to ten signs, she spontaneously began to combine them (showing *creativity*). Although she combined some signs in a consistent order (e.g. 'baby mine', rather than 'mine baby'/ 'tickle me' rather than 'me tickle'), she did not always seem to care about sign order (e.g. she was as likely to sign 'go sweet' as 'sweet go'). So, the evidence for *structure-dependence* is much weaker. Why should this be so?

Aitchison (1998) suggests four reasons:

1   The Gardners' overeagerness may have led them to reward her every time she signed correctly (regardless of order), so that the idea that order is important may never have been learned.

2   It may be easier to preserve order with words than with signs: deaf adults are also inconsistent in their word order.

3   This may have been a temporary, intermediate stage before she eventually learned to keep to a fixed order. The Gardners (1971, 1975, 1978, 1980) claim that this is indeed what happened.

4   She did not and could not understand the essentially patterned nature of language.

This inconsistent pattern is largely confirmed by the other studies: Sarah, Lana, Koko and Nim Chimpsky all showed a *statistical preference* for putting certain signs in a particular order, but none showed any evidence of understanding any *rules*.

Even semanticity, which seems to be the one generally agreed criterion of language, is problematical. Is the correct use of a sign to refer to something a sufficient criterion? The Gardners describe Washoe's first use of 'toothbrush' as the first and clearest example of her using a sign purely for the sake of communication, that is, to *name* something. But not only is this a very isolated example when compared with how young children use language, Savage-Rumbaugh *et al.* (1980) seriously doubt whether any of the apes (including their own, Lana) use the individual elements in their vocabularies as 'words'. Terrace (1987) hypothesizes that the deceptively simple ability to use a symbol as a name required a cognitive advance in the evolution of human intelligence at least as significant as the advances that led to grammatical competence.

Much of a child's initial vocabulary of names is used to inform another person that s/he has noticed something (MacNamara, 1982); often, the child refers to the object spontaneously, showing obvious delight from the sheer act of naming. But it is just this aspect of uttering a name which is missing from apes' use of signs. MacNamara believes that no amount of training could produce an ape with such ability, because this is not an acquired ability, but a 'primitive of cognitive psychology' (and a necessary precursor of naming). Chimps usually try to 'acquire' objects (approach it, explore it, and so on) and show no signs of trying to communicate the fact that they have noticed it as end in itself (Terrace, 1987) (but see **Subsequent research**).

Patterson (1978) claims that 'language is no longer the exclusive domain of man', and Rumbaugh (1977) argues that 'neither tool-using skills nor language serve qualitatively to separate man and beast any more'. However, Chomsky (1980) believes that the higher apes 'apparently lack the capacity to develop even the rudiments of the computational structure of human language'. Aitchison (1998) agrees with Chomsky, saying, 'The apparent ease with which humans acquire language, compared with apes, supports the suggestion that they are innately programmed to do so'.

Subsequent research

All these criticisms and conclusions (both in support of and against non-human language) are based on *production-based* training: putting the chimp through rote-learning of symbols, starting from scratch and gradually building up a vocabulary, one symbol at a time. As Rumbaugh and Savage-Rumbaugh (1994) point out, this is clearly *not* how children usually acquire language; so perhaps any comparison between children and chimps is simply invalid and tells us very little about the fundamental question: is language unique to human beings?

Matata (born in the wild and introduced to the research aged five) was the first bonobo involved in Savage-Rumbaugh's alternative to production-based training (starting in 1981). Instead of ASL, Savage-Rumbaugh used an extensive 'lexigram', a matrix of 256 geometrical shapes and symbols, on a board, each representing verbs and nouns. Whenever a symbol is touched, the English sentence is simultaneously spoken. Matata was a slow learner, but her six-month-old 'kidnapped' son, Kanzi, spontaneously learned whatever symbols Matata knew. This stimulated an even greater effort to place language learning in a naturalistic context.

By age ten (1991), Kanzi had a vocabulary of 200 words; but what is really impressive is not the number of words, but their apparent meaning for him and his grasp of certain grammatical rules and complexities of spoken English. He was the first to demonstrate that *observational exposure* is sufficient to provide for the acquisition of lexical ('lexicon' = dictionary) and vocal symbols. This exposure takes place in the context of routines that form part of the chimps' specially constructed daily life (such as social play, visits to interesting places, structured testing time, nappy changing, bathing, riding in the car, looking at a book, and so on).

Savage-Rumbaugh *et al.* (1993) compared Kanzi's comprehension of human speech with that of a child, Alia, who had also learned to use the keyboard. When tested on over 400 novel sentences (which required them to perform some rather unusual actions, or referred to unpredictable places or situations), Kanzi scored 74 per cent correct, and Alia (aged two and a half) 65 per cent.

Clearly, Kanzi demonstrated language comprehension as well as production, without formal training; he had simply responded to the communication going on around him. As with a child, his responses were not pure imitation, but showed an understanding of the use of symbols. Control chimps (raised without exposure to the lexigram) failed to develop any understanding of speech, despite later exposure; this suggests a *critical period* in chimps for language acquisition (Clamp and Russell, 1998).

Savage-Rumbaugh believes that there is only a *quantitative* difference between humans' and chimps' grasp of language (one of degree only).

Applications and implications

When Washoe was five years old, she was sent away with Roger and Deborah Fouts to a primate station (she had grown large and potentially dangerous). The Gardners next saw her 11 years later: when they unexpectedly entered the room Washoe was in, she signed their name, then 'Come, Mrs G', led her to an adjoining room and began to play a game with her which she had not been observed to play since she had left the Gardners' home (Singer, 1993).

Observations like this, as well as supporting the argument that non-humans really are capable of language, also raise some important *ethical* questions:

● How justifiable is the whole attempt to study language in non-humans, whether through production-based or more naturalistic methods, since, either way, they are removed from their natural habitat in which they do not spontaneously use language? (The Gardners state that newborn laboratory chimps are very scarce, and Washoe was a 'wild-caught infant'. See **Exercises**.)

● What happens to the chimps (and other non-humans) when they have served their purpose as experimental subjects?

EXERCISES

1   **Explain the difference between language and communication.**

2   **What does 'anthropomorphize' mean? (See** Methodological issues**.)**

3   **In the** Theoretical issues **section, comparisons have been made between children and chimps. Can you identify some important *differences* between Washoe and children acquiring language under normal circumstances?**

4   **Can you think of a more valid comparison group for the 'experimental group chimps' than 'normal children'?**

5   **Does it matter that different studies have used different training methods involving different kinds of language?**

6   **How reliable were the reports of Washoe's acquisition of new signs? Were the criteria strict enough?**

7   **Is there anything ethically wrong with the way Washoe was 'acquired' for the study? What do you think about the very attempt to teach her something that is 'unnatural' for a chimp?**

4 Pictorial perception and culture

Deregowski, J.B. (1972)

Scientific American, 227: 82–8

BACKGROUND AND CONTEXT

A major advantage of *cross-cultural studies* is that they act as a buffer against generalizing from a comparatively small sample of the Earth's population (Price-Williams, 1966). Unless we study a particular process in *different* cultures, we cannot be sure what the contributory influences on that process are, especially heredity and environment. If we find consistent differences between different cultural groups, then unless we have good, independent reasons for believing these differences are biologically caused, we must attribute them to environmental factors (whatever these may be).

But what exactly do we mean by 'culture'? According to Segall *et al.* (1990):

> Those social stimuli that are the products of the behaviour of other people essentially constitute culture. Briefly, we employ culture – as did Herskovits (1948) – to mean 'the man-made part of the environment'. These products can be material objects, ideas, or institutions. They are ubiquitous; it is rare (perhaps even impossible) for any human being ever to behave without responding to some aspect of culture.

Relating this to perception, cross-cultural studies enable us to discover to what extent perceiving is structured by the nervous system (and so common to all human beings) and to what extent by experience. These factors are emphasized, respectively, by nativists and empiricists (see Gross, 2005).

A common method is to present members of different cultural groups with *visual illusions* (such as the Müller-Lyer and horizontal-vertical). The pioneering study by the Cambridge Anthropological Expedition to the Torres Straits (Rivers, 1901) found that, compared with English adults and children, the Murray Islanders were less prone to the Müller-Lyer, but the horizontal-vertical was *more* marked among the Murray Island men, and *very* marked in children. Rivers attributed these findings to some physiological or, at least, some simple and primitive psychological condition (Price-Williams, 1966).

A later and more extensive study (Segall *et al.*, 1963) presented illusions to samples of non-European children and adults, mainly African, but also from the Philippines. Their findings for the Müller-Lyer largely replicated those of Rivers (when all the Europeans were compared with all the non-Europeans). But the horizontal-vertical had a different cultural distribution: the Batoro and Bayankole peoples of Africa (who both live in high, open country) proved the most susceptible, while the Bete (who live in a jungle environment) were the least susceptible. Europeans and Zulus fell somewhere in between.

One influential explanation of such cultural differences is Segall *et al.*'s (1963) *carpentered-world hypothesis* (CWH). According to the CWH, the visual world of Western culture is largely man-made, consisting of straight lines, and in which there is a bias towards interpreting acute and obtuse angles as right angles extended in space. Since we tend to interpret illusion figures (which are two-dimensional/2-D drawings) in terms of our past experience, we 'add' the third dimension (depth), which is not actually present in the drawing. This misleads us as to the true nature of the stimulus, resulting in what we call an illusion.

According to Berry *et al.* (1992), 'If the hypothesis is correct, people in industrial urban environments should be more susceptible to illusions such as the Müller-Lyer'. However, a number of studies failed to support the CWH (e.g. Mundy-Castle and Nelson, 1962; Gregor and McPherson, 1965; Jahoda, 1966). As a result, psychologists began to move away from environmental (or ecological) explanations of cultural differences towards considering 2-D pictures as cultural products in their own right. The *interpretation of pictures* came to be seen as an acquired skill of considerable complexity.

AIM AND NATURE

● METHOD/DESIGN

The aim of Deregowski's article was to present a summary of some of the findings from studies of pictorial perception in different cultural groups, including his own and that of others (e.g. Hudson, 1960, 1962). It is not always obvious where Deregowski is referring to his own research (and that of his co-researchers) rather than someone else's, and it is only through reading other sources (e.g. Serpell, 1976) that this becomes clear.

The overall nature of the studies discussed is *cross-cultural*: a comparison is made between the interpretation of 2-D pictures by members of Western cultures (unspecified) and various African countries (e.g. Zambia). However, the method used to actually make these comparisons is a form of experiment, in which the *independent variable* is either the participant's nationality or the characteristic of being a 2-D or 3-D perceiver (based on, say, Hudson's picture tests).

In either case, the investigator is, of course, unable to manipulate the independent variable: it is a characteristic or ability the participant already possesses and is selected accordingly. This method is sometimes called *ex post facto* experimentation (see Coolican, 2004). (Note that cross-cultural studies as such are *not* a method of collecting data, but an overall *approach* to the study of human behaviour. Exactly how data are collected will depend on the purpose of the study, the age of the participants, the kind of behaviour under investigation, and so on; experiments, observation, psychometric testing or some combination of methods may be used.)

● RESULTS

Some of the earliest evidence regarding the way pictorial information is interpreted cross-culturally came from missionaries, explorers and anthropologists working with members of remote, illiterate peoples. For example, Mrs Donald Fraser, who taught health care to Africans in the 1920s, described an African woman slowly discovering that a picture she was looking at portrayed a human head in profile:

> *She discovered in turn the nose, the mouth, the eye, but where was the other eye? I tried by turning my profile to explain why she could only see one eye but she hopped round to my other side to point out that I possessed a second eye which the other lacked.*

But there were also accounts of vivid and instant recognition of animals in pictures, so the evidence from these unsystematic observations is inconclusive. However, examples like those of Mrs Fraser suggest that some form of learning is required to recognize pictures. Yet it has been shown that an unsophisticated African adult from a remote village is unlikely to choose the wrong toy animal when asked to match the toy to a picture of, say, a lion. But given a photograph of a kangaroo, s/he is unlikely to choose at random from the toys. This suggests that even people from cultures where pictorial material is uncommon will recognize items in pictures, provided that the pictures portray *familiar* objects.

Conventions for depicting the spatial arrangement of three-dimensional/3-D objects in a flat (2-D) picture can also make perception difficult. These conventions provide depth cues which tell the observer that the objects are not all the same distance from him/her. Inability to interpret such cues inevitably creates misunderstanding of the meaning of the picture as a whole. Hudson came across this difficulty when testing South African Bantu workers, and this led him to construct a pictorial perception test, comprising a series of pictures, such as those shown in Figure 4.1.

AIM AND NATURE

Figure 4.1. Pictorial depth perception is tested by showing subjects a picture such as the illustration on the left. A correct interpretation is that the hunter is trying to spear the antelope, which is nearer to him than the elephant. An incorrect interpretation is that the elephant is nearer and is about to be speared. The picture contains two depth cues: overlapping objects and known size of objects. The illustration on the right depicts the man, elephant and antelope in true size ratios when all are the same distance from the observer.

These pictures contain various combinations of three pictorial depth cues:

● familiar size;

● overlap (superimposition);

● linear perspective.

Hudson's test has been used in many parts of Africa, with participants drawn from a variety of tribal and linguistic groups. Participants were shown one picture at a time and asked to name all the objects in the picture in order to determine whether or not they were recognized correctly. Then they were asked about the relationship between the objects: What is the man doing? What is closer to the man?

Those who gave the 'correct' answers (i.e. took account of the depth cues) were classified as having 3-D perception; otherwise, they were said to have 2-D perception. The results from African tribal groups were unequivocal: both children and adults found it difficult to perceive depth in the pictures, and this seemed to apply through most educational and social levels.

Further testing showed that these results were not simply a reflection of the particular pictures used by Hudson. Primary schoolboys and unskilled workers in Zambia were shown a drawing of two squares, one behind the other and connected by a single rod. They were also given sticks and modelling clay and asked to build a model of what they saw. If Hudson's test is valid, the 2-D perceivers should have built flat models of the squares, while 3-D perceivers should have built a cube-like object. A few of the 3-D perceivers made flat models, while a substantial number of the 2-D perceivers built 3-D models. This suggests that Hudson's pictures, although more demanding than the construction task, appear to measure the same variable.

A group of Zambian primary school children were classified as 3-D or 2-D perceivers based on the construction task. As predicted, the 3-D perceivers spent longer than the 2-D perceivers looking at the *two-pronged trident* shown in Figure 4.2, before trying to copy it; they also spent more time looking at it than they did a control trident (with three simple prongs). The 2-D perceivers spent equal amounts of time looking at both trident figures. (See **Exercises**.)

Do people who find pictures that use linear perspective depth cues difficult to interpret prefer pictures that depict the essential characteristics of an object, even if all those characteristics cannot be seen from a single viewpoint? Again, Hudson was the first to carry out systematic cross-cultural studies which tried to answer this question. He showed African children and adults pictures of an elephant: one view was like a photograph seen from above (perspective drawing); the other was a top view of an elephant, with its legs unnaturally split to the sides (split drawing) (see Figure 4.3). With one exception (who said the elephant was jumping about dangerously), all the participants preferred the split-drawing.

Other studies have shown that preference for split drawings also applies to geometric representations. Unskilled Zambian workers were shown a wire model and asked to make a drawing of it; most drew a flat figure of the split type. They also preferred the split drawing when shown the model and asked to choose between this and a perspective drawing. When they were asked to choose the appropriate wire model after looking at a drawing, only a few chose the 3-D model after looking at the split drawing; most chose a flat wire model that resembled the drawing.

Although preference for split drawings has only recently been studied systematically, indications of such a preference have been apparent for a long time in the artistic styles of certain cultures, such as the Indians of the north-western coast of North America. Other examples are rock paintings in the caves of the Sahara, and primitive art found in Siberia and New Zealand. The style is universal, being found in children's drawings in all cultures, including those where the style is considered 'wrong' by adults.

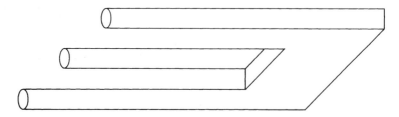

Figure 4.2. Ambiguous trident is confusing to observers who attempt to see it as a three-dimensional object. Two-dimensional perceivers see the pattern as being flat, and are not confused.

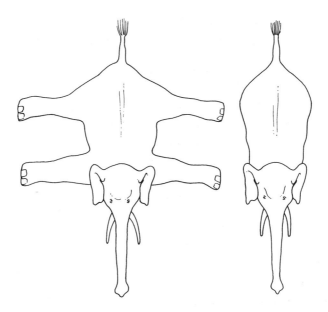

Figure 4.3. The split-elephant drawing (left) was generally preferred by African children and adults to the top-view perspective drawing (right). One person, however, did not like the split drawing because he thought the elephant was jumping around in a dangerous manner.

Figure 4.4. This stylized bear rendered by the Tsimshian Indians on the Pacific coast of British Columbia is an example of a split drawing developed to a high artistic level. According to anthropologist Franz Boas, such drawings are ornamental, and are not intended to convey what an object looks like. The elements represent specific characteristics of the object.

AIM AND NATURE

● CONCLUSIONS

If we accept that certain perceptual processes can be found in all human beings, then based on the evidence above, it can be concluded that in all societies, children have an aesthetic preference for split drawings. But in most societies, this preference is suppressed, because the drawings do not convey information about the depicted objects as accurately as perspective drawings do. Aesthetic preference is sacrificed on the altar of efficient communication.

In some societies, however, the split drawing has been developed to a high artistic level; either they are not regarded as a means of communication about objects, or the drawings incorporate cues/symbolic elements that compensate for this lack of communication value and enable the viewer to interpret the artist's intention. But people from outside these societies find it hard to understand this kind of stylized art. Perhaps the basic difficulty involves the observer's inability to integrate all the picture's elements into a coherent whole. However we try to explain them, we cannot deny the significant differences in how pictures are interpreted between cultures.

EVALUATION

Methodological issues

(Before reading on, try to identify *pictorial depth cues* which are missing from the Hudson pictures. What about non-pictorial depth cues? See **Exercises**.)

One of the things the experienced picture perceiver has learned is the Western artist's use of *relative size* to represent distance. So, in Hudson's pictures, a major cue to the relationship between the man, the elephant and the antelope is their relative size against the background knowledge of their normal sizes (what Deregowski calls 'familiar size'). Hudson also uses the cues of *overlap* (or *superimposition*) and *linear perspective*. For example, in one drawing, the elephant and a tree were shown near the apex of a pair of converging straight lines representing a road. Since the laws of perspective were a late discovery in European art (Gombrich, 1960), and the assumption of parallel edges to a road is promoted by a 'carpentered' environment, it is not too surprising that African children seldom understand this cue. Hudson (1960) found overlap (if noticed) to be the most effective of his three cues – confirmed by Kilbride *et al.* (1968) with a sample of Ugandan schoolchildren.

Also, there is a contradiction between these depth cues and others in the real world, namely *binocular disparity* and *motion parallax*, both of which are missing from Hudson's pictures (and, indeed, from *all* pictures). Also missing is *gradient of density* (or *texture gradient*). Gibson (1950) and Wohlwill (1965) found all these to be more important as depth cues in pictures than in 3-D displays for Western participants over a wide age range.

Serpell (1976) refers to an unpublished report (by Kingsley *et al.*), in which an artist redrew one of Hudson's pictures, adding pebbles on the road and grass in open terrain; each surface had a gradient of density, while everything else remained unchanged. Under these conditions, 12-year-old Zambian children gave 64 per cent 3-D answers, compared with 54 per cent on Hudson's original. When colour and haze around distant hills were added, the figure rose to 76 per cent.

Berry *et al.* (1992) point out that texture gradient is a powerful depth cue in photographs, but is hardly ever used in stimulus material in cross-cultural studies. To the first-time observer, therefore, these pictures may display unusual qualities. Another depth cue missing from Hudson's pictures is *elevation* (or *height in the horizontal plane*: the position of a figure higher or lower in the picture). McGurk and Jahoda (1972, in Berry *et al.*, 1992) used a test in which elevation was the crucial cue. Using non-verbal responses, participants were asked to place models of people on a response board in similar positions to those occupied by the figures in the stimulus pictures. Using this method, even four-year-olds from Ghana, Hong Kong and Zimbabwe showed evidence of depth perception. All this points to the original Hudson pictures making the perception of depth difficult for non-Western participants.

Theoretical issues and other relevant research

In light of the criticisms made above of Hudson's pictures, perhaps cultural differences can be attributed not so much to the ability to identify 2-D pictorial representations of the real, 3-D world, but to the conditions under which the recognition of objects in pictures is made. Specifically:

● Do the studies Deregowski describes make it difficult for the African participants to give 'correct' responses? Is learning to 'read' pictures as necessary as it appears to be?

● Could it be that the drawings used by Hudson emphasize certain depth cues while ignoring others, thereby putting non-Western perceivers at a double disadvantage? (This has been dealt with in **Methodological issues** above.)

● Is it also possible that what is taken as a difference in perception is really a matter of stylistic preference? (See **Applications and implications** below.)

Regarding the first point, Deregowski *et al.* (1972) studied the Me'en tribe of Ethiopia, living in a remote area and still largely unaffected by Western culture. Members of the tribe were shown drawings of 5cm-high animals, and they responded by feeling, smelling, tasting or rustling the paper, showing no interest in the visual content of the picture itself.

However, when the unfamiliar paper was replaced by 30cm-high pictures painted on (familiar) cloth, they responded to the drawing of the animal. Without exception, despite almost certainly never having seen a picture before, seven out of ten correctly identified the first cloth picture as a buck, and ten out of ten correctly identified the second as a leopard. As Serpell (1976) says:

> Given a sufficiently salient stimulus, with distracting cues removed such as the novelty of paper or the distinct white band of the border, immediate recognition may be possible simply by stimulus generalization, one of the most basic characteristics of learning.

In some cases, recognition seems to have been built up gradually, by helping the participant to trace the outline of the animal with a finger. Deregowski *et al.* (1972) note the similarity in this aspect of their participants' verbal responses to those of young US children in a task presenting increasingly clear images of objects, starting with a completely blurred image (Potter, 1966).

Another way of simplifying the task is to ask participants to identify an object without them having to name it. Deregowski (1968) gave a recognition task to boys and men in a 'relatively pictureless' Bisa community (a region of Zambia remote from main roads). They had to select from an array of 18 model animals the one depicted in a black-and-white photo. Six were commonly seen in the area, while the rest were very exotic. The boys were better at finding the strange animals than the men were (they had received more schooling), but the men (mainly hunters) were better with familiar animals. Under optimal conditions, pictures do seem to be recognizable without any prior learning. Unlike words, most pictures are not entirely arbitrary representations of the real world; their arbitrariness 'lies in what features they choose to stress and what features to leave out and it is these conventions governing this choice which the experienced picture perceiver must learn' (Serpell, 1976).

Applications and implications

Much of the research seems to imply a belief that the Western style of pictorial art represents the real world in an objectively correct fashion: by implication, the participant who does not understand it is 'deficient' in some way. But since 'artistic excellence' is not identical to 'photographic accuracy', Gombrich (1960, in Serpell, 1976) asks if it may be possible that people in different cultures 'reject' Western art forms on *aesthetic* grounds and that all the research has mistakenly described a stylistic preference as a difference in perception.

Hudson (1962) and Deregowski (1969, 1970) found that African people with limited Western education slightly preferred unfolded, split, developed or chain-type drawings (as in the left-hand elephant: see Figure 4.3) to *orthogonal* or perspective drawings (as in the right-hand elephant). This is often because the perspective drawing fails to show some of the important features (literally, in the case of the African woman shown the photograph by Mrs Fraser, above).

The importance of artistic convention increases the more symbolic and abstract the art is: the convention is part of the fund of common experience shared by artist and audience. Duncan *et al.* (1973) point out that the small lines used by cartoonists to imply motion are the least understood of all the pictorial conventions which have been shown to rural African schoolchildren; where the artist had drawn a boy's head in three different positions above the same trunk to indicate that the head was turning round, half the children thought he was deformed! Similarly, Western observers require guidance from an anthropologist to understand the art forms of American Indians (Boas, 1927, in Serpell, 1976) or Nuba personal art in the Sudan (Faris, 1972, in Serpell, 1976).

Serpell and Deregowski (1980) describe picture perception as a set of *skills*, which includes the ability to treat pictures as representations of real space (the Me'en had some initial difficulty with this), and interpreting impoverished or ambiguous cues. Berry *et al.* (1992) ask if these skills might be organized hierarchically in some way, ranging from general perceptual phenomena to knowledge of specific symbols and conventions.

Based on their review of the evidence concerning susceptibility to visual illusions, Segall *et al.* (1999) conclude by stating:

> *people perceive in ways that are shaped by the inferences they have learned to make in order to function most effectively in the particular ecological settings in which they live ... we learn to perceive in the ways that we need to perceive. In that sense, environment and culture shape our perceptual habits.*

EXERCISES

1 (a) According to Gregory (1983), what kind of illusion is the two-pronged trident?

   (b) Explain why the 3-D perceivers spent longer looking at the two-pronged trident than the control trident, and why the 2-D perceivers spent equal amounts of time looking at each figure.

2 Hudson's pictures include the depth cues of familiar size, overlap (superimposition) and linear perspective. Deregowski also refers to gradient of density (texture gradient). Serpell says that binocular (retinal) disparity and motion parallax are missing. Briefly explain what is meant by each of these.

3 Briefly describe *three* other depth cues.

4 Most depth cues are both *pictorial* and *monocular*. What do you understand by these terms?

5 In Hudson's study, how was 3-D perception operationalized?

6 (a) How was the validity of Hudson's test of 3-D perception established?

   (b) What kind of validity does this involve?

7 What would be the (directional) hypothesis which predicts that Hudson's test is valid?

5 Levels of processing: A framework for memory research

Craik, F.I.M. and Lockhart, R.S. (1972)

Journal of Verbal Learning and Verbal Behaviour, 11: 671–84

BACKGROUND AND CONTEXT

The view that memory comprises a number of separate stores, between which information passes, has a long history. It was James (1890) who originally distinguished between *primary memory* and *secondary memory* (corresponding to short- and long-term memory, respectively), although Ebbinghaus (1885), one of the pioneers of memory research, would have accepted such a distinction.

Hebb (1949), Broadbent (1958), and Waugh and Norman (1965) have also made the distinction. But probably the most discussed and influential distinction between short-term memory (STM) and long-term memory (LTM) is Atkinson and Shiffrin's, made within their *multi-store model* (MSM, or 'dual memory' theory, 1968, 1971), so named because of its emphasis on these two types of memory. This became – and in many ways remains – an extremely influential model of memory, generating a huge amount of empirical research.

Note that in Table 5.1 (page 51), Craik and Lockhart make reference to 'short-term store' (STS) and 'long-term store' (LTS); these refer to the two relevant storage *systems* (as used in the name of Atkinson and Shiffrin's model), while STM and LTM refer to *experimental situations.*

In the model, STS and LTS are referred to as permanent *structural components* of the memory system, and represent intrinsic (fixed) features of the human information-processing system. The memory system also comprises relatively transient processes (*control processes*), a major example being *rehearsal.* This serves two main functions:

● It acts as a buffer between sensory memory (a briefly held literal copy of sensory information) and LTS, by maintaining incoming information within STS.

● It transfers information to LTS (see Table 5.1, page 51).

The MSM emphasizes the sequence of stages that information passes through as it moves from one structural component to another while being processed.

AIM AND NATURE

This is a *review paper*, which summarizes and discusses theory and research conducted by other investigators. Craik and Lockhart's aims were to:

1   examine the reasons for proposing multi-store models (the case in favour), that is, review the evidence *for* multi-store models;

2   question their adequacy (the case against);

3   propose an alternative framework in terms of levels of processing (LOP) – this offers a new way of interpreting existing data and provides a heuristic framework for further research. (See **Exercises**.)

● MULTI-STORE MODELS

The case in favour

When humans are viewed as information processors (Miller, 1956; Broadbent, 1958), it seems necessary to propose holding mechanisms or memory stores at various points in the system. For example, based on his dichotic listening experiments, Broadbent (1958) proposed that information must be held temporarily before entering the limited-capacity processing channel: perceived items could be retained in the short term by recycling them, before being transferred into and retained in a more permanent LTS.

Broadbent's ideas were extended by Waugh and Norman (1965), and Atkinson and Shiffrin (1968), and it became widely accepted that memory can be understood in terms of three levels of storage: sensory, STS and LTS. (See **Background and context** above.)

Craik and Lockhart summarize the evidence for the differences between these three levels of storage in Table 5.1. Much of this evidence comes from studies by the researchers cited above.

The case against

Some criticisms were general (e.g. Melton, 1963), while others objected to specific aspects; for example, Tulving and Patterson (1968, in Craik and Lockhart) argued against the idea of information being transferred from one store to another, while Shallice and Warrington (1970) found evidence that information could enter LTS

Table 5.1

Commonly accepted differences between the three stages of verbal memory

Feature	Sensory registers	Short-term store	Long-term store
Entry of information	Pre-attentive (requires no attention)	Requires attention	Rehearsal
Maintenance of information	Not possible	Continued attention; rehearsal	Repetition; organization
Format of information	Literal copy of input	Phonemic; probably visual; possibly semantic	Largely semantic; some auditory and visual
Capacity	Large	Small	No known limit
Information loss	Decay	Displacement; possibly decay	Possibly no loss; loss of accessibility or discriminability by interference
Trace duration	½ to 2 seconds	Up to 30 seconds	Minutes to years
Retrieval	Readout	Probably automatic; in consciousness; temporal/phonemic cues	Retrieval cues; items possibly search process

without 'passing through' STS first. Craik and Lockhart took exception to the criteria for distinguishing between STS and LTS as shown in Table 5.1.

Capacity

Exactly what is meant by the term 'limited capacity' is unclear: does the limitation refer to processing capacity, storage capacity or some interaction between the two? In terms of the *computer analogy* on which the MSM is based, does the limitation refer to the storage capacity of a memory register or to the rate at which the processor can perform certain operations? (See **Exercises**.) Broadbent's (1958) limited-capacity channel seems to imply the latter, while later models (e.g. Waugh and Norman 1965) appear to imply the former; both are present in Miller's (1956) interpretation (but the relationship between them is not spelled out).

As far as the storage capacity of STS is concerned, different researchers have found evidence for different values: for example, Baddeley (1970) put it at two to four words; memory span is given as typically five to nine items (depending on whether the items are words, letters or digits); and if the words in a span list form a sentence, young participants can accurately recall strings of up to 20 words

(Craik and Masani, 1969). So, if capacity is a critical feature of STS operation, the MSM must account for this very wide range of capacity estimates.

The most widely accepted explanation is that capacity is limited in terms of chunks and that the number of items that can be chunked depends on how meaningful the material is. But how can a chunk be defined independently of its effects on memory?

According to Craik and Lockhart, STS's limited *storage* capacity is a direct consequence of its limited *processing* capacity.

Coding

Based on studies with verbal material, Conrad (1964) and Baddeley (1966) concluded that information in STS is coded acoustically, while in LTS coding is predominantly semantic. However, STS coding can be either acoustic or articulatory (e.g. Levy, 1971); even with verbal material, STS can sometimes be visual (Kroll *et al.*, 1970, in Craik and Lockhart).

When traditional procedures are used for STM, STS seems incapable of coding information semantically (Kintsch and Buschke, 1969; Craik and Levy, 1970). But Schulman (1970, 1972) believes it can do so.

Coding no longer seems to be a satisfactory basis for distinguishing between STS and LTS. Although it could be argued that STS is flexible, this removes an important basis for distinguishing one from the other.

Forgetting characteristics

If this is to be used as a way of distinguishing between STS and LTS, there must be consistency across different designs and experimental conditions. But this does not appear to be the case. For example, in paired-associate-learning, STS remembering extends to 20 intervening items, while in free-recall and probe experiments (Waugh and Norman, 1965), STS information is lost much faster. Different researchers have reported that the memory trace for visual stimuli lasts for between 1 and 25 seconds.

Given that we recognize pictures, faces, melodies and voices after long periods of time, we clearly have LTM for relatively literal non-verbal information. This makes it difficult to draw a line between 'sensory memory' and 'representational' or 'pictorial' memory.

Whatever the limitations of the MSM, there are some basic findings that any model must accommodate; these include the different ways in which information is encoded, the different lengths of time that differently encoded information lasts in memory, and the limited capacity at some points in the memory system.

AIM AND NATURE

● LEVELS OF PROCESSING

Many theorists now agree that perception involves the rapid analysis of stimuli at several different levels or stages (Selfridge and Neisser, 1960; Treisman, 1964). Earlier stages are concerned with analysing the physical or sensory features (e.g. lines, angles, brightness, pitch and loudness); later stages match the input against stored abstractions from past learning (i.e. pattern recognition and the extraction of meaning).

This idea of a series or hierarchy of processing stages is often referred to as 'depth of processing', where greater 'depth' implies a greater degree of semantic or cognitive analysis. After the stimulus has been recognized, it may be further processed through elaboration; for example, a word may trigger stored associations or images based on past experience of the word. Such 'elaboration coding' (Tulving and Madigan, 1970) is not limited to verbal material, but also applies to sounds, sights, smells, and so on.

The coding characteristics and persistence of the memory trace are by-products of perceptual processing (Morton, 1970). Specifically, trace persistence (how long the memory lasts) is a function of depth of analysis, with deeper levels associated with more elaborate, longer-lasting and stronger traces.

Highly familiar, meaningful stimuli are, by definition, compatible with existing cognitive structures. So, pictures and sentences will be processed to a deep level more quickly than less meaningful material, and will be retained. Retention is a function of depth, not speed of analysis; how deeply something is processed is determined by various factors (such as the amount of attention given to a stimulus, and the processing time available).

Although different levels may be grouped into stages (e.g. sensory analyses, pattern recognition, stimulus elaboration), Craik and Lockhart prefer to think of them as a continuum. Stimuli can also be retained in memory through recirculating information at one level ('keeping the items in consciousness'/'holding the items in the rehearsal buffer'/'retention of the items in primary memory').

Craik and Lockhart distinguish between two kinds of repetitive processing:

● Type I (as when you verbally rehearse a telephone number to keep it 'in mind' – say it out loud – before calling the number), which demonstrates primary memory;

● Type II, which involves deeper analysis.

While Type I merely prolongs an item's high accessibility without leading to a more permanent memory trace, Type II should improve memory performance.

AIM AND NATURE

● EXISTING DATA RE-EXAMINED

Incidental learning

The LOP approach is interested in systematically studying retention following different orienting tasks given within the *incidental learning* paradigm (i.e. where participants are not told explicitly that they need to remember the material and so do not expect to be tested on it). Under incidental learning conditions, the experimenter has control over the processing that participants use (the orienting task), which is missing when participants are merely instructed to learn (*intentional learning*); in the latter, they use unknown coding strategies (the experimenter does not know *how* they are learning).

Tresselt and Mayzner (1960, in Craik and Lockhart) tested free recall after incidental learning under three different orienting tasks: crossing out vowels, copying the words and judging how far the word illustrated the concept of 'economic'. Four times as many words were recalled under the last condition compared with the first, and twice as many compared with the second. Similar results were found by several other studies, including Hyde and Jenkins (1969) and Johnston and Jenkins (1971, in Craik and Lockhart), supporting the general conclusion that memory performance is a positive function of the LOP required by the orienting task. However, beyond a certain point, the effectiveness of a particular LOP depends on how the remembering is tested (e.g. free recall or recognition). (See **Subsequent research** below.)

Selective attention and sensory storage

Moray (1959) showed that words presented to the non-attended channel in a dichotic listening test were not recognized in a later memory test, and Neisser (1964) found that non-target items in a visual search task left no recognizable trace. So, if stimuli are only partially analysed, or processed only superficially, they do not stay in memory very long. Treisman (1964) played the same prose passage to both ears dichotically, but staggered in time, with the unattended ear leading: the lag had to be reduced to 1.5 seconds before participants realized that the messages were identical. When the attended (shadowed) ear led, a mean lag of 4.5 seconds would still allow this recognition to occur. So even though participants were not trying to remember the material in either case, the extra processing required by the shadowing was sufficient to treble the durability of the memory trace.

Many studies of sensory memory are also consistent with the LOP approach.

The SLS/LTS distinction

According to the LOP approach, the proposed limited-capacity holding mechanism (Miller, 1956; Broadbent, 1958) is taken to be a flexible central processor that can be used at one of several levels in one of several coding dimensions; it can only deal with a limited number of items at once (items are kept in consciousness/ primary memory (PM) by rehearing them at a fixed level of processing). At deeper levels, we can make greater use of learned cognitive structures, making the items more complex and semantic.

The depth of PM will depend on both the usefulness of continuing to process at that level and how easily the material can be processed more deeply. For example, if the participant's task is merely to reproduce a few words, seconds after hearing them, then phonemic analysis will do; but if the words form a meaningful sentence, deeper levels are needed – and longer units can be dealt with. According to Kintsch (1970), PM deals at any level with units or 'chunks' (e.g. objects, a sound, letter, word, idea or image) rather than with 'information' (i.e. collections of attributes).

Craik and Lockhart believe that acoustic errors will predominate only to the extent that analysis has not processed to a semantic level. Much of the data on acoustic confusions in STM is based on material such as letters and digits which have relatively little semantic content. So the material itself constrains processing to a structural level and, not surprisingly, structural errors result.

The serial position curve

In free recall, the recency effect has been taken to reflect output from STS, and the primacy effect, output from LTS (Glanzer and Cunitz, 1966). According to Atkinson and Shiffrin (1968), initial items receive more rehearsals and so are better registered in LTS. In LOP terms, since participants know they must stop attending to initial items in order to perceive and rehearse later items, they use Type II processing on the early items (deeper semantic processing), while late items can survive on Type I (phonemic processing). Several studies (e.g. Craik, 1972) have shown that it is the type – rather than the amount – of processing which determines recall of the last few items in a list.

Repetition and rehearsal effects

The effects of repetition depend on whether the repeated stimulus is merely processed to the same level or encoded differently as it is repeated. For both audition (Moray, 1959; Norman, 1969) and vision (Turvey, 1967, in Craik and Lockhart), repeating an item only at a sensory level does not improve memory. It has also been shown that repetition without intention to learn does not facilitate learning (Tulving, 1966), which indicates that the MSM's claim that rehearsal both maintains information in STS and transfers it to LTS may not hold.

AIM AND NATURE

● CONCLUDING COMMENTS

If the memory trace is viewed as a by-product of perceptual analysis, then future research will need to specify the consequences for memory of various types of perceptual operations. Since deeper analysis will usually involve longer processing time, it is crucial to disentangle such variables as study time and amount of effort from depth.

The LOP approach is *not* a theory of memory, but a conceptual framework within which memory research might proceed. The MSM has often been taken too literally, while the LOP approach (as outlined here) is speculative and incomplete: it looks at memory purely from the input or encoding end, and no attempt has been made to specify either how items are organized or how they are retrieved. LOP provides an appropriate framework within which these processes can be understood.

EVALUATION

Theoretical issues

According to Rutherford (2005), Craik and Lockhart's article had a huge influence on memory research; indeed, the LOP approach changed the nature of psychological accounts of memory. It remained the most influential theoretical approach during the 1970s, but rapidly went out of favour after that (Eysenck, 1984, 1986). While most psychologists believe it is a gross oversimplification, we should bear in mind Craik and Lockhart's own concluding comment: LOP is *not* a theory of memory, but a *heuristic framework* for memory research. Despite this, many people regarded it as a theory (for example, it allows several specific predictions to be made) and, as such, it became the target for criticism (Eysenck and Keane, 2000; Parkin, 2000: see below).

LOP is basically concerned with the role of encoding in learning, and the relationship between how material is processed and the probability that it will subsequently be remembered. As such, it is primarily a theory of LTS (Baddeley, 1999). Craik and Lockhart did not reject the STS/LTS distinction, but they argued that it failed to reveal anything new about human memory. While the MSM begins with structural components, LOP begins with encoding processes; in fact, LOP assumes a PM/STS system that actually does the coding, but details of this are left so unspecified that the 'levels' approach has often, mistakenly, been taken to represent a unitary approach to memory (i.e. there is no STS/LTS distinction) (Baddeley, 1999).

Craik and Tulving (1975) carried out a series of experiments which demonstrated that the deeper the level of processing required by the orienting task, the better the retention. So, for example, being asked:

- 'Is the word in capital letters?' (TABLE/table) represents a *structural/orthographic* level of processing;

- 'Does the word rhyme with wait?' (hate/chicken) represents a *phonetic/phonemic* level;

- 'Is the word a type of food?' (cheese/steel) or 'Would the word fit the sentence: He kicked the ____ into the tree?' (ball/rain) both represent a *semantic* level.

A consistent finding was that, when participants were given an unexpected test of recognition (a test of incidental learning), semantic processing produced the best retention, followed by phonetic, with structural producing the poorest.

However, Lockhart and Craik (1990) accept that much of their original LOP model was oversimplified. For example:

- Originally, Craik and Lockhart saw processing as under the control of a *central processor*, with limited but flexible capacity to deal with new information. Retention depended on how the central processor was used during learning (deeper levels produce better retention). Embodied in this idea was the *coordinality assumption*, according to which the nature of the processing undertaken in response to an orienting task was directly related to the overt demands of the task. So, if you were asked whether 'TABLE' was in upper- or lower-case letters, your processing was taken to be *restricted* to the structural or orthographic level.

  In its extreme form, this assumption is patently wrong: there is abundant evidence that when we look at a word, we are automatically aware of its *meaning* (Parkin, 2000). The classic demonstration of this is the *Stroop effect* (see **Exercises**), although there is no definitive explanation of the Stroop effect: 'what we can conclude is that human beings are not able to orient their attention precisely to task demands and that irrelevant information, particularly meaning, is processed regardless of instructions' (Parkin, 1993).

  Because of phenomena like Stroop, Craik and Tulving (1975) proposed that any stimulus first undergoes a *minimal core encoding*, which includes a degree of semantic analysis, followed by consciously directed processing appropriate to the task's demands. The latter are *effortful* (i.e. they depend on some conscious effort).

- The original model implied that processing takes place in an ordered sequence, from shallow through to deeper. But instead of this continuum, the levels are seen as constituting separate 'domains'. This reflected the logical point that it is not possible to pass gradually from, say, structural to phonetic levels, because they contain *qualitatively* different dimensions of information-processing which do not overlap in any way (Parkin, 1993).

Methodological issues

Probably the most serious problem with LOP is the difficulty of measuring or defining depth *independently* of the actual retention score: if 'depth' is defined as 'how many words are remembered', and if 'how many words are remembered' is taken as a measure of 'depth', we are faced with a *circular* definition.

Craik and Tulving (1975) were well aware of this problem and they proposed a solution in the form of *processing time*. Based on their observation that semantic orienting tasks always took longer to perform, they devised a non-semantic task that took longer than a semantic one, and reasoned that if processing time were a valid independent measure of depth, the former should produce the best retention. But it didn't: despite taking *less* time, the semantic task still produced the best results. This was good news for LOP: if the non-semantic task had proved more effective, it would have meant that what matters is simply how long we spend attending to the stimulus (instead of one of LOP's core ideas that memory can be affected by qualitative differences in encoding).

Hyde and Jenkins (1973) proposed a different independent measure of depth in terms of five orienting tasks; these were meant to vary in the amount of processing of meaning involved. As predicted, they found that (a) rating words for pleasantness and (b) estimating the frequency with which the words are used in English would both produce significantly higher retention than other orienting tasks. However, others have challenged their assumption that (a) and (b) both involve thinking of the word's meaning, while (c) deciding the part of speech appropriate to each word (noun/verb/adjective/other) does not. An assumption is all it is and, as we noted above, it is impossible to completely control participants' processing activities.

Parkin (1979, in Parkin, 1993) took up the circularity problem in a series of experiments using *associative priming*. This refers to the observation that if two words are presented one after the other, identification of the second word is enhanced if it is associatively related to the first (e.g. table, chair). Semantic tasks should allow this to occur, because they direct conscious processing into the semantic domain (which is where word association resides). While these experiments suggested a solution to the circularity problem, they have not been followed up (Parkin, 1993).

Subsequent research

Eysenck (1984, 1986) argues that learning and memory are affected by at least four factors:

1   the nature of the task;

2   the kind of stimulus material used;

3   participant characteristics (e.g. idiosyncratic knowledge);

4   the nature of the retention test used to measure memory.

In many LOP experiments, several orienting tasks are used, but only one kind of stimulus material (usually words), one fairly homogeneous set of participants, and one kind of retention test (e.g. Hyde and Jenkins, 1973, used only free recall).

However, there are often significant *interactions* between the four factors, as demonstrated in a study by Morris *et al.* (1977). They predicted that stored information (deep or shallow) will be remembered only to the extent that it is *relevant* to the memory test used. So, deep or semantic information would be of little use if the memory test involved learning a list of words and later selecting other words that rhymed with the stored words; but shallow rhyme information would be very relevant. Participants given a *standard recognition test* (they had to say 'yes' if the words had been presented originally, and 'no' if they hadn't) showed the usual LOP effect (i.e. better recognition). But the reverse was true for those given a *rhyming recognition test* ('yes' to the new words that rhymed with the original targets, and 'no' to those that didn't).

These findings represent an experimental disproof of LOP, specifically the idea that deep processing is *intrinsically* more memorable than shallow processing. They also demonstrate that how memory is tested must be taken into account when we are trying to predict the outcome of any given retention activity. As Parkin (1993, 2000) puts it, different orienting tasks vary in the extent to which they require participants to regard the stimulus *as a word* (e.g. 'Is "tiger" a mammal?' compared with 'Does "tiger" have two syllables?'). But retention tests *always* demand that participants remember *words*. So a semantic orienting task and a retention test are both concerned with the same kind of information (*transfer-appropriate processing*: Morris *et al.*, 1977), while a structural or phonemic task and a retention test are not. This rather deflated the LOP approach (Parkin, 1998).

More recently, attempts have been made to extend and modify (or even replace) the original LOP model, using the concepts of *elaboration* and *distinctiveness* (see Eysenck and Keane, 1995).

Applications and implications

Prior to Craik and Lockhart's article, most accounts of memory emphasized the nature of the structures holding the information to explain memory performance (Rutherford, 2005). Memory theorists paid little attention to the relationship between perception and memory, or to the extent to which flexibility in the learning process could affect retention of the material being learnt. LOP showed the enormous variation in encoding that could occur, and all theorizing about memory now takes this basic observation into account.

Craik and Lockhart's aim that LOP should serve as a framework for memory research has only been partially fulfilled. Baddeley (1997) believes that it has limited theoretical power, and attempts to apply it to memory deficits in elderly and amnesic patients have proved disappointing. However, LOP indirectly stimulated research into *working memory* (see Gross, 2005), although LOP emphasizes factors influencing retrieval from LTM:

> Short-term memory studies became more closely associated with problems of attention, and with the role of short-term memory in other tasks such as reading and mental arithmetic. This led to the concept of a unitary short-term memory being replaced by that of a multi-component working memory. (Baddeley, 1999)

EXERCISES

1   The third of Craik and Lockhart's aims (see Aim and nature) **refers to providing a *heuristic* framework for further research. What is a *heuristic* and how does this differ from an *algorithm*?**

2   **When discussing *capacity* in relation to the case against the MSM, Craik and Lockhart state that the MSM is based on the *computer analogy*. What does this refer to?**

3   **What is the Stroop effect?**

4   **Apart from displacement, what other theories of STM forgetting are there?**

5   **What is meant by 'chunking' (as a way of increasing STM capacity)?**

6   **What kind of retention test is being used in:**

    (a) **essay-based exams?**

    (b) **multiple-choice tests?**

7   **Give two examples of an orienting task used to study LOP.**

8   (a) **What is the difference between *incidental* and *intentional* learning?**

    (b) **Why is it important for participants in LOP experiments to be tested under incidental conditions?**

6 Reconstruction of an automobile destruction: An example of the interaction between language and memory

Loftus, E.E. and Palmer, J.C. (1974)

Journal of Verbal Learning and Verbal Behaviour, 13: 585–9

BACKGROUND AND CONTEXT

In contrast with models of memory based on stimulus-response theory (associationist models), Bartlett (1932) saw memory as involving interpretation and reconstruction of the past. We try to fit past events into existing *schemas* (or *schemata*: our mental models or representations of the world), making them more logical, coherent and generally 'sensible'; this involves drawing inferences or deductions about what *might* or *should* have happened (all part of our 'efforts after meaning'). So, rather than human memory being computer-like (where output matches input), Bartlett saw it as an active attempt to understand – an 'imaginative reconstruction' of experience.

What is now referred to as *schema theory* (e.g. Rumelhart and Norman, 1983) regards what we already know about the world as a major influence on what we remember. The use of past experience to deal with new experience is a fundamental feature of how the human mind works (Cohen, 1993). The knowledge we have stored in our memory is organized as a set of schemas, each relating to a given type of object or event, acquired from past experience. They operate in a top-down direction to help interpret the bottom-up flow of information from the world. New experiences are not just passively copied or recorded into memory; rather, a memory representation is actively constructed by processes that are strongly influenced by schemas (Cohen, 1993).

Schema theory is not just interesting from an academic perspective. When applied to real-life situations such as eyewitness testimony (EWT), these ideas about the reconstructive and interpretative nature of memory assume critical importance. The greater the unreliability (inaccuracy) of human memory, and the greater the importance of EWT in cases of crimes and accidents, the greater the likelihood that people will be wrongly accused and convicted (a false positive error) and that the guilty will not be brought to justice (a false negative error).

Elizabeth Loftus is a pioneer (and still a leading figure) in the field of EWT research, which represents an application of cognitive psychology to real-world, social phenomena. Her basic procedure (paradigm) has been to manipulate the questions that participants are asked about a film or slides of an automobile accident, or a staged crime, in order to see how these can affect what they remember of the incident. This procedure is an attempt to simulate real-world situations, in which witnesses are asked (often very misleading) questions by police and lawyers.

AIM AND NATURE

● HYPOTHESIS

The study was conducted to investigate the influence of the wording of the question used to tap participants' estimates of speed (how fast two cars involved in an accident were travelling) on the actual speed estimate.

Loftus and Palmer define a *leading question* as one that, either by its form or content, suggests to the witness what answer is desired, or leads him/her to the desired answer. So, the leading question constitutes the independent variable, while the speed estimate is the dependent variable.

The study actually comprises two separate, but related, experiments.

Hypothesis 1 (Experiment 1)

There is no *explicit* hypothesis or statement of expected results (as there is for Experiment 2). But by *implication* it was expected that the verbs used to refer to how the two cars touched ('contacted', 'hit', 'bumped', 'collided' or 'smashed') would produce increasingly higher speed estimates (i.e. 'contacted' would produce the *lowest* and 'smashed' the *highest*).

Hypothesis 2 (Experiment 2)

Participants asked about the speed of the cars that 'smashed' would be more likely to say they had seen broken glass than participants who were asked about the cars that 'hit'.

● METHOD/DESIGN

Experiment 1

Forty-five students, divided into five groups, watched seven different films of traffic accidents (the films lasting between 5 and 30 seconds). Following each film, participants were asked a series of specific questions about the accident, the critical question being the one about the speed at which the cars were travelling.

What Loftus and Palmer manipulated was the verb used to refer to how the cars touched. Each of the five groups received the same form of the question ('About how fast were the cars going when they _____?'), but the missing word varied (either 'contacted', 'hit', 'bumped', 'collided' or 'smashed').

The specific verb used in the critical question was the *independent variable*, and the average (mean) speed estimate given in response to this question was the *dependent variable*. The experimental design was *independent groups*.

Experiment 2

One hundred and fifty students, divided into three groups, watched a film of a car accident (lasting just 4 seconds). As in Experiment 1, they were then asked a series of questions, one of which was the critical speed question. But this time, only 'hit' and 'smashed' were used; the third group was not asked about speed at all.

A week later, the participants returned, and without seeing the film again, answered a series of questions about the accident. This time, the critical question was 'Did you see any broken glass?', and participants had to answer 'yes' or 'no' (the *dependent variable*).

There was *no* broken glass in the accident.

● RESULTS/FINDINGS

Experiment 1

Table 6.1 shows the speed estimates for the various verbs.

The mean speed estimates are significantly different from each other and are consistent with Hypothesis 1.

AIM AND NATURE

Table 6.1

Speed estimates for the verbs used in Experiment 1

Verb	Mean speed estimates (mph)
smashed	40.8
collided	39.3
bumped	38.1
hit	34.0
contacted	31.8

Experiment 2

Table 6.2

Distribution of 'yes' and 'no' responses to the question: 'Did you see any broken glass?'

Response	Verb condition		
	smashed	hit	control
Yes	16	7	6
No	34	43	44

The important result in Table 6.2 is that the probability of saying 'yes' to the broken glass question is significantly greater when the verb 'smashed' is used than when 'hit' is used. A separate analysis revealed that 'smashed' was not just affecting the speed estimate.

● CONCLUSIONS

The results of Experiments 1 and 2 indicate that the form of a question (in this case, changing a single word) can markedly and systematically affect a witness's answer to the question. This could be a result of either response-bias factors (e.g. 'smashed' biases the participant's response towards a higher estimate), or the verb 'smashed' changes the participant's memory representation of the accident (s/he 'sees' the accident as being more serious than it actually was).

Experiment 2 was designed to test this second interpretation. By testing participants a week after seeing the film of the accident, it was shown that they 'remembered' other details (broken glass) that did not actually occur, but which are consistent with an accident occurring at higher speeds.

EVALUATION

Methodological issues

Cohen (1993) argues that many of the errors found in EWT experiments occur because participants are forced to give 'yes' or 'no' answers to direct questions. In real-life situations, where open-ended questions are used and witnesses can respond with 'don't know' and 'not sure', testimony is often much more accurate.

Several studies have found that the type of questions asked can have a dramatic influence on the accuracy of witness answers (Kebbell and Gilchrist, 2004). People tend to provide the most accurate answers (i.e. where the proportion of correct to incorrect information is greatest) to *open questions* (e.g. 'Describe your attacker'). The more *closed questions* (e.g. 'What colour was his shirt?' and 'Was his shirt red?') can reduce the accuracy, although they can add detail. As a general rule, as questions become increasingly specific, responses become less accurate (Kebbell and Wagstaff, 1999, in Kebbell and Gilchrist, 2004).

Laboratory studies on the accuracy of face recognition (which show very high accuracy, at least for same-race faces) are contradicted by real-world research on EWT: people often do little better than chance when trying to identify an alleged criminal in an identity parade (Fiske and Taylor, 1991).

Theoretical issues

There is a good deal of support for the *reconstructive hypothesis*. (See **Background and context** above.) EWT can easily be distorted, and modified, by information which becomes available *subsequent* to the actual event – even to the extent of 'remembering' things which were not actually seen in the original event. So in Experiment 2, the leading question regarding the type of contact between the cars ('hit' or 'smashed') influenced the degree to which participants 'remembered' seeing the non-existent broken glass.

The question regarding broken glass provides new information, which, Loftus believes, becomes incorporated into the memory, updating it and erasing any of the original information which is inconsistent with it (the *substitution hypothesis*). This subsequent information can be presented either in the form of *leading questions* (as in the Loftus and Palmer study), or through questions which introduce *after-the-fact information* (e.g. Loftus, 1975; see **Subsequent research** below).

According to the idea of *memory as reconstruction*, the memory itself is transformed as it is being retrieved – what was originally encoded changes at the point of recall. Loftus believes that the false, misleading information displaces or transforms the original, accurate information, which is then irretrievably lost.

According to the *coexistence hypothesis*, however, both the original, true version and the false, misleading version of the event are retained in memory. Participants usually give the latter version: this is the more recently presented and so is more accessible. However, if the two versions are inconsistent, it is unlikely that the original memory could, even in principle, be recovered: people would have to believe two contradictory things at the same time.

The Loftus and Palmer study appears to support the substitution hypothesis. If the 'smashed' participants really saw the accident as more serious than the other groups, then they might also 'remember' details (such as broken glass) that were not actually present, but which are consistent with an accident occurring at high speed. The results suggest that the answer to the broken glass question was determined by the earlier question about speed, which had *changed* what was originally encoded when seeing the film.

According to Baddeley (1995), 'the Loftus effect is not due to destruction of the memory trace but is due to interference with its retrieval'. Indeed, some of Loftus's own research has shown that witnesses cannot always be misled so easily. Loftus (1979) found that integration does not occur if the misleading information is 'blatantly incorrect'. In one experiment, participants saw colour slides of a man stealing a red purse from a woman's bag; 98 per cent remembered the colour of the purse correctly. When they later read a description of the event that referred to a brown purse, all but two continued to remember it as red.

In this example, the colour of the purse is the focus of the whole incident – not an incidental detail. Loftus (1991) herself recognized that changes in the original memory probably only happen to a limited extent.

The substitution hypothesis is consistent with schema theory. (See **Background and context** above.) According to Alba and Hasher (1983), the EWT research tends to support schema theory. Cohen (1993) believes that Loftus's misled witnesses are not only integrating prior knowledge from internal schemas about car accidents, and so on, with knowledge derived from recent observed events, but that they are also combining information from two *different external sources*:

● the observed event;

● subsequent verbal information about the event.

Clearly, memories are not simple copies of events, but may sometimes be composites based on different sources of information.

According to Fiske and Taylor (1991), the distinction between *episodic* and *semantic* memory (Tulving, 1972) is useful in understanding EWT. A leading question might refer to things which were not actually present at the scene of the crime (*episodic*), but which would be a perfectly reasonable inference to make in those circumstances (*semantic*, which includes all our schemas and stereotyped beliefs). It is easy to see how a witness could confuse the mention of something in a question with its actual presence at the crime scene, *if that something is commonly found in such situations.*

Subsequent research

According to Garry *et al.* (1994), there are four different kinds of memory distortion studies. First, there are those concerned with the effects of leading questions (e.g. the Loftus and Palmer experiment; Loftus and Zanni, 1975). Loftus and Zanni showed participants a short film of a car accident. Afterwards, some were asked if they had seen 'a' broken headlight, while others were asked if they had seen 'the' broken headlight. The latter were far more likely to say 'yes' than the former. The findings from these and other similar studies are disturbing given the large number of leading, potentially suggestive questions that are asked in cross-examination in real trials (Kebbell and Gilchrist, 2004).

A second type is those in which new items are inserted by suggestion into a previously observed scene (e.g. Loftus, 1975; Loftus and Hoffman, 1989). Loftus showed participants a short film of a car travelling through the countryside. One group was then asked: 'How fast was the white sports car going when it passed the "Stop" sign while travelling along the country road?' (There *was* a stop sign in the film.) A second group was asked: 'How fast was the white sports car going when it passed the barn while travelling along the country road?' (There was *no* barn.) 'The' barn implies that there actually was a barn in the film, which is what makes it misleading. A week later, all the participants were asked 'Did you see a barn?' Only 2.7 per cent of the 'stop sign' group said yes, compared with 17.3 per cent of the 'barn' group.

Third, there are those which manipulate details of an object that appeared in the previous scene (e.g. Belli, 1989).

These three types are to do with distorting a memory, or at least the report of an event which participants *actually witnessed.*

Applications and implications

A fourth type of memory distortion study is that which attempts a much more radical effect: the suggestion of an entire episode that *supposedly happened*, but which in fact did not occur in the participant's past. This amounts to the creation of a completely *false memory.* One example is the 'shopping mall' study (Garry *et al.*, 1994). Fourteen-year-old Chris was convinced by his older brother, Jim, that he had been lost in a shopping mall as a small child. Chris was given summaries of childhood events (three actual events and the false shopping mall incident), and asked to write about each one. Jim repeatedly provided Chris with false details about the shopping mall. Two weeks later, Chris could 'remember' details, such as the appearance of the elderly man who rescued him. When Chris was debriefed, he expressed dismay.

Loftus (1997) refers to a small number of similar studies, involving larger groups of participants, all showing that it is possible to 'implant' false memories. This is related to *false memory syndrome*. (See **Exercises** and Chapter 22.)

In a review of the literature of children's susceptibility to misleading questioning, Gathercole (1998) concluded that 'mere exposure to adults asking you about events that did not take place is clearly sufficient under some circumstances to yield false memories'.

If children really are more susceptible to the effects of false, post-event information, it might be because of their failure at *source-monitoring* (the ability to distinguish between memories from different sources). One practical implication of this is that the incorporation of source-monitoring questions (e.g. Did you see that happen or did somebody tell you that it happened?) into interviews should increase the reliability of children's testimony (Poole and Lindsay, 1995). Fundudis (1997) believes that, despite younger children's greater susceptibility to the effects of suggestion, they do not appear to be subject to false-memory syndrome.

In a review of studies of the older adult eyewitness, Memon *et al.* (2004) conclude that there is no clear evidence to suggest an age-related vulnerability to misinformation. However, older adults tend to recall fewer correct details than younger adults, particularly when they have had only a brief exposure to an eyewitness event; and they are consistently more prone to making false identifications from identity parades. Memon *et al.* recommend that research be conducted to see if eyewitness evidence obtained from older witnesses is given the same weight by investigating officers and jurors as the testimony of younger adults.

While most EWT research has set out to show its unreliability (Cohen, 1993), one noteworthy attempt to improve witness recall is the *cognitive interview* (CI) (Geiselman *et al.*, 1985; Harrower, 2001). This was defined primarily for use by the police. It maximizes the number of possible retrieval routes by, for example, reactivating/reinstating the context of the original incident. Most studies evaluating use of the CI have shown that it can elicit more information without any loss of accuracy, compared with standard interview techniques; it is most effective when used by specially trained police officers with cooperative adult witnesses (Harrower, 2001).

However, it has also proved successful with quite young children, and according to Memon (1998), it emerges as 'probably the most exciting development in the field of eyewitness testimony in the last 10 years'.

According to Wagstaff (2002), research suggests that the CI shares a number of characteristics with hypnotic memory facilitation procedures, which probably accounts for much of the alleged effectiveness of hypnosis as an interview procedure. (See Chapter 19.) The main limitation of the CI in practice is that it is very time-consuming, in terms of the time spent both interviewing witnesses and training interviewers. Consequently, researchers are now investigating how to streamline the interview by examining the relative contribution of the individual components (Kebbell and Wagstaff, 1999).

EXERCISES

1   In Methodological issues, **Kebbell and Gilchrist (2004) state that as questions become more specific (more closed), responses tend to become less accurate. They say that this finding can be understood in terms of the relative demands of the questions. How might the demands differ between different kinds of questions?**

2   **In Experiment 1:**

   (a) **Why were the films presented in a different order for each group of participants?**

   (b) **How might the order of the films for each group have been determined?**

   (c) **Was there a control condition? If so, what was it? If not, is this necessarily a design fault?**

3   **In Experiment 2, the 'broken glass' question was embedded in a list of ten questions, and it appeared in a random position in the list. Why was this done?**

4   *How* **do the different verbs used to denote 'touching' cars influence the subsequent estimates of speed?**

5   **How might Loftus and Palmer have tried to rule out other possible explanations for their results apart from the substitution hypothesis? (See** Theoretical issues.**)**

6   **How useful is the shopping mall study (Garry** *et al.***, 1994) for understanding the creation of false memories (especially of child sexual abuse) by suggestion during psychotherapy (the** *false memory syndrome* **issue)? (See** Subsequent research.**)**

7 Another advanced test of theory of mind: Evidence from very high-functioning adults with autism or Asperger syndrome

Baron-Cohen, S., Jolliffe, T., Mortimore, C. and Robertson, M. (1997)

Journal of Child Psychology and Psychiatry, 38(7): 813–22

BACKGROUND AND CONTEXT

Autism was first identified (quite independently of each other) by Kanner in the USA (1943) and Asperger in Austria (1944). It is usually detected from the age of four upwards, and diagnosis depends on the presence of characteristic behaviours that reflect a specific social, affective and cognitive profile (Mitchell, 1997: see below).

Autism is often described as the most severe of all child psychiatric disorders, because people with autism seem to be living in 'a world of their own'. This is why it is sometimes categorized as a *psychosis*, outside the normal range of experience (Baron-Cohen, 1995).

The current edition of the *Diagnostic and Statistical Manual of Mental Disorders* (DSM-IV-TR, 2000), published by the American Psychiatric Association, stresses three fundamental impairments:

● *Qualitative impairments in social interaction*: impaired non-verbal behaviours (especially eye contact), failure to engage in genuinely social games (such as turn-taking), no attempt to share interests through *joint-attentional behaviours*, and a failure to develop any friendship beyond the most superficial acquaintance. A lack of empathy is often seen as the central feature of the social deficit (Baron-Cohen, 1988; Kanner, 1943).

● *Qualitative impairments in communication*: failure to develop language and communication in a normal way (such as delayed and restricted language development, inappropriate use of language as a means of communication), and a failure to gesture properly.

- *Repetitive and stereotyped patterns of behaviour and lack of normal imagination*: an inflexible adherence to specific routines, becoming quite distressed if prevented from performing repetitive rituals, lack of spontaneous make-believe/pretend play (Leslie, 1987), and engaging in play which is often lacking in creativity and imagination (Baron-Cohen, 1987).

According to Smith *et al.* (1998):

> The challenge for any researcher investigating autism is trying to explain how one syndrome can lead to the specific combination of impairments which typify a person with autism…how different people with autism can be affected in markedly different ways; and how it is that people with autism can sometimes have better than average abilities in one or two areas (the 'islets of ability').

The Baron-Cohen *et al.* study is related to the first of these challenges, or at least to providing a partial solution. (The 'islets of ability' challenge is addressed in Chapter 8.)

During the 1980s and 1990s, the most influential theory of autism maintained that what all autistic people have in common (the core inability) is *mind-blindness* (Baron-Cohen, 1990), a severe impairment in their understanding of mental states and in their appreciation of how mental states govern behaviour (e.g. Baron-Cohen, 1993, 1995). They lack a 'theory of mind' (ToM), a term originally coined by Premack and Woodruff (1978), based on their work with chimpanzees (including Sarah: see Chapter 3). They defined ToM as the ability to attribute mental states (knowledge/wishes/feelings/beliefs) to oneself and others. The claim that a lack of ToM is at the core of autism is referred to as the *ToM hypothesis*.

As a direct test of the ToM hypothesis, Baron-Cohen *et al.* (1985) tested children with Down's syndrome, normal children (control group) and autistic children (the experimental group), using a *false-belief task* (the Sally-Anne test). Sally placed a marble in her basket, then Sally left the scene, and Anne took the marble and hid it in her box. Then, when Sally returned, children were given the Sally-Anne test; success or failure depended specifically on their response to the question:

> 'Where will Sally look for her marble?' (*belief question*)

The *correct answer* required the child to attribute a *false belief* to Sally (she will look in the *wrong place*).

As predicted, the autistic children were significantly less likely to pass the false-belief question (20 per cent) compared with the normal children (85 per cent) and those with Down's syndrome (86 per cent). Those who failed pointed to where the marble *really* was, rather than to any of the other possible locations.

These findings strongly support the ToM hypothesis: autistic children are unable to attribute beliefs to others, which puts them at a serious disadvantage when having to predict other people's behaviour. Baron-Cohen *et al.* (1985) regard this failure as representing a specific deficit; it cannot be attributed to the general effects of mental retardation, since the more severely retarded Down's syndrome children performed almost as well as the normal children.

Despite the ToM hypothesis being both convincing and powerful, a substantial amount of evidence has accumulated which is undermining it (Mitchell, 1997):

- Even in successful replications of the Sally-Anne study (and in the study itself), a minority of autistic children reliably succeed in answering the belief question correctly (or acknowledging false belief in some other way).

- While the Sally false belief task involves a *first-order belief* ('I think Sally thinks the marble is in the basket'), a second-order belief involves understanding that someone else can have beliefs about a third person ('I think that Anne thinks that Sally thinks the marble is in the basket'). Baron-Cohen (1989) found that *all* the autistic children failed this second-order belief task. However, many adults with Asperger's syndrome/AS (an autistic spectrum disorder not associated with retarded language development) *pass* such second-order ToM tests (Bowler, 1992; Ozonoff *et al.*, 1991). Both studies contradict Baron-Cohen's (1989) claim that lack of ToM is the core cognitive deficit in autism.

However, these studies cannot be taken as conclusive evidence for an *intact* ToM in these individuals, because such second-order tests can easily produce *ceiling effects* if used with participants whose mental age (MA) is above six years (Baron-Cohen *et al.*, 1997). This is because children with normal intelligence pass second-order tests at about six years (Perner and Wimmer, 1985). Unfortunately, second-order tests have often been regarded as a 'complex' or high-level test of ToM. While they are more complex than first-order tests, normal four-year-olds pass these. Both types of test are simply *probes* for four- or six-year-old-level skills, respectively; we cannot simply assume that they are suitable as tests of whether an *adult* (with autism, AS or any other condition) has a fully functional ToM.

Happé (1994b) tested adults with autism or AS on an 'advanced' ToM task, which involved story comprehension (the strange stories task): the critical questions concerned either a character's mental states (the experimental condition) or physical events (the control condition). The task was pitched at the level of a normal eight- to nine-year-old, making it more advanced than previous tests. She found that adults with autism or AS had more difficulty with the mental states questions than did matched controls; they used fewer appropriate mental state terms in their explanations of why characters behaved as they did.

AIM AND NATURE

● HYPOTHESIS

The study involved the use of a new, advanced *adult* test of ToM, for use with high-functioning adults (either with autism or AS), thus extending Happé's line of research.

Hypothesis 1

Participants with autism or AS will show a significant impairment in their ability to accurately choose words describing what a person in a photograph might be thinking or feeling, compared with both normal adults and those with Tourette's syndrome.

Hypothesis 2

The participants had taken part in a separate study, using Happé's strange stories task (Happé, 1994b – see above; Jolliffe, 1997). It was predicted that if both the new adult test and the strange stories task were measures of a relatively advanced ToM, then if participants had difficulties with one, they would also have difficulties with the other.

Hypothesis 3

Based on the 'folk psychology' belief that normal females may be superior to normal males with regard to social sensitivity or empathy, it was predicted that normal females would perform better than males on the eyes task of ToM.

● METHOD/DESIGN

The 'reading the mind in the eyes' task (eyes task, for short) involved looking at photographs of the eye region of 25 different faces (male and female), and making a forced choice between which of two words best described what the person in the photograph might be thinking or feeling.

Items from the eyes task were first described by Baron-Cohen (1995) as an adult test of the 'language of the eyes'. The faces were taken from magazines and were all standardized to one size (15 x 10cm). They were all black and white, with the same region of the face selected for each photo – from midway along the nose to just above the eyebrow. Each photo was shown for three seconds, with a forced choice between two mental state terms printed under each picture. Participants were asked: 'Which word best describes what this person is feeling or thinking?' Table 7.1 shows the mental state terms that participants had to choose between for each photograph.

Three groups of participants were tested:

● 16 adults (13 male, 3 female) with high-functioning autism or AS (the difference being that the latter showed no clinically significant language delay). They were all of average intelligence (making them relatively uncommon).

Table 7.1

Target mental state terms and their foil terms

Number of photograph	Target term	Foil term
1	Concerned	Unconcerned
2	Noticing you	Ignoring you
3	Attraction	Repulsion
4	Relaxed	Worried
5	Serious message	Playful message
6	Interested	Disinterested
7	Friendly	Hostile
8	Sad reflection	Happy reflection
9	Sad thought	Happy thought
10	Certain	Uncertain
11	Far away focus	Near focus
12	Reflective	Unreflective
13	Reflective	Unreflective
14	Cautious about something over there	Relaxed about something over there
15	Noticing someone else	Noticing you
16	Calm	Anxious
17	Dominant	Submissive
18	Fantasizing	Noticing
19	Observing	Daydreaming
20	Desire for you	Desire for someone else
21	Ignoring you	Noticing you
22	Nervous about you	Interested in you
23	Flirtatious	Disinterested
24	Sympathetic	Unsympathetic
25	Decisive	Indecisive

AIM AND NATURE

● 50 normal adults (matched for age; 25 male, 25 female). They were all assumed to have intelligence within the normal range.

● 10 adults with Tourette's syndrome (a clinical control group). They were also age-matched with the other two groups; the sex ratio (8 males, 2 females) matched the ratio in the first group. They too showed average intelligence.

The eyes task also involved basic aspects of emotion recognition and face perception. In order to test if difficulties on the eyes task were specific to the attribution of mental states rather than these other processes, Baron-Cohen *et al.* included two control tasks:

1   A *basic emotion recognition task*: participants were asked to judge photographs of whole faces displaying basic emotions (Ekman, 1992).

2   A *gender recognition task*: participants were shown the same sets of eyes used in the experimental task, but this time they had to identify the person's gender.

The eyes task, the strange stories task and the two control tasks were presented in random order to all participants.

● RESULTS

Hypothesis 1

Both control groups (the normal adults and those with Tourette's syndrome) performed significantly better (mean of 20.4) than the experimental groups (those with autism or AS: mean of 16.3) on the eyes task. Those with Tourette's syndrome did not differ from the normal participants.

Hypothesis 2

Participants with autism or AS performed significantly worse than control participants on the strange stories task. The pattern of results from the eyes task mirrored the pattern of performance on the strange stories task.

Hypothesis 3

Normal female participants performed significantly better than the normal male participants on the eyes task (means of 21.8 and 18.8, respectively).

● CONCLUSIONS

● As predicted, adults with autism or AS, despite being of normal or above-average intelligence, performed poorly on the eyes task, which represents a subtle ToM

AIM AND NATURE

test. The findings provided experimental evidence for ToM deficits at later points in development, and at higher points on the intelligence scale, compared with previous research.

- The similar pattern of results on the strange stories and eyes tasks supports the claim that the eyes task is a valid measure of ToM, since the former is an accepted, existing advanced ToM task.

- The finding that all groups were successful on the control tasks showed that the poor performance on the eyes task of the participants with autism or AS was not due to the stimuli being eyes, or to a deficit in extracting social information from minimal cues, or to a subtle perceptual deficit, or to basic emotion recognition. Since some of these participants had university degrees, this aspect of social cognition is clearly independent of general intelligence.

EVALUATION

Methodological issues

Baron-Cohen *et al.* point out that even this 'very advanced test' of ToM is still more simple than the real demands of live social situations. For one thing, their stimuli were static, unlike the real social world. A closer approximation might be based around a task assessing comprehension of films. Many of their participants with autism or Asperger's Syndrome told them that going to the movies is often a frustrating experience, a waste of their time. The social action proceeds rapidly, and they find it hard to work out why a character did or said something (their intentions or motives), who knows what and who doesn't, and why the audience laughs at particular points in the film. It just happens too fast.

However, movies are *not* pure tests of mind-reading, because they involve both (i) *central coherence*, which relies on contextual information being taken into account and integrated with other relevant information, and (ii) *executive functions* – the ability to plan behaviour, impulse control and working memory (see Chapter 5). Weak central coherence (Frith, 1989; Frith and Happé, 1994a, b) and impaired executive function (Frith, 1996) have both been proposed as explanations of autism which correct some of the limitations of the ToM hypothesis (see Gross, 2005). For these reasons, Baron-Cohen *et al.* decided to use the eyes test instead.

How do we know that the eyes task is a valid test of ToM? According to Baron-Cohen *et al.*, there are four reasons for believing that it is:

1 The target words refer to mental states.

2   These are not just emotion terms, but include terms describing cognitive mental states. This makes it more than simply a test of emotion perception.

3   The pattern of results from the eyes task mirrored that on Happé's strange stories – an existing advanced ToM test.

4   Poor performance by participants with autism or AS on the eyes task was not correlated with poor performance on the control tasks; this suggests that their deficit was not due to the stimuli being eyes, or to an inability to extract social information from minimal cues, or to a subtle perceptual deficit, or to basic emotion recognition.

However, Baron-Cohen *et al.* (2001) identified a number of problems with the eyes task:

● Its forced-choice nature meant that participants had to score 17 or above to be significantly above chance (i.e. what they could achieve by guessing). This left a very narrow range of scores (17–25) for identifying individual differences.

● Similarly, the narrow range of scores that are significantly above chance could lead to a score in the normal range being closer to the ceiling for the test. *Ceiling effects* are obviously undesirable, because this too reduces the ability to detect individual differences. (See **Background and context** above and **Exercises** below.)

● The items that related to basic emotions may have been too easy (contributing to the ceiling effect). They are 'basic' in the sense that they are recognized in all cultures, can be recognized as emotions without attributing a belief to the person, and are recognized even by very young, normally developing children (e.g. Ekman and Friesen, 1971). In contrast, complex mental states involve attribution of a belief or intention (a cognitive mental state).

● Some items could be answered correctly simply by checking the gaze-direction of the face, such as 'noticing' or 'ignoring' (mental states linked to perception). These might be too easy a clue for someone with a subtle mind-reading difficulty.

● There were more female than male faces, which may have biased the test in some way.

● The target words and their foils were always *semantic* opposites (opposite in meaning), such as 'sympathetic' vs 'unsympathetic'. Again, this made the test too easy, asking participants to distinguish between positive and negative mental states.

● Participants with high-functioning autism (who had suffered language delay) may have had difficulty mapping a word onto a picture.

Theoretical issues

According to Leslie (1987, 1994; Leslie and Roth, 1993), underlying ToM is an independent mental module (the *theory-of-mind mechanism*/ToMM). This is innately determined and begins to mature from about 12–18 months to four years. It processes information in the form of *meta-representations*: it is specialized for representing *mental* representations ('beliefs about beliefs', etc.) This is a *domain-specific* account.

The alternative, *domain-general* account of the child's acquisition of ToM is Piaget's concept of *egocentrism* (although the term ToM post-dates his work: see Samuel and Bryant, 1984: Chapter 25). Before the age of seven, children are unable to put themselves in someone else's psychological shoes because they lack reversible thought processes (Bryant, 1998).

In order to choose between these alternative accounts, we need experiments that contrast how children make inferences about other people's beliefs with their success in making very similar inferences which are *not* about beliefs. If the specific modular approach is correct, there should be very little developmental connection between the two types of inference. The little evidence there is (e.g. Zaitchik, 1990) suggests the opposite conclusion: there does not appear to be a 'switching on' of a module precisely set to work out what other people know. It is much more likely that young children's difficulties lie in making a clear distinction between what was true in the past and what is true now (Bryant, 1998).

Ironically, both approaches are subject to the same criticism, namely that they see the child as a 'solitary thinker', whose mental abilities develop in a social vacuum. According to Fonagy *et al.* (1997), 'mind-reading' does not suddenly develop at three to four years of age, independently of the child's social relationships. Too much happens between the infant-toddler and its caregiver which is difficult to account for, unless we assume a primitive ability to adjust his/her actions in the light of others' assumed mental states. Adults interacting with babies consistently assume that they possess a rudimentary representation of their own and others' minds; this assumption is probably critical to how this capacity actually develops between 33 and 40 months (Bartsch and Wellman, 1995).

Subsequent research

Based on their identification of problems with the eyes task (see **Methodological issues** above), Baron-Cohen *et al.* (2001) used a revised version of the test. The main changes were as follows:

● The total number of items (photographs) was increased from 25 to 36, and the number of response options (forced-choice words) was increased from two to four per trial. This means that participants only had to score 13 or above to be performing at significantly above chance. This provides a bigger window of 24 points (13–36) in which individual differences can be revealed. This also decreases the ceiling effect.

- The items were confined to complex mental states to make the task more challenging.

- The 'gaze-direction' items were excluded.

- There was an equal number of male and female photographs.

- The three foil words had the same emotional strength as the target word. For example, if the target word was 'serious', the foils might be 'ashamed', 'alarmed' and 'bewildered'. Having to choose between three similar words and the target word made the task more challenging and increased the possibility of revealing subtle individual differences.

- A glossary of all the mental state terms was included, which participants could consult if they were unsure of the meaning of a word.

This revised version of the eyes task was used with:

(i)   adults with high-functioning autism or AS;

(ii)   normal adults from a range of occupational backgrounds;

(ii)   normal students with high IQs (Cambridge University undergraduates);

(iv) randomly selected individuals from the general population.

The results basically replicated those of the 1997 study: the adults with autism or AS performed poorly compared with the normal controls. The revised test improved the power to detect subtle individual differences in social sensitivity in otherwise normally intelligent adults.

A team of Scandinavian researchers (Kaland *et al.*, 2002) developed a new 'advanced' ToM test ('stories from everyday life') for use with children and adolescents with AS of normal intelligence. The test was designed to assess participants' ability to infer a *mental state* (e.g. understanding social communication such as a *lie, white lie, figure of speech, misunderstanding, double bluff, irony, persuasion, contrary emotions, forgetting, jealousy, intentions, empathy* and *social blunders*) as distinct from a *physical/mechanical event.*

As predicted, participants with AS showed significantly more problems attributing mental states compared with the control groups; they performed considerably better when inferring physical states – but still did less well than the controls. They showed a tendency to interpret behaviour and speech literally, without regard to context, and to choose a physical explanation when one in terms of mental state was more appropriate.

According to Ramachandran and Oberman (2006), saying that people with autism cannot interact socially because they lack a ToM does not go very far beyond restating the symptoms. What Ramachandran and his colleagues (and other researchers) have been doing since the late 1990s is trying to identify the brain mechanisms whose known functions match those that are disrupted in autism. The key mechanism may already have been found, in the form of *mirror neurons.*

Originally identified in the premotor cortex (part of the frontal lobe) of macaque monkeys, mirror neurons were detected in the same regions of the human brain using brain-imaging techniques (see Chapter 29). They enable humans to determine other people's intentions by mentally simulating their actions (i.e. the same neurons that would fire when performing a certain action also fire when we watch another person performing the same action). In other parts of the brain, mirror neurons may play a role in empathetic emotional responses: when studying the anterior cingulated cortex of awake human participants, it was found that certain neurons that typically respond to pain also responded when seeing someone else in pain.

According to Ramachandran and Oberman (2006), mirror neurons seem to be performing the precise functions that people with autism fail to perform. So it seems logical to hypothesize that the mirror neuron system in such people is deficient in some way. Oberman *et al.* (2005) took electroencephalogram (EEG) measurements of the brains of ten high-functioning autistic children and compared them with ten age- and gender-matched controls. Their findings supported the hypothesis that there is a lack of mirror neuron activity in the brains of autistic children.

Applications and implications

It follows from Oberman *et al.*'s (2005) findings that, if treatments could be developed to restore mirror neuron activity, then at least some of the symptoms of autism could be alleviated (Ramachandran and Oberman, 2006).

It also follows from the ToM hypothesis that if the core problem involved in autism is a lack of ToM, then we should try to *teach* it to children with the disorder. Baron-Cohen *et al.* (2004) developed a DVD (*Mind-Reading: The Interactive Guide to Emotion*) for teaching emotion-recognition to people on the autistic spectrum aged eight and above. While highly successful (Golan and Baron-Cohen, 2006), it required users to be able to play a computer game, clicking a mouse, or to be supervised to do this. Since then, Baron-Cohen and the Department of Culture have collaborated in producing *The Transporters*, an animated series aimed at relatively 'excluded' autistic spectrum groups: those with significant learning difficulties, and preschoolers. Neither has the ability (or interest) to use a computer, but both enjoy watching animated films about vehicles.

Vehicles whose motion is determined only by physical rules (such as back and forth along linear tracks) would be greatly preferred by children with autism over planes and cars and other vehicles whose motion is highly variable. *The Transporters* is based around eight characters, all vehicles, all using this rule-based motion (including two trams, two cable cars and a funicular railway) and with real-life faces of actors grafted on to them.

The characters are toys in a child's bedroom, which 'come to life' when he goes off to school; they get caught up in dramatic stories that enable the child who watches to see different key emotions on the faces of the vehicles. These include basic emotions (happy/sad/angry/disgusted/afraid/surprised), as well as more complex ones (e.g. ashamed/joking/jealous/proud). Each of the 15 episodes lasts five minutes and is narrated (by actor Stephen Fry). Results so far are very encouraging (Baron-Cohen *et al.*, 2007).

According to Frith (in Gold, 1995), belief in ToM has practical benefits for teachers, parents and carers of autistic people: it 'explains the inexplicable. And it means you can adjust their environment to them, to suit their needs'; for example, the child whose unprovoked tantrums were explained once his father realized that he pointed at the sweet cupboard and expected to be given sweets – even when no one else was in the room to see him pointing.

EXERCISES

1 In the Baron-Cohen *et al.* (1985) study, the autistic children were compared with both normal children and Down's syndrome children.

   (a) Why were these two other groups used?

   (b) Can you suggest other groups that might have been used, and why?

2 In the 1997 study, what type of experimental design was used?

3 Why do you think that people with Tourette's syndrome might have been chosen as a (clinical) control group? (Try to think of *similarities* between the two groups that Baron-Cohen *et al.* may have thought important when predicting the difference on eye task performance between them and those with autism or AS.)

4 Towards the end of the Background and context **section, it is stated that the second-order tests used in studies such as that of Ozonoff *et al.* (1991) can easily produce 'ceiling effects' if used with participants whose mental age is over six years. What is meant by this term and what is the opposite effect?**

5 In relation to Hypothesis 1:

   (a) What are the 'basic' emotions identified by Ekman (1992)?

   (b) Based on your first answer, what broad difference can you spot between the mental state terms and their foil terms as they appear in Table 7.1?

6 In relation to Hypothesis 2, what is another (technical) way to describe the claim that if participants had difficulties on one, they will have difficulties on the other.

7 In relation to Hypothesis 3, what do you think Baron-Cohen *et al.* mean when they refer to 'folk psychology'?

8 While ToM is very similar to Piaget's concept of *egocentrism*, can you identify any *differences* between them?

8 Inside the mind of a savant

Treffert, D.A. and Christensen, D.D. (2005)

Scientific American, 293(6): 88–93

BACKGROUND AND CONTEXT

The study of *gifted children* really began with Terman's (1925) Stanford longitudinal study. Terman defined giftedness as an IQ (intelligence quotient: see Chapters 34 and 35) score of around 140, and on this basis, teachers nominated 643 ten-year-olds. Their mean IQ turned out to be 151. They were followed up over the next 60 years (Holahan, 1988).

Terman described the children as superior not just intellectually, but also in terms of their health, social adjustment and moral attitude (i.e. *globally* gifted – evenly talented in all academic and other areas). According to Winner (1998), this helped create the myth that gifted children are happy, well adjusted by nature, requiring little special attention, and easy to teach.

However, giftedness comes in many different forms, and contrary to the myth that Terman helped to create, one characteristic is its *unevenness*. Certain gifted children can leap years ahead of their peers in one area, yet fall behind in another. While some do fit the stereotype of the all-round high achiever, many children display giftedness in one area but are unremarkable, or even disabled, in others. This unevenness is surprisingly common.

Winner (1998) cites a survey of over a thousand highly academically gifted adolescents, which found that over 95 per cent had a strong disparity between mathematical and verbal abilities. Extraordinarily strong mathematical and spatial abilities often accompany average or even deficient verbal skills. Two famous examples are Albert Einstein and Thomas Edison.

Many children who struggle with language may have strong spatial skills, and the association between verbal deficits and spatial gifts seems especially strong among visual artists (such as Stephen Wiltshire: see Gross, 2005). The most unevenly gifted of all are the *savants*.

The term 'idiot savants' was first used by Langdon Down (best known for having identified Down's syndrome) in 1887. It refers to individuals who have a serious mental disability (such as autism: see **Theoretical and methodological issues** below) and some island of genius, a remarkable ability in some specific domain. Such individuals appear to be able to use processing strategies within a particular domain that seem independent of their overall (very low) level of intelligence. *Savant syndrome* has been recognized for almost 200 years, being reported mainly in the form of descriptive case histories.

AIM AND NATURE

● HYPOTHESIS

While no specific hypothesis was being tested, a question (raised by the skills of all savants) that the study is trying to throw light on is: does brain damage stimulate compensatory development in some other area of the brain, or does it simply allow otherwise latent abilities to emerge?

● METHOD/DESIGN

This is basically a case study of a single savant, Kim Peek (KP), born in 1951. He provided the inspiration for Dustin Hoffman's character, Raymond Babbit, in *Rain Man* (1988) (Treffert and Wallace, 2004). One of the present authors (Christensen) studied KP's brain, using magnetic resonance imaging (MRI: see Chapter 29). This was first carried out in 1988 and has been continued ever since.

● RESULTS/FINDINGS

In almost all savants, their memory has been linked to a specific domain, such as music, art or mathematics. But in KP's case, phenomenal memory itself is the skill (his friends call him 'Kim-puter'). He really can extract a fact from his mental library as fast as a search engine can mine the Internet.

He began memorizing books at the age of 18 months, as they were read to him. He has learned 9,000 books by heart to date. He reads a page in 8 to 10 seconds and places the memorized book upside down on the shelf to signify that it is now on his mental 'hard drive'.

KP's memory extends to at least 15 interests, including world and American history, sports, movies, geography, space programmes, actors and actresses, the Bible, church history, literature, Shakespeare and classical music. He knows all the area and zip codes in the USA, plus all the TV stations in each area. He learns the maps in the front of phone books and can provide Yahoo-like travel directions within any major US city or between any pair of cities. He can identify hundreds of classical compositions, say where and when each was composed and first performed, name the composer and provide many biographical details, and even discuss the formal and tonal components of the music. Most intriguing of all, he appears to be developing a new skill in middle age. Whereas before he could only talk about music, in the past two years he has been learning to play it.

His talents would be remarkable in any person, but they seem all the more so in contrast with his severe developmental problems. He walks with a sidelong gait, cannot button his clothes, cannot manage the chores of daily life, and has great difficulties with abstraction.

An unusual brain

Imaging studies of KP's brain have so far revealed considerable structural abnormality:

- His head and brain are very large. He was born with an encephalocele, or a baseball-size 'blister' on the back of his head. This spontaneously shrank and disappeared.

- The most striking feature is the complete absence of the corpus callosum, which normally connects the left and right hemispheres (see Figure 8.1). Although it is rare to have no corpus callosum, it is not always associated with any obvious functional problems. In adults who have their corpus callosum cut as a last-resort treatment for severe epilepsy, 'split-brain' syndrome is produced, in which each hemisphere works independently of the other (see Chapter 20). In people born without a corpus callosum, the two hemispheres may operate as one giant hemisphere, putting functions that are usually separate 'under one roof'.

- Also missing are the anterior and posterior commissures, which usually link the hemispheres as well. The cerebellum, which is responsible for certain motor functions, is smaller than average and malformed: fluid occupies much of the surrounding space, which might explain some of KP's difficulties with coordination and mobility.

These findings cannot yet be linked directly to any of his skills, but fMRI (functional MRI, which shows the brain *in action*) should provide insights.

In 1988 (when the MRI scans began), KP was also given psychological tests. His overall IQ score was 87 (the average being 100), but the verbal and performance sub-tests varied greatly: some fell within the superior range of intelligence, while others fell in the mentally retarded range. His overall diagnosis was 'developmental

AIM AND NATURE

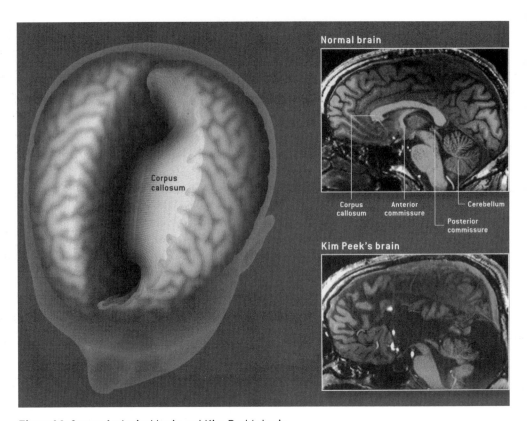

Figure 8.1. Scans of a typical brain and Kim Peek's brain.

disorder not otherwise specified – *not* autistic (which his inspiration for *Rain Man* suggests he is). Unlike autistic people, KP is outgoing and quite personable. (See Chapter 7 and **Theoretical and methodological issues** below.)

Memory and music

One thing that seems essential for the full development of savant skills is a great interest in the subject matter in question. In KP's case, all the interests began in rote memory, but later progressed to something more. He generally has a limited capacity for abstract or conceptual thinking: for example, he cannot explain many commonplace proverbs. But, unusually for savants, he does understand much of the material he has committed to memory. Down himself coined the term 'verbal adhesion' to describe the savant's ability to remember huge quantities of words without comprehension.

Sometimes his answers to questions or directions are quite concrete and literal. Once, when asked by his father in a restaurant to 'lower his voice', KP merely slid lower into his chair, thus lowering his voice box. But he is also capable of answers that are quite ingenious, (intentionally) witty and creative. Such creative use of material that had originally been memorized by rote can be seen as the verbal equivalent of a musician's improvisation. Like the musician, KP thinks so quickly that it can be difficult to keep up with his intricate associations. Often he seems to be two or three steps ahead of his audience.

In 2002, KP met April Greenan, Professor of Music at the University of Utah. She helped him to quickly learn to play the piano and to enhance his discussion of compositions by playing passages from them. He could now demonstrate on the keyboard many of the pieces he recalled from his massive mental library. He also has remarkable long-term memory of pitch, remembering the original pitch level of each composition.

Although KP is still physically awkward, his manual dexterity is improving. When seated at the piano, he can play the piece he wishes to discuss, sing the passage of interest or describe the music verbally. He shifts seamlessly from one mode to another. According to Greenan (a Mozart scholar):

> Kim's knowledge of music is considerable. His ability to recall every detail of a composition he has heard – in many cases only once and more than 40 years ago – is astonishing. The connections he draws between and weaves through compositions, composers' lives, historical events, movie soundtracks and thousands of facts stored in his database reveal enormous intellectual capacity.

She even compares him to Mozart, who had an enlarged head, a fascination with numbers and uneven social skills. She wonders whether KP might even learn to compose.

Life after Rain Man

The filming of *Rain Man* and its subsequent success proved to be a turning point in KP's life. Before then, he had been reclusive, retreating to his room when company came. Afterwards, the confidence he gained from contact with the film-makers, together with the celebrity provided by the film's success, inspired him and his father to share his talents with many audiences. They became enthusiastic emissaries for people with disabilities, and have shared their story with more than 2.6 million people.

● CONCLUSIONS

Treffert and Christensen recommend that family and other caregivers of people with special needs who may have some savant skill 'train the skill', rather than dismissing such skills as frivolous. This way, the savant may learn to connect with other people and reduce the effects of the disability. This is not an easy path,

AIM AND NATURE

because disability and limitations still require a great deal of dedication, patience and hard work.

KP possesses one of the most extraordinary memories ever recorded. Until we can explain his abilities, we cannot pretend to understand human cognition. Further exploration of savant syndrome will provide both scientific insights and stories of immense human interest. KP provides ample evidence of both.

EVALUATION

Theoretical and methodological issues

When Down introduced the term 'idiot savant' in 1887, 'idiot' was an accepted classification for people whose IQ was below 25; 'savant' ('knowledgeable person') was derived from the French *savoir*, meaning 'to know'. So, there was nothing 'politically incorrect' about the term at the time. However, it was actually a misnomer, since almost all cases occur in people with IQs over 40. In the interests of accuracy and dignity, the term 'savant syndrome' has been substituted and is now widely used (Treffert, 2006).

As noted above, KP's overall IQ score was 87 (well below the average of 100), but the verbal and performance sub-tests varied greatly. (See **Exercises**.) Based on these scores, it was concluded that 'Kim's IQ classification is not a valid description of his intellectual ability'. According to Treffert and Christensen, KP's case supports the 'multiple intelligences' argument, as opposed to the 'general intelligence' argument. (Again, see **Exercises**.)

Savant syndrome is seen in about 1 in 10 people with autism, and in about 1 in 2,000 people with brain damage or mental retardation. So, savantism is more commonly linked with autism than with any other single disorder. But only about half of all savants are autistic. The rest have some other kind of developmental disorder. As we have seen, KP was actually diagnosed with 'developmental disorder not otherwise specified' (i.e. *not* autism or autistic spectrum disorder).

Savant skills are typically confined to an intriguingly narrow range of special abilities, namely *music* (usually playing the piano); *art* (usually drawing, painting or sculpting); *calendar counting/calculation* (KP can tell you what day of the week you were born on and on what day you will celebrate your 65th birthday); *maths* (including lightning-fast calculating or the ability to compute prime numbers, for example, in the absence of other simple arithmetical abilities); *mechanical/spatial abilities* (such as the ability to estimate distances precisely without the benefit of instruments, the ability to construct complex models/structures with great accuracy, and map making and direction finding).

These skills tend to be *right hemisphere* (RH) in type, that is, non-symbolic, artistic visual and motor abilities, more concrete and directly perceived. In contrast, *left hemisphere* (LH) skills are more sequential, logical and symbolic, including language specialization (see Chapter 20).

A related finding is that males outnumber females in savant syndrome (four to six males for every female), as they do in autism. In explaining this finding, Geschwind and Galabjurda (1987, in Treffert, 2006) point out that the LH normally completes its development later than the RH. This means that the LH is subject to prenatal influences (some of which can be detrimental) for a longer period. In the male foetus especially, circulating testosterone (which can reach very high levels) can slow down growth and impair neuronal function in the more vulnerable LH. This, in turn, may cause the RH to become enlarged and dominant over the LH (a 'pathology of superiority').

In autistic disorder, LH dysfunction, compared with RH activity, has been demonstrated in several studies (Treffert, 2006). This finding, together with those relating to savant syndrome skills and sex differences in incidence of savant syndrome and autism, has led to the *left hemisphere hypothesis* (LHH). This is currently the most powerful explanation of savant syndrome, claiming that some injury to the LH causes the RH to *compensate* for the damage.

Perhaps the most convincing piece of evidence supporting the LHH is the discovery of 'acquired' savants. Miller *et al.* (1998, in Treffert, 2006) described five previously normal patients with fronto-temporal dementia (FTD), who acquired *new* artistic skills. They had no particular artistic abilities before the onset of the FTD, but as it progressed, so their artistic skills emerged. Brain scans revealed LH injury and dysfunction.

Miller *et al.* (2000, in Treffert, 2006) have also described seven other FTD patients who acquired new *visual* or *musical* skills, despite the progression of their dementia. All 12 patients with these newly emerged savant-type abilities were compared with FTD patients who did not develop such skills. Scans showed that 9 of the 12 had abnormalities only in the LH; they also performed better on tasks assessing right frontal lobe functions, but worse on verbal abilities.

Applications and implications

According to Snyder and Mitchell (1999, in Treffert, 2006), we are all potential savants. Savant brain processes occur in each of us, but they are overwhelmed by more sophisticated conceptual cognition (regulated for most of us by the LH). They conclude that autistic savants 'have privileged access to lower levels of information not normally available through introspection'.

It follows that if you can reduce or stop electrical activity in the LH, it might be possible to unlock the 'little Rain Man' in each of us (Treffert and Wallace, 2004). Snyder has attempted this, using a technique called repetitive trans-cranial magnetic stimulation (rTMS). This is used routinely in neurology departments and hospitals as a research tool to test for side effects of brain surgery, and to establish the function of different brain regions. It basically uses a strong magnetic field to switch off activity in the nearby part of the brain.

Snyder has found some evidence of the 'switching on' of RH abilities when the LH is switched off; Treffert and Wallace (2004) agree with Snyder's claims, concluding that 'we tend to be a left brain society'. This limits our access to the savant skills we all possess.

Although *Rain Man* is purely fictional and does not tell KP's life story (Barry Morrow was inspired to write the screenplay after a chance meeting with KP in 1984), there is one remarkably prophetic scene. When Raymond (the savant) instantly computes square roots in his head, his brother (played by Tom Cruise) responds by saying, 'He ought to work for NASA or something'.

It is possible that this might happen. NASA has proposed making a high-resolution 3-D anatomical model of KP's brain architecture. NASA hopes that this detailed model will enable doctors to improve their ability to interpret output from far less capable ultrasound imaging systems (currently the only kind that can be carried into space and used to monitor astronauts).

Treffert and Christensen believe that PK's transformation has general applicability. Much of what scientists know about health comes from study of pathologies, and certainly much of what will be learned about normal memory will come from the study of unique or unusual memory.

EXERCISES

1   What do you consider to be some of the strengths of this as a case study?

2   Treffert and Christensen refer to KP's 'inability to explain proverbs'.

   (a) Give two examples of a proverb.

   (b) Describe what form that inability might take in relation to both your examples (there is a clue in the paragraph which follows that reference in the text above).

   (c) How do you think children (under 11 years) might explain proverbs?

3   Despite the dedication, patience and hard work shown by KP's father in caring for him, and the fact that the two travel together on their lecture tours, do you feel that KP has been exploited in any way? Is there a 'circus act' aspect to his fame, such that people come to hear him out of some semi-morbid curiosity?

9 Cognitive consequences of forced compliance

Festinger, L. and Carlsmith, J.M. (1959)

Journal of Abnormal and Social Psychology, 58: 203–10

BACKGROUND AND CONTEXT

According to Festinger's (1957) *cognitive dissonance theory* (CDT), whenever we hold simultaneously two cognitions (a belief, idea, attitude, or awareness or memory of some aspect of our behaviour) which are psychologically inconsistent, we experience *dissonance*. Festinger defined dissonance as a negative drive state of 'psychological discomfort or tension'. This motivates us to reduce dissonance by achieving consonance. A major way of achieving this is through changing one or more of our cognitions, as in attitude change.

According to the principle of *cognitive consistency* (which is fundamental to the theory), human beings are internally active information processors, who sort through and modify a large number of cognitive elements in order to achieve some kind of cognitive coherence. It is really a part of human nature, a basic human need, thus making CDT not just a theory of *attitude change*, but also an account of human *motivation*. Two other influential theories of cognitive consistency are Osgood and Tannenbaum's (1955) *congruity theory* and Heider's (1958) *balance theory*.

To appreciate why CDT was regarded as so innovative and why it became so influential within social psychology, it needs to be seen in the context of the particular period in the history of psychology as a whole. When it first appeared (1957), the dominance of behaviourism in American psychology was waning, and the cognitive revolution was gaining momentum (Moghaddam, 1998: see Gross, 2005). CDT challenged at least two of behaviourism's fundamental tenets:

1   'Mental life' has no place in psychology.

2   Behaviour is shaped by reinforcements.

Researchers were beginning to look for alternative sources of inspiration for experimental studies, and within a few years dozens of studies had been carried out.

One of the earliest – and still one of the most famous – is the present one.

CDT has been tested under three main headings:

- *Dissonance following a decision* (post-decisional dissonance, e.g. having to choose between two equally attractive alternatives, with the prediction that we will devalue the alternative we reject).

- *Dissonance resulting from effort* (e.g. deciding to put yourself through an embarrassing or stressful situation, only for it to turn out to be trivial and not warranting the embarrassment/stress, with the prediction that the situation will be judged as more important and worthwhile the greater the embarrassment, etc.).

- Engaging in *counter-attitudinal behaviour* (e.g. if we act or express an opinion that is contrary to our private opinion (what we 'really' believe), we will be likely to change our opinion to bring it in line with what we said or did). The present study falls under this heading.

AIM AND NATURE

● HYPOTHESIS

The aim of the study was to test CDT, specifically the following hypothesis: the larger the pressure on participants to elicit particular overt behaviour (beyond the minimum needed to elicit it), the weaker will be the tendency to change their opinions so as to bring them in line with that behaviour.

(A more concise, less complex version of this is: the larger the reward given to the participant, the smaller will be the subsequent opinion change.)

● METHOD/DESIGN

The reward in question was either $1 or $20 for telling another participant (actually a stooge of the experimenter) that the task they were waiting to perform was really interesting.

The real participants had just performed this task themselves. (The task involved putting 12 spools onto a tray, emptying the tray, refilling it with spools, emptying it again, and so on. After doing this for 30 minutes, the participant was given a board containing 48 square pegs; the task was to turn the pegs a quarter-turn clockwise, then another quarter turn, and so on. This also took 30 minutes.) The hour spent on these repetitive, monotonous tasks was meant to provide participants with an experience that they would have a rather negative opinion about.

The participants were 71 male students in the introductory psychology course at Stanford University, and they volunteered for this study as part of the course requirement that they spend a certain number of hours as participants. It was advertised as a 'two-hour experiment dealing with "Measures of Performance"'. Students were also told about a study being conducted by the psychology department to evaluate the experiments that students were required to volunteer for, so as to improve them in the future.

After completing the tasks, participants in the *control condition* were not asked to do anything else, except that they were going to be interviewed as part of the departmental study. Those in the two *experimental conditions* were asked if they would be willing to stand in for the student volunteer whose role was to tell waiting participants about the tasks; they were shown the 'script' he used, in which he says, 'It was very enjoyable'. 'I had a lot of fun'. 'I enjoyed myself'. 'It was very interesting'. 'It was intriguing'. 'It was exciting'.

Once participants had agreed to this request, they were paid either $1 or $20; this was the amount they had been told they would receive when they were first asked. Participants had been randomly allocated to the three conditions.

After signing a receipt for the money, the participant was taken by the experimenter into the secretary's office (where he had previously waited), where a female stooge was waiting. The participant then made some positive remarks about the experiment, to which the stooge responded by saying she was surprised because a friend of hers had done it the week before and found it really boring. Most participants responded by saying something like, 'Oh no, it's really very interesting. I'm sure you'll enjoy it.'

Like control participants, those in the $1 and $20 groups were taken to another office, where an interviewer was asked if he wanted to interview them as part of the departmental study. In all cases, of course, he did. The interviewer was always unaware of which condition the participant was in. The interview consisted of four questions; participants were encouraged to talk about them first, before rating their opinion on an 11-point scale:

1   Were the tasks interesting and enjoyable?

2   Did the experiment give you an opportunity to learn about your own ability to perform these tasks?

3   From what you know about the experiment and the tasks involved in it, would you say that the experiment was measuring anything important? That is, do you think the results may have scientific value?

4   Would you have any desire to participate in another similar experiment?

AIM AND NATURE

Table 9.1

Average ratings on interview questions for each condition

Questions on interview	Experimental condition		
	Control (n=20)	$1 (n=20)	$20 (n=20)
How enjoyable tasks were (rated from –5 to +5)	–0.45	+1.35	–0.05
How much they learned (rated from 0 to 10)	3.08	2.80	3.15
Scientific importance (rated from 0 to 10)	5.60	6.45	5.18
Participate in similar experiment (rated from –5 to +5)	–0.62	+1.20	–0.25

All the participants were then debriefed (which included meeting the female stooge) and asked to return the money (which they all did willingly).

● RESULTS

Data for 11 of the 71 participants had to be discarded (for various reasons), leaving 60 participants (20 in each of the three conditions).

The control condition represented a baseline from which to evaluate the results of the other two conditions: it provided participants' reactions to the tasks and their opinions about the experiment as falsely explained to them, without the experimental introduction of dissonance.

The question regarding how enjoyable the tasks were was the most important result, because it was most directly relevant to the experimentally induced dissonance. The control group scores confirmed that the tasks were rather boring and monotonous (–0.45). For the two experimental groups, the dissonance produced by telling someone how interesting and enjoyable the tasks were could be reduced most directly by persuading themselves that they really were interesting and enjoyable. The difference between the scores for the $1 condition (+1.35) and the control condition was significant. But the –0.05 for the $20 group was *not* significantly higher than the control group's score. The difference between the $1 and $20 groups was significant.

AIM AND NATURE

● CONCLUSIONS

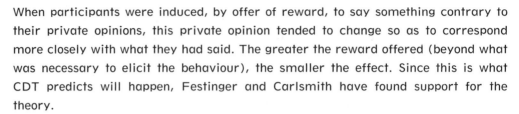

When participants were induced, by offer of reward, to say something contrary to their private opinions, this private opinion tended to change so as to correspond more closely with what they had said. The greater the reward offered (beyond what was necessary to elicit the behaviour), the smaller the effect. Since this is what CDT predicts will happen, Festinger and Carlsmith have found support for the theory.

EVALUATION

Theoretical issues

One of the strengths of CDT is that the predictions it makes are *counter-intuitive* (that is, contrary to what 'common sense' would predict). The common-sense prediction of the $1–$20 experiment is, surely, that the participants offered the $20 should be *more* likely to change their opinion about the task than the $1 group. The results, of course, go in the opposite direction.

These findings have been replicated by several studies in which children are given either a mild or a severe threat not to play with an attractive toy (e.g. Aronson and Carlsmith, 1963). If children obey a *mild* threat they will experience *greater* dissonance, because it is more difficult for them to justify their behaviour compared with children receiving a severe threat. Similarly, it is assumed that the $1 group experiences the greater dissonance. How can they justify lying about the boring task for a mere $1? The solution is to see the tasks as actually being interesting and enjoyable!

What is referred to here as the common-sense view corresponds to *incentive theory* (based on the notion of reward: Janis *et al.*, 1965). It seems that both theories can be true, but under different conditions, and a key variable involved is whether or not the counter-attitudinal behaviour is *volitional* (voluntary/when we feel we have acted of our own free will). If we believe we had no choice, there is no dissonance, and, hence, no attitude change. (See **Methodological issues** below.)

However, Bem claims that dissonance is neither a necessary nor sufficient explanation, and he rejects any reference to hypothetical, intervening variables. According to Bem's *self-perception theory* (SPT) (1967, 1972), any self-report of an attitude is an inference from observation of one's own behaviour and the situation in which it occurs. If the situation contains cues (e.g. offer of a large $20 incentive) which imply that we might have behaved that way regardless of how we felt personally (we lie about the task being interesting even though it was boring), then we do not infer that our behaviour reflected our true behaviour. But in the absence of obvious situational pressures ($1 condition), we assume that our attitudes are what our behaviour suggests they are.

Put another way, the $20 participants could easily make a *situational attribution* ('I did it for the money'), whereas the $1 participants had to make a *dispositional attribution* ('I did it because I really enjoyed it'). (See Chapter 15.)

Bem's own research shows only that Festinger and Carlsmith's participants *could have* inferred their attitudes from their own behaviour, not that they *actually* went through such a process of inference (Stroebe and Jonas, 1996). According to Eiser and van der Pligt (1988), SPT has not fulfilled its promise as a general alternative to CDT.

It may be (as with incentive theory), that both CDT and SPT hold, but to different extents in different contexts. For example, CDT may apply when we behave contrary to our initial attitude (counter-attitudinal behaviour, *outside* our 'latitude of acceptance'), while SPT may apply better when our behaviour and initial attitude are broadly consistent (attitude-congruent behaviour, *inside* our latitude of acceptance) (Hogg and Vaughan, 1998). According to Pennington *et al.* (1999), SPT may be very useful for helping us to understand attitude *formation*, but much less so in relation to attitude *change*.

Methodological issues

The Festinger and Carlsmith study is called 'Cognitive consequences of *forced compliance*'. This implies *lack* of choice, and therefore we would expect incentive theory (and not CDT) to hold. (See **Theoretical issues** above.) The title is rather misleading, because lying to the waiting stooge, in theory at least, was something the participant *chose* to do (albeit as a favour to the experimenter). This is illustrated by the fact that three participants did, indeed, refuse to take the money and be hired. So the dilemma for the $1 participants was, 'I chose to lie for just $1! How can I justify that?'

The crucial point here is that Festinger and Carlsmith deliberately created an *illusion of freedom*, by taking advantage of people's insensitivity to subtle situational prods. The real reasons for participants agreeing to lie about the tasks were contained in the powerful situational trappings of the experiment. Politely, but firmly, an authority figure (the experimenter) asked a favour of the participant (to deceive the next participant, for scientific purposes: Zimbardo and Leippe, 1991).

The compliance pressure was very subtle: the participant, who was already involved in the situation in which the favour was to be done, was being asked to 'step in', to fill a role without which the experiment could not proceed. The request to 'lie' was, ostensibly, *not part of the experiment*. 'Favour' implies choice, and this is what participants were meant to believe they had. But 'objectively', the situation was 'stacked' against them so that they were highly likely to 'agree'. Having agreed, the size of the inducement to lie then determined the degree of dissonance, and the corresponding degree of attitude change. Stroebe and Jonas (1996) believe that this 'choice' feature was intuitively built in to the experimental situation, despite not being specified in the original theory. As we have seen above, this has proved to be essential for dissonance arousal.

An objection that can be made to Festinger and Carlsmith's experiment is that it involves *circular reasoning*: the only evidence for the greater dissonance of the $1 group was their rating of the tasks as more interesting; and the fact that they rated the tasks as more interesting is evidence of their greater dissonance. Is there any *independent* evidence for the existence of dissonance? What kind of evidence would we accept? Croyle and Cooper (1983) found a more persistent increase in physiological arousal (as measured by galvanic skin response/GSR) in participants who wrote a counter-attitudinal essay under high-choice instructions (compared with low-choice or those who wrote an essay consistent with their own opinion).

Subsequent research

Another variable found to influence dissonance (and which interacts with voluntary/involuntary behaviour) is degree of *commitment*. Carlsmith *et al.* (1966) used a procedure similar to the $1/$20 experiment and confirmed Festinger and Carlsmith's findings. However, the dissonance effect was only found when participants lied in a highly committing, face-to-face situation (they had to make an identifiable video recording). Where they merely had to write an essay and were assured of complete anonymity, an incentive effect occurred. (This face-to-face variable was not manipulated by Festinger and Carlsmith.) Other variables thought to be *necessary* for dissonance to occur are:

● anticipating that our attitude-discrepant behaviour will have certain negative consequences;

● feelings of personal responsibility for those consequences (Cooper and Fazio, 1984).

Presumably, only if we believe we have chosen to act that way will we feel responsible. Stroebe and Jonas (1996) consider this to be another feature that Festinger and Carlsmith intuitively built in to the experimental situation: the stooge hinted that she had intended not participating (based on what another participant had told her) until the real participant's 'lie' misled her.

Although lying to another participant may contravene the norms of many cultures, other commonly used dissonance paradigms may *not* induce the same level of dissonance in all cultures (Cooper *et al.*, 2004). For example, using the *dissonance following a decision* procedure (see **Background and context**), Heine and Lehman (1997) asked Japanese and Canadian participants to rate a selection of Western rock and pop CDs; they then had to choose between two that they had rated similarly. The Canadians showed the usual dissonance effect, but the Japanese did not. Heine and Lehman concluded that Japanese people may not be as concerned about the inconsistency that arises when they 'lose' the positive aspect of the unselected option and 'accept' the negative aspects of the chosen one.

The tendency to change one's attitude or behaviour in order to be more consistent (and so reduce dissonance) reflects a need to view behaviour as driven by *internal* factors. But members of *collectivist* cultures (non-Western) do not demonstrate these tendencies: they are willing to sacrifice consistency to maintain a sense of harmony with others (Nagayama Hall and Barongan, 2002). It may even be considered selfish to act according to one's own desires, or to express one's attitudes, if they make others feel uncomfortable (Fiske *et al.*, 1998).

Applications and implications

Totman (1976) gave patients the illusion of choice over the medication they received. This seemed to have beneficial effects: the medicine is more effective because the individual is more committed to it. Although going beyond CDT, this interesting demonstration of 'mind over matter' is consistent with the prediction that individuals committed by their own choice will manifest their beliefs in the medication to a greater extent than those who are less committed (Stephenson, 1996).

Cooper and Axsom (1982) analysed the benefits of psychotherapy in terms of the *justification of effort* (such as embarrassment, financial cost, and so on). See **Background and context** above.) In line with the predictions from CDT, Cooper and Axsom found that riding an exercise bike to the point of exhaustion was as beneficial as implosive therapy in treating phobias (see Chapter 30), and those given a 'choice' of treatment benefited most of all.

The controversy between CDT, incentive theory and SPT is valuable, not so much because one of them is 'correct' and the others 'in error', but as an example of the development of method and theory in social psychology (Shaver, 1987). As Shaver says:

> *What begins as a simple statement (that is, dissonance will be produced whenever one cognitive element implies the opposite of another) becomes, through continuous refinement, a more complex but more accurate statement... Along the way, new methods are developed...new pitfalls are discovered, and new areas of research grow out of attempts to resolve theoretical controversy. Perhaps the greatest compliment that can be paid to the theory of cognitive dissonance is the recognition of its extensive role in this continuing process.*

Both CDT and SPT see attitudes 'following' behaviour (people often behave in a certain way, then report attitudes consistent with that behaviour); to this extent, they imply that viewing people as 'rational individuals' is limited (Moghaddam, 1998: see Chapter 22).

EXERCISES

1   What kind of experimental design was used?

2   What were the independent and dependent variables?

3   (a) Was the sample biased?

    (b) In light of your previous answer, how significant is it that the stooge was female?

4   Why was it important that the interviewer did not know which conditions participants had been allocated to?

5   In an experiment by Zanna and Cooper (1974), participants wrote a counter-attitudinal essay under instructions which implied either high or low choice. As predicted, high-choice participants changed their opinions more than low-choice participants. But they were also given a placebo pill, which they were told would either make them feel tense or relaxed – or were told nothing about it at all. The CDT prediction was supported when no information was given, and even more strongly when told it would relax them. But for those told the pill would make them tense, there was no difference between the high- and low-choice conditions. How do you explain Zanna and Cooper's findings?

6   How might the impact of situational pressures towards compliance have been tested?

7   Are there any ethical issues raised by the experiment?

10 Behavioural study of obedience

Milgram, S. (1963)

Journal of Abnormal and Social Psychology, 67: 371–8

BACKGROUND AND CONTEXT

In a very real sense, it is the horrific events of the Nazi concentration camps which form the background to this study. Milgram was originally attempting to test the 'Germans are different' hypothesis (GADH), used by historians to explain the systematic destruction of millions of Jews, Poles and others in the 1930s and 1940s. This maintains that:

● Hitler could not have put his evil plans into effect without the cooperation of thousands of others;

● the Germans have a basic character defect, namely a readiness to obey without question, regardless of the acts demanded by the authority figure, and it is this readiness to obey which provided Hitler with the cooperation he needed.

It is the second of these which Milgram was trying to test.

As Milgram (1963) says:

> It has been reliably established that from 1939 to 1945 millions of innocent persons were slaughtered on command; gas chambers were built, death camps were guarded, daily quotas of corpses were produced with the same efficiency as the manufacture of appliances.

He had originally planned to take the experiment to Germany; the 1963 study, conducted at Yale University (in New Haven, Connecticut), was really intended as a pilot study (a dummy run). The results clearly made the trip to Germany unnecessary: the GADH was clearly false.

AIM AND NATURE

● HYPOTHESIS

As we have said, the original hypothesis was the GADH, specifically the second part, and the 1963 experiment at Yale was designed to be a pilot study to iron out procedural and other practical problems before the experiment proper was carried out in Germany.

On the assumption that Milgram expected to collect data in Germany that would support the GADH, the 1963 study, by implication, predicted that there would be very low levels of obedience when American participants were instructed to deliver increasingly intense electric shocks (the highest shock level being life-threatening) to a fellow participant.

The 1963 study should be understood in the context of a series of experiments (of which it was the original). It represents a kind of baseline situation, with subsequent experiments systematically varying different variables, intended to throw light on the findings of the 1963 study. This first study came to be called the 'remote-victim' experiment; the next one ('voice-feedback') became the baseline for all subsequent experiments (Milgram, 1974). This series of experiments was not planned: as we have seen, the GADH implies that American participants would show very low levels of obedience (a finding which does not need explaining, unlike very high obedience).

Milgram had asked 14 psychology students to predict what would happen for 100 participants in the remote-victim experiment. They thought that very few would continue up to the highest shock level. Similarly, 40 psychiatrists predicted that less than 1 per cent would administer the highest voltage.

● METHOD/DESIGN

Within the 1963 study, the experimental situation was the same for all participants: there were no experimental and control conditions as such, but the experimenter's 'prods and prompts' to carry on giving shocks for wrong answers by the 'learner' (an actor pretending to be another naive participant) could be thought of as an *independent variable*. The rate of obedience (how far up the shock scale the participant went) constituted the *dependent variable*.

The study might be more accurately described as a *controlled observation* than an experiment. Indeed, observation was used as a technique for collecting data within the overall experimental design. Tape recorders, photographs and (sometimes) observers behind a one-way mirror were used to record participants' unusual behaviour. Later studies also made film records of the proceedings. This, together with post-experimental interviews with every participant, generated a great deal of *qualitative data* (such as their emotional responses to the situation and things they said about what they were being asked to do); these complemented the *quantitative data* (the number of participants continuing to shock up to different shock levels).

The participants were 40 males, aged between 20 and 50, from a wide range of educational and occupational backgrounds. They answered advertisements which were sent by post or appeared in local newspapers, asking for volunteers for a study of memory and learning, to be conducted at Yale University. It would take about an hour, and volunteers would be paid $4.50.

When participants arrived at Yale University psychology department, they were met by a young man in a grey technician's coat who introduced himself as Jack Williams, the experimenter. Also present was a Mr Wallace, introduced as another participant. In fact, Mr Wallace was a stooge, trained for the role, a 47-year-old accountant, whom most observers found mild-mannered and likeable.

Everything that happened after this was pre-planned, staged and scripted – except the degree to which the real participant obeyed the experimenter's instructions.

The participant and Mr Wallace were told that the experiment was concerned with the effects of *punishment* on learning. One of them was to be the teacher, and the other the learner. Their roles were determined by each drawing a piece of paper from a hat: it was rigged so that the naive participant was always the teacher (both slips of paper had 'teacher' written on them).

They all went into an adjoining room, where Mr Wallace was strapped into an 'electric chair' apparatus. The experimenter explained that the straps were to prevent excessive movement while the learner was being shocked. An electrode was attached to the learner's wrist and electrode paste applied 'to avoid blisters and burns'. The electrode was attached to the shock generator situated next door. The teacher and experimenter then moved into the room with the generator. The teacher was given a 45-volt shock to convince him that it was real, as he was to be operating it during the experiment. However, this was the *only* real shock that would be delivered at any point in the experiment which followed (in other words, the learner did *not* receive a single actual shock).

The generator (which looked very authentic) had a number of switches, each clearly marked with voltage levels and verbal descriptions, starting at 15 volts and going up to 450 in intervals of 15:

● 15–60 Slight shock

● 75–120 Moderate shock

- 135–180 Strong shock

- 195–240 Very strong shock

- 255–300 Intense shock

- 315–360 Intense to extreme shock

- 375–420 Danger: severe shock

- 435–450 XXX

The teacher had to read out a series of word pairs (e.g. 'blue-girl', 'nice-day', 'fat-neck'), then the first of one pair (the stimulus word) followed by five words, one of which was the original paired response. The learner had to choose the correct response to the stimulus word by pressing one of four switches, which turned on a light on a panel in the generator room. Each time he made a mistake, the teacher had to deliver a shock, and each successive mistake was punished by a shock 15 volts higher than the previous one. Before delivering each shock, the teacher had to announce the voltage level.

Mr Wallace was scripted to pound loudly on the wall at 300 volts and, after 315 volts, to stop pounding and give no further answers. If the learner failed to respond, the teacher was to take this as an error; this ensured that shocks could still be given up to 450 volts.

The experimenter had specially prepared 'prods' for whenever the teacher refused to continue or showed any resistance or reluctance to do so:

- Prod 1 'Please continue' or 'Please go on'.

- Prod 2 'The experiment requires that you continue'.

- Prod 3 'It is absolutely essential that you continue'.

- Prod 4 'You have no other choice, you *must* go on'.

The prods were always made in that order and delivered in a firm, but not impolite, tone of voice. There were also 'special prods' to reassure participants that 'Although the shocks may be painful, there is no permanent tissue damage, so please go on'.

● RESULTS

As shown in Table 10.1, the scores were radically different from what was expected. Every participant shocked up to at least 300 volts; five refused to go beyond 300, four more gave one further shock before refusing, two broke off at 330 volts, and one each at 345, 360 and 375. This makes a total of 14 *defiant* participants (35 per cent).

AIM AND NATURE

Table 10.1

Distribution of break-off points

Verbal designation and voltage indication	Number of participants for whom this was maximum shock
Slight shock 15 30 45 60	0 0 0 0
Moderate shock 75 90 105 120	0 0 0 0
Strong shock 135 150 165 180	0 0 0 0
Very strong shock 195 210 225 240	0 0 0 0
Intense shock 255 270 285 300	0 0 0 5
Extreme intensity shock 315 330 345 360	4 2 1 1
Danger: severe shock 375 390 405 420	1 0 0 0
XXX 435 450	0 26

These participants were often extremely agitated and sometimes even angry; sometimes they just got up from their chair and indicated that they wished to leave.

The rest (26 participants, or 65 per cent) were *obedient* participants; that is, they went all the way up to 450 volts. Many did so under extreme stress, some expressed reluctance to shock beyond 300 volts, showing many of the fears that the defiant participants displayed. At the end of the experiment, many heaved sighs of relief, mopped their brows, some shook their heads in regret. Some had remained calm throughout.

● CONCLUSIONS

One of the striking findings was the sheer strength of the tendency to obey. Despite having learned from childhood that it is morally wrong to hurt other people against their will, 65 per cent of this cross section of an ordinary American town abandoned this principle in following the instructions of an authority figure who had no special powers to enforce his commands – they would not have been punished or suffered any material loss had they disobeyed.

The other striking finding was the extraordinary tension and emotional strain caused by the procedure – in both the defiant and the obedient participants.

EVALUATION

Theoretical issues

Milgram's obedience studies are just as likely (if not more so) to be discussed in relation to the *ethics* of psychological research as in the context of the social psychological processes in which Milgram himself was interested (and which led him to conduct them in the first place). The ethical implications are discussed at length in **Applications and implications** below.

However, the studies do raise fundamental issues about human behaviour, such as how we come to accept responsibility for our actions and the relationship of this to our overall self-concept, the power of social situations to make us act in uncharacteristic ways, the influence of others over our actions, how we are socialized into playing submissive roles, and the different valuations we place on different kinds of social influence (such as obedience versus conformity). Many of these issues are also raised by Haney *et al.*'s (1973) prison simulation experiment (see Chapter 13).

Milgram's findings are extremely unsettling: how can it be that 'ordinary', law-abiding, non-sadistic Americans in the 1960s can deliver electric shocks to an undeserving fellow American severe enough to make him unconscious – or even kill him? Surely they must have been acting or pretending in some way (the results are not what they seem)? (See **Methodological issues** below.) Alternatively, Milgram is to blame for exposing his unsuspecting participants to such an emotionally distressing experience: they were not 'responsible' for their actions. But Milgram would stand this argument on its head: rather than claiming that they were not responsible (they obeyed) because they were so distressed, Milgram would argue that they were distressed because they found themselves obeying!

Milgram explains obedience in terms of the *agentic state*, in which the obedient participant comes to see him/herself as an agent of external authority. This is the opposite of the *autonomous state*, in which we see ourselves as being in control of our actions ('responsible'). Loss of this sense of being in control can be disturbing, especially when the authority figure is instructing us to behave in ways that conflict with our normal sense of 'justice' and right and wrong. Milgram believes that his studies hold a mirror up to us: his participants' behaviour reflects how most of us would behave under those same circumstances. We do not always like what we see!

Moghaddam (1998) cites Turnbull's (1972) study of the Ik, a traditional hunter-gatherer people now living in Uganda, near the Kenya border. Social life involves extreme selfishness and total concern with personal survival, to such an extent that parents deprive their children of food, and children even refuse water to aged parents. Cheating and stealing food is common. Why? The explanation seems to lie in the terrible conditions in which they live. Formerly hunter-gatherers roaming freely in search of game, they were forced by modernization and national boundaries to live in a confined territory with very limited natural resources. Life became a fierce struggle for survival to the extent that they seemed to have completely abandoned the value we associate with human social life. Such extreme conditions, similar to those in Nazi concentration camps where many of the values we normally associate with 'human nature' disappeared, underline the power of the situation to shape behaviour: 'our behaviour, it seems, is much more dependent on the social context than the dominant Western model of "self-contained individualism" assumes' (Moghaddam, 1998).

Methodological issues

A central methodological dilemma faced by social psychologists in particular is how to make their experiments have the maximum impact on participants without sacrificing control over the situation (Aronson, 1988). Aronson and Carlsmith (1963) distinguished between two kinds of realism:

1   If an experiment has an impact on the participants, forces them to take the situation seriously and involves them in the procedures, it has *experimental realism*.

2   The similarity of the laboratory experiment to the events which commonly occur in the real world is called *mundane realism*.

Aronson (1988) claims that Milgram's experiment is high in the first kind of realism, but lower in the second. There is no question that the participants took the experimental situation very seriously. However, Milgram argues that his experiment also has great mundane realism: the essential process involved in complying with the demands of an authority figure (the agentic state) is the same, whether the setting is contrived (as in the laboratory) or occurs naturally in the outside world.

Orne and Holland (1968) were major critics of the methodology of the obedience experiment. In their paper entitled 'On the ecological validity of laboratory deceptions', they use the term 'ecological validity' to cover both experimental and mundane realism (it is commonly used to refer *only* to mundane realism: see Chapter 1). According to Orne and Holland, Milgram's experiments lack *both*.

As far as *experimental realism* is concerned, they claim that participants do not take the situation at face value; in particular, they fail to believe that the learner is actually receiving painful shocks. But Milgram (1977, 1992) points to several sources of evidence that they took it very seriously indeed:

● In the 1963 study, participants were asked to rate how painful to the learner were the last few shocks they administered. The modal response on a 14-point scale was 14 and the mean 13.42 (14 = extremely painful/1= not at all painful).

● Participants' obvious tension and distress makes Orne and Holland's claim that they were merely *pretending* to sweat, tremble and stutter so as to please the experimenter 'pathetically detached from reality'. Baumrind's attack on the *ethics* of the experiment is, of course, based on the reality of their distress.

● In the follow-up questionnaire sent to all participants a year later, one item dealt with shocks given to the learner. Of those who responded, 80 per cent believed they were giving painful shocks. 'I fully believed …'/'Although I had some doubts, I believed the learner was *probably* …'), while only 2.4 per cent were 'certain the learner was not …'. The rest were either uncertain but leaning on the side of 'not', or 'just weren't sure'.

A replication by Rosenhan (1969) included steps that tried to ensure that the post-experiment interviewer was seen as independent of the study itself and was interested in the participants' true beliefs about what had happened ('You mean you really didn't catch on to the experiment?'). Fully 68.9 per cent of his high-school student sample completely accepted the experiment's authenticity.

According to Orne and Holland (1968), a major 'giveaway' that was bound to have made participants suspicious was the very fact that they were being asked to administer the shocks when the experimenter could so easily have done it himself. The answer is actually provided in the experimental instructions:

> we don't know how much punishment is best for learning, and we don't know
> how much difference it makes as to who is giving the punishment... So in this
> study we are bringing together a number of adults of different occupations and
> ages... We want to find out just what effect different people have on each other as
> teachers and learners.

Orne and Holland (1968) claim that Milgram's participants were responding to the *demand characteristics* of the experimental situation. (See Chapter 1.) The experimenter's prods (such as 'You have no other choice, you *must* go on') made the situation no different 'from the stage magician's trick where a volunteer from the audience is strapped into the guillotine and another volunteer is required to trip the release lever'. But wouldn't the demand cues have been read as instructing the participant to *break off the experiment*?

As far as *mundane realism* is concerned, Orne and Holland (1968) argue that the experimental situation is unique as a context for eliciting behaviour, and so we cannot generalize from it. When people agree to participate, they implicitly give the experimenter a free hand to ask almost anything of them for a limited time; in return, they will come to no harm (although there may be some discomfort or inconvenience). The willingness of Milgram's participants to carry out seemingly destructive orders reflects this implicit trust in the experimenter – and so does not tell us about how they will behave outside the experimental situation.

Milgram's (1977, 1992) response is to argue that psychology experiments are essentially the same as other social situations in which an authority figure gives orders to those in a subordinate position. The nature of those orders matters less than the relationship ('relationship overwhelms content'). This mirrors Milgram's claim that obedience is essentially the same process regardless of where it takes place and the circumstances in which it occurs (psychology laboratory or concentration camp). (See **Applications and implications**.)

Subsequent research

As we noted in the **Background and context** above, the 1963 study was the inspiration for a series of experiments (18 in total), which are described in Milgram's (1974) *Obedience to Authority*. One of these included an all-female sample, and the obedience rate was very similar to that for males. This finding has been replicated in numerous studies by other researchers.

Several *cross-cultural* replications have been conducted, for example in Germany (Mantell, 1971), Australia (Kilham and Mann, 1974), the UK (Burley and McGuiness, 1977) and Holland (Meeus and Raajimakers, 1986). Obedience rates ranged from 16 per cent (female students in Kilham and Mann's study) to 92 per cent (a sample of the general population in Meeus and Raajimakers' study).

However, it is very difficult to compare these studies, because of methodological discrepancies between them (Smith and Bond, 1998). For example, they have used different types of stooge, some of whom may have been perceived as more vulnerable or more deserving of shock punishment than others. For example, Kilham and Mann's female participants were asked to shock a *female* learner (while Milgram's stooge learner was always male).

Also, with the exception of Jordan (Shanab and Yahya, 1978), all the countries studied have been advanced industrialized nations; this suggests that we need to be cautious about concluding that we have identified a universal feature of social behaviour. However, Smith and Bond (1998) point out that in none of these countries is obedience to authority the kind of blind process that some interpreters of Milgram's work have implied. Obedience rates vary greatly, depending on social context (which defines the meaning of the orders given by the authority figure). Culture teaches people in certain roles to expect to be obeyed by others (Moghaddam, 1998).

Applications and implications

According to McGhee (2001), Milgram's obedience studies are 'probably the most…disturbing, most discussed, most criticized, and most notorious in the history of psychology'. He also believes that we cannot legitimately say that we have thought about social psychology unless we have thought carefully about Milgram's studies of 'destructive obedience'. They have also helped to shape the 'ethics debate' within psychology as a whole. In the early 1960s, most of the ethical principles we now take for granted (such as informed consent, use of deception only as a last resort, which Milgram himself discusses) were less clearly documented and enforced.

Baumrind (1964) expressed concern for the participants' welfare: were adequate measures taken to protect them from the stress and emotional conflict they undoubtedly suffered? Milgram argues that Baumrind is confusing the (unanticipated) outcome with the basic experimental procedure: the stress and conflict was not intended or deliberate – or expected. You cannot know your results in advance.

Indeed, the GADH, together with the predictions of students and psychiatrists (see **Hypothesis** section above), suggested that there would be very little obedience (and, therefore, little reason for conflict). Aronson (1988) asks if we would question the ethics if none of the participants had gone beyond the 'moderate shock' level. Apparently not.

So, could it be that underlying the criticism of Milgram is the shock and horror of the 'banality of evil' (the subtitle of Hannah Arendt's book on the Israeli trial of Adolf Eichmann, the Nazi in charge of the deportation of Jews to the death camps)? To believe that 'ordinary people' could do what Eichmann did (or what Milgram's participants did) is far less acceptable than that Eichmann was an inhuman monster, or that participants were put under immorally high levels of stress by an inhuman psychologist!

Milgram (1977, 1992) acknowledges that the use of 'technical illusions' (a term he prefers to 'deception' because it is morally neutral) poses ethical dilemmas for the researcher. By definition, they prevent participants from giving their *informed consent*, and so they should never be used unless they are 'indispensable to the conduct of the inquiry'.

Finally, to return to the beginning, Blass (1992) suggests that Milgram's research may have left the impression that situational pressures completely outweigh personality factors in determining obedience: 'I was only following orders' was, of course, the main defence made by Nazi war criminals at the Nuremberg trials. The plea of not guilty on grounds of 'obedience' was duly rejected, which suggests that there is more to obedience than the agentic state.

Eichmann is a case in point. Not only was he not the sadistic, evil psychopath that our horror at his crimes would make him out to be, but neither was he the puppet-like instrument of Hitler's 'final solution' to the 'Jewish problem'. He took pleasure and pride in his efficiency at transporting millions of Jews to the death camps, displaying 'eliminationist anti-Semitism', the primary motivation for the actions of Holocaust perpetrators (Goldhagen, 1996, in Cardwell, 2005). Equivalent hatreds (and related belief systems) can also help to explain the atrocities committed during the war in Bosnia in the early 1990s and the Rwandan genocide in 1994.

These and other crimes against humanity can only happen if individuals are predisposed in some way to respond to the demands of those in authority. As Blass (1992) says, an accurate picture of the obedience-to-authority process must recognize the interaction between external *and* internal influences.

EXERCISES

1 Putting yourself in the obedient participant's place, how might you have justified shocking all the way up to 450 volts? What features of the experimental situation could have made it more likely that you obeyed?

2 What kind of sample were Milgram's participants? Can they be considered a *representative* sample?

3 (a) What is the difference between conformity and obedience?

   (b) What do they have in common?

Good Samaritanism: An underground phenomenon?

Piliavin, I.M., Rodin, J. and Piliavin, J.A. (1969)

Journal of Personality and Social Psychology, 1(4): 289–99

BACKGROUND AND CONTEXT

The major inspiration for research into *bystander intervention* was the real-life murder of Kitty (real name Catherine) Genovese in the Queens district of New York in 1964. The first studies, conducted by Latané and Darley in 1968, were laboratory experiments, and it is ironic that Piliavin *et al.* wanted to take the research out of the laboratory (where the victim was only heard and only other participants were seen) and into the real world, where it had all begun. Not only was Kitty Genovese heard, but she and her murderer were also seen.

> For more than half an hour, 38 respectable, law-abiding citizens in Queens watched a killer stalk and stab a woman and didn't call the police. After she was stabbed the first time, she screamed 'Oh, My God, he stabbed me! Please help me! Please help me!' After the murderer had first grabbed her, lights went on in the ten-storey apartment block and windows were opened. From one of the upper windows, a man called down: 'Let that girl alone'. He walked off a little way up the street; lights went out. He returned to stab her a second time. 'I'm dying', she shrieked, 'I'm dying'. Windows were opened again, lights went on in many apartments. The assailant got into his car and drove off. He returned to stab her a third time, this time fatally. It was all over by about 3.30 a.m., but the first call to the police was recorded at 3.50 a.m. Witnesses had watched from behind their curtains: one couple pulled up chairs to the window and turned the light out to see better. The caller was a man who did not want to 'get involved'.

This extract from the *New York Times* (27 March 1964) suggests that there was no doubt people knew a serious crime was taking place (*defining the situation*). The repeated stabbings must have conveyed to any witnesses that no one else had gone for help, making it difficult to use *diffusion of responsibility* as a justification for not intervening themselves. The actual caller's not wanting to get involved suggests that the *costs of intervention* might be the key variable. Other reasons witnesses gave for their inaction included: 'We thought it was a lovers' quarrel', 'Frankly, we were afraid', and 'I was tired'. It would seem that 'bystander apathy' (Latané and Darley, 1970) is too simple a label to attach to the (non-)behaviour of the 38 witnesses.

AIM AND NATURE

● HYPOTHESIS

The main focus of Piliavin *et al.*'s study was on the type of victim (drunk or ill) and the race of the victim (black or white) (the *independent variables*); and on the speed of helping, the frequency of helping and the race of the helper (*dependent variables*). Other independent variables included movement out of the 'critical area' (of the train compartment), and spontaneous comments.

Based on previous research into similarity and liking, as well as on race and social distance, it was predicted that:

● an individual would be more inclined to help someone of the same than of a different race;

● help would be offered more often and more quickly to the apparently ill victim than to the apparently drunk victim.

The study was also concerned with the impact of *modelling* (another independent variable) in emergency situations, that is, the effect on others of seeing someone go to the aid of the victim.

A final aim was to examine the relationship between the size of the group (the number of potential helpers), frequency (how often) and latency (time between the emergency occurring and someone intervening), with a victim who was both seen and heard.

● METHOD/DESIGN

Before 1969, most studies of bystander intervention (a form of helping, and hence *pro-social* behaviour) were laboratory experiments. Piliavin *et al.*'s *field experiment* took place in the natural setting of a New York subway train ('a laboratory on wheels'), with *participant observation* being a major method for collecting data.

Four teams of students, each comprising a victim, a model and two observers, staged standardized collapses, in which the type of victim, race of victim and presence or absence of a model were manipulated.

Participants

The collapses (emergencies) were staged during the approximately 7½-minute journey between 59th and 125th Street stations. About 4,450 men and women who travelled on this stretch of the subway, between 11 a.m. and 3 p.m. on weekdays, during the period 15 April to 26 June 1968 were the unsolicited participants.

The racial composition of a typical train travelling through Harlem to the Bronx was about 45 per cent black and 55 per cent white. The mean number of people per compartment during these hours was 43, and the mean number in the 'critical area' where the incident was staged was 8.5.

Field situation

The incident occurred 70 seconds into the journey. The critical area was the end section of any compartment whose doors led to the next compartment. There were 13 seats and some standing room on all trains (see Figure 11.1).

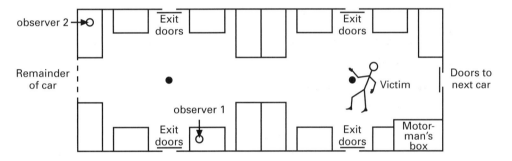

Figure 11.1. Layout of adjacent and critical areas of subway car.

Procedure

On each trial (the 7½-minute journey), two male and two female students boarded the train using different doors. Four different teams collected data for 103 trials. Each team varied the location of the experimental compartment from trial to trial. The females sat outside the critical area and recorded data as unobtrusively as possible, while the male model and victim remained standing. The victim always stood next to a pole in the middle of the critical area.

The victim staggered forward and collapsed, 70 seconds into the journey. Until receiving help, he remained on his back, looking at the ceiling. If he received no help by the time the train slowed to a stop, the model helped him to his feet. When the train reached the station, the team got off and crossed to another platform to board a train going in the opposite direction. Six to eight trials were run on any given day.

Victim

The four victims (one from each team) were 26- to 35-year-old males, three white, one black, all identically dressed in casual clothes.

● In 38 trials, the victim smelled of alcohol and carried a bottle wrapped tightly in a brown bag (*drunk condition*).

● In 65 trials, the victim appeared sober and carried a black cane (*cane condition*).

In all other respects, they behaved identically and each victim participated in both conditions.

Model

The models were four white males (aged 24–29). There were four model conditions used across both drunk and cane conditions:

1   *critical area – early*: model stood in critical area and waited approximately 70 seconds after the collapse;

2   *critical area – late*: as for 1, but waited 150 seconds;

3   *adjacent area – early*: model stood in middle of the compartment, adjacent to critical area, and waited 70 seconds;

4   *adjacent area – late*: as for 3, but waited 150 seconds.

The model helped by raising the victim to a sitting position and staying with him for the remainder of the trial.

There were equal numbers of *no-model* trials in each of the four model conditions.

● RESULTS

The frequency of help the victim received was impressive, at least compared with earlier laboratory studies. The cane victim received spontaneous help (i.e. before the model acted) on 62 out of 65 trials, and even the drunk was helped on 19 of 38 trials.

In all but three of the cane trials planned to be model trials, the victim received help before the model was scheduled to intervene; this happened less often with the drunk victim, where sometimes even the late model intervened.

There was more immediate, spontaneous helping of the cane victim than the drunk, and this applied equally to black and white victims.

On 60 per cent of the 81 trials on which the victim received help, he received it from two, three or even more passengers. There were no significant differences between black/white or cane/drunk victims in the number of helpers who came to his aid subsequent to the first.

Characteristics of spontaneous first helpers

On average, 60 per cent of the people in the critical areas were male, and men made up 90 per cent of the spontaneous first helpers. Of the first 81 helpers, 64 per cent were white (but this was not significantly different from the expected 55 per cent based on racial distribution in the compartments). However, on the 65 trials where spontaneous help was offered to white victims, 68 per cent of the helpers were white; this is significantly different from the expected 55 per cent. On the 16 trials where the black victim was spontaneously helped, 50 per cent of the first helpers were white. This represents a slight (non-significant) trend towards 'same-race' helping.

When race of helper was analysed separately for cane and drunk conditions, another non-significant, though interesting trend emerged. With both black and white cane victims, the proportion of helpers of each race was consistent with the expected 55 per cent/45 per cent split. But with the drunk, it was mainly members of *his own race* who came to his aid.

Modelling effects

Overall, the early model (70 seconds) elicited significantly more help than the late model (150 seconds).

Other responses to the incident

On 21 of the 103 trials, 34 people left the critical area; this was more likely to happen on the drunk trials and when no help had been offered during the first 70 seconds.

Passengers were most likely to make comments on drunk trials where no help was offered after 70 seconds. Many women said things such as, 'It's for men to help him', or 'I wish I could help him – I'm not strong enough'.

A test of the diffusion of responsibility hypothesis

Response times (latencies of response) were consistently faster in groups of seven or more passengers than in groups of one to three. This is clearly contrary to what the diffusion of responsibility hypothesis predicts.

● CONCLUSIONS

1   An individual who appears to be ill was more likely to receive help than one who appeared to be drunk, even when the immediate help needed was of the same kind.

2   In mixed groups of men and women, with a male victim, men were more likely to help than women were.

3   In mixed racial groups, there was some tendency for same-race helping to be more frequent, especially when the victim seemed drunk rather than ill.

4   There was no diffusion of responsibility: help was no less frequent or slower in coming from larger compared with smaller groups of bystanders (potential helpers); if anything, the effect was in the opposite direction.

5   The longer the emergency continued without help being offered:

   (a) the less impact a model had on bystanders' helping behaviour;

   (b) the more likely bystanders were to leave the immediate area in order to avoid the situation;

   (c) the more likely bystanders were to discuss the incident.

EVALUATION

Methodological issues

Given mixed groups of men and women, and a male victim (as in the Piliavin *et al.* study), men are more likely to help than women. In terms of the *arousal: cost–reward model* (see **Subsequent research** below), costs of helping are higher for women, and costs of not helping are lower. So what if the victim had been female? According to Eagly (1987), there is good reason to believe the results would not have been very different.

Eagly suggests that helping behaviour is at least as much determined by conforming to gender roles as by the demands of the situation. Social psychological studies of helping, whether laboratory or field, are confined to short-term encounters with strangers, which seems to increase the chances that men will be the helpers rather than women. This is because such encounters are more consistent with the traditional male gender role: men are 'heroes', who perform altruistic acts of saving others from harm with some risk to themselves. Related to this is the notion of chivalry: going to the aid of 'helpless females' or the 'damsel-in-distress syndrome'. So male (*agentic*) helping is often directed towards strangers and women; in addition, men are expected to be dominant (compared with the submissive female) and assertive, making helping an assertive act of intervention.

Women, by contrast, are expected to place the needs of others (especially family members) before their own. Their orientation is towards listening, sympathizing, showing kindness and compassion (rather than direct action), and this female (*communal*) type of helping is expressed most effectively through long-term relationships.

Combined with the female role encouraging avoidance of strangers (particularly men), this means that men and women should differ in their perception of whether providing aid is likely be dangerous for themselves as helpers. Especially in situations with an element of risk, men should be more likely to help; where there is also an audience to witness the helping act and other potential helpers available, this tendency will be even greater. Moghaddam (1998) makes an equivalent distinction between *heroic* (male) and *nurturant* (female) helping.

According to Eagly, the research literature (including the Piliavin *et al.* study) mainly confirms these predictions:

● men are more likely to help than women;

● men are more likely to help women than other men;

● women help men and other women more or less equally.

But since these findings are based largely on studies that require agentic/heroic helping (including the New York subway study), we cannot draw any general conclusions about gender differences. Role theory predicts that in other kinds of situations, women will be the greater helpers. Moghaddam (1998) believes that the neglect of communal/nurturant helping reflects a cultural bias in the research.

Whatever the advantages of a field experiment like the New York subway study may be (compared with laboratory studies), an unavoidable feature is that all the participants are unsolicited: since they are unaware that an experiment is taking place, they cannot give their consent – let alone their informed consent. Nor is it possible to debrief them, for obvious, practical reasons. Can researchers justify putting 'innocent' (non-volunteer) people through what, for some, might be a distressing episode (whether they help or not), when it is not possible to explain to them its false nature and its purpose?

Subsequent research

Piliavin *et al.* try to account for their findings in terms of a model of response to emergency situations (intended as a 'heuristic device': see **Exercises** at the end of the chapter), which was later revised and expanded to cover both emergency and non-emergency helping (Piliavin *et al.*, 1981). The *arousal: cost–reward* (ACR) *model* identifies two conceptually distinct, but functionally interdependent influences on helping:

1   *Arousal* in response to the need or distress of others is an emotional response and is the basic *motivational construct.* When arousal is attributed to the distress of the victim, it is experienced as unpleasant and the bystander is motivated to reduce it.

2   The *cost–reward* component involves *cognitive processes* by which bystanders assess and weigh up the anticipated costs and rewards associated with both helping and not helping.

The ACR model has generated a large amount of research, which has concentrated largely on the relative costs of helping and not helping (for reviews see Dovidio *et al.*, 1991; Gross, 2005; Schroeder *et al.*, 1995).

There are many different kinds of costs and rewards for helping and not helping, including *psychological aversion.* This relates to helping different kinds of victim. In a follow-up to the 1969 study, the victim bit off a capsule of bloodlike dye, which trickled down his chin. The helping rate dropped from 90 to 60 per cent. Passengers were much more likely to get someone else to help, especially someone they thought might be more competent in an emergency (Piliavin and Piliavin, 1972). Similarly, Piliavin *et al.* (1975) found that when the victim had an ugly facial birthmark, the rate of helping dropped to 61 per cent.

The cost–reward analysis is related to *attribution theory.* (See Chapter 14.) One of the major influences on the decision to help is the perceived *cause* of the need for help (Weiner, 1992). According to Piliavin *et al.*, the drunk victim is 'partly responsible' for his own plight. But note that they offer this only as an 'after-the-fact interpretation'. Is there any evidence that perceived causes are an element of the cost–reward matrix?

A common experimental paradigm is for a student to be asked for academic help from a supposed classmate, with the reasons for the request being manipulated. Applying the findings of studies using this paradigm (e.g. Barnes *et al.*, 1979; Berkowitz, 1969) to the Piliavin *et al.* study, getting drunk is perceived as a *controllable* cause of a need: people are typically held responsible for their alcohol consumption. When alcoholics are rated along with other stigmatized groups (such as the mentally ill, homosexuals and obese people), they are often seen as the most responsible for their own plight (Weiner, 1992). This is highlighted in campaigns against drink-driving: although the driver is clearly not intentionally harming his/her victim, because the harm is a consequence of a freely chosen, controllable act, s/he is held responsible (both legally and morally) for those consequences.

According to Weiner, perceived *uncontrollability* makes witnesses respond more sympathetically, which, in turn, makes helping more likely. By contrast, perceived controllability induces feelings of anger, which make neglect (non-helping) a more likely response. The cane victim, by implication, is ill and so is not responsible: his need for help is beyond his control and so he is more likely to receive help for this reason. Weiner (1988, in Weiner, 1992) found that people suffering from Alzheimer's disease, blindness, cancer, heart disease, paraplegia and Vietnam War syndrome were all rated as low on responsibility, high on liking and pity, and were much more likely to be 'promised' help. The reverse was true for those with AIDS or drug addictions, and for obese people and child abusers.

The degree of perceived responsibility can be altered by providing additional information: for example, someone with heart disease resulting from smoking is much more likely to be blamed. (Note the ongoing debate in the UK about the rights of patients who have already received a liver transplant and who then continue drinking, to go on the waiting list for another liver.) Similarly, someone who contracted AIDS from a blood transfusion is likely to be judged very differently from someone who engaged in unprotected sex.

Theoretical issues

A common response to the Kitty Genovese murder is to say, 'this could only have happened in a large metropolis like New York – it wouldn't have happened in a small town or village'. The implication is that people who live in cities are much less caring (whether because city life makes them like that or because uncaring people are attracted to city life).

In either case, the focus is on people and their dispositions, rather than the situational forces which influence behaviour. The need to explain the failure of those 38 witnesses to save Kitty's life is so strong that we may take the cognitively easy option and make the *fundamental attribution error*. (See Chapter 14.) Even if it were true that city dwellers are more callous and indifferent to others' needs, this alone could not account for such incidents where bystanders fail to intervene.

According to Milgram and Hollander (1964), living in towns and cities means that our friends and 'allies' are not constantly at hand. Kitty Genovese required immediate help, but those who might have rushed to her aid were miles from the scene of the tragedy.

In addition, Milgram (1977, 1992) observes that a rule of urban life is respect for other people's emotional and social privacy, perhaps because physical privacy is so hard to achieve. The diverse nature of city life encourages people to withhold their help for fear of antagonizing the people involved or 'crossing a line'. Also, as Milgram puts it: 'There are practical limitations to the Samaritan impulse in a major city. If a citizen attended to every needy person … he would scarcely keep his own affairs in order'.

The 'street' has a symbolic significance for the middle-class mentality: everything that is vulgar and dangerous in life, the very opposite of privacy and the security derived from living among one's prized possessions. Kitty's murder took place on the street, a place that was largely irrelevant to those 38 witnesses (Milgram and Hollander, 1964).

They also warn us that 'In our righteous denunciation of the 38 witnesses, we should not forget that they did not commit the murder; they merely failed to prevent it …' Is it possible that they failed to act *despite* what they believed was the right thing to do? We know how the 'press of circumstances' often makes us behave differently from how we ought to behave.

At a Catherine Genovese Memorial Conference on Bad Samaritanism (1984), the *New York Times* quoted a law professor who said, 'looking at those 38 people, we were really looking at ourselves. We might not have done anything either. That's the ugly side of human nature'.

Applications and implications

In terms of the ACR model, one of the costs of not helping someone of the opposite race is the threat to one's self-concept as a fair, non-prejudiced individual. This helps to explain why race did not have a significant effect on helping the cane victim, while there was a trend in the direction of same-race helping in the drunk condition. (See **Exercises**.)

Milgram (1977, 1992) suggests a rather different explanation for help across racial lines. He suggests that:

> ethnic allegiance may well be another means of coping with overload: the city dweller can reduce excessive demands and screen out urban heterogeneity by responding along racial lines; overload is made more manageable by limiting the 'span of sympathy'.

Moghaddam (1998) identifies several models of helping behaviour, placing them on a continuum that runs from 'assumes least self-centredness' at one extreme, to 'assumes most self-centredness' at the other. The ACR model comes very close to the 'selfish' end of the scale, with sociobiological accounts (e.g. Rushton, 1991) coming at the *very* end (see Gross, 2005; Schroeder *et al.*, 1995).

At the 'unselfish' end comes the *empathy-altruism model* (Batson, 1991, 1995): when people feel empathy, they become motivated to act, with the ultimate goal of benefiting the victim (i.e. altruistic). This contradicts the commonly held view within psychology that all motivation is ultimately directed towards the *egoistic* goal of increasing our own welfare, and the underlying assumption that human nature is fundamentally *self-serving* (as made by the ACR model). This view of people is known as *universal egoism*, which maintains that even behaviour that *appears* altruistic always turns out to be self-interest in disguise. According to Batson (2000), 'it's not true that everything we do is directed towards the ultimate goal of benefiting ourselves. It seems that we are capable of being altruistic as well as egoistic'.

Moghaddam (1998) believes that *culture* (not biology) is the major source of the great variety of motives (from absolute egoism to true altruism) underlying human pro-social behaviour. Under some conditions, people in the USA can be *more* helpful to members of *out-groups* compared with people living in traditional societies. This may be because the higher mobility and individualism in the USA (and other Western countries) brings Americans into contact with out-group members, and leads them to be both dependent on, and helpful towards, strangers in general. In less mobile, collectivist, non-Western societies, interaction with outsiders is less common, and less help is offered.

Finally, Moghaddam discusses the *meaning* of help. Culture provides the norms and rules that tell us when and how it is appropriate to seek and offer help; related to this is how people respond to *receiving* it. For example, older people (in certain Western countries, anyway) tend to be especially sensitive about independence and being able to cope alone ('help' is often perceived as 'charity'). Women both seek more help than men and receive more offers of help – but these conclusions are based on studies involving *agentic/heroic* helping. (See **Methodological issues** above.)

EXERCISES

1   In terms of the *arousal: cost–reward model*, try to account for the
    following findings from the Piliavin *et al.* study:

    (a) The drunk model was helped less than the ill model.

    (b) Women helped less than men.

    (c) The tendency towards same-race helping (particularly of the
        drunk).

    (d) No diffusion of responsibility on cane trials.

    (e) The longer the emergency continued (the victim receives no help),
        (i) the less likely helping became; (ii) the more likely people were to
        leave the critical area; (iii) the more likely people were to discuss it.

2   Aside from the ethical issues involved, briefly describe *two* advantages
    and disadvantages of field experiments compared with laboratory
    experiments.

3   Piliavin *et al.* describe the *arousal: cost–reward model* as a 'possible
    heuristic device'. What do you understand by this term?

4   How was participant observation used in the study?

5   Distinguish between the following:

    (a) pro-social behaviour;

    (b) helping behaviour;

    (c) altruism.

12

Experiments in intergroup behaviour

Tajfel, H. (1970)

Scientific American, 223: 96–195

BACKGROUND AND CONTEXT

According to Brown (1986), it is quite fitting that the study of *minimal groups,* and the subsequent *social identity theory* (SIT) designed to explain the results of these studies, should have occurred in Europe. This is because Europeans have plenty of experience of group conflict. Tajfel himself was a European Jew who, unlike the majority of his fellow Jews, survived the Second World War. There is a tragic irony (or perhaps prophecy) to Tajfel's reference in the article to his Slovenian friend's description of the stereotype held in Yugoslavia of Bosnians: not only does Yugoslavia no longer exist, but even in that part of Europe, with such a long history of ethnic conflict, who could have predicted the scale and intensity of hostility between the different ethnic groups, especially the 'ethnic cleansing' perpetrated by Muslims, Serbs and Croatians alike? How can we account for prejudice, discrimination and hostility between groups or between individuals as members of those groups?

One psychological approach is to regard prejudice and out-group rejection as 'residing' within the personality structure of individuals, the most influential theory of this kind being Adorno *et al.*'s (1950) *authoritarian personality.* Because they defer to authority, such people are likely to *conform* to societal norms, and would project their aggression onto out-groups which are already perceived as such in their society (Brown, 1985).

Conversely, if societal norms of prejudice and discrimination are sufficiently powerful, many people who do not have most or any of the characteristics of the authoritarian personality may engage in discriminatory behaviour. So, in practice, cultural or societal norms may be much more important than individual personality in accounting for ethnocentrism, out-group rejection, prejudice and discrimination. Brown (1985) gives the example of Nazi Germany, where many people became openly anti-Semitic who might not have held such views privately, or, if they did, would not have expressed them or acted on them until anti-Semitism became 'acceptable'. In other words, discrimination can occur in the absence of prejudice: prejudice is *not* a necessary precondition for discriminatory behaviour, just as prejudice does not guarantee that discrimination will occur (it is not a *sufficient* condition either).

So how can we account for the rise in prejudice and discrimination? One fairly obvious place to look is the relationship that exists between different social groups. This was the approach taken by Sherif, his wife and other colleagues during the 1950s and early 1960s (Sherif and Sherif, 1953; Sherif *et al.*, 1955; Sherif *et al.*, 1961). These studies all involved 12-year-old boys at summer camps in the USA, the best known being the last of these, the Robbers Cave experiment. Brown (1986) describes this as the most successful field experiment ever conducted on intergroup conflict.

Sherif and his colleagues created what Brown calls 'real ethnocentrism, real stereotypes, and real perceived injustice', by assigning previously unacquainted strangers to groups, allowing them to establish a group identity, and then putting these groups into competition with each other (see Gross, 2005). According to Sherif's (1966) *realistic group conflict theory*, objective competition between groups is a *sufficient condition* for prejudice and discrimination.

However, even assuming that it is sufficient (and Tyerman and Spencer's (1983) study involving English boy scouts at annual camp challenges this conclusion), we still need to ask if it is actually *necessary*. In other words, can prejudice and discrimination occur (or be created) in situations where there is *no* competition? Another way of asking this question is: does the fact of belonging to one nationality, religion, ethnic group or social class *in and of itself* generate predictable orientations towards members of other nationalities, and so on (Brown, 1996)? If so, what is the 'minimal case' for producing them?

Tajfel's (1970) study was designed to answer these two important questions.

AIM AND NATURE

● HYPOTHESIS

The same hypothesis was tested in two separate experiments, the first involving the task of estimating the number of dots on a screen, the second involving preference for slides of paintings by Klee or Kandinsky. The hypothesis stated that: 'discriminatory intergroup behaviour can sometimes be expected even if the individual is not involved in actual (or even imagined) conflicts of interest and has no past history of attitudes of intergroup hostility'.

● METHOD/DESIGN

This article is an early report of laboratory experiments carried out at the University of Bristol by Tajfel and his colleagues into intergroup discrimination. A more commonly cited reference is an article by Tajfel *et al.* (1971), entitled 'Social categorization and intergroup behaviour', which appeared in the *European Journal of Social Psychology*. Almost all the subsequent articles first appeared in this journal, and SIT (see **Background and context** above and **Applications and implications** below) is a very 'European' theory (Brown, 1986).

The actual experiments reported here are the same as those reported in the 1971 article. Despite the fact that the term *minimal group* is never used in either, this is how the experiments are usually referred to. Indeed, Tajfel established a basic procedure for investigating intergroup discrimination and in-group favouritism (the *minimal group paradigm*).

The whole point of the paradigm is to establish the '"baseline condition" for intergroup discrimination' (Schiffman and Wicklund, 1992), that is, the demonstration that merely putting people into groups, however arbitrary or meaningless the allocation may be, is sufficient for people to discriminate in favour of their own group and against members of the other group.

The participants were 64 boys, aged 14 and 15, attending a state (comprehensive) school in a Bristol suburb. They all knew each other well before the experiment.

Experiment 1

The first part of the experiment was designed to establish an intergroup categorization. The boys were brought together in a lecture room and told that the researchers were interested in the study of visual judgements. Forty clusters of varying numbers of dots were flashed on a screen and the boys were asked to estimate the number of dots in each cluster and to record their estimates on prepared score sheets.

In one condition, after the boys had completed their estimates they were told that on judgements of this kind some people consistently overestimate and some consistently underestimate the number of dots; these tendencies are in no way related to accuracy. In a second condition, they were told that some people are consistently more accurate than others. Four groups of eight served in each condition.

The second part of the experiment was designed to assess the effects of intergroup categorization on intergroup behaviour. After the estimates had been made and ostentatiously 'scored' by one of the experimenters, the boys were told that the researchers were going to make the most of the boys' presence by investigating other kinds of judgements. To make coding easier, they would be grouped according to the visual judgements they had just made. Actually, they were assigned to groups *randomly*, half to 'underestimators', and half to 'overestimators' (first condition), half to 'better' and half to 'worse' accuracy (second condition).

The new task would consist of giving to others rewards and penalties in real money, without knowing the identity of the boys receiving them. They were taken into another room, one by one, and had to work on their own in separate cubicles, where they found a pencil and a booklet containing 18 sets of ordered numbers, one set per page. It was stressed that on no occasion would they be rewarding or penalizing themselves – only others. At the end of the task, they would be paid the amount of money the other boys had awarded them. Each point they were awarded was worth one-tenth of a penny.

On each page in the booklet there was a matrix, comprising 14 boxes, each containing two numbers. (See Figure 12.1.)

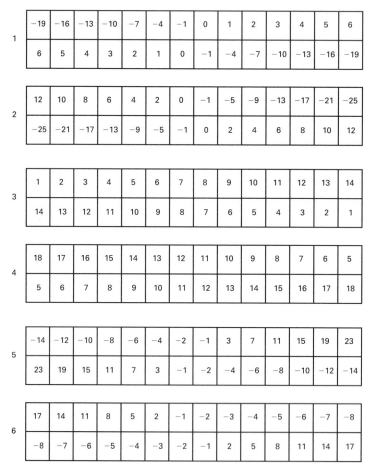

Figure 12.1. The six matrices used in the first experiment. The top line in each matrix represents the points that could be allocated to the boy's own group, and the bottom line, the points to the other group (e.g. in Matrix 4, 18/5 and 12/11, and so on).

The numbers in the top row were the rewards and penalties to be awarded to one person, and those in the bottom row were those to be awarded to another. Each row was labelled 'These are rewards and penalties for member No. __ of your group' or '... of the other group'. The participants had to check one box in each matrix.

As Figure 12.1 shows, there were six different matrices, each appearing three times in the booklet – once for each of three types of choice:

● *in-group* choices (the top and bottom row denoting the rewards and penalties to be awarded to two members of boy's own group);

● *out-group* choices; and

● *intergroup/'differential'* choices (one row indicating rewards and penalties to be awarded to an in-group member, and the other row indicating those for an out-group member).

(The top and bottom positions of in-group and out-group members were varied randomly.)

Results

The intergroup choices were first scored in terms of ranking of choices:

● Rank 1 stood for the choice that gave the in-group member the minimum possible number of points.

● Rank 14, at the opposite extreme, stood for the choice that gave the maximum number of points to the in-group member.

Comparable (but more complex) scoring methods were used for the other kinds of choice.

The results were striking. A large majority of participants, in all groups in both conditions, gave more money to members of their own group than to out-group members. All the results were above both Rank 7.5 (the point of maximum fairness) and the mean ranks of the in-group and out-group choices. In contrast, the in-group and out-group choices were closely distributed around the point of fairness. Intergroup discrimination was the deliberate strategy adopted in making intergroup choices.

Experiment 2

Due to the results of Experiment 1 being highly statistically significant in all eight groups of boys, Tajfel decided to analyse further the phenomenon of discrimination in favour of the in-group.

Three new groups, each of 16 boys, were tested, and this time the criterion for inter-group categorization was preference for the paintings of Klee or Kandinsky. Six slides of each artist were presented and the boys had to say which they preferred. Once again, they were assigned randomly to the 'Klee' or 'Kandinsky' group.

The procedure was the same as for Experiment 1, but the matrices were new. Tajfel looked at three variables:

● *maximum joint profit* (MJP): the largest possible joint award to both people;

● *maximum in-group profit* (MIP): the largest possible award to an in-group member;

● *maximum difference* (MD): the largest possible difference in gain between an in-group and an out-group member, in favour of the former.

There were four new matrices. As in Experiment 1, there were three types of choice:

1   between an in-group and an out-group member;

2   between two members of the in-group;

3   between two members of the out-group.

Results

● A comparison of the boys' choices in the various matrices showed that MJP exerted hardly any effect at all.

● The effect of MIP and MD combined against MJP was strong and highly significant.

● The effect of MD against MJP and MIP was also strong and highly significant.

In other words, when participants had a choice between maximizing the profit for all and maximizing the profit for members of the in-group, they acted on behalf of their own group. With a choice between profit for all and for their own group combined, as against their own group winning *more* than the out-group at the expense of both these utilitarian advantages, it was the maximization of *difference* that seemed more important.

Similar findings emerged from the two other types of choice. *In-group* choices were consistently and significantly nearer to the MJP than were the out-group ones. This was so despite the fact that giving as much as possible to two members of the out-group did not conflict with the in-group's interests: it simply would have meant giving more to 'the others' without giving any less to 'your own'.

Fairness was also an important influence: most choices were compromises between fairness and in-group favouritism.

● CONCLUSIONS

Although out-group discrimination is very easy to trigger, unlike Sherif *et al.*'s Robbers Cave experiment, neither an objective conflict of interests nor hostility had any relevance whatsoever to what Tajfel's participants were asked to do. It was enough that they saw themselves as clearly categorized into an in-group and an out-group – despite the fact that the criteria for the categorization were completely random. This was true despite the fact that the boys knew each other well beforehand, their own individual gains were not involved, and their choices could have been aimed at achieving the greatest common good.

The boys' choices were influenced by two major social norms – 'groupness' and 'fairness'. They managed to achieve a neat balance between the two in this experimental situation, but in real life, socialization into 'groupness' is powerful and unavoidable.

EVALUATION

Theoretical issues

Tajfel argues that in order to simplify and bring order to our 'social construction of reality', we gradually learn to classify social groups as 'we' and 'they' (in-groups and out-groups, respectively). This combines with the hostility inherent in many of the group stereotypes we are constantly exposed to, to produce 'generic norms' of behaviour towards out-groups (discriminating against the out-group in favour of the in-group). Tajfel sees this as a process that is both more general and goes deeper than either the learning of value judgements about a specific group or conformity. It has three consequences:

1   There may be discrimination against an out-group even if there is no reason for it in terms of the individual's own interests (what s/he can gain from any such discrimination).

2   Such discrimination may occur in the absence of any previously existing hostility or dislike towards the out-group.

3   This generic norm may manifest itself directly in behaviour towards the out-group *before* any prejudice or hostility has developed.

The usual conclusion drawn from Sherif *et al.*'s Robbers Cave experiment is that prejudice and hostility between the two groups of boys at summer camp were a *consequence* of the competition between them. But when the two groups first learned of each other's existence, they immediately expressed a wish to challenge the other group. This intergroup rivalry occurred *before* the actual competitive activities had been announced: just being in one group and becoming aware of a second group seemed to trigger feelings of competitiveness.

This, together with other experimental findings, strongly suggests that 'conflictual goal relationships are not actually necessary to elicit in-group bias in people's judgements' (Brown, 1988). However, we cannot conclude that *mere* group membership is the crucial variable; we must first remove all the other variables that serve as potential influences on attitudes and behaviour. The minimal group paradigm (MGP) is an attempt to create experimental conditions that would enable us to assess the effects of *intergroup categorization* as such – uncontaminated by other variables.

Methodological issues

Schiffman and Wicklund (1992) identify the following criteria for *minimal groups*:

● There should be no face-to-face interaction between group members.

● Complete anonymity of group membership should be maintained.

● There should be no instrumental or rational link between the criteria for inter-group categorizations and the nature of the in-group/out-group responses required from participants.

● The responses should not represent any utilitarian value to the participant.

● The strategy of intergroup differentiation should conflict with a strategy based on more 'rational' or 'utilitarian' principles.

● The responses should comprise real decisions about the distribution of concrete rewards (and/or penalties) to others.

How do these criteria apply to Tajfel's experiments?

● The boys worked on their own in separate cubicles when actually allocating the points (but they had initially assembled as one large group when estimating the dots or choosing between Klee and Kandinsky).

● They only knew of other in-group/out-group members by a code number (e.g. 'member 74 of Klee group') – they did not know the personal identity of these group members. Although they very likely belonged to the same sports teams, friendship groups, and so on, these groups had no connections with the imposed, arbitrary experimental groups: 'As underestimators and overestimators the boys had no prior history' (Brown, 1986). This is also relevant to the next point.

● The groups were actually determined randomly, although the boys believed their categorization depended on their dot estimation or artistic preferences. The point is that there is no obvious link between being, say, an overestimator and having the opportunity to award more points to fellow overestimators than to underestimators.

This is the criterion that relates most directly to what 'minimal' means. But is it possible to get even more minimal than this? Billig and Tajfel (1973) went much further (as far as it is possible to go!) in creating arbitrary, artificial groups: they actually *told* participants that they were being assigned purely randomly and, in front of them, tossed a coin or drew lottery tickets which determined their membership of 'As' or 'Bs' or 'Kappas' or 'Phis'. The same results were found as for the 1970/1971 experiments.

● The boys could only award points to *others* (either in-group or out-group members), never to themselves. They would receive the number of points allocated to them by others and they could not influence in any way how others behaved in order to maximize self-gain.

● As we have see, there were three basic strategies that could be used for awarding points: *maximum joint profit* (MJP), *maximum in-group profit* (MIP) and *maximum difference* (MD). These were tempered by *fairness/even-handedness*: it prevented in-group favouritism (MIP and MD) from taking extreme values. For example, in Matrix 3 (B) in Experiment 2, if the top line represents a member of the Klee group and the bottom line a member of the Kandinsky group, if the main goal were MIP for the Klee group, Klees should choose the extreme right-hand box (19 is the highest number of points available to Klees). In doing this, they would earn *fewer* points than Kandinskys (25 points). But in fact, boxes towards the left-hand end were much more likely to be chosen: fewer *absolute* points for Klees (e.g. 7 instead of 19), but the *difference* now favours the Klees (MD).

It is important to note that different matrices differed according to how 'transparent' they were in relation to these strategies (i.e. it was sometimes very obvious, and sometimes much less obvious, exactly how one could benefit an in-group member relative to an out-group member: see **Exercises**). Matrix 3 (B) in Experiment 2 is less transparent than others used by Tajfel.

● The experimental task involved displaying intergroup *behaviour*: allocating points to be exchanged for money at the end, rather than expressing attitudes (which do not necessarily translate into discriminatory acts: see **Background and context** above). But Schiffman and Wicklund (1992) see this as a major problem for the MGP:

psychological factors (such as degree of ego involvement, needs and conflict) are excluded from a group situation in which they might manifest themselves. They regard it as a fundamentally *reductionist* approach: 'By excluding psychological variables, *differentiation between groups* was ultimately shown to be dependent on *differentiation between groups*.'

In other words, as it stands, the minimal group experiment really tells us very little – at least nothing we did not know already.

Subsequent research

Much subsequent research, not surprisingly, has been concerned with aspects of the methodology of the MGP. For example, although, in principle, different strategies for allocating points are available to participants, the standard procedure suggests that discrimination might be the most appropriate strategy. Schiffman and Wicklund (1992) ask what else participants can do except discriminate. This relates to the *demand characteristics* of the task.

Also, the task has a kind of *forced-choice* format, in which case the results may be due to this rather than categorizing people into groups (Brown, 1986). Locksley *et al.* (1980) created random minimal groups (with American participants), giving each person five piles of poker chips to distribute instead of points (thus removing the forced-choice element). Despite this, the results confirmed those of studies using the standard set-up.

Perhaps schoolboy culture encourages an interest in group membership: if boys are divided by adults into groups (on whatever basis), they might automatically interpret these groups as 'teams' and think in terms of competition (Brown, 1986; Pennington *et al.*, 1999). However, the fact that many different national, cultural and age groups, of both genders, have all been tested, producing essentially the same results, strongly suggests that 'English schoolboy norms' play very little part in explaining the original findings.

If in-group favouritism is such a reliable, pervasive phenomenon, can it be generalized to the distribution of penalties and aversive stimuli? Hewstone *et al.* (1981) modified the standard MGP by asking participants to *subtract* money from in-group/out-group members (who had previously been allocated an initial sum). Despite some evidence of in-group bias, this was less pronounced than in the standard procedure.

Mummendey *et al.* (1993) extended this principle by asking participants to distribute (what they thought would be) durations of an unpleasantly high-pitched tone. This seemed to completely eliminate in-group favouritism: both fairness and minimizing the total amount of aversive stimulation were much more common. Mummendey *et al.* suggest that perhaps in the relatively 'neutral' laboratory conditions, a strong social desirability norm against harming fellow participants prevails; this raises the threshold for displaying in-group favouritism.

Applications and implications

Despite these methodological problems with the MGP, the minimal group data were the starting point for a major *theory* of intergroup discrimination, ethnocentrism and hostility, namely *social identity theory* (SIT) (Tajfel, 1978; Tajfel and Turner, 1979, 1986). Dividing the world into a manageable number of categories not only helps us to simplify and make sense of it, but also serves to help us define who we are. Our sense of identity is closely bound up with our various group memberships (Brown, 1988). A positive social identity is achieved and maintained by: 'favourable comparisons that can be made between the in-group and some relevant out-groups; the in-group must be perceived as positively differentiated or distinct from the relevant out-group' (Tajfel and Turner, 1979). The driving force behind such processes is the general striving for maintaining and enhancing our self-esteem.

How can SIT account for the minimal group experiments on which it is based? According to Brown (1996), code numbers for group members produce a feeling of anonymity in a meaningless group. The only possible source of identity is the in-group (primitive as it is), and the only way to make it distinguishable in a positive way from the out-group is to allocate more points to in-group members. But if we have to favour the in-group *in order* to distinguish it from the out-group, isn't this the *reverse* of what happens under 'normal' circumstances? Groups which we have already identified as 'in' or 'out' (they are already distinguished) are favoured (or not) *because* they are 'in' or 'out'?

This relates to the very 'status' of the MGP. The arbitrary/artificial nature of minimal groups is so far removed from our real-life group memberships that it can be asked if they have any ecological validity at all. In turn, how valid can SIT be if it is derived from the minimal group data?

SIT has been criticized on the grounds that it presents racism (and other forms of prejudice) as 'natural', helping to justify it. Stemming from Allport's (1954) claims that stereotypes are 'categories about people' and that 'the human mind must think with the aid of categories', Tajfel (1969; Tajfel *et al.*, 1971) saw the process of *categorization* as a basic characteristic of human thought. From this, racism (conceived as a form of intergroup hostility or in-group favouritism) may also be construed as natural. In terms of the distribution of resources, racism is thus justified as the norm ('charity begins at home') (Howitt and Owusu-Bempah, 1994). Of course, Tajfel never intended SIT to be seen as justifying racism, having lost his family and community in the Holocaust.

While there is plenty of evidence of intergroup discrimination, this appears to stem from raising the evaluation of the in-group (a *positive in-group bias*), and *not* derogatory attitudes or behaviour towards the out-group (which is what we normally understand by 'prejudice') (Vivian and Brown, 1995). Indeed, SIT suggests that prejudice consists largely of liking 'us' more than disliking 'them': favouring the in-group is the *core* phenomenon (Brewer, 1999; Hewstone *et al.*, 2002).

Despite these problems, SIT (and *self-categorization theory*, an extension of it: Turner, 1985; Turner *et al.*, 1987) has been a major influence on European (especially British) social psychology (Pennington *et al.*, 1999). According to Burr (2002), regardless of the debate over the relevance of minimal group experiments and SIT in explaining intergroup conflict, SIT

> is one of the few theories ... to postulate a thoroughly social understanding of the person and to regard the social realm as more than a set of variables which may come to influence the ready-made person.

EXERCISES

1   What is the difference between prejudice and discrimination?

2   The matrices below are very transparent.

   (a) What does 'transparent' mean here?

   (b) Briefly describe the four basic strategies for awarding points in the minimal group experiments.

   (c) Indicate how, for the matrices below, a member of the Klee group could award points according to these four strategies.

No.74 Klee	1	2	3	4	5	6	7	8	9	10	11	12	13	14	A
No.44 Kandinsky	14	13	12	11	10	9	8	7	6	5	4	3	2	1	

	23	22	21	20	19	18	17	16	15	14	13	12	11	B
	5	7	9	11	13	15	17	19	21	23	25	27	29	

(For each matrix, A and B, the Klee member must choose *one* box, e.g. in A, the fourth box from the left, 4/11, would mean 4 points awarded to no. 74 Klee and 11 points awarded to no. 44 Kandinsky.)

3   Explain the difference between *intra*group and *inter*group choices. How do these differ in terms of participants' typical allocation of points?

4   As well as matrices differing in their degree of transparency, the same matrix appeared three times, once for each kind of intra- and intergroup choice.

   (a) Why was this done?

   (b) Name the method by which this was done.

13

A study of prisoners and guards in a simulated prison

Haney, C., Banks, C. and Zimbardo, P. (1973)

Naval Research Reviews, 30(9): 4–17

BACKGROUND AND CONTEXT

For such a famous psychological study to have appeared in *Naval Research Reviews* may seem rather odd, but there is a good reason for it.

Brown (1985) observes that Western governments and military authorities were shocked by, and totally unprepared for, attempts at mass indoctrination by the Chinese during the Korean War in the early 1950s. This 'thought reform' (from the Chinese word for the psychological techniques used by Chinese Communists to bring about changes in political attitudes and self-concept) was used on United Nations prisoners of war (Korea), as well as Chinese intellectuals and Western civilians living in China. It represented a totally new form of warfare: instead of merely 'containing' enemy soldiers, the Communists actively tried to convert them to their 'side'. It also raised questions about loyalty, treason, and the preparation of soldiers for captivity and, in turn, freedom.

As a result, returning prisoners were studied extensively by military psychologists and psychiatrists, and a great deal of subsequent research was undertaken in the USA, the UK and elsewhere, often financed by the military authorities. (Although not prisoners of war, Western hostages, such as Brain Keenan, John McCarthy and Terry Waite, underwent a 'debriefing' period by military doctors and psychologists following their release and prior to their return to everyday life.)

Brown (1985) also points out that research by Hebb *et al.* (1952) into the disorienting effects of sensory and sleep deprivation (a technique much used in 'thought reform') was conducted on behalf of the Defence Research Board in Canada. Similarly, when discussing the ethics of the study (see **Applications and implications** below), Zimbardo (1973) refers to approval being officially sought and received in writing from the sponsoring agency – the Office of Naval Research (ONR) – which explains the publication of the 1973 study in the *Naval Research Reviews*. So, part of the impetus for the study was a very practical, military concern with the effects of thought control and indoctrination.

We should note that (unusually) this is one of several accounts of what is widely referred to as the 'prison simulation experiment' (PSE) or the 'Stanford prison experiment' (SPE). Others include:

● Zimbardo, P. (1971) 'The psychological power and pathology of imprisonment'. Statement prepared for the United States House of Representatives Committee on the Judiciary: Sub-Committee No. 3: Hearings on Prison Reform. (This is cited by Aronson, 1992. The study was actually carried out between 14 and 21 August 1971 (Murphy *et al.*, 1984).)

● Zimbardo, P., Banks, C., Haney, C. and Jaffe, D. (1973) A Pirandellian prison: The mind is a formidable jailor. *New York Times Magazine*, 8 April, 38–60. (Craig is sometimes given instead of Haney, and the order of the names may differ.)

● Haney, C. and Zimbardo, P. (1973) Social roles, role-playing and education: On the high school as a prison. *Behavioural and Social Sciences Teacher, 1*: 24–45.

● Haney, C., Banks, C. and Zimbardo, P. (1973) Interpersonal dynamics in a simulated prison. *International Journal of Criminology and Penology, 1*: 69–97.

AIM AND NATURE

● HYPOTHESIS

The basic hypothesis being tested was the *dispositional hypothesis*, the claim that the 'deplorable conditions of our penal system and its dehumanizing effects upon prisoners and guards' is due to the 'nature' of the people who administrate it, or the 'nature' of the people who populate it, or both. Guards are 'sadistic, uneducated and insensitive', which is, presumably, why they are attracted to the job in the first place, while the antisocial attitudes and behaviour of prisoners will prevail whether they are living 'in society' or 'in prison', so force is needed to keep them under control.

It follows that nothing need be done about prisons themselves: if the people in them are responsible for everything that is wrong (a *dispositional* or *internal attribution*), then changing conditions inside prisons will not make any difference.

Haney *et al.* expected to find evidence that would allow them to *reject* the dispositional hypothesis in favour of the view that it is the conditions (physical, social and psychological) of prison that are to blame, not the people in them (a *situational* or *external attribution*).

More specifically, they predicted that:

assignment to the condition 'guard' or 'prisoner' [will] result in significantly different reactions on behavioural measures of interaction, emotional measures of mood state and pathology, attitudes towards self, as well as other indices of coping and adaptation to this novel situation.

● METHOD/DESIGN

Haney *et al.* point out that:

the dispositional hypothesis cannot be critically evaluated directly through observation in existing prison settings, because such naturalistic observation necessarily confounds the acute effects of the environment with the chronic characteristics of the inmate and guard populations.

In order to separate the two sets of factors, a 'new' prison had to be constructed, 'comparable in its fundamental social psychological milieu to existing prison systems, but populated by individuals who are undifferentiated in all essential dimensions from the rest of society'. In other words, if you control for the characteristics of the individuals by deliberately selecting only non-criminal, non-sadistic, psychologically well-adjusted (in this case) young men, then any negative, pathological behaviour can be attributed to the 'prison'. This assumes that the simulated ('mock') prison accurately captures the *functional* (as opposed to the literal) characteristics of a real prison.

As well as being a *simulation*, the study involved detailed *observation* of the behaviour of prisoners and guards (using video, audiotape and direct observation); this provided essential *qualitative* data.

Participants

An initial pool of 75 respondents answered a newspaper advertisement asking for male volunteers for a psychological study of 'prison life' in return for payment of $15 per day. Based on a detailed questionnaire, the 24 most physically and mentally stable, mature and least involved in antisocial behaviours were selected for the study (22 participants, plus two standbys). They were all male college students living in the Stanford area.

The participants were randomly allocated to one of two 'conditions': the prisoner role or the guard role (the *independent variable*), in order to observe the resulting pattern of behaviour (the *dependent variable*).

Physical aspects of the prison

The prison was built in the basement of the psychology department at Stanford University. Three small cells (6 x 9 feet) were created, each containing a mattress, sheet and pillow. A small closet (2 x 2 x 7 feet) served as a solitary confinement facility.

Operational details

The prisoners remained in the prison 24 hours a day for the entire study. Three were randomly assigned to each of the three cells. The guards worked on three-man, eight-hour shifts and went about their normal lives at other times.

Role instructions

It was made clear in the contract that prisoners would have little or no privacy and that some of their basic civil rights would be suspended – excluding physical abuse. Once assigned, they were informed by telephone to be available at their homes on a given Sunday, when the experiment would begin.

The guards attended an orientation meeting, where they met the main researchers, the 'superintendent' of the prison (Zimbardo) and an undergraduate research assistant who assumed the role of 'warden'. Their task was to 'maintain the reasonable degree of order within the prison necessary for its effective functioning', although no details of how this might be achieved were given. They were deliberately given only minimal guidelines for the role of guard, so that their behaviour would reflect their genuine reactions to the experimental prison situation – rather than their ability to follow instructions. However, the experimenters stressed that they must not use any physical aggression or punishment.

Uniforms

The guards carried a whistle and a police baton, and wore plain khaki shirts and trousers, and reflective sunglasses, which made eye contact impossible. The prisoners wore loose-fitting, muslin smocks, with ID numbers front and back, no underclothes, rubber sandals and caps made from nylon stockings. They each had a light chain and lock around one ankle. They were each issued with a toothbrush, soap, soap-dish, towel and bed linen, but no personal belongings were allowed.

Induction procedure

With the cooperation of the Palo Alto Police Department, all the prisoners were unexpectedly 'arrested' at their homes. A police officer charged them with suspected burglary or armed robbery, read them their rights, handcuffed them and took them to the police station, where they were fingerprinted and placed in a cell.

AIM AND NATURE

They were then blindfolded and driven by one of the experimenters and a guard to the mock prison.

On arrival, each prisoner was stripped, 'deloused' (sprayed with deodorant) and made to stand alone, naked, for a while in the cell yard. After being given their uniform and having a mugshot taken, they were put in a cell and ordered to remain silent.

Administrative routine

The warden greeted the prisoners and read them the prison rules (devised by the guards and the warden). Prisoners were to be referred to only by their numbers.

● RESULTS

In general, both guards and prisoners showed a marked tendency towards increased negative emotions, and their overall outlook became more and more negative. Self-evaluations of both groups also became more disapproving.

Overt behaviour was generally consistent with the subjective self-reports and expressions of how they felt. Despite being free, in theory, to interact in any way they wished, their interactions were typically hostile, insulting and dehumanizing. Prisoners immediately became very passive, while guards were very active in giving orders (the most common form of verbal behaviour); verbal exchanges were strikingly impersonal, with few references to individual identity. Although it was clear to all participants that no physical violence would be tolerated, various kinds of more indirect aggression, such as verbal insults, were quite common (especially on the part of the guards).

Prisoners

Even when they thought they were not being observed, the prisoners' 'private' conversations were 90 per cent concerned with the immediate conditions in the prison, such as food, privileges, punishment, guard harassment and so on; only 10 per cent of the time did they talk about their lives outside the prison.

The most dramatic evidence of the impact of the situation on the participants was seen in the reactions of five prisoners who had to be released because of extreme depression, crying, rage and acute anxiety. This began as early as the second day. The fifth prisoner was released after being treated for a psychosomatic rash which covered various parts of his body. Of the remaining prisoners, only two said they were not willing to forfeit the money they had earned in return for being 'paroled'.

The experiment, due to last for two weeks, was terminated after just six days. All the remaining prisoners were delighted by their unexpected good fortune.

AIM AND NATURE

Guards

In contrast, most of the guards seemed to be distressed by the decision: they had apparently become sufficiently involved in their roles that they were enjoying the extreme power and control they exercised over the prisoners and were reluctant to give it up. Although one guard reported being upset at the prisoners' suffering, they all arrived for work on time and often stayed on duty voluntarily – without additional pay.

Like the prisoners, they rarely exchanged personal information – they either talked about 'problem prisoners', other prison topics, or did not talk at all.

Post-experimental data revealed that when individual guards were alone with a single prisoner and out of range of any recording equipment (such as on the way to the toilet), harassment was even greater than it was in the 'yard'. There was a daily escalation of guard aggression, even after most prisoners had stopped resisting/'rebelling', and despite the prisoners' distress, which became obvious as early as the second day. After the first day, almost all prisoner rights (including time and conditions of sleeping and eating) came to be redefined by the guards as 'privileges', which had to be earned by obedient behaviour. Watching movies and reading (constructive activities that had been planned and suggested by the experimenters) were arbitrarily cancelled until further notice – and subsequently never allowed.

Individual differences

Although the extremely pathological reactions in both groups testify to the power of the social forces that were operating, there were still individual differences in styles of coping and in degrees of successful adaptation to this novel experience. Half the prisoners endured the oppressive atmosphere, and not all the guards resorted to hostility. Some guards were tough but fair ('played by the rules'), some went way beyond what was permitted and showed 'creative' cruelty and harassment, but most exercised coercive control over the prisoners.

As noted above, half the prisoners coped by becoming 'sick' (extremely emotionally disturbed). Others became excessively obedient, siding with the guards against a solitary fellow prisoner who coped by refusing to eat. Instead of supporting this final and major act of rebellion, the other prisoners treated him as a troublemaker who deserved to be punished.

● CONCLUSIONS

Although it was difficult to anticipate exactly how prisoners would react to incarceration, and how guards would deal with having to supervise it (especially in a mock prison), the results of the SPE support many commonly held conceptions of prison life and confirm anecdotal evidence provided by ex-convicts.

By randomly allocating normal, healthy, male college students to the role of prisoner or guard, Haney *et al.* were able to separate the influence of personal characteristics and the power of the social situation. In light of the emotional and behavioural responses of their participants, they concluded that the dispositional hypothesis can be rejected in favour of the view that 'social, institutional forces ... make good men engage in evil deeds' (Zimbardo, 1973). Haney *et al.* end by saying:

> *If our mock prison could generate the extent of pathology it did in such a short time, then the punishment of being imprisoned in a real prison does not 'fit the crime' for most prisoners – indeed, it far exceeds it! Moreover, since both prisoners and guards are locked into a dynamic, symbiotic relationship which is destructive to their human nature, guards are also society's prisoners.*

EVALUATION

Theoretical issues

What exactly is it about prisons that induces destructive, dehumanizing and pathological behaviour? Haney *et al.* identify the following as critical factors in their mock prison:

● loss of personal identity;

● arbitrary control;

● dependency and emasculation.

These mirror very closely key aspects of 'total institutions' (Goffman, 1968) and 'extreme situations' (Bettelheim, 1960). Based largely on his study of psychiatric hospitals, Goffman defined a total institution as 'a place of residence and work where a large number of like-situated individuals, cut off from the wider society for an appreciable period of time, together lead an enclosed and formally administered round of life'.

A central feature of such institutions is the breakdown of the 'normal' boundaries between living, work and leisure. This allows high levels of psychological control over inmates, since every aspect of their lives is controlled. The basis of the coercive power of staff is the creation and maintenance of the *inequality* and *social distance* between inmates and themselves. On admission, inmates are robbed of their 'identity kit': personal possessions, clothes and name. Being put into uniforms, which are the same for all inmates, helps to create a loss of personal identity (or *de-individuation*), which is reinforced by the use of numbers instead of names.

The net effect of these characteristics of total institutions (together with loss of control over basic activities such as when to eat, sleep and go to the toilet) is that the self which existed prior to admission loses its significance, and a new institutional identity takes its place. The inmates are treated as a group, based on the idea of institutions as 'people-processing' factories (Cohen and Taylor, 1972). This represents an extreme *situationalist* approach, which sees situational variables as the *only* significant influences on behaviour.

However, some institutions are more 'total' than others. For both ethical and practical reasons, the mock prison lacked the racism and enforced homosexuality of most real prisons. In turn, prisons for offenders in the USA and the UK are rather more humanitarian than those experienced by Korean prisoners of war or Nazi concentration camp inmates during the 1930s and 1940s. The differences may be seen in terms of how 'extreme' the deprivation suffered by inmates is. Describing conditions in Dachau and Buchenwald concentration camps, where he was an inmate, Bruno Bettelheim (1960) states that:

> Every single moment of their lives was strictly regulated and supervised. They had no privacy whatsoever, were never allowed to see a visitor, lawyer or minister. They were not entitled to medical care… No prisoner was told why he was imprisoned, and never for how long.

Bettelheim's previous training and experience as a psychoanalyst helped him to protect himself against the disintegration of his personality which he so dreaded, and which he observed in so many of his fellow inmates:

> By destroying man's ability to act on his own or to predict the outcome of his actions, they [the camps] destroyed the feeling that his actions had any purpose, so many prisoners stopped acting. But when they stopped acting, they soon stopped living.

In Bandura's terms (1986), extreme situations destroy a person's sense of *self-efficacy*, inducing a sense of *learned helplessness* (Seligman, 1975), and this is what makes such situations so harmful. But even if this could explain the behaviour of Haney *et al.*'s prisoners, we would still need a different explanation for the manner in which the guards behaved.

Methodological issues

While the mock prison had many features of a total/extreme situation, there is still an issue regarding the interpretation of the findings from the SPE.

As we have seen, Haney *et al.* confidently rejected the dispositional hypothesis in favour of the situational explanation. Ordinary people can readily be induced to perform abusive and antisocial acts if they are put in a situation where they feel relatively anonymous and where such behaviour is expected of them (Zimbardo, 1975). (See **Applications and implications** below.)

However, Banuazzi and Mohavedi (1975) argue that the behaviour of both guards and prisoners may have reflected their pre-existing *stereotyped expectations* about how guards and prisoners behave. These 'mental sets' or 'culturally conditioned images' were brought to the situation and influenced their response to the mock prison environment: they were 'merely' *role-playing*. How could supporters of the situational hypothesis respond to this criticism?

● At what point does 'mere' role-playing become a 'real' experience? According to Zimbardo (1971, in Aronson, 1992):

> what we saw was frightening. It was no longer apparent to us or most of the subjects where they ended and their roles began. The majority had indeed become 'prisoners' or 'guards', no longer able to clearly differentiate between role-playing and self. There were dramatic changes in virtually every aspect of their behaviour, thinking and feeling.

● Even if the role-playing argument has some validity when applied to the guards, this is much less obvious in relation to the prisoners: just how *are* prisoners meant to act? Brown (1985) believes that very few people would have anticipated their extreme reactions. Besides, even if they were role-playing, were they really so different from first-time actual prisoners?

● It follows from the previous point that those participants allocated to the prisoner role were less well prepared psychologically than either the guards or hardened criminals. But doesn't this make Haney *et al.*'s findings difficult to generalize to real prisons?

One reply to this is to say that we normally *underestimate* the distress of real prisoners: if, as we have seen, the mock prison did not allow physical brutality, racism or involuntary homosexuality (and if the participants knew the study was to last only two weeks), and yet well-adjusted students reacted in such extreme, pathological ways, then the experience of real prisoners must be terrible.

Subsequent research

Because of the pathological reactions of the participants and the ethical repercussions (see **Applications and implications** below), Zimbardo urged that the SPE should never be repeated. But this created a dilemma for Reicher and Haslam (2006), two British psychologists who questioned Haney *et al.*'s explanation of their findings. If it is 'natural' to abuse power in groups, why did only *some* guards do so? Could it have been a product of Zimbardo's leadership? After all, he instructed his guards by telling them:

> You can create in the prisoners…a notion of arbitrariness, that life is totally
> controlled by us, by the system, you, me – and they'll have no privacy… We're
> going to take away their individuality in various ways. In general, what all this leads
> to is a sense of powerlessness.

Reicher and Haslam argue that there are also moral reasons for doubting the 'role' explanation: it suggests that all of us would mindlessly abuse others if given roles that appeared to demand this, which denies the capacity for human agency and choice. Bullies and tyrants come to be seen as victims who cannot be held accountable for their actions; in this way, psychological analysis easily ends up excusing the inexcusable (Haslam and Reicher, 2006).

Exactly 30 years after the PSE, Reicher and Haslam collaborated with the BBC to produce *The Experiment* (conducted in 2001 and screened in four hour-long documentaries in May 2002). A newspaper advert appealed for volunteers to take part in a 'university-backed social science experiment to be shown on TV', which would involve 'exercise, tasks, hardship, hunger, solitude and anger'. There was no financial incentive, but participation would 'change the way you think' (Brockes, 2001).

Like the SPE, the 15 male volunteers were randomly divided into prisoners and guards. But unlike the SPE, Reicher and Haslam did not act as prison superintendents who instructed the guards how to act. They simply set up a situation in which the guards had authority and the tools of power, and better conditions (food, living quarters, etc.) than the prisoners. The intention was to create a situation that was harsh and testing, but not harmful. The study was overseen by clinical psychologists and an independent ethics committee chaired by an MP.

Although the study was set in a prison-like environment (a converted studio at Elstree), the primary goal was not to mimic a real prison (both impossible and unethical). But the power differences between the two groups are characteristic of a wide range of institutional environments, such as offices, schools and factories. The critical questions were:

1   When do the powerful embrace inequality and abuse their power?

2   When do the powerless succumb to oppression or reject and resist it?

3   What is the role of the group in these processes?

Based on social identity theory (SIT) (Tajfel and Turner, 1979: see Chapter 12), a series of interventions were planned, designed to impact on the level of shared social identity among the prisoners, thereby increasing their willingness to resist the guards' regime and any tyranny associated with it. Systematic observation (aided by unobtrusive filming) and daily testing (psychometric and physiological) were used to observe both groups' behaviour.

Reicher and Haslam initially allowed opportunities for promotion from prisoner to guard. They expected that prisoners would try to reject their prisoner identity and work independently to improve their position, which, in turn, would allow the guards to reassert their greater power (and so maintain the status quo). But after these opportunities for promotion were later withdrawn (day three), the prisoners, as predicted, started collaborating to resist the guards' authority. At first they were compliant and worked hard to improve their situation, but they started to see themselves as a group and became uncooperative with the guards once they knew that, however hard they worked, they would remain prisoners. What is more, this shared identity led to improved organization, effectiveness and mental well-being: as the study progressed, the prisoners became more positive and empowered.

The guards, by contrast, threw up surprises. Several thought that groups and power are dangerous, and they were reluctant to exercise control. They disagreed among themselves about what their role should be and never developed a sense of shared identity. This produced poor organization which, in turn, made them increasingly ineffective at maintaining order, despondent and 'burned out'.

After six days, the prisoners collaborated to challenge the guards, leading to an organized breakout and the collapse of the prisoner–guard structure. The two groups then spontaneously established a 'self-governing, self-disciplining commune'. But some participants were still reluctant to discipline those who broke the commune's rules, which led to its collapse. In response, several former prisoners and guards proposed a coup in which they would become the new guards. They asked for black berets and sunglasses as symbols of a new authoritarian management they wanted to impose, which would ensure that prisoners 'toed the line', using force if necessary.

The coup never occurred. For ethical reasons, Reicher and Haslam could not risk the type of aggression observed in the SPE and they ended the study two days prematurely, after eight days. However, Reicher and Haslam believe that their study has generated more peer-reviewed publications than any previous social psychological field study. One of the insights it has provided is that groups give people choice rather than take it away, which is good for our well-being; but every member of a group is responsible for determining what the group stands for and the type of world it seeks to create.

Conversely, the failure of groups removes people's choice, which is bad for the well-being of individuals – and for the health of society – because it makes us more likely to be seduced by tyranny. Groups and power do not corrupt in and of themselves, but the failure of groups does corrupt absolutely.

Not everyone agrees with these claims, of course, especially Zimbardo. He objects strongly to the made-for-television/reality TV nature of *The Experiment*, and argues that it should not be considered serious social science. He claims that what was broadcast was a re-cut version that the prisoners had demanded after seeing a preview screening. Reicher and Haslam reply that the TV documentaries were not the full scientific story, but were designed to provide 'a window on the science'. (See **Exercises.**) Zimbardo (in Swain 2005) has also accused Reicher and Haslam of creating an 'artificial subtext of European social identity theory pitted against American role theory'.

Applications and implications

The PSE provoked almost as much controversy regarding its ethics as Milgram's obedience experiments (see Chapter 10). Zimbardo himself (1973) believes that the ethical concerns are even greater in the PSE:

> *Volunteer prisoners suffered physical and psychological abuse hour after hour for days, while volunteer guards were exposed to the new self-knowledge that they enjoyed being powerful and had abused this power to make other human beings suffer.*

Zimbardo (in McDermott, 1993) acknowledges that it took someone not directly involved in the SPE (who had been invited to interview the participants) to point out these abuses and the suffering it was causing. By playing the role of prison superintendent, Zimbardo became too involved in the 'prison' and lost sight of the research he was conducting.

According to Savin (1973), the benefits resulting from the study do not justify the mistreatment and degradation suffered by the prisoners: the end does not justify the means. Zimbardo (1973) defends the PSE in several ways:

- The only deception involved related to the prisoners' arrest by the Palo Alto police, who only gave their final approval minutes before it happened. Haney *et al.* wanted the arrest to come as a surprise, but Zimbardo recognizes that this was a breach of the informed consent contract signed by every participant, giving their permission for invasion of privacy, loss of civil rights and harassment.

- Approval was officially sought, and received in writing, from the Office of Naval Research (see **Background and context**), the Psychology Department and the University Committee of Human Experimentation.

- Group and individual debriefing sessions were held, and all participants returned post-experimental questionnaires after several weeks, then several months later, and subsequently at yearly intervals.

- Zimbardo (in Flanagan, 2005) claims that the benefits were greater than from any other study. A number of the participants were permanently affected in positive ways, making career decisions that benefited society and science (one became a clinical psychologist).

- More generally, as a consequence of congressional testimony, a US federal law was passed which forbids the housing of adolescents in pre-trial detention with adult prisoners.

Zimbardo believes the findings can be applied to any secretive prison system, where guards and prison officials are not routinely accountable to the public whose taxes pay for their salaries. Just after the SPE came to an end, there was a prisoner rebellion at Attica Prison in New York; their main grievance was that they were being dehumanized. The Governor's response was to send in the National Guard, killing many prisoners and guards who had been taken hostage.

Zimbardo also sees direct parallels between the SPE and Abu Ghraib prison in Iraq. He has testified as a defence expert witness for one of the US guards who abused helpless Iraqi prisoners. One of the investigative reports of the abuses at the prison (chaired by James Schlesinger) indicated that the results of the SPE should have been a forewarning to the US military: compared with the mock prison, Abu Ghraib was far more extreme and thus potentially at risk of the kind of abuses by American guards that eventually occurred. A detailed account of the SPE appeared as an Appendix to the Schlesinger report (Zimbardo, in Flanagan, 2005).

The SPE has led to research into a range of social situations that generate pathological conditions. These include the social psychology of madness and cults, shyness as a kind of self-imposed prison, and time-perspective – how people come to be controlled by their overuse of past, present or future timeframes (Zimbardo, in O'Toole, 1997).

EXERCISES

1   Identify some of the characteristics of the mock prison which make it a 'total institution'.

2   The *dispositional hypothesis* sees the behaviour of people in prisons as attributable to their personal characteristics (as opposed to conditions in the prison). What kind of *attribution bias* does this demonstrate? (See Chapter 14.)

3   In the Methods/design section, Haney *et al.* say that 'naturalistic observation [in existing prison settings] necessarily confounds the acute effects of the environment with the chronic characteristics of the inmate and guard populations'. What do they mean by this?

4   What is the major advantage of using video/audio recording compared with direct observation?

5   What were (a) the scientific and (b) the ethical reasons for choosing participants who were strangers at the beginning of the experiment?

6   How *scientifically valid* can television programmes such as *The Experiment* be?

Behaviour as seen by the actor and as seen by the observer

Nisbett, R.E., Caputo, C., Legant, P. and Maracek, J. (1973)

Journal of Personality and Social Psychology, 27(2): 154–64

BACKGROUND AND CONTEXT

According to Fiske and Taylor (1991), *attribution theory* deals with the general principles which govern how the social perceiver selects and uses information to arrive at causal explanations or judgements for behaviour. The backbone of attribution theory is formed, collectively, by six different theoretical traditions:

1 Heider's (1958) *common-sense psychology*;

2 Jones and Davis's (1965) *correspondent inference theory*;

3 Kelley's *co-variation model* (1967) and *causal schemata* (1972, 1983);

4 Schachter's (1964) *cognitive labelling theory*;

5 Bem's (1967, 1972) *self-perception theory*;

6 Weiner's (1979, 1985) *attribution theory of emotion and motivation*.

Schachter's theory is discussed in Chapter 18; Bem's theory is discussed in Chapter 9 (in relation to Festinger's cognitive dissonance theory); and Weiner's is discussed in Chapter 11 (in the context of bystander intervention). Heider's theory was clearly the spearhead for attribution theory as a whole (Fiske and Taylor, 1991).

Like Asch (famous for his research into conformity and interpersonal perception), Heider emigrated to the USA from Europe. They were both influenced by gestalt psychology and tried to apply this account of physical object perception to the perception of people (social perception). *The Psychology of Interpersonal Relations* (Heider, 1958) marked a new era in social psychology (Leyens and Codol, 1988).

For Heider, the starting point for studying how people understand their social world is 'ordinary' people. How do people usually think about and infer meaning from what goes on around them? How do they make sense of their own and other people's behaviour? These questions relate to what Heider called *common-sense psychology* or *naive epistemology* (epistemology is the branch of philosophy concerned with the nature of knowledge). He saw the 'ordinary' person (or layperson) as a *naive scientist*, who links observable behaviour to unobservable causes.

Perhaps Heider's major contribution to attribution theory was the identification of two basic, potential sources or causes of behaviour:

● *personal* or *dispositional* (internal);

● *situational* or *environmental* (external).

Fundamental to the question, 'Why do people behave as they do?', is whether the locus of causality is *inside* or *outside* the actor (the person whose behaviour we are trying to explain); the perceiver's task is to decide what kind of cause a given action is due to. Internal causes include motivation, ability, attitudes and personality, while external causes include other people's behaviour and traits, the demands of the social situation, and physical aspects of the environment. Understanding which set of factors should be used to interpret another person's behaviour will make the perceiver's world more predictable, and will provide a greater sense of control over it.

These insights provided the blueprint for later theories (Hewstone and Antaki, 1988). According to Fiske and Taylor (1991), Heider's major contribution was to define many of the basic issues that later theorists would explore. One of these, the underlying view of the person as a naive scientist, has been shown by research to be a misrepresentation: perceivers do *not* act like scientists, following detailed, formal, logical rules. Rather, they make attributions quickly and show clear preferences for certain sorts of causal information over others. We need more *descriptive* models, which show how people *actually* make attributions, rather than the *normative* models of Jones and Davis, and Kelley, which propose how people *should* make accurate causal attributions.

This has been partly achieved by examining the *biases* involved in the attribution process. A major form of bias is the *actor–observer effect* (AOE).

AIM AND NATURE

● HYPOTHESIS

The article describes three separate, but related, experiments carried out in order to test different aspects of the AOE (or the *actor–observer divergence* or *hypothesis*). The overall hypothesis (first proposed by Jones and Nisbett, 1971) states that actors tend to perceive their own behaviour as a response to situational cues, while observers tend to perceive the actor's behaviour as the manifestation of a disposition or quality possessed by the actor.

Each of the three experiments tested a different aspect of this general hypothesis:

1   Observers tend to assume that actors have a disposition to behave in the future in similar ways to those just observed (here, to volunteer for some further charity work or 'social service task', namely to canvass for the United Fund), while actors do not share this assumption.

2   Actors tend to attribute the cause of their behaviour (choice of girlfriend and college major) to properties of the chosen entity, while they are more likely to attribute their best friend's similar choices to the friend's dispositional qualities.

3   Actors tend to believe that they have fewer personality traits than other people do (including others who are similar and different in age, and others who are familiar and unfamiliar to the actor).

● METHOD/DESIGN

Study 1

Sixty-six female college students were recruited to participate in an experiment on 'decision making'. Present at each session were two real participants and two confederates. One of the real participants was randomly selected to be the observer, the other to be the actor. The confederates played the same role as the actor.

'Before the experiment began', the actor and confederates were requested to volunteer some of their time to serve as weekend hostesses for the wives of potential financial backers of a university institute concerned with the learning disabilities of disadvantaged children. The confederates always volunteered (either for about 4 hours, or for about 12 hours), thus serving as models and agents of social pressure.

The participant actor was asked by the experimenter if she was willing to volunteer and gave her answer verbally, face to face (high social-pressure condition). About half the participant actors indicated their willingness (or otherwise) to volunteer on a card (low social-pressure condition). (This variation did not have a significant effect on compliance rate, and so the data were pooled for the two conditions.)

In some sessions, $0.50 per hour was offered as a token payment for the weekend's work; in others, $1.50 was offered.

After the actor had either volunteered or refused to volunteer, both actor and observer were taken aside and quizzed about their perceptions of the actor's behaviour. They were told that the experimenters had decided to use the decision to

AIM AND NATURE

volunteer/not volunteer in the experiment (since it was more akin to everyday decisions than those used in the experiment). The actor was given 'a list of the reasons that people give us for volunteering for this task' and asked to decide how big a part each reason played in her decision to volunteer (on a scale of 0–8). The observer was given the same measures to judge why the actor had volunteered (if she had), or why the confederate actor had volunteered (if the actor had not done so).

Both actor and observer were then asked how likely they felt it would be that the actor would volunteer to canvass for the United Fund (also on a scale of 0–8).

Results

The financial incentive was a major determinant of the actor's choice to volunteer or not. Only 24 per cent of those offered $0.50 volunteered, compared with 68 per cent of those offered $1.50. However, among volunteers, the amount of money had little effect on the number of hours they volunteered for.

The actor's behaviour prompted the observers to make dispositional inferences. If she volunteered, observers saw her as more likely to help the United Fund than if she had not volunteered. Conversely, volunteers saw themselves as less likely to help than the observers did; and observers of non-volunteers tended to see them as less likely to help than did the non-volunteers themselves.

Study 2

Thirty male undergraduates were offered $1.50 to participate in 'Person Perception Surveys' in groups of 6–20. They had all previously completed the personality trait questionnaire used in Study 3 (below).

Thirty participants wrote four brief paragraphs describing why they liked the girl they had dated the most frequently in the past year or so, why they had chosen their college major, why their best friend liked the girl he had dated most often in the past year or so, and why he had chosen his major. They were also asked to put themselves in their best friend's position and try to write as he might, describing why the *participant* had chosen his girlfriend and major.

Order of answering for self, best friend and self as best friend were counter-balanced.

What they had written was scored for the degree to which it stressed 'entity' versus 'dispositional' reasons. Each reason was coded as being either a pure entity (e.g. 'She's a relaxing person'; 'Chemistry is a high-paying field') or as pure disposition (e.g. 'I need someone I can relax with'; 'I want to make a lot of money'). Reasons were coded as dispositional if they referred in any way to the person doing the choosing, which included many that could be described as entity x disposition interaction reasons (e.g. 'We have complementary personalities'; 'We can relax together').

Results

When explaining why they liked their own girlfriend, participants gave more than twice as many reasons phrased in terms of their own needs, interests and traits. In contrast, when explaining why their best friend liked his girlfriend, they gave almost equal numbers of reasons referring exclusively to the girl and the friend's dispositions.

When explaining their own choice of major, they gave an almost equal number of entity and dispositional reasons. When explaining their best friend's choice, they gave almost four times as many dispositional as entity reasons. (See Table 14.1.)

Table 14.1

Number of entity and dispositional reasons given by participants as explanations of their own and their best friend's choices of girlfriend and college major

Explanation	Reasons for liking girlfriend		Reasons for choosing major	
	Entity	Dispositional	Entity	Dispositional
Own behaviour	4.61	2.04	1.52	1.83
Friend's behaviour	2.70	2.57	0.43	1.70

The tendency to give relatively more entity reasons for self was found regardless of the order in which participants wrote their paragraphs.

When asked to write from their best friend's perspective, they virtually reproduced the pattern for explanations of their friend's choices: for girlfriend, 2.65 entity/2.57 dispositional reasons; for college major, 0.39 entity/2.22 dispositional reasons.

Study 3

Twenty-four participants filled out questionnaires indicating which of three descriptions best fitted five stimulus people: a trait term (e.g. reserved/intense/cautious), its polar opposite (emotionally expressive/calm/bold), or the phrase 'depends on the situation'.

There were 20 such three-choice items for each stimulus person: self, best friend, father, an admired acquaintance ('some individual of your own age and sex whom you like, but have known less than three months'), and Walter Cronkite (well-known television commentator).

AIM AND NATURE

Results

Participants were significantly more likely to apply the 'depends on the situation' category to themselves than to any other stimulus person. This difference was unaffected either by the order in which they completed the task for self, or by familiarity with or similarity in age to the stimulus person. The tendency to attribute more traits to others was as stable across participants and trait dimensions as it was across stimulus persons.

● CONCLUSIONS

All three studies provided evidence in support of the hypothesis that actors attribute causality to the situation, while observers attribute causality to the actor's dispositions.

Observers in Study 1 believed that actors would behave in the future in ways similar to those they had just witnessed, while actors did not share this belief. In Study 2, participants tended to describe their choices of girlfriend and college major in terms that referred to the properties of the chosen 'object', but were more likely to describe their friend's similar choices in terms that referred to his dispositional qualities. Participants in Study 3 seemed to see themselves as having relatively fewer traits (broad behavioural dispositions) compared with others; this implies that they are relatively more likely to behave in response to the demands of specific situations.

EVALUATION

Methodological issues

Nisbett *et al.* refer to their three experiments as 'demonstrational studies' which illustrate the divergent perspective of the actor and observer. They also say that the findings could be explained without resort to the original Jones and Nisbett (1971) hypothesis. (See **Background and context** above.) The studies are interesting in their own right, 'consistent with a proposition that is too widely applicable to be either proved or disproved by anything short of a very large and extremely diverse research programme'.

Clearly, these studies were some of the very first to be conducted in relation to this feature of the attribution process. So Nisbett *et al.* were wisely and understandably cautious about the claims that could be made for the general hypothesis based on the studies alone. Their use of the word 'tend' in each of the three predictions conveys this cautious approach.

However, two points of caution of our own should be added to theirs:

1   If the hypothesis is very general (as a 'theory' usually is), evidence is likely to accumulate that supports certain parts (or specific predictions) and not others: we normally only accept or reject very specific predictions – not 'general' ones, which the AOE is – or whole theories.

2   It is very rare – and dangerous – to use the terms 'prove' and 'disprove' (as they do): this implies 'certainty', when in psychology (and, indeed, science as a whole) we are dealing only with 'probability'. Chance always plays some part in any particular investigation (hence the use of statistical tests to tell us how much 'faith' we can put in our results: how great a part did chance play on this occasion?). It is always possible that we would obtain a *different* result if we repeated the investigation.

Weiner (1992) believes that the status of the AOE remains uncertain. Part of the problem is that dispositional and situational attributions are not always clearly separable. For example, if female X says that she dates male Y because he is sensitive, does this indicate a situational (entity) attribution (he 'causes' her to like him) or a dispositional attribution (she likes sensitive people)?

In Study 2, Nisbett *et al.* give as an example of a *pure entity* reason (i.e. situational) for liking the girl they dated most often, 'She's a relaxing person'; 'I need someone I can relax with' is given as a *dispositional* reason. However, a much more ambiguous example (in relation to choice of college major) is, 'I want to make a lot of money' (classified as dispositional because it refers to the person who is choosing), and 'Chemistry is a high-paying field' (situational). They are ambiguous in the sense that the two statements convey very similar information and, in fact, imply one another (Hewstone and Fincham, 1996).

This distinction between dispositional and situational causes is really at the heart of attribution theory (see **Background and context** above); while it has much intuitive appeal, in practice it is often difficult to achieve. Indeed, some studies have shown that many participants fail to understand the difference, and/or do not find it meaningful. The result is that the reliability and validity of such measures are now challenged rather than assumed (Hewstone and Antaki, 1988).

Theoretical issues

As we saw above, Jones and Nisbett's (1971) original hypothesis states that actors tend to perceive their own behaviour as a response to situational cues, while observers tend to perceive the actor's behaviour as a manifestation of a disposition or quality possessed by the actor. The second part of this hypothesis (i.e. the *observer's* bias) corresponds to the *fundamental attribution error* (FAE; Ross, 1977).

Put another way, the FAE (or *lay dispositionism*; Ross and Nisbett, 1991) is one component of the AOE. Heider's (1958) original theory can account for both components equally well:

> *behaviour ... has such salient properties that it tends to engulf the field rather than be confined to its proper position as a local stimulus whose interpretation requires the additional data of a surrounding field – the situation in social perception.*

In other words, the actor represents the 'figure' against the 'ground', constituted by the social situation (similarly, in the Rubin vase reversible figure illusion, when you perceive the vase as the figure, the two faces constitute the ground/background). People are active, dynamic, constantly moving and changing, and these properties make them interesting and attention-grabbing. By contrast, the situation is normally fairly static, constant and much less interesting: it is behaviour that usually stands out from the background of social context, social roles and situational demands.

So, *salience* is a crucial influence on the kind of attribution we make: if you are observing someone else, it is their *behaviour* that is most salient for you. According to Ross and Nisbett (1991), the claim that what you *attend to* (what is salient) is what you *attribute to*, is the best supported generalization in the whole attribution literature.

But what is salient for the actor? In Ross and Nisbett's terms, 'rampant dispositionism is kept in check when it's the self that is in question'. Now what is salient are all the features of the situation which were not attended to by the observer: the observer's 'ground' is the actor's 'figure'. This, of course, constitutes the actor component of the AOE.

In support of this *perceptual salience* explanation, Nisbett *et al.* cite the study by Storms (1973), which has become something of a classic. Two actor-participants at a time engaged in a brief, unstructured conversation, while two observer-participants looked on. Later, a questionnaire was used to measure the actor's attributions of their own behaviour in the conversation, and the observers' attributions of the behaviour of one of the two actors to whom they had been 'matched'. Visual orientation was manipulated by the use of videotapes of the conversation:

- the *no video* (*control*) group simply completed the questionnaire;

- the *same orientation* group simply saw a video of what they saw during the original conversation (before completing the questionnaire);

- the *new orientation* group saw a video that *reversed* the original orientation: actors saw themselves and observers saw the other actor (again, before completing the questionnaire).

As predicted, the first two groups displayed the usual AOE. But, also as predicted, the AOE was *reversed* in the third group: actors made more dispositional attributions than did observers. Visual orientation is an index of perceptual salience, which is a determinant of perceived causality (Brown, 1986).

The fact that it is *possible* (using the artificial means of a video camera) to change the kind of attribution one makes, shows that under 'normal' circumstances:

> attribution is guided to a very substantial degree by one's focus of attention and a
> primary reason that actors and observers have different causal interpretations is
> simply because actors and observers typically are attending to different things.
> (Ross and Nisbett, 1991)

However, as Hewstone and Fincham (1996) point out, dispositional attributions were very high in *all* the conditions of Storms's experiment, and the control condition actually failed to show the normal situational attributions for actors. It seems that, while the person in the centre of the visual field *is* rated as more causally important, this weighting does not always have a clear effect on the type of attribution that is made.

In Nisbett *et al.*'s Study 2, participants had to write five separate paragraphs, including one on how their best friend would explain the participant's choice of girlfriend and college major. The results for this virtually duplicated those for two other paragraphs – why their best friend had made his choice of (a) girlfriend and (b) college major. This shows the ability to 'reverse perspective': participants were 'remarkably capable of adopting the perspective of an outside observer of their own behaviour'. This can be seen as equivalent to Storms's finding. But while Storms *literally* changed people's perspective by using a video camera, Nisbett *et al.*'s participants changed perspective *mentally* (perceptual versus psychological, respectively).

Nisbett *et al.* discuss a second explanation of the AOE, namely the *informational* explanation. As an actor, we literally cannot see ourselves behaving, so what is salient for us are all the situational forces impinging on us. 'Superimposed' on this difference is *access to information* (Jones and Nisbett, 1971). Actors know how they feel about an event, about their intentions and about factors giving rise to those intentions, so they can more appropriately attribute their behaviour to these (often) short-term factors. They also have direct access to their own history, including how they have behaved in similar situations in the past. Knowing how we can behave differently on different occasions, and in different situations, may discourage us from making dispositional attributions. All these factors, as well as subtle contextual factors, may be inaccessible to the observer.

While Hewstone and Fincham (1996) consider the informational explanation to be less interesting and less researched than the salience explanation, both salience and informational factors are probably involved (Fiske and Taylor, 1991).

Subsequent research

In a study by Regan and Totten (1975, in Brown, 1986), observers were instructed to empathize with one of two women engaged in a real 'get acquainted' conversation. Compared with observers who merely observed, the empathizers were much more likely to make *situational* attributions.

Brown explains this finding by saying that normally observers notice actors' 'gross' behaviour, their 'large muscle movements' and actions. But Regan and Totten's observers were focusing more on expressive behaviour, the finer muscle movements and more subtle aspects of behaviour: effectively, they were observing the actor's *mental state*.

Applying this to Study 1, the actors 'knew their minds', they knew what did and did not appeal to them about the original request to volunteer, and how much the United Fund resembled it for them. The observers could not have known any of these things about the actors, who were strangers being observed in a 'non-empathizing' way (in terms of their 'gross' decision to volunteer or not to volunteer).

A major limitation of the AOE is that it sometimes fails to fit the facts: it is sometimes *reversed* (e.g. Chen *et al.*, 1988). If something goes wrong, or we receive negative feedback about something we have done, we typically blame it on the situation (or another person), as the AOE predicts. But what about *positive* feedback and achievements? Do we normally attribute these to the situation as well? No! We usually want to take the credit for our successes (*self-enhancing bias*), but do not want to accept the blame for our failures (*self-protecting bias*). Together, these are referred to as the *self-serving bias* (SSB; Miller and Ross, 1975); this seems to explain certain attributions that actors make which the AOE cannot handle.

An interesting exception to the SSB is the clinically depressed person, who believes that when things go wrong, the causes are internal, stable over time and reflect a global deficiency (Abramson and Martin, 1981). (See Chapter 18.) Another exception is the unhappily married couple, who make the same attributions about their partner's negative behaviour as depressed people do about their own failures; Bradbury and Fincham (1990) call this relationship pattern *distress-maintaining*.

Another exception involves culture and gender. The SSB is not found among Asians, who are more likely to attribute their successes to external factors (such as luck) and their failures to internal factors (such as lack of effort) (Kitayama and Markus, 1995). This, in turn, reflects a bias towards *self-effacement*, which is more likely to maintain one's self-esteem in a *collectivist* (mainly non-Western) culture (where the achievement of the individual is minimized). This strategy for maintaining self-esteem is also often used by women in *individualist* (mainly Western) cultures, who 'value relationships, put other people's needs before their own, and define themselves in terms of their connectedness to others' (Nagayama Hall and Barongan, 2002).

The AOE may also be partly determined by cultural factors. In collectivist cultures, people are more likely to attribute other's behaviour to situational factors; they do not expect people to behave consistently because different behaviours may be required when the situation calls for it (Nagayama Hall and Barongan, 2002).

Applications and implications

According to Zimbardo and Leippe (1991), Western cultures stress the 'cult of the ego':

> It is no wonder that we tend to look for the person in the situation more than we search for the situation that makes the person. Indeed, one of the major lessons of social psychology is that human behaviour is much more under the influence of situational variables than we normally recognize or are willing to admit.

By failing to account adequately for the power of subtle situational forces (such as roles, rules, uniforms, symbols and group consensus), we become vulnerable to those very forces: we *overestimate* our dispositional strength to resist them and *underestimate* their power over us. Zimbardo and Leippe (1991) cite the 40 psychiatrists who predicted that only psychopathic participants (less than 1 per cent) would go on giving shocks up to 450 volts in Milgram's obedience experiment. (See Chapter 10.) These 'experts' were making a dispositional attribution which their professional training had caused them to overuse.

Haney *et al.*'s Stanford prison experiment (see Chapter 13) was designed to test the *dispositional hypothesis* in relation to the pathological behaviour typically displayed in such total institutions. They rejected it in favour of a *situational* explanation.

If Western culture is guilty of the 'cult of the ego', then it is also true that US social psychologists may have been guilty of *ethnocentrism*, or at least a failure to recognize the variability between cultures and subcultures with regard to how people make attributions (Ross and Nisbett, 1991). (See **Subsequent research** above.) Different cultures construe the world in truly different ways, suggesting that marked cognitive differences may have fundamentally *social* origins.

Smith and Bond (1998) discuss the AOE in the context of communication breakdown between members of different cultural groups. They argue that until people from different cultures become more knowledgeable about each others' cultural codes, the 'cycle of misattribution' will continue.

EXERCISES

1   In Background and context, **reference is made to the gestalt psychologists. What does 'gestalt' mean and who are the main figures associated with this school of psychology?**

2   **In Study 2:**

(a) **What are the independent and dependent variables?**

(b) **What experimental design was used?**

(c) **By what method were the paragraphs scored for the degree to which they stressed 'entity' versus 'dispositional' reasons?**

(d) **How was 'dispositional' defined?**

3   **In a follow-up to Study 2, participants were presented with reasons in a questionnaire. Alternate forms of the questionnaire were constructed (such that for every reason which appeared in entity form on one, there was a dispositional form of that reason on the other, and vice versa).**

(a) **What is another term for 'alternate forms'?**

(b) **What is it a measure of?**

(c) **What other, equivalent measures are there?**

4   **In Study 3, there were 20 three-choice items (trait term/polar opposite/'it depends on the situation') for each of the five stimulus persons (including self). For the group of participants as a whole, the question for each stimulus person preceded the question for every other stimulus person equally often.**

(a) **What is this arrangement called?**

(b) **Why was it used in this particular case?**

5   **In Study 3, 'The tendency to attribute more traits to others was as stable across subjects and trait dimensions as it was across stimulus persons.' What does this mean?**

6   **Nisbett *et al.* refer to Brehm's (1966) concept of *reactance*: 'man's desire to see himself as free and able to control events that are important to him'. Do you agree that seeing ourselves as motivated by traits/dispositions makes us *less* free, and that freedom lies in seeing ourselves as acting in accordance with the demands and opportunities of each new situation as it occurs?**

Romantic love conceptualized as an attachment process

Hazan, C. and Shaver, P.R. (1987)

Journal of Personality and Social Psychology, 52(3): 511–24

BACKGROUND AND CONTEXT

According to Ainsworth (1989), an attachment is an affectional bond: 'a relatively long-enduring tie in which the partner is important as a unique individual and is interchangeable with none other'. As with other affectional bonds, there is a desire to stay close to the partner, to be in their company and spend time with them (*proximity maintenance*). A unique feature of attachments, though, is that the attachment figure provides a sense of security, a *safe base* from which to explore the environment, including what is unfamiliar, unknown and even threatening.

This feature of attachments can be seen very clearly in the case of *securely attached* one-year-olds in the 'Strange Situation' (Ainsworth *et al.*, 1978). This is an observational technique designed to assess the nature of the child's relationship with the mother. Emphasis is given to how the child reacts to the mother's return after she has been out of the room for a three-minute period.

Securely attached (Type B) children seek immediate contact with her when she returns; they quickly calm down in her arms (having been clearly distressed when she left), and start playing again. In contrast, *anxious-avoidant* (Type A) children positively ignore or avoid the mother on her return (having shown little or no distress when she left), and *anxious-resistant* (Type C) children seek contact with her when she returns, but simultaneously show anger and resist contact. Type C children generally cry a lot more than the others and are very distressed when the mother leaves.

The mother's ability to comfort the child when s/he is upset represents the third major feature of attachments, namely providing a *safe haven*, a source of support and reassurance at times of threat and distress. When we become separated from our attachment figures (temporarily or permanently), we display *separation protest* (the fourth major feature of attachments).

According to Weiss (1991), 'In adults as well as children, attachments appear to be relationships critical to continuing security and so to the maintenance of emotional security'.

Ainsworth was originally a student of Bowlby, arguably the most famous and influential of all attachment theorists. Both are best known for their study of attachment in young children. However, Bowlby made repeated references to attachment as a lifespan phenomenon (e.g. 'attachment behaviour is held to characterise human beings from the cradle to the grave' (Bowlby, 1977). Attachment theory, which Ainsworth and Bowlby developed both independently and together, leads to two very significant hypotheses (Bartholomew, 1993):

1   Attachment behaviour characterizes human beings throughout life.

2   Patterns established in childhood parent–child relationships tend to structure the quality of later bonds in adult relationships and may account for why some people seem to avoid this presumably 'natural' inclination.

AIM AND NATURE

● HYPOTHESES

The aims of the study were:

● to explore the possibility that attachment theory offers a valuable perspective on adult romantic love;

● to create a coherent framework for understanding love, loneliness and grief at different points in the life cycle.

Hazan and Shaver argued that attachment theory can help explain both healthy and unhealthy forms of love, encompassing both positive emotions (caring, intimacy and trust) and negative emotions (fear of intimacy, jealousy, and emotional ups and downs).

More specifically, they predicted:

1   About 60 per cent of adults will classify themselves as securely attached, with the other two (insecure) types (anxious-avoidant and anxious-ambivalent) being fairly evenly split (but a few more anxious-avoidant). (This is in line with Ainsworth *et al.*'s (1978) findings with one-year-olds using the Strange Situation; see **Background and context** above.)

2   There is a correlation between adults' attachment style (securely attached, anxious-avoidant, anxious-ambivalent) and the type of parenting they received

as children. (This is also consistent with Ainsworth *et al.*'s (1978) findings.)

3   Adults with different attachment styles will display different characteristic *mental models* (internal representations) of themselves and their major social-interaction partners. (This relates to the child's *expectations* regarding the mother's accessibility and responsiveness (Ainsworth *et al.*, 1978), and to Bowlby's (e.g. 1969) concept of *inner working models* (IWMs).)

● METHOD/DESIGN

The three attachment styles identified by Ainsworth *et al.* (1978) (based on observational studies of young children) had to be 'translated' in a way that would make them suitable for the study of adult attachments. This was done as shown in Table 15.1 (opposite), where respondents to a 'love quiz' in a local newspaper were asked to indicate which of three descriptions best applied to their inner feelings about romantic relationships. (This relates to hypotheses 1 and 3.)

They were also asked to complete a simple adjective checklist describing their childhood relationships with their parents. (This relates to hypothesis 2.) (See Table 15.2 on page 168.)

Hazan and Shaver tested two separate samples:

1   *Sample one* comprised 205 men and 415 women, aged between 14 and 82 (mean age 36), 91 per cent of whom described themselves as 'primarily heterosexual'. At the time of the survey, 42 per cent were married, 28 per cent were divorced or widowed, 9 per cent were 'living with a lover', and 31 per cent were dating. (Some checked more than one category.)

2   *Sample two* comprised 108 undergraduate students – 38 men and 70 women (mean age 18). They completed the questionnaire as a class exercise. They answered additional items that focused more on the *self* side of the mental model (as opposed to the partner), as well as additional items measuring loneliness. (These extra items relate to hypothesis 3.)

(Strictly, the use of two different samples corresponds to two separate studies conducted by Hazan and Shaver, both of which were reported in the same article. But here the findings are described as if for a single study.)

● RESULTS/FINDINGS

Hypothesis 1

Table 15.1 shows the percentage of respondents classified as either securely attached (56 per cent in both samples), anxious-avoidant (23 per cent in sample one

AIM AND NATURE

Table 15.1

Responses to the question, 'Which of the following best describes your feelings about romantic relationships?'

Classification	Percentage of respondents	Response
Securely attached	56	I find it relatively easy to get close to others and am comfortable depending on them and having them depend on me. I do not worry often about being abandoned or about someone getting too close to me.
Anxious-avoidant	23–25	I am somewhat uncomfortable being close to others; I find it difficult to trust them completely, difficult to allow myself to depend on them. I am nervous when anyone gets too close, and often, love partners want me to be more intimate than I feel comfortable being.
Anxious-ambivalent	19–20	I find that others are reluctant to get as close as I would like. I often worry that my partner does not really love me or will not want to stay with me. I want to merge completely with another person, and this desire sometimes scares people away.

and 25 per cent in sample two) or anxious-ambivalent (19 per cent in sample one, 20 per cent in sample two). The classification is based on which of three descriptions the respondents chose.

Both samples were also asked to describe:

> the most important love relationship you have ever had, why you got involved in it, and why it turned out the way it did... It may be a past or a current relationship, but choose only the most important one.

The responses from both samples were very similar. Those classified as secure described this special relationship as especially happy, friendly and trusting, being able to accept and support their partner despite his/her faults. Their relationships also tended to last longer and, if married, were less likely to end in divorce.

AIM AND NATURE

Hypothesis 2

Table 15.2

Correlation between adult attachment style and type of parenting respondents received as children

Attachment style	Type of parenting
Securely attached	Readily available, attentive, responsive
Anxious-avoidant	Unresponsive, rejecting, inattentive
Anxious-ambivalent	Anxious, fussy, out-of-step with child's needs, only available/responsive some of the time

Hypothesis 3

Questions designed to measure the mental model of self and relationships were answered in line with the prediction only in sample one, whose items were more focused on the partner or relationship than on the self:

● The *securely attached* expressed belief in lasting love. Even though romantic feelings wax and wane, only sometimes reaching the intensity experienced at the start of the relationship, genuine love is enduring. They also generally find others trustworthy and have confidence in themselves as likeable.

● The *anxious-avoidant* are much more doubtful about the existence or durability of romantic love: the kind of head-over-heels love portrayed in fiction does not happen in real life, and it is rare to find a person you can really fall in love with. They also maintain that they do not need a love partner in order to be happy.

● The *anxious-ambivalent* fall in love easily and often, but they rarely find what they would call true love. They also express more self-doubts (compared with both the other types), but compared with the anxious-avoidants, they do not repress or try to hide their feelings of insecurity.

The two insecure types, compared with the secure, were found to be the most vulnerable to loneliness; the anxious-ambivalent (sample two) were the most vulnerable of all.

● CONCLUSIONS

Support was found for all three hypotheses.

● Based on Ainsworth *et al.*'s (1978) original studies and later studies involving young children, the percentages falling within each of the three attachment style

AIM AND NATURE

categories were closely matched by the percentages of adults in Hazan and Shaver's study.

- The correlation between adults' attachment style and their recollections of the kind of parenting they received was remarkably similar to Ainsworth *et al.*'s (1978) findings. (In Ainsworth *et al.*'s study, the child's attachment style was correlated with the degree of *sensitivity* shown by mothers.)

- The mental models of adults differed according to their attachment styles. The securely attached were far more positive and optimistic about both themselves and (potential) love partners, compared with either of the insecurely attached.

- The two insecure groups, compared with the secure, were the most vulnerable to loneliness.

EVALUATION

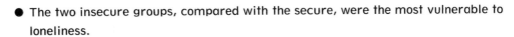

Methodological and theoretical issues

Hazan and Shaver acknowledge several methodological and theoretical limitations of their study. One of these relates to the continuity between early childhood and adult experience. At least from the point of view of the insecurely attached person, it would be overly pessimistic if continuity were the rule rather than the exception (i.e. if an insecurely attached child inevitably became an insecurely attached adult).

Correlations between current attachment style and parent variables (see Table 15.2) were statistically significant, but they were not strong. Also, they were higher for sample two, who were much younger than sample one. This suggests that continuity *decreases* as one goes further into adulthood. The average person participates in several important friendships and love relationships, which provide opportunities for revising mental models of self and others.

A study by Main *et al.* (1985) provides support for this more optimistic view. They found a strong association between adults' attachment history and the attachment styles of their own young children. However, some adults who reported being insecure in their relationships with their parents managed to produce securely attached children (assessed at one and six years). They had mentally worked through their unpleasant experiences with their parents, and now had mental models of relationships more typical of the securely attached (Hazan and Shaver, 1987).

If mental models can change, can the attachment styles they underlie also change? This question mirrors one of the criticisms made of the attachment styles identified by Ainsworth *et al.* (1978). Patterns of attachment to mothers and fathers are *independent*, so the same child might be securely attached to its mother, but insecurely attached to its father (Main and Weston, 1981). This shows that attachment patterns derived from the Strange Situation reflect qualities of unique relationships, rather than characteristics of the child. In the same way, adults' choice of paragraphs describing attachment styles might reflect the state of a current relationship (or lack of one). For example, if you have just got out of a relationship that ended badly, you are more likely to perceive relationships *in general* in a negative way.

Hazan and Shaver recognize that their measures (of attachment styles, relationships with their parents, mental models, etc.) were brief and simple. In the case of the paragraphs describing attachment styles, participants had to choose just one (a forced-choice, self-report measure). Is this a valid way of measuring such a complex aspect of behaviour?

According to Parkes (2006), although these three categories appear to be distinct from each other, one of the weaknesses of the Strange Situation used by Ainsworth *et al.* (1978) is its failure to measure the *strength* of the attachment styles. Infants are forced into all-or-nothing categories according to defined cut-off points. But common sense suggests that there must be degrees of attachment security/insecurity; the use of graded measures would provide more subtle results. It seems reasonable to apply this same criticism to the paragraphs used by Hazan and Shaver.

Despite these limitations, Hazan and Shaver succeeded in providing both a *normative* account of romantic love (i.e. an account of typical processes of romantic attachment) and an understanding of *individual differences* in adult relationship styles (Feeney, 1999). They provided a bridge between infant attachment theory and theories of romantic love; this generated intense interest among relationship researchers.

Subsequent research

Hazan and Shaver's findings have been replicated and extended in several studies. According to Bartholomew (1993), their method of operationalizing adult attachment patterns as self-report measures has stimulated thriving new research areas, such as attachment patterns among dating couples, the process of giving up parents as attachment figures, attachment patterns and work satisfaction, and attachment styles and religious beliefs and fear of death.

Bartholomew (1990, in Bartholomew, 1993) conducted a series of intensive interviews with young adults about their close relationships. As a result, she distinguished between two types of *patterns of avoidance* in adults:

- *fearful avoidant*, where the desire for social contact is inhibited by fear of rejection;

- *dismissive avoidant*, where the individual defensively denies the need or desire for intimate contact.

This distinction reflects different *models of the self*:

● people who fearfully avoid intimacy view themselves as undeserving of the love and support of others;

● those who dismiss intimacy have a positive model of the self that minimizes subjective awareness of distress and social needs.

Only the fearful-avoidant type corresponds to Hazan and Shaver's anxious-avoidant style.

According to Collins and Read (1990), when *both* members of dating couples are asked about their mental models, the securely attached tend to choose partners who are also securely attached. But the anxiously attached are no more likely to choose one another than one of the other types. The least happy among young dating couples seem to be:

● any combination involving an anxiously attached woman (perhaps because she tends to be clingy and jealous, thereby producing the unstable, unhappy relationship she expects);

● any combination involving an avoidant man (again, because his mental model may result in fulfilment of the expectation that relationships have little to offer (Bee, 1994).

According to Fletcher (2002), 'Love is … an evolutionary device to persuade couples to stay together for long enough to give their children a good shot at making it to adulthood …'. In our hunter-gatherer ancestral environment, two parents were better than one. Attachment bonds between procreative partners would have greatly enhanced the survival of their offspring (Zeifman and Hazan, 2000).

Bowlby (1969) identified three basic behavioural systems that bond male–female pairs together: attachment, caregiving and sex. Shaver *et al.* (1996) have proposed a theory of adult romantic love in terms of these three systems. So, whenever we say 'I love you', we can mean any or all of the following:

● *Love as attachment*: 'I am emotionally dependent on you for happiness, safety and security; I feel anxious and lonely when you're gone, relieved and stronger when you're near. I want to be comforted, supported emotionally, and taken care of by you'.

● *Love as caregiving*: 'I get great pleasure from supporting, caring for and taking care of you; from facilitating your progress, health, growth and happiness'.

● *Love as sexual attraction*: 'I am sexually attracted to you and can't get you out of my mind. You excite me, "turn me on", make me feel alive … I want to see you, devour you, touch you, merge with you, lose myself in you, "get off on you"'.

Applications and implications

Work can be seen as the adult counterpart of the child's exploration of its environment (using the mother as a safe base). They are functionally equivalent, both representing a major source of actual and perceived competence. Based on this aspect of attachment theory and their 1987 study, Hazan and Shaver (1990) derived and tested three hypotheses regarding the relationship between attachment style and orientation towards work. Using questionnaires, they found:

● In line with hypothesis 1, securely attached respondents approach their work with the confidence associated with secure attachments. They enjoy work activity and are relatively free of fear of failure. Although they value their work, they tend to value relationships more, and generally do not allow work to interfere with those relationships. They do not, typically, use work to satisfy unmet needs for love, nor do they use work to avoid social interaction.

● In line with hypothesis 2, anxious-ambivalent respondents reported that love concerns often interfere with their work performance and that they often fear rejection for poor performance. They also tend to ease up after receiving praise, which suggests that their main motivation at work may be to gain others' respect and admiration.

● Consistent with hypothesis 3, anxious-avoidant respondents use work activity to avoid social interaction. Work interferes with having friends and a social life.

Although this study is subject to many of the criticisms of the 1987 study, the findings suggest that one's approach to work is deeply affected by the strengths or weaknesses of one's mental model of attachments and relationships in general (Bee, 1994). Hazan and Shaver believe that attachment theory offers a way of explaining why love and work, traditionally treated as entirely separate areas of research, are so closely interrelated.

According to Kirkpatrick (1999), many aspects of religious belief and experience, especially those related to perceived relationships with God, reflect (at least in part) attachment processes. God can be regarded as demonstrating all the defining features of an attachment figure. For example, many believers use prayer as a way of maintaining contact with God (*proximity seeking*), and belief in the existence or presence of God seems to allay fear and anxiety, and provide a sense of confidence and emotional security (*secure base*). Perhaps most strikingly, religion plays an important role in times of stress (such as the loss of a loved one), providing comfort, support and strength (Kirkpatrick, 1992, 1994).

Despite the research interest in adult attachments inspired by the groundbreaking 1987 study, little attention has been paid to attachment specifically among older adults. The rapid growth of the Western world's elderly population has prompted many social scientists to seek greater understanding of issues such as:

- the role of attachment bonds in caregiving and chronic illness;

- the influence of attachment in coping with bereavement and loss;

- the relationship of attachment to adjustment and well-being in old age (Bradley and Cafferty, 2001; see Gross, 2003).

EXERCISES

1 (a) **What kind of sampling was involved in the two samples used by Hazan and Shaver?**

   (b) **Name *one* advantage and *one* disadvantage of each type.**

   (c) **Are there any characteristics of the two samples that might be considered biased?**

2 **The last finding in Hazan and Shaver's study was that the two insecurely attached groups, compared with the securely attached, were more likely to experience loneliness; the anxious-ambivalent (in sample two) were the most vulnerable of all. Try to account for this finding based on your knowledge of what the different attachment styles involve and their related mental models.**

16

Positive reinforcement produced by electrical stimulation of septal area and other regions of rat brain

Olds, J. and Milner, P. (1954)

Journal of Comparative and Physiological Psychology, 47: 419–27

BACKGROUND AND CONTEXT

In the context of psychologists' early attempts to study motivation, during the 1920s the concept of instinct (borrowed from biology) was largely replaced by the concept of *drive*. The term was first used by Woodworth (1918), who compared human behaviour with the operation of a machine: the mechanism of a machine is relatively passive and drive is the power applied to make it 'go'.

The concept of drive has taken two major forms:

1   *Homeostatic drive theory* (Cannon, 1929), which is a physiological theory. Cannon coined the term *homeostasis* (derived from the Greek *homos* meaning 'same' and *stasis* meaning 'stoppage') to refer to the process by which an organism maintains a fairly constant internal (bodily) environment – that is, how body temperature, blood sugar level, salt concentration in the blood, and so on, are kept in a state of relative balance or equilibrium.

2   *Drive reduction theory* (Hull, 1943), which is primarily a theory of learning. Drive reduction theory was intended to explain the fundamental principle of *reinforcement*, both *positive* (the reduction of a drive by the *presentation* of a stimulus) and *negative* (the reduction of a drive by the *removal* or *avoidance* of a stimulus).

Hull was interested in the *primary* (physiological) *homeostatic* drives that include hunger and thirst. He believed that all behaviour (human and non-human animal) originates in the satisfaction of these drives. His basic premise was that learning *always* and *only* occurs through primary drive reduction, based on Skinner's (1938) principle that operant (i.e. voluntary, non-reflex) behaviour is shaped by reinforcement.

Hilgard *et al.* (1979) report that in 1953, Olds was investigating the reticular activating system (RAS) of the rat's brain, part of the midbrain which controls the overall level of arousal or awareness, using microelectrodes. These tiny electrodes can be implanted permanently in specific brain areas without disturbing the rat's normal health or activity. When connected to an electrical source, they can supply electrical stimulation of varying intensities. Olds accidentally stimulated an area near the hypothalamus (part of the forebrain) and found that after receiving a mild current through the electrodes, the animal repeatedly returned to the place where it had been stimulated.

Further stimulations at the same location in the cage caused the rat to spend most of its time there. Later, Olds found that other rats with electrodes implanted in the same brain region leaned to press a lever in a Skinner box to produce their own electrical stimulation: each lever press closed a circuit that automatically produced a brief current. This is called *electrical self-stimulation* of the brain (ES-SB) or *intracranial self-stimulation* (ICSS; Toates, 2001).

AIM AND NATURE

● HYPOTHESIS

There were no specific hypotheses being tested. The aim of the study was to explore the reinforcing properties of the implantation of electrodes which deliver shock to the rat's brain. While previous studies had focused on the eliciting functions of electrical brain stimulation (i.e. studying the responses produced by the stimulation – *respondent/classical* conditioning), Olds and Milner focused on the responses which *precede* it and are *instrumental* in producing it (i.e. *operant/instrumental* conditioning).

The *research questions* being asked were:

1   Can direct brain stimulation be used to reinforce behaviour, specifically lever pressing in a Skinner box, in the same way that food can?

2   Are there particular brain sites where such stimulation will be effective and others where it won't be?

● METHOD/DESIGN

This was a highly controlled laboratory experiment, using rats as experimental subjects.

General

Fifteen male hooded rats were individually tested in a Skinner box, where lever pressing produced an electric current (ranging from 0.5V to 5V). This was delivered through a loose lead, suspended from the ceiling, which connected the stimulator to the rat's electrode. Subjects were given a total of 6–12 hours of training to press the lever (acquisition testing), where each lever press produced an electric shock, and 1–2 hours of extinction testing (where the stimulator was switched off).

After testing, the animal was sacrificed.

Electrode implantation

The electrodes consisted of two silver wires (0.01 inch diameter) cemented together to form a needle. This was cut to the correct length to reach the desired brain area, and stimulation occurred only at the tip. While the rat was anaesthetized, the electrode was inserted and held in place using jeweller's screws. Each subject was allowed to recover for three days before testing began.

Testing

The lever in the Skinner box activated a micro-switch in the stimulating circuit, so that when it was pressed, the rat received electrical stimulation, which continued for as long as the lever was pressed. Responses were recorded automatically on a paper strip.

At no time during the experiment were the rats deprived of food or water, and no reinforcement was used except for ES-EB.

● RESULTS

Locus

The highest scores were found together in the central portion of the forebrain. This is the *septal area*. Acquisition scores ranged from 75 to 92 per cent, and all subjects spent less than 22 per cent of their extinction time responding.

Acquisition scores for regions outside the septal area (either towards the caudate nucleus or towards the corpus callosum) dropped abruptly to 4–6 per cent. Above the corpus callosum, in the cingulate cortex, there was an acquisition score of 37 per cent and an extinction score of 9 per cent.

Behaviour

The lowest-scoring septal area rat gave a total of just over 3,000 responses in 12 hours of acquisition. When the current was turned on, the rat responded at the rate

AIM AND NATURE

of 285 responses an hour, compared with almost zero responses when it was turned off.

The highest-scoring septal area rat stimulated itself over 7,500 times in 12 hours. Its average response rate during acquisition was 742 responses an hour; during extinction there were virtually none.

 ## CONCLUSIONS

Clearly, electrical stimulation in certain parts of the brain, particularly the septal area, produces an effect apparently equivalent to that of a conventional primary reward as far as the maintenance of a lever-pressing response is concerned.

Stimulation of the cingulate cortex and the mammillothalamic tract also seems to be rewarding (although less so), while electrode stimulation in other brain regions is either neutral or punishing.

This electrical stimulation of the brain seems to have a primary rewarding effect (not associated with the reduction of any primary drive state); the phenomenon represents strong pursuit of a positive stimulus, rather than escape from some negative condition. If this is so, the septal area might represent a system whose unique function is to produce a rewarding effect on behaviour.

EVALUATION

Methodological issues

During the pre-testing session, if the rat did not respond regularly from the start, it was placed on the lever periodically (about every 5 minutes). Subsequently, it spent about 3½ hours per day in the Skinner box (3 hours of acquisition, 30 minutes of extinction). During acquisition, the rats were allowed to stimulate themselves with a voltage just high enough to produce some noticeable response in the resting animal.

The first few subjects were tested in this way for four days, but as there seemed to be little difference between the results on different days, this period was reduced to three and then two days for subsequent subjects. When calculating the scores, only the first six hours of acquisition for all subjects were used, so the scores are strictly comparable.

Periods when the rat was lever pressing regularly (at least one response every 30 seconds) were counted as periods of *responding*; intervals of 30 seconds or longer without a response were counted as periods of *no responding*.

The septal area (or septum pellucid) is part of the limbic system, which also includes the cingulate gyrus, thalamus, hypothalamus, hippocampus and amygdala. The limbic system as a whole is closely involved with behaviours which satisfy certain motivational and emotional needs, such as feeding, fighting, escape and mating. It also represents the meeting place between the cortex (or neocortex) – the most recent part of the (human) brain to have evolved – and older parts of the brain such as the hypothalamus (shared by all mammals).

It was Walter Hess who developed the technique of implanting electrodes in animal brains while investigating the RAS of the rat's brain (Roediger *et al.*, 1984). He accidentally implanted an electrode in an area near the hypothalamus known to be involved in sleep and arousal. The rat repeatedly returned to the place where it had been stimulated; further stimulation at the same cage location resulted in the animal spending most of its time there.

Theoretical issues

Olds and Milner's findings challenge Hull's homeostatic drive reduction theory (see above). Remember that Hull was trying to explain the principle of reinforcement in terms of homeostatic drive reduction. This rests on the assumption that some bodily need arises through some lack or deficiency (as in hunger, thirst or sex). But what do rats lack in the case of ES-SB?

ES-SB is an example of how drives can occur in the absence of any obvious physiological need (i.e. a *non-homeostatic drive*). Hull's theory emphasized primary (homeostatic) drives to the exclusion of secondary (non-homeostatic) drives. Primary drives are based on primary (innate) needs, but much human (and, to a lesser extent, non-human) behaviour can only be understood in terms of secondary (acquired) drives.

Several behaviourist psychologists – notably Miller (1948), Mowrer (1950) and Dollard and Miller (1950) – modified Hull's theory to include acquired drives (in particular, anxiety). This led to a great deal of research into avoidance learning in the 1950s (see Gross, 2005).

Just as ES-SB cannot be accommodated by drive reduction when considering only non-human motivation, so non-humans also seem to have other non-homeostatic drives that they share, to some degree, with humans. These include *competence motives*, such as seeking stimulation, the curiosity drive (Butler, 1954), the manipulative drive (Harlow *et al.*, 1950) and play.

While ES-SB may represent an important non-homeostatic drive, are there any important differences between the effects of ES-SB and (other) primary reinforcers? LeFrançois (1983) believes there are four:

1   Animals eventually become satiated following repeated food or water reinforcement – but not with ES-SB. (See **Exercises**.)

2   ES-SB seems to take precedence over other types of reinforcement: rats would rather die of hunger or thirst than go without it (e.g. Routtenberg and Lindy, 1965; Spies, 1965); they are prepared to cross an electric grid floor (Olds and Sinclair, 1957); and females will abandon their squealing newborn pups (Sonderegger, 1970).

3   When ES-SB is discontinued, extinction is remarkably more rapid than when food or water are used (although this does not quite square with Olds and Milner's findings: see **Locus** above). Lever pressing stops very abruptly, but reappears very rapidly when given just one or two shocks.

4   *Partial reinforcement* is much less effective (relative to a *continuous schedule*) compared with food or water, and it is usually impossible to train maze-running in rats using just ES-SB. (See **Exercises**.)

Panksepp (1998, in Toates, 2001) adds a fifth important difference. Rats' outward behaviour often displays an 'invigorated exploratory attitude' (i.e. they seem to be trying to get something behind the lever). This is not the type of behaviour seen when rats are pressing a lever to obtain food rewards or when they are actually eating them.

Subsequent research

Olds (1956) reported that one rat self-stimulated more than 2,000 times per hour for 24 hours consecutively! Later (1958), he found that rats which normally press a lever 25 times per hour for a food reward will press 100 times *per minute* for a reward of ES-SB. In all these cases, it is the septal area that is thought to be involved.

An even more dramatic demonstration of the power of the drive to self-stimulate is the finding that a male rat with an electrode in its lateral hypothalamus (LH) will self-stimulate in preference to eating if hungry, drinking if thirsty, or having access to a sexually receptive female. This effect has also been found in cats, monkeys and pigeons.

According to Green (1980) and Beaumont (1988), the main reward site for ES-SB is the median forebrain bundle (MFB), a fibre running from the brainstem up to the forebrain, through the LH, and the effects seem to depend on the presence of the synaptic transmitters dopamine and noradrenaline (the *catecholamines*). These neurotransmitters have been shown to be released from limbic structures during rewarding brain stimulation, and drugs which interfere with the operation of these pathways reduce the effect of ES-SB (Beaumont, 1988). Dopamine came to be described as a pleasure-neurotransmitter and a loss of dopamine as 'anaerobia' (Wise, 1982, in Toates, 2001).

Olds (1956) is credited with discovering the so-called 'pleasure centre'. Whether it is the septal area or the MFB, these reward or pleasure centres are generally thought of as the neural substrate of 'pleasure': any behaviour defined as pleasurable involves their activation. ES-EB is a 'short-cut' to pleasure, 'eliminating the need for natural drives and reinforcers' (Green, 1980).

However, two important qualifications need to be made:

1   Rather lower down in the hypothalamus, ES-SB produces pain and rats will go to great lengths to avoid it; often a single lever-press is sufficient for the rat to avoid the lever subsequently. Other sites seem to produce both reward *and* punishment. For example, Bower and Miller (1958) trained rats to press one lever for ES-SB and then another to turn it off, and it seems that prolonged brain stimulation might be aversive (Roediger *et al.*, 1984). An *intermediate* level of stimulation (moderate intensity and fairly brief) seems to be the most pleasurable (Hilgard *et al.*, 1979).

2   The actual region in the hypothalamus which will produce self-stimulation is considerably more diffuse than those involved in other hypothalamic drive centres (such as hunger and thirst). Also, other parts of the limbic system can produce pleasure responses (Rose, 1976).

Applications and implications

According to Rose (1976), although rats seem to enjoy ES-SB, their observed behaviour does not correspond to any obvious or easily identifiable behavioural state (such as rage, fear or sexual arousal). Is there a human equivalent?

During the mid 1960s and 1970s, reports came from the USA of electrodes being implanted in the pleasure centres of human beings (usually inmates of psychiatric hospitals, in particular people with schizophrenia or low intelligence). They were prepared to give themselves several hundred shocks per hour and gave vague descriptions of their subjective experiences ('feeling good'). This does not seem to have been a sexual feeling, but was sometimes described as feeling like an orgasm or the relaxed feeling which follows orgasm (Olds, 1958, 1962).

According to Campbell (1973), psychotics, epileptics and cancer patients have all reported relief from pain and anxiety, feeling 'wonderful', 'happy' or 'drunk' following stimulation of certain parts of the limbic system. Those who received more than a thousand stimulations per hour are content to do nothing else for six hours (the maximum period allowed). Rose (1976) asks how such experiments could be construed as 'treatment' and wonders if they can be compared with Nazi concentration camp 'experiments'. He believes that the idea of implanting electrodes into a person's brain (regardless of who does the stimulating) raises possibilities which are almost universally regarded as repugnant (such as mood and thought control).

According to Nestler and Malenka (2004), neurobiologists have known for a long time that drugs have their effect because they ultimately boost the activity of the brain's reward system: a complex circuit of neurons which evolved to make us feel 'flush' after eating or sex. At least initially, stimulating this system makes us feel good, which encourages us to repeat whatever induced the pleasure (the feeling is a powerful reinforcer). But recent research has indicated that chronic drug use can actually produce *structural* and *functional changes* in the system's neurons that last for weeks, months or years after the fix.

A key part of the circuit is the pathway extending from dopamine-producing neurons of the ventral tegmental area (VTA) to dopamine-sensitive neurons in the nucleus accumbens (NA), situated deep beneath the frontal cortex. Changes to these neurons contribute significantly to the tolerance, dependence and craving that fuel repeated drug use and lead to relapses, even after long periods of abstinence (Nestler and Malenka, 2004).

There are also pathways linking the NA and VTA with other brain regions that can help make addicts highly sensitive to reminders of past highs (such as drug paraphernalia – the 'equipment' used in drug-taking – and places where they have scored), vulnerable to relapse when stressed, and unable to control the urge to seek drugs.

The VTA-NA pathway acts as a 'rheostat of reward': it tells other brain centres how rewarding an activity is. The more rewarding, the more likely the organism is to remember it well and repeat it. Brain scans (see Chapter 29) show that the NA in cocaine addicts' brains 'lights up' when offered a snort, or when shown a video of someone using cocaine or even a photograph of white lines on a mirror. The amygdala and some areas of the cortex also respond. While being scanned, addicts rate their feelings of rush and craving on a scale of 0–3. Such studies show that the VTA and sublenticular extended amygdala are important to the cocaine-induced rush; and that the amygdala and NA influence both the rush *and* the craving for more of the drug, which becomes stronger as the euphoria wears off (Nestler and Malenka, 2004).

EXERCISES

1 In the Method/design **section, we are told that after testing, the subjects were 'sacrificed'.**

 (a) **What do you understand by this term?**

 (b) **What are the ethical implications of such a practice?**

2 **What was the purpose of the pre-testing session?**

3 **Why was it necessary to have periods of extinction testing?**

4 **What does LeFrançois (1983) mean when he says that animals become satiated if given repeated food or water reinforcement?**

5 **What is meant by:**

 (a) **partial reinforcement;**

 (b) **continuous reinforcement?**

17

The relation of eye movements during sleep to dream activity: An objective method for the study of dreaming

Dement, W. and Kleitman, N. (1957)

Journal of Experimental Psychology, 53(5): 339–46

BACKGROUND AND CONTEXT

Dreaming has always fascinated human beings, although it is only very recently that it (and its relationship to sleep) has been studied scientifically. Although theories of sleep and theories of dreaming have been proposed separately, it is difficult to discuss one without the other. For example, sleep deprivation is a common way of studying the normal functions of sleep, and the findings are often expressed in terms of how the dreaming process is disrupted.

Conversely, the scientific study of dreams and dreaming has been conducted mainly in relation to physiological variables during sleep. This required a reliable method of determining precisely when dreaming occurs. Ultimately, this knowledge always depends on the subjective report of the dreamer (there is no independent way of establishing that a dream has taken place). However, this becomes relatively objective if such reports can be reliably linked to physiological phenomena, which in turn can be measured by physical techniques.

Aserinsky and Kleitman (1955) were the first to report such a relationship in adults (based originally on their study of sleeping children). They observed periods of rapid, connected eye movements during sleep and found a high incidence of dream recall in participants woken during these periods; when woken at other times (non-rapid eye movement/NREM sleep), there was a very low incidence of dream recall. The relationship between the occurrence of this *rapid eye movement* (REM) *sleep* and dreaming was confirmed in both normal participants and diagnosed schizophrenics (Dement, 1955). REM sleep was also shown to appear at regular intervals in relation to a cyclical change in the depth of sleep during the night, as measured by the electroencephalograph (EEG) (Dement and Kleitman, 1955).

The present (1957) study reports the results of a rigorous testing of the relationship between eye movements and dreaming.

AIM AND NATURE

● HYPOTHESIS

The three main hypotheses being tested were:

1   There is a significant relationship between REM/NREM sleep and dreaming, such that (based on previous research) REM sleep is associated with dreaming and NREM sleep is not.

2   There is a significant positive correlation between the subjective estimate of the duration of dreams and the length of eye-movement period prior to awakening.

3   There is a significant association between the pattern of eye movement and the content of the dream, such that the former actually reflects the visual experience of the dream.

● METHOD/DESIGN

Participants (seven adult males and two adult females) were studied under controlled laboratory conditions. They spent a night in the sleep laboratory, being woken at various intervals, and physiological recordings were made of:

● changes in corneoretinal potential fields as the eyes moved;

● brainwaves (as a criterion of depth of sleep).

This was done by attaching two or more electrodes near the eyes, and two or three electrodes to the scalp.

Participants were woken by the ringing of an ordinary doorbell placed near the bed, loud enough to ensure immediate awakening in all levels of sleep. Participants had to speak into a recording device near the bed, first stating whether or not they had been dreaming, and then, if they could, to relate the content of the dream.

There was no communication between participants and the experimenter until it had been judged that the former had been dreaming; this depended on the participant relating a coherent, fairly detailed description of dream content. Then, and only then, the experimenter would enter the room to ask for further details.

Participants were never told, of course, whether they had been woken from a period of REM or NREM sleep.

● RESULTS/FINDINGS

REM sleep was characterized by a low-voltage, relatively fast EEG pattern. In between the REM periods, EEG patterns indicating deeper sleep were either predominantly high-voltage, slow activity, or frequent, well-defined sleep spindles with a low-voltage background. No REMs were ever observed during the initial onset of sleep. These findings were identical to previous observations on uninterrupted sleep (Dement and Kleitman, 1955).

REM periods which were not terminated by awakening varied between 3 and 50 minutes (mean of 20 minutes); they tended to increase the later in the night they occurred. The eyes were not in constant motion; rather, the activity occurred in bursts of one or two, up to 50 or 100 movements. A single movement generally took 0.1–0.2 seconds and was followed by a fixation pause of varying duration.

The REM periods occurred at fairly frequent intervals throughout the night. The frequency varied between individual participants, the average being one REM period every 92 minutes.

In all, 21 per cent of the awakenings occurred in the first two hours of sleep, 29 per cent in the second two hours, 28 per cent in the third two, and 22 per cent in the fourth two.

Despite the considerable disturbance of being woken several times, the frequency and regularity of REM periods was almost exactly the same as for uninterrupted sleep (Dement and Kleitman, 1955). A wakening during an REM period generally terminated the REMs until the next period, and the sequence of EEG changes (excluding the brief period of wakefulness) was the same as that following an REM period that ended spontaneously.

Hypothesis 1

Participants uniformly showed a high incidence of dream recall following REM awakenings and a very low incidence following NREM awakenings – regardless of how the awakenings were chosen. (See **Exercises**.)

The incidence of dream recall dropped dramatically almost immediately REMs stopped. In 17 awakenings carried out within eight minutes of the end of an REM period, five dreams were recalled; when NREM awakenings occurred within more than eight minutes, dream recall was much lower (six dreams recalled in 132 awakenings).

AIM AND NATURE

In general, participants were most confident that they had not dreamed when the NREM awakenings took place during an intermediate stage of sleep (i.e. spindling with low-voltage background). When aroused during deep sleep (high-voltage, slow waves), participants often awoke rather confused; they often felt they must have been dreaming but could not remember the dream.

When participants could not recall a dream following REM awakenings, this was usually early in the night (most during the first two hours).

Hypothesis 2

Participants were woken either 5 or 15 minutes (decided randomly) after the onset of REMs and, based on their recall of the dream, had to decide which was the correct duration. All but one was able to do this very accurately.

There was a significant correlation between the minutes of REMs and lengths of dream narratives (the number of words used to describe the dream). Narratives for dreams recalled after 30 or 50 minutes were not a great deal longer than those after 15 minutes, although participants had the impression of having been dreaming for an unusually long time.

Hypothesis 3

Since it was impossible for participants to say in what order and direction they had gazed during the dream, they were woken as soon as one of four predominant patterns of eye movement had persisted for at least one minute:

1   mainly vertical;

2   mainly horizontal;

3   both vertical and horizontal;

4   very little or no movement.

Of 35 awakenings, there were only three periods of either pure vertical or horizontal movements. One participant dreamed of standing at the bottom of a tall cliff operating some sort of hoist, looking up at climbers at various levels, and looking down at the hoist machinery. Another dreamed of climbing up a series of ladders, looking up and down as he climbed. The third dreamed of throwing basketballs at a net, first shooting and looking up at the net, then looking down to pick up another ball from the floor. In the only instance of pure horizontal movement, the dreamer was watching two people throwing tomatoes at each other.

On ten occasions when participants were woken after little or no eye movement, their dreams involved the dreamer watching something at a distance or just staring at an object. In two of these cases, about one minute of ocular inactivity was followed by several large movements to the left just before awakening. The corresponding dream content was almost identical in both cases: in one, the dreamer was driving a car, staring at the road ahead and, as he approached a crossroads, was startled by a car that suddenly appeared, speeding towards him from the left; in the other, the dreamer was also driving a car and staring at the road ahead, when he saw a man on his left who hailed him as he drove past.

In the 21 awakenings following a mixture of movements, participants were always looking at people or objects close to them (e.g. talking to a group of people, looking for something, fighting with someone).

● CONCLUSIONS

Regularly occurring periods of REMs were observed every night in a sleep laboratory for nine adult participants.

As predicted:

● A high incidence of dream recall was obtained from participants when woken during REM periods, and only a very low incidence when woken at other times.

● When a series of awakenings was conducted either 5 or 15 minutes after the REMs (dreaming) had begun, participants judged the correct dream duration very accurately.

● The pattern of REMs was related to the visual imagery of the dream.

Recording REMs during sleep represents an objective measure of dreaming. This contrasts with the forgetting, distortion and other factors involved in relying on subjective recall of dreams.

EVALUATION

Methodological issues

Is it possible that the difference between REM and NREM sleep with regard to dreaming is actually an artefact of the ability to *recall* the dreams following the 'rude awakening'?

Beaumont (1988) argues that being woken from NREM (or S-) sleep may lead to the dream being forgotten before the participant is sufficiently awake to report it. This is a deeper kind of sleep, in which the brain is much less active, with EEGs that are very different from those of the waking state. By contrast, being woken from REM (or D-) sleep may allow the ongoing dream to be remembered and then reported: the brain is much more active and EEGs are much like those of the waking state.

Clearly, if this is so, then we have stumbled on a major confounding variable which challenges the very basis of Dement and Kleitman's sleep/dream research. Herman *et al.* (1978, cited in Smith *et al.*, 1986) claim that an appreciable amount of mental activity occurs during NREM sleep, and there are no completely consistent differences between dream reports obtained when people are woken from either kind of sleep.

Foulkes (cited in Klosch and Kraft, 2005) showed that equating REM sleep with dreaming and NREM sleep with a dreamless state was an oversimplification. Only 5 to 10 per cent of sleepers who were woken during a NREM phase reported dreams. But when he reformulated the standard question of sleep research from 'Were you dreaming just now?' to 'What was going through your head just now?', 70 per cent described dreamlike impressions during NREM sleep. Also, it is now established that dreaming occurs not only in the lighter levels of NREM sleep, but also in the *hypnogogic period* of sleep onset, as well as in 'daydreaming' as studied under laboratory conditions (Foulkes, 1993).

However, people woken from REM sleep commonly report that they were dreaming (Hobson, 1999), and dreaming is associated primarily with REM sleep (McCarley, 1995). According to Mueller and Roberts (2001), dream reports from REM sleep have remained the principal focus of empirical investigations of dreaming (but see **Subsequent research** below).

Theoretical issues

While we are awake, our thought is strongly influenced by external sources, while dreaming involves a mainly endogenous (internal) generation of mental activity (Hobson, 1990). Some psychologists might think of sleep as 'non-behaviour', while others regard the cognitive richness of dreaming as a prime candidate for investigation (Toates, 2001). Indeed, one of psychology's most famous controversies concerns what interpretation, if any, should be placed on dreaming, and thereby what is the function of sleep. (See **Subsequent research** and **Applications and implications** below.)

It is widely accepted that sleep is *not* a passive process (a 'default state') corresponding to neuronal fatigue (Dement, 1994). Indeed, in REM sleep the nervous system can display as much activity as during waking. Sleep is an active process, the output of specific activity in a specific neuronal pathway (Hobson, 1986; Moruzzi, 1996).

In support of the REM sleep–dreaming relationship, evidence has been found for the *REM rebound* phenomenon. When people are deprived of approximately two hours of REM sleep (but otherwise allowed to sleep normally), the following night there is an *increase* in REM sleep as compensation for the previous night's loss (Webb and Bonnet,

1979). Dement (1960) woke volunteers from their REM sleep on five successive nights (while a control group was only woken during their NREM sleep). Dement reported that the REM-deprived group became nervous, irritable, unable to concentrate, and paranoid – they attributed sinister motives to the experimenter, developing all kinds of unreasonable suspicions and even hallucinating.

However, he later maintained that these symptoms were not really caused by the lack of REM sleep; they were more likely to have been caused by his own expectations, communicated (ironically) through concern for their welfare. Dement had told his participants what he thought the probable results would be, and that a psychiatrist would be available constantly. After the third day, participants were sleeping very little: they were having more frequent periods of REM sleep and so were being woken more often.

Dement replicated the study in 1965 and found no evidence of psychiatric disturbance with REM sleep deprivation. When allowed to sleep normally (without interruption), they did 60 per cent more dreaming until they had made up their lost REM time. These and other results demonstrating the REM rebound are consistent with the idea that REM sleep and dreaming is perhaps the most important function of sleep (Empson, 1993).

Subsequent research

Contrary to this view of the function of sleep, research in the 1990s indicated that REM sleep might not be the driving force behind dreams. Dreaming seemed to be more of a continuous process, not confined to periods of REM sleep. Rather than seeing NREM sleep as 'dream-free', research suggested that NREM dreams are relatively short and rationally constructed in terms of facts and logic, compared with the more visual, emotional and detailed REM dreams (Klosch and Kraft, 2005).

Some researchers even questioned whether REM sleep was *necessary* for dreaming to take place. Since Jouvet's (1967) research with cats, it had been believed that the pons – a small bundle of neurons in the brainstem – was responsible for REM sleep. But Lavie (1982, in Klosch and Kraft, 2005) reported the case of an Israeli man who had suffered damage to precisely the part of the pons responsible for REM sleep. Despite never entering REM sleep, he continued to suffer from terrible nightmares. Solms (in Klosch and Kraft, 2005) identified several other similar cases in the literature, as well as over 100 cases of people who said they never dreamed, despite having an intact pons and sleeping through completely normal REM phases (Klosch and Kraft, 2005).

However, these 100-plus people did have lesions in other brain regions. What seems clear from this research is that dreaming often takes place independently of REM sleep and of its generation in the pons. Only damage to the frontal lobes of the higher cortex causes dreams to disappear; damage to lower-level information-processing areas, such as the visual system, may only affect the quality of visual imagery.

This view of dreams as being generated by higher-level areas of the cortex completely inverted the theories which had largely dominated throughout the 1980s and 1990s. According to Klosch and Kraft (2005), by 2002, neuroscientists, psychiatrists and psychologists were falling into one of two camps, led by Solms on the one hand, and Hobson on the other.

According to the *activation-synthesis model* (Hobson and McCarley, 1977; McCarley, 1983; Hobson, 1988; Mamalek and Hobson, 1989), REM sleep results from activation of the 'REM-ON' area located in the pontine reticular formation (at the base of the brain). This prevents most sensory information from reaching the brain. The motor cortex is highly active, generating activity that would normally produce movement, but these commands are 'switched off', so that we are effectively *paralysed* during REM sleep. Parts of the brain that control emotion and store memories may also be activated.

Dreaming takes place when these simultaneously *activated* systems are *synthesized*, in essentially the same way as in the waking brain. When we are awake, sensory and motor information is integrated with information about our emotional state, and memories of similar experiences; we draw on past experience to make sense of what is going on now (Moorcroft, 1993). Sensory and motor events follow one another in an orderly way and seem 'normal', but when we are asleep, this orderly sequence breaks down (due to the largely *internal* and *random* nature of the activity), resulting in bizarre shifts that are characteristic of dreams (Mueller and Roberts, 2001).

Dreams normally arise from activity within the visual system (McCarley, 1995), and dream content is primarily visual and involves movement (Hobson, 1988). Many dreams involve vigorous physical activity, such as running, jumping and struggling (see hypothesis 3 above). Again, many common dream experiences can be thought of as an *interpretation* of bodily states; for example, being chased, locked up or frozen with fear may well reflect the blocked motor commands to our muscles; floating, flying and falling may reflect vestibular activation (balance centres in the ear); and the sexual content of dreams may reflect vaginal engorgement and penile erection (Ornstein, 1986).

Partly based on the activation-synthesis model, Crick and Mitchison (1983) proposed the idea of *reverse learning*: we dream in order to forget! A complex associational network such as the neocortex might become overloaded by vast amounts of incoming information, leading to the formation of false ('parasitic') thoughts (out-of-date, but persistent, views of the world). REM sleep serves to erase these false thoughts ('unlearning') on a regular basis.

Trying to remember our dreams, so crucial for psychodynamic theories such as those of Freud and Jung, are not a good idea according to Crick and Mitchison: dreams are the very patterns of thought the system is trying to tune out. But in their 1986 revision of the model, unlearning only applied to bizarre dream content: nothing could be said about dream narrative (the more coherent, sequential, 'story-like' content). Dreaming to forget was now better expressed as dreaming to reduce fantasy or obsession.

This revision of reverse learning suggests that the truth of the activation-synthesis model (and other *neural* models, such as reverse learning) does not necessarily *exclude* other theories of dreams. While the activation-synthesis model may account for 'where dreams come from' (the activation component), it fails to explain 'what dreams are for'. *Psychological* theories focus on the synthesis component and try to explain dreams' significance for the dreamer: dreams are inherently *meaningful*. Freud (1900), like Jung (1967), saw *symbolism* as of central importance: dreams can put the dreamer in touch with parts of the self that are usually inaccessible during waking life. Hall (1966) saw dreams as 'personal document, a letter to oneself', and, like Jung, he advocated the study of dream *series* rather than single, isolated dreams.

Applications and implications

REM sleep may have *evolved* to help animal species to access repeatedly the information most needed for their survival (such as the location of food, and means of predation or escape). To maintain sleep, locomotion had to be suppressed by inhibiting motor neurons, but suppressing *eye movements* was not necessary, because this does not disturb sleep. So, this information needed for survival could be accessed visually and integrated with past experience to provide an ongoing strategy for behaviour (Winson, 1997).

Humans may have inherited the same basic mechanism from lower species, and information crucial for our survival may constitute the core of the unconscious. Because other species have no language, the information processed during REM sleep is necessarily *sensory*. Consistent with our early mammalian origins, our dreams are also sensory (primarily visual: see above): they do *not* take the form of verbal narratives. But while there is no functional need in non-humans for this material to become conscious, in humans there is no reason for it *not* to become conscious: we *can* remember our dreams (Winson, 1997).

Dreams clearly have a deep psychological core, and they often concern life's difficulties that may threaten our psychological safety and survival. Consistent with this view is the finding that we tend to dream more when under stress; this suggests that dreams provide an endless variety of ideas and options (Panksepp, 1998).

Freud's theory contains a profound truth: there *is* an unconscious and dreams are indeed the 'royal road' to its understanding. However, rather than a cauldron of untamed passions and destructive wishes:

> the unconscious is a cohesive, continually active mental structure that takes note of life's experiences and reacts according to its own scheme of interpretation. Dreams are not disguised as a consequence of repression. Their unusual character is a result of the complex associations that are called from memory. (Winson, 1997)

Broadly agreeing with Winson, Hobson (2002) argues that dreams are highly emotional. Our level of emotional competence has a high survival value and underlies the more precise information needed to function socially:

> we need, first and foremost, to know when to approach, when to mate, when to be afraid, and when to run for cover. These are the skills that sleep refreshes every night of our lives by activating our brains.

On a more practical note, it is generally accepted that a characteristic symptom of mood disorders is sleep disturbances (typically, depressed patients fall asleep easily but wake early and are unable to get back to sleep). Kupfer (1976) found that depressed people tend to enter REM sleep sooner than non-depressed, and spend increased time in it during the last half of sleep. Vogel *et al.* (1980) deprived depressed patients of REM sleep over a period of several weeks and found, remarkably, that this reduced their depression relatively permanently (Carlson and Buskist, 1997).

According to Hobson (2002), the claim that dreaming has no function as such is extreme but scientifically tenable, because there is no evidence that the content of dreams has a significant influence on waking behaviour. However, in addition to its cognitive function, the activation of the brain during sleep may have a lifelong developmental role. The fact that newborns engage in far more REM sleep than adults do suggests that one function of brain activation is construction of the brain itself: we go on throughout our lives needing to reconstruct our brains and our minds (Hobson, 2002).

EXERCISES

1   Does it matter that seven of the nine participants were males and only two were females?

2   Participants were asked to abstain from alcoholic or caffeine-containing drinks on the day of the experiment. Why do you think this was done?

3   Why was it important that participants were never told, after awakening, whether their eyes had been moving or not?

4   Different participants were woken from REM sleep according to a variety of schedules:

    ● random number tables (x 2);

    ● three REM, three NREM, etc. (x 1);

    ● told only woken from REM, but actually woken from REM and NREM randomly (x 1);

    ● at the experimenter's whim.

    Why was this done?

18 Cognitive, social and physiological determinants of emotional state

Schachter, S. and Singer, J.E. (1962)

Psychological Review, 69(5): 379–99

BACKGROUND AND CONTEXT

Exactly what emotion is and how it can be explained has been a matter of controversy during most of psychology's history. It is useful to think of every emotion as comprising:

1   a subjective experience (e.g. happiness, anger);

2   a set of physiological changes involving the nervous system and the endocrine (hormonal) system, over which we have little, if any, conscious control (although we may become aware of some of their effects, such as 'butterflies' in the stomach, sweating);

3   associated behaviour (e.g. crying, running away, screaming).

Similarly, research interest has focused on four broad classes of emotional variable (Parkinson, 1987), namely:

● cognitive appraisal of the situation (individuals react emotionally to stimulus events to the extent that they are perceived as relevant to their current goals/interests);

● the body's internal reaction (as in (2) above);

● overt behaviour (as in (3) above);

● facial expressions (which can be thought of as a subset of the previous point).

All the above are characteristic features of 'emotion' as understood by both psychologists and laypeople; but none is a necessary condition of emotional experience. For example, Zajonc (1980) argues that emotion is possible without cognitive appraisal; Valins (1966) believes it is possible without physiological arousal; and Leventhal (1980) claims that it is possible without facial expression.

However, according to Schachter's (1964) *cognitive labelling theory* (or two-factor theory), *both* physiological arousal *and* cognitive interpretation (or cognitive labelling) are necessary (and sufficient) – but neither on its own is sufficient. The Schachter and Singer study provides the cornerstone for that theory.

AIM AND NATURE

● HYPOTHESIS

The aim of the study was to test, experimentally, three propositions regarding the *interaction* between physiological and cognitive factors in the experience of emotion:

1   If an individual experiences a state of physiological arousal for which s/he has no immediate explanation, s/he will 'label' this state and describe it in terms of the cognitions available. So precisely the same state of arousal could receive different labels (e.g. 'joy'/'anger'), depending on the cognitive aspects of the situation.

2   If an individual experiences a state of physiological arousal for which s/he has a completely appropriate explanation (e.g. 'I've just had an injection of epinephrine'), s/he will 'label' this state accordingly.

3   Given the same circumstances, an individual will react emotionally, or describe his/her feelings as emotions, only to the extent that s/he experiences a state of physiological arousal.

These three propositions constitute the basic hypotheses that were tested.

● METHOD/DESIGN

The hypotheses were tested by manipulating, separately:

● physiological arousal;

● appropriateness of the explanation;

● situations from which descriptive explanations could be derived.

The experiment was presented as a study of the effects of vitamin compounds and supplements on vision ('In particular, we want to find out how the vitamin compound called Suproxin affects your vision').

1   Physiological arousal.

Out of 195 participants (all male college students taking introductory psychology), 184 agreed to the injection (described as 'mild and harmless'). Depending on the condition they had been assigned to, participants received one of two forms of 'Suproxin' (a fictitious name):

● *Epinephrine* is a sympathomimetic drug whose effects almost always mimic perfectly stimulation of the sympathetic nervous system: marked increase in systolic blood pressure, slight increase in heart rate, decrease in cutaneous blood flow, increase in muscle and cerebral blood flow, blood sugar and lactic acid concentrations, and slight increase in respiration rate. The major subjective symptoms are palpitation, tremor and sometimes a feeling of flushing and accelerated breathing. These effects usually begin 3–5 minutes after the injection, and typically last for 15–20 minutes.

● *Placebo*: same quantity of saline solution (which has no side effects at all).

2   The extent to which participants had an appropriate explanation of their bodily state.

'Appropriate' here means the extent to which participants had an authoritative, unequivocal explanation of their bodily condition: they knew precisely what they would feel and why.

● *Epinephrine informed (Epi Inf)*: the participant was told the actual side effects of the injection and that they would last 15–20 minutes. This information was reinforced by the doctor who came to give the injection once the participant had agreed.

● *Epinephrine ignorant (Epi Ign)*: the experimenter said nothing about side effects and simply left the room once the participant had agreed to the injection. The doctor said that the injection was mild and harmless and would have no side effects.

● *Epinephrine misinformed (Epi Mis)*: the experimenter told the participant that some people have experienced side effects from Suproxin, which last 15–20 minutes; these include the feet feeling numb, an itching sensation over parts of the body and a slight headache. The doctor confirmed these symptoms. Since none of these is actually a side effect of epinephrine, the explanation was completely inappropriate. This represented a kind of *control condition*. (See **Exercises**.)

● *Placebo*: apart from being injected with saline solution, participants in this condition were treated exactly the same as those in the Epi Ign condition.

3   Situations from which explanatory cognitions could be derived.

● *Euphoria*: immediately after the injection, the doctor left the room and the

AIM AND NATURE

experimenter returned with a stooge, whom he introduced as another participant. He said that both had had the Suproxin and that they had to wait 20 minutes while it was absorbed into the bloodstream; after this, they would both be given the same vision test.

Once the experimenter had left, the stooge began acting according to a 'script' consisting of 15 behaviours involving rough paper, rubber bands, folders and hula hoops (such as a 'basketball' game, making paper aeroplanes and playing with the hula hoop).

● *Anger*: this began as the euphoria condition did, but the participant and stooge were asked to spend the 20 minutes answering questionnaires. Before they started, the stooge said he thought it was unfair to be given injections and they should have been told about them when they were first called.

The five-page questionnaire began innocently enough, but then grew increasingly personal and insulting. Keeping pace with the participant, the stooge made a series of standardized comments about the questions, becoming increasingly argumentative and angry. Eventually, he ripped up his questionnaire and stormed out of the room.

Participants in the Epi Ign, Epi Inf and placebo conditions all experienced one or other of the stooges (who never knew the condition any particular participant was in). The Epi Mis condition was not run with the angry stooge. This makes seven conditions in all.

Participants were allocated randomly to one of the seven conditions, making the design *independent groups*.

The dependent variable was the participant's *emotional state*, measured by:

● standardized observation through a one-way mirror (during the experiment in the company of the stooge); for example, did the participant join in with the euphoric stooge's games, or did s/he agree with the angry stooge's criticisms of the questionnaire?

● scores on a number of self-report scales (following the experiment, but before the debriefing); for example, 'how [irritated, angry or annoyed], [good or happy] would you say you feel at present?'

(Note that what is known as epinephrine in the USA is called adrenaline in the UK; hence, the study is often referred to as the adrenaline experiment.)

AIM AND NATURE

● RESULTS

Effects of the injections on bodily state

On all items, participants in the epinephrine conditions showed significantly more evidence of sympathetic arousal than those in the placebo condition, as measured by pulse rate and self-ratings on palpitation, tremor, numbness, itching and headache.

Effects on the manipulations of emotional state

● In relation to *euphoria*, the mean self-rating scores of both Epi Ign and Epi Mis were significantly greater than the mean of Epi Inf; placebo participants were less euphoric than either Epi Mis or Epi Ign, but rather more so than Epi Inf participants (none of these differences was statistically significant).

As far as behaviour was concerned, the same pattern of results was found as for self-ratings.

● In relation to *anger*, the self-ratings revealed very little anger (in any condition). It seems that participants were afraid to admit their irritation to the experimenter's face or on the self-rating scales, in case this endangered the extra points on their final exam that participation in the experiment would provide. So Schachter and Singer were forced to rely on the behavioural measures.

The Epi Ign participants displayed significantly more angry behaviour than the Epi Inf participants, as did the Epi Ign compared with those in the placebo condition. However, the difference between the Epi Inf and the placebo conditions was non-significant.

● CONCLUSIONS

In relation to both euphoria and anger, the emotional level in the Epi Mis and Epi Ign conditions was considerably greater than in the Epi Inf condition. These results are in line with predictions.

However, the results for the placebo condition were ambiguous – they consistently fell between the Epi Ign and Epi Inf participants. This makes it impossible to evaluate unambiguously the effects of the state of physiological arousal. (See **Methodological issues** below.)

In both the euphoria and anger conditions, placebo participants who showed signs of sympathetic arousal also showed considerably more anger than those who showed no such signs. Consistent with expectations, therefore, sympathetic arousal

AIM AND NATURE

accompanies an increase in emotional level. Also, the emotional level of placebo participants showing no signs of arousal was very similar to that of Epi Inf participants; this implies that both sympathetic arousal and appropriate cognition are necessary for the experience of emotion.

EVALUATION

Methodological issues

While the results are usually cited as supporting the hypotheses (and, by implication, cognitive labelling theory as well), Schachter and Singer are themselves a little more cautious.

They acknowledge that the results for the placebo condition are 'troublesome'. They also offer an explanation, by way of evaluating their experimental design: the disguised injection of Suproxin was far from ideal as a way of manipulating the absence of an immediate explanation of bodily state, because some participants would inevitably attribute their feelings to the injection – regardless of what they were told. The assumption that the placebo condition involves no sympathetic arousal is, they admit, completely unrealistic: the injection is quite a dramatic event which will inevitably make many participants anxious.

In a similar way, participants in the Epi Ign and Epi Mis conditions could still attribute their arousal to the injection (e.g. 'the shot gave me the shivers'), making the stooge less of an influence. Schachter and Singer identified and removed the data for these 'self-informed' participants (who were not at all euphoric or angry); the effect of this was that the difference between the Epi Ign and the placebo conditions for anger became significant, as was the difference for euphoria between the Epi Mis, Epi Ign and placebo conditions.

These are examples of 'experimental artefacts', whose effects they had to try to separate out from the data; this made their conclusions 'rather tentative'. Elsewhere, they imply that the experiment *on its own* does *not* support the hypotheses (especially hypothesis 1 and the self-report data in the anger condition: see above). According to Hewstone *et al.* (1997), the behavioural data in the anger condition cannot be compared directly with those from the euphoria condition. Since they are measuring quite different aspects of behaviour, a direct test of hypothesis 1 is impossible.

Hilgard *et al.* (1979) identify some additional problems:

● Epinephrine does not affect everyone in the same way; Schachter and Singer, in fact, removed from their analysis five participants who later reported that they had experienced no physiological symptoms.

● No assessment was made of participants' mood *before* the injections; presumably, someone in a better mood to begin with might respond more positively to a playful stooge.

● How comparable are arousal states created by drugs and manipulated in the laboratory to naturally occurring, real-life emotions?

Theoretical issues

Schachter's (1964) *cognitive labelling theory* assumes that the physiological arousal associated with different emotional states is essentially the same; this represents one of the most controversial aspects of emotion theory and research, both before and since Schachter and Singer's adrenaline experiment.

Schachter and Singer state that James' (1890) theory of emotion (usually referred to as the James-Lange theory) implies that different emotions 'will be accompanied by a variety of distinguishable bodily states'. (It also implies that physiological arousal is *sufficient* for emotional experience.) Cannon's (1929) theory (usually called the Cannon-Bard theory) claims the *opposite*: 'the same visceral changes occur in very different emotional states'.

According to Levenson (1994), it is a 'myth' that every emotion is autonomically different. It seems far more likely that reliable differences will only be found between emotions for which there are different associated typical behaviours; and even here it is quite unlikely that each will be unique (i.e. not sharing any features). For example, Levenson *et al.* (1990) identified a small number of fairly reliable differences in patterns of autonomic nervous system (ANS) activity, both between negative emotions (anger, disgust, fear and sadness) and between these and happiness.

These findings imply that we cannot draw general conclusions about the specificity of the body's response to emotional stimuli: it depends partly on which emotion (positive or negative – and which positive or negative emotion) we are talking about.

Pinel (1993) advocates a position that falls between the extreme views represented by the James-Lange and Cannon-Bard theories: while there is insufficient evidence for the former's claim that every emotion has a distinct pattern of ANS activity, the latter's claim that the ANS responds in exactly the same way to all emotional stimuli is clearly incorrect.

Dalgleish (1998) argues that there *is* now good evidence to support the James-Lange claim (which suggests that Schachter and Singer's participants must have made some emotional 'selection', at least partly, at a pre-physiological stage). But this evidence need not be too damaging to cognitive labelling theory, which claims that physiological arousal is only *necessary* and *not sufficient*; even if there are distinctive patterns of arousal, emotional experience can still be affected by how that arousal is interpreted (Power and Dalgleish, 1997).

According to Parkinson (1987), the focus of the adrenaline experiment is an atypical state of affairs, where the participant is unsure about the cause of his/her arousal (Epi Ign/Epi Mis). But Schachter (1964) admitted that usually we *are* aware of a precipitating situation prior to the onset of arousal (which takes approximately one to two seconds to reach consciousness), and so it is normally perfectly obvious to us what aspects of the situation have made us feel that way. But even here some cognitive analysis is needed before the emotion can be labelled. Schachter believes that the *quantitative* aspect of emotion can arise without cognitive mediation ('Am I in a state of emotional arousal?'), but the *qualitative* aspect requires prior cognition ('What emotion is it that I'm experiencing?'). According to Zajonc (1980), 'this view that affect [emotion] is post cognitive is now probably the most popular attitude among emotion theorists'.

Subsequent research

Are environmental cues (such as euphoric or angry stooges) as easily accepted as the basis for inferences about our own feelings as Schachter claims (Fiske and Taylor, 1991)? Using the adrenaline experiment approach, several studies (e.g. Maslach, 1979; Marshall and Zimbardo, 1979) concluded that participants' efforts to understand an unexplained state of arousal is more extensive than a quick examination of relevant cues in the immediate environment.

When trying to account for a current state of arousal, we often try to think of *past* occasions on which we felt like this. Others' behaviour may suggest or dictate how we should behave in that situation, but it does not provide information as to why we *feel as we do*. At the very least, others' behaviour must, in some way, be *appropriate* (Weiner, 1992).

These researchers also found that such arousal is more likely to be interpreted *negatively* (as unease or nervousness, similar to free-floating anxiety). This suggests that arousal cannot be labelled as easily as one emotion or another (*emotional lability*) as Schachter maintains. Also, if the dosage is high enough, adrenaline seems to produce an unpleasant mood – even in the Epi Mis condition, and in the presence of the euphoric stooge.

Despite criticisms of their work, the real impact of the adrenaline experiment was that it revived an old idea (implicit in the work of philosophers including Aristotle, Descartes and Spinoza), namely that emotions might be cognitive interpretations of situations (LeDoux, 1998).

What was missing from cognitive labelling theory (i.e. an account of what generates an emotional response in the first place) has been 'put back' by *cognitive appraisal theorists* (e.g. Frijda, 1988; Oatley and Johnson-Laird, 1996; Power and Dalgleish, 1997; Scherer, 1997). Probably the first appraisal theory was that of Arnold (1960), who defined appraisals as the mental assessment of the potential harm or benefit of a situation (Arnold and Gasson, 1954). According to LeDoux (1998), appraisal remains the cornerstone of contemporary cognitive approaches to emotion.

Applications and implications

According to Hewstone *et al.* (1997), the claim that emotion arises from an interaction between a 'coarse type of physiological arousal and finely differentiated cognitions' appealed greatly to social psychologists, who were becoming increasingly interested in the role of cognition. The experiment was also quickly seized on by attribution theorists (such as Nisbett and Valins, 1972), who regarded it as evidence that attributions made about emotion help to shape emotion.

Cognitive labelling theory implies that emotional reactions induced by a threatening experience can be *reattributed* to a neutral or less threatening source. For example, blaming your lack of success on some external stimulus (e.g. another person) may be less threatening than recognizing your own inadequacies – but it probably won't help you to become more successful.

One of the most important aspects of Schachter's work is the demonstration that our attributions for arousal are malleable (but, as we have seen, not as malleable as he proposed). In other words, it is possible for us to mislabel our feelings and to draw mistaken conclusions about the causes of those feelings (the *misattribution effect*: Ross and Nisbett, 1991). In the adrenaline experiment, participants in the Epi Ign and Epi Mis conditions attributed their arousal to something other than the adrenaline which was the real cause.

This has profound *clinical* implications: inducing people to reattribute their arousal from a threatening source to a less threatening one can help them to function more effectively in settings that currently cause anxiety (Fiske and Taylor, 1991). The *misattribution paradigm* (Valins, 1966), which began as a laboratory-based, experimental approach to emotional arousal, provides the potential for a general model for the treatment of emotional disorders (Valins and Nisbett, 1972).

EXERCISES

1   In what way can the Epi Mis condition be considered a kind of control condition?

2   The Epi Mis participants were 'somewhat (but not significantly)' more euphoric than the Epi Ign participants. How might you account for this?

3   The participants were all male, as were the stooges.

    (a) Can you think of any reasons why these results would not generalize to females?

    (b) What might be the effect of having an opposite-sex stooge?

4   Is it ethically acceptable to mislead participants about the side effects of the injection (either Epi Mis or Epi Ign)?

5   LeDoux (1998) criticizes appraisal theories for their failure to capture the unique aspects of emotion that make it different from cognition. He also says that these theories have based their understanding of appraisal processes largely on self-reports, that is, people's introspective verbal reflections. Why do you think he sees this as a (further) limitation of appraisal theories?

19

Hypnosis, motivation and compliance

Orne, M.T. (1966)

American Journal of Psychiatry, 122: 721–6

BACKGROUND AND CONTEXT

A crucial distinction in the discussion of hypnosis is that between the 'state'/'special process' view, and the 'non-state'/social psychological view (Wagstaff, 1987, 1995). This corresponds to what Orne (in the present article) refers to as the subjective experience theory and the motivational theory, respectively. The state/subjective experience theory is commonly referred to as the 'traditional' approach.

According to Wagstaff, this controversy as to the nature of hypnosis has raged since the late eighteenth century. Although it was once thought that hypnosis is a special sort of sleep (the Greek *hypnos* = sleep), not all modern state theorists subscribe to this view. However, they continue to see hypnosis as an altered state of consciousness with various depths; it is assumed that the deeper the hypnotic state, the more likely it is that the hypnotized person will display hypnotic phenomena (Hilgard, 1978; Bowers, 1983).

The state of hypnotic trance (supposedly qualitatively different from a normal waking state) is usually brought about through *induction procedures* such as *fixating on* a coloured drawing pin on the wall and/or soothing words about relaxation and suggestions to concentrate (the 'induction patter': Nash and Benham, 2005). In academic research, susceptibility to hypnosis is usually measured by means of standardized scales. The yardstick for all these scales is the Stanford Hypnotic Susceptibility Scale, Form C (referred to by Orne) (plus Forms A and B). This typically suggests to the participant that 'your hand is heavy and falling' (hand lowering), 'you cannot bend your arm' (arm rigidity), 'you will find it difficult to remember' (amnesia) and 'there is a fly buzzing round your head' (hallucination).

The traditional view also makes two fundamental assumptions:

1   Hypnotized people experience their responses as 'happening to them' (Bowers, 1983) or involuntary 'happenings' (as implied by the instruction given during the induction procedure).

2 Individuals will be capable of doing things while hypnotized which they would not
be able to do in the waking state (or at least their performance is superior),
including the ability to control pain (Hilgard and Hilgard, 1984) and displays of
amnesia and hallucinations (Orne, 1979; Kihlstrom, 1980; Bowers, 1983).

Although most academic state theorists do *not* accept claims that hypnotized people
can actually be regressed, going back before their birth, to former lives in Roman
Britain or medieval York, the state view has dominated the popular image of hypnosis.
This may be due partly to its portrayal in films and on television, including 'media
hypnotists' such as Paul McKenna.

Non-state theorists are mainly social and cognitive psychologists (Wagstaff being the
UK's leading exponent of this view), who see the hypnotic situation as a *social-
psychological interaction*. The hypnotist and participant act out social roles: the
participant's role is to act according to previous expectations and to cues provided by
the hypnotists, and to try very hard to act *as if* hypnotized.

AIM AND NATURE

● HYPOTHESIS AND METHOD/DESIGN

This is primarily a review article, in which Orne attempts to reconcile what seem
to be the contradictory findings from:

● experimental studies of hypnosis;

● clinical experience (the use of hypnosis with patients in a therapeutic setting).

While presenting data from his own studies, Orne also describes the findings of several
other researchers and clinicians – no one study is considered in any great detail.

Orne suggests two alternative ways of looking at hypnosis:

1 Hypnosis involves a change in the individual's motivation to please the
hypnotist, making him/her unusually compliant (the non-state view).

2 Hypnosis involves a change in the individual's subjective experience (the state
approach).

In relation to the first, he cites a number of studies (including his own) which argue
against the hypothesis that 'being susceptible to hypnosis leads to a generalized
tendency to comply with requests from the hypnotist'.

Regarding the second, the criteria used by trained observers for establishing that a
participant is actually hypnotized all focus on the critical variable of his/her ability

to respond to suggestions (ideomotor/challenge/hallucinations and memory distortions/post-hypnotic behaviour). Although this suggestibility refers at one level to overt *behaviour*, more importantly, at another level, it refers to an assumed change in the individual's *experience*: 'a subject is genuinely hypnotized not because he is willing to report certain things, but because his report really describes his personal subjective experience'. An example would be a *compulsion* to carry out a post-hypnotic suggestion, regardless of whether s/he actually recalls it. Further, the wider the range of distortions in the participant's perceptions or memory which can be induced by appropriate cues, the more deeply hypnotized the individual is said to be.

● RESULTS

As far as the motivational view is concerned, hypnotized individuals certainly *appear* to do things they would not normally do. They are also quick to comply with the hypnotist's requests, even when unusual or bizarre behaviour is requested. However, the source of the participant's motivation need not be the hypnotic state itself. When Orne asks students in a lecture, for example, to take off their right shoes or give him their wallets, they do so. If the same behaviour had occurred after a hypnotic induction, it would have seemed that the students were under hypnotic control (i.e. while these behaviours are admissible requests in a hypnosis situation, it is unusual for lecturers to make such 'unreasonable' requests, and therefore it is tempting to assume – incorrectly – that only hypnotized persons would comply with them).

Similarly, Orne and Evans (1965), replicating earlier experiments, found that deeply hypnotized participants can be compelled to carry out antisocial and self-destructive acts, such as picking up a rattlesnake, lifting a coin out of fuming nitric acid, and throwing the acid at an assistant. But Orne and Evans also found that this behaviour could be obtained equally well from *non-hypnotized* participants in the waking state. The latter were fully aware of the nature of the behaviour they were being asked to perform. But post-experimental interviews revealed that they were convinced (correctly) that appropriate safeguards would be taken to protect them and the assistant from any real harm.

There does not appear to be any behaviour which participants will perform under hypnosis which they would not perform in the waking state. What this shows is that people tend to do *anything* which might conceivably be required of them in an experimental setting.

Effect on performance of difficult tasks

If participants believe the experimenter is trying to show that hypnosis increases performance of difficult, tiring tasks, they may readily provide supporting data –

AIM AND NATURE

not necessarily by *increasing* their hypnotic performance, but by *decreasing* their waking performance (Evans and Orne, 1965; Orne, 1959). It has also been shown that with proper motivation, waking participants can surpass their own hypnotic performance. However, these studies failed to use the same instructions in the two conditions, which is very difficult to achieve in such experiments.

London and Fuhrer (1961) got round this difficulty by giving a large number of participants an initial test of susceptibility to hypnosis, and then selecting the extreme responders (highly hypnotizable) and the non-responders (unhypnotizable). They were *all* told that they were sufficiently deeply hypnotizable for the purposes of the experiment. If hypnosis makes participants more compliant, the performance of the extreme responders (on a motor task) should be superior to the latter's. But in several experiments, London and Fuhrer (and others) found that, if anything, it was the poor responders who performed better under hypnotic conditions. Evans and Orne (1965) found *no* difference between good and poor responders.

The further findings, that:

- high responders tend to arrive *late* for the experiments, while the poor responders tend to be *early*;

- poor participants are willing to tolerate significantly *higher* shock levels;

support the conclusion that hypnotizable participants are not more motivated to comply with or please the hypnotist.

Criteria for hypnosis

Probably the most widely used objective scale of hypnotic depth is the Stanford Hypnotic Susceptibility Scale, Form C (Weitzenhoffer and Hilgard, 1962). (See **Background and context** above.) Scores agree very well with the judgements of trained observers.

Hypnotic suggestions can be classified into four groups:

- *Ideomotor*: in the sway test, the participant is told: 'You are falling backwards...you feel yourself falling further and further backwards'. The response is defined as positive by the extent to which s/he actually falls; but it is implicitly assumed that this is because *s/he feels drawn backward*, rather than because of the conscious voluntary decision to do so (which would not count as an ideomotor response). If we were merely measuring behavioural compliance, we would use the simple instruction: 'Fall backwards now'.

- *Challenge:* for example, 'Your eyes are tightly glued together; you cannot open them. Try to open them. You cannot'. The same criteria apply as with ideomotor suggestions. The response measures 'depth of hypnosis' only in so far as it

AIM AND NATURE

reflects an *experienced* inability on the participant's part to open his/her eyes (i.e. the extent to which s/he *cannot* comply even when challenged to do so).

● Suggestions dealing with *hallucinations*, *amnesia* or other *memory distortions*; again, the same criteria apply.

● *Post-hypnotic phenomenon*: this is the most difficult to deal with here, since the criterion is *purely behavioural*. However, it is still assumed that participants feel *compelled* to carry out the suggested behaviour, regardless of whether they actually recall the suggestion. Despite this subjective compulsion, a post-hypnotic suggestion is likely to be *less* effective than a simple request to carry out the behaviour. So, clearly, post-hypnotic suggestion is not merely a matter of behavioural compliance.

Thus, the essence of hypnosis is not so much a way of manipulating a person's behaviour (as so often portrayed in popular literature and patients' fantasy) as of creating distortions of perception and memory.

In a *clinical context*, the therapist is often more interested in changing the patient's behaviour than in studying his/her experience. 'Hypnotic' therapy has been found to change habit patterns and to suppress a wide range of neurotic symptoms. Therapists have often defined suggestions as 'hypnotic' if they are followed by changes in the patient's behaviour; this clearly involves a different criterion from the subjective criterion discussed above. It is quite possible that patients do not become hypnotized in the experiential sense, and yet respond to a therapeutic suggestion; conversely, other patients may be *deeply hypnotized and fail to respond to such suggestions*.

It is highly likely that there is a low correlation between the experiential definition of hypnotizability and response to therapeutic suggestion. This is indicated by the puzzling phenomenon of 'light hypnotic trance' (such as the patient closing his/her eyes in response to the therapist's request to do so), which may be sufficient to produce therapeutically marked behaviour changes.

Effects on role relationship

Such therapeutic effects may not be primarily a function of hypnosis itself, but may be a consequence of the change in relationship when a therapist assumes the role of 'hypnotist', and shares with the patient the expectation that hypnosis involves unlimited compliance. This is certainly a different relationship from the usual therapeutic one: not only does the patient attribute magical powers to the therapist, but the therapist's behaviour tends to reinforce these fantasies.

Even in individuals who fail to become hypnotized, the relationship itself may still alter their motivation and dramatically affect their responses to certain types of suggestion.

AIM AND NATURE

● CONCLUSIONS

A simple motivational theory of hypnosis is inconsistent with an experiential definition. Tasks which could, in principle, be carried out by non-hypnotized individuals
are not performed any better under hypnosis; experiments have failed to find evidence for the hypothesized 'motivation to please the hypnotist', which ought to
produce 'better' performance.

The clinical effectiveness of the hypnotic induction procedure seems to result from
the changed relationship between patient and therapist.

EVALUATION

Methodological issues

Most experiments have compared groups of hypnotized participants (those given a
hypnotic induction procedure) with various control groups, set up to test alternative,
non-state explanations:

● in the *simulating group* (Orne, 1959, 1979), participants are told to fake hypnosis, but
are not told *how* to do this;

● in *task-motivated groups*, participants might be instructed to try hard to imagine and
experience suggestions, but they are not given a formal hypnotic induction
procedure (Barber, 1969).

The rationale is that if hypnotized participants respond no differently from non-
hypnotized controls, then there is no need to postulate a special state to explain the
former's behaviour. Conversely, if controls *cannot* reproduce the behaviours of
hypnotized participants, then it seems that hypnosis *does* involve an additional, unique
element.

So, do hypnotized participants display *physiological changes* not shown by controls?
Although EEG, blood pressure, blood-clotting time, breathing rate, skin and oral
temperature may all *change* when participants are given hypnotic induction, equivalent
changes also occur when they are asked to close their eyes, relax or imagine various
effects. Also, these changes are different from those involved in sleep or sleepwalking
(Spanos, 1982; Wagstaff, 1981). Most researchers of both 'camps' now seem to agree
that the search for a unique physiological correlate of the hypnotic state has largely
failed (Wagstaff, 1995). (See **Subsequent research** below.)

But are there any more subtle measures of hypnotic responding? Wagstaff (1987)
believes that probably the most significant demonstration of the differences between

hypnotic ('real') and simulating behaviour is what Orne (1959, 1979) calls *trance-logic*. Two key examples are:

- If it is suggested to hypnotized participants ('reals') that they cannot see an object actually in front of them (e.g. a chair), although some will claim they cannot see it, they will still walk round it rather than bump into it. But simulators tend to bump into it while claiming they cannot see it. Again, if shown a chair and asked to hallucinate a man sitting in it, reals will tend to report that the image is transparent (they can still see the chair through the man!). But simulators tend to report it as opaque, and so cannot see the chair through the man.

- If reals view a person and, at the same time, receive a suggestion to hallucinate that person standing in a different location, they tend to report seeing *both* the actual person and the hallucinated image. Hardly any simulators do this. Orne (1959) called this the 'double hallucination' response.

According to the state view, reals have little need for logical consistency and can tolerate illogical responses: this is trance-logic.

Theoretical issues

The most popular contemporary state theory, which provides a powerful explanation of trance-logic, is *neo-dissociation theory* (NDT) (Hilgard, 1974, 1977, 1978, 1979; Bowers, 1983). In the chair example, NDT maintains that the 'part' which does not see the chair is dissociated from the 'part' which knows it is there and walks round it. These parts are unaware of each other because they are separated by 'amnesia barriers'; but they can break through simultaneously, so that participants report logical inconsistencies.

Basically, NDT maintains that we have multiple control systems, not all conscious at the same time, but which can be brought into consciousness 'under hypnosis'. This is best illustrated by Hilgard's demonstration of the *hidden observer*. The participant is hypnotized and then given the following instruction:

> When I place my hand on your shoulder, I shall be able to talk to a hidden part of you that knows things are going on in your body, things that are unknown to the part of you to which I am now talking. The part to which I am now talking will not know what you are telling me or even that you are talking... You will remember that there is a part of you that knows many things that are going on that may be hidden from either your normal consciousness or the hypnotized part of you. By doing this, you can contact another system of control or 'part' of you, which will then speak, unaware of the normal 'waking part' or 'hypnotized part'.

NDT, specifically the hidden observer, is relevant to understanding *hypnotic analgesia* (the control/elimination of surgical and non-surgical pain through hypnosis alone). (See **Applications and implications** below.)

Both state and non-state theorists recognize the problem of compliance or faking, largely as a result of Orne's pioneering work (starting in 1959). He stressed the extent to which participants in *any* experimental situation may modify their behaviour in an attempt to please the experimenter, save themselves embarrassment or bolster self-image. For example:

● Milgram (1974) claims that the desire not to commit a social impropriety and not ruin an experiment can be extremely powerful (more so than we realize). (See Chapter 10.)

● Sheridan and King (1972) found that 72 per cent of ordinary people were prepared to give high levels of *real* shock to a *real*, innocent puppy (see Gross, 2005).

● Orne (1962) found that participants will agree to ridiculous requests if the context is appropriate. (See the discussion of *demand characteristics* in Chapter 1.)

For some non-state theorists, compliance is an integral component of much hypnotic responding (Spanos, 1991; Wagstaff, 1991).

Subsequent research

PET scans have been used to study blood-flow changes linked to hypnosis. Concar (1998) cites one study in which hypnotized participants were told to manipulate in their mind's eye pieces of artwork shown on a computer screen inside the scanner. They either had to 'colour in' grey images or become 'colour-blind', seeing only in shades of grey when faced with images containing real colours.

The scans of those who claimed they could colour in the grey images differed from those who said they could not; some of these differences were in specific and highly relevant brain areas. Among those who claimed they had become 'colour-blind', there was *reduced* blood flow to a part of the occipital lobe, while it *increased* in those who claimed they could colour in the grey images.

Rainville *et al.* (1997, in Nash, 2001) asked hypnotized volunteers to place one hand in painfully hot water. It was suggested that the water was either more or less unpleasant than it really was, which produced large changes in their anterior cingulate gyrus (part of the limbic system involved in the control of attention, emotion and motivation). This sets the volume/tone of the emotional 'soundtrack' the brain attaches to thoughts and perceptions, and is the precise brain area where you would expect to find changes if hypnosis really helped take the sting out of the participants' pain. The changes were highly correlated with what they claimed to be feeling: the more painful the water, the greater the *increase* in blood flow, and the less painful, the greater the *decrease* (Nash, 2001). (See **Applications and implications** below.) The activity of the somatosensory cortex – where pain sensations are processed – was not affected.

According to Gruzelier (1998), hypnosis impairs verbal fluency and other skills linked to the left frontal lobe; this might be one way of suspending the brain's logical, critical faculties. (See Chapter 20.) More recently, Gruzelier (2002) found changes in the limbic system during hypnosis, especially the inhibition of the amygdala and the excitation of the hippocampus, which seem to relate to processing in the auditory cortex. These changes were only found in participants susceptible to hypnosis, as was reduced attentional processing.

Gruzelier has also studied an 'error detection system' (EDS) in the frontal lobe and limbic system, which monitors ongoing activities and changes in behaviour in response to novel stimuli (such as when the brain receives conflicting information, as can happen in hypnosis). The EDS seems able to dissociate from other cognitive processing, such as in trance-logic situations (see **Methodological issues** above); it is aware of the mismatch between what it knows and what it is being told. The EDS could be the location in the brain of Hilgard's 'hidden observer'.

Applications and implications

The role of hypnosis in pain relief is demonstrated by Rainville *et al.*'s study (1997, in Nash, 2001) described above. According to Nash and Benham (2005), a huge number of clinical studies have indicated that hypnosis can reduce the pain of cancer patients, burn-wound debridement (peeling off the dead skin), children undergoing bone marrow aspiration and women in labour. They refer to one meta-analytic study (a study of studies), which concluded that hypnotic suggestions relieved the pain of 75 per cent of 933 participants in 27 different experiments. The pain-relieving effect of hypnosis is often substantial, sometimes matching or exceeding that provided by morphine.

However, the American Society for Clinical and Experimental Hypnosis says that hypnosis cannot and should not stand alone as the sole medical or psychological intervention for any disorder (Nash and Benham, 2005). Also, non-state theorists argue that pain relief *could* occur for various reasons other than those proposed by state theorists such as Hilgard. Wagstaff (1995) points out that:

● pain is a complex psychological sensation and can be alleviated through relaxation, reduction of stress and anxiety, and the use of strategies such as distraction and reinterpretation of the noxious (painful) stimulus (all these are often used in cases of hypnotic surgery);

- many surgical procedures are less painful than might be commonly predicted; for example, many internal organs are insensitive to pain, and it is not true that the deeper you cut into the body the more it hurts (but pulling and stretching of damaged tissue is painful);

- cases of surgery with hypnosis alone are rare, and there are important individual differences in pain thresholds.

Wagstaff concludes by saying that although disagreements about the mechanisms involved in hypnotic pain control continue, it is widely accepted that human beings have a considerable capacity to control and tolerate pain without chemical painkillers (analgesics).

Nash and Benham (2005) cite evidence that hypnosis can boost the effectiveness of psychotherapy (such as cognitive behaviour therapy/CBT) for some conditions (such as obesity, insomnia, anxiety and high blood pressure). (See Chapter 30.) It can also be an effective component in the broader treatment of asthma, some skin disorders, irritable bowel syndrome/IBS, haemophilia and the nausea associated with chemotherapy. However, drug addiction and alcoholism do not respond well to hypnosis, and the evidence in relation to quitting smoking is equivocal.

Perhaps the most controversial use of hypnosis is in relation to *recovered memories* (the *false memory syndrome* controversy). (See Chapters 6, 22 and 31.)

EXERCISES

1   In the Criteria for hypnosis **section above, referring to the Stanford Hypnosis Susceptibility Scale, Orne says that scores on the scale agree very well with the judgement of trained observers. What is another term for 'agree'?**

2   **Orne refers to Form C of the Stanford Scale. Wagstaff (1995) refers to Forms A and B. What is the purpose/advantage of having different forms of the same test?**

3   **Non-state theorists have criticized many studies of pain inducement, in which the same participants are tested in both the hypnotized and non-hypnotized conditions.**

   (a) **Why is this a (potential) problem?**

   (b) **How could it be prevented?**

4   **What is meant by** *demand characteristics* **and why are they important for understanding human psychological experiments in general?**

5   **While the clinical use of hypnosis may be ethically as acceptable as any other therapeutic procedure, do you find anything wrong with the experimental use of hypnosis?**

20 Hemisphere deconnection and unity in conscious awareness

Sperry, R.W. (1968)

American Psychologist, 23: 723–33

BACKGROUND AND CONTEXT

According to Ornstein (1986), the cerebral cortex appeared in our ancestors quite recently, about 50 million years ago. It performs the functions which have greatly increased our adaptability as a species. A feature of the brain in all primates is its division into hemispheres, but only in the human brain are the hemispheres specialized for different functions (*lateral specialization or functional lateralization*). This represents the most recent development in human evolution (less than four million years old) and is uniquely human.

According to Bogen (1969), scientists have been trying to characterize the nature of the left and right hemispheres for well over 100 years. The great physiologist, Hughlings Jackson (1964, in Bogen), distinguished between the expressive left and the perceptual right hemisphere. Zangwill (1961, in Bogen) proposed that the left is predominantly symbolic, while the right is predominantly visuospatial.

Sperry's work has made a tremendous contribution to our understanding of functional lateralization. According to Levy-Agresti and Sperry (1968), the

> mute, minor hemisphere [right] is specialized for Gestalt perception, being
> primarily a synthesist in dealing with information input. The speaking, major
> hemisphere [left], in contrast, seems to operate in a more logical, analytic,
> computer-like fashion.

A dramatic experimental breakthrough in the study of hemisphere specialization came when a new surgical technique for treating some forms of epilepsy was developed. Epileptic seizures are caused by a sort of electrical storm which spreads across the cortex, causing millions of neurons to fire. A seizure occurs when this wave of electricity sweeps over the centres that control various parts of the body, producing violent spasms, and, eventually, loss of consciousness. In extreme cases, seizures occur almost continuously (*status epilepticus*), representing a medical emergency with a fairly high mortality risk. In some patients, *both* hemispheres are involved, each amplifying the action of the other and contributing to the seizure (Coren, 1992).

It had been observed that if a patient had suffered damage to the corpus callosum (which connects the two hemispheres), the frequency and severity of the seizures were often reduced. This led to a surgical procedure that involves cutting this connecting tissue (the *split-brain operation*). Sometimes, as well as cutting the corpus callosum, the smaller anterior and hippocampus commissures, and in some cases the massa intermedia, are also cut. These more drastic operations are called *commissurotomies* (Coren, 1992).

The first commissurotomies involving human beings were performed by two neurosurgeons, Vogel and Bogen, in California. Not only did the operations produce dramatic medical benefits (the epilepsy was eliminated or markedly reduced), but there were no noticeable effects on personality, intelligence, ability to converse, perception, motor performance or coordination of the two halves of the body when performing skilled tasks (Coren, 1992; Stevens, 1998).

Sperry, a neuropsychologist, had developed a split-brain operation for use with monkeys in the early 1950s, which allowed him to test each hemisphere separately. He realized that such testing in humans might provide the definitive answer as to whether there are any differences between the abilities of the two hemispheres. Sperry's laboratory began extensive testing of Vogel and Bogen's patients (in 1961); the present article is one of several that reports the findings. Sperry was awarded the Nobel Prize for his work on split-brain patients in 1981.

AIM AND NATURE

● HYPOTHESIS

As mentioned above, this is one of a series of articles published by Sperry and his colleagues (e.g. Gazzaniga), reporting their findings concerning the 'functional outcome' of commissurotomy: the behavioural, neurological and psychological effects of having the two cerebral hemispheres disconnected.

It is important to spell out (although it should be clear enough from the **Background and context** above) that in no way was the surgery performed *for the purposes* of psychological research: Sperry's participants were patients suffering from severe epilepsy, which could not be controlled through medication, and who, as a last resort, underwent a commissurotomy. Sperry merely took the opportunity to study these split-brain patients: what better way to study the functioning of the two hemispheres than to present tasks to each hemisphere separately in people whose hemispheres cannot 'communicate' with each other?

● METHOD/DESIGN

Sperry's investigations are a kind of *natural experiment*: the experimental manipulation is either done literally by nature (e.g. someone is born without a corpus callosum), or in the 'natural' course of a person's life (epileptic patients undergo surgery for their epilepsy which disconnects the two halves of their brain).

Because they were not randomly assigned to a 'commissurotomy' condition, and because there was no 'non-commissurotomy' condition, this cannot be considered a true experiment. However, participants were presented with a series of tasks under carefully controlled laboratory conditions, and they acted as their own controls.

Method 1

The apparatus shown in Figure 20.1 allowed for the lateralized testing of the right and left halves of the visual field, separately or together, and the right and left hands (and legs), with vision excluded.

To test vision, with one eye covered, the participant focused on a designated fixation point on the upright translucent screen. Visual stimuli were back-projected at one-tenth of a second or less, too fast for eye movements to move the stimulus into the wrong half of the visual field. Figure 20.2 shows that everything seen to the left of the vertical meridian (the line bisecting the eye from top to bottom) through

Figure 20.1. Apparatus for studying lateralization of visual, tactual, lingual and associated functions in the surgically separated hemispheres.

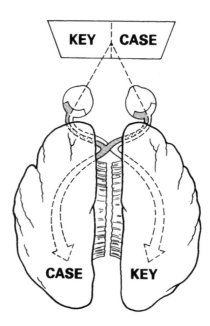

Figure 20.2. Things seen to the left of a central fixation point with either eye are projected to the right hemisphere and vice versa.

either eye is projected to the right hemisphere and vice versa, without significant gap or overlap.

● RESULTS

1   After a projected picture of an object had been identified and responded to in one half of the visual field, it was recognized again only if it reappeared in the same half-field. When visual material was projected to the right half of the field (and hence, typically for right-handed people, to the left hemisphere), participants were able to describe it in speech and writing, quite normally. But when the same material was projected into the left half of the visual field (and hence to the right hemisphere), they typically insisted they had not seen anything or that there was only a flash of light on the left side. However, if Sperry asked them to use their left hand to point to a matching picture or object, presented along with various other pictures or objects, they could choose the correct item quite consistently.

2   If two different figures were flashed simultaneously to both visual fields (e.g. '$' on the left and '?' on the right) and participants were asked to draw what they saw using their left hand (but with the hand concealed from their vision), they regularly reproduced the '$'. If asked what they had just drawn, they said without hesitation that it was '?'.

AIM AND NATURE

3   When part of a word was flashed to the left field and the rest of the word to the right, the letters on each side were perceived and responded to separately. In the key/case example (see Figure 20.2), participants would sometimes first reach for and select with the left hand a key from among a collection of objects (indicating perception through the right hemisphere). Then with their right hand they would spell out the word 'case', or speak the word if asked to give a verbal response. When asked what kind of 'case' they were thinking of, the answer (coming from the left hemisphere) might be something like 'in *case* of fire', 'the *case* of the missing corpse' or 'a *case* of beer' – depending on the particular mental set the left hemisphere was in at the time.

4   When an object was placed in their right hand for identification by touch, participants readily described it or named it in speech or writing; but when the same object was placed in the left hand, they would make wild guesses and often seemed unaware that anything was present at all. However, if the object was taken from the left hand and placed in a grab bag or scrambled with a dozen other test items, participants successfully searched for and retrieved it, even after a delay of several minutes.

If two objects were placed simultaneously, one in each hand, and then removed and hidden in a scrambled pile of test items, each hand hunted through the pile and searched for its own object. In the process, each hand explored, identified and rejected the item the other hand was searching for.

5   After a picture of some object (e.g. a cigarette) had been flashed to the right hemisphere via the left visual field, participants could retrieve the pictured object from a collection of objects using blind touch with the left hand (mediated through the right hemisphere). However, unlike the normal person, they had to use the corresponding hand (i.e. the left, in this case) for retrieval, and failed when asked to search out the same item with the right hand (see Figure 20.3). Using the right hand, participants recognized and could call out the names of each object as they came to it – but the right hand or its hemisphere does not know what it is looking for, and the hemisphere that can recognize the correct answer gets no feedback from the right hand. Hence, the two never get together, and the performance fails.

It also works the other way round: if participants were holding an object in their left hand, they could point out a picture of this object or its printed name when these appeared in a series presented visually. But again, the latter had to be seen through the corresponding half of the visual field (i.e. the left). This applies to vision, hearing, touch and smell.

Instead of selecting objects which match exactly the pictured item, the right hemisphere was able to select related items or ones that 'go with' the target

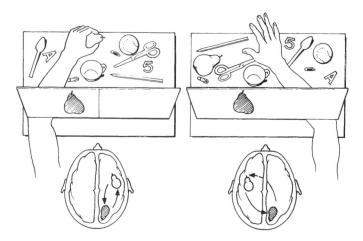

Figure 20.3. Visuotactile associations succeed between each half of the visual field and the corresponding hand. They fail with crossed combinations in which visual and tactual stimuli are projected into opposite hemispheres.

item. For example, if a picture of a wall clock had been flashed, and the closest item that could be found tactually by the left hand was a toy wristwatch, the watch was chosen.

If a word such as 'eraser' was flashed to the left visual field, participants were able to search out an eraser from among a collection of objects using only touch with the left hand. But if they were asked to name the object they had just chosen, they were unable to do so. The *talking* (left) hemisphere clearly does not know the correct answer, so the right hemisphere must, in this case, have read and understood the test word. Other tests showed that the right could understand fairly complex spoken definitions, such as 'shaving instrument' (razor), 'dirt remover' (soap) and 'inserted in slot machine' (coin). It also expresses genuine annoyance at errors made by the left hemisphere, when it 'knows' the answer but cannot say it.

6   When a pin-up of a nude was interspersed unexpectedly with a series of geometric shapes flashed to the right and left fields at random, (male) participants denied seeing anything, but a sneaky grin and sometimes blushing and giggling on the next couple of trials demonstrated that the right hemisphere is capable of appropriate emotional reactions.

● CONCLUSIONS

1   There appears to be a doubling in most aspects of conscious awareness. Instead of the normally unified single stream of consciousness, split-brain

patients behave in many ways as if they have two independent streams of consciousness, one in each hemisphere, each cut off from the other (i.e. each hemisphere seems to have its own separate and private sensations, perceptions, concepts and impulses to act, with related volitional, cognitive and learning experiences). Following surgery, each hemisphere also has its own chain of memories, which become inaccessible to the other.

2 Unlike normal people, split-brain patients have to retrieve an object with the same hand used to initially identify it. They fail at *cross-retrieval* (i.e. they cannot recognize with one hand something identified only moments before with the other hand. The second hemisphere does not know what the first hemisphere has been doing. While the dominant (left) is usually in control, the right can sometimes take over temporarily.

3 Contrary to the traditional belief that the right hemisphere becomes 'word-blind', 'word-deaf' and 'tactually alexic' following commissurotomy, it is capable of understanding both written and spoken words to some extent, but it cannot express this understanding verbally.

4 The right hemisphere is a second conscious entity, which is characteristically human and runs along in parallel with the more dominant stream of consciousness in the left. The quality of mental awareness in the right is comparable to that of some types of aphasic patients following damage to the motor and main language centres. Under normal conditions, the left hemisphere may be unaware of the presence of the right.

EVALUATION

Methodological issues

Although there are only a few of them, split-brain patients offer the advantage of being able to target the information to one hemisphere which does not then transfer that information to the other hemisphere (as happens via the corpus callosum in the intact brain). By projecting sensory information to one or other hemisphere, the mode of processing by that hemisphere can be studied in what is as near to controlled within-participant conditions as we could hope for (Toates 2001). (See **Exercises**.)

The brain damage is under surgical control and targets a defined, circumscribed area of the brain (Kosslyn *et al.*, 1999). However, Toates (2001) argues that any conclusions drawn from such studies should be considered in light of the following qualifications:

● the role of either hemisphere might be different when the information is projected to both and there is communication between them;

- behaviour is normally the product of an interaction between the hemispheres (Sperry, 1974) – the performance of one in isolation might be deceptive regarding its role prior to surgery when it interacts with the opposite hemisphere (as Toates says, 'There might be reorganization of processing systems following surgery (particularly if the patient is young), so that the performance of a hemisphere is changed');

- the surgery is a last resort after years of suffering and failed medication (Kosslyn *et al.*, 1999); we cannot just assume that these patients are like controls in all other respects;

- even split-brain patients would normally not act in such a way that information is projected only to one hemisphere.

A certain amount of the tactile information arising from either hand is projected to *both* hemispheres, and so is available to both hemispheres even in split-brain patients. But in the absence of communication between the hemispheres, the fine-grained processing of detail by the somatosensory cortex (as in object discrimination) is available only to the *contra-lateral* (opposite side) hemisphere. So, the experimenter can project visual information to one hemisphere and tactile information to the other, and split-brain patients will not be able to integrate these two sources (Kosslyn *et al.*, 1999).

However, the nature of sound, the ear, and the fact that auditory information is projected to both hemispheres, means that a comparable procedure for targeting auditory information to only one hemisphere is not possible (Toates, 2001).

According to Bogen (1969), lateralization is *relative*; for example, we cannot simply say that the left hemisphere is 'verbal' and the right hemisphere is 'non-verbal'. As Sperry found, the right does have *some* language ability. Ornstein (1986) observes that the primary factor involved in lateralization is not the type of information (words or pictures versus sounds or shapes) which is processed, but *how* it is processed. For example, in one study, participants were given a technical passage and two folk tales. There was no change in the level of activity in the left hemisphere, but the right was more activated while the participant read the stories than while reading the technical material.

Much of what we know about normal brain function in general (and lateralization in particular) is based on the study of those who have suffered brain damage or, in the case of split-brain patients, undergone drastic surgery for epilepsy. As regards the former, we assume that the damaged area has stopped working correctly, but that the rest of the brain carries on more or less as normal. This may or may not be a reasonable assumption (Beaumont, 1988). In the case of the latter, long-standing pre-surgical pathology might have caused an abnormal reorganization of the patients' brains, making generalizing from them to normal brains invalid (Cohen, 1975; see Toates' qualifying points above).

Cohen argues that, far from 'doing their own thing', the two hemispheres work very much together. Similarly, Fernald (1997) claims that the terms 'right- and left-brained' are grossly inaccurate when used in the same way as 'handedness': the hemispheres are *integrated*, separate but complementary information-processing subsystems. While damage to the right hemisphere causes difficulties in reading maps, perceiving spatial relationships and recognizing complex geometrical forms (all right-brain abilities), such patients will also have trouble *talking about* such things as maps (a left-brain ability). But they will also have problems understanding others' speech, which involves a recognition of emotion in the tone of the voice (right-brain) (Carlson, 1992). Clearly, *both* hemispheres contribute to language abilities. According to Kosslyn *et al.* (1999), 'some popular dichotomies, such as the left hemisphere being analytic and verbal whereas the right is holistic, artistic, creative and perceptual need careful qualification'.

Theoretical issues and subsequent research

The most common way of distinguishing between the hemispheres has been the claim that the left is specialized for verbal processes, while the right is specialized for visuospatial processes. But this is rather oversimplified, and the distinction is most accurate in relation to *higher-order* cognitive processes within these domains. For example, while the basic processes of language may be present in both (e.g. the right hemisphere may sometimes possess a vocabulary that is roughly equivalent to that of the left), only the left has the specialized neural processes needed to carry out the complex linguistic functions of everyday life (Gazzaniga, 2000). In the vast majority of intact brains, only the left hemisphere retains the ability to speak, enabling verbal report of conscious experience (Colvin and Gazzaniga, 2007). (See **Methodological issues** above.)

One of the difficulties associated with generalizations in psychology (even with something as 'biological' as cerebral function) is the existence of *individual differences*. Some people seem to have much more literalized brains than others; others have language more or less equally represented on both sides (*bilateral representation*: Beaumont, 1988).

As far as the left hemisphere being dominant for language, this seems to be true for 95 per cent of right-handed patients, while only 5 per cent had their right hemisphere dominant. But with left-handers, things are much less clear-cut: 75 per cent had their left hemisphere dominant, none had the right dominant, but 25 per cent showed bilateral representation (based on a review by Satz (1979) of all studies between 1935 and 1975, cited in Beaumont, 1988).

Over and above this left-/right-handed difference, it has been widely assumed that men's hemispheres are *more asymmetrically organized* (less symmetrical) for speech and spatial abilities than women's. It follows that left–right specialization will be most prevalent in right-handed men (and not all people; Ornstein, 1986).

● Kimura (1992, 1999) studied the ability of patients with damage to one hemisphere to mentally rotate objects. As expected, damage to the right hemisphere produced lower scores for *both* sexes compared with damage to the left. Also as expected, women did less well overall than men on a block rotation task. But, *contrary* to expectations, women were at least as much affected as men by damage to their right hemisphere. In other words, men and women seem to be equally 'asymmetrical' as far as right-side damage interference with spatial ability is concerned. This suggests that normal sex differences on such tasks are *not* caused by the dominance of the right hemisphere, but that some other brain system(s) must be involved.

● Men suffer *aphasia* (impairment of the ability to produce speech) from left hemisphere damage more often than women do. The implication here is that speech must be more *bilaterally organized* (more symmetrical) in women. This would mean that women with right-sided damage are almost as likely to become aphasic as women with left-sided damage. But in over 20 years of working with brain-damaged patients, Kimura has not found this to be the case.

● Cahill (2005) cites a number of studies using PET and *f*MRI scanning, which reveal that anatomical variations occur between males and females in an assortment of regions throughout the brain. These include parts of the frontal and parietal cortex, and the amygdala. These sex differences are generally consistent with the average differences in male/female abilities; for example, parts of the parietal cortex involved in space perception are bigger in men than women (but bear in mind Kimura's observations above). However, Cahill points out that these (and other) size differences are *relative*: they refer to the volume of the particular brain structure compared with the brain's overall volume.

● Cahill also describes an experiment he conducted which found an almost immediate hemispheric difference between the sexes in response to emotionally unpleasant photographs (such as a decaying animal). In men who reported the strongest responses and showed the best recall two weeks later, the greatest activity was in the right-hemisphere amygdala; for women, it was the left-hemisphere amygdala. In both cases, the response occurred within 300 milliseconds of seeing the images – before people have had much, if any, chance to consciously interpret what they have seen.

● Women, on average, excel at word recall, finding words that begin with a specific letter, rapidly identifying matching items, and performing certain precision manual tasks (such as placing pegs in designated holes on a board). However, some of these average sex differences in cognition vary from slight to quite large, and 'men and women overlap enormously on many cognitive tests that show average differences …

On the whole, variation between men and women tends to be smaller than deviations within each sex' (Kimura, 1999).

Even if we accept male superiority in visuospatial tasks (especially those involving mental rotation), this is still open to interpretation. For example, Brosnan (1998) gave sixth-form students a standard test of visuospatial ability (the embedded figure test), but it was presented in one of two ways:

1   in the traditional way (as an explicit test of visuospatial ability);

2   as a test of 'empathy'.

While the boys' performance was not affected by how it was presented, girls underperformed in (1). But girls who scored high in masculinity also scored more highly than those scoring high in femininity. For Brosnan, these results indicate that some sex differences may be attributable to 'psychological gender differences' which determine an individual's motivation. This *psychological* interpretation contrasts sharply with *biological/neuropsychological* explanations which focus on differences in brain anatomy (see Chapter 41).

Age is another factor that seems to be associated with hemispheric asymmetry. Colvin and Gazzaniga (2007) point out that there is a growing body of work suggesting that the strength of asymmetries shifts across the lifespan, possibly reflecting the extent to which the corpus callosum becomes myelinated. (See Chapter 29.)

Applications and implications

One fascinating hypothesis suggests that the right hemisphere's greater ability to process and mentally manipulate visual images may form the basis for other, more complex functions. For example, individuals with right-hemisphere damage often report an inability to dream; this is also mentioned by split-brain patients. However, when talking to a split-brain patient, you are speaking only to the left hemisphere. So, perhaps 'I cannot dream' should be interpreted as meaning that the *left hemisphere does not dream*: it is possible that the right hemisphere dreams but cannot talk about it. After all, dreams are predominantly a sequence of thoughts dominated by visual imagery (Coren, 1992). (See Chapter 17.)

This leads on to what is, arguably, the most interesting and controversial of all the issues relating to lateralization in general, and split-brain patients in particular: do the two halves of the brain represent two kinds of consciousness (two minds)?

Ornstein (1986) cites reports of an entire hemisphere (right or left) being removed for the treatment of certain types of epilepsy (hemispherectomy), without destroying the 'person'. So, if possession of a 'mind' requires only one hemisphere, does having two hemispheres make it possible that we have two minds? Indeed, do split-brain patients have two minds, two separate, distinct modes of consciousness? Ornstein and Sperry certainly think so.

According to Sperry (1964, in Apter, 1991), 'when the brain is bisected, we see two separate "selves" (essentially a divided organism with two mental units, each with its own memories and its own will) competing for control over the organism'. Does this mean that the normal role of the corpus callosum is to keep the two hemispheres in exact synchrony, so that we normally have one, unified mind?

Ornstein asks if commissurotomy produces a splitting or doubling of the mind (that was not there before), or if it reveals the duality that is really there all the time? This argument is an example of the *double brain theory*, which essentially 'reduces' the mind (or the 'self' or personality) to a hemisphere of the brain (Apter, 1991). (This theory is also used to explain multiple personality disorder; see Chapter 31.)

Based on his work with split-brain patients, Gazzaniga (1998) has proposed the concept of 'the interpreter'. This refers to a capacity, or set of mechanisms, residing in the left hemisphere of human brains. Its function is to enable us to make inferences and to form beliefs about both interior events (internal bodily states) and external events, including our own actions and other people's. The interpreter frees us from the immediacy of the present environment; it allows us to remember and to plan, and to do so in inventive and unique ways.

When a split-brain patient is presented with information that can only be properly conceptualized by what is received by the right hemisphere, the left hemisphere will recontextualize and make good sense of that information. In one experiment, the left hemisphere is visually presented with a picture of a chicken claw, and the right with a scene involving snow. The patient is asked to select from an array of pictured images associated with the presented pictures. As expected, using their right hand (controlled by the left hemisphere), patients point to a chicken, and, with their left hand (controlled by the right hemisphere) to a snow shovel. When asked to explain why they chose those items, they respond: 'Oh, that's simple. The chicken claw goes with the chicken, and you need a shovel to clean out the chicken shed' (Gazzaniga, 1998).

In the intact brain, the snow-related information would be communicated to the left hemisphere via the corpus callosum. The interpreter integrates that information and produces a rational, coherent 'story', drawing on other current and remembered experience. Gazzaniga regards this capacity for rational invention as what distinguishes the human from the non-human brain (Gallagher, 1998).

EXERCISES

1 Referring to the section on Methodological issues, why should there be a difference between the two hemispheres in their respective levels of activity in response to the technical passage and the folk tales?

2 Ornstein (1986) reports an experiment in which brain activity was recorded while participants mentally rotated objects in space. They were then asked to perform the task analytically, by counting the number of boxes. Which hemisphere would be mainly involved in each case?

3 In what ways could split-brain patients be considered unrepresentative of adults in general?

4 Why can split-brain experiments not be considered *true* experiments?

5 What does Toates (2001) mean when he says that split-brain studies come as close to controlled within-participant conditions as you might hope for?

6 Explain the difference between *localization* and *lateralization* of brain function.

21 Visions from the dying brain: Near-death experiences may tell us more about consciousness and the brain than about what lies beyond the grave

Blackmore, S. (1988)

New Scientist, 5 May, 43–6

BACKGROUND AND CONTEXT

According to Greyson (2000), near-death experiences (NDEs) are: 'profound psychological events with transcendental and mystical elements, typically occurring to individuals close to death or in situations of intense physical or emotional danger'.

NDEs (and the related *out-of-body experience*/OBE) represent one type of *paranormal* phenomenon, which, collectively, form the subject matter of *parapsychology*. Colman (1987) defines parapsychology as: 'a branch of psychology devoted to examining and seeking to explain…apparently supernatural or paranormal (beside or beyond the normal) phenomena'.

Watt (2001) explicitly rejects any reference to 'supernatural' in her definition, because this implies that such phenomena are incompatible with scientific theorizing and investigation. She defines parapsychology as 'the scientific study of paranormal phenomena and experiences', where 'paranormal' means that:

> the phenomena appear to suggest that organisms can interact with the environment in ways that are not explicable within current scientific understanding. This does not mean that paranormal phenomena can never be understood, but it may mean that some of our present scientific knowledge and theories would need to be adjusted to accommodate them.

NDEs were popularized by Moody, an American psychiatrist, in his book *Life After Life* (1975). Based on accounts of numerous survivors of cardiac arrest and other life-threatening situations, Moody presented a description which included:

● experiences of floating along a dark tunnel with a bright light at the end;

● leaving the body and being able to watch the proceedings from above (an OBE);

● meeting a 'being of light' who helped them review their past life;

● feeling as if they were passing into another world (the light) where some final barrier marked the return from joy, love and peace to pain, fear or sickness. In these cases, the person had to choose between carrying on into the light and returning to life's pain or suffering.

Although these experiences were often difficult to talk about, they frequently left people feeling that they had changed for the better – less materialistic and with reduced fear of death.

These accounts promoted the popular view that NDEs must be evidence for life after death. But many scientists and doctors rejected the experiences as, at best, drug-induced hallucinations or, at worst, pure invention. However, the 'truth' seems to lie somewhere in between these extremes (Blackmore, 2005).

AIM AND NATURE

● HYPOTHESIS AND METHOD/DESIGN

The 'study' is primarily a *review article*, in which Blackmore considers alternative explanations of NDEs in terms of known or hypothesized *physiological processes*, in particular those relating to brain mechanisms. She argues that before interpreting NDEs as evidence of life after death, we need to rule out explanations – both physiological and psychological: not only can we apply what we already know (about the brain) to these experiences, but they can also teach us much about the brain. Such scientific explanations allow testable predictions to be made, but they must also make sense to the people who have had NDEs.

Blackmore cites research – both that of others and her own conducted in the Brain and Perception Laboratory at the University of Bristol Medical School – but the article is *not* an account of specific research. Here is a brief example of an NDE sent to Blackmore by a woman in Cyprus:

> *An emergency mastectomy was performed. On the fourth day following the operation I went into shock and became unconscious for several hours …*

Although thought to be unconscious I remembered, for years afterwards, the entire, detailed conversation that passed between the surgeon and anaesthetist present… I was lying above my own body, totally free of pain and looking down at my own self with compassion for the agony I could see on the face; I was floating peacefully. Then … I was going elsewhere, floating towards a dark, but not frightening, curtain-like area … then I felt total peace … Suddenly it all changed – I was slammed back into my body again, very much aware of the agony again.

These experiences seem very real. The tunnel is so convincing that people often assume it is some 'real' passageway to the next life. The OBE is so realistic that people are convinced that their spirit has left their body and can see and move without it. The positive emotions are so strong that many do not want to 'come back'. For those who reach the final stage, it often seems as though a conscious decision has been made to return to life and responsibilities rather than remaining in bliss and peace.

Explaining the tunnel

According to the astronomer Carl Sagan, the only way of explaining the universal nature of NDEs is by reference to the one experience all human beings share – namely, birth. The tunnel is 'really' the birth canal, and the tunnel experience and the OBEs are a reliving of one's birth. Similar arguments have given rise to the 'rebirthing' business, regression, and all sorts of other 'New Age' techniques.

But the birth canal is nothing like a tunnel, even if the fetus were actually face-first and open-eyed into it. Also, the newborn's cognitive abilities would not allow us to remember our birth in a meaningful way as adults. Studies of so-called 'age regression' under hypnosis show that people generally invent superficially plausible experiences.

However, at least the 'birth theory' can be tested. If tunnels and OBEs are a re-experience of birth, then people born by Caesarean section (CS) should not have them. Blackmore gave a questionnaire to 254 people, 36 of whom had been born by CS. Both groups reported the same proportion of OBEs and tunnel experiences. It could be that these experiences are based on the *idea of birth in general* – but this drastically weakens the theory.

The tunnel seems to have a rather interesting origin in the structure of the visual system. It is not confined to NDEs, but can occur in epilepsy and migraine, when falling asleep, meditating or just relaxing, when pressure is put on both eyes, or with certain drugs (such as LSD, psilocybin or mescaline). Why do such different conditions produce the same hallucinations?

The visual cortex, which processes both visions and visual imagination, is usually in a stable state; this is a result of neurons that inhibit the action of others. But many of the conditions listed above reduce or interfere with these inhibitory neurons. LSD, for example, suppresses the action of the raphe cells, which regulate activity in the visual cortex. Any interference with inhibition may produce a highly excitable state: there will be *random* firing of cells. The visual cortex is organized so that many cells are devoted to the centre of the visual field, and a few to the periphery. Random firing of cells will produce the effect of a bright light in the centre fading out towards darkness; in other words, a tunnel effect. But no one has yet tested this hypothesis.

However, this does not explain why the tunnel experience, if it is a hallucination, seems so real. Blackmore suggests that the answer may lie in asking what makes *anything* so real. The distinction between 'out there' and 'in my mind' is not an easy one as far as the nervous system is concerned. Almost as soon as visual or auditory processing starts, information from memory is mixed in with the sensory input. It seems unlikely that any simple tag could be attached which says 'this came from outside' or 'this is a hallucination'. Blackmore believes the decision is made at a much higher level. The system simply takes the most stable model of the world it has at any one time and calls that 'reality'. Normally, there is one 'model of reality' that is overwhelmingly stable, coherent and complex. It is the one built up from sensory input – 'me, here, now'.

Visions from the dying brain

But what about the dying system, a brain with massive disinhibition, beset with noise and danger or failing altogether to produce a workable model of reality? The system will try to restore stability as soon as possible, and one way of doing this would be to rely on memory: to ask, as it were: Who am I? Where am I? What am I doing? The answers will be there in memory, provided enough capacity remains for processing. One interesting feature of memory models is that they are often in bird's-eye view.

So let us suppose that a dying woman's system constructs a model of what she knows should be happening: her body on the operating table, the surgeons around her, the lights above and the apparatus around. This may well be in a bird's-eye view – from the ceiling. This model may work rather well. It may also incorporate some input, such as the sounds of the people talking or the clink of instruments on the trolley, as well as the jolts of attempts to resuscitate her. In this way, a mental model could be produced which is not only convincing, but actually contains some correct details about the events going on at the time – and is a bird's-eye view. If this is the best model the system has at the time, it will seem perfectly real.

This explanation suggests several testable predictions. For example, people who have OBEs ought to be those who can more easily imagine scenes from a bird's-eye view, or more easily switch viewpoints mentally. Blackmore (1987, in Blackmore, 1988) found support for this in several experiments. Blackmore and Irwin (in Blackmore, 1988) also found that people with OBEs tend to recall dreams in bird's-eye view – though not events from waking life. Although the reasons for this are unclear, this approach seems to be more productive than the belief that something leaves the body.

However, Sabom (1982), an American cardiologist, has claimed that patients have seen things during NDEs that they could not possibly have reconstructed from hearing or from what they previously knew about resuscitation techniques. As well as collecting anecdotes, such as that of a shoe seen on an inaccessible window ledge, he asked participants to imagine going through a resuscitation procedure and to tell him what they 'saw'. They represented a control group. What they told him was nothing like the detailed and correct descriptions of apparatus or the movement of needles on dials which people with NDEs saw from out of the body.

A better control group in Sabom's work would be composed of people who had actually been through the full procedure and experienced the actions and conversations of staff. The behaviour of the needles should be recorded precisely for comparison with the patient's account.

● CONCLUSIONS

There are good physiological and cognitive reasons why NDEs seem so real and have such a profound and lasting effect on the people who have them. But they are not as mysterious as they might appear. NDEs may tell us more about consciousness and the brain than about what may or may not happen beyond the grave. Its many components can be seen as changes in mental models brought about by disinhibition of the cortex and the breakdown of the usual model of normality driven by sensory input. But they should not be dismissed as 'just hallucinations': they are life-transforming and important hallucinations that we should try to understand.

EVALUATION

Methodological issues

NDEs have been reported following resuscitation (after the person had been pronounced clinically dead); by people who actually died but were able to describe their experiences in their final moments; and by individuals who, in the course of accidents or illness, simply *feared* that they were near to death (Greyson, 2000). According to Roe (2001), in all three types of case it could be claimed that the experience has more to do with the *process* of dying than with the end point of death itself. Roe poses the fundamental question: Are people who have NDEs really dead? The answer he gives is: 'It depends on how you define "dead"'.

Initially, doctors determined death by checking for pulse, respiration and pupil reaction to light. With the invention of the stethoscope, the focus shifted to the heart. Later, cardiopulmonary resuscitation showed that people who had been pronounced dead could be brought back to life. So attention has shifted to brain function. Yet a lack of cortical activity – and even brainstem quiescence – may only be symptomatic of *dying*, rather than an indicator of actual death. In each case, there may be a suspicion that some remnant of life may be going undetected which is capable of maintaining some kind of phenomenological experience. These shifts in focus show how difficult it is to identify any single event as defining death. As Roe (2001) points out, 'death is a process that takes time, and if the appropriate action is taken then the dying process can be reversed'.

Roberts and Owen (1988) give an extreme definition of death, involving an irreversible – and permanent – loss of organ functions. Accordingly, all NDE reports refer to the experiences of people who have remained alive. If NDEs really do indicate what happens after we die (as many who report them believe), then we might expect to find differences between those who were actually near death and those who merely *thought* they were. But there is very little evidence to support this claim. The fact that virtually identical NDEs can be induced by perceived threat (i.e. fear of being near death) needs to be taken into account in any potential explanation (Roe, 2001). (See **Subsequent research** below.)

By their very nature, NDEs and OBEs are *spontaneous* occurrences: people are unlikely to volunteer for experiments in which they are brought to the brink of death, and most researchers would not think such experiments ethically acceptable, even if such volunteers could be found!

According to Colman (1987), spontaneous cases are not generally regarded as scientific evidence for the existence of 'psi', a general term for any paranormal phenomenon or the hypothesized mechanism underlying them (Blackmore, 1995). There are three major reasons for this:

1   They are unrepeatable, making it impossible for independent researchers to check them (unlike general psychology or experimental parapsychology). There is also a lack of theory as to when and where spontaneous psi should occur.

2   It is impossible to *exclude* a normal explanation; that is, some perfectly normal process (such as falling asleep and dreaming) could account for the apparently

paranormal experience. In 27 years of psychoanalytic work with patients, Freud never encountered a paranormal dream. Also, the accumulation of similar cases does not necessarily strengthen the case for psi. However, in the case of NDEs, reports have been widespread through many ages and cultures (Blackmore, 2005). Long before Moody's *Life After Life* (1975), there had been similar descriptions of deathbed experiences (when the patient did go on to die) in the psychical research literature. Dying patients often described wonderful visions to those sitting at their bedside; these included heavenly scenes, bright light, and deceased friends or relatives coming to help them. As far as culture is concerned, the evidence for consistency is patchy. Blackmore (1993) refers to studies carried out in India, Africa and Mesopotamia, which found some important differences in the content of NDEs compared with those reported by Moody. For example, American NDEs typically involved images of the person's dead mother, while female figures were extremely rare among Indians, especially males. Indians usually saw religious figures, who differed according to their particular faith. Also, while Americans were usually happy to go with their dead relatives or visionary angels (Gabriel or St Peter at his gates), Indians were more likely to refuse to go. Blackmore (1993) concludes that NDEs seem to be *universal* in the sense that something like the modern NDE has been reported in many ages and cultures. They are also reported by children. However, even if the content of NDEs were *consistent* across time and culture, this would not in itself point to any particular *explanation*. (See **Theoretical issues** below.)

3   Most importantly, cases of spontaneous psi rely unavoidably on the testimony of those who report them. Colman believes that since paranormal events are literally contrary to the laws of nature, there are never good grounds for believing the testimony. But this argument is based on his definition of paranormal, which, as we saw in the **Background and context**, is not accepted by most researchers in the field.

Theoretical issues

Blackmore (2005) considers a number of alternative explanations in addition to those discussed in the 1988 article.

1   *Expectation* certainly affects NDEs, in two ways. First, as we have seen above, they often happen to people who *think* they are dying: you do not have to be physically close to death to have an NDE. Indeed, some aspects of the NDE, such as the OBE, can occur at any time and to perfectly healthy people. The examples given above of cultural and religious differences in the content of NDEs reflect differences in expectations about death. But since the general pattern seems to be similar across cultures, religious expectations cannot be responsible for the entire experience or most of its common features. We might also expect suicide

attempters to have more hellish experiences, but their NDEs are much like those of others – and they tend to reduce future suicide attempts.

2   When under stress, the brain releases chemicals that act to reduce pain or help us to cope with the stress. These include *endorphins*, the brain's own morphine-like drugs. It has been suggested that endorphins could account for the NDE. Stressors can include both actual physical trauma and extreme fear – such as the fear of dying. Endorphins can block pain and induce feelings of well-being, acceptance and even intense pleasure. While this might account for the positive experiences that are characteristic of NDEs, some researchers argue that 'hellish' NDEs are far more common than has been thought previously. Also, it has been argued that serotonin plays a more important role than endorphins, and that the drug ketamine can induce states similar to NDEs.

3   *Anoxia* (lack of oxygen to the brain) has been put forward as causing NDEs. But this is implausible, given that so many NDEs occur in the absence of anoxia (such as when people only *think* they are dying). However, anoxia causes disinhibition in the cortex, which Blackmore argues may be responsible for the tunnel and the light. In other words, it is the disinhibition (not the anoxia itself) which is responsible for much of the NDE (Blackmore, 1993). Hypercarbia (increased carbon dioxide in the blood) is also thought to play a role in NDEs and has long been known to induce visions, lights, mystical experiences and OBEs.

4   The *temporal lobe* is sensitive to anoxia, and stimulating it artificially induces hallucinations, memory flashbacks, body distortions and OBEs. The limbic system is also sensitive to anoxia and is involved in the organization of emotions and memory. Endorphins increase the chance of seizures in the temporal lobe and limbic system, so they might produce the same effects as anoxia. Also, research looking for an 'NDE-prone personality' has found that those most likely to have NDEs may have more unstable temporal lobes (high lability); but it is unclear whether this is a cause or an effect of NDE.

Subsequent research

According to Roe (2001), NDEs are much more common than was originally thought, with up to one-third of people who come close to death reporting them. Although this may be an overestimate, it is certainly not a rare experience. This could reflect improvements in resuscitation techniques, such that 'more people survive the kinds of close brush with death (e.g. heart attack, drowning, road traffic accident) that would previously have been fatal' (Roe, 2001). Alternatively, it could just mean that the notion of NDE has become part of popular culture, and so may provide the basis for some fantasized experience produced while unconscious or in crisis. Roe observes that its portrayal in films such as *Flatliners* has made the classic NDE almost archetypal (Roe, 2001). (This has parallels with the 'epidemic' in reported cases of multiple personality disorder, especially by psychiatrists in the USA: see Chapter 31.)

Moody's main purpose was to convince researchers that NDE was a topic worthy of serious study, and in that he certainly succeeded (Roe, 2001). Not only is there the International Association for Near-Death Studies and its *Journal of Near-Death Studies*, but more detailed research since Moody's pioneering study has confirmed that the experience takes a consistent form and has explored several proposed explanations. (See **Theoretical issues** above.)

Ring (1980) took Moody's largely anecdotal research a step further by using a structured interview and measurement scale, with 102 survivors of life-threatening injuries or illnesses. Of these, 49 survivors (48 per cent) met his criteria for deep or moderate NDEs, the other 53 (52 per cent) being 'non-experiencers'. The vast majority had suffered a sudden episode, such as coronary infarction (heart attack) or haemorrhage. Ring identified a 'core experience', comprising five stages (feelings of deep peace and well-being, a sense of separation from the body/OBE, entering darkness/passing through a tunnel, seeing the light, and entering the light/beautiful garden). Fenwick (1997) collected over 300 accounts, and his findings are strikingly similar to Ring's.

However, Orbach (1999) cites reports of negative NDEs by Evans-Bush and Greyson (1996), in which people are frightened by the prospect of entering the tunnel, experience an emptiness and loss of meaning, and a 'wailing and gnashing of teeth, grotesque sub-human creatures, tormented and tormenting'.

Ring and Cooper (1997, in Blackmore, 2005) found that some members of their sample of 31 blind people (some blind from birth) reported classic NDEs similar to those of sighted people; a few claimed to have obtained visually based knowledge that they could not have gained by any normal means. Ring and Cooper concluded that these people cannot see in the ordinary physical sense, but have attained 'transcendental awareness'.

Kübler-Ross (1991), internationally renowned for her work as a doctor with terminally ill patients, collected over 25,000 cases of NDEs from a wide range of cultural and religious (and non-religious) backgrounds all over the world during the 1980s (including a 2-year-old child and a 97-year-old man). She concluded that:

> *At the moment of death, all of you will experience the separation of the real immortal You, from the temporary house, namely the physical body ... the soul or the entity ... the butterfly in the process of leaving the cocoon. When we leave the physical body there will be a total absence of panic, fear or anxiety.*

Applications and implications

As a neurophysiologist and neuropsychiatrist, Fenwick (1997) argues that all thoughts and feelings result from neuronal activity in the brain. 'Mind' is merely a product of the brain, and 'certainly cannot act at a distance from it, or independently of it'. Like Blackmore, he believes that our models of the world are created in our brains from the messages that come via the sense organs. When we are deeply unconscious, there can be *no* model building, no experiencing and no memory. Yet NDEs are remarkably lucid and clearly remembered. How is this possible?

According to Corbett (1996):

> *The psychologist cannot definitively answer the question of whether consciousness is literally able to move out of the body into another realm of reality. But ... to insist on a purely organic explanation of these events [NDEs] is to abandon true openness in the face of an unanswerable question.*

Jung (1967) believed in a psychic reality beyond the narrow ego-consciousness. He speculated on its continuation after the individual death of our body. If we assume that life continues in some mysterious 'there', since 'there' can have no location, the only way of continuing is in the psyche – free from the limits of space and time. Like Fenwick (1997), Jung was astonished at what happens when the cortex has stopped functioning. He had an NDE himself and he refers to cases of severe brain injury, during which both dreaming and perception of the outside world can take place. Against all the odds, some sort of consciousness seems to remain possible in apparent unconsciousness (Orbach, 1999).

According to Blackmore (2005):

> *At our present state of knowledge it probably remains a matter of personal preference whether to interpret the NDE as a glimpse of the life beyond or the product of the dying brain. Either way the NDE is clearly an interesting and potentially life-changing experience that can teach us much about living as well as dying.*

Key Studies in Psychology

EXERCISES

1   When discussing Sagan's account of the tunnel component of the NDE
    in terms of reliving one's birth, Blackmore cites a study in which she
    found the same proportion of OBEs and tunnel experiences reported by
    people born normally and by Caesarean section. She takes this as
    evidence against Sagan's account.

    (a) Are the data consistent with her prediction?

    (b) Are there different types of memory which could explain the link
         between the birth experience and tunnel experiences?

    (c) Does Sagan's theory (and related New Age techniques) necessarily
         overestimate the capacities of newborns?

2   What are LSD, psilocybin and mescaline? What properties do they
    share?

3   When discussing why experiences such as tunnel experiences, if they
    are hallucinations, seem so real, Blackmore states that the nervous
    system cannot easily distinguish between 'out there' and 'in my mind'.
    What other distinction, commonly made in cognitive psychology's
    discussion of information processing, does this correspond to?

4   What does it mean to say that Blackmore's explanation of NDEs and
    OBEs is *reductionist*? Does her account in terms of neuropsychological
    mechanisms necessarily exclude other explanations? (If hers is true,
    must the others be false?) More generally, is the scientific 'model of
    reality' inherently more 'true' than others, and if so, by what criteria?

22 Analysis of a phobia in a five-year-old boy

Freud, S. (1909)

Pelican Freud Library, Volume 8, Case Histories 1 (1977)

BACKGROUND AND CONTEXT

Freud's work represents many things (often just referred to as 'psychoanalysis'). It is a theory of personality and personality development (hence a theory of child development, including moral development), an account of motivation and dreams, and an approach to the treatment of (certain kinds of) mental disorder. It is useful to refer to all the theoretical aspects of his work as 'psychoanalytic theory', reserving 'psychoanalysis' for the related form of psychotherapy.

The five-year-old boy who was the subject of this case study was called Hans, hence 'The case of Little Hans's (this is how Freud himself refers to the child). This is an important study because of the claims Freud made for it, namely that it confirmed the Oedipal theory already set out in *Three Essays on the Theory of Sexuality* (1905). The case study gave the abstract theory a personality (Ward, 2001). It also demonstrates Freud's explanation of the origin of phobias (in contrast with, say, explanations based on conditioning; see Chapters 23 and 30).

Little Hans was the only child patient Freud reported on, and this assumes particular significance in light of a standard criticism of his theorizing, namely that he built up a whole theory of *child development* around his (almost) exclusive treatment of *adult* patients.

AIM AND NATURE

● HYPOTHESIS

As we have noted above, Freud believed that the Hans case study confirmed and illustrated his Oedipal theory, which had been formulated four years earlier. Indeed, Freud observed that:

> *In his attitude towards his father and mother, Hans really was a little Oedipus who wanted to have his father 'out of the way', to get rid of him, so that he might be alone with his beautiful mother and sleep with her.*

So, an *implicit* hypothesis may have been that a five-year-old boy's phobia (of being bitten by a horse) can be interpreted in terms of castration anxiety, as set out in the Oedipal theory of psychosexual development.

● METHOD/DESIGN

The study reports the findings of the psychoanalytic treatment of a five-year-old boy. In fact, the actual account of the analysis comprises the middle section of the report as a whole, the others being Introduction, in which a great deal of background information is provided, and Discussion. (The account given here draws on all three sections.)

This is a *case study*, sometimes misleadingly referred to as a 'case history'. The latter is really just the collection of background information as a necessary preliminary to the primary aim of the study, which is to understand and/or treat the subject. Most case studies take place in a *clinical* context: they are reports of attempts by doctors, psychiatrists, psychologists and others in the caring professions to help those with brain damage/injury or some mental disorder.

For Freud, there is no real distinction to be made between the case study as a form of helping and as a piece of scientific research (a point made by Freud himself in defence of the criticism that the method is *unscientific*). (See **Methodological issues** below.)

● FINDINGS

Part 1

Hans showed an unusually lively interest in his 'widdler'; he discovered that the presence or absence of a widdler allowed him to differentiate between animate and inanimate objects. He assumed that all animate objects were like himself and possessed this important bodily organ, including both his parents; he was not deterred by watching Hanna, his newborn sister having a bath: 'But her widdler's still quite small... When she grows up, it'll get bigger all right'.

This belief that everyone has a widdler was part of Hans's *Weltanschauung* (world view), so it would have been very distressing for him to have acknowledged that Hanna did not have one after all. It also explains why he suppressed a threat made by his mother that related to his widdler (and which he only recalled some time later): when Hans was three and a half, she found him with his hand on his penis. She threatened him by saying, 'If you do that, I shall send for Dr. A to cut off your widdler. And then what'll you widdle with?' His answer was, 'My bottom'. Hans had started masturbating (the commonest – and most normal – form of auto-erotic sexual activity) from quite a young age.

His masturbation was associated with liking to exhibit his penis, as well as curiosity about other people's. One of his dreams, dating from the beginning of his period of repression, expressed a wish that one of his little girlfriends should assist him in widdling (i.e. that she should share the spectacle). He repeatedly expressed to both his parents his regret at never having seen their widdlers (probably motivated by his need to make a comparison). Hans had observed that large animals had widdlers that were proportionately larger than his, so he suspected that the same was true of his parents and was anxious to check this out. He thought his mother must have a widdler 'like a horse' and that his would grow with him: his wish to be bigger seemed to become focused on his genitals.

The only other erotogenic (erogenous) zones that afforded him similar pleasure were those associated with excretion. However, during the time that he was troubled by his phobia of horses (see below), these two aspects of his sexuality were repressed.

His Oedipal wish (see **Hypothesis** above) had originated during one summer holiday, when his father was sometimes away, leaving Hans to enjoy the intimacy with his mother that he longed for. At that time, he wished that his father would 'go away'. But later, after they had returned to Vienna and his father was around much more, he wished that his father were *permanently* away, that he were 'dead'. The fear induced by this death wish against his father formed the main obstacle to the psychoanalysis.

The most important influence on the course of Hans's psychosexual development was the birth of a baby sister when he was three and a half years old. He had been told that 'the stork' would be bringing a little girl or boy. His father tells how, after Hanna was born:

He was then called into the bedroom. He did not look at his mother, however, but at the basins ... filled with blood and water, that were still standing about the room. Pointing to a blood-stained bedpan, he observed in a surprised voice, 'But blood doesn't come out of my widdler'. Everything he says shows that he connects what is strange in the situation with the arrival of the stork ... Hans is very jealous of the new arrival, and whenever anyone praises her ... he at once declares scornfully: 'But she's not got any teeth yet'. During the first few days, he was naturally put very much in the background. He was suddenly taken ill with a sore throat. In his fever he was heard saying: 'But I don't want a baby sister!'

He became consciously afraid that yet another baby might arrive. His hostility towards Hanna manifested itself as a fear of the bath:

I: *[his father] asked him whether he was afraid and if so, of what.*

Hans: *Because of falling in.*

I: *When you went in a boat at Gmunden [holiday resort], weren't you afraid of falling into the water?*

Hans: *No, because I held on... It's only in the big bath that I'm afraid of falling in.*

I: *But Mummy baths you in it. Are you afraid of Mummy dropping you in the water?*

Hans: *I'm afraid of her letting go and my head going in.*

I: *But you know Mummy's fond of you and won't let go of you.*

Hans: *I only just thought it.*

I: *Why?*

Hans: *I don't know at all.*

I: *Perhaps it was because you'd been naughty and thought she didn't love you any more?*

Hans: *Yes.*

I: *When you were watching Mummy giving Hanna her bath, perhaps you wished she would let go of her so that Hanna should fall in?*

Hans: *Yes.*

During the analysis, he gave undisguised expression to his death wish against Hanna; but he did not consider this as wicked as the one against his father, even though they both took his mummy away from him.

Part 2

One day, while Hans was in the street, he had an anxiety attack. He did not know what he was afraid of, but he revealed to his father that it was a way he could stay

AIM AND NATURE

close to his mother and 'coax' (cuddle) with her. However, he was still anxious even when she was with him. He then expressed the quite specific fear that he would be bitten by a white horse.

In fact, the anxiety attack was not as sudden as it first appeared; a few days earlier, Hans had had an anxiety dream in which his mother had gone away, so that he had no mother to coax with. But the origins of his fear went even further back. During the preceding summer, he had had periods of mixed longing and apprehension, which had gained him the advantage of being taken into his mother's bed. This appeared to intensify his sexual excitement for his mother, and this was demonstrated by his two attempts at 'seducing' her (the second of which occurred just before the outbreak of his anxiety, when he encouraged her to touch his penis after his bath).

Hans suggested an explanation of his fear of being bitten by a horse. While at Gmunden, a father seeing his daughter off on her journey home warned her not to 'put your finger to the white horse or it'll bite you'. The phrase 'don't put your finger to' was similar to the words used to warn him against masturbating.

Because it appeared that Hans's repressed wish might be to see his mother's widdler at all costs, his father enlightened him by telling him that women do not have one. Hans's reaction was to produce a fantasy that he had seen his mother showing her widdler; he also maintained that his widdler was 'fixed in, of course'. These two things suggested that his mother's threat of castration (some 15 months earlier) was now having a delayed effect on him: the fantasy was a protective or defensive one.

Having partly mastered his castration complex, Hans was now able to communicate his wishes regarding his mother. He did this, still in a distorted way, by means of the fantasy of the two giraffes:

Hans: *In the night there was a big giraffe in the room and a crumpled one, and the big one called out because I took the crumpled one away from it. Then it stopped calling out, and then I sat down on top of the crumpled one.*

I: *[father] (puzzled): What? A crumpled giraffe? How was that?*

Hans: *Yes. (He quickly fetched a piece of paper, crumpled it up and said:) It was crumpled like that.*

I: *And you sat down on top of the crumpled giraffe? (He again showed me by sitting down on the ground.) … Why did you come into our room?*

Hans: *I don't know myself.*

I: *Were you afraid?*

Hans: *No, of course not.*

I: *Did you dream about the giraffe?*

Hans: *No, I didn't dream. I thought it all. I'd woken up earlier.*

I: *What can it mean: a crumpled giraffe? You know you can't squash a giraffe together like a piece of paper.*

Hans: *Of course I know. I just thought it; of course there aren't any really and truly. The crumpled one was all lying on the floor, and I took it away – took hold of it with my hands.*

I: *What? Can you take hold of a big giraffe like that with your hands? … What did you do with the crumpled one?*

Hans: *I held it in my hand for a bit, till the big one had stopped calling out. And when the big one had stopped calling out, I sat down on top of it.*

I: *Why did the big one call out?*

Hans: *Because I'd taken away the little one from it.*

His father recognized the fantasy as a reproduction of the bedroom scene which used to take place every morning between Hans and his parents. His mother and father were the two giraffes.

Freud now put to Hans that he was afraid of his father because he had jealous and hostile feelings towards him. In doing so, he had partly interpreted Hans's fear of horses for him: the horse must be his father, which interpretation was supported by the fact that the black on horses' mouths and the things in front of their eyes [blinkers] match a grown-up man's moustache and eye glasses.

This seemed to act as a release for Hans, who volunteered a great deal of information about his phobias. He was not only afraid of being bitten by horses, but also of carts, furniture vans and buses (all horse-drawn at that time), all heavily loaded, of horses that started moving and that looked big and heavy, and of those that were driven quickly. Hans himself explained the meaning of all these examples: he was afraid of horses *falling down*.

What had triggered his first anxiety attack was going for a walk with his mother and seeing a bus horse fall down and kick about with its feet. This terrified him and he thought the horse was dead. From that time, he thought all horses would fall down. His father suggested that when he saw the horse fall down, he must have thought of him – his father – and wished that he might fall down in the same way and be dead. Hans did not dispute this interpretation, and a little later played a game that involved biting his father; this demonstrated his acceptance that he had identified his father with the horse he was afraid of.

EVALUATION

Theoretical issues

One of the most serious problems faced by much of Freud's theory in general, and the case of Little Hans in particular, is that of *alternative explanations*. Among those who offer alternative interpretations to Freud's 'little Oedipus' account are two eminent psychoanalysts, Erich Fromm and John Bowlby.

1   According to Fromm (1970), Freud wanted to find support for the theory of sexuality based on adults by directly reviewing material drawn from a child. Freud paints a very positive picture of Hans's parents, who were:

both among my closest adherents, and they had agreed that, in bringing up their first child, they would use no more coercion than might be absolutely necessary for maintaining good behaviour. And, as the child developed into a cheerful, good natured and lively little boy, the experiment of letting him grow up and express himself without being intimidated went on satisfactorily.

He adds:

Considering the education given by his parents, which consisted essentially in the omission of our usual educational sins, [undoubtedly they] were determined from the very beginning that he was neither to be laughed at nor bullied.

But what about his mother's threat of castration (far stronger than 'very slight allusions', as Freud describes them), her threats not to come back, and the lies they told (such as those about the stork, and not telling Hans that women do not have a penis)? Fromm believes that Freud had a 'blind spot': he was a liberal, rather than a radical critic of bourgeois society, criticizing the severity of educational methods, but not condemning the principles of force and threat. Consistent with this non-radical attitude, his original claim that his adult patients were the victims of child sexual abuse (the 'seduction theory') was replaced by the Oedipus complex account: by emphasizing the child's incestuous desires, he was able to defend the parents against such claims.

But wasn't Hans's mother guilty of actively seducing him? She liked to have him in bed with her, and to take him with her to the bathroom. Hans actually wanted to sleep with Maried (their landlord's 13-year-old daughter). (See **Applications and implications** below.)

Freud's extreme patriarchal attitude prevented him from believing it possible for a woman to be the main cause of fear. But Fromm maintains that 'clinical observation amply proves that the most intense and pathogenic fears are indeed related to the mother; by comparison, the dread of the father is relatively insignificant'. It seems that Hans needed his father to protect him from a menacing mother. Fromm believes that the fear of horses was the result of:

- fear of the mother (due to her castration threat);

- fear of death (he had witnessed a funeral at Gmunden, then the fallen horse which he thought was dead).

To avoid both fears, he developed a fear of being bitten; this protected him from horses and from experiencing both types of anxiety.

Fromm suggests that Hans's hostility was aimed at his *mother* (based on her castration threat, her 'treason' at giving birth to Hanna, and his desire to be free from fixation on her), rather than his father (as the Oedipus theory claims). Therapy succeeded not so much because of the interpretations made of Hans's fear, but as a result of the father's protective role and that of the 'super father' (Freud). There was great warmth and friendship in Hans's relationship with his father. Fromm concludes that 'this was a slight phobia, such as occurs in many children, and it would probably have disappeared by itself without any treatment, and without the father's support and interest'.

2 Bowlby (1973) reinterprets Hans's fear in terms of attachment theory: did his anxiety about the availability of attachment figures play a larger part than Freud realized? Agreeing with Fromm, Bowlby argues that most of Hans's anxiety arose from his mother's threats to desert the family. The main evidence for this claim comes from:

- the sequence in which the symptoms developed and statements made by Hans himself;

- evidence in the father's account that the mother was in the habit of using threats of an alarming kind to discipline Hans – including the threat to abandon him.

The symptoms did not come out of the blue; Hans had been upset throughout the preceding week. He woke up one morning in tears. Asked why he was crying, he told his mother: 'When I was asleep I thought you were gone, and I had no Mummy to coax with'.

Some days later, his nursemaid had taken him to a local park, as usual. Hans started crying in the street and asked to be taken home, so he could coax with his mother. During that evening, he became very frightened and cried, demanding to stay with his mother. But this was not the first time he had expressed the fear that his mother might disappear; on a previous occasion, six months earlier, he had said: 'Suppose I was to have no Mummy. Suppose you were to go away'.

When Hanna was born, Hans was kept away from his mother. His father interpreted Hans's anxiety about leaving the house as 'in reality the longing for [his mother] which he felt then'. Freud endorsed this by describing Hans's 'enormously intensified affect' for his mother as 'the fundamental phenomenon in his condition'.

Clearly, distinct from and preceding any fear of horses, Hans was afraid that his mother might go away and leave him (Bowlby, 1973). As we have seen, she threatened to cut off his widdler; a year later, when the phobia was first reported, she 'warned him' not to touch his penis. Three months later, Hans came into his father's bed one morning and told him:

Hans: *When you're away, I'm afraid you're not coming home.*

Father: *And have I ever threatened you that I shan't come home?*

Hans: *Not you, but Mummy. Mummy's told me she won't come back.*

Father: *She said that because you were naughty.*

Hans: *Yes.*

Even the fear of being bitten by a horse is consistent with Bowlby's interpretation: it was closely linked in Hans's mind to someone leaving after hearing his father at Gmunden warn his daughter not to put her finger near the white horse (see above).

Table 23.1 summarizes the different interpretations of Freud and Bowlby.

Table 23.1

Differences of interpretation between Freud and Bowlby

Item	Freud	Bowlby
Hans's insistent desire to remain with his mother	Expression of sexual love for mother, having reached extreme 'pitch of intensity'	Anxious attachment ('separation anxiety')
Dreams that she had gone away and left him	Expression of fear of punishment for incestuous wishes	Expression of fear that she would carry out threat to desert family
White horse will bite	Fear of castration as punishment for wanting father 'out of the way' (i.e. dead)	Fear of mother's desertion
Mother's displays of affection and allowing him to come into her bed	Action which might have encouraged Hans's Oedipal wishes	Natural and comforting expression of motherly feelings

Gay (1988) refers to an article by Slap, an American psychoanalyst, entitled *Little Hans' Tonsillectomy* (1961). In it, he describes how, in February 1908, in the second month of the neurosis, Hans had his tonsils out. The phobias worsened and, shortly afterwards, he explicitly identified *white* horses as biting horses. Based on this and related evidence, Slap proposed that Hans probably added his fear of the surgeon (white mask and coat) to his fear of the moustached father.

This additional fear is most easily explained in terms of the acquisition of a conditioned fear response through classical conditioning (see the case of Little Albert: Chapter 23). Eysenck (1985), probably Freud's most outspoken critic (see Chapter 30), wanted to *replace* Freud's account with one based on classical conditioning. He cites Wolpe and Rachman's (1960) evaluation of Little Hans, in which they claim that the incident which Freud describes as merely the 'exciting cause' (i.e. trigger) of Hans's phobia was really the cause of the *entire* disorder, namely the moment when the horse collapsed in the street. In Hans's own words: 'I only got it [the phobia] then. When the horse and the bus fell down, it gave me such a fright, really! That was when I got the nonsense [phobia].' This was confirmed by Hans's mother. His initial fear response generalized to all horses, horse-drawn buses, and so on.

Ironically, these (apparently conflicting) explanations can be accommodated within the psychoanalytic account of phobias. According to Freud, phobias (child or adult) typically represent the conscious manifestation of *several* unconscious (latent) sources of anxiety, which become focused on/compressed into the single (manifest) phobic object or situation (through *condensation, transformation* and other unconscious processes: Ward, 2001). As Ward says, what Freud saw in Hans was a little boy full of many fears, albeit castration anxiety was the predominant one. (See **Exercises**.)

Methodological issues

Freud was aware of the methodological objections which could be raised to the fact that Hans was being analysed by his father (Max Graf, an eminent music critic and an early member of the psychoanalytic society). His wife (Hans's mother) had been treated by Freud before her marriage to Hans's father. How could the father be objective in his observations and psychoanalysis of someone with whom he was so emotionally involved? Also, Hans must have been susceptible to his father's suggestions. Doesn't this immediately invalidate the case study as an *independent* test of Freud's Oedipal theory?

Freud seemed to agree with this criticism, saying that Hans's father did have to put into words things Hans could not say himself. However, although this 'detracts from the evidential value of the analysis', the 'procedure is the same in every case' (i.e. with adult patients too): 'For a psychoanalysis is not an impartial scientific investigation, but a therapeutic measure. Its essence is not to prove anything but merely to alter something'.

While this may meet the immediate criticism outlined above, doesn't it at the same time condemn the whole of Freud's work to the realm of 'non-science'? (The foundation on which all his theories are constructed is his analysis of neurotic patients.) Isn't the consulting room his laboratory, his patients the participants, and what they say about themselves (especially their childhood) the data?

The answer is provided by Storr (1987), a popularizer of psychoanalytic theory and himself a trained psychoanalyst. Storr claims that, although a minority of Freudian hypotheses can be tested scientifically (they are refutable), most are based on observations made in the course of treatment, which cannot be regarded as a scientific procedure (see Freud's quote above). Such observations are inevitably contaminated by the subjective experience and prejudice of the observer (however detached s/he tries to be), and so cannot be regarded in the same light as observations made during a chemistry or physics experiment. While experimental psychology studies human beings as if they were objects responding to the stimuli impinging on them, psychoanalysis (or any form of psychotherapy) *cannot* be conducted in this way.

But if people are not mere objects responding to external stimuli, then it is both unethical and inaccurate (i.e. unscientific) to study them as if they were. Perhaps Freud comes closer to treating people as they 'really' are – and so is *more* of a scientist than most experimental psychologists! However, even if the case of Little Hans, like all psychoanalytic treatments, cannot be thought of as 'an impartial scientific investigation', it still has some rather distinctive features:

1   It was conducted not by the therapist author (Freud), but by a second party (the father), who acted as an intermediary between Freud and the patient (Hans); Freud actually met Hans twice, once for a 'therapeutic session', and once to take him a birthday present (Gay, 1988).

2   Very little was said in the case study about technique (*how* the psychoanalysis was conducted).

However, it demonstrated what all psychoanalytic therapy has in common, namely the 'excavation' of childhood foundations of adult neurosis (Gay, 1988). But because of Hans's age, compared with adult therapy, there was relatively little 'digging' that needed to be done. It also shared another feature of Freud's reports of his therapeutic work: 'Freud's case histories read like individual stories, but he used them to put forward more general hypotheses, in his wish to be regarded as a serious scientist' (Jacobs, 1992).

This relates to the *idiographic-nomothetic* debate in psychology, which, in turn, is part of the more general debate about the nature of science. (See **Exercises**.)

Applications and implications

As we noted above, Freud's Oedipal theory (1905) replaced the earlier (1896) 'seduction theory' (or, more accurately, the sexual abuse theory of hysteria; Mollon, 1998). While the earlier theory claimed that adult neurotics were victims of actual incest and other sexual abuse suffered in childhood, the later one argued that what patients believed were memories of abuse, were, in fact, merely *fantasies*.

Freud has been condemned in recent years for this retraction of his original theory, which recognized abuse as real. Alice Miller (1986), for example, holds the Oedipal theory partly responsible for society's reluctance to acknowledge the extent of incest and sexual abuse in general. According to Masson (1992), 'fantasy – the notion from Freud that women invent allegations of sexual abuse because they desire sex – continues to play a role in undermining the credibility of victims of sexual abuse'.

However, Freud did not totally abandon the seduction theory and recognized the reality of abuse at various points in his career (Jacobs, 1992; Mollon, 1998).

More seriously, according to Esterson (1998, 2001), Israels and Schatzman (1993) and others, Masson's account of the seduction theory (which first appeared in *Assault on Truth*, 1984) is *mistaken*, based on a fundamental misconception. In Freud's theory, the fantasies are *unconscious* and so must be analytically uncovered by the therapist: reports of child sexual abuse (CSA) that the patient had always remembered *do not fall into this category*. The cornerstone of Masson's attack on Freud's abandonment of the 'truth' (that most of his female patients told him they had been sexually abused in early childhood, usually by their fathers) is contradicted by contemporary documentary evidence (Esterson, 1998, 2001).

Freud is regarded by many as responsible for so-called *false memory syndrome* (FMS). In 1993, false memory *societies* were established, both in the UK and the USA, providing support for people (typically parents) who believed they had been falsely accused of sexually abusing their now adult children. The latter typically 'recovered' memories of CSA during the course of psychotherapy, and therapists were accused by the parents of having 'implanted' these (false) memories into their vulnerable patients.

However, according to Mollon (1998), the Freud condemned (especially) by US critics such as Crews (1997) is a Hollywood caricature. Freud stressed the unreliability and reconstructive nature of memory (see Chapter 6), and 'to assume that psychoanalysts search for buried memories, analogous to lost video-recordings, is to misunderstand profoundly the analytic endeavour'.

Finally, there is a fascinating postscript to the case study (Freud 1922), which tends to support various aspects of both Fromm's and Bowlby's interpretations. (See **Theoretical issues** above.) He lost touch with Hans after 1911. Critics of Freud at the time predicted that Hans would suffer as a result of 'losing his innocence' and being made the victim of psychoanalysis. However:

> *Little Hans was now a strapping youth of 19. He declared that he was perfectly well and suffered from no troubles or inhibitions. Not only had he come through his puberty without any damage, but his emotional life had successfully undergone one of the severest of ordeals. His parents had been divorced, and each… had married again … he lived by himself, but he was on good terms with both of his parents.*

His only regret was that he had been separated from Hanna. When the parents first separated, he had gone with his father. He remembered nothing of his analysis or that period of his life. Little Hans became Herbert Graf, a well-known producer and director of operas.

EXERCISES

1 Ward (2001) refers to *condensation* and *transformation* as unconscious processes by which various different unconscious sources of anxiety become focused on/compressed into a single phobic object/situation.

   (a) What do you understand by these terms?

   (b) What were the different fears that, in Hans's case, were all brought together in the single fear of being bitten by a horse?

2 Briefly explain the difference between *idiographic* and *homothetic* theories (of personality). Give *two* examples of each.

3 Why is the case study considered to be the least scientific of all empirical methods used by psychologists?

4 Apart from your answers to (3), is there anything about the case of Little Hans which makes it 'less scientific' that it might otherwise have been?

5 Is it possible – or necessary – to choose between Freud's, Fromm's and Bowlby's interpretations? Can they all be (partially) true?

23 Conditioned emotional reactions

Watson, J.B. and Rayner, R. (1920)

Journal of Experimental Psychology, *3*(1): 1–14

BACKGROUND AND CONTEXT

John Broadus Watson was the American founder of *behaviourism* (1913), the school of thought which claims that behaviour – the overt, observable and measurable aspects of human activity – is the only appropriate subject matter for the scientific discipline of psychology. Watson was reacting against the attempts of the early psychologists, such as Wilhelm Wundt in Germany, to study the conscious human mind through *introspection* (inspection of one's own mind) in order to establish general laws of human thought. Watson saw this as a futile pursuit, since only the individual has access to his/her mind: no one else can inspect it in order to check the accuracy of what the introspections 'reveal'. The mind is 'private', while behaviour is 'public' (accessible to other observers), and this is a basic requirement of science.

If behaviour is a valid subject for psychology, we must have some way of defining and analysing it: Watson found the key in the concept of the *conditioned reflex* (or conditioned response). All behaviour can be broken down into a number of such conditioned responses: however complex it may appear, it is always composed of these simple units, all of which, in turn, are based on three inborn human emotions, namely rage, fear and love (sex).

The conditioned reflex had been discovered in the first few years of the twentieth century by Ivan Pavlov, the Russian physiologist, in the course of his investigation of the digestive system of dogs. Through associating a stimulus (unconditioned stimulus/UCS) which naturally produces a particular response (unconditioned response/UCR) with a neutral stimulus which does not (this is the conditioned stimulus/CS), the latter eventually comes to produce the response on its own: when it does, it is called a conditioned response/CR (it is now produced by a conditioned stimulus).

Watson was the first psychologist to apply this process of classical (or respondent or Pavlovian) conditioning to human behaviour, with 11-month-old Albert B. (better known as 'Little Albert'), destined to become one of the most famous children in the whole of the psychological literature (along with Little Hans: see Chapter 22). The study was to become part of social science folklore, and clinched Watson's fame as the father of behaviourism (Simpson, 2000).

AIM AND NATURE

There was no hypothesis as such: the aim of the study was to provide an empirical demonstration of the claim that various kinds of emotional response could be conditioned (conditioned emotional responses/CERs); specifically, fear. Four separate but related questions were asked:

1   Could they condition fear of an animal (e.g. a white rat) by visually presenting it and simultaneously striking a steel bar?

2   If such a CER could be established, would this transfer to other animals or other objects?

3   What is the effect of time on such CERs?

4   If, after a reasonable period, such CERs have not died out, what laboratory methods could be devised to remove them?

● METHOD/DESIGN

The method used was a laboratory experiment involving a single participant, Albert B. His mother was a wet nurse in the hospital (Harriet Lane Home for Invalid Children) where Watson and Rayner happened to be working. This made Little Albert a convenient participant; far from being an invalid, he was strong, healthy and not easily upset ('stolid'), which made him especially suitable.

The study also represents a *diary study*, the detailed record of the behaviour of one child over a period of approximately six weeks (though not on each day during that period). But unlike the diary studies of Darwin and, to some extent, Piaget, the focus was on very specific behaviour, namely Little Albert's fear response to particular animals and objects.

When he was approximately nine months old, Watson and Rayner tested him to see what stimuli induced fear reactions. He was confronted suddenly with a white rat, a rabbit, a dog, a monkey, masks with and without hair, cotton wool and burning newspapers. At no time did he display fear in response to any of these stimuli. His mother and hospital staff confirmed that little, if anything, frightened him, and he hardly ever cried.

However, while Rayner got Little Albert to fixate her moving hand, Watson came behind him and struck a hammer on a suspended steel bar (four feet long and ½ inch in diameter). This startled Albert violently, and when the hammer was struck a second time, his lips began to pucker and tremble; a third hammer blow caused a sudden crying fit.

This sound stimulus provided Watson and Rayner with the means of trying to answer the four questions above. The attempts did not begin until Albert was 11 months and three days old, when he was tested again with all the stimuli to see if these produced any fear response; as before, only the sound of the hammer on the steel bar did so.

Throughout the period of testing, Albert's building blocks were given to quieten him and to test his general emotional state. They were always removed from sight before the conditioning process began.

● RESULTS

Establishing a CER to a white rat

11 months, 3 days

- White rat suddenly taken from the basket and presented to Albert. He began to reach for it with his left hand. Just as his hand touched the rat, the bar was struck right behind his head. He jumped violently and fell forward, burying his face in the mattress. But he did not cry.

- Just as his right hand touched the rat, the bar was struck again. Again Albert jumped violently, fell forward and began to whimper. No further tests were carried out for a week.

11 months, 10 days

- Rat presented suddenly without the sound. There was steady fixation but no tendency at first to reach for it. When it was then placed nearer, Albert began to reach, tentatively, with his right hand. When rat nosed his left hand, he immediately withdrew it. He started to reach for rat's head with forefinger of left hand, but withdrew it suddenly before contact. So, the two joint presentations (rat + hammer on steel bar) given the previous week had some effect. When presented with his building blocks, he started playing with them immediately.

- Three successive joint presentations (rat + hammer on steel bar) failed to produce crying, but when rat was suddenly presented on its own, Albert's face puckered, he whimpered and withdrew his body sharply to the left.

AIM AND NATURE

- Joint presentation: Albert fell over immediately to right side and began to whimper.

- Another joint presentation: started violently and cried (but did not fall over).

- Rat alone: *The instant the rat was shown, the baby began to cry. Almost instantly he turned sharply to the left, fell over on left side, raised himself on all fours and began to crawl away so rapidly that he was caught with difficulty before reaching the edge of the table.*

In all, seven joint presentations were given to produce the complete CER.

Would the CER transfer to other stimuli?

11 months, 15 days

- When presented with his blocks, Albert reached for them and played as usual.

- Rat alone: whimpered immediately, withdrew right hand, turned head and trunk away.

- Blocks again: smiled and gurgled as he played with them.

- Rat alone: leaned over to left side as far away from rat as possible, then fell over, got up on all fours and scurried away as quickly as possible.

- Blocks again: reacted as before.

  This showed that the CER had carried over completely for the five days since the last testing.

- Rabbit alone: it was suddenly placed in front of him on the mattress. He leaned as far away from it as possible, whimpered, then burst into tears. When it was placed in contact with him, he buried his face in the mattress, then got up on all fours and crawled away, crying as he went.

- Blocks alone: played with them even more energetically than usual.

- Dog alone: he immediately shrank back; as it approached, he tried to get on all fours, but did not cry at first. As soon as the dog moved out of his range of vision, he quietened down. The dog was then made to approach Albert's head (he was lying down now): he straightened up immediately, fell over to the opposite side and turned his head away. He then began to cry.

- Blocks alone: began to play immediately.

- Fur coat (seal) alone: withdrew immediately to left side and began to fret. When it was placed close to his left side, he began to cry and tried to crawl away on all fours.

- Cotton wool alone: concealed in paper package, but then became exposed. When placed on his feet, he kicked it away but did not touch it with his hands. When his hand was placed on it, he immediately withdrew it, but did not show the shock produced by the animals or fur coat. After playing with the paper, the negative reaction to the cotton wool began to weaken.

- Just in play, Watson put his head down to see if Albert would play with his hair. His reaction was completely negative. But he played quite happily with the hair of two observers. However, he reacted very negatively to a Santa Claus mask.

11 months, 20 days

- Blocks alone: played with them as usual.

- Rat alone: withdrew whole body, but no crying. Fixated it and followed it with his eyes. The response was much weaker than the previous week. It was decided to freshen it up with another joint presentation (rat + hammer).

- Rat alone: CER now strong again – but no crying.

- Rat alone: fell over to left side, got up on all fours and started to crawl away. No crying, and as he moved away, he began to gurgle and coo, even while trying to avoid the rat.

- Rabbit alone: leaned to the left as far as possible. Began to whimper, but reaction not as violent as previously.

- Blocks alone; began to play immediately.

So far, all the tests had been performed on a table with a mattress in a small, dark room. What would happen if the situation were markedly changed? Before testing this, Watson and Rayner freshened up the CER to both the rabbit and the dog by pairing each with the hammer on the steel bar (which had not been done before).

Once this had been achieved (although Albert still showed some conflicting tendency to fear the rabbit while trying to stroke it), Albert was taken into a large, well-lit lecture room. He was placed on a table in the middle of the room. He was tested with the rat alone (four times, with a rat + hammer pairing in between), the rabbit alone (twice), the dog alone (twice), and the blocks alone (twice). The CER still transferred to these other animals.

How persistent was the CER?

It had already been shown that the CER would continue for a week, but because of Albert's imminent departure from the hospital, it was not possible to make the interval longer than one month. During this time, he was taken to the laboratory weekly.

12 months, 21 days

- Santa Claus mask: withdrawal. Gurgling, then slapped at it without touching. When his hand was forced to touch it, he whimpered and cried. This happened on two further occasions. Eventually, he cried at the mere sight of the mask.

- Fur coat: wrinkled his nose and withdrew both hands, then began to whimper as the coat was brought nearer. Tentatively reached for it, but drew back before making contact. Touched it accidentally and started to cry immediately. When it was removed from sight and re-presented a minute later, he immediately began to fret.

- Blocks: began to play with them as usual.

- Rat: allowed it to crawl towards him without withdrawing. He sat very still and fixated it intently. When it touched his hand, he withdrew it immediately and leaned back as far as possible, but did not cry. When it was placed on his arm, he withdrew his body and began to fret. But he then allowed it to crawl against his chest, first fretting, then covering his eyes with both hands.

- Blocks: usual reaction.

- Rabbit: when placed directly in front of him, he showed no avoidance at first. But after a few seconds, his face puckered and he pushed the rabbit away with his feet. As it came nearer, he began pulling his feet away, nodding and wailing 'da da'. After about a minute, he reached out tentatively and touched rabbit's ear with right hand, then stroked it. Started to fret again and withdrew hands. When his hand was placed on the rabbit, he immediately withdrew his hand and began to suck thumb. When it was placed in his lap, he began to cry, covering his face with both hands.

- Dog: Albert fixated it intently, sitting very still. He began to cry, but did not fall over backwards as on last contact. When this very active dog came closer, he first sat motionless, then began to cry, covering his face with both hands.

How could CERs be experimentally removed?

Unfortunately, Albert was removed from the hospital the day these last tests were performed. If they had had the opportunity, Watson and Rayner say they would have tried several methods:

- constantly confronting the child with those stimuli which produced the responses, in the hope that habituation would occur corresponding to 'fatigue' of reflex;

- trying to 'recondition' by showing objects producing CERS (visual), while simultaneously stimulating the erogenous zones (tactual), first the lips, then the nipples, and, as a last resort, the sex organs;

- trying to 'recondition' by giving him candy or other food just as the animal is shown;

- building up 'constructive' activities around the object by imitation and making his hand stroke the animal.

● CONCLUSIONS

Seven joint presentations of the rat and hammer on steel bar produced as complete a conditioned fear response as was theoretically possible. It transferred spontaneously to a rabbit, a dog, a fur coat, cotton wool, a Santa Claus mask and Watson's hair; there was no transfer to his building blocks or the hair of two observers.

The CER continued intact for a week after conditioning, then persisted for another four weeks, but with a certain loss of intensity. This may have been because Albert was such an extremely phlegmatic child.

While Freud saw sex (what Watson and Rayner call 'love') as the principal emotion involved in CERs, they regard fear as primary. Many phobias are probably true CERs either of the direct or transferred type.

EVALUATION

Theoretical issues

Watson believed that the child's unconditioned responses (fear, rage and love) to simple stimuli are only the starting points in 'building up those complicated habit patterns we later call our emotions' (Watson, 1931). For example, the emotion of jealousy is not innate or inevitable, but rather 'a bit of behaviour whose stimulus is a [conditioned] love stimulus, the response to which is rage' (e.g. stiffening the whole body, reddening of face, pronounced breathing, verbal recrimination and possibly shouting). This is a good illustration of the *reductionist* nature of Watson's behaviourism (and of behaviourism in general): complex human emotions are broken down into (reduced to) simple CERs – a whole broken down into its constituent parts (see Gross, 2005).

Along with this reductionist account of emotional development, Watson was proposing a *quantitative* view of development: as the child grows up, its behaviour becomes increasingly complex, but it is basically the *same* kind of behaviour as it was earlier (i.e. a series of CERs that become added and re-combined). The same basic principles are involved at all ages (those of classical conditioning). By contrast, a *qualitative* view (such as that of Freud or Piaget) sees development as passing through a series of distinct stages, with different *kinds* of behaviour involved at each stage.

The case of Little Albert seems to support the general belief that (even) babies are not indifferent to their experience, and that nasty experiences, especially, may have peculiar after-effects (Walker, 1984). Here, Watson and Freud seem to be in agreement. However:

> In my view, it would be foolish to claim that experiences as extreme as those suffered by Albert are not likely to have some carry-over effects in infants, but even more ridiculous to assume that conditioning is a sufficient explanation for all adult emotions (Walker, 1984).

Methodological issues

Little Albert is often cited as an example of 'classic research', being reported in every textbook of psychology from generation to generation. But ironically (according to Cornwell and Hobbs, 1976), this 'classic' reputation has resulted in the details of the experiment being obscured, making psychologists less (rather than more) cautious, producing a false impression of familiarity with the details and a 'painting out of the warts'.

In 'The strange saga of Little Albert', Cornwell and Hobbs argue that the experiment is a classic example of how a piece of research can become *misreported/misrepresented* until it assumes 'mythical proportions'. In 1917, Watson was awarded a grant to carry out research into the development of reflexes and instincts in infants. As we have seen, he believed that there is a limited number of inborn emotional reactions which are the starting point for building the complex emotions of adulthood (through the process of conditioning). He began his experiments with Albert in 1919, attempting to show how conditioned emotional responses (CERs) come about and how they can be removed; the results were published in 1920.

Watson and Rayner stressed the limited nature of their evidence. They may have planned to study other children, but were unable to continue their research at the Johns Hopkins University (Baltimore). In 1920, in a sensationally publicized case, Watson was divorced by his wife and immediately married Rosalie Rayner. He was forced to resign from his academic post.

In 1921, Watson and Rosalie Rayner Watson published a second account of Little Albert (in *Scientific Monthly*). In it, they stated that Albert *did* show fear in response to a 'loss of support' (being held and then let go) – the opposite of what they claim in the 1920 article. Also, Watson subsequently referred to this 1921 paper as the original, although the 1920 article is the one that is usually cited. A third account was given in some lectures by Watson which were eventually incorporated into his book *Behaviourism* (1924). It is also recounted in other books and articles. Each of these accounts is referred to, at least once, as 'the original'.

In a survey of 76 'general psychology' books at Glasgow University, Cornwell and Hobbs found at least one distortion in 60 per cent of the 30 different reports of the experiment. They ask if all the mistakes are just the result of carelessness. There is no doubt that several accounts seemed to put the experiment in a more favourable light, both methodologically and ethically. For example:

- The implication is made that Albert was one of a number of studies of infants.

- On the assumption that a child will instinctively show a fear of rats, the rat is often reported as a 'rabbit', making Albert's initial *lack* of fear seem more plausible, and his conditioned fear more striking.

- Many accounts claim that Albert's conditioned fear was removed before he left the hospital; indeed, Watson and Rayner knew a month in advance that he would be leaving. Eysenck (1976), for example, gives details of a fictitious extinction involving pieces of chocolate! (See **Exercises**.)

This last 'myth' raises two major questions:

1   Did Watson and Rayner really intend to remove the CER as they say they did? (And even if they did, does this let them off the hook ethically?)

2   How might they have done it? (See **Applications and implications** below.)

Subsequent research

Not long after the Little Albert experiment, Watson supervised the treatment of Little Peter, a two-year-old living in a charitable institution, who had an extreme fear of rabbits, rats, fur coats, feathers, cotton wool, and so on. He showed no fear of wooden blocks and similar toys. The treatment was carried out by Mary Cover Jones (1924), who describes the case of Peter as a sequel to that of Little Albert ('Albert grown a bit older').

While the case of Albert showed how a fear could be *produced* experimentally under laboratory conditions through classical conditioning, Jones used the method of direct *unconditioning* in an attempt to *remove* Peter's naturally occurring phobias.

In unconditioning, the feared stimulus is paired with something pleasurable, and exposure to it is gradually increased. The rabbit was put in a wire cage in front of Peter while he ate his lunch in his high chair. At first, the caged rabbit anywhere in the room was sufficient to induce a fear response; the cage was gradually moved closer and Peter tolerated this (steps 1–4). By step 6, he could tolerate the rabbit being out of its cage, and by step 13 he could hold it on his lap. He then stayed alone in the room with the rabbit (14), allowed it in the play pen with him (15), fondled it affectionately (16), and, finally, let the rabbit nibble his fingers (17).

This is generally regarded as the first reported use of (what is now known as) *systematic desensitization* (the term first used by Wolpe in 1958), a commonly used method for the removal of phobias. (See **Applications and implications** below.)

Applications and implications

As noted above, two unanswered questions concern Watson and Rayner's intention to remove Albert's CER, and the method(s) they might have used to do so.

1   At the beginning of their article, they state that 'a certain responsibility attaches to such a procedure' (i.e. experimentally inducing a CER), and that they were very hesitant about doing so. They eventually decided to go ahead, since 'responsibilities would arise anyway as soon as the child left the sheltered environment of the nursery for the rough and tumble of the home'.

When they say 'responsibility' they seem to mean 'risk', thus giving a false impression of having grappled long and hard with the ethical issues involved. But what sort of justification is it to maintain that Albert would have acquired the CERs anyway? How likely is he to have encountered a rat, and is he likely at all to have encountered any of the other stimuli while his ears were being assaulted by the sound of a full-grown man striking a hammer on a large steel bar right behind his head?

The fact that he was stolid and unemotional, and the belief that the experiment could do him no harm, cannot be used in their defence either: some stimulus was needed which would frighten him, otherwise the experiment could not proceed, so Watson and Rayner knowingly decided to cause him distress. The ethics of Watson and Rayner's techniques seemed to draw little open criticism at the time – either from the university administration or from other psychologists. According to Hulse (in Simpson, 2000): 'Times were just different, people were trusted to behave themselves... It's only been in the last 20 to 30 years that issues of ethics in science have become profoundly part of the consciousness of scientists'.

2   Watson and Rayner state that that they would have attempted several methods to try removing the CER ('had the opportunity existed'). (See above.) The first, constantly confronting Albert with the feared stimulus, sounds like *flooding*, a form of *forced reality-testing*. Methods (2) and (3) sound like *systematic desensitization*, in which the fear is gradually extinguished by exposing the patient to increasingly frightening forms of the feared stimulus in combination with a pleasurable stimulus or activity (or, more commonly today, with deep muscle relaxation: see Chapter 30). Method (4) sounds like *modelling* (e.g. Bandura), in which the patient observes another person (the model), who interacts with the feared object but shows no fear (see Chapter 24).

According to Jones (1924), they *did* intend to uncondition Albert's fear. They also wished to discover if removing the fear of one animal/object (such as the rat) would 'spread without further training to other stimuli'). Jones found that this did, indeed, happen with Peter.

Eysenck and Rachman (1965), Wolpe and Rachman (1960) and other behaviourist psychologists and therapists, believe that the case of Little Albert exemplifies how *all* phobias (abnormal fears) are acquired, that is, through classical conditioning. According to Wolpe and Rachman:

> Any neutral stimulus, simple or complex, that happens to make an impact on an individual at about the time a fear reaction is evoked, acquires the ability to evoke fear subsequently ... there will be generalization of fear reactions to stimuli resembling the conditioned stimulus.

While there is evidence showing that *some* phobias are CERs, the claim that all phobias are acquired this way – and *only* in this way – is extreme and difficult to defend. For example, some phobias are easier to induce experimentally (in people who do not already have them), and it is common knowledge that certain 'naturally occurring' phobias (not deliberately induced) are more common than others: rats, jellyfish, cockroaches, spiders and slugs are consistently rated as frightening, while rabbits, ladybirds, cats and lambs are consistently rated as non-frightening (Bennett-Levy and Marteau, 1984).

These and similar findings are consistent with Seligman's (1970) concept of *biological preparedness*: different species are biologically equipped to acquire certain CRs more easily if they have high survival value. This implies that there is more to phobias than just classical conditioning. Indeed, Rachman (1977) maintains that direct conditioning of any kind accounts for relatively few phobias; rather, many phobias are acquired on the basis of information transmitted through observation and instruction (such as in *modelling*: see above). Interestingly, Jones (1924) thought that Peter's phobias probably were not directly conditioned fears; she wondered where his fear of white rats, for example, might have come from.

According to Harris (1997), Albert's fear was difficult to induce and transitory, and Watson and Rayner recognized that the whole experiment was a failure! Yet every textbook account tells us how easily they created a rat phobia, which then generalized into a lifelong fear of rabbits and other white, furry things. But *why* should textbook authors want to present the study in a more favourable light than it appears to deserve?

Harris claims that the study served as a celebratory 'origin myth' for behaviourists, who wanted their speciality to have a long and convincing past. Different accounts all suggested that Watson had tapped into the power of behaviourism as a theory and technology: the case of Little Albert helps to legitimize the whole behaviourist enterprise.

There is no suggestion that textbook accounts were *deliberately* altered; indeed, many (if not most) textbook authors have no special 'allegiance' to Watson. However, the strange saga of Little Albert can be seen as a case study in the creation of myths, even within a so-called 'science' of psychology. It also demonstrates the importance of reading *original material* (i.e. *primary sources*) whenever possible!

EXERCISES

1   According to Cornwell and Hobbs (1976), the material presented in the box below contains more than 20 mistakes. How many can you spot?

> In the 1920s, J.B. Watson did a series of experiments with children showing how emotional responses can be conditioned and reconditioned. Watson's first subject was an eight-month-old orphan, Albert B., who happened to be fond of rabbits, rats, mice and other furry animals. He appeared to be a healthy, emotionally stable infant, afraid of nothing except loud sounds, which made him cry. To establish a conditioned fear response in Albert, Watson selected a toy rabbit as a conditioned stimulus. Initially this rabbit evoked no fear in the child. Then the rabbit was displayed to Albert and, half a second or so later, Watson made a sudden loud noise (the unconditioned stimulus) by crashing metal plates together right beside Albert's head. The noise alarmed the infant and he began to cry. Thereafter the sight of the formerly friendly rabbit alone, without the loud noise, was sufficient to elicit crying – a conditioned fear response. This fear response to the toy rabbit did not die away after a day or two, but continued. Moreover, it spread to other stimuli that bore a resemblance to the rabbit, such as a glove, a towel, a man's beard, a toy and a ball of wool. Watson did not leave Albert with his conditioned fear. In the second part of the experiment, Alfred's fear response was reconditioned by pairing the rabbit with stimuli that had pleasant associations (such as mother, favourite dessert, and so on). By presenting the rabbit at mealtimes, at a distance which Albert could tolerate without whimpering, it was possible to gradually move the animal closer without any open signs of fear in the child. Eventually, Albert was once more able to stretch out his hand to feel the rabbit, and the two were happily reunited.

2   How does the single-participant design relate to other kinds of experimental design?

3   What is another word for 'transfer' (of the CR to other, similar, stimuli)?

4   The CER did not transfer to Albert's building blocks. What feature of conditioning does this illustrate?

5   What are the other *two* basic phenomena involved in conditioning (in addition to your answers to (3) and (4) above)?

24 Transmission of aggression through imitation of aggressive models

Bandura, A., Ross, D. and Ross, S.A. (1961)

Journal of Abnormal and Social Psychology, 63(3): 575–82

BACKGROUND AND CONTEXT

Albert Bandura is probably the most influential of the *social learning theorists*. While accepting the basic principles of classical (or respondent/Pavlovian) and operant (or instrumental/Skinnerian) conditioning, social learning theorists argue that:

- conditioning on its own is inadequate as an explanation of most human, social behaviour;

- reinforcement is not the all-important influence on behaviour that Skinner claimed it to be;

- learning cannot be explained properly without attributing cognitive processes to the learner (the S-O-R approach, as opposed to Skinner's S-R or 'empty organism' approach).

According to Howe (1980):

> If all learning depended upon the reinforcement of existing responses, it would be difficult for a person to acquire new behaviours. Fortunately, mechanisms ... exist ... making it possible for new things to be learned without it being necessary to wait for each activity to be produced by the individual learner. One way to learn is through watching other people behave, and in this way we can acquire habits, skills, and knowledge without having to directly experience the consequences of every single action ... People are able to learn from what they observe, and they thereby gain access to a much wider range of abilities than would be possible if all learning depended upon the reinforcement of behaviours.

So, *observational learning* (or *modelling*) represents a major alternative to conditioning as a basic form of human learning. It is much more efficient than trial-and-error learning (the basis of operant conditioning); for example, watching someone else (the *model*) perform some skill may prevent us having to painstakingly make mistake after mistake in our attempts to acquire the skill ourselves. Also, the model demonstrates the 'whole' skill, while, according to Skinner, each component of the skill must be learned separately, step by step, and then 'put together' (through 'chaining') at the end of the process. Language is a good example of a complex behaviour that could probably never be acquired unless children were exposed to 'model speakers'. (See Chapter 3.)

As Shaffer (1985) points out, modelling enables the young child to acquire many new responses from people who are simply 'going about their own business' and not trying to teach the child anything. But this is a double-edged sword: often the modelled behaviour is not what the parents (or society in general) would approve of (e.g. smoking, swearing, aggression). Children are continually exposed to a whole range of behaviours, both desirable and undesirable, through the same basic process of modelling. The Bandura *et al.* study focuses on one of these undesirable, antisocial behaviours, namely aggression. According to Howe (1980), experimental studies of modelling have concentrated on the influence of aggressive models because, compared with other social behaviours, aggressive acts are easy to identify and can be measured objectively.

AIM AND NATURE

While several earlier studies (e.g. Bandura and Huston, 1961) had shown that children readily imitate an adult model's behaviour in the presence of the model, Bandura *et al.* believed that a more crucial test of observational or *imitative learning* involves the generalization of imitative responses to new settings where the model is absent.

● HYPOTHESIS

The major, overall, hypothesis, was that:

1   Participants exposed to aggressive models will reproduce aggressive acts resembling those of the models to a significantly greater extent than both participants exposed to non-aggressive models and those not exposed to any models at all.

A secondary hypothesis, which follows from (1) and is 'contained' within it was:

2   Participants exposed to subdued, non-aggressive models will display significantly less imitative aggression than control group participants (i.e. those who are not exposed to any models at all).

3   Participants will imitate the behaviour of same-sex models to a greater degree than opposite-sex models.

4   Boys will be more likely to imitate aggression than girls, especially when they are exposed to aggressive male models.

● METHOD/DESIGN

Participants

The participants were 36 boys and 36 girls (age range 37–69 months, mean age 52 months), enrolled in the Stanford University Nursery School. One adult male and one adult female served as models. One female experimenter conducted the study for all 72 children.

Experimental design

The children were divided into eight experimental groups of 6 and a control group of 24. Half the experimental participants were exposed to aggressive models and half to subdued, non-aggressive models. These groups were further subdivided into male and female. Half the participants in the aggressive and non-aggressive conditions observed same-sex models, the other half observed opposite-sex models. The control group had no exposure to a model at all.

All the children were matched for their normal levels of aggressive behaviour in the nursery school. They were rated independently (for physical and verbal aggression) by the experimenter and a nursery school teacher, both of whom knew the children well. There was very high agreement between their ratings. The children were arranged in groups of three, after which each child was assigned randomly to one of the two experimental conditions or the control group.

Experimental conditions

Participants were initially brought individually by the experimenter into the experimental room; the model was invited by the experimenter to come and join in the game, which involved designing pictures using potato prints and stickers. The child sat at one end of the room, while the model sat at the opposite end, where there was a small table, a tinker-toy set, a mallet and a five-foot inflated Bobo doll.

In the *non-aggressive condition*, the model assembled the tinker toys in a quiet, subdued manner, totally ignoring the Bobo doll.

In the *aggressive condition*, the model began assembling the tinker toys, but after about a minute, turned to the Bobo doll and spent the rest of the time punching it (not counted as imitative responses if the child subsequently displayed them), then laying it on its side, sitting on it and punching it repeatedly on the nose. The model then raised Bobo, picked up the mallet and struck the doll in the head, tossed it up in the air and kicked it around the room. This sequence of aggressive acts was repeated about three times, interspersed with verbally aggressive responses such as 'Sock him in the nose', 'Hit him down', 'Throw him in the air', 'Kick him', 'Pow', and two non-aggressive comments, 'He keeps coming back for more' and 'He sure is a tough fella'. This lasted ten minutes in total.

Aggression arousal

Before being tested for imitation, all participants were subjected to mild aggression arousal to ensure that they were under some degree of instigation to aggression.

They were taken to another room which contained various attractive toys (including a fire engine and a doll set). The experimenter told them that the toys were there for the participant to play with, but once they had become sufficiently involved with them (usually after a couple of minutes), she stated that these were her very best toys and that she did not let just anyone play with them: she had decided to reserve them for the other children. However, they could play with any of the toys in the next room.

Test for delayed imitation

The experimental room contained a variety of toys, some that could be used in imitative or non-imitative aggression, and others that tended to elicit predominantly non-aggressive responses (such as a tea set, crayons and colouring paper). The former included a three-foot Bobo doll, a mallet and two dart guns.

Each child spent 20 minutes in the room. His/her behaviour was rated in terms of predetermined response categories by observers through a one-way mirror in an adjoining observation room. The observers had no knowledge of the conditions to which the children had been assigned.

Response measures

Three measures of imitation were:

- *Imitation of physical aggression*: e.g. acts of striking the Bobo doll with a mallet, sitting on it and punching it in the nose, kicking it and tossing it in the air.

- *Imitative verbal aggression*: e.g. 'Sock him', 'Hit him down', 'Kick him', 'Throw him in the air' and 'Pow'.

- *Imitative non-aggressive verbal response*: 'He keeps coming back for more' and 'He sure is a tough fella'.

AIM AND NATURE

Two responses counted as *partially imitative behaviour* were:

● *mallet aggression*: the child strikes objects other than the Bobo doll with the mallet;

● *sits on Bobo doll.*

In addition, *non-imitative aggressive responses* were:

● *punches Bobo doll*;

● *non-imitative physical and verbal aggression* (e.g. any aggressive acts directed towards objects other than the Bobo doll and hostile remarks that did not fall within the imitative verbal aggression above);

● *aggressive gun play.*

● RESULTS

Complete imitation of model's behaviour

Children in the aggressive condition reproduced a good deal of physical and verbal aggression similar to the model's; their mean scores were significantly greater than for those in the non-aggressive and control conditions (70 per cent of whom displayed almost *no* imitative aggression). There was no difference between the non-aggressive and control conditions.

Approximately one-third of the children in the aggressive condition also imitated the model's non-aggressive verbal responses, compared with none of those in the other two conditions.

Partial imitation of model's behaviour

Children in the aggressive condition partially imitated the model's aggressive behaviour (physical and verbal) to a significantly greater degree than those in the non-aggressive and control conditions. Again, these two latter groups did not differ from each other.

Non-imitative aggression

There were no differences between the groups in relation to aggressive gun play or punching the Bobo doll. But as far as non-imitative physical and verbal aggression was concerned, the aggressive groups displayed significantly more than the non-aggressive groups.

AIM AND NATURE

Influence of sex of model and sex of participants on imitation

The prediction that boys are more likely than girls to imitate an aggressive model was only partially confirmed. They imitated more physical aggression than girls, but no more verbal aggression.

There appeared to be a sex–model interaction, especially in the case of the male model. For example, boys showed significantly more physical and verbal imitative aggression, significantly more non-imitative aggression, and engaged in significantly more aggressive gun play following exposure to the aggressive male model than the girls did. In contrast, girls exposed to the female model displayed considerably more imitative verbal aggression and more non-imitative aggression than the boys (but not significantly so).

● CONCLUSIONS

Children who were exposed to aggressive models later reproduced a substantial amount of the model's physical and verbal aggression (as well as non-aggressive responses); the imitative responses were almost identical to the modelled behaviour. Children who were exposed to non-aggressive models or who had no exposure to any models, rarely produced such responses.

The fact that children expressed their aggression in ways which clearly resembled the model's novel behaviour (unusual behaviour purposely selected because it was unlikely to have been observed outside the experimental situation) provided striking evidence for the occurrence of learning by imitation.

Imitation was found to be influenced differently according to the model's gender. Boys showed more aggression than girls following exposure to the male model; this difference was especially marked in relation to highly sex-typed male behaviour (i.e. physical aggression), as opposed to verbal aggression.

EVALUATION

Theoretical issues

Bandura (1973), in common with other social learning theorists (e.g. Buss, 1971; Zillmann, 1978), sees aggression primarily as a specific form of social behaviour, both acquired and maintained in much the same way as other forms of behaviour. This contrasts sharply with instinct theorists, such as Freud (1920) and Lorenz (1966), and drive-reduction theories such as Dollard *et al.*'s (1939) frustration–aggression hypothesis.

According to social learning theory (SLT), a wide range of factors are responsible for the acquisition of aggression (including direct provocation by others and environmental stressors). But by far the most important is exposure to live and filmed (symbolic) models. Humans are not constantly driven towards violence by built-in, internal forces or ever-present external stimuli (as claimed by instinct theories and drive-reduction theories, respectively). Rather, people only aggress under appropriate social conditions which tend to facilitate such behaviour. SLT is also more optimistic about the possibility of controlling or preventing human aggression: since it is *learned* behaviour, it is open to direct modification by altering or removing the conditions which normally maintain it (Baron, 1977). (See **Applications and implications** below.)

For Skinner (e.g. 1938), no reinforcement equals no learning. But Bandura argues that learning *can* occur without reinforcement: exposure to a model's behaviour is sufficient for learning. However, reinforcement can influence the likelihood of the learned behaviour actually being *performed* (but is only one of several influences on actual behaviour). Reinforcement may either be *direct* (as when the *child* is reinforced for imitating the model) or *vicarious* (as when the *model's* behaviour is reinforced); for Skinner, there is only one kind of reinforcement, that is, direct.

This crucial distinction between learning and performance was demonstrated in another study by Bandura, Ross and Ross (1963b). Four-year-olds watched one of two films, both involving two men, Johnny and Rocky. In the first film, Johnny is playing with some attractive toys. Rocky asks if he can play too, but Johnny refuses and Rocky becomes very aggressive towards Johnny and his toys, eventually winning them away from Johnny. Johnny sits dejectedly, while Rocky celebrates with food and drink.

In the second film, things begin in the same way as in the first film, but Rocky is beaten up by Johnny. A control group did not see a film. Seeing Rocky rewarded (film one) resulted in the highest number of acts of imitative aggression, while seeing him punished (film two) produced the lowest number; the control group fell midway between the two.

Does this mean that the children actually *learned* more about aggression from film one than those who saw film two, or simply that they were more ready to *reproduce* the behaviour they had observed? Does failure to imitate mean that no learning has taken place?

A later study (Bandura, 1965) showed the answer to be 'no'. He tested children under three conditions (model rewarded, model punished, and model neither rewarded nor punished: phase one). As in the earlier study, the first group displayed more imitative aggression than the second group (but no more than the control group). In a second phase of the experiment, children were offered rewards for imitating the model's behaviour: under these conditions, all three groups produced the *same* number of imitative aggressive acts. Clearly, the children were *performing* differently in the first phase, but the second phase revealed that they had all *learned* equally about aggression from whichever model they had seen.

Vicarious reinforcement had influenced imitation (phase one) and *direct* reinforcement had influenced imitation (phase two), but *neither* had any influence over what the children had learned about the model's aggressive behaviour.

If learning can take place without being expressed through behaviour, exactly what is being learned in observational learning? 'What are children acquiring that enables them to reproduce the behaviour of an absent model at some point in the future – often the distant future?' (Shaffer, 1985).

Bandura's (1977) answer is *symbolic representations* of the model's behaviour, stored in memory and retrieved at a later date to guide the child's own attempts at imitation. They may take the form of images or verbal labels that describe the behaviour in an economical way.

Other cognitive processes relate to the very nature of reinforcement. While Skinner saw reinforcement working in an 'automatic' way to make the behaviour it follows more likely to be repeated, Bandura saw both direct and vicarious reinforcement as providing *information*. In the words of Mischel (1986), another social learning theorist:

> *Information that alters the person's anticipations of the probable outcomes to which a behaviour will lead changes the probability that he will perform the behaviour. Models inform us of the probable consequences of particular behaviours and thus affect the likelihood that we will perform them.*

While SLT can say how a child might acquire a particular behaviour pattern, it fails to take account of the underlying developmental changes that occur. For example, do three-year-olds and ten-year-olds typically learn the same amount or in the same way from modelling? Given Bandura's emphasis on cognitive aspects of the modelling process, a genuinely developmental SLT is possible, but has not yet been proposed (Bee, 2000). The importance of cognitive processes is reflected in Bandura's (1986, 1989) renaming of SLT as *social cognitive theory*.

Subsequent research

As in the 1961 study, Bandura, Ross and Ross (1963a) tested 96 three- to five-year-olds under three conditions, after first frustrating them by removing the promise of attractive toys, then observing them during a 20-minute play period. This time, however, the non-aggressive live model condition was replaced by a *filmed aggressive model*. The filmed model produced the most imitative aggression, closely followed by the live aggressive model. As in the 1961 study, the imitative aggression was a 'carbon copy' of the model's aggressive acts.

According to Baron (1977), Bandura's Bobo doll experiments constitute the 'first generation' (or 'phase one') of scientific research into the effects of media violence. With the exception of the 1961 experiment, all the Bobo doll studies used filmed models, usually presented via a television screen (as opposed to a projector screen). The basic finding was that young children can acquire new aggressive responses not previously in their behaviour repertoire, merely through exposure to a filmed or televised model. If children could learn new ways of harming others through such experience, then, by implication, mass media portrayals of violence might be contributing, in some degree, to increased levels of violence in society (Baron, 1977). (See **Applications and implications** below.)

Methodological issues

Bandura (1965) himself warned against this interpretation of his research in light of his finding that acquisition does not necessarily equal performance. Nevertheless, the mere *possibility* of such effects was sufficient to focus considerable public attention on his research. However, criticism of the Bobo doll 'paradigm' (both then and since) also suggests that public concern may have been premature:

- The films used differed in several important ways from standard television or movie material. They were very brief (typically three and a half minutes), often lacked a plot, provided no cause or justification for the model's behaviour, which was typically quite bizarre (deliberately, so that it was distinctive enough to grab – and keep – the child's attention).

- Similarly, the novelty of the Bobo doll itself was a crucial factor. For example, Kniveton and Stephenson (1970, in Cumberbatch, 1995) found that children not familiar with the doll imitated five times more than children who had been exposed to it previously. Indeed, Nobel (1975, in Cumberbatch, 1995) suggested that even young children participating in laboratory experiments understand that they are *expected* to play a particular role.

- Not only was exposure time very brief, but the effects (the dependent variable) were demonstrated almost immediately. Can a single exposure have long-term effects, as they might (so it is feared) outside the laboratory? According to Hicks (1965, 1968 in Baron, 1977), it can. He retested children six to eight months following a brief, single exposure (under ten minutes) and found that 40 per cent of the model's aggressive acts were reproduced.

- The dependent variable was operationalized as aggressive acts directed at an inanimate object (an inflated doll) specifically designed for such treatment. Since no living being was being harmed by such actions, should we really describe the behaviour as 'aggression' at all? Wouldn't it be more appropriate to interpret the behaviour as a form of play, especially as the Bobo doll is, essentially, a 'toy' (Klapper, 1968 in Baron, 1977)?

Bandura's (1973) response to this is to draw once more on the learning-versus-performance distinction. Procedures based on attacks against inanimate objects are useful for understanding how such behaviours are acquired: aggressive responses are often learned in contexts that are far removed from actual harm to others. He gives the example of boxers in training using punchbags, and hunters practising by shooting at inanimate targets.

● The situation in which the child reproduces the model's behaviour was very permissive: any realistic consequences, such as peer retaliation or adult punishment, were absent (Gunter and McAleer, 1997). But perhaps this criticism is only relevant to *performance* and not to learning.

● According to Gunter and McAleer (1990):

Although we can be quite certain about what occurs in the laboratory, we are left with a great deal of uncertainty concerning how much the process demonstrated in the laboratory accurately reflects what happens in children's lives.

According to Baron (1977), one response to these criticisms was 'phase two' of the television violence research, aimed at:

● using more realistic measures of aggression where behaviour would be directed against other people;

● removing the exact similarity between the model's behaviour and the context in which participants could themselves display aggression.

One of the leading figures in this second phase was Leonard Berkowitz. (See **Applications and implications** below.) However, the role of observational learning in explaining the impact of media violence (as well as pro-social behaviour: see Chapter 11; and gender-role stereotypes: see Chapter 41) is still considerable, along with arousal, disinhibition and desensitization (see Gunter and McAleer, 1997).

Applications and implications

Although Bandura was initially more concerned with developing theoretical issues than with applied aspects of the media, his (and Berkowitz's) laboratory-based experimental approaches stimulated many others to research media violence. Their theoretical orientations helped to shape the way later researchers conceptualized media effects (Cumberbatch, 1995).

As well as its relevance to symbolic models, SLT has always contr[...]
of the so-called 'cycle of violence' or, more technically, the 'inter[...]
transmission of violence'. The basic idea is that if you have been [...]
(physical) abuse as a child, you are very much more likely to be a [...]
than if you have not experienced abuse yourself. It also increases [...]
will be a wife- (or a husband-) batterer. Berkowitz (1993) refers t[...]
as a *risk factor* for the development of adult aggressiveness: it makes it more probable –
but it is never certain. Why should this be?

Many of the same factors which are proposed to explain the effects of television
violence are relevant here. For example, one feature of *disinhibition* is that you learn
the 'right' way to act in a given situation by observing what others do. When children
see adults fight, they learn that they too can solve their problems by attacking the
people who 'get in their way'.

As Berkowitz (1993) points out, you do not have to have been the victim of abuse
yourself: *witnessing* violence may be sufficient. However, when you are yourself the
victim, you are simultaneously suffering the painful effects *and* witnessing the
aggressive behaviour. Physical punishments demonstrate the very behaviour which
parents are often trying to eliminate in their child; ironically, the evidence suggests
that the child is likely to become *more*, not less, aggressive.

Copycat violence implies the role of observational learning, and Bandura (1973)
claims that documented cases of the contagion of television and movie violence,
although fairly rare, still occur with alarming regularity. Airline hijackings were
unknown in the USA until 1961; then some hijackings of Cuban airliners to Miami
were followed by a wave, reaching a peak of 87 in 1969 (Mischel, 1986). Then came
9/11 (2001).

Observational learning also influences emotional responses, through a process of
vicarious (classical) conditioning: 'by observing the emotional reactions of others to a
stimulus, it is possible to learn an intense emotional response to that situation'
(Mischel, 1986). This can help explain the learning of animal phobias in people who
have not suffered a traumatic incident with the animal themselves, but have *witnessed*
someone else's fear. These same basic principles can be used to *remove* phobias,
through *modelling therapy*.

Bandura *et al.* (1969) assigned teenage and adult volunteers, all with intense snake
phobias, to one of three treatment conditions (or a non-treatment control):

1   The *systematic desensitization* condition involved relaxation training while
    visualizing progressively stronger fear-arousing snakes.

2   *Symbolic modelling* involved showing films of fearless children and adults
    interacting in a progressively bold way, first with plastic snakes, and later with real

ones (holding them, then allowing the snakes to crawl all over them). They also received relaxation training.

3   *Live modelling and guided participation* involved observing a model, initially through an observation window, then directly in front of them. The model encouraged the volunteers to handle the snake themselves, first with gloves on, then with bare hands, guiding them physically, then gradually allowing the volunteer to 'take charge'.

Condition (3) proved to be the most powerful, being almost completely successful in removing phobias quickly and completely.

According to Newell and Dryden (1991), Bandura's SLT has facilitated a greater acceptance of *cognitive behaviour therapies* (CBTs). (See Gross, 2005.)

Kent (1991) believes that Bandura's concept of *self-efficacy* has helped to explain anxiety. Self-efficacy refers to our belief that we have control over our behaviour and can achieve our goals: we experience anxiety when we perceive ourselves as being ill-equipped to manage potentially painful events/situations. For example, a snake phobic may have a high sense of self-efficacy in most areas of his/her life, but perceives situations involving snakes as beyond his/her control.

Behavioural treatments, such as *in vivo* exposure (e.g. actually handling a snake) and modelling have important effects on patients' self-efficacy beliefs. Indeed, Bandura (1986) argues that various therapies may all be effective for the same reason: they serve to increase a patient's self-efficacy, that is, confidence in their ability to deal with situations that previously induced anxiety. (See Chapter 30.)

EXERCISES

1 What is the major difference between the 1961 study and earlier studies of modelling?

2 In relation to hypothesis (3), Bandura *et al.* say that 'as a result of differing reinforcement histories, tendencies to imitate male and female models thus acquire differential habit strength.' Put this into your own words to explain what they mean.

3 (a) Which experimental design was used?

 (b) What is the advantage *in this particular case* of using this design?

 (c) What alternative design could have been used?

4 Why was it felt necessary to deliberately subject all the children to 'mild aggression arousal' following exposure to the model?

5 Bandura *et al.* say: 'the mere observation of aggression, regardless of the quality of the model–subject relationship, is a sufficient condition for producing imitative aggression in children.' Does this need to be qualified in light of subsequent research?

6 Do you consider the study to be ethically sound?

Asking only one question in the conservation experiment

Samuel, J. and Bryant, P. (1984)

Journal of Child Psychology and Psychiatry, 25(2): 315–18

BACKGROUND AND CONTEXT

The ability to *conserve* represents one of the major landmarks within Piaget's (e.g. 1950) theory of cognitive development. It marks the end of pre-operational and the beginning of operational thought (at about age seven), a major *qualitative* shift from non-logical to logical thought (albeit still tied to actual, concrete situations).

Piaget's conservation experiments are probably his most famous. Essentially, they involve presenting the child with two identical quantities (say, two beakers of water), whose appearance is changed (transformed) in some way (the water from one beaker is poured into a beaker of a different size). The child is asked the same question ('Is there the same amount of water in the two beakers?') both *before* and *after* the transformation. According to Piaget, pre-seven-year-olds reliably fail conservation tasks (they maintain that there is no longer the same quantity following the transformation), because they lack the logical thinking (or 'operations') required (specifically, *compensation* and *reversibility*).

There have been many replications of Piaget's conservation experiments, sometimes with important modifications. For example, Rose and Blank (1974) dropped the *pre*-transformation question, and found that six-year-olds often succeeded on a test of number transformation (using rows of counters), compared with children tested using the standard (Piagetian) version. Significantly, when the first group of children was retested on the standard form of the task a week later, they made fewer errors than the second group. (Other modifications to Piaget's methods are discussed in **Theoretical issues** below.)

Samuel and Bryant's experiment represents one in a long line of studies which challenge Piaget's conclusions regarding conservation through criticizing his *methods*. What these studies have in common is their focus on the conditions under which children will display their ability to conserve, rather than whether or not they are actually capable of conservation.

AIM AND NATURE

● HYPOTHESIS

The study was a partial replication of the Rose and Blank study, in which only the *post*-transformation question in Piaget's conservation experiment was asked. But while Rose and Blank used only six-year-olds to study number conservation, Samuel and Bryant used five-, six-, seven- and eight-year-olds to study conservation of mass (or substance) and volume, as well as number.

Based on Rose and Blank's findings, Samuel and Bryant predicted that: children from five to eight years old, asked only the post-transformation question, are more likely to display conservation of number, mass (substance) and volume, compared with children tested using the standard (Piagetian) procedure.

● METHOD/DESIGN

The study used quite a complex experimental design.

1   Manipulating the form of the task (standard/Piaget or post-transformation question only).

2   There was a *fixed-array* control condition: the child did not see any transformation being made, but only saw the post-transformation display.

3   Age was an additional independent variable (though not manipulated, making this part of the study a *quasi-experiment*).

4   There was a mixed design, such that the four age groups (252 in total) constituted *independent samples*, with each being randomly split into three subgroups, closely matched in age (corresponding to (1) and (2) above); within each of these groups, participants were tested on all three types of conservation (*repeated measures*).

Materials

● Conservation of *mass* involved Play-Doh cylinder shapes. The transformation involved squashing one of these into a sausage or a pancake.

● Conservation of *number* involved two rows of counters. The transformation involved spreading out or bunching up one of the rows.

● Conservation of *volume* involved two identical glasses containing liquid. The transformation involved pouring the liquid from one of the glasses into a narrower or a shallow, wider one.

Every child was given four trials with each kind of material – two with equal and two with *unequal* quantities (e.g. the rows of counters contained six and five counters). The order of these trials, and the order in which the three types of material were introduced, were systematically varied between children.

● RESULTS

No systematic difference between equal and unequal quantity trials was found, so the results were pooled for the two types of trial.

As predicted, the one-judgement task (asking only the post-transformation question) was typically easier (i.e. fewer errors were made) than the standard conservation task; it also proved easier than the fixed-array control. This difference was generally true of all three types of material. However, there were significant age and materials differences:

● *Age*: there was a significant difference between every age group, such that the older groups did consistently better than the younger groups.

● *Materials*: the number task was significantly easier than the mass or volume tasks.

● CONCLUSIONS

Despite overall differences in the skills of the four age groups, and in the difficulty of the different conservation tasks, children were significantly more likely to succeed when only the post-transformation question was asked than when tested using the standard (two-question) form of the task. Thus, Rose and Blank's (1974) results held good.

Children who fail the traditional conservation task often *do* understand the principle of invariance (i.e. they *are* able to conserve). They make their mistakes for a quite extraneous reason: the experimenter's repetition of the same question about the same material makes them think they must change their answer the second time. The crucial question is not whether a child possesses a particular cognitive skill, but how and when s/he decides to apply that skill.

EVALUATION

Methodological issues

Samuel and Bryant's study represents a great advance on that of Rose and Blank: it involved four age groups (five-, six-, seven- and eight-year-olds), three conditions of testing (standard, one-judgement and fixed-array), and three kinds of conservation task (mass, number and volume). Each of these corresponds to an independent variable (with age being selected for, not manipulated). Success on the conservation task (number of errors made) was the dependent variable.

Where there is more than one independent variable, the design is referred to as a *factorial* design (4 x 3 x 3: four age groups x three conditions x three conservation tasks). The appropriate statistical test is the *analysis of variance* (ANOVA), one of the most useful and versatile of all statistics used in psychology (Solso and Johnson, 1989; see Coolican, 2004).

Each child was tested four times with each kind of material: twice with equal and twice with unequal quantities. No systematic difference was found between the two types of trial, so the results were pooled. Samuel and Bryant do not say *why* they did this, nor what can be inferred from the fact that there was no systematic difference. The fact that they were used at all suggests that they expected to find a difference. To take the example of number conservation, being able to count is a necessary, but not sufficient, condition of being able to conserve. So, if a child failed to conserve, it could be due to his/her basic inability to count. Using unequal quantities (presumably) was designed to identify children who could not conserve because they could not count (rather than because they lacked compensation and reversibility). (See **Exercises**.)

If the child's ability to conserve (the number of errors made) was not affected by whether equal or unequal quantities were used, then either the ability to count is irrelevant after all, or (as is more likely) the children who conserved recognized the unequal quantities. In the standard condition, if the child said 'No' to the pre-transformation question, then either the trial ended at that point, or the child who could conserve would say 'Yes' when asked again. In the one-question condition, being able to count should have been sufficient for all the children to have said 'No' on the unequal quantity trials.

Theoretical issues

Samuel and Bryant found that the number conservation task was significantly easier than the mass and volume tasks. This supports Piaget's concept of *horizontal décalage*.

conservation does not develop all in one go during the concrete operational stage, but in the invariant order of number and liquid quantity (6–7 years), substance (or mass) and length (7–8), weight (8–10) and volume (11–12). (Note that what Samuel and Bryant call volume is more accurately called liquid/continuous quantity; Piaget tested volume through *displacement* of liquid). (See **Exercises**.)

Another alternative to Piaget's method of testing conservation was the famous 'naughty teddy' experiment (McGarrigle and Donaldson, 1974), which was concerned with number and length conservation. In the case of number, it proceeded in the normal way up to the point where the child agreed that there was an equal number of counters in the two rows. Then naughty teddy (a glove puppet) emerged from a hiding place and swept over one of the rows of counters, rearranging them and disturbing the one-to-one correspondence. The child was invited to put teddy back in his box and the questioning resumed: 'Now, where were we? Ah, yes, is the number in this row the same as the number in that row?' Out of 80 four- to six-year-olds, 50 conserved under the naughty teddy condition, compared with 13 out of 80 tested using the standard form.

According to Piaget, it should not matter *who* rearranges the counters (or *how* this happens) – but it seems to be relevant to the child. However, Light *et al.* (1979) criticized naughty teddy on the grounds that the children were, non-verbally and unwittingly, being instructed to 'ignore the rearrangement': in a sense, the task itself may be 'lost'. In other words, they may have been so absorbed by naughty teddy's antics and putting him back in his box, that they did not actually *notice* the perceptual transformation.

A way of testing this hypothesis was designed by Moore and Frye (1986). They distinguished between an *irrelevant* perceptual change (which is what the traditional conservation procedure involves: nothing is added or subtracted) and a *relevant* one (something is actually added or subtracted). They predicted that if naughty teddy really is distracting, then children should do worse when a relevant change occurs (they *added* a counter to one row, so the correct answer became 'the two rows are now *unequal*'), and better when an irrelevant change occurs. This, indeed, is what they found, thus supporting the criticism of Light *et al.* and, indirectly, supporting Piaget.

A criticism made by several psychologists, including Margaret Donaldson (1978), is that Piaget focused on the child's understanding of the *physical world* to the exclusion of the *social world*. Cognitive development cannot be properly understood without examining the development of social understanding; by trying to understand cognitive abilities in isolation, Piaget systematically *underestimated* children's logical abilities.

According to Donaldson, when children are faced with a task or problem, they have to decide what is required of them, and they do this from two sources:

- the words that are spoken;

- the setting in which the words are spoken.

The former are interpreted in light of the child's interpretation of the latter. In Piaget's conservation tasks, these two sources of information can *conflict* with each other:

> Before the child has developed a full awareness of language, language is embedded in the flow of events which accompany it. So long as this is the case, the child does not interpret words in isolation, but instead interprets situations, more concerned to make sense of what people do when they talk and act than to decide what words mean. (Donaldson, 1978)

The fact that the experimenter asks the child essentially the *same* question twice (pre- and post-transformation) can confuse a child who understands that nothing has actually changed (can conserve), but who believes that *a different answer is expected* ('Why else would the experimenter ask me the question again?'). This is called the *extraneous question hypothesis*. (See **Subsequent research** below.) The child cannot disembed the verbal question from the situation as a whole, in which an adult, a stranger to the child and an authority figure, seems to require a particular response (a different answer).

While for Piaget social understanding is simply a manifestation of cognitive development, Donaldson sees it as both separate and more important (Smith and Cowie, 1992). Smith *et al.* (1998) point out that other investigators have not always replicated McGarrigle and Donaldson's (1974) main findings.

According to Meadows (1995), Piaget implicitly viewed children as largely independent and isolated in their construction of knowledge and understanding of the physical world (the 'child-as-scientist'). In contrast, Vygotsky (e.g. 1962) stressed the *social* nature of knowledge and thought (the 'child-as-apprentice'). (See Gross, 2005.)

Despite these (and other) criticisms, Piaget's 'theory set the agenda for most research in this area for the past thirty years and still serves as a kind of scaffolding for much of our thinking about thinking' (Bee, 2000).

Subsequent research

A partial replication of Samuel and Bryant's experiment was carried out by Porpodas (1987). With six- and seven-year-old Greek children, he used the same three conditions, plus volume and number conservation, and the results largely confirmed those of Samuel and Bryant (and Rose and Blank).

However, Porpodas was also interested in testing the *explanation* given by those investigators, namely the 'extraneous reason hypothesis' (ERH). (See **Theoretical issues** above.) The superior performance of children in the one-question condition, compared with the fixed-array children, suggests that they carry over information from the pre-transformation display: they use their working or short-term memory (STM) to help them realize that nothing changes during the transformation. This suggests, in turn, that in Piaget's form of the task, the child's failure may be due to interference in its STM, resulting from the experimenter talking to the child when asking the pre-transformation question.

If this hypothesis is correct, then children's difficulty in carrying over information from the pre-transformational display should be observed – even in the one-question condition – if something interferes with the child's STM. Accordingly, Porpodas selected a different sample of 186 six- and seven-year-old boys and girls, who were tested on number and volume conservation under one of three conditions:

1   standard;

2   one-question only;

3   one-question with interference (the experimenter started a short discussion with the child, irrelevant to the task, while performing the transformation, but without referring to it in any way).

As predicted, children of both age groups in condition (3) did *worse* than those in the other two conditions, for both number and volume (but significantly more so for the six-year-olds on volume and the seven-year-olds on number).

Porpodas concluded that asking one question does *not* guarantee the child will reveal its understanding of the principle of invariance; what is needed most is the uninterrupted functioning of the child's STM. This explanation is *complementary to* the ERH – *not* an alternative to it.

Applications and implications

According to Bryant (1998), despite studies like those of McGarrigle and Donaldson (1974), Light *et al.* (1979), and Rose and Blank (1974) (and indeed Samuel and Bryant), it would be too hasty to dismiss Piaget's conservation experiments 'as a clumsy manoeuvre whose results are based on a complete misunderstanding between the adult experimenters and the children whom they test'. For example, not all the children in the 'favourable' (accidental) naughty teddy study gave the correct answer: there was an appreciable number of conservation failures which need explaining. (See **Theoretical issues** above.)

Also, critics of Piaget take failures in the standard task to be *false negatives* (i.e. the children *can* conserve, but are being prevented from displaying their ability by the misleading form of the task). However, the Light *et al.* study strongly suggests that McGarrigle and Donaldson (1974) may have produced *false positives* (the children gave the correct answer, but for the wrong reason – they did not understand that nothing had really changed because they were distracted and probably would not have noticed if anything *had* changed).

What this underlines is the difficulty (if not impossibility) of trying to 'lay bare' any human ability (child or adult): a logical operation such as conservation cannot be understood independently of those methods used to tap or 'expose' it. In the same way, no human ability can be understood independently of the *cultural context* in which it is displayed and used.

Dasen (1994) cites studies he conducted in remote parts of the central Australian desert with 8- to 14-year-old Aborigines, involving conservation of liquid, weight and volume. The shift from pre- to concrete operational thought took place on average between the ages of 10 and 13. But on tests of spatial relationships, they performed way ahead of Western children. Dasen sees this as making good sense in terms of Aboriginal culture, where things are not *quantified* (measured). For example, water is essential for survival – but the exact amount matters little, and number words do not go beyond five (after which everything is 'many').

Conservation experiments have also been conducted with Eskimo, African (Senegal and Rwanda), Hong Kong and Papua New Guinea samples. Consistent with Dasen's findings, children from non-Western cultures often lag way behind Western samples in acquiring operational thought – unless they have attended white schools, for example. So, cultural factors can affect the *rate* of cognitive development, but *not* the developmental *sequence* (Schaffer, 2004).

As Dasen (1994) puts it, 'The deep structures, the basic cognitive processes, are indeed universal, while at the surface level, the way these basic processes are brought to bear on specific contents, in specific contexts, is influenced by culture'.

EXERCISES

1   What is meant by 'compensation' and 'reversibility' as logical operations necessary for conservation?

2   Why was the fixed-array condition used?

3   In relation to the order in which each child was tested with the three types of material, Samuel and Bryant say these were 'systematically varied' between children.

(a) What is another term for 'systematically varied'?

(b) Why was this necessary?

(c) How might this have been done?

4   The finding that conservation develops gradually through the concrete operational stage (number and liquid quantity, substance/mass and length, weight and volume) is an example of *horizontal décalage*. This refers to inconsistencies *within* a particular kind of ability. What do you think *vertical décalage* refers to? Give an example.

26 Children of the Garden Island

Werner, E.E. (1989)

Scientific American, 260: 106–11

BACKGROUND AND CONTEXT

The debate concerning the influence of nature and nurture (or heredity and environment) on human behaviour is one of the longest-running and most controversial, both inside and outside psychology. It deals with some of the most fundamental questions that human beings (at least those from Western cultures) ask about themselves, such as, 'How do we come to be the way we are?' and 'What makes us develop in the way we do?'

Sometimes, as in the case of language and perception, the focus of the debate is on an ability shared *by all human beings*; at others (as with intelligence and criminal behaviour), the focus is on *individual differences*. In both cases, however, certain assumptions are made about the exact meaning of 'nature' and 'nurture', as well as about how they are related. By distinguishing different types of environment, such as *shared* and *non-shared*, it is easier to understand the relationship between nature and nurture, including *gene-environment correlation* and *gene-environment interaction*.

The *shared environment* refers to factors such as overcrowding, poverty, socio-economic status (SES), family break-up and marital discord. In studies of intelligence, for example, children are often compared in terms of these environmental factors, and in making this comparison, it is assumed that children from the same family will be similarly and equally affected by them. But for the majority of characteristics, children within the same family are often quite *dissimilar*.

This substantial within-family variation does *not* mean that family environment is unimportant. Indeed, differences between children growing up together is exactly what we would expect to find, because it is the *non-shared environment* which has greater influence on development (Plomin, 1996). Different children in the same family have different experiences: they are treated differently by their parents and each occupies a different 'micro-environment' (Plomin and Thompson, 1987).

But how do non-shared environments arise? Why do parents treat their different children differently? How do children in the same family come to have different experiences? Two major answers to this question are the concepts of *gene–environment correlation* and *gene–environment interaction*.

Reactive gene–environment *correlation* refers to other people's responses to the child's *genetic* tendencies (Plomin *et al.*, 1977). For example, babies with a sunny, easygoing and cheerful disposition/temperament are more likely to elicit friendly reactions from others than miserable or 'difficult' babies. Some children are simply easier to love (Rutter and Rutter, 1992).

An often cited example of gene–environment *interaction* is *phenylketonuria* (PKU). This is a bodily disorder caused by the inheritance of a single recessive gene from each parent. The effect of these PKU genes is that phenylalanine builds up in the blood, depriving the developing nervous system of essential nutrients. The result is severe mental retardation and, eventually, death.

This relationship between what the child inherits (two PKU genes – the *genotype*) and the actual signs and symptoms of the disease (high levels of phenylalanine and mental retardation – the *phenotype*) seems quite straightforward: given the genotype, the phenotype will inevitably occur. However, routine blood tests soon after birth can detect the presence of the PKU genes, and an affected baby will be put on a low-phenylalanine diet. This prevents the disease from developing.

The interaction between genotype and phenotype is likely to be more complex in the case of more complex characteristics, such as intelligence, and academic and occupational achievement. One example of such a relationship is *cumulative deficit*. Dozens of studies have shown that children from poor families, or families where the parents are relatively uneducated, have lower IQ scores than those from middle-class families (Bee, 2000). However, these social class differences are not found before the age of two and a half to three, after which they widen steadily. This suggests that the longer a child lives in poverty, the more negative the effects on IQ and other measures of cognitive functioning become (Smith *et al.*, 1997). The effects of any genetic difference that may be involved are accentuated by environmental factors, especially poverty.

Another example of the complex relationship between genotype and phenotype is the concept of *facilitativeness*. According to Horowitz (1987, 1990), a highly *facilitative* environment is one in which the child has loving and responsive parents, and is provided with a wide range of stimulation. When different levels of facilitativeness are combined with a child's initial *vulnerabilities/susceptibilities*, there is an interaction effect. For example, a *resilient* child (one with many protective factors and a few vulnerabilities) may do quite well in a poor environment. Equally, a *non-resilient* child may do quite well in a highly facilitative environment. Only the *non-resilient* child in a *poor* environment will do really badly.

This interactionist view is supported by Werner's study of 'Children of the Garden Island'. More specifically, she was concerned with *resilience*, the term applied to children exposed to severe risk factors, who nevertheless thrive and excel. It is the ability to spring back from and successfully adapt to adversity (Leckman and Mayes, 2007).

AIM AND NATURE

● HYPOTHESIS

No specific hypotheses were tested. The two original main aims of the study were:

1   To assess the long-term consequences of prenatal and perinatal (around the time of birth) stress.

2   To document the effects of adverse early rearing conditions on children's physical, cognitive and psychosocial development.

As the study progressed, Werner and her fellow researchers began to take a special interest in certain 'high-risk' children, who, in spite of exposure to reproductive stress, discordant and impoverished home lives, and uneducated, alcoholic or mentally disturbed parents, went on to develop healthy personalities, stable careers and strong interpersonal relationships. The researchers decided to try to identify the protective factors that contributed to the resilience of these children.

● METHOD/DESIGN

This was a 30-year longitudinal study of a cohort of 698 children born on the Hawaiian island of Kauai (the Garden Island) in 1955 (the Kauai longitudinal study). In other words, every child born in that year was included in the study, and they were assessed at 1, 2, 10, 18, and 31 or 32 years of age. The majority (422 in all) were born without complications, following uneventful pregnancies, and grew up in supportive environments. It was the remaining 276 who became the focus of the study.

Public health nurses interviewed the women in each trimester of pregnancy, noting any exposure to physical or emotional trauma. Doctors monitored any complications during the prenatal period, labour, delivery and the neonatal period. Nurses and social workers interviewed the mothers in the post-partum period (immediately following the birth) and when the children were one and ten years old. Interactions between parents and offspring in the home were also observed. Paediatricians and psychologists independently examined the children at two and ten years of age, assessing their physical, intellectual and social development, and noting any handicaps or behaviour problems. Teachers evaluated the children's academic progress and their behaviour in the classroom.

From the outset, Werner and her fellow researchers recorded information about the material, intellectual and emotional aspects of the family environment, including stressful life events that resulted in discord or disruption of the family unit. In addition, they gained access to the records of public health, educational and social service agencies, and the local police and family court files. Werner also administered a wide range of aptitude, achievement and personality tests in elementary (primary) and high school (secondary) grades. The children were interviewed when they were 18 and again in their early 30s.

● RESULTS

Findings relating to the two original main aims

Of the 698 children in the 1955 cohort, 69 were exposed to moderate prenatal or perinatal stress, that is, complications during pregnancy, labour or delivery. About 3 per cent (23 individuals) suffered severe prenatal or perinatal stress; only 14 lived to the age of two. Of the 12 children who died before reaching two years of age, 9 had suffered severe perinatal complications.

Some of the surviving children became 'casualties' in the next 20 years. By the age of 18, 15 per cent of the young people had delinquency records and 10 per cent had mental health problems requiring either in- or outpatient care. There was some overlap between these groups. By the time they were 25, all those with long-term mental health problems had learning problems as well. Of the 70 with mental health problems at 18 years of age, 15 also had a record of repeated delinquency.

As these children were followed from birth to 18, two trends emerged:

● the impact of reproductive stress diminished with time;

● the developmental outcome of virtually every biological risk factor was dependent on the quality of the rearing environment. The better the home environment, the more competence the children displayed. This was already evident by two years old: toddlers who had experienced severe perinatal stress, but lived in middle-class homes or in stable family settings, did nearly as well on developmental tests of sensory-motor and verbal skills as toddlers who had experienced no such stress.

Pre- and perinatal complications were consistently related to impairment of physical and psychological development at ages 10 and 18 *only* when they were combined with chronic poverty, family discord, parental mental illness or other persistently poor rearing conditions. Children raised in middle-class homes, in a

AIM AND NATURE

stable family environment, and by a mother who had finished high school, showed few, if any, lasting effects of reproductive stress later in their lives.

Findings relating to 'high-risk' children: protective factors that contribute to their resilience

A total of 201 individuals (30 per cent of the surviving children) were designated high-risk, because they had experienced moderate to severe perinatal stress, grew up in chronic poverty, were raised by parents with little formal education, or lived in a family environment troubled by discord, divorce, parental alcoholism or mental illness. Children who were exposed to four or more of these risk factors before their second birthday were termed 'vulnerable'. Two-thirds of this high-risk group (129 in all) did develop serious learning or behaviour problems, or pregnancies by the age of 18.

Yet one out of three of these high-risk children (72 in total) grew into competent young adults who loved well and played well. None developed serious learning or behaviour problems in childhood or adolescence. They succeeded in school, managed home and social life well, and set realistic educational and vocational goals for themselves when they left school. By age 20, they had developed into competent, confident and caring people, with a strong desire to take advantage of any opportunity to improve themselves.

These 72 *resilient* individuals were compared with the other 129 in the high-risk group who developed serious and persistent problems in childhood and adolescence. A number of *protective factors* were identified which enabled these resilient individuals to resist stress:

- From infancy on, they displayed *temperamental characteristics* which elicited positive responses from family members and strangers alike. These include a fairly high activity level ('active'), a low degree of excitability and distress ('easygoing', 'even-tempered') and a high degree of sociability ('affectionate', 'cuddly'). Also, they had no eating or sleeping habits that were distressing to their caretakers.

- At 20 months, they were described as alert and responsive. They played vigorously and tended to seek out novel experiences and to ask for help when they needed it.

- At primary school, they concentrated well on their assignments and displayed good problem-solving and reading skills. Although not gifted, they used whatever talents they had effectively. They usually had a special hobby they could share with a friend; both boys and girls excelled at fishing, swimming, horseback riding and hula dancing.

AIM AND NATURE

- They tended to come from families with four or fewer children, with two years or more between themselves and the next sibling. Despite poverty, family discord or parental mental illness, they had the opportunity to establish a close attachment with at least one caretaker during their early years. This might be grandparents, older siblings, uncles or aunts, or a regular babysitter.

- Among the girls, maternal employment and the need to look after younger siblings seemed to contribute to their marked autonomy and sense of responsibility. This was especially so where the father had died or was absent because of divorce or desertion.

- Resilient boys were often firstborn sons who did not have to share their parents' attention with other siblings. They also had a male role model in the family (if not the father, then a grandfather or uncle). Structure and rules, and assigned chores, were part of the boys' daily routine during childhood and adolescence.

- They also found emotional support outside their immediate family. They were generally popular with classmates and had at least one close friend (usually several). They relied on an informal network of neighbours, peers and elders for advice and support in times of crisis and transition. School was a 'home away from home', a refuge from a disordered household. They often mentioned a favourite teacher who had become a role model, friend and confidante. For others, emotional support came from a church group, youth leader or favourite minister. Many also participated in extracurricular activities, which enabled them to be part of a cooperative enterprise.

The resilient children at age 30

In 1985 (at age 30), 545 individuals (80 per cent of the birth cohort) were traced, including 62 of the 72 in the resilient group.

- They seemed to be handling the demands of adulthood well: 75 per cent (46 individuals) had received some college education, 42 worked full-time and 75 per cent said they were satisfied with their jobs.

- Compared with their low-risk peers, a significantly higher proportion of the resilient individuals described themselves as being happy with their current life (44 per cent versus 10 per cent), but they did report a significantly higher number of health problems (46 per cent versus 15 per cent): men's tended to be stress-related, while the women's were mainly related to pregnancy and childbirth.

- While 82 per cent of the resilient women were married, only 48 per cent of the men were. Those who were married were strongly committed to their partners and children.

AIM AND NATURE

● Common characteristics were personal competence and determination, support from a spouse or partner, and a strong religious faith.

● CONCLUSIONS

Werner's findings seem to provide a more hopeful outlook than the extensive research into 'problem' children, who come to the attention of therapists, special needs teachers and social services agencies. Risk factors and stressful environments do not inevitably lead to poor adaptation. At each stage in an individual's development from birth to maturity, there is a shifting balance between stressful events which increase vulnerability, and protective factors which increase resilience. What matters is that the balance is favourable. But when stressful events outweigh the protective factors, even the most resilient child can have problems. It may be possible to shift the balance from vulnerability to resilience through appropriate intervention.

EVALUATION

Methodological issues

The Kauai longitudinal study faced a problem shared by all longitudinal studies, namely, *attrition* of the sample. (See **Exercises**.) Over a 30-year period, we expect members of the original sample to be 'lost' for one reason or another. Here, the dropout rate was very favourable:

● at the 2-year follow-up, 96 per cent of the living children were still on Kauai and available for study;

● 90 per cent for the 10-year follow-up;

● 88 per cent for the 18-year follow-up;

● 80 per cent for the 31/32-year follow-up, including 62 of the 72 who had been designated 'resilient' at age 18 (86 per cent).

Another problem is finding a community in the first place that is willing or able to cooperate in such a large-scale research project. Kauai was chosen for several reasons, not least of which was how receptive the island's population was to the project. Medical, public health, educational and social services provision was comparable to that of similar-sized communities on the US mainland at the time. The population of Kauai includes individuals of Japanese, Filipino, Portuguese, Chinese, Korean and northern European, as well as Hawaiian, descent. So, the study would take account of a wide variety of cultural influences on childbearing and child-rearing. All these factors helped to make the birth cohort fairly representative of the US population as a whole.

Theoretical issues

Several theorists, including Garmezy and Rutter (1983) and Masten and Coatsworth (1995, in Bee, 2000), broadly agree with Werner's interpretation of her results. Each child is born with certain *vulnerabilities*, such as difficult temperament, a physical abnormality, allergies or a genetic tendency towards alcoholism. Each child is also born with some *protective factors*, such as high intelligence, good coordination, an easy temperament or a lovely smile. These tend to make him or her more *resilient* in the face of stress. These vulnerabilities and protective factors then interact with the child's environment, so the *same* environment can have quite different effects, depending on the qualities the child brings to the interaction. As Bee (2000) says, 'Environments don't just "happen" to children, willy-nilly. Children interact with their environment'.

This account seems to be saying that protective factors are the cause, and resilience the effect. But the data that Werner presents are basically *correlational*: the greater the number of protective factors, the greater the child's resilience. It is possible that the more resilient the child (through temperament and other genetically influenced characteristics), the greater the number of protective factors it 'wraps round' itself. For example, the temperamentally more active and affectionate child (resilience) will elicit more favourable responses in others (a protective factor). In other words, might resilience be the cause, and protective factors the effect? The way that Werner lists the characteristics of the resilient child makes it difficult to know whether they are features of resilience or examples of protective factors.

Rutter (1990, in Smith *et al.*, 1998) believes that it is more useful to think of resilience as a *process* which is part of a complex social system at a particular point in time.

Subsequent research

According to Leckman and Mayes (2007): 'As images from Iraq haunt our media, we count our dead and prefer not to be reminded that as in World War II and the Vietnam conflict the number of civilian casualties far exceeds that of the military'. They note that Werner was a child in Germany during World War II; she subsequently wrote a series of books about children during that war (and the American Civil War), using first-person accounts recorded in personal diaries and letters. These are harrowing accounts of survival in the face of the brutality of war. But she is best known for her research on Kauai.

Masten and Coatsworth's review (1998, in Bee, 2000) provides a list of the key qualities of resilient children. The list closely matches Werner's and is divided into three sources:

- *individual*: good intellectual functioning, appealing, sociable, easygoing disposition, self-efficacy (our belief that we can act effectively and exercise some control over events that influence our life: Bandura, 1986), self-confidence, and high self-esteem, talents and faith;

- *family*: close relationships to a caring parent figure, authoritative parenting (warmth, structure, high expectations), socio-economic advantages, and connections to extended supportive family networks;

- *extra-familial context*: bonds to pro-social adults outside the family, connections to pro-social organizations and attending effective schools.

The way these characteristics are grouped suggests that resilience and protective factors are really one and the same: it is individuals who are resilient and individual, family and extra-familial characteristics that are protective. In other words, resilient individuals are those who manage to resist stressful events and conditions (in Werner's terms, high-risk) through protective factors/characteristics.

These characteristics are the same qualities that are linked to competence in children who are *not* growing up in poverty or other risky environments. For example, studies of boys raised in high-crime inner-city neighbourhoods show that high intelligence and at least a minimum level of family cohesion are key ingredients affecting their chances of creating a successful life pattern (Sampson and Laub, 1994 in Bee, 2000). Boys raised in poverty-level families where there was alcoholism, or who had parents with strong antisocial tendencies or low IQ, were much less likely to develop the competence needed to 'bootstrap' themselves out of these difficult circumstances.

A characteristic not included in Masten and Coatsworth's list is *gender*. Werner found that up to the age of 10, boys tended to be less resilient than girls when faced with a wide variety of physiological and psychosocial stressors. For example, more boys than girls experienced birth difficulties; of those with the most serious complications, a greater proportion of boys died. In later years, boys were more likely to develop behaviour problems, have difficulties at school, require medical treatment for serious illness, come to the attention of mental health services and become delinquent. But after age 10, this pattern reversed: by 18, more boys than girls had improved, and any new problems appeared more often in girls than in boys. However, females appeared to cope more successfully overall.

Applications and implications

Werner's findings suggest very clearly that some children growing up in adverse conditions need far greater assistance than others. If early intervention cannot be offered to every child at risk, priorities must be established for choosing those who should receive help. Priority should be given to infants and young children who lack – permanently or temporarily – some of the essential attachments that appear to buffer stress. Such children may have survived neonatal intensive care, spent long periods in hospital separated from their families, be the offspring of addicted, mentally ill, lone or teenage parents, have working mothers and not have stable child care, or be migrant and refugee children without permanent roots in a community (Werner, 1989).

Werner argues that all children can be helped to become more resilient if adults in their lives encourage their independence, teach them appropriate communication and self-help skills, and model as well as reward acts of helpfulness and caring. According to Werner:

> *The life stories of the resilient individuals on the Garden Island have taught us that competence, confidence, and caring can flourish even under adverse circumstances if young children encounter people in their lives who provide them with a secure basis for the development of trust, autonomy, and initiative.*

EXERCISES

1   Werner states that before the Kauai longitudinal study, investigators tried to reconstruct the events that led to physical or psychological problems by studying the history of individuals in whom such problems had already surfaced. This retrospective approach can create the impression that the outcome is inevitable, since it takes into account only the 'casualties' and not the 'survivors'.

  (a) What is meant by a 'retrospective' approach?

  (b) What is the term used to describe the kind of approach adopted by longitudinal studies?

  (c) Describe *one* advantage and *one* disadvantage of the latter approach.

2   Is there anything (potentially) unethical about the study?

3   In general terms, why is sample attrition a potential problem, and why was it not a problem here?

27 Social and family relationships of ex-institutional adolescents

Hodges, J. and Tizard, B. (1989)

Journal of Child Psychology and Psychiatry, 30(1): 77–97

BACKGROUND AND CONTEXT

The general context is the effect of early experience on later behaviour and development, specifically the effect of institutional upbringing on later attachment (to both adults and peers, within and outside the family). Related to this are several interconnected questions:

1   If the later environment continues to be deprived, we would expect a continuation of deprived behaviour. But if the environmental improvement is sufficiently great, is there a corresponding positive change in behaviour?

2   Can the effects of early deprivation be reversed, or at least modified?

3   Are some aspects of development (e.g. social, linguistic) more vulnerable than others?

4   Are there critical or sensitive periods for the development of behaviour?

According to Rutter (1989), during the 1950s the dominant view was of the consistency of personality and the lack of major change after early childhood. For example, Bowlby (1951) claimed that maternal deprivation caused permanent and irreversible damage. However, longitudinal studies failed to show high stability over time, and the claims regarding maternal deprivation were severely criticized. It became clear that people changed a good deal over the course of development; the outcomes of early adversities were quite diverse, depending heavily on the nature of subsequent life experiences (Clarke and Clarke, 1976). Even markedly adverse experiences in infancy carry few risks for later development – provided the subsequent rearing environment is good (Rutter, 1981).

Both continuities and discontinuities are to be expected (e.g. Rutter, 1987). Development is concerned with *change*, so it is unreasonable to suppose that the pattern will be set once and for all in early life. Physiological changes (such as puberty: see Chapter 29) and new experiences will both serve to shape psychological functioning. But continuities will also occur: children will carry with them the results of earlier learning and structural and functional change.

However, the *timing* may be as crucial as the nature of experiences. For example, very young infants (especially those younger than seven or eight months) are protected from separation experiences because they have not yet developed strong attachments; older children are protected because they have learned to maintain relationships over time and place. Toddlers are most at risk, because attachments are just becoming established and they lack the cognitive skills required to maintain a relationship with attachment figures in their absence (Rutter, 1981, 1987).

Tizard and her co-workers (e.g. Tizard and Tizard, 1971; Tizard and Rees, 1974; Tizard, 1977; Tizard and Hodges, 1978) followed a group of children who had experienced institutional care for the first years of their lives; most were subsequently adopted, fostered or restored to their biological families. They had received good physical care in the institutions, which also seemed to provide adequately for their cognitive development (as measured by intelligence tests).

However, staff turnover, and an explicit policy against allowing too strong an attachment to develop between children and their carers, meant that the children had little opportunity to form close, continuous relationships with an adult. By the age of two, they had been looked after by an average of 24 different caregivers; by age four, the average was 50. This seemed to fit Bowlby's (1951) description of maternal deprivation as 'not uncommonly almost complete in institutions ... where the child often has no one person who cares for him in a personal way and with whom he feels secure'.

As a result, the children's attachment behaviour was very unusual. At two, they seemed to be attached to a large number of adults (they would run to be picked up when anyone familiar entered the room and cry when they left). At the same time, they were more afraid of strangers than a home-reared comparison group. By four, 70 per cent of those children still in institutions were said 'not to care deeply about anyone'.

Their first opportunity to form a close, reciprocal, long-term attachment came when they left the institutions and were placed in families; this happened at ages ranging from two to seven years. Although most formed attachments to their parents, the ex-institution children showed several atypical features in social development. At four, they were no longer shy of strangers; indeed, about one-third of them were markedly attention-seeking and over-friendly towards strangers, and a few were indiscriminately affectionate to all adults.

AIM AND NATURE

The Hodges and Tizard article represents the latest in a series of reports on the development of these ex-institutional children.

● HYPOTHESIS

There is no hypothesis as such. The study is a 'progress report', characteristic of *longitudinal* studies (though not an inevitable feature), in which the same group of individuals is followed up over a period of time (usually several years). However, since the participants had been followed from early childhood until age 16, two major research questions were being asked:

1   How enduring are the effects of early experience (i.e. institutional upbringing), and could they be reversed after age eight?

2   How satisfactory is the outcome for adopted children and their families, especially compared with possible alternative placements?

● METHOD/DESIGN

Like *cross-cultural* studies (see Chapter 4), longitudinal studies represent an overall *approach*. They are conducted mainly in relation to developmental psychology, because they present ways of studying *change over time*. The actual collection of data can involve a variety of specific methods; Hodges and Tizard used interviews and questionnaires, both with the participants themselves (16-year-old ex-institution children), and with their parents and teachers.

Hodges and Tizard also refer to their study as a 'form of natural experiment': some change occurs in the natural course of events (here, the child's rearing environment: the *independent variable*), which is studied for its effect on some aspect of the child's development (here, social relationships: the *dependent variable*). These children are compared with (matched) controls, whose environment has not changed, so the design is *independent groups/samples*.

The independent variable had two 'values': adopted and restored (returned to biological family); this allowed the two ex-institution groups to be compared with each other, as well as with the control/comparison groups.

Attrition in, and whereabouts of, the sample

It was extremely difficult to locate the children after eight years without contact, but eventually they were all traced. Of the 51 studied at age eight, 9 were not available for study at age sixteen. These nine, added to the 14 unavailable after age four, meant that the losses over the 12 years (ages four to sixteen) amounted to 35 per cent.

Of the 28 adopted children seen at age eight, 26 were still in their adoptive homes at age sixteen, as were 12 of the 13 restored children who were still with their parents at age sixteen. Only one child had remained in residential care throughout the period. The rest of those who had been in residential or temporary foster care at age eight had experienced many changes, but 5 were back in residential care at age sixteen.

Altogether, 17 adopted boys and 6 adopted girls, 6 restored boys and 5 restored girls, 3 boys and 2 girls in institutional care were interviewed.

Comparison groups

A new, matched comparison group was formed to replace the one used in earlier stages of the study. The original comparison group of 30 working-class children from London was set up when the experimental group children were in institutions at age two; this no longer seemed appropriate either for the primarily middle-class adopted group, or for the restored group who often lived in disadvantaged homes. Also, the majority of ex-institution children were boys, while the original comparison group had been half boys and half girls.

Each of the ex-institution children was matched on gender, one- or two-parent family, socio-economic status, and position in the family. An additional comparison group was used to assess information obtained from the schools; this comprised same-gender classmate, nearest in age.

Assessment procedure

The ex-institution adolescents and their mothers (fathers too were occasionally present) or care workers were interviewed by one interviewer, and the matched comparisons by one of four others. The interviews took place in the family home or institution.

With the permission of the adolescent or adult concerned, the interviews were tape-recorded. The interviews lasted several hours; occasionally a second visit was needed. As well as being interviewed, the adolescents completed a questionnaire on 'social difficulty'; the parent or care worker completed a questionnaire regarding the adolescent's behaviour.

Permission was obtained from both the parents and the adolescents to contact the school via a postal questionnaire; this was a different form of the questionnaire given to parents or care workers, plus a specially designed questionnaire which focused on relationships with teachers and peers. Teachers completed one set for the ex-institution adolescent and one for the matched classmate.

● RESULTS

Relationships within the family

Attachments to parents. As at age eight, the vast majority (17 out of 21) of the adoptive mothers felt that their child was deeply attached to them at age sixteen, and this was true for all their comparisons. Of the 4 who felt their child was not closely attached to them at sixteen, one had felt the same at age eight; at sixteen, the relationship seemed mutually rejecting and hostile. The other 3 mothers had described their eight-year-olds as closely attached, but now doubted the strength of their attachment.

By contrast, only 5 out of 9 restored children were described as deeply attached to their mother (at age eight, the figure was 6 out of 13). Only 1 out of 7 mothers of restored children (who also had other children) felt they loved each child equally (compared with 6 out of 8 comparisons); 5 of the other 6 restored mothers preferred a sibling to the restored child. Out of 14 adoptive parents, 9 loved their children equally; for their comparisons the figure was 13 out of 16.

Adopted adolescents were more often said by their mothers to be attached to their fathers at sixteen than the restored group, who, in turn, were less attached to their fathers than their comparisons.

Relationships with siblings. The comparison adolescents reported fewer marked problems with siblings than the ex-institution group as a whole (as confirmed by the mothers). The restored group got on particularly badly with their siblings (as at age eight).

Showing affection. At age eight, the adopted children and those still in institutional care were found to be the most affectionate and cuddly, with restored children strikingly the least cuddly. As they grew older, 10 out of 22 adopted children had become less demonstrative, but the restored group were still strikingly less affectionate than both the adopted group and their own matched comparisons. There was also a clear (but not significant) tendency for adoptive parents to find it easier to show affection to their adolescents than parents of restored adolescents.

Confiding and support. The two ex-institution groups did not differ greatly from their comparison groups in the proportion who would turn to a parent if they felt depressed or miserable. But fewer of the former would confide in anyone, and fewer – at least of the adoptees – would confide in a peer.

For all groups, their choice of who, if anyone, they would confide in if worried about something depended on the nature of the particular cause of their anxiety. For example, 75–80 per cent would turn to a parent over financial difficulties, but only one ex-institution and two comparison adolescents would do so if worried about not being liked by the opposite sex; instead, they would either keep it to themselves, deny it or share it with a peer.

Disagreement over control and discipline. In all groups, both the adolescents and their mothers believed that disagreements over style of dress or hairstyle were very rare. Disagreements over staying out late, doing homework, helping round the house and pocket money were significantly less frequent in adoptive families than in their comparisons (according to the parents). But comparison adolescents themselves reported fewer rows than ex-institution adolescents, especially the restored group, significantly more of whom felt their parents were too strict compared with their own comparisons.

Peer relationships

Specific difficulties with peer relations. Overall, the ex-institution adolescents had poorer peer relationships than their comparisons. Six out of 30 of the former were described as 'friendly with anyone who's friendly towards him/her' as opposed to 'choosing his/her friends'. There were no differences regarding the number of contacts with same- or opposite-sex friends, or whether s/he currently had a boy/girlfriend (with adolescents and parents largely agreeing on this).

Ex-institution adolescents less often reported themselves as belonging to a 'crowd' of young people who generally went round together; this difference was significant in the case of the adopted group and their matched comparisons.

Teachers rated the ex-institution group as more often quarrelsome, less often liked by their peers and as bullying more than the comparison group.

Special friends. According to the mothers, the ex-institution adolescents were much less likely to have a definite special friend than their comparisons (11/31 compared with 24/31), but there was no difference between adopted and restored. Interviews with the adolescents showed a similar, but not significant, pattern.

Adolescents described as closely attached to the mother were less likely to be seen as 'friendly towards anyone who's friendly towards him/her' by peers. Although there was no overall relationship between being 'over-friendly' at age eight and friendliness towards strangers at sixteen, there was a clear tendency for 'over-friendliness' at eight to be associated with parents' rating at sixteen that the adolescent was friendly with any peer who was friendly towards them, rather than choosing their friends.

Relationships with teachers

As eight-year-olds, the ex-institution children were seen by their teachers as trying more than most to get their attention – and from a stranger entering the room. At 16, they were still 'trying to get a lot of attention from adults', significantly more often than the school comparison group – but not significantly more than their matched comparisons. The restored 16-year-olds were significantly more often aggressive than the adopted group and both their comparisons.

 ## CONCLUSIONS

The Hodges and Tizard study suggests that children deprived of close and lasting attachments to adults in their first years of life can form such attachments later. But these do not arise automatically just because the child is placed in a family; this depends on the adults concerned and how much they nurture such attachments.

The adopted adolescents were much more likely to develop attachments to their adoptive parents than the restored adolescents were to their biological parents. But both ex-institution groups continued to have difficulties in their peer relationships, as well as with adults outside the family; these seem to have originated in their early institutional experience.

These findings may have implications for the adolescents' future adult relationships.

EVALUATION

Theoretical issues

A major source of data regarding the whole continuity–discontinuity debate (especially in the context of early adversity) are studies of children who, in the natural course of events, have experienced major changes (for the better) in their environments. This allows us to determine the specific effects of early experiences, as distinct from those of later ones; this has proved difficult because of the strong associations between the two under normal circumstances (Rutter and the ERA study team, 1998). The Hodges and Tizard study is a major example of these studies that allows us to separate the effects of early and later experience.

Even more dramatic are studies of children who are discovered after having suffered severe and prolonged privation; the most famous cases include Anna (Davis, 1947, 1949), Isabelle (Mason, 1942), the Czech twins (Koluchova, 1972, 1976, 1991), Genie (Curtiss, 1977), Mary and Louise (Skuse, 1984), and Romanian orphanage children

(Rutter and the ERA study team, 1998; Rutter *et al.*, 2007: see **Subsequent research** below).

What all these case studies demonstrate is that theories which stress the overriding importance of early experience for later growth (i.e. *critical periods*) are inadequate (Clarke, 1972). Adverse early experience *may* (but not necessarily) have serious, lasting effects on development in *some* circumstances (Clarke and Clarke, 2000; Rutter, 1981). Individuals show great resilience and there is no simple connection between cause and effect.

Hodges and Tizard's results strongly support the view that Bowlby greatly oversimplified and overemphasized the effects of early deprivation, by overemphasizing the mother's role in what is a much broader and more complex set of relationships and influences. There does not seem to be a critical period for development (except, arguably, for language: but see **Applications and implications** below), although a *sensitive* period might exist. The fact that even the adopted children were not 'unscathed' supports the view that the first two years or so is still the *optimum* time for developing attachments (but not the *only* time).

Rutter and Rutter (1992) believe that Hodges and Tizard's data strongly suggest that the lack of depth and selectivity in the adolescents' peer relationships was a consequence of their early institutional experiences, with the lack of selective attachments being the key feature, However, while there may seem to be some sort of sensitive period for the development of close friendships in adolescence, we need to know whether this pattern of relationships persists into adulthood. (Again, see **Applications and implications** below.)

Further, there is an increasing tendency to see children as part of a social system in which they are in a mutually modifying relationship, with the mother no longer playing such a pivotal role (Skuse, 1984). 'Maternal deprivation' is too general and heterogeneous, and its effects too varied, to be of continuing value (Rutter, 1981).

Methodological issues

As we saw in the **Method/design** section above, Hodges and Tizard describe their study as a kind of natural experiment. What we do not know is how it was decided which children would be adopted and which restored to their biological parents. If it was because of certain characteristics of the children themselves (e.g. those who were adopted were seen as more socially responsive), wouldn't this have spoilt the logic of the 'experiment'? Hodges and Tizard deny this.

One of the major problems associated with any longitudinal study is *attrition* of the sample. As we noted above, the dropout over the 12 years of the study amounted to

35 per cent of the original institution sample. How representative is this? Turning the numbers round means that the 16-year-olds constituted 65 per cent of the original sample, a figure that Hodges and Tizard say is comparable with another, larger, longitudinal study. But how much further attrition could they afford over, say, another 20-year period? (Also, would this be within their professional lifetime? We seem to have discovered another problem with longitudinal studies!)

The data were collected mainly though interviews and questionnaires, and so can only be as reliable and/or valid as the particular methods used (and the skills of those administering them). Was there any way of independently checking the accuracy of the answers given? How objective can parents be about their children, and children about their parents, and, indeed, both groups about themselves? How objective could the teachers be, given that they knew which pupils were ex-institution children?

Subsequent research

As important as case studies such as those of Anna, Isabelle and the Czech twins may be, the numbers involved are, of course, very small. The opportunity to study the psychological effects of early global privation in a systematic way arose from the adoption by English families of a large number of children reared in extremely poor conditions in Romanian institutions (following the fall of the Ceauşescu regime). A high proportion of such children showed severe developmental retardation, growth failure and widespread infections.

Rutter and the ERA study team (1998) reported their findings from a study of 111 Romanian children who entered the UK before the age of two, and 52 control group children (within-UK adoptees, who had not suffered early privation). Both groups of adoptive parents were educationally and occupationally above general population norms, and were not significantly different from each other. Both groups of children were assessed at age four using the Denver scales (designed for use by parents to focus on readily observable attainments), the McCarthy scales (a general cognitive measure which correlates highly with both Stanford-Binet and Wechsler IQs: see Chapters 34 and 35), and detailed measures of socio-emotional and behavioural functioning.

Some of the residential institutions in which the Romanian children had been raised were officially called 'hospitals', others 'orphanages'; but in practice there was little difference between them. Conditions varied from poor to appalling: the children were mainly confined to their cots; there were few, if any, toys; very little talk from care givers; no personalized care-giving; gruel was fed by bottles often left propped up; and the general physical environments could be very harsh. As a whole, these children were more severely deprived, physically and psychologically, than almost any other sizeable group of children previously studied. The conditions were, in all respects, incomparably worse than those in the UK (or indeed most other industrialized countries).

At the time of entry to the UK, most of the children were severely malnourished and suffered from chronic and recurrent respiratory and other infections. In addition, 'considered as a whole, the evidence is entirely consistent in indicating that the Romanian adoptees as a group showed major developmental retardation' (Rutter and the ERA study team, 1998).

By age four, the physical catch-up was very substantial, although they remained (as a group) slightly lighter, shorter and smaller in head circumference than the control group. Their *developmental catch-up* was equally impressive (although those who were adopted *before* six months had a catch-up that was almost complete by age four). Despite their profoundly unpromising start in life (or in view of it?), the degree of cognitive catch-up was 'spectacular', and provides clear evidence that the initial developmental retardation was caused by the profoundly deprived circumstances of their early institutional rearing (Rutter and the ERA study team, 1998).

Other Romanian orphans were adopted by Canadian families between the ages of eight months and five and a half years (Chisolm *et al.*, 1995). It seems that some negative impact on the children's relationships with adoptive parents can be attributed to their institutional experiences. For example, their behaviour was often described as *ambivalent*: they simultaneously wanted contact and resisted it. Also, they were not easily comforted when distressed. Based on their intellectual recovery, Schaffer (1998) believes there are good reasons for being optimistic that they will eventually overcome this impairment.

However, two follow-up studies of the UK-adopted children suggest that there is a continuing strong effect of their early privation. In the first of these, the children were studied up to the age of six (Rutter and the ERA study team, 2004). Many children displayed *disinhibited attachment*, which in many ways resembles the attachment behaviour of Hodges and Tizard's ex-institution sample: a lack of close confiding relationships; rather indiscriminate friendliness; a relative lack of differentiation in response to different adults; a tendency to go off with strangers; and a lack of checking back with a parent in anxiety-provoking situations. Both DSM-IV-TR (American Psychiatric Association, 2000) and ICD-10 (World Health Organization, 1992), two of the major classifications of mental disorders (see Chapters 30, 31 and 33) have brought these features together in the concept of *reactive attachment disorder – disinherited type*.

This pattern persisted from ages four to six, and Rutter (2006) argued that it might reflect some form of biological programming, that is, an effect on brain structure and functioning which has arisen as a means of adaptation to the environmental circumstances operating at a sensitive period of development. If this were the case, we would expect strong persistence into middle childhood/early adolescence. Rutter *et al.* (2007) reported a further follow-up to age 11.

As reported by parents, and confirmed by the researchers, disinhibited attachment (DA) persisted from age 6 to 11, but it did become less frequent during that period. Although DA was strongly associated with institutional rearing, children adopted after six months did not display it to a significantly greater degree. However, DA constitutes a meaningfully distinct behavioural pattern, and a clinically significant disorder, which was evident in these Romanian orphans from the preschool years and did not first appear in middle childhood (Rutter *et al.*, 2007).

Applications and implications

What about long-term personality and social adjustment of those who experience early privation? The little evidence that exists is encouraging. Hodges and Tizard's research indicates that children who fail to enjoy close and lasting relationships with adults in the first years of life *can* form such attachments later on. The ex-institution adolescents have now been followed up into adulthood (average age 31 years), through postal questionnaires (Hodges *et al.*, in preparation; Jewitt, 1998) and interviews using the Adult Attachment Interview (AAI: Main *et al.*, 1985), with a sub-sample of the ex-institution group (Williams, 1999). There were few significant differences between them and the matched comparisons, including evidence of psychiatric disorder. However, the ex-institution group consistently reported difficulties in relationships with friends, partners and children, and significantly greater difficulties in relationships with their families of upbringing. In addition, they reported a tendency to be over-aggressive in their interpersonal relationships, and to be independent and self-reliant. But they also reported *more rewarding* intimate friendships, with higher levels of companionship and higher self-esteem than the comparison group (these differences were *not* statistically significant).

While acknowledging the small sample size (22 ex-institution, 23 comparison), Hodges (personal communication, 2000) states that: 'the evidence seems to support both the view that the effects of earlier adversity fade given the right later circumstances, and the view that there are some enduring effects producing continuities in personal characteristics'.

At the age of 29, the Czech twins studied by Koluchova (1991) had married, become fathers and were described as entirely stable, with no abnormalities and enjoying warm relationships.

Quinton and Rutter's (1988) study of women who had spent most of their childhood in group (residential) homes found that they experienced difficulties in close friendships, sexual/romantic relationships and parenting, especially if they went into care in infancy and stayed until at least age 16. According to Rutter and Rutter (1992), this suggests that 'a lack of early selective attachments may predispose to difficulties in all kinds of very close relationship in adult life'.

However, while *as a group* the institutionalized women were less sensitive, supportive and warm towards their children (compared with non-institutionalized controls), there was also considerable variability *within* the institution group; by no means did all of them make bad parents. For example, those who had had more positive school experiences were more likely to make proper plans and choices for their career and marriage partner; this made it very much more likely that they would marry for positive reasons and have a supportive marital relationship. In turn, this increased their chance of good social functioning – including being a caring parent.

These different *developmental pathways* represent a route for escaping early adversity: the 'same' early experience does not inevitably mean the same consequences later in life.

Most human characteristics (with the possible exception of language) are highly 'canalized' (Scarr-Salapatek, 1976); this makes them virtually resistant to obliteration by even the most dire early environments (Skuse, 1984).

EXERCISES

1   Briefly describe *three* advantages and *three* disadvantages of the longitudinal compared with the cross-sectional approach (*not* including the attrition of the sample in the former).

2   Briefly describe *two* ways in which a natural experiment differs from a laboratory experiment.

3   (a) Why did Hodges and Tizard think it necessary to form a new matched comparison group for the study of the ex-institution adolescents?

    (b) Who were they?

4   Why was it necessary to have a comparison group at all?

28 Sex reassignment at birth

Diamond, M. and Sigmundson, H.K. (1997)

Paediatric and Adolescent Medicine, 151: 298–304

BACKGROUND AND CONTEXT

Often the first thing we notice about other people is whether they are male or female (their *sexual identity*). The importance of sexual identity to our self-concept and interaction with others is reflected in the fact that every known culture distinguishes between male and female. (See Chapter 41.) Similarly, 'Is it a boy or a girl?' is usually the first question to be asked by and of new parents.

These two examples demonstrate the importance of sex as a social category. But, strictly, *sex*(ual identity) refers only to the *biological* facts about us, such as chromosomal make-up, genitalia, and reproductive anatomy and functioning. By contrast, *gender* (gender identity) is what culture makes out of the 'raw material' of biological sex: it is the *social equivalent* or *social interpretation* of sex.

Whether we choose to focus on sex or gender, we assume that they are *dichotomous*, in other words, each of us can only be one or the other. However, in reality, things are not always as straightforward as this assumption would imply. Although estimates vary, it has been suggested that around 1 in 4,500 live births involves an infant whose genitals are sufficiently ambiguous to make the immediate classification of male or female very difficult (Warne, 1998, in Liao and Boyle, 2004). The general term for such sexually undifferentiated infants is 'intersex'.

Two of the better-known causes of intersex are:

● *androgen insensitivity syndrome* (AIS) (or *testicular feminizing syndrome*), when a chromosomally normal male (XY) is born with normal-looking female external genitals and a shallow vagina.

● *adrenogenital syndrome* (AGS) (or *congenital adrenal hyperplasia*/CAH), when a chromosomally normal female (XX) is born with male-looking genitals (such as an enlarged clitoris that resembles a penis).

These are examples of *pseudo-hermaphroditism*. (See **Exercises**.)

Ever since the pioneering work of Money in the 1950s, the study of intersexuality has been of interest to psychologists. This is partly because of what it teaches us about gender identity in general; ironically, the study of intersex individuals has helped to reinforce the dichotomy between male and female.

Money's key contribution was to provide compelling evidence for the influence of nurture or socialization in the development of gender. According to Money and Ehrhardt's (1972) *biosocial theory*, it is the *interaction* between biological and social factors that matters, rather than the direct influence of biology alone. How an infant is labelled sexually determines how it is raised or socialized. In turn, this determines its gender identity, from which follow gender role and sexual orientation ('anatomy is destiny'). Some of the most apparently compelling evidence to support biosocial theory came from Money and Ehrhardt's study of an identical male twin (Bruce Reimer).

Bruce was not intersex at birth. At eight months, while undergoing a routine circumcision, his penis was accidentally burnt off (the 'penectomized twin'). After consulting Money, his parents decided it was in Bruce's best interests to raise him as a girl (Brenda). In 1967, orchidectomy (surgical castration: removal of the testicles) and preliminary surgery to facilitate feminization were conducted. Further surgery to create a full vagina was performed later in childhood. The child was seen by Money at yearly intervals at Johns Hopkins University in Baltimore, USA. Bruce/Brenda is often referred to John/Joan in the literature.

AIM AND NATURE

● HYPOTHESES

The aim of the article is to challenge two basic assumptions ('postulates') of Money and Ehrhardt's biosocial theory, namely:

1   Individuals are psychosexually neutral at birth.

2   Healthy psychosexual development is intimately related to the appearance of the genitals.

● METHOD/DESIGN

This is a *review article*, which re-examines the medical notes and impressions of therapists who were originally involved with the Reimer twins. New data also come from interviews with John himself, his mother and his wife in 1994 and 1995 (when John was 29 and 30). Diamond and Sigmundson conducted these interviews together.

Sigmundson was chief psychiatrist of the management team the case was referred to in the patient's home area in Winnipeg, Canada. Although the patient was assigned to the immediate care of female psychiatrists (intended as role models for Joan), Sigmundson maintained direct supervisory control of the case.

The unique nature of the case attracted the attention of the BBC, who invited Diamond (a biologist and long-time critic of the first postulate) to act as a consultant (1979–82).

● RESULTS/FINDINGS

Postulate 1: Individuals are psychosexually neutral at birth

John/Joan's mother recalls:

> *As soon as he had the surgery, the doctor said I should now start treating him as a girl, doing girl things, and putting him in girls' clothes. But that was a disaster. I put this beautiful little dress on him … and he [immediately tried] to rip it off; I think he knew it was a dress and that it was for girls and he wasn't a girl.*

But Joan could act in quite a feminine way when she wanted to, and at about age six was described as doing so. For example, the mother stated: 'One thing that really amazes me is that she is so feminine. I've never seen a little girl so neat and tidy as she can be when she wants to be.' But more often, she resisted such behaviour and would imitate her father more than her brother did. A typical example, from when the twins were four or five, was Joan putting on shaving cream and pretending to shave, rather than putting on lipstick like her mother.

Joan usually rejected girls' toys, clothes and activities when offered to her. Throughout childhood, she consistently preferred boys' games and activities. She liked to tinker with gadgets and tools, taking things apart to see how they worked. She also dressed up in men's clothes. She was regarded as a tomboy, not avoiding rough-and-tumble play or fights.

Joan's realization that she was not a girl gelled between the age of 9 and 11. As John relates:

> *There were little things from early on. I began to see how different I felt and was, from what I was supposed to be. But I didn't know what it meant. I thought I was a freak or something … I looked at myself and said I don't like this type of clothing. I don't like the types of toys I was always being given. I like hanging around with the*

guys and climbing trees and stuff like that and girls don't like any of that stuff. I looked in the mirror and [saw] my shoulders [were] so wide, I mean there [was] nothing feminine about me ... But that [was] how I figured it out. [I figured I was a guy] but I didn't want to admit it. I figured I didn't want to wind up opening a can of worms.

Joan already had suicidal thoughts and did not want additional stress. She fought the boys and girls who were always teasing her about her looks and girly clothes. She had no friends; no one would play with her. She was a good-looking girl, but, as her mother recalls: 'When he started moving or talking, that gave him away, and the awkwardness and incongruities became apparent.'

The other girls teased Joan so aggressively that she often retaliated forcefully. At age 14, she was expelled from school for grabbing another girl by the shirt and: '[ramming] her round the wall like this, threw her on the ground ... until the teacher grabbed me.'

Despite the lack of a penis, Joan often tried to stand to urinate. This made a mess and it was difficult to 'aim'. She persisted in this despite being told off about it. When she was 14, the other girls threatened to 'kill' her if she persisted in this behaviour in their toilets, and she sometimes went to the boys' toilets to urinate.

At age 12, Joan was given oestrogen (female hormone). But this made her 'feel funny' and she would often dispose of her daily dose of hormones. She was unhappy about her developing breasts and would not wear a bra. Things reached crisis point when she was 14. She confessed to her endocrinologist (the specialist in charge of her hormone treatment) that 'I suspected I was a boy since the second grade' (age seven). This doctor personally believed that she should continue with her medication and proceed as a girl, but discussed with her the possible male and female paths open to her. The local psychiatric team (in Canada) had noticed Joan's preference for boys' activities and refusal to accept female status, so they had already discussed among themselves the possibility of accepting Joan's change back to being male.

Shortly after this, at age 14, Joan decided to revert to living as a male. Knowing about her previous suicidal thoughts, the local therapists agreed to sex reassignment. John eventually persuaded his father to tell him the truth of what had happened when he was a baby. John recalls: 'All of a sudden everything clicked. For the first time things made sense and I understood who and what I was.'

John requested and received testosterone (male hormone) injections. He also had a mastectomy (removal of his breasts) at age 14 and phalloplasty (the surgical construction of a penis) at 15 and 16. He began to work out and blossomed into an attractive, muscular young man.

AIM AND NATURE

After these surgical procedures, John adjusted well. As a boy he was reasonably well accepted and popular with both boys and girls. Several girls had crushes on him. But he was very unsure of himself when it came to actual sexual contact. However, after his return to male living he felt that his attitudes, behaviours and body were in harmony as they had never been as a girl. At the age of 25, he met and married a much older woman and adopted her three children.

Postulate 2: Healthy psychosexual development is intimately related to the appearance of the genitals

Initially at Johns Hopkins, then with the local therapists prior to the sex reassignment, Joan's expressed feeling of not being a girl was treated with ridicule. She would be told things like, 'All girls think such things when they are growing up'. John recalls thinking: 'You can't argue with a bunch of doctors in white coats; you're just a little kid and their minds are already made up. They didn't want to listen.' She often just went along with them in order to ease the pressure to act as a girl.

Starting at age seven, Joan began to rebel against going for the consultations at Johns Hopkins. She was embarrassed about the forced exposure of her genitals, and it was also uncomfortable. After the age of eight, she strongly resisted attempts to persuade her to have more surgery to repair her vagina. At Johns Hopkins the consultants enlisted male-to-female transsexuals to convince Joan of the advantages of being female and having a vagina constructed. She was so disturbed by this that on one occasion she ran away from the hospital and was found hiding on the roof of a nearby building. After age 14, she adamantly refused to return to Johns Hopkins and came exclusively under the care of local paediatricians, paediatric surgeons, an endocrinologist and psychiatrists.

John recalls thinking, from preschool through primary school, that doctors were more concerned with the appearance of her genitals than Joan herself was. She thought they were making a big fuss about nothing: 'Leave me be and then I'll be fine... It's bizarre. My genitals are not bothering me; I don't know why it is bothering you guys so much.'

When asked what Joan thought of her genitals when she was younger, John replied, 'I didn't really have anything to compare myself against other than my brother when we were taking a bath.' Nudity was a rare sight in the very conservative religious community the family lived in. At the yearly visit to Johns Hopkins, the twins were made to stand naked for inspection by groups of clinicians and to inspect each other's genitalia. This experience was recalled with very negative emotions by both twins.

John recalls frustration, which remains, at not having his feelings and wishes recognized. Despite the obvious absence of a penis, Joan knew she was not a girl. When she tried to express such thoughts, the doctors would change the subject. At

AIM AND NATURE

the time, she described herself as feeling 'like a trapped animal'.

The teasing she received from other children was due to her clothes and behaviour, *not* her genitals. None of Joan's peers knew anything about her genitals. Added to this were the attempts by her local doctors, her parents and (mainly) female psychotherapists to prepare her for vaginal reconstruction and life as a female. John recalls, 'They kept making me feel as if I was a freak.'

At age 14, Joan started refusing to live as a girl. She took to wearing jeans and shirts, because these are gender-neutral, and she aspired to becoming a mechanic. Rorschach and thematic apperception tests at the time produced responses more typical of a boy than a girl. Her adamant rejection of a female role, and her improved appearance and disposition when acting as a boy, convinced the local therapists that sexual reassignment was the correct path to take. He immediately began having testosterone injections.

Following the phalloplasty, there was difficulty with urethral closure. Several attempts to repair this all failed. John now urinates through a fistula (hole) at the base of his penis while sitting down. Much of the penis lacks sensation.

John's first sexual partner was a girl, when he was 18. Intercourse with his wife happens only occasionally. He is capable of orgasm with ejaculation, and they mostly pleasure each other through physical affection and mutual masturbation. John recalls thinking it was small-minded of others to think that all his personality was summed up by the presence or absence of a penis:

> Doctor… said, 'It's gonna be tough, you're going to be picked on … you're not gonna find anybody [unless you have vaginal surgery and live as a female].' … I wasn't very old at the time, but it dawned on me that these people gotta be pretty shallow if that's the only thing they think I've got going for me; that the only reason why people get married and have children and have a productive life is because of what they have between their legs … If that's all they think of me, that they justify my worth by what I have between my legs, then I gotta be a complete loser.

● CONCLUSIONS

John is a mature and forward-looking man with a keen sense of humour and balance. Although still bitter about his experience, he accepts what happened and is trying to make the most of his life, with support from his wife, parents and family. He has job satisfaction and is generally self-assured.

This update to a case for so long accepted as a 'classic' completely reverses the conclusions and theory behind the original reports. Cases of infant sex reassignment need to be reviewed after puberty: five- and ten-year post-sex reassignment follow-ups are still not sufficient.

AIM AND NATURE

No support exists for the postulates that individuals are psychosexually neutral at birth or that healthy psychosexual development is dependent on the appearance of the genitals. Certainly long-term follow-up on other cases is needed.

EVALUATION

Theoretical issues

According to Ceci and Williams (1999), this article helps to redress the existing imbalance in the debate regarding the influences on the development of gender identity. As developmental psychologists, they believe that most textbooks stress the importance of how children are reared to the detriment of biological explanations.

The 'supremacy of socialization', of course, is what Money and Ehrhardt's biosocial theory is advocating. Their *Man and Woman, Boy and Girl* (1972) provides a large amount of research data (including the case of John/Joan), which they claim support the *nurture* side of the nature–nurture debate. Ceci and Williams state that perhaps the single most striking aspect of the account given by Diamond and Sigmundson is how quickly John, who spent the best part of 14 years being raised as a female, was able to adopt a male gender identity and role. This strongly suggests that biological influences are not as irrelevant as many psychologists seem to believe.

Until very recently, most people working within the psychology of women have taken as read the 'natural' or 'biological' separation of human beings into two (and only two) sexes. Basing their work on Money's research, feminist psychologists (e.g. Unger, 1979) have accepted his distinction between sex (which is biological) and gender (which is social). Biosocial theory's emphasis on the socialization of gender identity is consistent with feminist psychologists' beliefs that gender differences are learned (i.e. socially constructed). Accepting Money's distinction, if gender is socially constructed, then sex (male and femaleness) is a (non-constructed) biological category.

However, social constructionist approaches (commonly misunderstood as nothing more than the 'nurture' end of the nature–nurture debate) attempt to challenge (by deconstructing) the very notion of dichotomous biological sex (Kitzinger, 2004). This is an approach which some feminist psychologists have been developing for some time. Kitzinger quotes Kessler and McKenna (1978), who argue that:

> *To take the sexes for granted, to treat the existence of two sexes as an irreducible fact, obscures each individual's responsibility for creating the world in which she/he lives ... gender is a social construction, a world of two sexes is a result of the socially shared, taken-for-granted methods which members use to construct reality.*

The existence of intersexual individuals shows that our Western male/female dichotomy is *not* a biological given. Anthropologists have described 'third sex' categories in other cultures (see Chapter 41), and European and North American feminists have been criticized for assuming that all cultures organize their social world through a perception of human bodies as male or female (Kitzinger, 2004).

Kitzinger argues that instead of asking how successfully intersex people can be surgically and socially modified in order to become male or female, psychologists could be exploring how the myth of two biological sexes is reproduced, regulated – and sometimes resisted.

Methodological issues

According to Diamond and Sigmundson, the first postulate was derived not from the study of normal individuals, but from hermaphrodites and pseudo-hermaphrodites. Normal, here, of course, means unambiguously male or female. According to the social constructionist critiques of this dichotomy, these groups would fall into a third category of 'normality', namely intersexual individuals. Would Money's study of such groups, and the derivation of the first postulate from it, then become valid? (See **Exercises**.) The second postulate had only anecdotal support. (Again, see **Exercises**.)

Diamond and Sigmundson point out that long-term follow-up of case reports are unusual but often crucial. Perhaps the initial impressions of the consultants (Money and Ehrhardt, 1972; Money and Tucker, 1975) were appropriate at the time, and Joan's behaviour and thinking shifted in the course of development. However, clinical notes and the impressions of the local doctors at the time, as well as John's recollections in 1994–95, indicate that he never fully accepted sex reassignment. Only when it became obvious that the original management programme of maintaining Joan as a girl no longer proved viable and was psychologically damaging – even life-threatening – did the local team change their minds.

It is also possible, they say, that interpretations of Joan's behaviour from her early years were mistaken. If results do not fit one's hypothesis, they might be (unconsciously) presented in a way that makes them seem to support it. For example, 'tomboyish behaviour' is consistent with the first postulate (some 'normal' girls are known to be 'tomboys'), whereas 'typical male behaviour' is not (such behaviour can only be displayed by 'real' boys).

Furthermore, the second postulate reduces a person's total sexuality to just those behaviours and experiences that relate to the genitals. However, an individual's sexual profile comprises at least five levels: gender patterns, reproduction, sexual identity, arousal and physiological mechanisms, and sexual orientation (PRIMO). According to

Diamond and Sigmundson, John's reassignment to Joan addressed only the gender patterns; it was assumed that sexual identity and the other levels would follow. Joan did indeed become aware of what was expected of her as a girl, but did not feel comfortable with this – standing while urinating is a dramatic illustration of this. Sex reassignment also failed at the other four levels.

Subsequent research

Diamond and Sigmundson cite a study of 20 patients with micro-penises who were reared as boys. None had any doubt about being male. They also cite several studies of males originally reassigned as females who switched back and successfully lived as males, despite not having a normal penis. In many of these cases, the ages at which various milestones were reached, feelings developed and the reassignment challenged, were very similar to John/Joan's experience.

When John was 18, he tried to commit suicide on two separate occasions. Colapinto (2000) met John in 1997, when he was 31 and renamed David Reimer. According to Colapinto:

> The strongest impression I was left with was of John's intense, unequivocal masculinity. His gestures, walk, attitudes, vocabulary – none of them betrayed the least hint that he had been raised as a girl ... when conversation turns to his childhood ... his voice ... takes on a tone of aggrievement and anger, and he tends to drop the pronoun 'I' from his speech, replacing it with the distancing 'you' ... almost as if he were speaking about someone else altogether. Which, in a sense, he is.

In 2002, his brother committed suicide, for which he seemed to blame himself. In 2004, David Reimer committed suicide.

Applications and implications

According to Diamond and Sigmundson, having to make decisions in cases of ambiguous or severely damaged genitalia are some of the most difficult that doctors ever face. Traditionally, guidelines for making such a decision have been based on the two postulates that were examined in their review article. For example, because it is simpler to construct a vagina than a satisfactory penis, only the infant with a penis of adequate size should be considered for a male gender assignment. Such clinical advice, concerned mainly with surgical options, is fairly standard in medical texts.

Based on their review, Diamond and Sigmundson offer new guidelines. They believe that any chromosomally normal male (XY), born with a normal nervous system, should be raised as a male. Surgery to repair any genital problem, although difficult, should be conducted in keeping with this principle. Parents and the child should be referred for appropriate and long-term counselling, rather than immediate sex reassignment surgery.

In 1996, in the first public demonstration by intersexuals in modern history, 26 activists gathered outside the annual meeting of the American Academy of Paediatricians to protest against its continued support of 'intersex genital mutilation' (Kitzinger, 2004). They argued that cosmetic genital surgery on intersex infants whose genitals do not conform with the culture's male/female dichotomy violates the child's human rights.

Genital mutilation (clitoridectomy and infibulation) affects over 100 million girls and women worldwide, most of whom live in Africa. Intersex genital mutilation has been described as 'the homegrown version of female genital mutilation' (Wilchins, 1997, in Kitzinger, 2004).

EXERCISES

1   What do you understand by the terms 'hermaphrodite' and 'pseudo-hermaphrodite'?

2   In the Methodological issues section, it is suggested that inclusion of intersex as a third sexual category would make the first postulate valid after all. Do you agree or disagree with this claim? What are your reasons?

3   Diamond and Sigmundson claim that the second postulate is invalid because it is based on anecdotes. What is wrong with anecdotes as a source of scientific evidence?

4   Kitzinger (2004) describes other forms of body-altering techniques used to 'improve' bodies that are 'insufficiently dichotomized' by nature.

(a) What do you think she means by 'insufficiently dichotomized'?

(b) Try to think of some examples of body-altering techniques.

29 Development of the adolescent brain: Implications for executive function and social cognition

Blakemore, S.-J. and Choudhury, S. (2006)

The Journal of Child Psychology and Psychiatry, 47(3/4): 296–312

BACKGROUND AND CONTEXT

The word 'adolescence' comes from the Latin *adolescere* meaning 'to grow into maturity'. As well as being a time of enormous physiological change, adolescence is also marked by changes in behaviour, expectations, and relationships with both parents and peers.

In Western, industrialized societies, there is generally no single initiation rite signalling the passage into adulthood. This makes the transition more difficult than it appears to be in more traditional, non-industrialized societies. Relationships with adults in general, and parents in particular, must be renegotiated in a way that allows the adolescent to achieve greater independence. This process is aided by changing relationships with peers.

Compared with previous generations, adolescence begins five years earlier, marriage takes place six to seven years later, and cohabitation, perhaps as a prelude to marriage, is rapidly increasing (Coleman and Hendry, 1990).

Until quite recently, it was believed that the changes associated with adolescence, in particular the emotional changes (such as mood swings), were the result of the dramatic hormonal changes responsible for puberty. These, combined with the lack of clear boundaries between 'child' and 'adult' in Western societies, could explain the moodiness and 'teenage angst' that parents especially find so difficult. But what about the role of the brain in all this?

It was once widely accepted by neuroscientists that after the initial reorganization of its neural (brain cell) circuits in very early childhood, the brain remained much the same for the rest of a person's life. Except for the gradual loss of brain cells during the adult years, it was thought that the physical development of the brain stopped in childhood (Connor, 2006).

However, post-mortem studies of human brains beginning in the late 1960s, together with studies of non-human animals' brains starting in the mid 1970s, revealed that some brain areas continue to develop well beyond early childhood. But it was not until the advent of brain imaging that the true scale of the changes in the teenage brain became fully apparent.

- *Magnetic resonance imaging* (MRI) uses a very large magnetic field to produce high-quality, three-dimensional images of brain structures without injecting radioactive tracers. A large cylindrical magnet creates a magnetic field around the person's head, and a magnetic pulse is sent through the magnetic field. Different brain structures (such as so-called white matter, grey matter, blood vessels, fluid and bone) have different magnetic properties, and so appear different in the MRI image. Sensors inside the scanner record the signals from the different brain structures, and a computer uses this information to construct an image. MRI allows both surface and deep structures to be presented in great anatomical detail.

- *Functional MRI* (*f*MRI) allows scientists to observe the brain at work (interactions between brain and behaviour: Blakemore and Choudhury, 2006). When neurons (nerve cells) become active, they require a supply of oxygen to be carried to them in the blood. The *f*MRI scanner detects this oxygen carried in the blood because oxygen has magnetic properties; it measures the amount of oxygenated blood sent to particular regions in the brain. The information is used to make 'films' of changes in brain activity as participants perform various cognitive and perceptual tasks.

AIM AND NATURE

● HYPOTHESIS

Although this article does not describe a specific study, it is possible to identify a hypothesis based on a large amount of research evidence that is discussed. This states that, given the continued structural changes in the prefrontal cortex and parietal cortex during adolescence, cognitive abilities that rely on the functioning of these regions (and their complex interactions with other regions) should also change during this time.

● METHOD/DESIGN

This is a *review article*, which means that the authors are describing and evaluating research (mainly other people's), rather than testing any specific hypotheses of their own. However, the focus is on the use of brain imaging techniques (as described above) to demonstrate specific changes in the brain during puberty and adolescence compared with childhood. Blakemore and Choudhury also discuss the implications of brain development for executive function and social cognition. (These are described in the **Evaluation** section below.)

● RESULTS

The first experiments on adolescent brains

Post-mortem studies carried out in the 1970s and 1980s showed that the structure of the prefrontal cortex undergoes significant changes during puberty and adolescence. Two main changes were revealed in the brain before and after puberty:

1   As neurons develop, a layer of myelin (myelin sheath) is formed around the axon, from supporting glial cells. Myelin acts as an insulator and massively increases the speed of transmission (up to 100 times) of electrical impulses between neurons. Whereas sensory and motor brain regions become fully myelinated in the first few years of life, axons in the frontal cortex continue to become myelinated well into adolescence.

2   An adult brain has about 100 billion neurons; at birth, the brain has only a slightly smaller number. After birth, neurons get bigger. But the most significant change involves the wiring, the intricate network of connections between them (the *synapses*). Early in postnatal development, new synapses begin to form: the *synaptic density* (the number of synapses per unit volume of brain tissue) greatly *exceeds* adult levels. This process of synaptic proliferation (*synaptogenesis*) lasts up to several months, depending on the species of animal and the brain region. These early peaks in synaptic density are followed by several years of synaptic elimination (*pruning*): frequently used connections are strengthened and infrequently used connections are eliminated. This experience-dependent process reduces the overall synaptic density to adult levels.

The data for synaptogenesis and pruning came mainly from studies of sensory regions of the brains of cats and rhesus monkeys. But the time course for these processes differs according to the brain region involved. Histological studies of monkey and human prefrontal cortex have shown that synaptogenesis occurs during childhood and again at puberty, followed by a plateau phase and then a pruning after puberty. Pruning occurs throughout adolescence and results in a net decrease in synaptic density in the frontal lobes.

Synaptic pruning is believed to be essential for the fine-tuning of functional networks of brain tissue, making the remaining circuits more efficient. One example of this is babies' ability to categorize speech sounds. Newborns can distinguish between *all* speech sounds, but by 12 months, babies lose the ability to distinguish between sounds they are not exposed to (those not used in their native language). This fine-tuning of sound categorization is thought to rely on synaptic pruning in sensory areas involved in processing sound.

Viewing the adolescent brain with MRI

Before the advent of non-invasive brain imaging techniques, the structure of the human brain could only be studied after death. MRI provides detailed, three-dimensional images of the living human brain.

Linear increases in white matter during adolescence. One of the most consistent findings from MRI studies is that there is a steady, progressive increase in white matter in certain brain regions during childhood and adolescence. Myelin appears white in MRI scans, so the increase in white matter – and related decrease in grey matter – with age is taken to reflect increased myelination of axons in the frontal and parietal lobes.

One study of 111 children and adolescents, aged 4–17, found an increase in white matter specifically in areas that connect anterior speech regions (Broca's area) and posterior language regions (Wernicke's area). The corpus callosum (the dense mass of fibres that connects the left and right hemispheres) has also been found to undergo region-specific growth during adolescence and up to the mid twenties.

Non-linear decreases in grey matter during adolescence. While the increase in white matter in certain brain regions seems to be linear across all brain areas, changes in grey matter density appear to follow a region-specific, non-linear pattern. Several studies have shown that its pattern of development follows an inverted-U shape. How can we account for these findings?

● It is likely that axonal myelination results in an increase in white matter and a simultaneous decrease in grey matter as viewed by MRI.

● The increase in grey matter at the start of puberty might reflect a sudden increase in the number of synapses.

Similarly, the gradual *decrease* in grey matter density that occurs *after* puberty in certain brain regions has been attributed to post-pubescent synaptic pruning.

AIM AND NATURE

Changes in behaviour and cognition after puberty

Two of the brain regions that have consistently been shown to undergo continued development during adolescence are the *prefrontal cortex* and the *parietal cortex*. Given this continued development, it might be expected that cognitive abilities that rely on the functioning of these regions (and their complex interconnections with other regions) should also change during this time. Most studies to date have investigated the frontal lobes and *executive function*.

Development of executive function. *Executive function* describes the ability to control and coordinate our thoughts and behaviour (Luria, 1966; Shallice, 1982). These skills include selective attention, decision making, voluntary response inhibition and working memory. Each of these executive functions is involved in cognitive control, for example, filtering out unimportant information, holding in mind a plan for the future, and inhibiting impulses.

Lesion studies with monkeys, and functional imaging experiments with humans, have linked cognitive control with the frontal lobes. The small number of studies of changes in executive function skills during adolescence show that these do indeed continue to develop during adolescence. Some skills improve in a linear way, while others do not. It seems that the changes in performance are linked to the pruning and myelination processes occurring in the frontal cortex.

Viewing the adolescent brain in action with *f*MRI. Functional MRI (*f*MRI) provides a safe, non-invasive tool for studying interactions between brain and behaviour. It has been used in only a handful of studies to investigate the neural bases of cognitive development, using tasks designed to tap specifically into executive functions.

A popular paradigm for studying response inhibition is the go/no-go task. This involves inhibiting a response when a specific stimulus is presented. For example, participants are required to press a button when seeing letters of the alphabet, except for 'X' (the no-go stimulus). This task requires executive action: the command to inhibit a habitual response.

Using this method, one study showed that in both 7- to 12-year-olds and 21- to 24-year-olds, several regions in the frontal cortex became activated during the go/no-go task. However, while there was significantly greater activity in children than adults in the dorsolateral prefrontal cortex, adults showed greater ventral activity.

Development of social cognition in the brain. Recognition of facial expressions of emotion by adolescents is an aspect of social cognition which has not been studied extensively. However, while some research evidence confirms the role of the amygdala, other evidence implicates the role of the dorsolateral prefrontal cortex. In adolescent girls, the pattern of decreased amygdala and increased dorsolateral prefrontal cortex activation may reflect an increased ability to contextualize and regulate emotional experiences.

AIM AND NATURE

● CONCLUSIONS

The study of the development of executive function and social cognition beyond childhood is a new but rapidly evolving field. The finding that changes in brain structure continue into adolescence and early adulthood challenged accepted views. However, as important as developmental cognitive neuroscience may be, a richer account of changes in adolescent learning and social behaviour requires a multidisciplinary approach which recognizes the complex interactions between genetics, brain structure, physiology and chemistry, and the environment.

EVALUATION

Theoretical issues

In addition to executive functions, there is evidence that the prefrontal cortex is involved in several other high-level cognitive capacities, such as self-awareness (Ochsner, 2004) and theory of mind (Frith and Frith, 2003). (See Chapter 7.) These are both aspects of *social cognition.*

As well as neural development, there are major changes in hormones at puberty. While it is impossible to tease apart all the important influences on the social and emotional behaviour of adolescents, significant neural development and hormonal changes are both likely to influence social cognition.

The interaction between neural and hormonal influences and social cognition may be *two-way.* Changes in what we perceive as important in the social world around us (such as when we enter a new school or college) leave their imprint on the pruning process.

So far, very few studies have looked at the effect of puberty and adolescence on social cognitive abilities. However, one area that has been investigated is *perspective taking*: the ability to step into other people's 'mental shoes' in order to understand what they think, feel or believe (this is related to first-order theory of mind). Perspective taking includes awareness of one's own mental states (first-person perspective/1PP) and the ability to attribute mental states to others (third-person perspective/3PP). According to Choudhury *et al.* (2005), development of social perspective taking is disturbed during puberty (i.e. it is a more difficult task). This is consistent with the synaptic reorganization in the prefrontal cortex taking place at this time.

Underlying perspective taking are *mirror neurons,* first described by Rizzolatti *et al.* in the mid 1990s (Dobbs, 2006). These are found in various parts of the brain, including the premotor cortex and centres for language, empathy and pain. These mirror neurons were first observed in monkeys in relation to relatively simple actions, such as grasping a piece of food. Certain neurons in the monkey's motor cortex fired in the same way when it observed one of the researchers grasp a piece of food as when the monkey itself grasped the food. This pattern of neural activity associated with the observed action was a true representation in the brain of the act itself – regardless of who was performing it (Rizzolatti *et al.*, 2006). In both monkeys and humans, the mirror neurons are able to read another person's *intentions*.

By extension, mirror neurons seem to help us 'read' other people's *emotions* – an essential part of social cognition. As Rizzolatti *et al.* (2006) say:

> *Such a mirror mechanism for understanding emotions cannot, of course, fully explain all social cognition, but it does provide for the first time a functional neural basis for some of the interpersonal relations on which more complex social behaviours are built.*

Given that newborns can imitate actions (such as sticking out the tongue), it is highly likely that mirror neurons are present – and active – at birth. According to Ramachandran (in Dobbs, 2006), mirror neurons may help explain how humans took a 'great leap forward' about 50,000 years ago, acquiring new skills in social organization, tool use and language that made human culture possible. But little is known about how they develop in individual humans.

Methodological issues

According to Dobbs (2005), *f*MRI (first used in the mid 1990s) represented a huge improvement on earlier *functional* brain-scanning techniques (i.e. those which show not just how the brain is structured, but also how it *works*, such as positron emission topography/PET). Researchers have used it extensively to make bold claims about a wide range of human behaviour: psychologists have praised it for finally making psychology quantifiable, and cognitive neuroscientists have cited it frequently in the recent, vast expansion in understanding of the brain. However, just how reliable and valid are the findings from *f*MRI studies?

*f*MRI is much faster than PET, provides a much more detailed image, and does not require the person to be injected with radioactive material. However, a major problem with interpreting *f*MRI data is that they measure neuronal activity *indirectly* by detecting associated increases in blood flow (haemodynamic response). While neurons take milliseconds to fire, the blood surge follows two to six seconds later. This means that an increase in blood flow might be 'feeding' more than one operation. Also, thousands or even millions of neurons may have to fire to significantly light up a region: it is as if an entire section of a stadium has to shout to be heard (Dobbs, 2005).

Researchers also have to choose between and adjust many different methods (algorithms) of extracting an accurate image, as well as compensating for variations in skull and brain configuration, body movements, 'noise in the data', and so on. This chain of inferences makes errors much more likely.

For some critics, these limitations make *f*MRI too crude an instrument for the more ambitious work for which it is being used. For example, Faux (in Dobbs, 2005) claims:

> The beautiful graphics fMRI produces imply much more precision than there actually is. It's really a very gross, if not vague, physiological measurement that people are using to try to pin down some very complex behaviours. And in too many studies the authors way overinterpret the data. None of that advances the science.

One basic concern is that *f*MRI is being used to tie specific mental processes to particular brain regions. This relates to the long-standing debate regarding the *localization of brain function*. (See Chapter 20.)

Subsequent research

Recent MRI studies indicate that the brain may reach maturity much later than the end of adolescence. Blakemore and Choudhury (2006) cite a study by Sowell *et al.* (2001) of 7- to 30-year-olds, which found that the loss of grey matter in the frontal cortex accelerated during adulthood between the early twenties and up to the age of 30.

Blakemore and Choudhury cite a further MRI study by Sowell *et al.* (2003) of 7- to 87-year-olds, which revealed a reduction in grey matter density in the dorsal, prefrontal, parietal and temporal cortices. This was accompanied by an increase in white matter. The pattern of grey matter changes was non-linear during adolescence. Although the decrease in grey matter was most dramatic from childhood to young adulthood, white matter volume continued to increase well beyond this stage and even up to the age of 60. The non-linear decrease in grey matter was simultaneous with a linear increase in white matter, consistent with earlier MRI data and post-mortem studies.

Applications and implications

Based on their review of the research, Blakemore and Choudhury speculate that, as result of the synaptic reorganization that occurs in puberty, the brain might be more sensitive to the effects of experience. This may be seen especially in relation to executive function and social cognition. This sensitive period may be similar to that for early sensory development.

Blakemore and Choudhury believe that research into the cognitive implications of continued brain maturation beyond childhood may be relevant to the social development and educational achievement of adolescents. Further studies are needed to establish how axonal myelination and synaptic proliferation and pruning influence social, emotional, linguistic, mathematical and creative development. For example, how does the quality of the environment interact with brain changes in the development of cognition? Longitudinal studies of the effect of early privation on the cognitive development of Romanian children adopted in the UK have begun to investigate this question (O'Connor and Rutter, 2000). (See Chapter 27.)

Research within both psychology and cognitive neuroscience can also contribute to the debate about juvenile crime, such as the current use of antisocial behaviour orders (ASBOs) in England and Wales. ASBOs are civil orders which can be imposed on anyone aged ten or over who is deemed to have acted in a way that 'causes harassment, alarm or distress' to another person. If they are breached, they become criminal offences. But what is the significance of ten as the age at which a child can be held legally responsible for criminal behaviour in England and Wales?

This figure is one of the lowest in Europe. Comparable ages for responsibility are 13 in France, 14 in Germany, 15 in Italy, 16 in Spain and 18 in Belgium. According to Hooper (2006), the simple and single reason is that in 1993, the toddler James Bulger was murdered by Jon Venables and Robert Thompson when they were both aged ten. The media, having already worked themselves into a frenzy about 'evil child killers', demanded a change – and we got one.

Whatever age is chosen, underlying criminal law is the principle of autonomy: individuals are regarded as rational, autonomous human beings capable of choosing their actions. This is what makes individuals criminally responsible. Blakemore and Choudhury argue that neuroscientists and psychologists can evaluate the efficacy of ASBOs by drawing on recent evidence from cellular, behavioural and brain imaging studies, and asking:

1   What is the role of brain development in causing problem behaviour among adolescents?

2   Given that the brain is still developing, what might be the long-term psychological effects on the adolescent of receiving an ASBO?

3   What alternatives might there be to current punitive methods?

EXERCISES

1 Try to explain the link between the development of executive function and the pruning and myelination processes.

2 In a widely cited and much publicized study of adolescent emotional responsiveness (in Dobbs, 2005), the researchers used *f*MRI to scan adolescents as they were presented with black-and-white photographs of fear-struck, middle-aged faces. Compared with adults, adolescents showed less activity in their frontal lobes (where much analysis and judgement occurs) and more in the amygdala (which responds to emotion in a more direct way). The adolescents also scored poorly when trying to describe the facial expressions. The researchers concluded that the results suggested that the teenager's brain may be responding with more of a gut reaction than an executive or thinking kind of a response.

(a) What is the independent variable in this study?

(b) Can you suggest any design flaws which could point to a different conclusion?

(c) How might you redesign the study in order to remove this flaw?

3 Do you consider that ten is too young to be the age of criminal responsibility? Try to explain your answer in terms of what you know about cognitive development in general, and moral development in particular. What can be inferred from the fact that different European countries have different ages for criminal responsibility?

30 The effects of psychotherapy: An evaluation

Eysenck, H.J. (1952)

Journal of Consulting Psychology, 16: 319–24

BACKGROUND AND CONTEXT

All forms of psychotherapy stem from Freud's psychoanalysis. Eysenck was always one of Freud's most outspoken critics, of both his theory and techniques of psychotherapy (which are intimately connected). Eysenck was a leading advocate of treatment methods based on classical learning theory (i.e. conditioning), in particular, methods based on classical (respondent or Pavlovian) conditioning, known as *behaviour therapy*. From this perspective:

- all behaviour, whether adaptive or maladaptive, is acquired by the same principles of classical conditioning;

- the case of Little Albert (see Chapter 23) exemplifies how *all* phobias are acquired (i.e. through classical conditioning) (Eysenck and Rachman, 1965, although they have both modified their views since then);

- the medical model of psychological abnormality is completely rejected, including any distinction between 'symptoms' and underlying pathology; according to Eysenck (1960), if you 'get rid of the symptoms … you have eliminated the neurosis': what you see is what there is. However, MacKay (1975) observes that some behaviour therapists do use the formal diagnostic categories ('syndromes') and try to discover which techniques are most effective with particular diagnostic groups – key figures in this *nomothetic* approach (*behavioural technology*) are Eysenck, Rachman and Marks;

- the emphasis is on *current* behaviour and environmental influences: psychological problems are behavioural problems which need to be defined in terms of *observable behaviours* before any attempt can be made to change them.

Freud and Eysenck actually share the view that the same principles are involved in the development of both normal and abnormal behaviour; but the principles themselves are rather different. So, for example, neurotic symptoms and dreams (which have much in common 'structurally'), and defence mechanisms are all forms of compromise between the opposing demands made on the ego by the id and superego. Neuroses are maladaptive solutions to the individual's problems, but they involve basically the same defence mechanisms as are involved in adaptive behaviour (e.g. phobias involve repression, as do all neuroses, displacement and projection: see Chapter 22).

Also like Eysenck, Freud rejected the medical model. Although he distinguished between 'symptoms' and 'underlying pathology', the latter is defined in psychological (not genetic or biochemical) terms, and he was concerned with the individual (not the disorder). For example, a phobia is only the conscious, overt manifestation of an internal, unconscious conflict; the phobic object has become symbolically associated with the underlying source of conflict and anxiety. Although Freud used diagnostic labels, he did so as a linguistic convenience, rather than as an integral part of his theories: he focused on understanding the patient's problems in their life context rather than on clinical labelling (MacKay, 1975).

Unlike Eysenck, Freud emphasized *past events*, especially those from early childhood and of a sexual nature, and *unconscious* (and other *internal*) factors; the latter, at best, can only be *inferred* from the patient's dreams, free associations, and so on.

AIM AND NATURE

● HYPOTHESIS

Eysenck (1992) claims that, prior to his 1952 article, the *outcome problem* (trying to assess, empirically, whether psychotherapy actually *works*) had never been properly addressed by clinical psychologists. His study represents the first major scientific attempt to assess the effectiveness of psychotherapy.

The hypothesis being tested was that 'psychotherapy facilitates recovery from neurotic disorder', that is, increases the chances of recovery. Although this is 'open-ended' (technically, *non-directional*), knowing Eysenck's beliefs about the nature of neurosis and his rejection of Freud's approach, we can safely infer that he expected to be able to firmly *reject* the hypothesis.

● METHOD/DESIGN

The study was a survey of a large number of studies dealing with the improvement of neurotic patients following psychotherapy (either psychoanalytic or 'eclectic', i.e. 'mixed': a combination of different therapeutic techniques, not based on one particular approach, such as psychoanalysis).

In order to test the hypothesis, Eysenck compared patients who had received psychotherapy (the 'experimental' group) with two 'control' groups:

● patients who had been hospitalized for 'neurosis' in state mental hospitals (Landis, 1938);

● patients treated only by their GPs (Denker, 1946).

These control groups provided a baseline of *spontaneous recovery* (remission), that is, the percentage of patients who would recover without receiving any active psychotherapy. In Landis's case, over two-thirds of severe neurotics receiving mainly custodial care (and very little psychotherapy) recovered or improved to a considerable extent. In Denker's study, patients were seen regularly and treated by their own doctors with sedatives, tonics, suggestion and reassurance; this very superficial form of psychotherapy – the stock-in-trade of the GP – was all they offered. The recovery rate for these patients matched very closely that found by Landis.

The baseline for spontaneous recovery of 66 per cent was the 'figure to beat'.

Eysenck reviewed five studies of the effectiveness of psychoanalysis, and 19 studies of the effectiveness of eclectic psychotherapy. He evaluated the results of these studies in terms of four categories:

1   cured, or much improved;

2   improved;

3   slightly improved;

4   not improved, died or discontinued treatment.

● FINDINGS

Eysenck concluded that only 44 per cent of patients treated by means of psychoanalysis improved, while 64 per cent of those who received 'mixed' therapy did so.

● CONCLUSIONS

If the 44 per cent for psychoanalysis and the 64 per cent for eclectic therapy are compared with the 66 per cent spontaneous recovery rate, then there appears to be an *inverse* correlation between recovery and psychotherapy: the more psychotherapy, the smaller the recovery rate. In other words, the results fail to support the hypothesis that psychotherapy facilitates recovery from neurotic disorder.

However, in the psychoanalytic results, patients who stopped treatment were classified as 'not improved'. But when these 'dropouts' were considered separately,

AIM AND NATURE

and the percentages improved were based only on those who successfully finished treatment, the figure for those who benefited rose to 66 per cent.

Nevertheless, Eysenck concluded that these data fail to demonstrate that psychotherapy (Freudian or otherwise) facilitates the recovery of neurotic patients: roughly two-thirds of a group of neurotic patients will recover or improve to a marked extent within about two years of the onset of their illness, whether they receive psychotherapy or not. In view of these results, we should seriously question the inclusion of psychotherapy in the training of clinical psychologists.

EVALUATION

Theoretical issues

Where Freud and Eysenck disagree, they do so fundamentally. This is seen most clearly when we ask how to assess the effectiveness of psychotherapy, the crux of Eysenck's study. The criteria Eysenck refers to (as used by Denker) were:

● return to work and ability to carry on well in economic adjustments for at least five years;

● complaint of no further or very slight difficulties;

● making successful social adjustments.

These are all fairly tangible indicators of improvement, and even more so are the behaviour therapist's criteria that cure is achieved when patients no longer manifest the original maladaptive behaviour (e.g. the spider phobia is removed). If these more stringent (or more easily measured) criteria of actual behaviour change are required before the therapist can be viewed as successful, then behaviour therapists *do* seem to be more effective than psychoanalysts or humanistic therapists (with cognitive approaches in between: Rachman and Wilson, 1980; Shapiro and Shapiro, 1982).

But are these criteria appropriate for assessing 'cure' or improvement as applied to psychoanalysis? According to Jacobs (1984), the goals of therapy are limited by what the client consciously wants to achieve and is capable of achieving, together with his/her motivation, ego strength, capacity for insight, ability to tolerate the frustration of gradual change, financial cost, and so on. These factors, in turn, determine how cure is defined and assessed.

In practice, psychoanalysis ranges from 'psychoanalytical first aid' (Guntrip, 1968, in Jacobs, 1984) or symptom relief, to different levels of more intense work. However, Storr (1966) believes that a quick, complete 'cure' is very much the exception rather than the rule; most people who undergo psychoanalysis cannot expect their symptoms to disappear easily, or (even if this should happen) that they will be freed of emotional problems. This is because of what we noted earlier in the **Background and context**: neurotic symptoms are merely the outward and visible signs of an inner, less visible conflict. Exploration and analysis of the symptoms inevitably lead to an analysis of the whole person, his/her development, temperament and character structure. Symptom analysis, therefore, is usually just the *beginning* of the analytic process, and most patients do not have clear-cut symptoms anyway (Storr, 1966).

When asked 'Does therapy work?', psychoanalytic therapists may answer the question by saying that it is a misleading question (like asking whether friendship 'works'). It is an activity that people participate in, which is important to them, affects, moves, even transforms them (Oatley, 1984). But for Eysenck, if it cannot be demonstrated empirically that it has well-defined beneficial effects, it is worthless. Because he is interested in comparing recovery rates (measured statistically), his assessment of the effects of therapy is purely *quantitative*. This relates to what Eysenck (1992) refers to as the *outcome problem* (see above). By contrast, psychoanalysis and those who adopt other non-behavioural approaches (such as Rogers' client-centred therapy), are much more likely to be concerned with the *qualitative* aspects of therapy: *how* does it work? what is the nature of the therapeutic process? what is the role of the relationship between client and therapist? and so on. These questions relate to what is called *process research*. The point here is that there are different *kinds* of questions that one can ask regarding the effects of psychotherapy.

Methodological issues

Eysenck's 1952 study is largely responsible for the explosion of research into the effects of psychotherapy (Oatley, 1984); both the quantity and quality of this research has increased since 1952, especially since the 1970s (Garfield, 1992). However, psychotherapy research as a whole involves a crucial distinction between the *efficacy* of a therapy (the results it achieves in the setting of a research trial) and its *clinical effectiveness* (the outcome of the therapy in routine practice) (Roth and Fonagy, 2005).

Most outcome research relies on research trials, and so is concerned with efficacy. Outcome research uses therapist *manuals* (hence 'manual research'): these are detailed guidelines about how to conduct a particular therapy, which stipulate specific procedures to be followed at different stages of treatment. Specifying what therapists are to do via a manual in a controlled study (*randomized clinical trial*/RCT) allows someone reading a study to know what actually happened to patients in a given experimental condition.

The use of manuals is designed to achieve a high degree of *internal validity*: we can confidently infer that any changes in patients' behaviour, mood etc., were the result of the particular therapeutic techniques used. But this begs the question: do the results from manual-based studies generalize to the actual practice of psychotherapy outside the constraints of the RCT (Davison *et al.*, 2004)?

According to Roth and Fonagy (2005), achieving internal validity requires the use of techniques rarely seen in everyday practice, such as studying highly selected, diagnostically homogeneous patient populations (i.e. patients are chosen because they have all been given the same diagnosis), randomly allocating these patients to different treatment conditions – including control (no-treatment) conditions – and using extensive monitoring of both patients' progress and the types of therapy used by therapists. All this detracts from the research's *external validity*: being able to generalize the results to everyday practice. As Roth and Fonagy put it, this is the problem of inferring clinical effectiveness from any demonstrations of efficacy.

Most therapists describe themselves as *eclectic*, which suggests that controlled studies of *specific* techniques and treatments are limited in what they can tell us about the nature and outcomes of therapy *as actually practised* (Lambert and Bergin, 1994). If most practising therapists rarely behave strictly in line with a particular theoretical orientation, then RCTs can tell us little about the effectiveness of psychotherapy available to patients who are not participating in such studies (Davison *et al.*, 2004). As Marzillier (2004) puts it, the very procedures designed to improve the research distance it from the realities of clinical work.

The use of manuals is also designed to minimize the influence of differences between therapists. But even in RCTs there is great variability between therapists (Teyber and McClure, 2000), and, in general, therapist differences are *greater* than treatment differences (Beutler, 1997). In client-centred therapy, therapist qualities are all-important, but also, more generally, we must not let the focus on treatment variables blind us to the importance of therapist empathy, sensitivity and ability to inspire trust (Davison *et al.*, 2004).

Psychotherapy is a highly complex interchange in which a number of factors interact, any one of which could significantly influence the outcome. Patients differ along many dimensions, including social class, background, the stage of their disorder at the time they present for treatment, and how well they were functioning before the disorder appeared. Therapists also differ in their personality, skills, motivation, ability to understand their patients' problems, and how closely they follow specific techniques. Service provision also varies in important ways, including the length of treatment offered, and the quality of liaison with other services. These examples of interacting factors largely reflect process research. But Orlinsky *et al.* (1994, in Roth and Fonagy, 2005) note that the distinction between process and outcome research can become blurred, with each contributing to and influencing the other.

Eysenck does not explicitly make the distinction between outcome and process research, and, as we have seen, the focus of the 1952 article was very much on outcome. However, one of his later criticisms of psychoanalysis relates to process factors: he states that patients who undergo psychoanalysis are nearly always YAVIS (young, attractive, verbal, intelligent and successful). They tend to have a favourable prognosis regardless of treatment. Selection criteria exclude seriously disturbed people (including sexual deviants and alcoholics), those who do not request a 'talking therapy', and those not considered suitable for psychotherapy for other reasons. In *Decline and Fall of the Freudian Empire* (1985), Eysenck claims that as a result:

> psychoanalysts would seem to have loaded the dice in their favour. Failure to do
> better than no treatment or eclectic forms of psychotherapy, when no or few
> patients are excluded, seems to suggest, if anything, that psychoanalysis does less
> well than eclectic psychotherapy or no treatment at all.

He does not produce any evidence regarding these claims of selectivity for psychoanalysis, although it is widely accepted that the nature of the therapy, together with its duration and cost, makes it accessible only to the privileged few, namely the well-educated, articulate and reasonably well-off middle classes.

Could Eysenck's 1952 conclusions be undermined by the control groups that provided the 66 per cent baseline figure? Landis (1938) pointed out a number of differences between psychotherapy patients and those state hospital patients he used as a control group. He concluded by saying that these differences 'all argue against the acceptance of [this] figure … as a truly satisfactory baseline, but in the absence of any other better figure this must serve'.

Eysenck (1985) says that it was *because* of the poverty of the evidence that in his 1952 article he did not say that psychoanalysis/psychotherapy had been proven to be useless; to have done so would have involved going way beyond what the evidence justified. What he did conclude was that psychoanalysts had failed to demonstrate their claim that psychoanalysis is superior to no treatment at all.

According to Rachman and Wilson (1980), the evidence that had accumulated since Eysenck's 1952 article did not challenge his figure of 66 per cent (for spontaneous remission). However, they qualify this in two ways:

● the 66 per cent figure needs to be revised for specific categories of neurotic disorder (e.g. obsessive disorders seem to have a much lower rate of spontaneous remission than anxiety disorders, with hysterical symptoms in between);

● there is a serious lack of controlled evaluations of the effects of psychoanalysis.

Subsequent research

Bergin (1971) reviewed some of the studies included in Eysenck's review, and concluded that, by choosing different criteria of 'improvement', the success rate of psychoanalysis could be raised to 83 per cent. Bergin also cites certain studies (not included by Eysenck) which showed 30 per cent spontaneous remission. Not surprisingly, Eysenck was very critical of Bergin's re-analysis; he argued (1985) that the widely cited 30 per cent figure should be disregarded, because it is based on inadequate evidence. But is it any more inadequate than that on which Eysenck's own 66 per cent was originally based?

Bergin and Lambert (1978) reviewed 17 studies of untreated 'neurotics', and found an average spontaneous remission rate of 43 per cent. Also, the rate varied widely depending on the disorder (largely agreeing with Rachman and Wilson, above). Eysenck (1985) makes no reference to Bergin and Lambert's review.

Smith and Glass (1977) reviewed 400 studies of a wide variety of therapies (including psychodynamic, gestalt, client-centred, transactional analysis, systematic desensitization, and eclectic). It was one of the first large-scale examples of *meta-analysis*, defined by Matt (1993) as 'a type of literature review that makes explicit use of quantitative methods to sum up a body of separate but similar studies [i.e. primary studies] for the purpose of integrating the findings'.

They concluded that *all* these therapies were more effective than no treatment. For example, the 'average' client who had received therapy scored more favourably on the outcome measures than 75 per cent of those in the untreated control groups. There also seemed to be no significant differences between behavioural and non-behavioural therapies. Luborsky *et al.* (1975) found all forms of therapy to be equally effective.

Smith *et al.* (1980) extended the earlier study to include 475 studies (an estimated 75 per cent of the published literature). A strict criterion for inclusion in their meta-analysis was that there should be a comparison between a treated group (given a specified form of therapy) and a second group (drawn from the same population) either given no therapy, put on a waiting list or given some alternative form of therapy. Again, therapy was shown to have a significant effect: the average client was better off than 80 per cent of the control groups on the outcome measures. Smith *et al.* confirmed their earlier findings that, overall, neither behavioural therapy nor psychoanalytic therapy was superior, but different treatments did seem to be more effective with different kinds of disorder.

Once again, Eysenck (1985) is very critical of the Smith *et al.* (1980) study. In their assessment of 18 different types of therapy, and using *effect size* (ES) scores (equivalent to the percentages quoted above), systematic desensitization emerged with an ES of 1.05, psychodynamic therapy with 0.69, and placebo treatments with 0.56. Eysenck argues that instead of regarding placebo treatment as a treatment, it is more appropriate to see it as a proper control against which to compare other, *real* treatments. On this basis, the difference between the psychodynamic and placebo 'treatments' was negligible – undermining the argument that psychodynamic therapy is beneficial. (See **Exercises**.)

Furthermore, there was no evidence in the Smith *et al.* (1980) study that better trained or more experienced therapists increased the chances of successful outcomes, or that the longer therapy lasted, the more effective it was likely to be. Eysenck (1985) believes that this seriously undermines the psychodynamic approach:

> *Even now, 30 years after the article in which I pointed out the lack of evidence for therapeutic effectiveness, and some 500 extensive investigations later, the conclusions must still be that there is no substantial evidence that psychoanalysis or psychotherapy have any positive effect on the course of neurotic disorders, over and above what is contributed by meaningless placebo treatment.*

A German study by Wittman and Matt (1986), originally designed as a replication – and extension – of the Smith *et al.* (1980) study, found that the effects of psychotherapy based on German-language studies were *less than half* the size of those reported by Smith *et al.* Matt (1993) concluded that the average ESs for psychotherapy outcome studies 'depend on, and have to be interpreted in, the cultural context in which the research is being conducted and reviewed'.

According to Lilienfeld (1995), the question 'Is psychotherapy effective?' could be seen as remarkably complex in some respects, but also too simple in others. As Paul (1966) observed, what we need to ask is: *What* treatment, by *whom*, is most effective for *this* individual, with what specific problem, and under *which* set of circumstances? This is to do with the matching of client, therapy and setting, and the question still haunts psychotherapy research and disturbs therapists (Wilson and Barkham, 1994).

Applications and implications

According to Eysenck (1992):

> *if there were no positive effects of psychoanalysis as a therapy, then it would be completely unethical to apply this method to patients, to charge them money for such treatment, or to train therapists in these unsuccessful methods.*

Clearly these are very important issues which need to be taken very seriously. Smith *et al.* (1980) concluded that the therapist's qualifications, training and length of experience were irrelevant, and several other reviews have reached the same conclusion (e.g. Christensen and Jacobson, 1994). Dawes (1994) claims that any sensitive person can perform insight-oriented psychotherapy, provided s/he shows empathy, just as all that is needed for behaviour therapy is some knowledge of behavioural principles.

However, Strupp (1996) points out some important differences between professional therapists and non-professionals:

- training enhances common factors, such as warmth, listening skills and commitment to patients' welfare;

- training equips the therapist to manage the way patients' problems manifest themselves in the therapeutic relationship (such as hostility, dependency and idealization), and to avoid playing a complementary role (such as becoming responsible for a dependent patient).

Similarly, Seligman (1996) argues that trained expertise becomes important when the patient's problem is more complex, when there is no training manual to follow, and when clinical judgement is needed (as in formulating the problem in the first place).

The value of training in psychotherapy is, perhaps, the most important *specific* factor involved in the effectiveness of therapy (MacLeod, 1998), and is related more to process than to outcome research. (See **Theoretical issues** above.) Strupp (1996) estimates that about 85 per cent of the variability in therapeutic outcomes is attributable to *common* factors (such as the therapist's personality, his/her ability to help patients gain insight into their problems, and encouraging them to face up to things they find difficult).

According to Westen and Morrison (2001), the greatest innovation in clinical training and practice in the past decade has been the expectation that treatment for mental disorder (as for medical trials) should be empirically validated or supported (i.e. evidence-based).

EXERCISES

1 Why was it necessary to establish a baseline?

2 What are the three basic techniques used in psychoanalysis?

3 Briefly describe the differences between *systematic desensitization*, *implosion* and *flooding* as forms of behaviour therapy.

4 Explain what is meant by 'symptom substitution'. (**See** Background and context.)

5 Explain the difference between *psychodynamic* and *psychoanalytic* theory/therapy.

6 In Subsequent research, **Eysenck (1985)** is cited as claiming that placebo treatment is more appropriately seen as a proper control against which to compare other, real treatments.

(a) What is meant by a 'placebo effect'?

(b) Describe what the placebo condition in a drug trial might be.

(c) Is it possible to devise a placebo control in a study of therapeutic effectiveness in the way Eysenck suggests?

31 A case of multiple personality

Thigpen, C.H. and Cleckley, H. (1954)

Journal of Abnormal and Social Psychology, 49: 135–51

BACKGROUND AND CONTEXT

According to the World Health Organization's (WHO, 1992) tenth revision of the International Classification of Diseases (ICD-10), *multiple personality disorder* (MPD) falls under the heading of 'Neurotic, Stress-Related and Somatoform Disorders'. In the USA, the American Psychiatric Association's official classification system (also used in the UK) is the Diagnostic and Statistical Manual of Mental Disorders (DSM: see Chapter 33). Originally published in 1952, the current edition is DSM-IV-TR (American Psychiatric Association, 2000). The category 'neurosis' has been dropped and neurotic disorders are dispersed among several categories, such as Anxiety Disorders, Somatoform Disorders, and Dissociative Disorders; the last includes MPD, which since 1994 is officially called *dissociative identity disorder* (DID).

Dissociative neurosis involves psychological dysfunction, such as disturbances in identity, memory, perception and awareness. One part of the self separates – or becomes dissociated – from the other parts (which has led to the common confusion between MPD and schizophrenia, in which a splitting occurs within the personality: see Gross, 2005).

According to DSM-IV-TR, the diagnostic criteria for DID are:

- the presence of two or more distinct identities or personality states (*alters*), each with its own relatively enduring pattern of perceiving, relating to and thinking about the environment and the self;

- at least two of these alters recurrently take control of the person's behaviour;

- inability to recall important personal information that is too extensive to be explained by normal forgetting;

- the disturbance is not due to the direct physiological effects of substance abuse or a general medical condition.

Typically, the 'presenting personality' (or *host*) – the one who seeks medical help – claims to be unaware of any other personalities (*alters*) and is amnesic for events which took place when other alters were 'out', that is, in control of the person's body. (Generally, it is a concern about such 'blackouts' that leads the presenting personality to seek help.) However, the alters often know about the presenting personality (Stephens and Graham, 2007), and some of them are aware of the others.

In the past, people with DID reported relatively few alter personalities, but the average number now reported is 15 – and some exhibit more than 100 (Bennett, 2006). The 'original' case was the fictional *Dr Jekyll and Mr Hyde* by Robert Louis Stevenson (a 'dual' personality). A more recent, real-life case, even more dramatic and remarkable than the subject of Thigpen and Cleckley's 'Eve White', is *Sybil* (Schreiber, 1973), who had 16 separate personalities. (See **Theoretical issues** below.)

AIM AND NATURE

Thigpen and Cleckley, two American psychiatrists, reported on the psychotherapeutic treatment of a 25-year-old woman ('Eve White' – the host/presenting personality), referred to them because of 'severe and blinding headaches'. The receipt of a letter marked the beginning of the treatment of her DID.

● METHOD/DESIGN

At first, Thigpen and Cleckley used hypnosis to 'contact' the alter, Eve Black, but she then 'outed' spontaneously. The major method of treatment seemed to be simply talking to one or other personality (there is no reference to the use of medication, for example), especially trying to encourage them to talk about childhood memories.

The case study also includes the report by an independent expert who gave the two Eves four psychological tests: the Wechsler-Bellvue intelligence scale (now known as the Wechsler adult intelligence scale/WAIS), the Wechsler memory scale, drawings of human figures, and the Rorschach ('ink blot') test. (The Rorschach is a *projective* test, in which the testee supposedly projects unconscious feelings and wishes into their interpretations of a series of ambiguous drawings – resembling ink blots.) An electroencephalogram (EEG) was also used.

At the first interview, Eve White mentioned 'blackouts' following the headaches. Her family was unaware of anything that might suggest a real loss of consciousness or serious mental condition. In subsequent interviews, she came across as an ordinary case with commonplace symptoms and a relatively complex, but familiar, set of marital conflicts and personal frustrations.

Several days after a treatment session, a letter was received (see Figure 31.1).

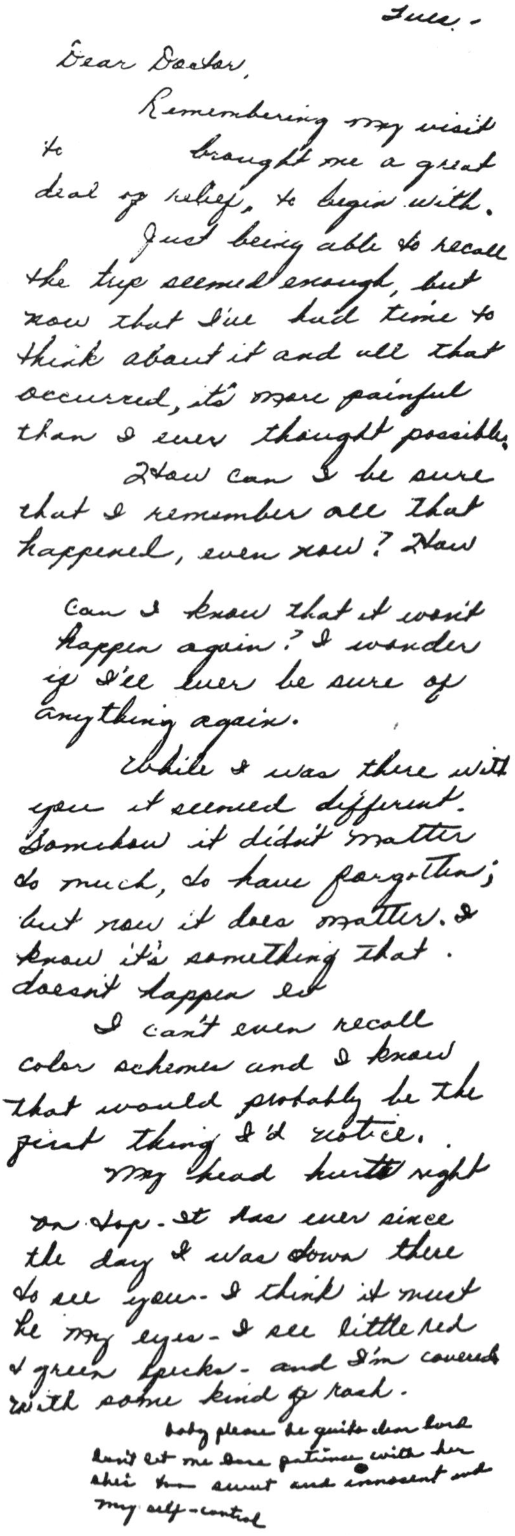

Figure 31.1. 'This letter in retrospect was the first intimation that our patient was unusual. The dramatic and unexpected revelation of the second personality shortly followed' (Thigpen and Cleckley).

Though unsigned, the postmark, content and the familiar handwriting pointed to this having been written by Eve White. But the handwriting in the final paragraph looked like a child's. If Eve White had written this herself, what motive could she have had for such a prank? She seemed to be a cautious, matter-of-fact, meticulously truthful person, consistently taking her troubles seriously.

On the next visit, she denied sending the letter – though she recalled having started one that she never finished (she thought she had destroyed it). During this session, this usually excessively self-controlled woman began to become distressed and agitated. Apprehensively and reluctantly, she asked: did the occasional impression of hearing an imaginary voice mean she was 'insane'? There was nothing to suggest an early schizoid change or that she was having 'ordinary' auditory hallucinations. Yet she insisted, with painful embarrassment, that she had heard a voice addressing her, briefly but distinctly, on several occasions over the last few months. Then, a strange expression came over her face, apparently involuntarily. As if seized by pain, she put both hands to her head; after a moment of tense silence, her hands dropped and in a bright, sparkling voice she said, 'Hi there, Doc!'

This 'newcomer' had a childishly daredevil air and gave an erotically mischievous glance. She spoke casually of Eve White and her problems, using *she* or *her* every time she referred to her; when asked her own name, she immediately replied, 'Oh, I'm Eve Black'. Her manner, gestures, expressions and posture all convinced Thigpen and Cleckley that this could only be another woman.

Over the next 14 months and 100 hours of treatment, extensive material was obtained about the behaviour and inner life of both Eves. Following her original spontaneous appearance, Eve Black would still 'pop out' at unpredictable times; Thigpen and Cleckley had to hypnotize Eve White when they wanted to speak to her. But after a few hypnotic sessions, they merely had to request Eve White to let them speak to Eve Black. Then they called Eve Black's name, and she would come out. The reverse was true when Eve Black was out and they wished to speak to Eve White.

● FINDINGS

Eve Black had apparently enjoyed an independent life since Eve's early childhood (she was not a product of disruptive, emotional stresses experienced in recent years). Eve White had no knowledge or suspicion of the other's existence until some time after she made her surprise appearance in that therapy session; she still did not have access to the latter's awareness. When Eve Black was 'out', Eve White remained quite oblivious of what the former did; but Eve Black was aware of Eve White's thoughts and actions even when absent. For example, she regarded Eve White's genuine and natural distress about her failing marriage as silly, and her

AIM AND NATURE

warm and consistent love and concern for her four-year-old daughter as trite, bothersome, insignificant and 'pretty corny'.

Eve White was temporarily separated from her husband, and her daughter was living with her grandparents in a village, while Eve worked and lived in a city about 100 miles away. She was very lonely and frustrated by the separation from her daughter, fearing that over time she would become a stranger to her daughter. Under hypnosis, her unhappiness became clearer.

Eve Black had little or no real compassion for her, but neither did she seem purposefully cruel; she appeared to be immune to major emotional events in human relationships. She spoke freely of episodes in childhood when she emerged, usually to engage in acts of mischief or disobedience. Although Eve Black's account could not be trusted, Eve White's memory provided considerable indirect evidence of Eve Black's stories, through conformation of reports of punishments she had received and accusations made against her for things she knew nothing about (but which were described by Eve Black). Some stories were corroborated by Eve's parents and her husband – but she managed to conceal her identity from all of them. Although she had often 'come out' in front of all of them, she went unrecognized until she agreed to reveal herself to them in the therapists' office.

Eve Black's adult behaviour was typically irresponsible, displaying a shallow hedonistic desire for excitement and pleasure. She denied being married to Eve's husband, whom she despised, and any relation to Eve's daughter. During her longer periods 'out', she avoided her family and friends, seeking the company of strangers.

Psychological consultation report

As noted above, an independent expert gave both Eves a number of psychological tests.

- Eve White obtained an IQ score of 110, and Eve Black 104 on the Wechsler-Bellvue intelligence scale. Eve White's memory function was far above her IQ (even though she complained of a memory disturbance), while Eve Black's was on the same level as her IQ.

- Eve Black's Rorschach record was by far the healthier of the two, showing a hysterical tendency; Eve White's showed anxiety, an obsessive-compulsive tendency, rigidity and an inability to deal with her hostility.

- The projective tests indicated regression in Eve Black and in Eve White. The dual personality seemed to be the result of a strong desire to regress to an early period of life, namely the one before marriage (Miss Black was actually the maiden name of Mrs White). So, these were not two distinct personalities with completely different ways of thinking, but rather one personality at two stages of her life.

● The Rorschach and drawings indicated conflict and resulting anxiety in Eve White's roles of wife and mother; she regressed in order to avoid the guilt associated with the hostility she felt about these roles. Since Eve Black was free from marital and maternal conflicts, she had escaped from the impossible situation Eve White found herself in. She felt contempt for Eve White, who allowed herself to get into such a situation due to lack of foresight and cowardice.

The problem actually began much earlier in life, with a strong sense of rejection by her parents – especially after the birth of her twin sisters, whom Eve White loved dearly and Eve Black despised.

Although Eve Black had been able, since childhood, to disappear at will, the ability to displace Eve White's consciousness, and emerge to take control, had always been limited: sometimes she could 'get out', sometimes not. Once Eve White had learned of the other's existence during treatment, her willingness to step aside and 'release the imp' played an important part in the alter's ability to appear and express herself directly.

Believing that they had a reasonably complete and accurate history of Eve White's life since early childhood, Thigpen and Cleckley were astonished to learn (via a distant relative) that Eve had been married before. Eve denied all knowledge. Eve Black eventually admitted that *she* was the bride: although there was no formal record of a marriage, she did live with a man during a period when she was largely in control.

She had no wish for sex, but often enjoyed denying her husband his conjugal rights. In turn, he beat her savagely, but she avoided most of the pain by 'going in' and leaving Eve White to feel the blows. She was able to 'pick out' or erase certain items of memory of Eve White, including that of the beatings. This explains why Eve White did not remember them.

After about eight months of treatment, Eve seemed to have made encouraging progress. She had not had headaches or 'blackouts' for a long time; nor had she heard the imaginary voice since the other Eve had revealed herself. She felt better about her daughter and was hopeful of sorting out her marital problems eventually. But then the headaches returned and became worse and more frequent, as did the 'blackouts'. Eve Black denied all responsibility and seemed to be affected by them in the same way as Eve White, who was found two or three times lying unconscious on the floor by her roommate (which had not happened before).

On one particular occasion, Eve White was discussing (under hypnosis) a very early recollection of being scalded by water from a washbasin and sustaining a painful injury. As she spoke, her eyes closed, her speech stopped, and her head dropped back on the chair. After two minutes, her eyes opened, blankly staring around the room, and when they finally met the therapists', an unknown husky voice asked, 'Who are you?' This marked the first appearance of Jane, who lacked Eve Black's obvious faults, and was far more mature, bold and interesting than Eve White.

Report of electroencephalogram

- Eve Black's record showed evidence of restlessness and muscle tension; her EEG was distinct from that of the other two and could be classified as borderline normal.

- Eve White's and Jane's EEG records could not be distinguished from each other; both were clearly normal.

Jane had awareness of what both Eves did and thought, but incomplete access to their knowledge and memory prior to her appearance. But through her, the therapist knew when Eve Black was lying. Jane was free of Eve White's responsibilities and attachments, but was capable of compassion and learned to take over many of her tasks both at work and home in order to relieve and help her. She stayed 'out' more, but could only emerge through Eve White, being unable to displace Eve Black or communicate through her.

● CONCLUSION

While some would claim that they had been hoodwinked by a skilful actress, Thigpen and Cleckley believe that this was very unlikely. While they do not, obviously, constitute three quite separate people, Thigpen and Cleckley argue that the three personalities had become split off from a once unified whole.

What we mean by *multiple personality* begs the question of what we mean by *personality*. If Jane could have remained in full possession of that integrated human functioning called personality, Eve would probably have regained full health, adjusted satisfactorily and found her way to a happy life.

EVALUATION

Theoretical issues

Traditionally, reported cases of DID were extremely rare; the earliest is usually taken to be Prince's (1906) Miss Beauchamp. But there seems to have been an 'epidemic' in DID diagnosis in the USA during the last few decades. According to Lilienfeld (1995), between 1934 and 1971 there were only 12 reported cases, while several investigators have recently claimed to have seen 50 or more cases. Significantly, DID (then called MPD) was included in DSM for the first time in 1980 (DSM-III), and this marked the beginning of an explosion of reported cases during the 1980s. Before 1980, there were just 200 cases in the entire world literature – by 1984, there were more than 1,000 in the USA alone (Mair, 1999). This explosion has continued and extends far beyond the USA, including Holland, Germany, Switzerland, Turkey, South America and Japan (Cohen, 1995).

One reason for the very low frequency of reported cases (prior to 1980) is that the existence of the alter personalities is often discovered (initially) only through hypnosis, used by just 10 per cent of psychotherapists. (Eve Black made her first appearance quite spontaneously, although after that she could only be 'summoned' through hypnosis; Altrocchi, 1980.) Critics have argued that, instead of additional personalities being 'discovered' through hypnosis, they are being *created* by it (Fahy, 1988; Lilienfeld, 1998).

How can we account for this 'epidemic'?

- The rise and fall of reported cases seems to be correlated with the impact of Freud's psychoanalytic theory (at least among psychotherapists and psychiatrists in the USA). Freud was an *antirealist* in relation to DID: he rejected the 'received view' of the late nineteenth and early twentieth centuries which claimed that the distinct personalities are separate, unique persons with their own identities. As Freud's psychoanalysis became less influential from the 1950s onwards, so the 'received view' resurged (Apter, 1991).

- Apter (1991) also believes that the surge of reported cases of child sexual abuse (CSA) contributed to the DID epidemic. Child abuse (in general) has always featured prominently in the DID literature (there are some horrendous examples reported in the case studies, Sybil being a notable example); indeed, one of the two dominant theories of DID is that it is the result of childhood trauma. Boon and Draijer (1993, in Bennett, 2006) found that 94 per cent of those diagnosed with DID in their sample reported a history of childhood physical and/or sexual abuse.

Supporters of this childhood trauma model (e.g. Gleaves, 1996, in Bennett, 2006) suggest that the experience of severe trauma during childhood produces a mental 'splitting' or dissociation as part of a defensive reaction. The abused child learns to enter a self-induced hypnotic state, placing the memory of the abuse into the unconscious as a means of coping with it. These dissociated parts of the individual 'split' into alter personalities which, in adulthood, manifest themselves to help cope with stressful situations and express resentments or other feelings that are unacceptable to the host personality. (See Chapter 19.)

According to Mair (1999), this view of DID as caused by childhood abuse (in particular, CSA) has only emerged in the last 30 years or so, and seems to have been greatly influenced by the publication of *Sybil* in 1973. The number of alters per case has also increased in that time. (See **Background and context**.) Patients are more likely to be female, depressed or suicidal, and far more likely to report increasingly extreme and bizarre abuse (including ritual abuse that involves gang rape, torture, bestiality, human sacrifice and cannibalism). Rieger (1998, in Davison and Neale, 2001) claims that Sybil's alters were created during therapy by a therapist who gave substance to her different emotional states by giving them names.

(It is ironic that the decline of psychoanalysis and the surge in reported CSA should both be seen as contributing to the DID epidemic, in view of the claim that Freud rejected his own 'seduction theory' of neurosis: see Chapter 22.)

● DID could be regarded as a largely North American phenomenon of the twentieth century (especially the second half). Aldridge-Morris (1989) wrote to the British Psychological Society (BPS) and the Royal College of Psychiatrists in 1987, asking whether British professionals had experience of DID comparable to their American counterparts. Of the very few replies received, only four testified to having seen such patients (a total of six between them), and even these were very tentative. Aldridge-Morris concluded that 'it is clear that some therapists have an astronomically higher probability of meeting such patients than their colleagues and the vast majority (dare one say "all"?) are in the United States'.

As we saw above, the epidemic has spread to several other parts of the world, but not (yet) to the Czech Republic (CSSR), New Zealand, Australia or India (Aldridge-Morris, 1989). All the countries where cases are reported may have certain features in common that make DID more likely to occur. According to Varma et al., (1981, in Aldridge-Morris), twentieth-century Western people are fascinated with role-playing, largely created, and certainly reinforced, by show business/the entertainment industry in general, and movies in particular. These include portrayals of Eve White (*The Three Faces of Eve*), *Sybil* and *When Rabbits Howl*, all of which provide 'stage directions' about the role of the DID patient; therapists provide additional direction, encouragement and, perhaps most importantly, 'official validation' for the different alters.

There is no suggestion of deliberate deception or fabrication (Spanos et al., 1986). Rather, there is a much greater awareness of DID in the USA than in the UK, for example. There are more source data to provide role models, and, more generally, a greater acceptance/love of psychiatrists, psychotherapists and psychologists, together with a de-stigmatization of psychotherapy – at least among the educated middle class (Aldridge-Morris, 1989). So it is plausible that the DID epidemic reflects an increase in the public's ability to mimic the symptoms of DID (Lilienfeld, 1995).

If DID were a naturally occurring state, the prevalence of cases would not change over time; this strongly supports the view of the socio-cognitive theorists (e.g. Lilienfeld et al., 1999; Spanos, 1994), which represents the major alternative to the childhood trauma model. According to socio-cognitive theory, DID is a set of beliefs and behaviours constructed by the individual in response to personal stress, therapist pressure and society's legitimization of the construct 'multiple personality'. DID has become a legitimate way for many people to understand and express their failures and frustrations, as well as a tactic for manipulating others.

Subsequent research

During several months of therapy following Jane's appearance, Eve White (real name Chris) learned about the other two. A crucial moment was when Eve White was able to recall and deal with her feelings about a traumatic incident at age six: her aunt forced her to kiss her dead grandmother. By this time, Eve and her first husband had divorced and Jane had married Don Sizemore, her (Chris's) present husband. During a crisis in Jane's life, a fourth personality emerged, Evelyn. She had all the memories of the other three, accepted responsibility for their actions, and seemed to be a much more mature and complex person than any one of them.

For almost 20 years, except for the movie *The Three Faces of Eve*, the public knew nothing of the case. Then, in January 1975, Mrs Chris Sizemore revealed that she had been not only both Eves, Jane and Evelyn (all fictitious names), but many others besides, both before and after 1954 – at least 9 before Eve Black and about 22 altogether. She had had role models for denial, repression and dissociation while growing up, such as her grandmother, who tended to faint at times of stress (such as funerals). Chris also fainted at times of stress and repressed memories of events such as her grandfather's funeral.

Chris believes she began to develop separate personalities as a safety valve mechanism as young as two. By then she had seen a man drown, and another cut into three pieces by a saw at a limber mill (her personalities tended to exist in groups of three). In a personal communication to Altrocchi (1980), she describes the time she witnessed her mother cut her arm badly: she could not cope with this and thought her mother was going to die. She ran to her bed, stuck her head under the pillow and felt herself receding into space, watching 'the other little girl' go to get her father: 'It wasn't me, I was watching'.

Together with her cousin, Elen Pitillo, Chris Sizemore wrote *I'm Eve* (Sizemore and Pittillo, 1977); in it, they say:

> *Paradoxically, to survive intact, she splintered; she created other selves to endure what she could not absorb, to view what she could not comprehend, to do what she had been forbidden, to have what she had been denied.*

When the pain became unbearable, Chris disappeared, and someone else took her place. But this contributed to making her even more inhibited and withdrawn, and prevented her developing a coherent self-concept. She decided to reveal herself as the famous Eve as part of her therapy with Dr Tsitos, whose major strategy was to deal only with Chris, and to make it difficult for the others to come out. Over the years, as a personality died, she assimilated aspects of it.

Methodological issues

Is there any independent evidence (separate from the case study) for the existence of DID as a distinct mental disorder?

1   Thigpen and Cleckley gave the *semantic differential* attitude scale (Osgood, 1952; Osgood *et al.*, 1957) to both Eves and Jane, on two separate occasions, two months apart. Eve White emerged as socialized, construing the world 'normally', but showing an unsatisfactory attitude towards herself. Eve Black achieved a 'violent kind of adjustment', saw herself as perfect and the world 'abnormally'; her construct system was the least stable over time. Jane had the 'healthiest' perception of the world and the most satisfactory self-evaluation. The scores had been calculated (using a blind analysis) by Osgood and Luria, who took them as evidence of the existence of three distinct personalities.

2   London *et al.* (1969, in Thigpen and Cleckley, 1984) analysed, frame by frame, a 30-minute film of Eve, looking for possible facial regularities and other transformations of expressive behaviour. All three personalities 'appeared' in the film, and all showed *transient micro-strabismus* (the deviation of one eye from the axis of the other, such as one moving to the left, the other to the right, or one moving while the other does not). Each personality showed a different pattern of micro-strabismus.

While this (and other) objective data might seem quite convincing, some fundamental criticisms of the use of tests (especially – but not exclusively – psychological tests) have been made by Orne *et al.* (1984):

● the objectivity of the blind tester is always doubtful: we cannot take the assessment of 'separate personalities' at face value because the tester starts off by *assuming* the scores come from 'different' individuals;

● the tests that are used have not been standardized on DID populations (only on 'normal' populations);

● there needs to be control group data, allowing a demonstration of clinicians' ability to distinguish between scores derived from 'genuine' patients and from participants who are faking/simulating.

Some people may be highly suggestible and prone to fantasy (making them susceptible to cues from others, including psychotherapists); in turn, this may give them a talent for adopting and enacting roles. However, this would not itself mean that role-playing is what goes on in diagnosed cases of DID (Davison and Neale, 2001).

Applications and implications

How does a diagnosis of DID stand as a legal defence in a court of law? Altrocchi (1980) cites the case of Arthur D. Wayne Bicknall, who was acquitted by a Californian judge in 1976 of drink-driving, after his psychiatrist, Allison, testified that one of the accused's alters ('Johnnie') was the true criminal. Allison actually summoned, under hypnosis, two of Bicknall's alters as character witnesses!

Such cases highlight the concept of moral responsibility. At the very least, one has to be performing the criminal act *knowingly* in order to be held responsible, and in the case of DID, this 'one' means the host personality. But if we went out and got drunk and committed a crime 'under the influence', could we not also plead 'not guilty'? Presumably, however, getting drunk would have been done knowingly; the person with DID cannot knowingly switch personalities in order to escape responsibility (even though one or more alters may be able to do so, as Eve Black did when trying to get Eve White into trouble). This, of course, presupposes that (conscious) role-playing, acting, hypnotic suggestion, and so on, have been ruled out.

Saks (1997), an American lawyer, argues that a new legal principle should be established, namely, 'irresponsibility by virtue of multiple personality disorder'. Her argument centres around defining *personhood* (what is a person): unlike most people, for the individual with DID there is a discrepancy between 'me' and 'my body'. The law should be concerned with the body *as a container for the person*: it is the person who may/may not be guilty, *not* the body, so that if the alter put on trial is different from the one that occupied the body at the time the crime was committed, the former should not be held responsible. However, if the former was aware of the latter's criminal intentions and did nothing to try to prevent the crime, then the former would be complicit in the crime and would be at least partly responsible.

Thigpen and Cleckley (1984) point out that, since Eve, they have come across only *one* case of DID among the tens of thousands of patients they saw in the ensuing 30 years of practice. They urge psychiatrists and other mental health professionals to reserve the diagnosis only for those very few individuals 'who are truly fragmented in the most extreme manner'.

According to Mair (1999), both the British Psychological Society (1995) and the Royal College of Psychiatrists (1997) have warned of the ease with which therapists may, unwittingly, encourage *false memories* of childhood abuse. They should be particularly aware of the unreliability of memories reported by patients suffering from dissociation. Even some supporters of the childhood trauma model (e.g. Kluft, 1996; Ross, 1997; see **Theoretical issues** above) acknowledge that false memories are a problem, one of which is corroborating the claims of childhood abuse (Mair, 1999). While it is likely that some adults with DID have suffered some abuse, the presence of a known history of abuse may sometimes be used as the basis for the diagnosis! The abuse may well have contributed to the patient's current problems, but this does not mean that *only* the abuse is responsible – or that the mechanisms involved are properly understood. According to Mair, the view that DID is caused by severe childhood trauma 'can neither be proved nor disproved. It is dogma, not science'.

EXERCISES

1   Do you believe that psychologists and psychiatrists should be used as expert witnesses in criminal cases?

2   If the testimony of an expert witness is accepted as showing that the defendant has DID, should this necessarily lead to a verdict of 'not guilty'?

3   Are there any advantages which Thigpen and Cleckley's case study has over Freud's way of working with his patients (such as Little Hans: see Chapter 22)?

4   Briefly describe *two* important differences between DID and schizophrenia.

5   (a) What is meant by a 'blind tester'?

    (b) What advantages are usually claimed for using a blind tester?

6   Briefly describe the *semantic differential* attitude scale.

The hallucinations of widowhood

Rees, W.D. (1971)

British Medical Journal, 4: 37–41

BACKGROUND AND CONTEXT

Death of a spouse is at the top of the list of 'life events' (producing the highest Life Change Unit score) in Holmes and Rahe's (1967) *Social Readjustment Rating Scale* (SRRS). Traditionally, this has been the most commonly used measure of stress.

Loss of a husband or wife is a major life change that many elderly people will experience – especially if they are female. Most married women will outlive their husbands (Hendricks and Hendricks, 1977), so there are many more widows than widowers. Among people over 65, widows outnumber widowers by four to one. By the age of 65, 50 per cent of women have lost their husbands, and by 75, the figure is 66 per cent (Botwinick, 1984).

Widowhood puts a severe financial strain on the survivor (especially women). But loss of a spouse can also shatter the person's social world, leading to social and physical isolation, with 75 per cent of widowed adults living alone. Significantly, Gubrium (1973) found that people who had remained single all their lives felt more satisfied in late adulthood than widows or widowers of the same age. Widowers, in particular, feel more lonely, have a harder time with routine household chores, and are generally less happy with their lives. Given that men benefit more from marriage than women do (it is more psychologically protective for men: Bee, 1994), it is not surprising that widowers are considerably more likely to remarry (and do so sooner) than widows.

According to Parkes (2006), there is plenty of research into the psychological consequences of losing a partner. In fact, most of the research into the prediction of risk following bereavement has been carried out on widows and widowers in the English-speaking world. Loss of a spouse has come to be seen as the norm for grief (i.e. reaction to loss of spouse has become the 'standard' against which other types of loss are measured).

The loss of a spouse is the most frequent type of bereavement to lead to psychiatric referral. While hallucinations have traditionally been taken to indicate serious mental disorder (psychosis: see Chapter 33), they may be regarded as perfectly normal in the context of the loneliness suffered by many widows and widowers.

AIM AND NATURE

● HYPOTHESES

There were only two clear-cut (explicit) hypotheses:

1   The incidence of hallucinations would be greater for those who had been happily married for many years, and the period of living together would be directly related to the incidence of hallucinations.

2   Widowed people with a hysteroid personality would be more likely to hallucinate than those with an obsessoid personality.

Because there had been no previous research into the hallucinatory experiences of bereaved spouses, Rees thought it worthwhile to determine the incidence of these experiences. Rees wanted to find out if there is an association between incidence of hallucinations and any of the following:

● age when widowed;

● duration of widowhood;

● place of death;

● marital harmony;

● remarriage;

● being widowed twice;

● childless marriages;

● husband's occupation;

● personality (hysteroid/obsessoid: see hypothesis 2 above);

● previous disclosure of hallucinations;

● the helpfulness of hallucinations;

● time of occurrence of hallucinations;

● duration of marriage (see hypothesis 1 above). (This was actually tested using a separate sample from the main survey: see **Method/design** below.)

Other variables that might be related to the incidence of hallucinations included sex (gender), age when interviewed, factors associated with death, cultural background, residence when bereaved, change of residence after bereavement, social isolation and depression requiring treatment.

● METHOD/DESIGN

This was a survey study, in which 227 widows (age range: twenties to nineties) and 66 widowers (age range: thirties to eighties), all living within a defined area of Mid-Wales (Llanidloes) and all attending the same group medical practice, were interviewed about their hallucinatory experiences of their dead spouse. This sample formed 80.7 per cent of all widowed people within this area of Mid-Wales (363), and 94.2 per cent of those suitable for interview (311). There were 52 people excluded from the sample due to serious physical or mental defects, and two women refused to be interviewed (a much lower rate than is usual in studies of bereavement).

Each person was interviewed (in 359 cases with no one else present) in a 'semi-rigid' manner, that is, the interviewee was encouraged to talk freely about the deceased spouse, 'but enough direction was given to ensure that all items listed on a standardized form were covered', in particular, whether the widowed person had experience of *hallucinations* (visual, auditory or tactile) or *illusions* (sense of presence) of the deceased.

During the course of the interview, participants were also asked to complete the hysteroid–obsessoid questionnaire (Caine and Hope, 1967). The purpose of using this questionnaire was to determine whether a relationship exists between post-bereavement hallucinations and personality type. Some of the older participants were unable or unwilling to complete the questionnaire; results were obtained for 54 men and 199 women.

A separate sample of 104 widows and 23 widowers was used to collect data to test hypothesis 1 (see above).

● RESULTS

'Hallucination' is used to include all hallucinations *and* illusions (unless otherwise stated). Almost half (46.7 per cent) of the sample reported post-bereavement hallucinations, which often lasted many years, and at the time of interview, 106 people (36.1 per cent) were still experiencing them.

The most common type of hallucination was the illusion of feeling the presence of the dead spouse. Auditory hallucinations were slightly less common than visual ones; more than one person in ten reported speaking to the deceased. The least common hallucination was the feeling of being touched by the dead spouse.

AIM AND NATURE

The proportions of men and women having hallucinations were similar: 50 per cent of men, 45.8 per cent of women. But widows were significantly more likely than widowers to have auditory hallucinations, while widowers were significantly more likely than widows to have spoken to the dead spouse.

All the following factors were found to affect the incidence of hallucination:

● *Age when widowed*

Most people were in the older age groups when widowed: 57.6 per cent of men and 96 per cent of women were 60 or over. Only 4.5 per cent of men and 13.7 per cent of women were below 40. Those widowed before 40 were the least likely to hallucinate. Of those widowed below the age of 60, 7.7 per cent conversed with the dead, and 10.6 per cent visually hallucinated, compared with 17.2 per cent and 19.4 per cent of those widowed at an older age. All these differences were statistically significant.

● *Duration of widowhood*

A significantly higher proportion of people widowed for less than 10 years hallucinated compared with those widowed for a longer period. Of those widowed for over 20 years, 4.5 per cent visually hallucinated, compared with 16.8 per cent of those widowed for less than 20 years. Significantly more of the former also conversed with their dead spouse compared with those widowed for less than five years.

● *Place of death*

There was no association between where the spouse died (at home, in hospital, or some other place) and the total proportion of widowed people who hallucinated. However, 34.6 per cent of the widowers whose wives died in hospital hallucinated, compared with 60.8 per cent of those whose wives died outside hospital. Conversely, 55.4 per cent of widows whose husbands died in hospital hallucinated, compared with 25.7 per cent of those whose husbands died elsewhere. Both differences were statistically significant.

● *Marital harmony*

Surviving spouses of unhappy marriages were significantly less likely to hallucinate than those describing their marriage as happy.

● *Remarriage*

Those who hallucinated were significantly less likely to accept an offer of marriage than those who did not (the dead spouse 'was opposed to it').

- *People widowed twice*

Of the 11 participants widowed twice, neither of the two men hallucinated. One of the women had illusions of the presence of both dead husbands. Another reported having had visual hallucinations of her first husband, but none of her second. An 80-year-old widow had visual hallucinations of a son who had died in early adulthood, but no hallucinations of her two husbands, one of whom she was very fond of, while the other she disliked intensely.

- *Childless marriages*

Widowed spouses of childless marriages hallucinated significantly less often than those who had had children.

- *Husband's occupation*

Widows of men classified as professional or managerial hallucinated significantly more often than those of men in other categories.

- *Hysteroid–obsessoid questionnniare*

As the hysteroid type is more imaginative than the obsessoid, more of the former would be expected to hallucinate than the latter: 61.5 per cent of the former hallucinated, compared with 45.2 per cent of the latter. This difference was significant.

All the following factors had no effect on the incidence of hallucination:

- age when interviewed;

- factors associated with death (sudden; inquest; necropsy (post-mortem); relatives present; relatives expected death);

- cultural background (ability to speak Welsh; sectarian allegiance with Christian faith; regularity of church attendance; Wales outside Llanidloes area; outside Wales);

- change of residence after bereavement;

- social isolation (feeling lonely; living alone; relatives nearby; regular job);

- depression requiring treatment (before bereavement; after bereavement);

- previous disclosure of hallucinations;

- help from hallucinations;

- time of occurrence of hallucinations;

- duration of marriage (using one statistical test – chi-squared): the association between duration of marriage and incidence of hallucinations proved non-significant; but when regression analysis was used, which takes the time sequence into account, a significant result was found (i.e. the longer the marriage lasts, so the predicted increase in hallucinations occurs).

● CONCLUSIONS

It seems reasonable to conclude from the Mid-Wales study that hallucinations are normal experiences after widowhood, providing helpful psychological phenomena to those experiencing them. They are common experiences after loss of a spouse, occur regardless of gender, race, creed or place of residence, do not affect overt behaviour, tend to disappear with time, are not associated with illness or abnormality, are more common in people whose marriages were happy and who became parents, and can be integrated by people and kept a secret. Most people feel they are helped by their hallucinations and, significantly, among those *least* likely to hallucinate are those widowed before the age of 40 – the very group which is most likely to die soon after widowhood (Kraus and Lilienfeld, 1959).

EVALUATION

Methodological issues

Perhaps one of the more confusing aspects of the study concerns the use of the word 'hallucination' to include all hallucinations and illusions. Rees distinguishes between hallucinations (visual, auditory, tactile) and illusions (a sense of the presence of the deceased). But he later states that 'The most common type of hallucination is the illusion of feeling the presence of the dead spouse'. He then says: 'The incidence of various illusions is shown in Table 4' (not reproduced here). The title of Table 4 is 'Incidence of various hallucinations'. So, is there a difference between hallucinations and illusions?

Parkes (1986) refers to his study of 22 widows in London. They often described illusions of having seen or heard their dead husband. These illusions usually involved the misinterpretation of some existing sight or sound, such as mistaking a man in the street for their husband, or a creak in the night being mistaken for the husband moving around the house. These examples suggest that there is a real difference: illusions are misinterpretations of actual, existing sensory stimulation, while hallucinations (as commonly understood) are 'Perceptions in any sensory modality without relevant and adequate external stimuli' (Davison *et al.*, 2004). We could add to this definition that the perception is as real as any 'normal' perceptual experience, but Parkes goes on to say that 'they are sometimes of such vividness that people need to be reassured that they are not an unusual feature'. However, he confirms Rees's conclusion that these experiences are no more common among psychiatrically disturbed widows and are simply part of the normal reaction to bereavement.

One of Rees's conclusions is that hallucinations are common experiences following widowhood, and occur regardless of race, creed or place of residence. In the actual results section, 'cultural background' is one of the factors that was found *not* to affect incidence of hallucinations. (See **Exercises** at the end of the chapter.) He addresses the question of culture further in the Discussion.

He points out that it is generally believed that the Celtic (including Welsh) character is highly imaginative and perceptive, which might suggest that post-bereavement hallucinations would be more common in Mid-Wales than elsewhere in Britain. But he gives four reasons for believing that this is *not* so:

1   There was no association between incidence of hallucination and place of residence when the death occurred.

2   There was no variation in incidence of hallucination between the cultural groups studied.

3   The proportion of hysteroid people studied was considerably smaller than the proportion of less imaginative, obsessoid people.

4   Marris (1958) interviewed 72 young widows in south-east London and found that half had experienced hallucinations or illusions of the dead spouse. This is very close to the 45.8 per cent found in Mid-Wales.

But what about countries with very different cultural traditions? Rees cites a study by Yamamoto *et al.* (1969), who wanted 'to examine the process of mourning in a culture whose religions sanction the implied presence of the deceased through ancestor worship'. Of 20 widows living in Tokyo who were interviewed, 18 (90 per cent) reported feeling the presence of the dead husband. None worried about their sanity: religion helped this aspect of their grieving.

Theoretical issues and subsequent research

Hallucinations related to death have been portrayed in several films. These include *Don't Look Now*, where Donald Sutherland 'sees' the red shiny raincoat worn by his young daughter when she drowned, and *Truly, Madly, Deeply*, in which the ghost of the dead lover, Alan Rickman, represents Juliet Stephenson's continuing attachment to him.

According to Archer (1999), a widely held assumption is that grief proceeds through an orderly series of stages or phases, with distinct features. While different accounts vary in the details of particular stages, the two most commonly cited are those of

Bowlby (1980) and Kübler-Ross (1969). According to Bowlby, adult grief is a form of *separation anxiety* in response to the disruption of an attachment bond. (See Chapter 15.) The initial reaction is numbness and disbelief, which can be interspersed with outbursts of extremely intense distress and/or anger. This is followed by yearning and searching for the deceased, which can last for months or even years. Hallucinations (including sensing the presence of the deceased) can be understood in the context of this yearning and searching phase.

Several studies have reported a decline in clear visual memory of the dead spouse over time. For example, Parkes (1970, 1972) found a consistently high reporting (77 per cent) of a clear visual memory over 13 months in his London study. Grimby (1993, in Archer, 1999) reported figures of around 50 per cent for feeling the presence of the deceased, 30 per cent for hearing them, and 26 per cent for seeing them, among a sample of people in their seventies in Sweden. These figures were for one month after the death, and there was a steady decline over the next 11 months.

If hallucinatory experiences are normal for grieving widows and widowers, how can we account for them? Benthall and Slade (1985, in Archer, 1999) found that people who report more frequent hallucinatory experiences show a greater bias towards detecting voices when these are absent in a signal detection task (which involves discriminating the presence or absence of voices). These findings suggest that there are individual differences among the 'normal' (non-schizophrenic), non-grieving population in proneness to hallucinations.

However, different situations can make it more or less likely that hallucinations will be experienced, because of differences in the ease of making the necessary attribution about the source of stimulation (Archer, 1999). After a bereavement, intrusive thoughts and a clear visual image of the deceased will both provide a much stronger source of *internal* stimulation than is usually the case. This, combined with reduced external stimulation, such as sitting in a darkened room late at night, will make it more likely that a misattribution will occur. These are the conditions under which hallucinations are most commonly reported by widowed people.

In *Totem and Taboo* (1913), Freud attributed the widespread fear of ghosts (spirits of the dead) to the projection of unconscious hostility towards the deceased. But this is much more likely to arise from the general inability of human beings to understand and accept the reality of death.

Applications and implications

Several studies have shown that among the factors which predict problematic reactions to the death of a spouse is an ambivalent or dependent relationship with him or her. For example, in Parkes and Weiss's (1983) Harvard bereavement study (a longitudinal study of young widows and widowers), high levels of reported marital conflict were associated with little distress during the first few weeks of bereavement. But after the first month, the grief of the conflicted group tended to become severe and protracted; two to four years later, these widows and widowers still expressed a surprising amount of pining. Dependent relationships were also associated with long-lasting grief, but in this case the grief was intense from the outset.

Waukomis and Chartier (2003, in Parkes, 2006) found that widows and widowers classified as insecurely attached to their spouse suffered more anger, social isolation, guilt, death anxiety, somatic (bodily) symptoms, despair and depersonalization than more securely attached people. (See Chapter 15.) These assessments were made an average of 8.6 years after the death.

However, it is not only the relationship with the spouse that influences the reaction to the loss. The support of family and friends can also reduce loneliness, and lack of support is particularly common in old age; grown-up children have their own home and family, and decreased mobility makes it more difficult to maintain social relationships outside the home. Fulton and Owen (1977, in Parkes, 2006) compared reactions to the death of a spouse, parent and child. They found that, although people who had lost a child were more grief-stricken and preoccupied by thoughts of the loss, it was those who had lost a spouse who were most lonely. This reflects the fact that widows and widowers are more likely to be living on their own following the loss.

Bromley (1988) distinguishes between isolation and desolation in old age. Elderly people may experience isolation from their contemporaries by physical incapacity, or disengagement from younger adults by cultural change and social mobility. All this makes social contact less frequent than it was before (*isolation*). Far more serious is *desolation*, which is to be left alone, neglected, forsaken by the person one deeply wants to be with, a kind of emotional deprivation, having no one to confide in or trust (in particular, one's spouse).

EXERCISES

1 How might participants' reports of their hallucinatory experiences have determined what counted as hallucinations? In other words, how might Rees have *operationalized* 'hallucinations'?

2 How might it have been a disadvantage if Rees had made the interview more rigid?

3 (a) How does Rees define 'cultural background'?

   (b) Is this definition adequate as a basis for his conclusions regarding race, creed and place of residence?

4 Although Rees found no significant gender differences in incidence of hallucinations, there were only 66 widowers compared with the 227 widows in the sample. Does this make the sample gender-biased?

33 On being sane in insane places

Rosenhan, D.L. (1973)

Science, 179: 250–58

BACKGROUND AND CONTEXT

The attempt to classify mental illness is an integral part of the *medical model* of mental disorder (or psychological abnormality) on which traditional psychiatry is based. Psychiatrists, as medically trained practitioners, regard mental illness as comparable to other kinds of (physical) illness, but the symptoms are behavioural and cognitive rather than bodily. (But any hard-and-fast distinction between these two broad categories soon begins to break down: many symptoms of anxiety, for example, take a physical form, such as vomiting, sweating, gooseflesh and headaches; conversely, physical illness often makes us feel tired or depressed, lowers self-esteem, and so on.)

The vocabulary used by psychologists and other non-psychiatrists, as well as the layperson, to refer to mental disorder is borrowed from medical terminology: deviant behaviour is referred to as *psychopathology* and is classified on the basis of *symptoms*, the classification being called a *diagnosis*, while the methods used to try to change the behaviour are called *treatments* or *therapies*, and these are often carried out in psychiatric *hospitals*. If the deviant behaviour ceases, the *patient* is said to be *cured* (Maher, 1966). The use of such language reflects the pervasiveness of a 'sickness' model of psychological abnormality (together with terms such as 'syndrome', 'prognosis' and 'in remission'). We tend to think about abnormal behaviour *as if* it were indicative of some underlying *disease*.

All systems of psychiatric classification stem from the work of Emil Kraepelin (1913), who claimed that certain groups of signs and symptoms occur together sufficiently often to merit the designation 'disease' or 'syndrome'; he then described the diagnostic indicators associated with each syndrome.

One of the two major classification systems currently used in the UK is the Mental Disorders Section of the Tenth Revision of the International Classification of Diseases (ICD-10), published by the World Health Organization in 1992. There is considerable overlap between ICD-10 and the system used in the USA, the Diagnostic and Statistical Manual of Mental Disorders (DSM), published by the American Psychiatric

Association, originally in 1952, revised in 1968 (DSM-II), then again in 1980 (DSM-III), with a minor revision in 1987 (DSM-III-R). The most recent major revision was in 1994 (DSM-IV), with a minor (text) revision in 2000 (DSM-IV-TR).

However, the systems differ regarding the number of major categories they use. For example, ICD-10 has a single category for *schizophrenia, schizotypal states* and *delusional disorders*, which corresponds to three separate DSM categories, namely *schizophrenia, delusional disorders* and *psychotic disorders not elsewhere classified*. They agree, however, that schizophrenia is the most serious mental disorder, and the whole debate surrounding the reliability and validity of the medical model has focused on schizophrenia.

AIM AND NATURE

● HYPOTHESIS

Rosenhan's study was an experimental test of the hypothesis that psychiatrists cannot reliably tell the difference between people who are sane and those who are insane.

Rosenhan claimed that if the hypothesis were supported it would follow that the classification system used to make such a diagnosis cannot be valid: unless we can reliably differentiate the sane from the insane, we cannot be sure that a particular diagnostic label, such as schizophrenia, actually describes a patient's mental disorder.

● METHOD/DESIGN

The hypothesis was tested in two ways:

1. The major experiment (what most of the article describes and discusses, and the one usually cited by others) involved pseudo-patients (participants complaining of hearing voices – auditory hallucinations) trying to gain admission to various US hospitals. Complaining of hearing voices was the manipulated *independent variable*, and the *dependent variable* was whether or not psychiatrists admitted the pseudo-patients – and, if so, what diagnostic label they used.

2. A secondary experiment (whose aim was to see whether the tendency towards diagnosing the sane as insane – based on the first experiment – could be reversed) involved misinforming members of hospital staff that pseudo-patients would be trying to gain admission (based on accurate information regarding the first experiment); this false information was the manipulated

independent variable. The *dependent variable* was the number of patients whom staff subsequently suspected of being pseudo-patients (all of whom, in fact, were genuine patients).

Both experiments took place in actual psychiatric hospitals, so the study was a *naturalistic/field* experiment. The first experiment also involved a large measure of *participant observation*: once admitted, the pseudo-patients kept written records of how the ward as a whole operated, as well as how they were treated personally.

Experiment 1 (main study) – pseudo-patients and their settings

The eight pseudo-patients comprised a psychology graduate student in his twenties, three psychologists (one of whom was Rosenhan), a paediatrician, a psychiatrist, a painter and a housewife (three women, five men). All used pseudonyms. Those in the mental health professions claimed other occupations.

Apart from Rosenhan, whose presence was known to the hospital administrator and chief psychologist, the presence of pseudo-patients (and the nature of the research) was unknown to the hospital staff.

In order to be able to generalize the results, a variety of hospitals was chosen. The 12 hospitals in the sample (some of the pseudo-patients were admitted to more than one hospital) were located in different states on the east and west coasts of the USA; some were old and shabby, some quite new; some were research-orientated, others not; some had very good staff:patient ratios, others were quite understaffed. All but one were state- or federal-funded.

After calling the hospital for an appointment, the pseudo-patient arrived at the admissions office complaining of hearing voices; while often unclear, they seemed to be saying 'empty', 'hollow' and 'thud'. The voices were unfamiliar and of the same sex as the pseudo-patient. Apart from 'the voices' and falsifying their name and employment, everything else they said about themselves was true, including their life history, relationships with parents and siblings, spouse and children, work colleagues and people at school, as well as the things that upset or frustrated them and brought them joy and satisfaction. None showed any signs of psychopathology.

As soon as they had been admitted to the psychiatric ward, the pseudo-patients stopped simulating *any* symptoms of abnormality. Apart from a brief period of nervousness (many had never visited a psychiatric ward before and they were all afraid that they would immediately be exposed as frauds), they behaved 'normally' on the ward, speaking to patients and staff as they might ordinarily. When asked by staff how they were feeling, they indicated that they were fine and no longer experienced symptoms. They did what was asked of them, including taking their medication (which was not swallowed). In addition to the activities available on the ward, they spent their time writing down their observations about the ward, the patients

(vertical margin text:) AIM AND NATURE

and staff; initially this was done 'secretly', but it soon became clear that no one else cared, so they did it quite openly (e.g. in the day room).

Like a true psychiatric patient, the pseudo-patients were admitted without knowing how long they would be in hospital. They would have to get out using their own devices, essentially by convincing the staff that they were sane. They were highly motivated to be discharged as soon as possible, and so behaved as 'sanely' and cooperatively as possible.

● RESULTS

The normal are not detectably sane. Despite their public 'show' of sanity, the pseudo-patients were never 'found out' by staff. In 11 out of 12 cases, they were admitted with a diagnosis of schizophrenia, and discharged with a diagnosis of 'schizophrenia in remission'.

Although there were considerable variations between the hospitals, several were considered excellent. Length of hospitalization ranged from 7 to 52 days (average = 19 days).

It was quite common for the real patients to 'detect' the pseudo-patients' sanity. During the first three hospital admissions (based on accurate accounts), 35 out of 118 patients on the admissions ward voiced their suspicions (such as, 'You're not crazy. You're a journalist, or a professor [referring to the continual note-taking]. You're checking up on the hospital'). So were patients better at detecting normality than psychiatrists?

Rosenhan suggested that doctors are strongly biased towards *type-two errors* (Scheff, 1966), that is, they are more inclined to call a healthy person sick (a *false positive*) than a sick person healthy (a *false negative*, or *type-one error*). It is clearly more dangerous to misdiagnose illness than health, so it is better to err on the side of caution.

The stickiness of psychodiagnostic labels. Many of the pseudo-patients' normal behaviours were entirely overlooked or seriously misinterpreted. Diagnoses were in no way affected by the relative health of the circumstances of their lives. Rather, the reverse was true: how their circumstances were perceived was shaped entirely by the diagnosis. For example, one pseudo-patient had had a close relationship with his mother, but was rather remote from his father during early childhood. But during adolescence and beyond, his father became a close friend, while his relationship with his mother cooled. His present relationship with his wife was close and warm: apart from occasional angry exchanges, friction was minimal. The children had rarely been smacked. This was 'translated' in the case summary prepared for the patient's discharge as follows:

AIM AND NATURE

This white, 39-year-old male ... manifests a long history of considerable ambivalence in close relationships, which begins in early childhood. A warm relationship with his mother cools during his adolescence. A distant relationship to his father is described as becoming very intense. Affective stability is absent. His attempts to control emotionality with his wife and children are punctuated by angry outbursts and, in the case of the children, spankings. And while he says that he has several good friends, one senses considerable ambivalence embedded in these relationships also.

Nursing records for three pseudo-patients indicated that their note-taking was seen as an aspect of their pathological behaviour. 'Patient engages in writing behaviour' was the daily nursing comment on one of them who was never asked about his note-taking. Pseudo-patients' notes were full of patient behaviours which were misinterpreted by well-intentioned staff as stemming from within the patient, rather than the complex of environmental stimuli surrounding him/her. For example, it was not uncommon for a patient who had been mistreated by an attendant to go 'berserk'; if a nurse came on the scene at this point, s/he would assume that this stemmed from the patient's pathology.

The experience of psychiatric hospitalisation. Mental health professionals displayed ambivalence towards psychiatric patients, reflecting the labels they give to patients and the settings they live and work in. Typically, patients and staff were strictly segregated, with their own dining facilities, bathrooms and communal areas. Staff emerged from the glassed quarters (the 'cage') mainly for caretaking purposes: to give medication, conduct a therapy or group meeting, instruct or reprimand a patient. Otherwise, staff kept very much to themselves.

Doctors, especially psychiatrists, were even less accessible than nurses and attendants, and were rarely seen on the wards. When pseudo-patients politely asked any member of staff, 'When am I likely to be discharged?', they were typically given a brief reply while 'on the move' and with head averted, or they were not responded to at all. Often the reply was, 'Good morning [Dave]. How are you today?' (moves off without waiting for an answer).

Patients were deprived of their legal rights by virtue of being psychiatric inpatients: their freedom of movement was restricted; they could not initiate contact with staff; personal privacy was minimal (some toilets had no doors); and their personal history was available to any staff member who chose to read their file. Some pseudo-patients felt they were invisible, as when they were first assessed in a semi-public room, where staff went about their business as if they were not there. On the ward, attendants sometimes gave out verbal and even serious physical abuse to patients in front of other patients – but not in front of other staff members. All this contributed to the patients' sense of *powerlessness*.

AIM AND NATURE

The heavy reliance on psychotropic drugs implicitly contributed to a sense of *deper-sonalization*: staff are convinced that treatment is being given and that further patient contact is not necessary.

Experiment 2 (secondary study)

The staff in a research and teaching hospital, who had heard the results of experiment 1, doubted that such errors could be made in their hospital. They were informed that at some time during the next three months, one or more pseudo-patients would try to gain admission. Each member of staff was asked to rate each patient (on a ten-point scale) who presented him/herself at admissions or on the ward, as to the likelihood that s/he was a pseudo-patient.

Findings

All the staff (attendants, nurses, psychiatrists, doctors and psychologists) were asked to make judgements (on a ten-point scale) about 193 patients admitted for treatment with whom they had had sustained contact, or for whom they had had major responsibility:

- 41 patients were confidently judged to be pseudo-patients by at least one staff member;

- 23 were suspected by at least one psychiatrist;

- 19 were suspected by one psychiatrist *plus* one other staff member.

In fact, all patients during this period were genuine.

● CONCLUSIONS

According to Rosenhan, the results of both experiments showed that psychiatrists cannot distinguish the sane from the insane. Psychiatric hospitals impose a special environment in which the meaning of behaviour can easily be distorted. Patients suffer powerlessness, depersonalization, segregation and self-labelling, which are all counter-therapeutic.

A type-two error in psychiatric diagnosis does not have the same consequences as in medical diagnosis: while a misdiagnosed cancer, for example, is a cause for celebration, misdiagnosed schizophrenia is rarely found to be in error because the label sticks.

EVALUATION

Theoretical issues

The medical model, including the classification of mental disorders, has been fiercely attacked and defended during the past 40 years or so. During the 1960s, what became known as the 'antipsychiatry' movement emerged: a group of psychiatrists and psychotherapists, among them R.D. Laing, Aaron Esterson, David Cooper and Thomas Szasz. Schizophrenia became the focus of their attack.

Arguably the best-known – and most radical – challenge to the medical model was Szasz's (1972) claim that the traditional distinction between organic and functional mental illness is really one between 'disease of the brain' (*not* the mind) or neuropsychological disorder, and 'problems in living'. In other words, there is no such thing as 'mental illness': the term makes no sense. Bailey (1979) makes a similar distinction between *physical* illness and *disorders of psychosocial or interpersonal functioning*. This way, the concept of *mental* illness is, effectively, disposed of.

According to Laing's (1967) *conspiratorial model*, schizophrenia is a label, a form of violence perpetrated by some people on others. The family, GP and psychiatrists conspire against the schizophrenic in order to preserve their definition of reality (the *status quo*). They treat schizophrenics as if they were sick and imprison them in mental hospitals, where they are degraded and invalidated as human beings.

Rosenhan discusses the effects of *diagnostic labelling* at great length. His results demonstrate what several authors (e.g. Scheff, 1966) have hypothesized, namely that psychiatric labels tend to become *self-fulfilling prophecies*. Not only do psychiatric labels stick in a way that other (medical) labels do not, but, more seriously, *everything* the patient says and does is interpreted in terms of that label (such as the 'writing behaviour' of the pseudo-patients). According to Lilienfeld (1995), Rosenhan's study 'provides a sorely needed reminder of the human mind's propensity to rearrange or reframe facts to achieve consistency with pre-existing beliefs'.

Rosenhan states that mental illness is a purely *social* phenomenon, the consequence of a labelling process. As Scheff argues, the label 'schizophrenia' influences how the person will continue to behave (based on stereotyped ideas of mental illness), and how others will react to him/her. The labelling process creates a *social role*, which *is* the disorder.

Lindsay (1982) found that schizophrenic patients were rated by ordinary people as more abnormal regardless of whether they had been told correctly or incorrectly who was schizophrenic and who was not. (See **Exercises**.) These results 'strongly indicate that the label is far from an empty one, and that there is a reality of some kind behind it' (Miller and Morley, 1986). Miller and Morley also point out that the patients videotaped by Lindsay were all fairly new cases, so they had not had long to adapt to the label and change their behaviour accordingly (as an extreme supporter of labelling theory would claim). They believe that to argue for 'labelling' as against the medical model is a *false dichotomy* (it is *not* one or the other).

While Rosenhan's study and labelling theory have usefully highlighted how people labelled as mentally ill are treated, they cannot account for why someone begins to show deviant behaviour in the first place (MacCleod, 1998). Also, if diagnostic labels are really so powerful, why were the genuine patients in Rosenhan's study not deceived by them? The pseudo-patients' actual behaviour seems to have been more powerful than whatever adverse effects the labels may have exerted on these observers' perceptions (Lilienfeld, 1995).

According to McLeod (1998), labelling theory is an example of a theory that fitted the practices of a particular place and time; for example, it seems to be especially applicable to *involuntary* hospital admissions. When Scheff conducted his research in the USA in the 1960s, 90 per cent of all psychiatric admissions were involuntary. When Bean (1979) replicated Scheff's study in the UK, the figure was just 18 per cent. Not only will there be national and cultural differences in admission rates, but the US figure is likely to have fallen in that time.

Labelling theory also implies that definitions of abnormality will vary between cultures, reflecting different social norms and values. For example, the only difference between the visions of a shaman and the hallucinations of a diagnosed schizophrenic is that shamans are perceived by their culture as wise. Contrary to labelling theory, both the Eskimo and Yoruba peoples have a concept of being crazy that is quite similar to our definition of schizophrenia. The Eskimo's *nuthkavihak* includes talking to oneself, refusing to talk, delusional beliefs and bizarre behaviour; the Yoruba's *were* encompasses similar symptoms. Both cultures also have shamans, but they draw a clear line between their behaviour and that of crazy people (Murphy, 1976).

Subsequent research

The debate about the medical model has taken place at many different levels, often less 'fundamental' than Szasz's rejection of the very concept of mental illness. In defence of classification, Kendell (1983) claims that every psychiatric patient has attributes at three levels:

1   those shared with *all* other psychiatric patients;

2   those share with *some* other psychiatric patients;

3   those that are unique to them.

Classification is feasible provided there are attributes at level (2): the shared attributes are what constitutes one category as distinct from others. The value of classification depends on the relative size in importance of the attributes at (2) compared with (1) and (3). According to Miller and Morley (1986), most psychiatrists and psychologists believe that there *are* important attributes at level (2).

The question of the *reliability* of classification (i.e. how consistently psychiatrists identify level (2) attributes) is at the heart of Rosenhan's study: he was trying to show that psychiatrists cannot be 'trusted' to correctly identify genuine patients (who share certain attributes with other patients) as distinct from pseudo-patients (who are only *pretending* to share these attributes with other patients). Reliability is usually assessed by measuring the diagnostic agreement between two or more psychiatrists who have examined the *same* patients. Generally, agreement is quite high when discriminating between organic and functional disorders, but can be very poor for specific diagnoses.

Early studies regularly showed low reliability: psychiatrists varied widely in how much information they elicited at interview, as well as in their interpretations of that information. Variations were also found between groups of psychiatrists trained in different countries. For example, the US-UK Diagnostic Project (Cooper *et al.*, 1972) found that New York psychiatrists who were shown videotaped clinical interviews were twice as likely to diagnose schizophrenia as their London counterparts (shown the same videotapes). The International Pilot Study of Schizophrenia (World Health Organization, 1973) confirmed that US psychiatrists (and those in the former USSR) had unusually broad concepts of the disorder.

However, little attempt was made in any of these reliability studies to ensure that the different psychiatrists used agreed criteria (Cooper, 1983). When attempts are made to construct special instruments or interview procedures for reaching a diagnosis based on operational criteria (and psychiatrists trained to use them), fairly impressive levels of reliability are achieved (especially for schizophrenia and psychotic depression). Such instruments include the present-state examination (Wing *et al.*, 1974), the Feighner criteria (Feighner *et al.*, 1972), research diagnostic criteria (Spitzer *et al.*, 1978) and schedule for affective disorders and schizophrenia (Endicott and Spitzer, 1978).

The second and third of these helped to shape DSM-III; see **Background and context** above), which addressed itself largely to the whole problem of unreliability, especially the lack of clear criteria. It covered a broader range of disorders, and used more specific categories and more precise language than earlier versions. The use of checklists also helped to increase reliability: the patient had to show a specified number of observable symptoms before being given a particular diagnosis.

Methodological issues

Crucially, it was DSM-II that was in use at the time of Rosenhan's study. It seems much less likely that psychiatrists using any of the later versions of DSM would have been misled by pseudo-patients, since a characteristic hallucination must be repeated on several occasions, whereas Rosenhan's colleagues basically made one such report (Sarbin and Mancuso, 1980). Reliability has undoubtedly improved since the publication of DSM-III, aided by the use of 'decision trees' and computer programs that lead the psychiatrist through the tree (Holmes, 1994). Despite some categories (still) having greater reliability than others, this is now quite acceptable for most of the major categories (Davison *et al.*, 2004).

However, problems remain. For example, reliability may not be as high in everyday practice as it is when psychiatrists know they are taking part in a formal reliability study, and there is still room for subjective interpretation on the psychiatrist's part (as when comparison is made, at one point, between the patient and an 'average person'). As Davison *et al.* (2004) say: 'Such judgements set the stage for the insertion of cultural biases as well as the clinician's own personal ideas of what the average person should be doing at a given stage of life'.

However, much more attention is now paid to how symptoms of a given disorder may differ depending on the *culture* in which they appear. For example, guilt is common in Western societies, but rare in Japan or Iran. In the USA, depression among Latinos is more likely to involve *somatic* (bodily) symptoms (such as headaches and 'nerves') than among the white population. In DSM-IV-TR, cultural differences are dealt with:

● in descriptions of each disorder in the main body of the manual;

● in an appendix that provides a general framework for evaluating the role of culture and ethnicity;

● by describing *culture-bound syndromes* (CBSs) in the appendix. (See Gross, 2005.)

Applications and implications

While the early reliability studies involved *inter-rater/judge reliability*, Rosenhan's study, technically, did not, since each patient was assessed by a single psychiatrist. Nevertheless, his findings have significant implications for the reliability of psychiatric diagnosis: if mental health professionals cannot distinguish between the mentally ill and the healthy, the question of whether they can distinguish between different varieties of mental illness seems premature and, perhaps, even pointless (Lilienfeld, 1995).

In defence of those psychiatrists involved in Rosenhan's study, Kety (1974, in Sarbin and Mancuso, 1980) poses the following (rather unsettling) scenario:

> *If I were to drink a quart of blood and, concealing what I had done, had come to the emergency room of any hospital vomiting blood, the behaviour of the staff would be quite predictable. If they labelled and treated me as having a bleeding peptic ulcer, I doubt that I could argue convincingly that medical science does not know how to diagnose that condition.*

But as Sarbin and Mancuso point out, Kety does not go on to ask what the doctors would say when no bleeding was observed the next day and all the tests proved negative. Would they discharge him with a diagnosis of 'bleeding peptic ulcer in remission'? This, of course, is meant to parallel the situation that the pseudo-patients were in once they had been admitted.

One of Rosenhan's fiercest critics, Spitzer (1976), notes that the discharge diagnosis 'schizophrenia in remission' is hardly ever given to *real* patients given an admission diagnosis of schizophrenia; therefore, the diagnoses were a function of the pseudo-patients' *behaviour*, and *not* the setting (psychiatric hospital) in which they were made (as Rosenhan claims). In other words, these psychiatrists successfully recognized that the individuals who showed symptoms of a disorder that rarely disappears completely, had in fact experienced 'remission'. Thus, far from condemning diagnostic labelling, Rosenhan's study suggests that mental health professionals *can* actually distinguish psychotic from non-psychotic people with surprisingly high levels of accuracy (Lilienfeld, 1995).

However, Neisser (1973) sees this as a 'heads I win, tails you lose' situation: the psychiatrist can never be wrong. But Lilienfeld believes that 'in remission' is more informative than 'normal', because it implies the increased risk of subsequent schizophrenic episodes.

Finally, Spitzer points out that Rosenhan, as a professor of psychology (and law), should know that the terms 'sane' and 'insane' are *legal* – not psychiatric – concepts; no psychiatrist makes a diagnosis of 'sanity'/'insanity'. This is ironic given Rosenhan's condemnation of the use of psychiatric labelling.

EXERCISES

1   Why was it important to use a range of hospitals, and in what respects did they differ?

2   According to Rosenhan, the results of experiment 2 indicated that the tendency to label some people as insane can be reversed when the stakes are high (prestige and diagnostic acumen).

   (a) What do you think he means by 'the tendency to label some people as insane can be reversed'?

   (b) Explain this reversal in terms of type-one and type-two errors.

   (c) What do you think he means by 'when the stakes are high (prestige and diagnostic acumen)'?

3   Linsdsay (1982) showed videotaped recordings of participants alleged to have schizophrenia, and of normal controls, to a sample of patients in a general hospital. One group was told nothing about the people in the video, while two other groups were told either correctly or incorrectly who were the schizophrenics and who were not. The participants had to rate the degree of abnormality shown by each person on the video. What would Rosenhan have predicted?

4   If Rosenhan had used control groups in the two experiments, what might they have been?

5   Is there anything unethical about the concealment of the true identity of the pseudo-patients and the inevitable deception involved?

34 Familial studies of intelligence: A review

Bouchard, T.J., Jr. and McGue, M. (1981)

Science, 212: 1055–9

BACKGROUND AND CONTEXT

The relative influence of nature and nurture/heredity and environment represents the most controversial issue in the behavioural sciences, and 'nowhere are the weapons more poised to be fired than with respect to the question of the extent to which measured intelligence is a product – wholly or in large measure – of genetic endowment' (Gardner *et al.*, 1996).

The nature–nurture/heredity–environment debate has raged for most of psychology's history. Some of the major figures in this controversy (especially hereditarian theorists, who favour the nature/heredity side) are discussed in Chapter 35. According to Sternberg and Grigorenko (1997), virtually all researchers accept that:

- Both heredity and environment contribute to intelligence.

- Heredity and environment interact in various ways.

- Extremely poor, as well as highly enriched, environments can interfere with the realization of a person's intelligence, regardless of his/her heredity.

However, there is very little agreement beyond these very general beliefs.

Arguably one of the stickiest aspects of the whole debate is the attempt to separate out the effects of heredity and environment: given agreement about the first point above, the question becomes '*How much* does each contribute?' Most of the major attempts to 'parcel out' these two types of influence (twin studies, adoption studies and other 'family resemblance' studies) have been conducted by *behaviour geneticists* (leading examples of whom include Thomas Bouchard and Robert Plomin).

Behaviour-genetic theory, derived from evolutionary theory, focuses on the causes of individual *variation* in intelligence (and other characteristics) within populations.

According to Scarr (1997), behaviour-genetic theorists regard four major sources of variation as crucial for explaining individual differences in intelligence:

1   *Additive genetic effects*: these are the combined effect of many genes (the *genotype*), each contributing a small amount to differences in measured intelligence (the *phenotype*).

2   *Non-additive genetic effects*: these include the effect of dominant genes and other major gene effects, and gene–environment correlations and interactions. (See **Applications and implications** below.)

3   *Between-family non-genetic effects*: these refer to psychosocial environmental differences between one family and another, making siblings more similar than children reared in different families. Examples include social class and parental differences in child-rearing styles.

4   *Within-family non-genetic variances*: these refer to those aspects of the environment, both biological and social, that make siblings in the same family different from one another. Examples include both pre- and post-natal influences that affect one sibling differently from another.

At a general level, behaviour-genetic theory claims that genetic differences are a major source of intellectual differences among children, regardless of parental rearing styles (unless parents are abusive or seriously neglectful: Scarr 1992, 1993). Specific predictions focus on observations of intellectual resemblance among family members. Similarity in intelligence is predicted to the extent that parents and children, and siblings, are genetically related, with little/no similarity among those who are genetically unrelated – even if they are reared together. Observations of families with different degrees of genetic and environmental relatedness provide critical tests of these predictions (Scarr, 1997).

AIM AND NATURE

● HYPOTHESIS

The explicit aim of Bouchard and McGue's study is to update an earlier review by Erlenmeyer-Kimling and Jarvik (1963). Although it is not explicitly intended to find support for behaviour-genetic theory, *implicitly* it is; that is, partly based on the findings of the earlier review (which became widely cited as strong evidence for genetic determination of IQ), Bouchard and McGue expected to find that the closer the genetic resemblance between family members, the closer their measured intelligence would be.

● METHOD/DESIGN

The article reports the findings of a comprehensive survey of the world literature on familial resemblance and measured intelligence, that is, IQ correlations between relatives. Several new studies were reported since the earlier review (59 in all), and Burt's twin study data were *removed* (following the revelation in the 1970s that he fabricated many of his results – although the controversy was reopened by Joynson in 1989).

Altogether, 140 studies were found, but these were reduced to 111 by the application of explicit selection criteria. They produced 526 familial correlations based on 113,942 pairings.

● FINDINGS

Figure 34.1 shows correlations between relatives, both biological and adoptive, in the 111 studies. The median correlation in each distribution is indicated by a vertical bar, and the small arrow indicates the correlation that would be predicted by a genetic model with no dominance, no assortative mating, and no environmental effects.

In general, the pattern of average correlations was consistent with the pattern that would be predicted on the basis of polygenic inheritance (i.e. the higher the proportion of genes two family members have in common, the higher the average correlation between their IQs).

The data contained considerable heterogeneity (variability); in an attempt to identify the factors that contributed to this, Bouchard and McGue analysed the data in terms of (1) opposite-sex and same-sex pairings; and (2) male and female pairings.

1   Among dizygotic (DZ) (non-identical or fraternal) twins, the IQs of same-sex twins were more similar than those of opposite-sex twins. This may have reflected a social-environmental effect (for example, parents may treat same-sex twins more similarly than opposite-sex twins). The difference between non-twin same-sex and opposite-sex siblings and between same-sex and opposite-sex parent–offspring pairings was negligible.

2   There were no consistent trends for the male–female comparison. For example, the average correlations were larger in male than female twins, but the reverse was true for other siblings. These findings are consistent with a polygenic theory of inheritance, which does not propose the existence of sex linkage.

AIM AND NATURE

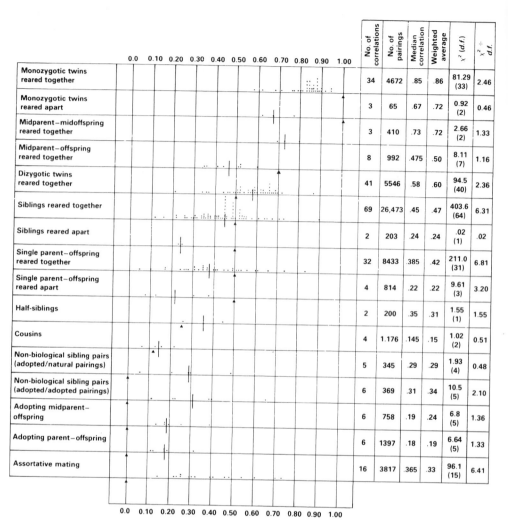

Figure 34.1. Familial correlations for IQ. The vertical bar in each distribution indicates the median correlation; the arrow indicates the correlation predicted by a simple polygenic model.

Another possible source of the heterogeneity was the intelligence test used. There was great diversity in the IQ tests used in different studies. For example, the 34 correlations for monozygotic (MZ) identical twins reared together were based on results from 22 different tests; and the 42 correlations for DZs were based on results from 25 tests. Bouchard and McGue compared correlations for individually administered tests and group-administered tests, for MZs and DZs separately; in neither case was the difference significant.

The 34 correlations based on 4,672 MZ twin pairs reared together produced a weighted average of 0.86, which is very close to what was reported in earlier reviews; this was about the same for male and female pairs. Of the reported correlations, 79 per cent were above 0.80.

After omitting the Burt data, there were data for just 65 pairs of MZ twins reared apart (in three separate studies). The weighted average of 0.72 was much lower than that for the MZs reared together, suggesting the importance of between-family environmental differences. But the size of the correlations would be difficult to explain in terms of any strictly environmental hypothesis.

The average correlation for mid-parent–mid-offspring based on three studies was 0.72; the genetic expectation could not be determined, because this would depend on the number of offspring. However, the mid-parent–individual offspring correlation has a simple genetic expectation of 0.707; the observed weighted average was only 0.50.

The weighted average of the 41 correlations in DZ pairs was 0.60, considerably higher than for non-twin siblings, and same-sex DZ pairs showed somewhat greater similarity than opposite-sex DZ pairs (0.62 vs 0.57); males were slightly more similar than females (0.65 vs 0.61).

The weighted average for siblings reared together was 0.47; although this was close to the simple genetic expectation of 0.50, the range of correlations was from 0.13 to 0.90. Opposite-sex and same-sex siblings were almost identical, as were female and male siblings. Based on just 203 pairs of siblings reared apart, a weighted average of 0.24 was found; this was much less than the expected value.

The weighted average correlation between individual parent and individual offspring was 0.42 (based on just 32 correlations). There was a broad range of correlations, which could not be attributed to either a sex effect (opposite-sex and same-sex pairings produced similar averages) or a maternal effect (average correlation of mother–offspring was the same as father–offspring). The simple genetic expectation is 0.50. This is also the expectation for parent and separated offspring; the weighted average was 0.22.

For cousins, the average (of four correlations) was 0.15 – very similar to the simple genetic expectation.

The average adopted–natural sibling correlation should be higher than the adopted/adopted sibling pair, but Bouchard and McGue found the reverse to be true.

● CONCLUSIONS

As in the Erlenmeyer-Kimling and Jarvik review, the pattern of averaged correlations was remarkably consistent with polygenic theory. This is not to discount the importance of environmental factors: MZ twins reared apart were far from perfectly correlated, DZ twins were more similar than other biological siblings, and adoptive parents' IQs showed a consistent relationship with those of their adoptive offspring. However, Bouchard and McGue found no evidence for sex-role and maternal effects, sometimes thought to be important.

It is indisputable that the data supported the inference that IQ is partially determined by genetic factors, but it is doubtful whether they told us to what degree. Because of the large amount of unexplained variability within the different relationships, any models used to explain the data should be used cautiously.

EVALUATION

Theoretical issues

Behaviour-genetic theorists mostly take it for granted that IQ tests are reliable and valid measures of intelligence. However, there are good reasons for challenging this assumption:

- It is possible for two IQ tests, A and B, to have different *standard deviations* (a measure of dispersion or variability of scores around the mean, and how IQ scores are usually expressed); this means that the same individual could score differently on the two tests. But both tests claim to be measuring the same thing, namely intelligence. This suggests that while intelligence is a *psychological* concept, IQ is a *statistical* concept. If it is possible for the same characteristic to be assigned different values according to which test is used to measure it, then perhaps instead of asking, 'How intelligent is this person?', we should ask, 'How intelligent is this person as measured by this particular test?' This is relevant in discussing the Bouchard and McGue review, in which they note the diversity of tests used in the 111 studies. We cannot just assume that the scales are equivalent, which makes the procedure of finding the median correlation for different studies problematical.

- Expressing intelligence as a *number* creates the (misleading) impression that IQ tells us something 'absolute' about an individual's intellectual ability (in the same way as metres and centimetres tell us about height). But whereas height is measured on a *ratio scale* (and, by implication, an *interval* scale too), many psychologists believe that intelligence can only be measured on an *ordinal* scale: IQ can tell us how intelligent we are *relative* to others (higher or lower), but we cannot be more precise about the size of those differences (Ryan, 1972). (See **Exercises**.)

The idea that intelligence is hereditary (i.e. *differences* in IQ are inherited) is deeply embedded in the theory of IQ testing itself, because of its commitment to the measurement of something intrinsic and fixed. From the very beginning of the American and British mental testing movements, it was assumed that IQ was biologically heritable (Rose *et al.*, 1984; see Chapter 35). Rose *et al.* point out what they consider to be certain mistaken senses of 'heritable', as used by psychometricians;

these have become mixed up with geneticists' technical meaning of the term and contribute to false conclusions about the consequences of heritability:

1   *Genes do not determine intelligence:* there is no one-to-one correspondence between the genes inherited from one's parents and even physical characteristics. What we inherit is the *genotype,* the genes which are involved in the development of a particular trait; the *phenotype* is the actual trait as it manifests itself in the organism. While the former is fixed, the latter develops and changes constantly. The first principle of developmental genetics is that every organism is a unique product of the interaction between genes and environment at every stage of life.

2   Even allowing that genes alone do not determine the phenotype, it is claimed that they determine the *effective limits of the phenotype:* genes determine capacity or potential. However, Ryan (1972) rejects the whole idea of innate potential on the grounds that it is impossible to measure potential separately from actual behaviour/performance.

The first point is related to one of the areas of agreement among all researchers, namely that there is interaction between heredity and environment. (See **Background and context** above.) For Wahlsten and Gottlieb (1997), the complex sequence of bidirectional and interacting causes makes it almost impossible to assign a definite role to the genotype unless a major gene can be identified. But the prevalent model in human behaviour genetics assumes that heredity and environment are *additive,* separately acting causes whose contributions to any phenotype can be neatly divided up statistically. Wahlsten and Gottlieb regard this assumption as biologically unrealistic given our present state of knowledge.

Methodological issues

In general, *heritability* is estimated from the correlation of a trait between relatives (Rose *et al.,* 1984). However, most of the results of family resemblance (or *concordance*) studies can be interpreted as supporting *either* the genetic *or* the environmental theory. This is because relatives resemble each other not only in terms of their genes, but also in terms of their environments: the closer the genetic relationship (blood tie), the more likely they are to share the same environment. This is why psychologists and behaviour geneticists take advantage of the 'natural experiments' of twin studies (especially the separation of MZ twins) and adoption studies: they present an opportunity to study the relative influence of the two (normally inseparable) variables: heredity and environment.

With Burt's twin studies excluded from Bouchard and McGue's review, the three remaining studies of separated MZs are (presumably):

1   Newman *et al.* (1937);

2   Shields (1962);

3   Juel-Nielsen (1965).

One of the criteria Bouchard and McGue used for selection (in their Notes), was that 'the procedure for zygosity determination was both objective and valid. Use of a validated questionnaire was considered an acceptable procedure'. In other words, it should be possible to establish objectively whether or not any of the volunteers are MZ or DZ twins. But this was clearly *not* so in the case of Newman *et al.*'s study (see Kamin 1977): in 1937, there was no reliable/valid medical test for zygosity, which, surely, is the only kind of test that *should* be used.

Perhaps more seriously, the whole rationale of these studies is that MZs are reared separately (in truly uncorrelated environments). But this is also flawed, since several kinds of correlated environments can occur for supposedly separated twins, such as the prenatal and early post-natal environments: they are womb-mates, and selective placement after separation is likely to produce low to moderate correlations of their childhood environments. In addition, there may be similarity of adult environments if and when the twins are reunited prior to psychological testing (as in the Minnesota twin study – see **Subsequent research** below – where the twins were tested on average ten years following reunion!). This is an unacceptable confounding of the two factors (Wahlsten and Gottlieb, 1997).

Howe (1997) also argues that being separated at birth is *not* the same as being reared *completely* apart, which is, of course, impossible:

> no two individuals who began life in the identical uterus can be said to have been reared apart to the extent that would be essential in order for an investigation based on separated twins to yield entirely unambiguous evidence about the effects of genes on intelligence. In practice, however, separation at birth is the best that can be done.

To share a womb is to share nine crucial formative months of one's life, and differences in prenatal environments can have powerful effects on post-natal development. For example, maternal smoking and drinking during pregnancy can adversely affect the child's intelligence.

The greater correlation/concordance of MZs compared with same-sex DZs is taken to be the strongest evidence in favour of the genetic theory. This conclusion depends on the validity of the *equal environments assumption* (EEA), according to which both types of twin experience (roughly) equal environments. However, most people (including leading twin researchers) understand that MZs' physical and social environments are much more similar. This means that the higher concordance for MZs can tell us little about genetic influences on differences in intelligence (or any other psychological trait).

However, supporters of the EEA (e.g. Kendler *et al.*, 1993; Scarr, 1968; Shields, 1954) argue that this greater similarity of MZs' environments is *caused by* their genetic similarity: twins 'create their own environment' (Plomin *et al.*, 1977). According to Joseph (2003), this is a 'heads I win, tails you lose' argument, which, even if valid (which he denies) is *irrelevant*: the *reasons* that they experience more similar environments does not matter. He gives the hypothetical example of a twin study into possible genetic influences on lung cancer. Let us assume there is a genetic basis for the desire to smoke tobacco. Because of their greater genetic similarity, it is likely that MZs would be more concordant for cigarette smoking. According to Plomin *et al.*'s logic, since the tendency towards *smoking* is 'driven genetically', the higher MZ concordance for *lung cancer* is evidence of a genetic predisposition for lung cancer. This is clearly mistaken: lung cancer could still be *completely* explained by exposure to tobacco smoke – an *environmental* event (Joseph, 2003).

The problem with the early *adoption studies* (e.g. Burks, 1928; Leahy, 1935) was that adoptive families differ, as a group, in various ways, from the 'matched control group' of ordinary biological families (see Kamin, 1977). The obvious improvement on this 'classical' design was to study adoptive parents who also had a biological child of their own: two genetically unrelated children will have been reared in the same environment by the same parents (and the adopted child will also be genetically unrelated to the adoptive parents).

Scarr and Weinberg (1977, 1983) and Horn *et al.* (1979) used this new design, the former involving *transracial* adoptions (the mother and her biological child were white, while the adopted child was black). In both studies, there was no significant difference between (i) the correlation of the mother's IQ and her biological child's IQ, and (ii) the correlation of the mother's IQ with the adopted child's IQ. According to Rose *et al.* (1984):

> The child's race, like its adoptive status, had no effect on the degree of parent–child resemblance in IQ. These results appear to inflict fatal damage to the notion that IQ is highly heritable ... children reared by the same mother resemble her in IQ to the same degree, whether or not they share her genes.

Howe (1997) argues that the adoptive homes involved in adoption studies have tended to be very similar in the degree to which they provide intellectually stimulating environments; this makes it possible that the data have under-represented the range of differences that can occur in children's everyday experiences. Had there been greater variety, the conclusions might have given more weight to the role of environmental factors and less to genetic ones (the reverse of the usual conclusions that are drawn).

Subsequent research

The Minnesota twin study (Bouchard *et al.*, 1990) has been going on since 1979, accumulating pairs of separated MZs (MZAs) during that time; the latest figure stands at 56. They have also studied 30 pairs of separated DZs, but the data are presented almost exclusively in terms of MZAs compared with MZTs (MZs reared together). This represents a different 'methodology' from earlier studies, where the crucial comparisons were between MZAs and same-sex DZTs. In either case, the aim is to separate two normally interrelated variables.

Once recruited, the twins were subjected to a week (50 hours) of intensive physiological and psychological assessment (including measures of personality and temperament, occupational and leisure interests, and social attitudes, as well as intelligence). It is the most 'international' twin study to date, recruiting from all over the USA, the UK, Australia, Canada, New Zealand, China, Sweden and Germany.

Regarding IQ, Bouchard found a *heritability estimate* of 70 per cent: 70 per cent of the variance between the IQ scores of individuals is attributable to genetic factors. This is higher than the 48 per cent proposed in the 1981 study, and by Loehlin (1989) and Plomin and Loehlin (1989). However, virtually the entire literature on IQ similarity in twins and siblings is limited to studies of children and adolescents. The mean age of the MZAs in the Minnesota study was 41 years (with a range of 19–68).

Summarizing their findings as a whole, Bouchard *et al.* claim that adult MZs are about equally similar on most physiological and psychological traits, regardless of whether they were brought up together or apart; they are strikingly similar because they are genetically identical. They rule out the significant effect of socio-economic status (SES) or other environmental factors on twins' IQ scores, but some of their methods for measuring environmental variables were dubious, to say the least. For example, as an 'index of cultural and intellectual resources', they provided a checklist of available household facilities, such as power tools, sailboat, telescope, unabridged dictionary and original artwork.

Horgan (1993) points out some additional criticisms that have been made of the Minnesota study:

● Some of the 'eerie', 'bewitching' and 'remarkable' parallels between some of the reunited MZs have been greatly exaggerated.

● The method used to select twins may have been biased: much of the recruitment came through media coverage, with 'self-referrals' or relatives and friends telling twins about the study. It has created considerable publicity, both in the USA and other parts of the world, attracting people who want to be 'famous'; this makes them an atypical sample of twins (let alone people in general).

- The MZAs may actually have had more extensive contact with each other while growing up than at least the media make out.

Bouchard *et al.* claim that any shared experience they may have had as adults is unimportant: they had already passed through the early 'formative years' (critical or sensitive period) for intelligence. However, Wahlsten and Gottlieb (1997) comment:

> The distinction between hardware and software that is so obvious in a computer is not present in the living human brain, where experience continues to alter the connections throughout life. If brain structure can be altered significantly in adult animals, it seems likely that the intelligence of adult humans is also modifiable.

Applications and implications

More important than the specific size of the heritability estimate (HE) is the fact that it is *not* a fixed value, but a *relative* index, referring to a particular population at a particular time. If everyone's environment were to become very similar, the higher the HE would become: relatively more of the variance between people's IQ scores would be attributable to genetic differences. This is another example of the *interaction* between heredity and environment: it is perhaps much more fruitful to consider *how* and *in what ways* they act to produce the phenotype of intelligence, than it is to measure *how much* each contributes. (See **Background and context** above.)

Bouchard *et al.* suggest that children have different experiences, partly because they elicit different parenting responses, partly because they will seek out different environments which match their temperaments. (These are examples of *gene–environment correlation*.) When different individuals pay different attention and respond differently to the same objective experience, *gene–environment interaction* is taking place. If this view is correct, then the developmental experience of MZs is more similar than that of DZs, as environmentalist critics of twin research have argued. If the genotype influences development through dictating the characteristics, selection and impact of experience (nature *via* nurture), then it may be possible to change even highly heritable traits, especially if any intervention is tailored to each child's talents and inclinations (Bouchard *et al.*, 1990).

Ironically, these views are echoed to some extent by Gould (1981), a major critic of the genetic theory (see Chapter 35). What he calls the *hereditarian fallacy* involves equating 'heritable' with 'inevitable'. Equally serious, and equally mistaken, is the confusion of *within-* and *between-group heritability*, that is, assuming that if heredity explains a certain percentage of variation among individuals *within* a group (e.g. white Americans), it must also explain a similar percentage of variation *between* groups (e.g. white and black Americans) on the trait in question (e.g. IQ). These are entirely *separate* phenomena: knowing one tells us nothing about the other.

Twin and adoption studies provide data on which the HE for *within*-group differences is based, but this has then been used by hereditarian theorists like Jensen (1969) to explain *between*-group differences in the same genetic terms.

Genetic or hereditarian theorists believe in the *direct* influence of genetics on intelligence: this is more or less fixed from birth, so any attempt at increasing an individual's intelligence is pointless (although Bouchard *et al.* recognize that change *is* possible: see above). Only population control (*eugenics*) can restrain the swift growth of a permanent underclass of people with low IQs (Herrnstein and Murray, 1996). However, if the influence of genetics is *indirect*, then change is possible and a particular IQ is not determined once and for all at birth. It may be no more difficult to change IQ than those mental skills known to be acquired through experience and learning (Howe, 1997); in turn, this is consistent with the view that there is nothing unique or fundamental about those abilities that determine an individual's performance on an IQ test (Howe, 1998).

Agreeing with Bouchard *et al.*, Gardner (1993) argues that, while there is considerable plasticity and flexibility in early development, this is mediated by strong genetic constraints which guide development along some paths rather than others. However, he also challenges one of the basic assumptions of the hereditarian argument:

> Genetics has made its greatest progress in accounting for simple traits in simple organisms ... But when it comes to more complex human abilities – the capacities to solve equations, to appreciate or create music, to master languages ... we are still woefully ignorant about the genetic component and its phenotypic expression ... any complex trait reflects many genes ... when it comes to human intelligence, it is questionable whether one ought to speak of 'traits' at all.

According to Segall *et al.* (1999):

> Dual inheritance theory [Boyd and Richardson, 1985] shows that the nature versus nurture (or genetics versus culture) controversy is an inappropriate conceptualization of the relationship between biological and cultural forces. While they may have different outcomes, and involve different processes, they are parallel rather than competing forces. And, they interact with each other when applied to any particular individual human being.

EXERCISES

1 (a) What is the biggest single problem associated with family resemblance studies in general? (Looking at Figure 34.1, which two variables change together as you work down from the top?)

   (b) Which specific type of family resemblance study attempts to overcome this problem?

2 What is meant by a *polygenic* theory of intelligence?

3 What is meant by genetic *dominance*?

4 What is meant by *assortative mating*?

5 Why might Bouchard and McGue have chosen the median as the measure of the average?

6 What is the difference between individual and group tests of intelligence? Give at least *one* example of each.

35 A nation of morons

Gould, S.J. (1982)

New Scientist, 6 May: 349–52

BACKGROUND AND CONTEXT

An early and striking example of the 'tenacity of unconscious bias and the surprising malleability of "objective" data in the interest of a preconceived idea' (Gould, 1981) is Binet's discovery of a positive correlation between head size and intelligence. When he first decided to study intelligence, it was 'natural' that Binet should use craniometry (the measurement of skulls, first used by Broca). But he suspected that, unconsciously and unknowingly, he would distort the actual measurements, producing the results he expected (*experimenter bias*). He concluded that 'The idea of measuring intelligence by measuring heads seemed ridiculous' (Binet, 1900 in Gould, 1981).

In 1904, Binet was commissioned by the French minister of public education to perform a study for a specific, practical purpose, namely to develop ways of identifying those children whose lack of success in normal classrooms suggested the need for some form of special education. Consequently, he brought together a large series of short tasks, related to everyday life problems (e.g. counting coins, assessing the 'prettier' face), but supposedly involving such basic reasoning processes as 'direction (ordering), comprehension, invention and censure (correction)' (Binet, 1909 in Gould, 1981).

The result was the first recognized test of intelligence (1905), with tasks arranged in ascending order of difficulty. In 1908, the concept of mental age (MA) was introduced, and a child's general intellectual level was calculated as chronological age (CA) *minus* MA. Children whose MA was sufficiently behind their CA could then be recommended for special education. Finally, the German psychologist, Stern (1912), pointed out that *division* is more appropriate than subtraction: it is the *relative* (not the absolute) size of the difference that matters, hence MA/CA x 100/1 (multiplying by 100 gives a whole number). The IQ (intelligence quotient) was born!

Binet refused to speculate on the *meaning* of the IQ score: intelligence is too complex to capture with a single number and represents the average of many performances, *not* an entity with an independent, objective existence. Not only did he refuse to label IQ as a measure of innate intelligence, but Binet also rejected it as a general device for ranking *all* pupils in terms of mental ability (as opposed to those needing special education).

Also, whatever the cause of poor school performance, Binet's aim was to identify these children in order to help and improve, *not* to label in order to limit. It is this, rather than belief in/denial of innate intellectual differences, which differentiates strict *hereditarians* and their opponents (Gould, 1981). (See Chapter 34.) Ironically, many US school boards have come full circle, and now use IQ tests only as Binet originally recommended: as instruments for assessing children with specific learning difficulties.

However, returning to the early twentieth century, and crossing from France to the USA, it was H.H. Goddard who first introduced Binet's scale to America, translated Binet's articles into English, applied his tests and advocated their general use. He agreed with Binet that the tests worked best in identifying those just below the normal range, but Goddard regarded the scores as measuring a single, innate entity. His purpose in using the tests was to recognize people's limits so that they could be segregated, to curtail breeding so as to prevent further decline of the American 'stock'; this was already threatened by immigration from without and by the prolific reproduction of the feeble-minded from within (Gould, 1981).

Two categories of mental deficiency were already well established at this time: *idiots* (MA below 3) and *imbeciles* (MA between 3 and 7). But what about 'high-grade defectives' (MA between 8 and 12), who could be trained to function in society? Goddard called them *morons* (from the Greek for foolish). This, of course, explains the title of Gould's article: Boring (1923, in his analysis of Yerkes' 1921 data) found the average MA of white, American adults to be 13 – just above the upper limit of moronity.

AIM AND NATURE

The 1981 references above are from Gould's *The Mismeasure of Man*, and the 1982 article is an edited extract from that now classic book. In it, he traces the history of the measurement of human intelligence, from nineteenth-century craniometry to today's highly technical and sophisticated methods of IQ testing. (Incidentally, the book won the American National Book Critics' Circle Award for 1982; a second edition was published in 1996.) So, the basic *method* is *historical analysis*.

More importantly, the book is an attempt to expose the fundamental problems involved in trying to measure intelligence (problems which, by implication, apply to other aspects of complex human functioning, such as personality), and so offers an extremely thorough and lucid critique of intelligence testing. As a biologist, Gould is in a very sound position when arguing against one of the fundamental beliefs on which the IQ-testing movement is based: the view that differences in IQ are largely determined by biological (i.e. genetic) differences between people, differences which cannot be modified. This belief that 'biology is destiny' is commonly referred to as the *genetic* or *hereditarian theory of intelligence*, and the book as a whole is devoted to a refutation of this theory – both because of its scientific/methodological inadequacies, and (perhaps more critically) because of the racist social policies which it breeds and reinforces.

The IQ test can be regarded as an ideological weapon, used by white-dominated society to oppress minority groups, especially (but by no means exclusively) African Americans and people of African-Caribbean origin in the UK. As scientists, psychologists responsible for the construction and use of IQ tests are meant, and are seen by society at large, to be objective and value-free. However, as Gould convincingly demonstrates, their theories and instruments have too often been dangerous reflections of their own personal motives and racial, class and sexual prejudices. (It is more accurate to refer to this as the *thesis* of the book, rather than any attempt to test a specific *hypothesis*.)

● 'A NATION OF MORONS'

Robert Yerkes (referred to in **Background and context** above) was frustrated by psychology's image as a 'soft' science, if a science at all. He wanted to prove that it could be as rigorous a science as physics (i.e. it must involve measurement and quantification). The most promising source of such quantification lay in the embryonic field of mental testing. But there were many internal contradictions, with different tests producing very different results, even when properly administered.

With the approach of World War I, Yerkes got one of those 'big ideas' that propel the history of science: could psychologists possibly persuade the army to test all its recruits? This could be the opportunity psychology had been waiting for to change itself from dubious art into respected science. Yerkes campaigned, within both the government and the field of psychology, and finally got his way. As Colonel Yerkes, he supervised the testing of 1.75 million recruits during World War I.

He brought together all the major figures from the hereditarian school (notably, Terman and Goddard), and they wrote the new army mental tests between May and July 1917.

● The *Army Alpha* test was designed for literate recruits and consisted of a written examination. It included eight parts and could be given to large groups, taking less than an hour. The items have become familiar to generations of test takers ever since (analogies, filling in the next number in a sequence, and so on): the Army Alpha is the 'granddaddy, literally as well as metaphorically, of all written mental tests'.

- The *Army Beta* was designed for illiterates and those who failed the Army Alpha. It comprised a pictorial test (see Figure 35.1).

Those who failed the Army Beta would be recalled for an individual examination. Army psychologists would then grade each man from A to E (with pluses and minuses) and offer suggestions for proper military placement. For example, those given a D or an E could not be expected 'to read and understand written directions'.

Yerkes asserted that the tests 'measure native intellectual ability' (i.e. unaffected by environmental factors, such as acquired knowledge and education). Could this claim really justify the inclusion of, for example, 'Washington is to Adams as first is to ...'? One part of each test is simply ludicrous: how could Yerkes *et al.* attribute the low scores of recent immigrants to innate stupidity when their multiple-choice tests consisted entirely of questions such as:

- Crisco is a: patent medicine, disinfectant, toothpaste, food product?

- The number of Kaffir's legs is: 2, 4, 6, 8?

- Christy Mathewson is famous as a: writer, artist, baseball player, comedian?

Recruits had to be allocated to the appropriate test. Men illiterate in English (either by lack of schooling or foreign birth) should have taken Army Beta (either by direct assignment or via failure on Alpha). But there was considerable inconsistency between camps in their ability to allocate recruits appropriately. The persistent logistical difficulties created a systematic bias that substantially lowered the mean scores of black people and immigrants. For two major reasons, many men took only Alpha and scored either zero or close to zero, not because they were innately stupid, but because they were illiterate and should have taken Beta by Yerkes' own protocol:

1   Recruits and draftees had, on average, spent fewer years in school than Yerkes had anticipated. Queues for Beta began to grow and, at many camps, men were sent in droves to Alpha by lowering the requirements: schooling to age nine was sufficient in one camp, and in another, anyone who said they could read (at whatever level) took Alpha.

2   Pressure of time, and the hostility of regular officers, often precluded a Beta retest for men who had mistakenly taken Alpha. The stated protocol (of taking Beta after failing Alpha) hardly applied to black people, who, as usual, were treated with less concern and more contempt by everyone. Failure on Beta should have led to an individual examination. Half the black recruits scored D− on Beta, but only 20 per cent of these were recalled. When the protocol was followed, the scores for black people improved dramatically.

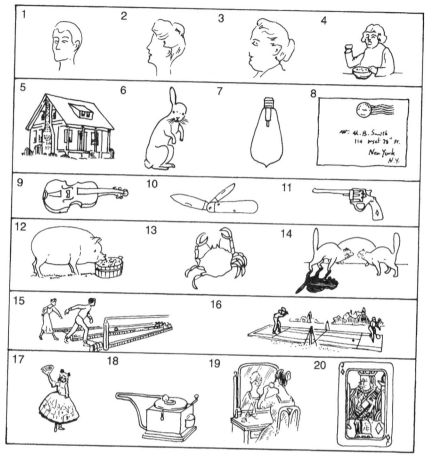

Figure 35.1. The Army Beta for testing innate intelligence. But were recent immigrants familiar with phonographs, tennis courts and light bulbs? Could they spot the missing rivet in the knife (10) or the ball in the right hand of the man (15)?

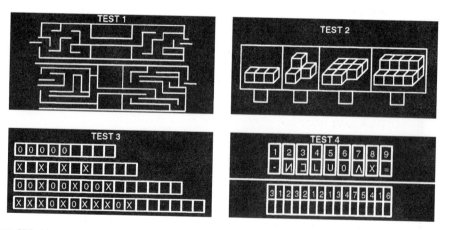

Figure 35.2. More examples from the Beta test for army recruits. Test 1: running a maze. Test 2: count the numer of cubes. Test 3: find the next in the series. Test 4: translate the numerals into symbols. Remember, this was a test for illiterate people – and they had to *write* their answers.

The effects of this systematic bias are evident in one of Boring's analyses of the data. He converted the scores of 4,893 men who had taken both Alpha and Beta, and calculated an average MA of 10.775 for Alpha and 12.158 for Beta. He only used the Beta scores in his summaries; Yerkes' procedure worked. But what about the huge numbers who should have taken Beta, but were given only Alpha and scored terribly low – primarily poorly educated black people and immigrants with an imperfect command of English?

What was it like to be an illiterate black or foreign recruit, anxious and confused by the (for them) novel experience of taking an examination, never told why, or what would be made of the results – expulsion? the front line? One examiner recalled (in 1968) his administration of Beta: 'It was touching to see the intense effort ... put into answering the questions, often by men who never before had held a pencil in their hands.'

Although Beta comprised only pictures, numbers and symbols, it still required pencil work and, in three of its seven parts, a knowledge of numbers and how to write them. Yerkes had overlooked – or consciously bypassed – this crucial aspect of test taking. Most of the men must have ended up either utterly confused or terrified. The conditions of testing, and the basic character of the test, make it ludicrous to believe that Beta measured any internal state deserving the label 'intelligence'.

Although the tests had a strong impact on screening men for officer training, their major impact was felt outside the military. They were the first mass-produced written tests of intelligence, and enquiries flooded in from schools and businesses. In his *Psychological Examining in the United States Army* (1921), Yerkes stated that tests could now rank and stream *everybody* (not just those with special educational needs): the era of mass testing had begun.

Boring (1923) selected 160,000 cases from the files and produced data that reverberated through the 1920s with a hereditarian ring. The scales of Alpha, Beta and individual examinations were converted to a common standard, so that racial and national averages could be constructed from samples of men who had taken the tests in different proportions (for example, few black men took Alpha). From his analysis, three 'facts' surfaced, which continued to influence social policy in the USA long after their source had been forgotten:

● The average MA of white American adults was a shocking 13 – just above the edge of moronity. Terman had previously set the standard at 16. The new figure became a rallying point for *eugenicists*, who lamented the decline of American intelligence, caused by the unconstrained interbreeding of the poor and feeble-minded, the spread of Negro blood through interbreeding, and the swamping of an intelligent native stock by the immigrating dregs of southern and eastern Europe.

- European immigrants could be graded by their country of origin. The average man of many nations was a moron. The darker people of southern Europe and the Slavs of eastern Europe were less intelligent than the fair people of western and northern Europe. The average Russian had an MA of 11.34, the Italian, 11.01, and the Pole, 10.74.

- The Negro lay at the bottom, with an average MA of 10.41. Some camps tried to carry the analysis further, by dividing black people into three groups, based on the intensity of their skin colour; as might be expected, the lighter groups scored higher!

The overall average of 13 had political impact, but Yerkes' figures for racial and national differences gave hereditarians licence to claim that the fact and extent of group differences in innate intelligence had finally been established. Brigham, Yerkes' disciple, published *A Study of American Intelligence* (1923), which became a primary vehicle for converting the army results into social action.

Yerkes divided recruits by country of origin into English, Scandinavian and Teutonic on one side, and Latin and Slavic on the other, and stated, 'the differences are considerable (an extreme range of practically two years mental age)', favouring the Nordics. But he saw a potential problem: most Latin and Slavic people had arrived recently and spoke English either poorly or not at all, while the main wave of Teutonic immigration had passed some time before. According to Yerkes' protocol, it should not have mattered (those without English took Beta, which supposedly measured innate ability independent of literacy and language). But the data still showed an apparent disadvantage for those unfamiliar with English.

An even more potentially disturbing correlation showed that average test scores for foreign-born recruits rose consistently with years of residence in the USA. Did this

Figure 35.3. The results of the Army intelligence tests influenced immigration policy in the USA in the 1920s. The quotas were based on the arrivals before 1890. Immigrants up to that year were mainly Nordic, and supposedly more intelligent than the southern and eastern Europeans who arrived later.

AIM AND NATURE

not indicate that familiarity with American culture, and not innate intelligence, determined differences in the scores? While Yerkes admitted this possibility, he concluded that recent immigration had drawn the dregs of Europe, lower-class Latin and Slavic peoples, while immigrants of longer residence belonged primarily to superior northern stock. The correlation with years in America was an artefact of genetic status.

The army data had their most immediate and profound impact on the great immigration debate, a major political issue in the USA at that time. Although the 1924 Restriction Act may have been passed without scientific backing, the timing, and especially its peculiar character, clearly reflected the lobbying of eugenicists, using the army data as their major weapon (Congressional debates continually cited the army data). Eugenicists not only wanted limits to immigration, they also wanted to impose harsh quotas against nations of inferior stock – a feature of the Act that might never have been implemented, or even considered, without the army data and eugenicist propaganda. The eugenicists battled and won one of the greatest victories of scientific racism in US history: 'America must be kept American' proclaimed Coolidge as he signed the bill.

Brigham had a profound change of heart in 1929, but he could not undo what the tests had achieved. The quotas stood and slowed immigration form southern and eastern Europe to a trickle. Throughout the 1930s, Jewish refugees, anticipating the Holocaust, sought to emigrate, but were not admitted – even when quotas from western and northern Europe were not filled. Estimates suggest that the quotas barred up to six million southern, central and eastern Europeans between 1924 and 1939. We know what happened to many who wished to leave but had nowhere to go. The paths to destruction are often indirect, but ideas can be agents as surely as guns and bombs.

Figure 35.4. Jews came out badly in the tests. Notable Jews were explained by the fact that the public noticed the few great ones (for example, Einstein) because they were so rare.

EVALUATION

Theoretical issues

Terman, working at Stanford University, was the figure mainly responsible for standardizing Binet's test for use in the USA. From 1916 onwards, the *Stanford-Binet* became the standard for virtually all IQ tests that followed, including most of the written (group) tests. As Gould points out, the Army Alpha and Beta marked the beginning of mass testing in the USA, and soon became a multimillion-dollar industry.

Like Goddard, Terman agreed with Binet that the tests worked best in identifying 'high-grade defectives', and also like Goddard, but contrary to Binet's views, Terman emphasized people's limits in order to restrict their freedom to reproduce. Yerkes was the central figure in the Army Alpha and Beta tests, and together with Goddard and Terman, was the leading US hereditarian of his day. The Army tests had been constructed to measure innate intelligence, so, by definition, there was no room for the role of environmental factors. According to Gould (1981):

> As pure numbers, these data carried no inherent social message. They might have been used to promote equality of opportunity and to underscore the disadvantages imposed upon so many Americans. Yerkes might have argued that an average mental age of 13 reflected the fact that relatively few recruits had the opportunity to finish or even to attend high school. He might have attributed the low average of some national groups to the fact that most recruits from these countries were recent immigrants who did not speak English and were unfamiliar with American culture. He might have recognized the link between low Negro scores and the history of slavery and racism. But scarcely a word do we read through 800 pages of any role for environmental influence.

This quote from Gould seems to illustrate very clearly how dogma can determine the way that data are interpreted in order to produce scientific 'fact': once a theorist has formulated a view of something (in this case, the explanation of intellectual differences between national, ethnic and racial groups), all the data are moulded to fit the theory and, hence, apparently, to support it. The often claimed objectivity of science is sacrificed on the altar of a theory which the scientist must 'prove' at all costs.

Yerkes, Terman and Goddard were already committed hereditarians before they came together to work in the Army tests, and Gould gives some striking examples of the dogmatic nature of Yerkes' thinking:

● He found a correlation of 0.75 between test score and years of education for 348 men who scored below the mean on Alpha. Only one had ever attended college, four had graduated from high school, and only ten had ever attended high school. But Yerkes argued that men with more innate intelligence spend more time in school: that is *why* they spend more time in school.

● The strongest correlations of test score with schooling came from black–white differences. Once again, the fact that black people spend relatively little time in school compared with white people is explained in terms of a disinclination on the part of the former, based on low innate intelligence.

How can you argue against such reasoning? Yerkes seems to be illegitimately inferring a *cause* from a correlation, since (a) it may be lack of schooling which causes the low IQ scores, and (b) there may be some third factor which accounts for *both* the low IQ scores and the short period of schooling, such as racial segregation – at that time, officially sanctioned (if not mandated) – poor conditions in black schools, and economic pressures to leave school and find work among the poor (which black people usually are). You can only infer which of two correlated factors is the cause of the other based on some theory about how they are related (Deese, 1972); in Yerkes' case, this is the hereditarian theory. So, Yerkes is presenting data to support a theory, but for that to work, the data must first be interpreted according to that very same theory: a classic example of *circular reasoning*.

● Yerkes found that half the black people from Southern states had not attended school beyond the third grade (age nine), while half of those from Northern states had reached the fifth grade (age 11). Again, in the North, 25 per cent completed primary school, compared with only 7 per cent from the South, and the percentage of Alphas was very much smaller and the percentages of Betas very much larger in the Southern than the Northern group. Why? You can probably anticipate Yerkes' explanation: only the best Negroes had been smart enough to move North!

Gould (1981) said: 'Even by standards of their own era, the American hereditarians were dogmatists. But their dogma wafted upon favourable currents into realms of general acceptance, with tragic consequences'. Those tragic consequences were the immigration laws which condemned an estimated six million Europeans to the Holocaust.

Methodological issues

Yerkes and his team had blindly assumed that the Army tests were not biased (they did not favour one national or racial group more than another). Indeed, this assumption is essential to the hereditarian argument: test results can only reflect innate differences in intelligence if the tests are unbiased.

In the second half of the twentieth century, it was Jensen in the USA who revived the 'race and IQ' debate, with a highly controversial article, published in 1969 ('How much can we boost IQ and scholastic achievement?'). In it, he claimed that the failure of preschool compensatory programmes (such as Operation Headstart) was due to the innate inferiority of black children.

This was followed, in 1980, by his 800-page *Bias in Mental Testing*, in which (a little perversely given the title) he argued that IQ tests are *not* biased – consistent with the hereditarian position of his predecessors. In his review of Jensen's book, Gould (1987) notes that Jensen bypasses the whole issue of habitability, and he seems to advocate dropping the discussion of what causes differences on test scores. But the question of causation is the motivating theme of the 1969 article, and is *implicit* throughout the book. The crucial question is, what exactly does Jensen mean by 'bias'?

Gould (1987) distinguishes two meanings, one technical, one non-technical (or vernacular). Our ordinary understanding of the term, in the present context, is that the poorer performance of black people is the result of environmental deprivation relative to white people. It is linked to the idea of fairness, and maintains that black people have received a poor deal, for reasons of education and upbringing (i.e. nurture), rather than nature. This is the non-technical meaning (V-bias: see **Applications and implications** below).

The second, technical sense of 'bias' is far narrower in meaning, and Jensen confines his discussion exclusively to this statistical or S-bias. An IQ test is S-biased if the *same* IQ score predicts *different* school grades (or some other performance criterion) for black and white people (*intercept bias*). As shown in Figure 35.5, both groups have the *same slope*, but white people have a higher y-intercept (i.e. the same IQ score predicts *higher* school grades for white children than for black children).

As Gould points out, 'No sensible tester wants to construct an instrument in which the same score means different things for different kinds of people'. Jensen devotes most of his book to showing that S-Bias does not affect mental tests and that it can be corrected when it does. But in showing that tests are unbiased, all Jensen has managed to show is that the lower black and higher white average scores lie on the same line, as shown in Figure 35.6.

While acknowledging the difference between this and V-bias, Jensen argues that the culture-fairness of a test (or its degree of 'culture-loadedness': its V-bias) cannot be defined objectively, and so S-bias is the only kind that should be discussed. In doing this, he seems to be undermining the hereditarian position, since (as we saw in **Theoretical issues** above), only by *assuming* that tests have no V-bias can differences in IQ scores be taken to reflect innate, genetic differences. But if V-bias cannot be defined or measured objectively, it cannot be ruled out; nor can it be shown *not* to affect test scores.

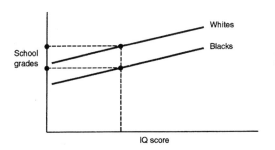

Figure 35.5. A test with S-bias (Gould, 1987).

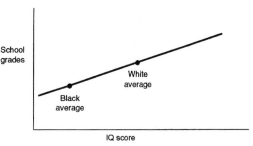

Figure 35.6. A test without S-bias (Gould, 1987).

> *In short, the primary content of this book is simply irrelevant to the question that has sparked the IQ debate and that Jensen himself addressed in his 1969 article: what does the lower average score of Blacks mean? His concept of bias (S-Bias) does not address the issue. (Gould, 1987)*

In the second edition of *The Mismeasure of Man* (1996), Gould claims that this same basic mistake (confusing S- and V-bias and explicitly addressing only the former) is made by Herrnstein and Murray in *The Bell Curve* (1994). This is just one of several more recent books promoting the hereditarian argument and right-wing social policies of a strongly racial nature (Howe, 1997).

Even more overtly racial is Rushton's *Race, Evolution, and Behaviour* (1995) and *The g Factor* (Brand, 1996), which achieved the rare notoriety of being withdrawn by its British publisher after Brand announced that he was 'perfectly proud to be a racist in the scientific sense'.

Applications and implications

While Jensen (1980) dismisses the question of the culture-fairness of a test (V-bias), others would regard it as crucial for interpreting black–white differences. Indeed, as we have seen, the hereditarian argument *depends* on the fairness of tests being established.

According to Segall *et al.* (1999), IQ tests are biased against those whose cultural background differs from that of the test's original normative sample. They argue that all attempts at constructing 'culture-fair' or 'culture-free' tests have failed; 'clearly, culturally mediated experience always interacts with test content to influence test performance'. (See **Exercises**.)

For Gardner (1993), *contextualization* is all-important:

> *Rather than assuming that one would possess a certain 'intelligence' independent of the culture in which one happens to live, many scientists now see intelligence as an interaction between, on the one hand, certain ... potentials and, on the other, the opportunities and constraints that characterize a particular cultural setting.*

This can be seen as an anti-hereditarian argument: Jensen, Yerkes and the others *do* assume that intelligence can be measured separately from its cultural expression because it is essentially *biological*. Another anti-hereditarian argument rests on the concept of *race*. According to Fernando (1991), the genetic differences between the 'classically described' races (European, African, etc.) are, on average, only slightly greater than those between nations within a racial group. This means that it is very difficult to discuss black–white differences in terms of *racial* differences, since this would account for only a small fraction of the *genetic* difference needed by hereditarians to explain the commonly found 15-point difference in IQ.

While the action of biological evolution (Darwinian selection) is very slow, 'cultural evolution' ('the inheritance of acquired characteristics': Gould, 1981) works quickly: differences between groups are likely to be more cultural than genetic in origin (Segall *et al.*, 1990).

According to the *cultural psychology perspective*, culture influences which behaviours are considered to be intelligent, the processes underlying intelligent behaviour, and the direction of intellectual development (Miller, 1997). (See Chapter 25.) While not rejecting all use of psychometric (mental) tests, Miller argues that:

> *all measures of intelligence are culturally grounded, with performance dependent, at least in part, on culturally based understandings. Thus, even in the controlled conditions of the experimental laboratory, intellectual performances reflect individuals' interpretations of the meaning of situations and their background presuppositions, rather than pure g.*

Psychological theories of intelligence must offer accounts that are *relative* to a particular time and context. But the hereditarians argue for a universal, culture-free, unchanging, objectively measurable, biologically determined property called 'g' or general intelligence (Miller, 1997). Furthermore, these 'universal' theories are associated with right-wing social philosophy, which their advocates are not afraid of revealing. For example in the Preface to *The Bell Curve*, Herrnstein and Murray (1994) claim that 'Affirmative action [positive discrimination], in education and the workplace alike, is leaking poison into the American soul', and, 'It is time for America once again to try living with inequality, as life is lived'. According to Kamin (1995):

> *This kind of sentiment, I imagine, is what led New York Times columnist Bob Herbert to the conclusion that The Bell Curve 'is just a genteel way of calling somebody a nigger'. Herbert is right. The book has nothing to do with science.*

EXERCISES

1 Yerkes is also famous for what other research?

2 To defend the use of the Army tests as a measure of innate intelligence, they would have to be seen as measuring *aptitude* as opposed to *attainment*. Explain the difference between these two terms and comment on why this argument may not be valid.

3 What is a *eugenicist*?

4 Is it ethically acceptable to restrict people's ability to reproduce?

5 How did Yerkes explain the correlation between the average test score for foreign-born recruits and length of residence in the USA in a way that was consistent with hereditarian theory?

6 Explain the difference between *culture-free* and *culture-fair* tests. (See Gross, 2005.)

36 Brain abnormalities in murderers indicated by positron emission topography

Raine, A., Buchsbaum, M. and LaCasse, L. (1997)

Biological Psychiatry, 42: 495–508

BACKGROUND AND CONTEXT

For a long time it has been suspected that violent behaviour is more likely to occur in people with generalized brain dysfunction. Studies using electroencephalographic (EEG), neurological, neuropsychological and cognitive techniques have repeatedly shown that violent offenders have poorer brain functioning than normal controls (e.g. Raine, 1993 in Raine *et al.*, 1997).

Although until recently it was not possible to localize the specific brain areas that may be dysfunctional in these offenders, it has long been thought that dysfunction of the *prefrontal cortex* may disrupt the regulation of aggression. This idea has been supported by neurological studies of patients with damage to the prefrontal cortex (e.g. Damasio *et al.*, 1990 in Raine *et al.*, 1997).

Other evidence suggests that violent individuals may have *functionally asymmetrical hemispheres* (the two halves of the brain do not function equally) and *reduced inter-hemispheric coherence* (the two hemispheres do not work together efficiently); these may be linked to dysfunction of the corpus callosum (which connects the two hemispheres).

Animal experiments, together with neurological studies of patients with brain injuries, also suggest that structures in the limbic system, such as the amygdala and hippocampus, as well as the thalamus, play a role in controlling aggression. As important as this research is, it is one step removed from the question of whether extremely violent offenders have specific brain dysfunction.

The advent of brain imaging techniques in the early 1970s (Raichle, 1998) made it possible, for the first time, to directly assess brain functioning in violent individuals.

Initial research again implicated the frontal lobe, as well as the temporal cortex. But the early research involved small samples of hospitalized patients and focused on aggressive personality as opposed to extreme violent behaviour.

Brain imaging techniques include *computerized topography* (CT or CAT scan), *magnetic resonance imaging* (MRI) and *positron emission topography* (PET). (See Chapter 29.) In PET, a radioactively labelled substance (a tracer) is added to a substance naturally used by the body (such as oxygen, fluorine, carbon, nitrogen or glucose). This is either injected or inhaled. When this material gets into the bloodstream, it goes to brain areas that use it. So, oxygen and glucose, for example, accumulate in brain areas that are metabolically active. When the radioactive material breaks down, it gives off a neutron and a positron. When a positron hits an electron, both are destroyed and two gamma rays are released. Gamma ray detectors record the brain area from where the gamma rays are emitted. This provides a functional view of the brain.

PET scans pinpoint in brilliant colour the brain regions where neurons are working during a particular mental task. They have shed new and exciting light on many brain diseases and pathological conditions, including epilepsy, Parkinson's disease, Alzheimer's disease, Huntington's disease and Down's syndrome. Because they are very sensitive to brain changes during episodes of schizophrenia, depression and other mental disorders, PET scans are being used extensively in psychiatry (Sabbatini, 1997). Most recently, and perhaps most controversially, they are being used to study the brain in relation to criminal behaviour, especially violent crime.

AIM AND NATURE

● HYPOTHESIS

The aim of the study was to provide direct evidence for the claim that murderers pleading not guilty by reason of insanity (NGRI) have brain dysfunction. Raine *et al.* expected to find differences between murderers pleading NGRI and matched controls only in specific brain areas:

1   As far as *cortical areas* are concerned, the murderers were expected to show *lower* glucose metabolism (and, hence, *less* activity) in the following areas:

   ● *prefrontal cortex* (both *lateral* – away from the centre – and *medial* – in the centre);

   ● the *superior parietal gyrus* (a gyrus is the structure between two sulci or fissures – the folds characteristic of the cortex; 'superior' means 'as seen from above'; Toates, 2001);

● *left angular gyrus* (a region of the parietal lobe behind the posterior end of the lateral fissure).

No differences were expected in the *temporal lobe* or the *cingulate*. (See **Evaluation** below.)

2   As far as the *subcortical* areas were concerned, the murderers compared with the controls were expected to show reduced glucose metabolism in the *corpus callosum*, as well as *abnormal asymmetries* in the *amygdala, thalamus* and the *medial temporal lobe* (including the *hippocampus*).

No differences were expected in the *caudate* (nucleus), *putamen* or *globus pallidus* (together comprising the *basal ganglia*), the *midbrain* or the *cerebellum*. All these have been linked to various psychiatric conditions – but not to violence.

● METHOD/DESIGN

AIM AND NATURE

The study is sometimes simply referred to as a PET-scan study of murderers' brains. In fact, it is a *correlational* study, in which the link between brain abnormalities and violent behaviour is being investigated using PET.

More specifically, the independent variable (IV) is being a murderer (pleading NGRI) or not being a murderer (at all), while the dependent variable (DV) is glucose metabolism levels in various parts of the brain (both cortical and subcortical). Clearly, the IV is *selected for*, rather than manipulated, so we cannot be sure that any differences in brain activity actually *cause* the violent behaviour. This makes the study a *quasi-experiment*.

Murderers who plead NGRI represent a particularly important group of offenders. The participants consisted of 41 such offenders (39 men, 2 women, mean age of 34.3 years) and 41 controls, matched for age and gender.

After being injected with a radioactively labelled substance (a tracer), participants were given a continuous performance task (CPT). After 32 minutes, they were transferred to the adjacent PET scanner room.

● RESULTS

In support of both hypotheses, the following key findings were shown for murderers pleading NGRI, compared with non-violent control participants:

● reduced glucose metabolism in bilateral prefrontal cortex (i.e. on both sides), the posterior parietal cortex (bilateral superior gyrus and left angular gyrus), and the corpus callosum;

- abnormal asymmetries of activity (left hemisphere lower than right) in the amygdala, thalamus and medial temporal gyrus, including the hippocampus;

- the areas where no differences were found (or expected) are all concerned with movement; for example, the cerebellum (along with the motor cortex, basal ganglia and some other regions) plays a role in the computation of the commands sent to effect motor action.

● CONCLUSIONS

Raine *et al.* conclude that their preliminary findings 'provide initial indications of a network of abnormal cortical and subcortical brain processes that may predispose to violence in murderers pleading NGRI'. However, they also comment that 'these findings cannot be taken to demonstrate that violence is determined by biology alone; clearly, social, psychological, cultural and situational factors also play important roles in predisposing to violence'. (See **Exercises**.)

EVALUATION

Methodological issues

PET scans depend on tracing the location of radioactive material. So, as McGhee (2001) points out, we need to be sure that sufficient radioactive material was injected in the first place for it to appear during a scan. This is especially important if we are looking at a small area of the brain or low-activity processes. If we predict activity in brain area X, but not in Y, we need to be sure that if we do see this pattern on the scan, it is because of different neural activity levels, *not* because there was insufficient radioactive material injected to show up at Y.

A problem shared by PET, MRI and functional MRI (*f*MRI; see Chapter 29) is the sheer computational load involved (McGhee, 2001). High-powered computers are needed to collect, store and present the data gathered from multiple scans. Special software is available to ensure that successive images are matched together correctly to produce accurate displays over time, without compromising the structural detail. Nevertheless, the faster that images are captured, the greater the amount of 'noise' which threatens to obscure the signal (Menon and Kim, 1999, in McGhee, 2001).

A further difficulty is that different studies identify different 'hot spots' (areas of greatest neural activity) for the same task. Farah and Aguirre (1999), for example, found that 17 separate studies indicated between them 84 different candidates for the precise brain region involved in object recognition.

Gabrielli (1998) has identified some additional technical and conceptual issues in the interpretation of neuro-imaging:

- The images generated by PET and *f*MRI scans are *not* images of neural activity as such, but of nearby (local) blood flow or metabolic changes (such as glucose metabolism), which are *indicative* of neural activity. This makes the images much more indirect evidence of brain activity.

- Residual activity can be found in parts of the brain that are severely damaged. These traces may be of processes not directly involved in those being studied, but merely correlated with them. It could be that in undamaged brains, much of the activity we observe is nothing to do with the critical processes that actually produce the behaviour the participant is displaying.

According to McGhee (2001), 'scans can only describe brain activity, not brain function. To describe brain function requires further interpretation of the stimuli presented to the subject and of the patterns of responses to those stimuli over several trials'.

(For discussion of some specific methodological limitations of the Raine *et al.* study, see **Method/design** above and **Exercises**.)

Subsequent research

Major damage to the prefrontal cortex (PFC) has been found to produce pseudo-psychopathic personality in adult patients. While this does not usually include violent and criminal behaviour, their altered social behaviour in many ways resembles that of lifelong developmental sociopathic (psychopathic) individuals (Damasio, 2000). However, until recently, no researcher had actually studied individuals with antisocial personality disorder (APD) – who have no detectable brain trauma – to see if they have subtle prefrontal deficits.

Raine *et al.* (2000) used MRI to study the brains of 21 volunteers with APD, comparing them with 34 healthy participants, a substance-dependent group and 21 psychiatric controls. These all-male groups were also assessed for autonomic activity (skin conductance and heart rate) during a social stressor in which they gave a videotaped speech about their faults and failures.

The APD group showed an 11 per cent reduction in prefrontal grey matter volume (see Chapter 29), but without any obvious brain lesions (injuries), as well as reduced autonomic activity during the stressor (they sweated less and showed lower heart rate). Raine *et al.* concluded that their findings provide the first evidence for structural brain deficit in APD.

According to Damasio (2000), the APD group's failure to display autonomic responses commonly seen in a normal population is evidence of the selective emotional disturbance of these individuals (embarrassment and guilt). This disturbance is similar to what Damasio and his colleagues have found in neurological patients with selective prefrontal damage. However, this prefrontal malfunction is probably associated with malfunction in various subcortical areas (such as the amygdala and brainstem), as well as higher-order association areas in other parts of the cortex.

More directly related to the 1997 study is a subsequent analysis of the data, which compared murderers who killed on impulse with those who had planned their crimes in detail and committed them in cold blood, apparently without conscience (Strueber *et al.*, 2006/2007). Only the former showed abnormalities in their PFC. This supports the belief that deficiencies in emotional control may fail to prevent impulsive violent offenders from acting. They do not stop to think about the consequences. In contrast, the cold, calculating criminal requires a largely intact PFC: long-term planning involves complex decision processes.

Raine *et al.* (2004) studied 29 violent criminals with APD, 16 of whom had been caught and convicted ('unsuccessful psychopaths') and 13 of whom had evaded the law ('successful psychopaths'). They were compared with 23 control participants. Raine *et al.* guaranteed the successful group absolute confidentiality and promised not to alert the authorities.

Using MRI, Raine *et al.* found that the volume of grey matter in the PFC was over 22 per cent lower among the unsuccessful group compared with the controls. For the successful group, the volume was within normal limits. Indeed, the latter's PFC performed above average on a variety of neuropsychological tasks. In the unsuccessful group, the hippocampus in either hemisphere differed in size, a difference which was thought to have arisen early in brain development. This asymmetry may impair the ability of the hippocampus and amygdala to work together, so that emotional information is not processed correctly.

So, PFC deficits may have more to do with the criminal's chances of being caught than with serious, chronic violence. Also, it is unclear whether the PFC hypothesis applies to females. Violent female offenders are rare, and so less well studied. However, there is no apparent connection in females between a decreased PFC volume and psychopathological tendencies, as has been shown in males. Women have more effective impulse control, which tends to fail only when the functioning of the PFC is massively impaired in childhood (Strueber *et al.*, 2006/2007).

Theoretical issues

Lower than normal activity in the PFC, parietal cortex and corpus callosum suggests a deficit in the integration of information needed to modify and inhibit behaviour. For example, increased blood flow to the PFC usually occurs when people are engaged in planning some future behaviour. Luria (1973) found that patients with PFC damage were often unable to carry out forward planning, living in the 'here and now', controlled by physically present stimuli and situations. Damage can also result in impulsive behaviour, loss of self-control, immaturity and the inability to modify behaviour; all of these can make aggressive acts more likely (e.g. Damasio, 1985, Damasio *et al.*, 1994, both in Raine *et al.*, 1997).

Abnormalities in the hippocampus and amygdala suggest deficiency in forming and utilizing emotionally coloured perceptions and memories (Toates, 2001). In the amygdala, for example, emotional significance is given to the cognitive processing about the world performed by the temporal cortex (to which it is connected) (LeDoux, 1998). The amygdala also receives, more directly from the senses, raw information about threats (such as loud noises), before elaborate processing takes place (LeDoux, 1989). Abnormalities in the amygdala have been repeatedly associated with aggressive behaviour in both humans and non-humans.

The hippocampus, amygdala and thalamus are also critically involved in learning, memory and attention; abnormalities in their functioning may relate to deficits in acquiring conditioned emotional responses and the failure to learn from experience displayed by criminal and violent offenders (e.g. Raine, 1993, in Raine *et al.*, 1997).

Reduced levels of activity in the left hemisphere compared with the right (in the amygdala, thalamus and the hippocampus) could account for violent conduct. The right hemisphere, which has been implicated in the production of negative emotion, may experience less regulation and control by left hemisphere inhibitory processes.

Raine *et al.* argue that this may contribute to the expression of violence, but only in individuals who are already *predisposed* towards violence. A predisposition towards violence may be related to one or more of the brain abnormalities described above. But equally, brain abnormalities may predispose the individual towards certain behaviours and/or abilities which represent predispositions in their own right. For example, reductions in glucose metabolism in the left angular gyrus have been correlated with reduced verbal ability, while damage to this area has been linked to deficits in reading and arithmetic. Such cognitive dysfunctions could predispose the individual affected to educational and occupational failure, which in turn predispose to crime and violence. Violent offenders with low verbal intelligence often have learning difficulties (Raine, 1993, in Raine *et al.*, 1997).

It is for these, and other similar reasons that Raine *et al.* conclude by saying that their findings do *not* demonstrate that violence is determined by biology alone. The findings have *not* shown that there is a direct causal link between certain brain abnormalities and violent behaviour, only that these can act as a *predisposition* to act violently.

It is likely that at least some of the murderers in Raine *et al.*'s study would be diagnosed as having *antisocial personality disorder* (APD: DSM-IV-TR, American Psychiatric Association, 2000) or *dissocial personality disorder* (ICD-10, World Health Organization, 1992). (These labels refer to what used to be called *psychopathic personality disorder* or *psychopathy*.) Typically, those with APD:

- act violently towards their marriage partners and their children;

- are impulsive and fail to strive consistently towards any goal, lacking a purpose in life;

- have low tolerance of frustration and a tendency towards violence, which often results in repeated criminal offences; their lack of guilt and failure to learn from experience leads to behaviour that persists, despite serious consequences and legal penalties;

- commit a disproportionate number of violent crimes.

Hare (1991) has identified two distinct, but correlated, factors involved in APD:

- *Factor 1*: affective and interpersonal characteristics, including superficial charm, pathological lying, manipulation, lack of empathy, shallow affect and lack of guilt.

- *Factor 2*: a chronic and versatile antisocial lifestyle, including proneness to boredom, a parasitic lifestyle, impulsivity, juvenile delinquency and a violation of release conditions.

According to Mitchell and Blair (2000), displaying the full APD seems to involve a complex *interaction* between social environment and biological predispositions. In particular, social environment (such as socio-economic status/SES) influences factor 2, while factor 1 is unrelated to SES. This suggests that biological make-up determines whether individuals show emotional difficulties, but these emotional difficulties are only *risk factors* (equivalent to what Raine *et al.* call *predispositions*): an adverse social environment provides the conditions needed for the disorder to develop.

Other conditions that make predisposed individuals more likely to actually commit murder include national culture. For example, Colombia's rate is 15 times that of Costa Rica, and the rate for the USA is 10 times that of Norway (Nisbett and Cohen, 1999). Nisbett and Cohen also note that there are marked differences *within* the USA. In small Southern towns, the murder rate for white males is about double the rest of the country. They attribute this difference to a 'culture of honour' in the South, according to which men think it is justifiable to kill to protect one's property, or to meet insults with violence. This is reflected in laws and social policies, which are more likely to exonerate people who shoot another person for 'property' reasons. According to Nisbett and Cohen, this North/South difference 'shows that violence is a matter of nurture as much as one of nature. Whether a man reaches for his gun or his civility when insulted is a matter of culture'.

Applications and implications

If it can be demonstrated that people with APD have a brain disorder (reduced grey matter in the PFC), then isn't it reasonable to explain their violent conduct – including murder – in terms of that brain disorder? In other words, the violence can be blamed on the disorder, absolving the offender of blame and responsibility ('He couldn't help himself – his relative lack of grey matter prevented him from controlling his behaviour as normal people can'; see Chapter 31). This is clearly relevant to the NGRI plea made by the 41 murderers in Raine *et al.*'s study.

This is a fundamentally important moral and legal issue. Is it right that the results of PET and MRI scans should be admissible as evidence in courts of law, as is happening in the USA? According to Mayberg (in Fillon, 2000), a Canadian professor of psychiatry and neurology, moves towards using such evidence are being led by defence attorneys, *not* by doctors. One of her concerns is the unscientific nature of scans as evidence of the claimed disorder.

However, even if we could be absolutely certain that the accused has a brain abnormality, we still cannot be certain that this abnormality actually *caused* the violent behaviour. Even Raine and Damasio, two of the leading researchers in the field, acknowledge the role of non-biological factors in violent behaviour. At the very least, the defence would have to show that the brain abnormality was the *major* contributor, a seemingly impossibly difficult thing to do.

But what if we are certain that the accused has the brain abnormality, and we also know that a high percentage of people with this abnormality commit violent crimes, including murder. Might the accused still be held (legally and morally) responsible (Grafton *et al.*, 2006/2007)? Perhaps Raine *et al.*'s distinction between successful and unsuccessful psychopaths comes into its own here: the former seem to know what they are doing and are acting deliberately and intentionally when they commit their crime.

There are cases – at least in the UK – where accepting evidence of psychiatric disorder does not necessarily result in a 'diminished responsibility' verdict. Peter Sutcliffe, the Yorkshire Ripper, was convicted of the murder of several prostitutes, despite his paranoid schizophrenia.

Given what is known about PFC, and other brain abnormalities, and APD, many people have been calling in recent years for the screening of *potential* violent criminals (Gibbs, 1995). Raine (1993) himself advocates a medical approach to crime control, based on screening, diagnostic prediction and treatment. One worry with this is that voluntary screening for the good of the individual child might lead to compulsory screening for the protection of society (Gibbs, 1995).

EXERCISES

1   In their Conclusions, why do Raine *et al.* warn against taking their findings to demonstrate that violence is determined by biology alone (i.e. abnormal brain processes)?

2   Is the sample sufficiently representative for us to be able to generalize the results to other types of violent offenders?

3   Gibbs (1995) claims that it is one thing to convict someone of an offence and then compel them to do something, and another to require someone who has not committed any offence to undergo the same treatment/screening. What are some of the ethical and practical issues that arise from this claim?

4   What do you understand by the terms 'aggression' and 'violence'?

5   In Theoretical issues, brain abnormalities are referred to as a biological predisposition towards violence, with psychological, social, cultural and situational risk factors acting as potential triggers for actual violence. What account of schizophrenia is this similar to?

6   Why do you think Gibbs (1995) is concerned that studying 'whites only' in the context of violence (as a result of political pressures) could inadvertently reinforce racial stereotypes?

37 Nurses' and students' perceptions of care: A phenomenological study

Bassett, C. (2002)

Nursing Times, 98(34): 32–5

BACKGROUND AND CONTEXT

According to Maes and van Elderen (1998), health psychology is:

> a sub-discipline of psychology which addresses the relationship between psychological processes and behaviour on the one hand and health and illness on the other hand ... however ... health psychologists are more interested in 'normal' everyday-life behaviour and 'normal 'psychological processes in relation to health and illness than in psychopathology or abnormal behaviour.

Turpin and Slade (1998), however, believe that health psychology is an *extension* of clinical psychology (see Chapter 30), focusing specifically on people with physical health problems and their associated psychological needs.

According to Ogden (2004), health psychology is based on the *biopsychosocial model* of health and illness (Engel, 1977, 1980). This is the major alternative to the *biomedical model*, which maintains that:

- diseases either come from outside the body and invade it, causing internal physical changes, or originate as internal, involuntary physical changes – such diseases can be caused by chemical imbalances, bacteria, viruses or genetic predisposition;

- individuals are not responsible for their illnesses, which arise from biological changes beyond their control – people who are ill are victims;

- treatment should consist of vaccination, surgery, chemotherapy or radiotherapy, all of which aim to change the physical state of the body;

- responsibility for treatment rests with the medical profession;

- health and illness are qualitatively different: you are either healthy or ill;

- mind and body function independently of each other – the abstract mind (feelings and thoughts) is incapable of influencing the physical body;

- illness may have psychological consequences, but *not* psychological causes.

In opposition to these ideas, the biopsychosocial model sees human beings as complex systems; illness is often caused by a combination of biological (e.g. viruses), psychological (e.g. behaviours and beliefs) and social (e.g. employment) factors. According to Stroebe (2000), the model reflects fundamental changes in the nature of illness, causes of death and overall life expectancy during the twentieth century. The influence of non-biological factors (e.g. improvements in medical treatment and changes in lifestyle) in major causes of death, such as cardiovascular disease and cancer, is incompatible with the biomedical model, which ignores the role of psychological and sociocultural factors.

According to Nichols (2005):

> Despite 20 years of major expansion and research in psychology – and in particular health psychology – the average-patient test will almost always reveal our failure to develop psychological care as part of the thinking, culture and routines of general hospitals and health centres.

The 'average-patient test' involves visiting your local hospital, picking a ward at random, going with the clinical nurse manager to the third bed on the left or right, and asking, 'Who is handling this patient's psychological care and how is it going?'

Despite nursing becoming more psychologically minded during the 1990s, along with publications encouraging the introduction of psychological approaches into health care, and psychologists producing specific local provisions (such as some stroke, intensive care or cancer units), 'psychological care is still not a common provision in hospitals' (Nichols, 2005).

According to Norris (1989, in Bassett, 2002), caring is expected to (i) change theories that guide practice; (ii) foster research that tests theories; and (iii) modify nursing practice. So greater insight into and understanding of caring has practical implications for nursing, and is not simply an academic exercise.

AIM AND NATURE

There was no hypothesis being tested. Rather, as with most studies that adopt a *phenomenological* approach, Bassett's aim was to *explore* some aspect of the participant's *experience*. (See **Theoretical issues** and **Methodological issues** below.)

Here, the focus was on 'the lived and expressed experiences' in relation to the phenomenon of care and caring; in other words, what do the participants (15 nurses and 6 nursing students – 2 for each year of a three-year advanced diploma) understand by the concepts of care and caring; what do they *mean* for these participants; and how do they put this understanding and meaning into practice when performing their nurse role?

● METHOD/DESIGN

Each participant was interviewed in depth and the interviews tape-recorded. Transcripts were made of the tape-recordings, which were then read to develop a 'feeling' for them and to make sense of them. The taped interviews were also listened to and categorized according to several emerging themes. Significant statements relating to the phenomenon of care and caring were collected. These statements were then categorized according to their perceived meanings.

Although Bassett does not use the term, the method he used sounds like *interpretative phenomenological analysis*. (See **Methodological issues** below.)

● FINDINGS

The formulated meanings from the categorized statements were arranged into the following themes:

● encouraging autonomy;

● giving of oneself;

● taking risks;

● supporting care;

● emotional labour.

Encouraging autonomy

The notion of *patient empowerment* seemed to be important, and was the only theme that could not be broken down into subcategories.

Anne: *I'd say it's definitely about providing the patient with something, but it's also about empowering that patient where possible.*

She seemed to want to allay patients' fears and anxieties by giving them greater autonomy and control over their care.

Jill: *To give the patients real independence and control of their own care, which is what modern nursing is about, rather than doing everything for them. Then you have to do a certain amount of teaching of patients in terms of health promotion,*

*health education, and in some cases teaching how to actually give physical care –
like for someone with diabetes, how to give their injections.*

Cathy, a psychiatric nurse, thought it was important, among other aspects of care,
to encourage patient autonomy:

> Cathy: *I'm quite interested in all the issues around what empathy really is and
> actually being able to demonstrate it, and how patients perceive that, and …
> actually being able to empower people… if you work in psychiatry you are dealing
> with a fairly down-trodden group of people in society so it's also really important
> to be able to make people have control and not feel controlled, and have choice
> and not feel as though choices are being made for them, and be able to influence
> what happens to them.*

Cathy linked empathy with empowerment. She seemed to have a strongly developed
sense of justice, and sometimes saw her patients as being at the powerless end of
the continuum.

Students also saw empowerment as an important basis for the care they gave their
patients – even those who are dying. But Bassett warns that some caution may be
necessary when trying to empower patients.

Giving of oneself

Nurses give to patients in terms of time, energy and effort. They spend time learning skills and gaining knowledge, both as students and throughout their nursing
careers. To simply provide mechanical care may not be sufficient in their eyes –
providing care without *genuineness* was seen as not caring adequately for patients.

It seems there may be at least two distinct levels of care that can be given to
patients: giving something of oneself or giving something up. For example:

> Jack: *Care is about giving up part of yourself, whatever that might be. It could be
> time, energy, commitment to other people – which a person either chooses to
> appreciate or not. So it's giving anything of yourself so that a person can benefit
> from it.*

Cathy had been a general nurse before becoming a psychiatric nurse. She also
described giving something of herself in the ways she cared for her patients. The
students seemed to be picking up the importance of different ways of caring from
their experienced colleagues on the wards.

> Carl: *[C]are, I think, is a whole range of things really. But I mean that if you want to
> kind of try and put it in a nutshell I think caring is basically identifying what
> people's needs really are, and that's not only the physical need, all sorts of different
> other needs – I suppose psychological and emotional needs as well.*

AIM AND NATURE

He went on to point out that what matters is the nurse's ability as a person to relate to patients with medical or psychological needs.

Taking risks

Taking risks in nursing is not about putting patients at risk by acting in an irresponsible way, or randomly experimenting with medications or care. It refers to testing the boundaries of accepted care, moving from the defined boundaries of the profession, and developing new and innovative ways of caring for patients.

Jack, for example, seemed to believe that nurses who truly cared sometimes took risks:

> Jack: *Because if you are really delivering care then you are not worried about what you do… In practice, if you are really caring then perhaps no one is going to trip you up… People recognize that you are caring… – she gives [of] herself, she stops afterward, she never has a break – you know you really think she is a caring person. But when it comes down to it – will I get a complaint or will I get anything said against me, or this might go to court – and you think: 'Oh, she's not caring.' It's a form of self-protection, and she's thinking about herself and not her patients.*

This indicates that an element of courage is needed to care for patients in a more radical way. To care fully, the courageous nurse meets the patient's needs in what some might consider a deeper way.

Cathy described a situation where she refused to give one of her psychiatric patients an injection, against the psychiatrist's wishes. In not obeying the doctor's order, she was taking a professional risk, but this is sometimes essential to protect patients from harm. (See Chapter 10.) Some nurses felt that on occasions they had to take a stand against their professional colleagues' interpretations of normal nursing procedures or protocols, in the cause of caring for their patients.

Students also saw taking risks as an essential part of caring. For them, this seemed to mean 'standing up' for patients when the care they had received was less than they deserved. For example, Alice, a first-year student, maintained that 'the key to good care is being strong enough to object if you don't agree with something'.

Supporting care

Participants identified certain supporting factors as essential to ensuring that care can be delivered effectively, namely managerial, organizational and psychological support systems.

Anne acted as operating theatre manager for half her working time. Her priorities for care incorporated a wider, more encompassing view than simply providing

AIM AND NATURE

hands-on patient care. She felt that to provide good care for patients, the members of her team needed to be cared for as well:

> Anne: *The first thing from a priority point of view would be the care of the patient, but thereafter my role is definitely to make sure that the staff are OK. There's this old adage 'Who cares for the carers?' And I don't think a lot of people do, and I don't think we are very good at caring for each other.*

Some participants considered a major part of their caring role to be the creation of a caring environment. According to Lynn, it was vital to have a system of organization in place to support care.

Emotional labour

This theme was unique to the student participants and seemed to reflect the fact that learning to nurse can constitute an emotional assault. Alice thought that when things become 'matter-of-fact' and 'hardened', the nurse may be defending him/herself, not wanting to be emotionally affected.

According to Joan:

> *I think there is a big difference between hardness and being able to bottle up your emotions until there is an appropriate time to let it all out ... hardness ... that's basically being desensitized ... and when you do that you don't treat the person as a person.*

Carl had experienced situations that seemed to upset him, particularly when he did not have enough time to do all he wanted to do for patients:

> Carl: *I've seen examples of, say, nursing staff who really give the individual patients the very minimum access to their time. That they perform the task or the clinical operation procedure that is required, and basically that is it. Don't go beyond that. Also, the use of rather abrupt language as well. That makes me sad.*

Anton spoke about ways of controlling his emotions when upset ('put them somewhere in a drawer').

⦿ CONCLUSIONS

Bassett's phenomenological study allowed nurses and nursing student participants to discuss personal examples of their roles, through which important insights into the ways they care for their patients could be identified. Five main themes were identified, based on analysis of the transcripts of tape-recorded interviews: encouraging patient autonomy, giving of oneself, taking risks on the patient's behalf, supporting care and emotional labour. All except the last of these were common to the qualified nurses and the students.

If the 15 nurses and 6 nursing students were representative of other British nurses and nursing students, then the study revealed that nursing care was alive and well in British health care, promising a bright future.

It is important for policymakers at all levels to accept that nurses want to provide quality care for their patients. To enable them to achieve this, the government, educators, managers and nurses themselves need to ensure that the necessary structures are in place.

EVALUATION

Theoretical issues

Along with social work, teaching and the police force, nursing is identified as a *high-stress* occupation. A study by Borrill *et al.* (1996, in Carson *et al.*, 1997) of 11,000 NHS staff found that nurses had the second-highest stress score among seven staff groups. Shift work, although not unique to nurses, is an inherently stressful aspect of the job; this is common to all those working in the emergency services (police, fire, ambulance, emergency medical teams and mountain rescue). They also share routine encounters with death, tragedy and horror. They are required to deal with people in pain and distress, and handle dead bodies; they may also face personal danger and injury.

These intrinsic sources of stress (which also include giving emotional support to patients' families) are made worse by the inadequate training nurses receive for handling such demands (Gaze, 1988). According to Mazhindu (1998), there has been little research into the effects that *emotional labour* in nursing has on the quality of nursing practice and on nurses' personal lives.

The term 'emotional labour' was first used by Hochschild (1983) in her study of flight attendants, who are able to maintain a cool, calm, caring and comforting exterior, often in quite deplorable and emotionally draining conditions. Being friendly, kind, courteous and smiling are all part of the job (and have financial value for the airline); hence 'labour' (rather than 'care'). Hochschild defined emotional labour as 'the induction or suppression of feeling in order to sustain an outward appearance that produces in others a sense of being cared for in a convivial safe place'.

Smith (1992, in Small, 1995) drew on Hochschild's work in her own study of student nurses' experiences of being socialized into nursing. She carried out her research on elderly care wards, an environment in which high-tech nursing tasks are few, but opportunities to listen to reminiscences (see Gross and Kinnison, 2007), provide companionship and clip toenails are many. In such wards, 'the functioning hearing-aid was just as much a lifeline to survival as the intravenous infusion to the post-operative patient in the acute surgical ward' (Smith, 1992, in Small, 1995).

However, while the demands of emotional work can be as tiring and hard as physical and technical labour, they are not so readily recognized and valued. Smith (1988, in Smith, 1995) found that, on most general wards, sisters tended to encourage nurses to involve themselves in physical and technical activities rather than emotional care; this was relegated to the quiet periods of the day, after the 'real' work was completed.

Emotional labour can be seen as related to the concept of *emotional intelligence* (EI):

> *a type of social intelligence that involves the ability to monitor one's own and others' emotions, to discriminate among them, and to use the information to guide one's thinking and actions. (Salovey and Mayer, 1990, in Evans and Allen, 2002)*

People who are able to manage their own feelings well, while reading and dealing with other people's emotions, are particularly suited to the caring professions, so it is surprising that most nurse education programmes fail to include this aspect of training (Evans and Allen, 2002).

Evans and Allen cite the work of Sims and Lindberg (1978), who argue that 'Negative self-concepts are barriers to the effective independent functioning vital to the successful performance of professional roles'. This is reflected in the notion of the *wounded healer* (Clarkson, 1997, in Evans and Allen, 2002): if you are a passive person, you will be a passive nurse. According to Evans and Allen:

> *Self-awareness is an important part of nursing. The key to self-knowledge lies in interpersonal [emotional] intelligence… If they [students] are able to deal with their own feelings well, they will be able to deal with others confidently, competently and safely.*

Methodological issues

Bassett notes that the expressed experiences recorded and interpreted were applicable only to each particular nurse at the time of the interview; as such, they can only throw some degree of light on their views of what care might be. Nurses are not all the same in how they care for their patients, and they reflect patients' changing needs by giving different types and intensities of care. These differences in care requirements and provision are dependent on the context.

The themes that emerged from the study are generally well represented in the literature. The findings and expressed beliefs certainly appear to underline and reinforce the complexity of the phenomenon of care (Bassett, 2002).

Bassett quotes Parahoo (1997), according to whom, with any study, the methodology is the key to success. In this case, Bassett provides very few details regarding the method used, except to say that it adopts a phenomenological approach; as we noted in the

Method/design section above, the few details he does provide suggest that he was using *interpretative phenomenological analysis* (IPA). The aim of IPA is to explore in detail how participants are making sense of their personal and social world; the main currency of an IPA study is the *meanings* which particular experiences, events and states hold for participants (Smith and Osborn, 2003). The approach is phenomenological in that it attempts to explore personal experience, and is concerned with an individual's personal perception or account of an object or event, as opposed to trying to define the object or event objectively. In Bassett's study, although 'care and caring' could be defined objectively, the abstract nature of the concepts lends itself to investigating personal meanings.

IPA also emphasizes that the research exercise is a *dynamic process*, in which the researcher is actively trying to get close to the participant's personal world (an 'insider's perspective'; Conrad, 1987, in Smith and Osborn, 2003). But this cannot be achieved completely or directly. IPA involves a two-stage interpretation process (a double *hermeneutic*): the participants are trying to make sense of their world, and the researcher is trying to make sense of the participants' efforts to make sense of their world. So, consistent with its phenomenological origins, IPA is concerned with trying to understand what it is like from the participant's perspective, to 'take their side' (Smith and Osborn, 2003).

While mainstream psychology is still strongly committed to *quantitative* and experimental methodology (à *nomothetic approach*), IPA uses in-depth *qualitative* analysis (an *idiographic approach*). However, Smith and Osborn (2003) stress that, as with qualitative research in general, there is no single, definitive way of doing IPA.

Applications and implications, and subsequent research

Some of the participants thought they sometimes had to step out of the normal parameters of nursing care to provide a high standard of care. The culture of nursing tends to be rigid, or even constricting, in the way it makes nurses conform to its norms. Bassett argues that nurses need to 'strike out' from positions of 'professional safety' and begin to take risks for their patients.

According to Nichols (2005), the neglect of psychological care has real – and serious – clinical consequences. (See **Background and context** above.) These include shock and even post-traumatic stress disorder, confusion and distress, loss of self-worth, lowered personal control and a collapse into dependency. Not only are these responses highly undesirable in themselves, but they can also undermine medical treatment and interfere with rehabilitation.

For example, Hemingway and Marmot (1999) found that the probability of cardiac patients suffering a second heart attack increased if they were in 'emotional disarray' and lacked support. Nichols believes that this is exactly what psychological care is about – monitoring for signs of such responses and intervening with basic care techniques, or referral to psychological treatment. Nurses, therapists (physio-, occupational) and anyone else involved in the patient's care, can all play a part under the guidance of psychologists.

Interestingly, a recent survey of 354 physiotherapists, chiropractors and osteopaths found that at least 10 per cent continued long-term treatment with patients, even after three months or more without demonstrable improvement. Follow-up interviews with a sample of these physical therapy practitioners revealed that many see it as their responsibility to provide psychological support and health advice to patients. Despite international guidelines for the treatment of lower back pain in primary care recommending that patients be referred back to their GP in the absence of any improvement, many of the interviewees were unhappy to discharge patients, and were uncertain about what would happen to them once they had left their care (The Psychologist, 2006).

Even though the theme of emotional labour was unique to students in Bassett's study, this does not mean that it is not an important issue for more experienced nurses. If his findings suggest that students are particularly vulnerable to the effects of emotional labour, this should be of concern: it is important to nurture newcomers to the profession. As Bassett (2002) says, 'If students experience sadness and emotional trauma that is unresolved or buried there may be a danger that they will leave nursing or may not develop the caring attributes necessary for quality nursing care.' Bassett believes that care has been displaced from its central position by various forces in recent years; it should be reaffirmed as the central and unifying tenet of nursing:

> *This involves placing care at centre stage, not just by referring to it constantly in lectures but also by identifying the need to provide real support for both nurses and students. Nurse educators need to remember what it is like to begin to learn to nurse and so help students to cope better with the emotional assaults that occur when they enter nursing.*

The government launched its first 'dignity in care' campaign at the end of 2006, aimed at creating a care system with zero tolerance of abuse and disrespect of older people. Although dignity in care is everyone's responsibility, nurses are absolutely crucial to the entire process: they have the most contact with patients and provide the most intimate care (Taylor, 2007).

EXERCISES

1   In relation to the first theme (*patient empowerment*), Cathy, the psychiatric nurse, refers to psychiatric patients as 'a fairly down-trodden group'. What do you think she means by this, and is there any evidence to support her claim? Do you agree with her statement?

2   Cathy says: 'so it's also really important to be able to make people have control and not feel controlled'. Is there anything contradictory in this statement?

3   Cathy's description of psychiatric patients corresponds closely to Seligman's (1974) concept of *learned helplessness*. Explain what Seligman means by this term.

4   In relation to the second theme (*giving of oneself*), participants stated that providing care without *genuineness* is not adequate. What do you understand by 'genuineness'? (This relates to one of three therapist attitudes necessary for Rogers' client-centred therapy; see Gross, 2005.)

5   Given the nature of IPA, do you consider that Bassett's sample was adequate?

38 Readiness to recover in adolescent anorexia nervosa: Prediction of hospital admission

Amettler, L., Castro, E., Serrano, E., Martinez, E. and Toro, J. (2005)

Journal of Child Psychology and Psychiatry, 46(4): 394–400

BACKGROUND AND CONTEXT

In the past 30 years, eating disorders (EDs) have become widespread in Western industrialized societies. This may be related to the overabundance of food, but it is likely to be influenced by societal norms that link attractiveness to being thin (American Psychiatric Association, 1994). Indeed, the popular and scientific assumption is that the preoccupation with thinness and dieting in Western societies is a direct cause of eating behaviours.

However, culture is just one of many factors that contribute to the development of EDs. Cultural factors have to interact with the psychology and biology of the vulnerable individual (Fedoroff and McFarlane, 1998).

Within the widely used classification of mental disorders employed by psychiatrists, both in the USA and elsewhere (DSM-IV-TR; American Psychiatric Association, 2000), *anorexia nervosa* (AN) has a 'diagnostic primacy'. In other words, other EDs (such as bulimia nervosa) are only diagnosed after AN has been ruled out (Roth and Fonagy, 2005).

The essential feature of AN (literally, 'nervous lack of appetite') is a refusal to maintain body weight at or above a minimally 'normal' body weight; this is defined as a body weight 15 per cent below that expected for the individual's age and height. For a diagnosis of AN, there must also be:

- an intense fear of gaining weight or becoming fat, despite being underweight;

- a severe restriction of food intake, often with excessive exercising, in order to achieve weight loss;

- a disturbance in how body weight or shape is experienced, and an undue influence of body weight or shape on self-evaluation;

- in post-menarchal females (those who have started menstruation), amenorrhoea (the absence of at least three consecutive menstrual cycles).

There are two specific subtypes of AN:

- *binge-eating/purging type*: during the AN episode, there is regular binge eating or purging (self-induced vomiting, or use of laxatives or diuretics);

- *restrictive type*: there is no such behaviour.

AN typically begins in the mid teens (mean age of onset 17 years). In some, the disorder is short-lived, but it becomes more severe in 10–20 per cent of individuals. Though a proportion of patients will recover, many continue to have disordered patterns of eating, with some moving to a more bulimic pattern. One representative study (Lowe *et al.*, 2001, in Roth and Fonagy, 2005) followed up 84 patients 21 years after initial hospital admission. Of these, 51 per cent were classified as fully recovered and 21 per cent as partially recovered; 10 per cent still met diagnostic criteria and 17 per cent had died of causes related to AN. Continued low weight was predictive of poorer outcome. AN has the highest mortality rate of *any* psychiatric disorder (including depression and alcoholism). According to the Eating Disorders Association (EDA), mortality is 13–20 per cent (Waterhouse and Mayes, 2000); death is caused both by the effects of starvation and by suicide.

AIM AND NATURE

● HYPOTHESIS

There was no explicit hypothesis. The aim was to assess in a sample of adolescent patients if the degree of motivation to change (specifically, the readiness to recover) is a predictor of the need for inpatient admission during follow-up. Based on previous research, readiness to recover at the start of treatment predicts weight recovery at follow-up. Another way of expressing this is to say that the *lower* the motivation to recover, the *greater* the need for inpatient admission.

● METHOD/DESIGN

This is a questionnaire study, involving 70 adolescents (69 females, 1 male, aged 13–19) who fulfilled the DSM-IV diagnostic criteria for AN at the point of starting treatment at the Eating Disorders Unit of the Child and Adolescent Psychiatry and Psychology Department of the University Hospital Clinic in Barcelona, Spain.

Patients were at different points of their treatment programme and at different levels of weight recovery. There were 30 inpatients, while others were outpatients or were attending the Day Hospital.

Treatment in this unit is based on a multidisciplinary approach that combines biological management, nutritional rehabilitation, a behavioural programme aimed at improving eating patterns and weight, individual and group cognitive treatment, and individual and group parent counselling. When physical risk is high, psychopathology is intense or collaboration in the outpatient setting is very poor, inpatient treatment is indicated. In addition, if weight and eating behaviour do not improve after several weeks, patients are admitted for complete hospitalization in order to avoid a long period of malnutrition.

Participants were given the Anorexia Nervosa Stages of Change Questionnaire (ANSOCQ) (Riegler *et al.*, 2000, 2002). This is a 20-item self-report questionnaire for evaluating readiness to recover in AN; it addresses weight, shape and eating behaviour, methods of weight control, and emotional and relationship problems.

Two other self-report questionnaires were employed. The Spanish version of the Eating Disorders Inventory-2 (EDI-2) (Garner, 1991) was used. This comprises 91 items for evaluating eating attitude and symptoms usually associated with eating disorders. The 11 scales are: drive for thinness, bulimia, body dissatisfaction, ineffectiveness, interpersonal distrust, interoceptive awareness, asceticism, perfectionism, social insecurity, maturity fears and impulse regulation.

The Beck Depression Inventory (BDI) (Beck *et al.*, 1961, 1996) comprises 21 items for evaluating depressive symptomatology. A score over 16 is taken to suggest a diagnosis of depressive disorder.

Patients were evaluated again six to nine months after the initial assessment.

● RESULTS/FINDINGS

After six to nine months of treatment, the sample was divided into those who needed hospital admission – due to poor outcome – during this period and those who did not. (The seven who had already left the unit were contacted by phone in order to find out if they had been admitted to another hospital.)

1. There were no differences in mean age or body mass index (BMI: a measure of body fat based on height and weight) between the two groups.

2. The group that needed hospital admission obtained a lower mean score on motivation to change, measured with the ANSOCQ.

3. On the EDI-2 scales, there were significant differences between the groups on bulimia, ineffectiveness, interpersonal distrust, interoceptive awareness and

maturity fears. On all these scales, the group that needed admission had higher mean scores than the group that did not.

4   The mean score on the BDI was also significantly higher for the group that needed admission.

Significantly, fewer patients who needed an admission during follow-up were already inpatients at the start of the study.

For each patient, averages of the total scores were calculated to classify them into stages of readiness to change. Figure 38.1 shows the percentage of patients needing admission and not needing it for each stage of change:

● pre-contemplation (score 20–29);

● contemplation (score 30–49);

● preparation (score 50–69);

● action (score 70–89);

● maintenance (score 90–100).

The percentage of patients who needed admission fell as patients entered a higher stage of change. Whereas 80 per cent at the pre-contemplation stage needed admission, at the preparation stage this fell to about 50 per cent, and at the maintenance stage the percentage fell to 0 per cent.

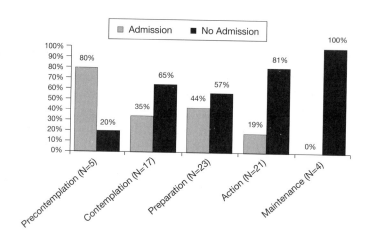

Figure 38.1. Percentage of patients who were admitted and not admitted during follow-up in each stage of change. Reproduced from Amettler *et al.* (2005), with permission from Wiley-Blackwell.

● CONCLUSIONS

The findings are consistent with the expected outcome. Patients who needed hospital admission during follow-up did not differ in age or BMI. The significant differences were on the BDI, some of the EDI-2 scales, the percentage of patients admitted on first evaluation, and motivation to change as measured by the ANSOCQ.

Depressive symptoms help to explain why some patients find it difficult to change their eating behaviour. In adolescents, maturity fears and other factors, such as lack of supportive family relationships, may have a special significance for motivation to change.

Probably the most important finding is that motivation to change was lower in patients needing hospital admission during follow-up: 80 per cent of patients in the pre-contemplation stage needed admission. In the other stages, the percentage fell progressively to zero for those in the maintenance stage. So, the closer a patient is to the action or maintenance stages, the lower the probability of hospitalization and the better the collaboration with outpatients' treatment. Motivation to change was found to be an independent predictor of hospital admission.

EVALUATION

Theoretical issues

Of the 70 patients, 60 (85.7 per cent) were of the restricting type, and the other 10 (14.3 per cent) of the purging type. This is consistent with what we most commonly associate with AN. But the binge-eating/purging type sounds more like bulimia nervosa (BN) than it does the restricting type of AN (Claridge and Davis, 2003). So, the DSM classification seems quite arbitrary, and some researchers have questioned whether these really are separate disorders (Mitchell and McCarthy, 2000). The only real difference between BN and restricting type AN is the patient's *body weight* (that of the former is either within normal limits or actually *over*). DSM has chosen to use body weight (in practice, BMI = weight (kg)/height (metres squared)) as the unifying characteristic for the AN subtypes, instead of classifying eating disorders according to their *psychobehavioural* similarities.

Among those with improved weight and menstrual functioning, some continue to have abnormal eating habits, some become overweight and some develop BN. The most useful predictor of poor outcome is a long history of AN at the point of first seeing a doctor (Gelder *et al.*, 1999).

According to Amettler *et al.*, collaboration with treatment and readiness to recover can be very low in AN, and it can be very difficult to establish an adequate treatment programme. Therapeutic interventions have been proposed to increase patients' motivation to change. The concept of motivation to change can be defined as a patient's willingness to introduce any change which leads to improvement in their condition. Prochaska and DiClemente's (1982) *stages of change* (SOC) model is intended to explain the process towards a real willingness of the patient to recover:

- *pre-contemplation*: the patient has no intention of making any change and may not even recognize the need for change;

- *contemplation*: recognizing the need to change and starting to consider possible ways of achieving this;

- *preparation*: planning how to make the change/making small changes;

- *action*: actively engaging in a new behaviour;

- *maintenance*: sustaining the change over time and trying hard not to relapse.

The model has been tested in several studies of motivation to change in relation to different health-related behaviours/disorders, including alcohol abuse, smoking, obesity and psychological problems in general.

Methodological issues

There have been very few controlled studies of the SOC model involving eating disorders, and the results vary depending on the diagnosis of the patients studied. The only study using an instrument designed to assess motivation specifically in AN was carried out by Riegler *et al.* (2000). They used the ANSOCQ. However, the sample comprised mainly adult patients.

The adolescent patients treated at the unit were asked to participate in the study and informed that all their responses would be kept confidential. Study procedures were approved by the University Hospital Ethics Committee.

The issue of hospital admission as the measure of motivation to changes is dealt with in the **Exercises**. Amettler *et al.* warn against drawing any general conclusions from their results, which rest on hospital admission as the key measure of motivation to change. They also claim that another limitation of the study is that only some variables have been studied; other factors, such as previous treatments, parental collaboration, family problems or personality disorders, also need to be taken into account.

Applications and implications

Amettler *et al.* claim that their data reveal some of the patient characteristics that need to be taken into account specifically during treatment for AN, at least in adolescents, in order to gain their collaboration and reduce the need for hospital admission. Perhaps more specific attention to motivation to change and depressive symptomatology will help to achieve a better involvement with and response to treatment.

According to Roth and Fonagy (2005), in routine practice, a range of individual therapies are used (including behavioural, cognitive-behavioural and psychodynamic). Family therapies are also common, usually aimed at improving the disruptions to family life created by the disorder. Most treatments recognize the critical importance of establishing an appropriate dietary regime, and this is usually a common element across interventions.

Questions about *how* to treat AN are more central than *where* this should take place (Crisp, 2002, in Roth and Fonagy, 2005). However, the relative cost of inpatient and outpatient programmes make treatment location a legitimate concern. Very few adequate randomized control trials (RCTs) have been conducted, one exception being the study by Crisp *et al.* (1991, in Roth and Fonagy, 2005). This reports one-year outcomes for 90 severe anorexics randomly allocated to one of four treatment conditions:

1   *Inpatient treatment* comprised a package of behavioural techniques aimed at restoring weight, plus weekly individual therapy, group therapy, family therapy, dietary advice and a range of milieu treatments. On discharge, patients were seen for 12 weeks of outpatient therapy.

2   *Outpatient treatment 1*: 12 sessions of psychodynamic individual or family therapy, plus dietary advice.

3   *Outpatient treatment 2*: 10 sessions of group therapy, plus dietary advice.

4   Patients were seen only for assessment and referred back to their GP or consultant. They then received a variety of unmonitored treatments.

After one year, patients in all conditions showed improvements. But this was most striking for both outpatient groups. The inpatient group showed the most relapse.

Although these findings suggest that even seriously ill anorexic patients can be treated as outpatients, clinicians actually have little research to guide them when admission is being considered as an option. In practice, the need for medical intervention may drive the treatment that is offered. But further research is needed to clarify the short- and long-term benefits of treatment location (Roth and Fonagy, 2005).

A number of factors have been linked to prognosis. Low weight at referral is associated with poorer outcome, and both speed of weight increase and how long patients can maintain their target weight have been linked to outcome. As we have seen, motivation is also a highly relevant factor. Although some studies have shown that it is possible to increase levels of motivation for change, this has not yet been linked to outcome (Roth and Fonagy, 2005).

EXERCISES

1   Why was it important to study a sample of adolescent patients, as opposed to adults?

2   Amettler *et al.* chose hospital admission to measure motivation to change (the 'real' measure), while other researchers have used dropout rate or weight recovery. Why do you think they chose hospital admission over the other two?

3   The adolescents were at different points in their treatment programmes and at different levels of weight recovery. Some were inpatients, some outpatients, and others were attending a day hospital. What reasons might the researchers have had for choosing such a sample, and what advantages could this variety of patient situation provide?

4   In the ED1-2 scales, what is meant by the terms *interoceptive awareness* and *asceticism*?

39 Abortion in young women and subsequent mental health

Fergusson, D.M., Horwood, L.J. and Ridder, E.M. (2006)

Journal of Child Psychology and Psychiatry, 47(1): 16–24

BACKGROUND AND CONTEXT

According to Raphael (1984), 'The loss of a child will always be painful, for it is in some way a loss of part of the self'. 'Child' here may refer to a baby, toddler, teenager or adult child. But it may also refer to *prenatal* loss, either through miscarriage (*spontaneous abortion*) or termination (*therapeutic* or *induced abortion*). It is in this latter sense that the term is most commonly used.

The 1967 Abortion Act (UK) defined therapeutic termination as one undertaken before the gestational age of 28 weeks (i.e. before the 28th week of pregnancy). But advances in technology have greatly improved the chances of survival for premature babies, and a reduction to 24 weeks was approved by Parliament in 1990. The Abortion Act made it possible for a woman to have an abortion legally, provided two doctors independently agree that the termination is necessary to prevent:

- the likelihood of the woman's death;

- permanent illness (physical or psychological);

- damage to a woman's existing children;

- abnormality in the baby.

The Act stopped far short of supporting the idea that a woman has an absolute right to control her body. Practically, the law relies on individual doctors exercising discretion as to who qualifies for an abortion (Timpson, 1966, in Hughes, 2003).

Despite its legality, abortion is still a very 'live' moral issue. But the debate has also involved empirical concerns about the links between unwanted pregnancy, abortion and long-term mental health. Specifically, several authors have proposed that abortion may have adverse mental health effects due to guilt, unresolved loss and lowered self-esteem. However, overall the evidence is quite weak (i.e. inconclusive).

AIM AND NATURE

● HYPOTHESIS

Rather than testing specific hypotheses, Fergusson *et al.* analysed the relationship between abortion in young women aged 15–25 and subsequent mental health in a birth cohort of young women studied to the age of 25. The specific aims of this analysis were:

1 to examine the extent to which mental health outcomes between the ages of 15 and 25 varied between three status groups: (a) not pregnant by age 25, (b) pregnant, no abortion, (c) pregnant, abortion;

2 to control for confounding pre-pregnancy factors (which could affect the association between mental health and pregnancy status), such as social background, childhood and family history, mental health and personality factors;

3 to compare the rates of mental disorders between (a) the pregnant, no abortion (PNA) and not pregnant (NP) groups, and (b) the pregnant, abortion group (PA).

● METHOD

The data used in this analysis were taken from the Christchurch Health and Development Study (CHDS). This is a longitudinal study of a birth cohort of 1,265 children born in the Christchurch urban region of New Zealand, who have been studied from birth to age 25.

The analysis is based on those female participants for whom information on pregnancy history and mental health outcomes are available. The sample sizes varied between 506 and 520, depending on the timing of assessment of pregnancy history and mental health (80–83 per cent of the original cohort of 630 females).

Pregnancy and abortion, 15–20 years

Participants were interviewed at ages 15, 16, 18, 21 and 25 about pregnancy and abortion occurring since the previous assessment. By age 25, 205 women (41 per cent of the cohort) had become pregnant at least once, and 74 (14.6 per cent) reported seeking and obtaining an abortion at least once. In total, 422 pregnancies were reported prior to age 25, of which 90 were terminated. Compared with figures for New Zealand as a whole, the rate of abortion reported here suggests some under-reporting.

These figures relate to all three specific aims outlined above.

Mental health, 15–25 years

At ages 16, 18, 21 and 25, participants were asked about mental health issues since the previous assessment, using questionnaires based on the Diagnostic Interview Schedule for Children (DISC) at age 16, and the Composite International Diagnostic Interview (CIDI) (World Health Organization, 1993) at ages 18–25. These were supplemented by additional measures.

Based on these questionnaires, it was possible to determine the proportion of participants who met the DSM-IV (Diagnostic and Statistical Manual for Mental Disorders; American Psychiatric Association, 1994) criteria during the intervals 15–18, 18–21 and 21–25 years for:

- major depression;
- anxiety disorders (including generalized anxiety, panic disorder, agoraphobia, social phobia and specific phobia);
- alcohol dependence;
- illicit drug dependence.

In addition to measures of DSM-IV disorders, measures of self-reported suicidal ideation and attempts were taken.

These measures relate to the second and third specific aims above.

Covariate factors

These relate to the second specific aim above and refer to the possible confounding factors that could distort the relationship between mental health and pregnancy status.

1. *Measures of family socio-demographic background*: (a) maternal education was assessed at the time of the participant's birth (no formal qualifications/ secondary qualifications/tertiary qualifications); (b) family socio-economic status was assessed at birth.

2. *Measures of family functioning*: (a) a measure of *family instability* was constructed, based on the number of changes of parents experienced by the participant from birth to age 15; (b) at age 15, participants were classified as having a *parental history of criminality* if any parent reported a history of offending; (c) at ages 18 and 21, participants were classified as having experienced *childhood sexual abuse* (before age 16) if they reported any episode of abuse involving physical contact with a perpetrator; (d) at ages 18 and 21, participants were classified as having experienced childhood physical abuse (before age 16) if they reported that at least one parent had regularly

used physical punishment, had used physical punishment too often or too severely, or had treated them in a harsh and abusive manner.

3   *Childhood conduct problems (7–9 years)*: at ages 7, 8 and 9, the extent to which participants exhibited tendencies to behave in disordered and oppositional ways was assessed using a scale that combined items from two other child behaviour rating scales. Separate ratings were obtained from the child's parent(s) and class teacher.

4   *Child educational achievement*: participants' class teacher was asked to assess their performance in each of five curriculum areas from 11 to 13.

5   *Measures of child personality*: (a) neuroticism was assessed at age 14 using a short form of the neuroticism scale of the Eysenck personality inventory; (b) self-esteem was assessed at age 15 using the Coopersmith self-esteem inventory.

6   *Measures of adolescent adjustment*: (a) at age 18, participants who reported having first had sexual intercourse before age 16 were classified as having early *sexual onset*; (b) at age 15, participants were questioned about their use of tobacco, alcohol and cannabis; (c) at age 15, participants were given a mental health interview, which combined components of the DISC (see above) and other measures to assess a range of DSM-III-R disorders over the previous 12 months (major depression and anxiety disorders (see above)). They were also asked about the frequency of suicidal thoughts in the previous 12 months.

7   *Young adult lifestyle factors*: at each assessment from 18 onwards, participants were asked about changes in their living arrangements, including (a) living with parents and age of leaving family home; (b) entry into cohabiting relationships.

● RESULTS

Associations between pregnancy/abortion history and mental health outcomes

(This relates to the first and third specific aim: see above.)

1   For all mental health outcomes except alcohol dependence, there were significant associations between pregnancy history and rates of disorder. Rates of mental disorder were highest among those having had abortions (PA), and lowest among those who had not become pregnant (NP). Rates for those who became pregnant but did not have an abortion (PNA) were intermediate between these extremes.

2   The differences between the NP and PNA groups were not significant. In all comparisons, the PA group had significantly higher rates of disorder than the NP group, and except for anxiety disorder, significantly higher rates than the PNA group.

Adjustments for confounding

(This relates to the second and third specific aim.)

There was a significant tendency for those who became pregnant by age 25 to have suffered greater childhood social and economic disadvantage, family dysfunction and individual adjustment problems. They were also more likely to have left the family home at a young age and to have entered a cohabiting relationship.

After controlling for these confounding variables:

1   For depression, suicidal ideation, illicit drug dependence and total mental health problems, the association with pregnancy/abortion history remained statistically significant. For anxiety disorder, the association was marginally significant.

2   The rate of mental disorder for the NP and PNA groups was not significantly different. But the PA group had significantly higher rates of disorder than the PNA group, and with the exception of anxiety disorder, significantly higher than the NP group.

● CONCLUSIONS

This study produced evidence consistent with the view that in young women, exposure to abortion (i.e. the experience of having an abortion) is associated with a detectable increase in risks of mental health problems – both at the time of the abortion (concurrently) and afterwards (subsequently). This conclusion is based on comparisons with same-aged members of the cohort group who had either not become pregnant by age 25 or had become pregnant without seeking an abortion.

EVALUATION

Theoretical issues

In New Zealand, legal abortion is controlled by legislation similar to the 1967/1990 Acts in the UK, but it also includes some additional grounds for granting an abortion:

● the pregnancy is the result of incest;

● the woman is severely mentally handicapped;

● the pregnancy is the result of rape.

An abortion is also considered on the basis of age. Another difference from the law in the UK is the requirement that all women considering an abortion should receive counselling. (See **Exercises**.)

In the UK, adolescents are becoming sexually active at an increasingly younger age. The Family Planning Association reports that nearly one in five young women says they have had sex before the age of 16 (Hughes, 2003). Much of this activity is risky; contraceptive use is often erratic and may result in unwanted pregnancies.

Within Western Europe, the UK has the highest teenage birth rate. This is twice that of Germany, three times that of France, and six times that of the Netherlands (Brennan, 2002, in Hughes, 2003). According to the National Assembly for Wales (2003), Wales has a considerably higher teenage birth rate than England. In 2000, the conception rate in Wales for under-18s was 47.3 per 1,000 females. Although the rate fluctuates from year to year, the latest figures are below the peak 1998 level.

Unwanted teenage pregnancy is clearly a health problem for Wales. Abortion remains a common approach to dealing with unwanted pregnancies, which is ideally performed in the first trimester (three months) because it is considered to be less traumatic. This is relevant to the Fergusson *et al.* study, because at what point in the pregnancy the abortion was performed was not taken into account. This is (another) potential confounding factor.

Compared with previous generations, adolescents in Western societies are enjoying greater freedom at a younger age. (See Chapter 29.) But this is double-sided: greater freedom brings more risks, and greater costs when errors of judgement are made. As Hendry (1999) says, '"dropping out" of school, being out of work, teenage pregnancy, sexually transmitted diseases, being homeless, drug addiction and suicide, are powerful examples of the price that some young people pay for their extended freedom'. Abortion is a further example of the price to be paid.

There are many biological, psychological and social reasons why women opt to terminate a pregnancy. In some sociocultural settings, premarital sexual activity is taboo, using contraception is forbidden among unmarried youth, and abortion is viewed as the only solution to premarital pregnancy (World Health Organization, 2002, in Hughes, 2003).

In the 1960s, teenage pregnancy in the UK began to be redefined as a social problem that could be studied and dealt with scientifically, rather than a moral problem of sexual transgression.

Methodological issues

According to Fergusson *et al.*, most previous studies compared only those who became pregnant but did not seek abortion and those who did. In other words, those women who were not (yet) pregnant were excluded from the analysis. This makes it more difficult to interpret the data. Specifically, the finding that rates of mental health problems are higher among the PA group than the PNA group is consistent with two quite different interpretations:

● exposure to abortion leads to an increased susceptibility to subsequent mental health problems;

● pregnancy without abortion is beneficial to mental health.

The only way to distinguish between these two alternative explanations is to include data for the NP group. This provides a reference point which helps to determine the *direction* of the association between abortion and mental health.

For this reason, Fergusson *et al.* conducted a *prospective analysis*. Most of the data were based on a *concurrent* assessment of pregnancy status and mental health. In other words, these assessments were made at the same point in time. This raises issues about the direction of any causal link. As with the limitations involved in comparing just PNA and PA groups described above, the results of a concurrent analysis may be interpreted in two ways:

● mental health problems increase the risk of abortion;

● abortion increases the risk of mental health problems.

To help choose between these interpretations, the researchers carried out a prospective analysis in which pregnancy/abortion history before age 21 was used to predict mental health outcomes from 21 to 25 years. This analysis was limited to the overall number of disorders.

The association between pregnancy/abortion history prior to 21 and mental health problems remained statistically significant. Also, and consistent with the previous analysis, the results show a clear pattern in which:

● the rates of disorder for the NP and PNA groups were not significantly different;

● the rates for the PA group were significantly higher than both of these groups.

Even after controlling for confounding factors, exposure to abortion before 21 was associated with increased risks of later mental health problems.

Applications and implications

While recognizing the methodological limitations of their study (see **Exercises**), Fergusson *et al.* believe that it raises the possibility that for some young women, exposure to abortion is a traumatic life event which increases longer-term susceptibility to common mental health disorders. These findings are inconsistent with the current consensus on the psychological effects of abortion. In particular, the American Psychological Association's statement on abortion (APA, 2005, in Fergusson *et al.*) concluded that:

> *well-designed studies of psychological responses following abortion have consistently shown that risk of psychological harm is low ... the percentage of women who experience clinically relevant distress is small and appears to be no greater than in general samples of women of reproductive age.*

This fairly strong conclusion about the absence of harm from abortion was based on a relatively small number of studies, which had one or more limitations, including:

● lack of comprehensive assessment of mental disorders;

● failure to compare all relevant groups.

Fergusson *et al.* also point out that the APA's statement appears to disregard the findings of several studies which claimed to show that abortion *does* have negative effects.

Fergusson *et al.* argue that the issue of whether or not abortion has harmful effects on mental health is far from resolved. It is difficult to disregard the real possibility that abortion in young women is associated with increased risk of mental health problems. But there is a clear need for further well-controlled studies to explore the issue before any firm conclusions can be drawn. They intend to study the participants at age 30, when it may be possible to gather further contextual information associated with decisions regarding abortion.

EXERCISES

1   In their Discussion, Fergusson *et al.* point out some of the limitations of their study which threaten its validity. One of these concerns is what they call *omitted covariates*. What they mean by this are possible confounding variables that they have not controlled. List some other possible confounding variables and give your reasons for choosing these.

2   Why exactly is it so important to understand the role of possible confounding variables in this study? (This requires you to look back at the Conclusions.)

3   Participants were only asked about sexual and physical abuse once they reached the ages of 18 and 21. Why do you think this was? Would it have been appropriate to ask them before these ages?

4   In relation to childhood conduct problems:

   (a) What is meant by 'disordered' and 'oppositional' behaviour?

   (b) Why was it thought necessary to obtain separate reports from parents and teachers?

5   Do you think it is a good idea that all New Zealand women considering an abortion are required to have counselling?

40 Black is beautiful: A reexamination of racial preference and identification

Hraba, J. and Grant, G. (1970)

Journal of Personality and Social Psychology, 16(3): 398–402

BACKGROUND AND CONTEXT

Racial (or ethnic) preference and identification are both related to *ethnic awareness*. These are, in turn, related to other aspects of social development, in particular, racial/ethnic prejudice and discrimination, and self-esteem. Hraba and Grant's study examines the interaction (at the level of the individual) between the developmental and social aspects of ethnic awareness and these related processes: how do prejudice and discrimination (usually discussed within social psychology) affect the *self-perception* (including self-esteem) of members of minority groups?

● Regarding *ethnic awareness*, by age four to five, children can make basic discriminations (such as black and white), and during the next few years more difficult ones (such as Anglo-American and Hispanic). By eight or nine, they understand that ethnic identity remains constant, despite age changes or superficial attributes such as clothing.

● *Ethnic identity* (or *self-identification*) involves awareness of one's own ethnicity, and closely parallels developing awareness of others' ethnicity. It has been assessed mainly by using dolls or photographs and asking children to point to one that looks most like them. Generally, children of four and over choose appropriately, although this is not always the case (Aboud, 1988).

● *Ethnic preference* (measured, for example, by children's choice of a doll or photograph that they would like to play with) is the main concern of Hraba and Grant's study. This is related to *evaluative attitude*: the child's feelings (positive or negative) about being a member of a particular group (Phinney, 1990).

Most research into ethnic preference has involved African American children's self-concept. Starting with studies by the African American couple Kenneth and Mamie Clark (1939, 1947), research up to the 1960s showed that black American children compared themselves unfavourably with white children, and grew up feeling 'inferior'. The attitude held by the majority towards one's ethnic group seemed to be consistently reflected in the child's developing attitude towards itself: the concept of *self-hatred* was even used to describe how such children reacted to the prejudice and discrimination they experienced (Allport, 1954).

According to Schaffer (1996):

> it is no wonder that children from minority groups become highly self-conscious about their status. Belonging to a particular social group, and being able to define oneself in terms of that group, may have many advantages for a child, but when that group is subject to adverse discrimination and is looked down upon by the rest of society there may be unfortunate consequences for the way in which children define and evaluate themselves.

While the idea of self-hatred originated in relation to Jews in the USA in the 1930s, it has survived in the form of *black negative self-identity*. Despite the mass of research it has stimulated, there is little conclusive evidence as to exactly what constitutes an identity problem in the black child (Owusu-Bempah and Howitt, 2000). (See **Theoretical issues** below.)

According to social identity theory (SIT: see Chapter 12), a major need in a competitive society like ours is to understand the complexity of the social world and locate oneself at an acceptable position within it. While negative racial attitudes may fulfil this function for the majority-group child in a multiracial society, by definition they cannot do so for the minority group. This can be seen in the phenomenon of *misidentification* (black children choosing a white doll when asked to select one that looks like them), as demonstrated by Clark and Clark.

This *self-denigration* by minority groups was addressed by civil rights and black politico-cultural movements in the USA during and after the 1960s, encouraging a positive view of being black. This was captured in slogans such as 'black is beautiful'.

AIM AND NATURE

● HYPOTHESIS

Hraba and Grant's study was a replication of Clark and Clark's (1939) famous doll study. The aim was to see if the Clarks' finding that the majority of black children preferred a white doll was still valid. (Note that the Clarks' 1947 study is probably the more commonly cited of the two, and Hraba and Grant refer to it in their Introduction. But their main results table makes it clear that they were replicating the 1939 study.)

● METHOD/DESIGN

The procedures used by Clark and Clark were followed as closely as possible. The participants (160 four- to eight-year-olds, 89 black children, 71 white children, in the public school system of Lincoln, Nebraska) were interviewed individually using a set of four dolls (two black and two white, identical in all other respects). They were presented with eight items (as originally used by Clark and Clark):

1 Give me the doll that you want to play with.

2 Give me the doll that is a nice doll.

3 Give me the doll that looks bad.

4 Give me the doll that is a nice colour.
(These items measured *racial preference*.)

5 Give me the doll that looks like a white child.

6 Give me the doll that looks like a coloured child.

7 Give me the doll that looks like a Negro child.
(These items measure *racial awareness/knowledge*.)

8 Give me the doll that looks like you.
(This item measured *racial self-identification*).

These represent three of the *dependent variables* (as assessed by Clark and Clark). Hraba and Grant added a fourth, namely asking the children to name and indicate the race of their best friends. This was an attempt to identify the behavioural consequences of racial preference and identification. They also asked teachers for the same information. The *independent variable* was the child's ethnic group membership ('race'), namely white or black, with the latter subdivided into light (practically white), medium (light brown to dark brown) or dark (dark brown to black). Participants were *selected* for these characteristics (race cannot be manipulated) and, for the same reason, they could not be randomly allocated to different conditions. So, the method involved was a *quasi-experiment*.

They controlled for race of interviewer: an equal number of black and white children were assigned to both black and white interviewers.

● RESULTS

Hraba and Grant made two comparisons:

1 between their (Lincoln) sample and the Clarks' sample (this represents the basic replication);

2   between black and white children in the Lincoln sample, with white children providing a benchmark.

Racial preference (items 1–4)

1   The differences in racial preference between the Clark and Clark and the Lincoln samples were highly significant: most of the black children in the Lincoln sample preferred black dolls, just as the majority of the white children preferred white dolls.

2   Black and white children in the Lincoln sample preferred dolls of their own race. The white children were significantly more ethnocentric (showed same-race preferences) on items 1 and 2; there was no significant difference on item 3; and the black children were significantly more ethnocentric on item 4.

Age. The Clarks found that black children preferred white dolls at all ages (3–7), although this decreased with age. A majority of the black children at all ages (3–8) in Hraba and Grant's sample preferred a black doll, and this preference increased with age. With white children, there was a similar age trend (except on item 4).

Skin colour. The Clarks found that the children of light skin colour showed the greatest preference for the white doll and the dark children the least. Hraba and Grant found that the light-skinned children were at least as strong in their preference for a black doll as the others.

Racial identification (racial awareness/knowledge: items 5–7; racial self-identification: item 8)

On items 5 and 6, the Clarks found that a majority of their participants correctly identified white and 'coloured' dolls (94 per cent and 93 per cent, respectively). Hraba and Grant's sample was comparable: 90 per cent and 94 per cent, respectively. On item 7, 86 per cent of Hraba and Grant's sample made the correct identification, compared with 72 per cent of the Clarks'.

Age. Like the Clarks, Hraba and Grant found an inverse relationship between misidentification (items 5–8) and age. This relationship also held for white children.

Skin colour. Like the Clarks, Hraba and Grant failed to find significant differences in misidentification (items 5–7) among black children, depending on their skin colour. While the Clarks found that more black children with light skin colour misidentified themselves (80 per cent on item 8), only 15 per cent of Hraba and Grant's black children with light skin colour did so; there was no significant difference in misidentification on item 8 by skin colour.

Race of interviewer. This was not related to choice of doll on any of the items for either black or white children.

AIM AND NATURE

Race of respondents' friends. For both black and white children, there was no apparent relationship between doll preference and race of friends. Of the black sample, 70 per cent had white friends, and 59 per cent of the white sample had black friends.

● CONCLUSIONS

The results indicate that black children in interracial settings are not necessarily white-oriented. One interpretation of this finding is that conditions specific to Lincoln, Nebraska had mediated the impact of the 'Black Movement'. Also, interracial contact may promote black pride, which, in turn, enhances black academic performance. Given the racial composition of the Lincoln schools, the interracial friendship patterns support this interpretation.

The lack of relationship between doll choice and friendship pattern suggests that we cannot simply assume that there is a correspondence between doll choice and interpersonal behaviour. If 'black is beautiful' is taken to mean a rejection of white people, then this clearly was not borne out by the friendship patterns: contrary to expectations, black children who, without exception, preferred black dolls did not have all black friends (this was not possible in predominantly white schools).

Alternatively, 'black is beautiful' might mean acceptance of and by whites. As expected, more black children with friends of both races preferred black dolls (except on item 4) than those with all black friends. This relationship approached statistical significance.

EVALUATION

Theoretical issues

As we noted in the **Background and context** above, Hraba and Grant's study is really concerned with the self-perception of minority group children in the context of a racist society. One aspect of self-perception is self-esteem, the value or worth which an individual attaches to him/herself.

According to Wilson (1978), despite the 'black is beautiful' revolution, American racism remains: white continues to be preferred, including 'belief in its inherent rightness and the hatred of black and belief in its inherent wrongness'.

The US Joint Commission on Mental Health of Children (1970) published a report indicating that discrimination can have damaging effects on the psychological adjustment of young children and adolescents; they grow up being subjected to derogatory views of the black American which produce negative self-images (Powell-Hopson and Hopson, 1992).

However, Schaffer (1996) maintains that:

> How children make sense of their membership of a minority group is … not just a reflection of the majority view in their society; more immediate experiences in the family constitute a more powerful source of influence. It is thus perfectly possible for minority children to be aware of their underprivileged status and yet not internalise these as part of their self-concept.

We need to distinguish between *group identity*, assessed by so-called preference measures indicating children's evaluation of their group, and *personal identity*, as assessed by self-esteem measures. (See **Subsequent research** below.)

According to Owusu-Bempah and Hewitt (2000), the notions of black self-hatred and identity conflict inevitably imply that black children will typically have low self-esteem. But there is little historical or contemporary support for this, and, indeed, they claim that it is a myth.

For over 20 years, research has shown that black people's self-esteem is no different from that of white people – but still the myth lives on.

Subsequent research

Milner (1975) studied five- to eight-year-olds (white, black and south Asian) in the UK, using very similar procedures to those of the Clarks. He used three dolls of different skin tones (white, black and south Asian), and when asked, 'Which doll looks the most like you?', all the white children chose the white doll, 76 per cent of the Asian children chose the Asian doll, while only 52 per cent of the African Caribbean children chose the black doll. The figures for racial misidentification were: white (0 per cent), Asian (24 per cent) and African Caribbean (48 per cent). When asked which of the dolls they would rather be, all the white children, 66 per cent of the Asian children and 80 per cent of the African Caribbean children chose the white doll. Milner interpreted these findings as apparently showing that they would rather be white than a member of their own (actual) racial group. The results essentially duplicated those of the Clarks.

However, a later study (Milner, 1983) failed to replicate this earlier trend among black children, as did another UK study by Davey and Mullin (1982). These British studies, together with Hraba and Grant's American study, might have encouraged the belief that black children growing up in a racist society could still like their race and themselves.

However, further US studies gave cause for concern. For example, Powell-Hopson and Hopson (1988) studied the choices of black youngsters between black and white Cabbage Patch dolls: about 65 per cent of the black children preferred the white doll. Similar results were found in a study comparing children in the USA and Trinidad (a predominantly black country) (Gopaul-McNichol, 1992). According to Owusu-Bempah and Howitt (2000), one obvious explanation for these contradictory findings is that the misidentification studies (including the Clarks') are seriously flawed. (See **Methodological issues** below.)

A study by Powell-Hopson (1985) used the Clark and Clark doll test *plus* a treatment intervention which involved modelling, reinforcement and learning colour meaning word associations. Although the results did not show that the black children wished they were white, it did indicate their awareness of society's preferences. These preferences are the result of conditioning and can be changed. The use of black role models (the researchers) seemed to have a definite positive impact on children's attitudes and choices (Powell-Hopson and Hopson, 1988).

Studies which have looked specifically at black children's self-esteem, compared with white children, have produced conflicting results, as have those looking at the relationship between racial preferences/attitudes and self-esteem (Clark, 1992). Black children seem to compartmentalize their racial attitudes and prevent them from influencing self-evaluation. According to Clark, these findings raise serious doubts about the construct validity of the doll tests, making them poor predictors of self-concept/self-esteem; they also contradict the 'black self-hatred doctrine' (see Schaffer's 1996 quote above).

According to Moghaddam (1998), the belief that black people who internalize society's negative racial group attitudes inevitably develop low self-esteem arose from the research tradition pioneered by the Clarks (although they were not directly testing self-esteem). It is possible to show a strong black doll preference and at the same time have low self-esteem. But Hraba and Grant's results (which do not include a direct measure of self-esteem) are consistent with more recent research showing that ethnic minorities, as well as other minorities (including women, homosexuals and physically disabled people) do *not* generally have lower self-esteem than other groups (Crocker and Major, 1989).

Methodological issues

The doll test represents a *forced-choice technique*. This has been criticized by many researchers (e.g. Aboud, 1988; Milner, 1981) for the following reasons:

- It fails to provide a measure of the *intensity* with which an attitude is held. When a child chooses a black doll, for example, it is unclear whether the preference is slight or very strong.

- It confounds *acceptance* of one group with *rejection* of another. If a child prefers the white doll, this does not necessarily mean that s/he is rejecting the black doll; the child may *marginally* prefer the white doll (see first point above).

- It provides no indication of the *salience* of race in children's everyday social categorization.

In relation to this last criticism, Bennett *et al.* (1991) studied 8- and 11-year-old British children, both white and from a number of ethnic minorities. When asked to indicate liking/disliking for photographs of children of various ethnic groups (a *non-forced-choice* technique), the older children showed a weaker ethnocentric bias and used a greater number of categorization strategies than the younger ones. The single most important finding was the generally greater significance given to *individual* rather than ethnic differences by the older children.

Owusu-Bempah and Howitt (2000) argue that a major flaw of doll studies is the *age* of the children typically involved (four- to eight-year-olds in Hraba and Grant's study). Such young children are not capable of experiencing racial self-hatred, because they do not adequately grasp the concept of race; what they appear to do is classify people in terms of their literal skin colour. For example, only people with very dark skin would be classified as black, while light-skinned black people and those from south Asia would be classified as white. Consistent with this, in the Clark and Clark (1947) study, 20 per cent of the light-skinned children, 73 per cent of the medium-skinned children and 81 per cent of the dark-skinned children said they were like the black doll. This suggests that a concept such as black self-hatred is unnecessary for explaining their doll choices. It is not until the age of eight to ten years that children begin to construe race in adult-related ways; before that, it has little or no *social* meaning for them.

Applications and implications

According to Schaffer (1996), it is primarily in adolescence that the issue of ethnic identity acquires importance and may become the focus of acute self-consciousness. The main challenge of ethnicity lies in the formation of an identity appropriate to one's group; this can be difficult when the group is a social minority, and for the mixed-race child (who has a 'foot in each camp') the strains will be even greater.

> *Mixed-race individuals have often been insultingly referred to as 'mulatto', 'half-caste', or 'half-breed', and throughout their history, mixed-race children in Britain*

have aroused strong feelings in the people around them. Attitudes have ranged from 'common-sense' doubt to extreme persecution, but they have never been indifferent. (Wilson, 1987, in Bradding, 1995)

Tizard and Phoenix (1993) studied a group of 58 individuals, aged 14–17 years, each with one white and one black (usually Caribbean) parent, all British-born, living in London. Less than half thought of themselves as 'black'; most of the rest described themselves as 'mixed' or 'brown', and a few as 'more white than black'. However, these were not fixed identities: many seemed to switch back and forth between identifications, often depending on the situation. Most resisted the pressure to be either black or white, because they felt that they were *both*. Neither did they want to alienate one parent by choosing the other, therefore settling for something in between.

However, compared with a group of adolescents with two black parents, twice as many wished they were another colour. Some described the hostility they sometimes met from both black and white people, which confused and upset them; this made the stress involved in their identity formation even greater than for the minority black group. Despite this, they seemed to 'emerge' during adolescence as well-balanced, emotionally healthy individuals: 60 per cent were classed as having a positive racial identity; 20 per cent expressed more anxieties about their status; and 20 per cent were considered to have a 'problematic' identity (unhappy and/or confused) (Tizard and Phoenix, 1993).

In terms of social identity theory (SIT: see Chapter 12), the extreme societal responses evoked by mixed-race individuals may be due to the fact that they 'strike at the very heart of a racist system. They threaten its existence by calling into question the categories upon which it is based' (Wilson, 1987, in Bradding, 1995).

Another group for whom racial identity is both especially salient and potentially difficult to establish are black children/adolescents growing up in a white family (*transracial placements*). Own-race adoption/fostering has been advocated as the ideal arrangement in both the USA and the UK (where the policy is fully embraced by the 1989 Children Act), but it continues to be debated, both among professionals and in the public domain (Owusu-Bempah and Howitt, 2000).

Gill and Jackson's (1983) study of mixed-race adolescent adoptees (mainly of Anglo-Asian origin) found that the vast majority had no particular problems at school; most were above average ability; and many were actually among the most able. Both this and the Tizard and Phoenix study showed that the children had no problems recognizing the physical differences between themselves and others (they accurately identified their skin tone), just as majority children do. Overall, they were satisfied with their physical appearance and racial identity.

However, in a review of both British and American research, Rushton and Minnis (1997) conclude that transracial placements continue to be difficult because the context is a racist one: ethnically matched placements will be in the best interests of both the child and the community in most cases.

Owusu-Bempah and Howitt (2000) claim that in order to help black children, professionals and all concerned must carefully distinguish between children's personal identity (and their 'private domain self-esteem') and their feelings about the black community in general (and their 'public domain self-esteem'). They argue that:

> Racism may negatively affect their perception or beliefs about their own race, but this does not automatically, nor necessarily, affect their sense of self-worth. Rather, it is their life chances which are restricted by racism … Institutional racism thwarts their efforts and aspirations, and very likely makes them feel embittered and angry. Our focus, therefore, must be on the racist system, rather than the individual psychology of the children.

But surely the problem needs to be tackled on *both* fronts. As Reicher (1999) says:

> The dangers of focusing on the systemic to the exclusion of the individual are every bit as serious as those of treating the individual to the exclusion of the systemic – and every bit as fatal to the fight against racism.

EXERCISES

1 Why was it important to control for race of interviewer?

2 What does 'benchmark' mean (when referring to the sample of white children), and why was it necessary to have a benchmark at all?

3 What does 'ethnocentric' mean?

4 Why should the preference for white (Clark and Clark) or black (Lincoln) dolls increase with age?

5 Regarding the section on Racial identification: Age, explain what is meant by 'Like the Clarks, Hraba and Grant found an inverse relationship between misidentification (items 5–8) and age'.

6 The two white and two black dolls were identical in all respects apart from colour. Why was this an important aspect of experimental control but which could potentially confound the results?

41 The measurement of psychological androgyny

Bem, S.L. (1974)

Journal of Consulting and Clinical Psychology, 42(2): 155–62

BACKGROUND AND CONTEXT

Prior to the 1970s, the prevalent view (both within psychology and in society at large) was that an individual could be *either* masculine *or* feminine. It was assumed that people who achieved a good fit with their sex type/sex role (i.e. a masculine male and a feminine female) were better adjusted psychologically/psychologically healthier than those who did not (Moghaddam, 1998).

According to Brown (1986), many widely used psychological tests (developed between the 1930s and the 1960s, such as the Terman and Miles scale) had this assumption built in to them. Because of the way they were designed and scored, it was impossible for an individual to register as both highly masculine *and* highly feminine: they were seen as *mutually exclusive,* in the sense that the nearer the masculine end of the scale you scored, the further away from the feminine end you were. So, it was impossible to find any *androgynous* people, that is, individuals who display *both* masculine *and* feminine characteristics ('andro' = male, 'gyne' = female). ('Mutually exclusive' usually implies 'either/or', one category or another).

When scores on these tests were factor-analysed (tested for inter-correlations between different parts of the test), the same temperamental factors kept emerging:

- independent, assertive, dominant and instrumental (masculine);

- interpersonal sensitivity, compassion and warmth (feminine).

These correspond closely with sociological (Parsons and Bales, 1955) and anthropological (Barry *et al.*, 1957) ideas of what might be universal masculinity and femininity, and until the early 1970s defined the dimensions most worth measuring (Brown, 1986).

By the early 1970s, several researchers had challenged this traditional view: the same individual could be high on both, low on both, or medium on both, since masculinity and femininity were *independent* dimensions. This shift in perspective owed a great deal to the feminist movement, including feminist psychologists such as Sandra Bem. To 'discover' androgyny, it was necessary to incorporate this new conception into a different sort of test, which would produce two logically independent scores: the Bem sex role inventory (BSRI) was the first and most influential of these tests (Moghaddam, 1998).

AIM AND NATURE

Bem's article describes the development of the BSRI. The implicit prediction is that it should be possible to design a questionnaire which reliably and validly measures a person's degree of masculinity, femininity or androgyny.

● METHOD/DESIGN

Item selection

As a preliminary to item selection for the masculinity and femininity scales, Bem compiled a list of about 200 personality traits that seemed to be both positive in value and either masculine or feminine in tone; this list served as the pool from which the masculine and feminine items were ultimately chosen.

An additional list of 200 traits was compiled which seemed to be neither masculine nor feminine in tone, half positive and half negative in value; from this, a social desirability scale was chosen.

The 'judges' (participants) were 40 Stanford University undergraduates who completed the questionnaire in 1972, and an additional 60 in 1973. In both samples, half were male and half were female.

Because the BSRI was designed to measure how much a person divorces him/herself from those characteristics that might be considered more 'appropriate' for the opposite sex, the final items were selected if they were judged to be more desirable in US society for one sex than the other. Specifically, judges used a seven-point scale, ranging from 1 (not at all desirable) to 7 (extremely desirable), to rate the (approximately) 400 personality characteristics. Each judge rated the desirability of all 400 traits either 'for a man' or 'for a woman'; no judge rated both.

A personality trait qualified as masculine if it was independently judged by both males and females in both samples to be significantly more desirable for a man than for a woman; similarly for feminine traits. Of those traits that met these criteria, 20 were chosen for the masculinity scale (including aggressive, competitive, and self-reliant) and 20 for the femininity scale (including compassionate, sensitive to the needs of others, and yielding). A neutral trait was one which:

● was independently judged by both males and females to be no more desirable for one sex than the other;

● did not produce significantly different desirability ratings by male and female judges.

Ten positive and ten negative traits met these criteria, and were chosen for the social desirability scale.

Once all the individual items had been selected, mean desirability scores were computed for the masculine, feminine and neutral items for each of the 100 judges. For both males and females, the mean desirability of the 40 masculine and feminine items was significantly higher for the 'appropriate' sex, while for the neutral items it was no higher for one sex than the other. These results, of course, were a direct consequence of the criteria used for selecting the items.

Scoring

The BSRI asks people to indicate on a seven-point scale how well each of the masculine, feminine and neutral traits describes themselves. The scale ranges from 1 (never or almost never true) to 7 (always or almost always true) and is labelled at each point. Each person receives a masculinity score, a femininity score and, most importantly, an androgyny score; in addition, a social desirability score can also be calculated.

The masculinity and femininity scores indicate how much a person endorses masculine and feminine traits as self-descriptive:

1   Masculinity = mean self-rating for all endorsed masculine items.

2   Femininity = mean self-rating for all endorsed feminine items.

    (Both can range from 1 to 7 and the two scores are independent.)

3   Androgyny = relative amounts of masculinity and femininity the person includes in his/her self-description; as such, it best characterizes the nature of his/her total sex role. One simple way of calculating androgyny is femininity score − masculinity score (the androgyny difference score).

    The greater the absolute value of the androgyny score, the more the person is sex-typed or sex-reversed: high positive scores indicate femininity and high negative scores indicate masculinity. A 'masculine' sex role thus represents not only the endorsement of masculine traits, but the simultaneous rejection of feminine ones; similarly with a 'feminine' sex role. By contrast, the closer the androgyny score is to zero, the more the person is androgynous (equal endorsement of both masculine and feminine traits).

4   The social desirability score indicates how much a person describes him/herself in a socially desirable way on neutral items; it can range from 1 to 7, with 1 indicating a strong tendency to describe oneself in a socially *undesirable* direction.

Psychometric analyses

The BSRI was given to 444 male and 279 female introductory psychology students at Stanford University, and to 117 male and 77 female paid volunteers. Their data represent the normative data for the BSRI and serve as the basis for all the analyses below.

- *Internal consistency*: all three scores were found to be highly reliable, in both samples.

- *Relationship between masculinity and femininity*: these are logically independent scores, and results for both samples showed them to be empirically independent as well.

- *Social desirability response set*: because the masculine and feminine items are all relatively desirable – even for the 'inappropriate' sex – it was important to verify that the androgyny score was not simply tapping a social desirability response set. Tests of correlation were conducted between the social desirability score and the masculinity, femininity and androgyny scores for the two samples separately. They were also calculated between the social desirability score and the absolute value of the androgyny score. As expected, both masculinity and femininity scores were correlated with social desirability. Near-zero correlations between androgyny and social desirability confirmed that the androgyny score was not measuring a general tendency to respond in a socially desirable direction. Rather, it was measuring a very specific tendency to describe oneself in terms of sex-typed standards of desirable behaviour for both men and women.

- *Test–retest reliability*: the BSRI was given for a second time to 28 males and 28 females from the Stanford normative sample, about four weeks after the first test. Participants were told that the researchers were interested in how their responses on the test might vary over time, and more explicitly instructed not to try to remember how they had responded originally. Correlations between first and second tests for all four scores showed them to be extremely reliable.

- *Correlations with other measures of masculinity–femininity*: during the second BSRI test, participants were also asked to complete (a) the masculinity–

femininity scales of the California psychological inventory and (b) the Guilford-Zimmerman temperament survey, both of which had been used quite often in previous research on sex roles. While the former was moderately correlated with the masculinity, femininity and androgyny scales of the BSRI, the latter was not correlated at all with any of the BSRI scales.

- *Norms*: in both samples, males scored significantly higher than females on the masculinity scale, and females scored significantly higher than males on the femininity scale. On the two measures of androgyny, males scored on the masculine side of zero, and females on the feminine side; this difference was significant for both measures in both samples.

○ CONCLUSIONS

The fact that the BSRI correlated only moderately with one of the other two measures of sex roles, and not at all with the second, indicated that the BSRI measures an aspect of sex roles that is not directly tapped by these other two scales.

Bem hoped that the development of the BSRI would encourage researchers in the areas of sex differences and sex roles to question the traditional assumption that it is the sex-typed individual who embodies mental health, and to begin focusing on the behavioural and societal consequences of more flexible sex-role self-concepts. Rigid sex-role differentiation has already outlived its usefulness; perhaps the androgynous person will come to define a more human standard of psychological health.

EVALUATION

Theoretical issues

As we noted in the **Background and context** above, the BSRI made it possible to measure androgyny by logically and empirically separating scores on masculinity and femininity: it comprises two *independent* scales. For a large sample (male and female), the mean score on masculinity is higher for males and the mean score for femininity is higher for females (the scales really do differentiate the sexes). Where all participants are either male or female, individual masculinity and femininity scales are *uncorrelated*, which means the two dimensions are empirically (i.e. factually) – and not just logically – independent (Brown, 1986).

The concept of androgyny implied that women were no longer expected or encouraged to restrict their behaviours to traditional gender-role-specific traits. Bem (1977), together with other feminist psychologists (e.g. Maracek, 1978), prescribed androgyny as a liberating force, leading women to fuller lives. However, while clearly an improvement over the traditional view that masculinity and femininity are opposites and mutually exclusive, the androgynous perspective still maintains that personality comprises feminine and masculine elements. Further, it implies that feminine and masculine elements are *equivalent*, when, in fact, masculine traits are more highly valued (Doyle and Paludi, 1991). As Hare-Mustin and Maracek (1988) argue:

> when the idea of counterparts implies symmetry and equivalence, it obscures
> differences in power and social value… Arguing for no differences between
> women and men, however, draws attention away from women's special needs and
> from differences in power and resources between women and men.

So, while the concept of androgyny is in some ways very radical, it retains aspects of the traditional view: masculinity and femininity are still implicitly seen as inherent characteristics of individuals, rather than socially determined ('constructed') categories. This focus on individuals (who may be androgynous regardless of biological sex or gender) detracts from considering social and political inequalities between gender groups (Paludi, 1992).

Bem herself seems to have taken some of these criticisms into account in her later work. (See **Applications and implications** below.) For example, in 1981 she wrote:

> the concept of androgyny is insufficiently radical from a feminist perspective
> because it continues to presuppose that there is a masculine and a feminine within
> us all, that is, that the concepts of masculine and feminine have an independent
> and palpable reality rather than being themselves cognitive constructs derived from
> gender-based schematic processing. A focus on the concept of androgyny thus fails
> to prompt serious examination of the extent to which gender organizes both our
> perceptions and our social world.

Eichler (1980, in Wetherell, 1997) sees androgyny as a meaningless ideal. If our society were actually androgynous, the concept itself would not exist: sex (apart from its strictly biological sense) would be considered an irrelevant variable and defunct as a term of reference for social organization. It is illogical to aim at achieving androgyny while simultaneously regarding it as the *combination* of highly desirable feminine and masculine qualities.

While conceding this point, Bem's *gender schema theory* (see **Applications and implications** below) implies that gender conventions persist because they are *internalized* by individuals. But according to Wetherell (1997), Bem's type of social psychology has effectively *decontextualized* sex: gender identity in the BSRI is viewed in the abstract, quite independent of the situations to which it might relate. In effect, a set of 'imaginary identities' is produced: the stereotypes or social consensus reflected by a small group of students become, in the BSRI, *reified* into a universal, normative standard.

> *Bem's attempt to discover gender as a literal state rather than to treat it as a metaphorical device could thus serve to bolster up the very ideological practice she hoped to defuse [through the concept of androgyny]. (Wetherell, 1997)*

In other words, the BSRI (as with other psychometric tests, whether of personality or intelligence) claims to show what people are 'like'. The human 'subject' is unitary, coherent, consistent across situations, an 'individual' separated from, but influenced by, the rest of society. The BSRI encourages the view that androgyny, femininity and masculinity are built-in traits which one either has or does not have. But according to Wetherell, 'This impression … is an illusion … A snapshot of a constrained either/or type of response at one moment in time is generalized to become a permanent psychological feature'.

Methodological issues

The BSRI is the most widely used measure of sex-role stereotyping in adults (Hargreaves, 1986), and probably the most popular modern social-psychological method for measuring gender identity (Wetherell, 1997). However, it is not the only test of androgyny. Quite independently of Bem, Spence *et al.* (1975) devised the Personal Attributes Questionnaire (PAQ), which consists of instrumental (masculine) and expressive (feminine) trait terms (largely derived from the stereotypes described by Broverman *et al.*, 1972), and produces two essentially independent scores.

However, the PAQ did not assess androgyny in the same way as the BSRI, and this underlined a major problem with the BSRI, which relates to the very concept of androgyny. By defining androgyny as the difference between an individual's masculinity and femininity scores, Bem (unwittingly, of course) allowed for the *same* androgyny score to be obtained in two very *different* ways: by an individual who scores either *high* on both scales or *low* on both. But surely two such individuals are likely to be very different kinds of people; in which case, what do their androgyny scores mean? By contrast, PAQ allowed for four categories of persons:

1   the highly sex-typed male: *high* masculinity, *low* femininity;

2   the highly sex-typed female: *low* masculinity, *high* femininity;

3   the androgynous person: *high* masculinity, *high* femininity;

4   the 'undifferentiated' person: *low* masculinity, *low* femininity.

The crucial difference is that Bem did not distinguish between (3) and (4): she confounded them. Consequently, she compared her original (1974) results with those of Spence *et al.* and concluded that the four categories (2 x 2) approach was superior: androgyny was now defined as only *high in both* masculinity and femininity (not low in both as well). Her revised (and shortened) version of the BSRI (1977) is considered to be equivalent to the PAQ (Lubinski *et al.*, 1983).

Hargreaves (1986) proposes that androgyny is most economically assessed as the *product* of an individual's masculinity and femininity scores (masculinity x femininity): they are conceptually distinct but *interacting* variables.

Best and Thomas (2004) describe an attempt to develop a sex-role inventory with Costa Rican university students. Using Spanish translations of 200 items, including the PAQ and BSRI (1974), the researchers found that only two of the 55 PAQ items and half of the 60 BSRI items discriminated between men and women. So, many trait terms representing masculinity–femininity in the USA do not do so in Costa Rica. Similar failures have occurred with BSRI items in southern India, Malaysia and Mexico. Clearly, evaluating masculinity–femininity across cultures requires careful attention to culture-specific definitions of the concepts (Best and Thomas, 2004).

Subsequent research

There are two main hypotheses derived from the BSRI: first, that scores on the BSRI predict certain kinds of behaviour preference; and second, that androgyny is a good indicator of psychological well-being/mental health.

1   Bem's research strategy is to assess sex-typing using the BSRI, then to relate this to behaviour in 'real-life' situations. For example, Bem and Lenney (1976) asked participants to indicate which of a series of paired activities they would prefer to perform, for payment, while being photographed: 20 activities were stereotypically masculine (e.g. nailing two boards together), 20 were stereotypically feminine (e.g. ironing cloth napkins) and 20 were neutral (e.g. play with a yo-yo). Sex-typed individuals expressed a clear preference for sex-appropriate activities, even though such choices paid less than cross-sex-typed activities.

2   Bem (1975) found that androgynous individuals show sex-role adaptability across situations: they will behave as the situation requires, even though this means behaving in a sex-inappropriate way. Lubinski *et al.* (1981) found that androgynous people report feeling greater emotional well-being, and Spence *et al.* (1975) found that they have higher self-esteem. However, a review by Taylor and Hall (1982) suggested that masculinity – in both males and females – may be

a better predictor than certain measures of androgyny. Psychological well-being (measured by, for example, self-esteem, adjustment, and absence of anxiety, depression and psychosomatic symptoms) is generally more strongly related to masculinity than femininity on the BSRI, and seems not to distinguish reliably between sex-typed and androgynous individuals (Taylor, 1986).

Spender (1980) called the general tendency for 'masculine' attributes and occupations to be valued, while 'feminine' ones are derogated or downgraded, the 'plus male, minus female' phenomenon. According to Hefner *et al.* (1975, in Taylor, 1986), 'both men and women are trapped in the prisons of gender ... but the situation is far from symmetrical; men are the oppressors and women the oppressed'.

So, what do the PAQ and BSRI really measure? According to Spence (1983), they primarily measure *instrumentality* and *expressiveness* and can no longer legitimately be thought of as assessing the all-embracing 'masculinity' and 'femininity'. Indeed, the latter was dropped from Bem's shorter BSRI (1977). It follows that androgyny is also inappropriate.

Applications and implications

During the 1980s, Bem (e.g. 1984) reformulated her ideas as *gender schema theory* (GST). Schemas are the internal (mental) conceptual frameworks we build up, through past experience, which impose some order on the world; they make an otherwise overwhelming range of apparently diverse events and objects predictable. In our everyday lives, we perceive the world *through* these schemas, so that the world as we know it is composed of the categories represented by our schemas (Edley and Wetherell, 1995).

The male/female distinction is one of the most important classification systems in human social life (Bem, 1987). The social world that children grow up in is thoroughly gendered and gender differentiation is everywhere imposed from 'outside' (toys, clothes, hairstyles, socialization practices, the media, and so on). Consequently, children soon learn to interpret their experiences through this same set of categories, including, importantly, their sense of self. However, while some children see themselves as entirely defined by a particular gender category (so that self and gender are almost synonymous), others can imagine at least some degree of difference between self and gender. Clearly, the former are strongly sex-typed compared with the latter (as measured by the BSRI).

For Bem, sex-typing essentially involves spontaneously thinking of things in sex-typed terms, whereas androgyny is a disposition to process information in accordance with relevant non-sex principles. In deciding whether a particular item on the BSRI is self-descriptive or not, the sex-typed person does not reflect on individual behaviour, but quickly 'looks up' the trait in his/her gender schemas, and responds accordingly. The essential difference between these two kinds of people is one of *cognitive style*. Even if androgynous *behaviour* cannot predict mental health in a sex-typed culture, Bem still believes that information-processing freed of the tyranny of sex-typing (i.e. androgyny) is desirable (Brown, 1986).

Hyde and Phillips (1979) gave the BSRI to 13- to 85-year-olds, and Sinnott (1982) tested a sample of 60- to 90-year-olds (comparing them with Bem's 1974 sample). Both studies found some evidence of reduced sex-typing in older men, but in older women it was stronger. Sinnott also found that androgyny was associated with better physical and mental health, compared with highly sex-typed females and undifferentiated men and women.

Finally, what would the consequences be of Bem's goal of an androgynous society? As she herself says (1979), 'When androgyny becomes a reality, the *concept* of androgyny will have been transcended'. Archer and Lloyd (1985) seriously doubt that there will ever be an androgynous society: some form of group differentiation seems essential to human social organization. We have seen how GST puts gender identity at the centre of mental life, and although the *content* of gender roles will continue to change, gender *categories* will continue to exist in some form (Archer and Lloyd, 1985).

One such content change relates to women's occupational roles, especially in professional occupations. According to Nicolson (2000):

> *The dilemma for many professional women is how to negotiate and give meaning to their sense of femininity and gender identity in the world of power and intellect, when that world has defined them as outside the main professional arena.*

Being child-bearers, as well as child carers, women who aspire to traditionally male occupational status run the risk of either being seen as 'unfeminine' (they have to 'toughen up' to succeed in male strongholds: Nicolson, 2000) or having to make terribly difficult choices between family and career which men do not have to face – except perhaps the few truly androgynous ones!

EXERCISES

1   Why was it important to have an equal number of male and female judges when deciding on items for the BSRI?

2   What is meant by the 'internal consistency' of a psychological test, and what is it a measure of?

3   In the assessment of test–retest reliability, why was it important that participants did not remember their answers on the original test?

4   A way of assessing the validity of the BSRI scores is to see if they are correlated with scores on other tests (such as the Guilford-Zimmerman temperament survey.

    (a) What kind of validity is this?

    (b) Name the other main kinds.

5   Can you name a famous test of personality which has a social desirability scale built in to it?

6   Explain why it is important to have a set of normative data for any psychological test.

ANSWERS TO EXERCISES

CHAPTER 2: MCGINNIES (1949)

1 McGinnies gives the following reasons: to get the participant used to the apparatus and to allow the level of resistance (i.e. the GSR) to stabilize. Perhaps more importantly, by allowing the level of resistance to stabilize, a baseline could be established against which to compare changes in response to the critical and neutral words.

2 There may have been gender differences in response to the critical words. So, if, for example, women respond more slowly to emotionally charged words (especially if these are sex-related) and gender was not controlled for, and if there had been more females, gender could have represented a confounding variable.

3 This is exactly what you would expect according to the perceptual defence hypothesis: words which are negatively charged emotionally are more likely to be distorted so that we do not have to consciously identify them. But this finding is also consistent with Bruner's claim that increased GSR could be caused by the greater effort involved in recognizing words that are unfamiliar (i.e. critical words), compared with the more familiar (neutral) words.

4 (a) The order was probably determined randomly, but the words were presented in this same random order for all participants.

(b) Order effects are always a potential problem in a repeated measures design. Counterbalancing is the alternative way of trying to reduce the effects of practice, fatigue, and so on.

5 Length (they were, in fact, all five-letter words), and familiarity (see **Methodological issues**).

6 This is something that you could debate in a class or seminar.

CHAPTER 3: GARDNER AND GARDNER (1969)

1 ● Language implies communication, but not vice versa.
● While many non-human species are, like human beings, able to communicate, many critics of studies like those of the Gardners argue that *language* is unique (it is a human *species-specific* behaviour: see text).
● Non-human communication systems are quite inflexible and, although usually well adapted to a particular habitat, can become inaccurate when the environment changes; by contrast, human language can be modified by experience and is adaptable to novel situations.
● Communication involves a two-way process, whereby a message (or signal) is conveyed from a sender to one or more recipients (receivers) – its reception is denoted by a change in the recipient – but the message/signal does not have to be deliberate, as in non-verbal/bodily communication (in both humans and non-humans).
● Language is an arbitrary system of symbols, 'which taken together make it possible for a creature with very limited powers of discrimination and a limited memory to transmit and understand an infinite variety of messages and to do this in spite of noise and distraction' (Brown, 1965).

2 The tendency to attribute human characteristics (motives, feelings, abilities, etc.) to non-human animals.

3

Washoe	Children
1. She was relatively old when training began (8–14 months).	1. They are exposed to language from birth.
2. She was raised in an unnatural environment.	2. They are (usually) raised in natural environments.
3. She was deliberately taught to sign, which chimps do not do spontaneously (i.e. language *training*).	3. They do not (usually) have to be deliberately taught language: it is spontaneous (i.e. language *acquisition*).
4. Only signs were taught (*not* grammar). The debate concerns whether chimps sign 'grammatically'.	4. *Both* words that denote objects/actions, etc., *and* purely grammatical terms are acquired spontaneously (although early *telegraphic speech* involves only the latter; Brown, 1965).

4 Deaf children learning ASL (Carroll, 1986).

5 Direct comparisons between studies can only be made if the same (or very similar) methods are used. For example, it is much easier to use signs spontaneously than, say, plastic symbols; so when evaluating a study's data regarding spontaneity (compared with children's spontaneous speech), this must be taken into account.

6 To some extent, this is a matter of opinion; I'll let you think about this one.

7 It could be argued that, in some ways, rearing chimps 'as children' and training them to use language (usually in isolation from other chimps) is as unacceptable as raising them in laboratories. Is it 'mental or emotional cruelty' for the sake of 'science'? The *Great Ape Project* is trying to extend the 'community of equals' beyond human beings to all the great apes: chimpanzees (including bonobos), gorillas and orang-utans. This refers to the moral community within which we accept certain basic moral principles and rights as governing our relationships with each other, and which are enforceable at law. According to the 'Declaration of Great Apes', it is ethically indefensible to deny them (a) the right to life; (b) protection of individual liberty; (c) prohibition of torture.

As with intellectually disabled people, the inability of the great apes to stand up and defend their own rights is no barrier to our recognition of those rights. According to Singer (1993), 'It is time to put the slavery of the apes behind us. The great apes need more than humane treatment. They need equality'.

CHAPTER 4: DEREGOWSKI (1972)

1 (a) The two-pronged trident is a *paradoxical figure* (or *impossible object*).
  (b) 3-D perceivers tried to interpret the trident in 3-D terms, but, by definition, this cannot be done, so the confused participants spent longer looking at it than at the control trident (which does not cause any confusion). The 2-D perceivers were not confused by the two-pronged trident, which they were able to remember as easily as the control trident.

2 ● *Binocular (retinal) disparity*: because our eyes are (approximately) 6cm apart, they each receive slightly different retinal images, and the superimposition of these two images is *stereoscopic vision*. Convergence is related to this.

● *Motion parallax*: this is the major *dynamic* depth cue and refers to the speed of apparent movement of objects nearer or further away from us. Generally, objects further away seem to move more slowly than nearer ones.

3 ● *Relative brightness*: brighter objects normally appear to be nearer.

- *Aerial perspective*: objects at a great distance appear to have a different colour (e.g. the hazy, bluish tint of distant mountains).
- *Height in the horizontal plane*: when looking across a flat expanse (e.g. across the sea), objects that are more distant seem 'higher' (closer to the horizon) than nearer objects, which seem 'lower' and closer to the ground.
- *Light and shadow*: 3-D objects produce variations in light and shade (e.g. we normally assume that light comes from above).
- *Accommodation*: the change in the shape of the lens of the eye depending on the distance of the object (it flattens for distant objects and thickens for closer ones.
- *Convergence*: the simultaneous orienting of both eyes towards the same object. When looking at a distant object (25 feet or more), the line of vision of our two eyes is parallel, but the closer the object, the more our eyes turn inwards, towards each other.

4   *Monocular* cues are those which can be detected with only one eye and so (a) are not primarily dependent on biological processes (except accommodation), and (b) are mainly *pictorial* (i.e. they are features of the visual field itself). (*Binocular* cues – subject to retinal disparity and convergence – are *non-pictorial*.)

5   If the participant took note of depth cues and made the 'correct' interpretation of the relationship between the components of the picture when asked 'What is the man doing?' and 'What is closer to the man?', then s/he was judged to be a 3-D perceiver.

6   (a)   Participants were asked to build a model of a drawing of two squares. Most 3-D perceivers (on Hudson's test) built a 3-D model, while most 2-D perceivers built a flat (2-D) model.
    (b)   Concurrent validity.

7   There will be a significant positive correlation between participants' response to the Hudson pictures (2-D or 3-D perception) and the kind of model they build of a drawing of two squares (flat or 3-D).

CHAPTER 5: CRAIK AND LOCKHART (1972)

1   An *algorithm* is a procedure which guarantees a solution to a given problem by systematically testing every alternative in turn until the correct response is produced and verified (e.g. a flow diagram or decision chart). By contrast, *heuristics* do not guarantee a solution, but they drastically reduce the amount of 'work' that must be done by selecting the most likely options from a possible set.

2   The *computer analogy* is one of cognitive psychology's central ideas, according to which people are seen as *information processors*. Cognitive psychology has been heavily influenced by computer science, with human cognitive processes being compared to the operation of computer programs. Cognitive psychology now forms part of *cognitive science*, which emerged in the late 1970s.

3   If you are asked to name the *colour of the ink* in which a word is written, there is an interference effect produced if the word is the name of a *different* colour (e.g. 'blue' written in red ink). The Stroop effect is also demonstrated if you are asked to state *the number of digits* in an array (e.g. '4444' is easier than '444').

4   Trace decay; interference.

5   Chunking is a way of reducing a large amount of unrelated information to a smaller number of meaningful items (e.g. letters into words/words into sentences/numbers into historical dates).

6   (a)   Free recall.
    (b)   Recognition.

7   In the Hyde and Jenkins (1973) experiment, five orienting tasks were used:
    - rating words for pleasantness (semantic/deep processing);
    - estimating the frequency with which words are used in English (semantic/deep);
    - detecting the number of 'e's and 'g's in the words (non-semantic/shallow);
    - deciding the part of speech appropriate to each word (non-semantic/shallow);
    - deciding whether or not the word fits various sentence frames (non-semantic/shallow).

8   (a)   *Incidental learning* takes place when participants are not expecting to be tested on the learned material: they are *not trying* to remember, because they are not expecting to be given a memory test (but it is retained despite this). *Intentional learning* takes place when the participants *are* trying to learn.

(b) In LOP experiments, it is the *orienting task* which is being manipulated, and nothing else is meant to influence retention (such as deliberate attempts to remember).

CHAPTER 6: LOFTUS AND PALMER (1974)

1   For more open questions, the task is to tell the interviewer what the witness *can* remember. For more specific, closed questions, the task changes to one of providing the interviewer with what s/he *wants* the witness to remember. One result of this is that witnesses tend to provide less accurate answers, because they fill memory gaps with distorted or inaccurate material (i.e. they may become *suggestible* to the demands of the interviewer). (See **Theoretical issues** and **Subsequent research** in Chapter 6.)

2   (a) Presumably, this was done to ensure that *order effects* did not influence the speed estimate. Participants may have become more accurate in their estimation of speed over the course of the seven films (*practice effect*), or they may have become mentally tired (*fatigue*). These possible effects need to be controlled for, since they may contaminate the effect of the independent variable.

(b) The order of films for each group was, presumably, *randomly* determined.

(c) There was *no* control condition as such. All five groups were given a different form of the critical question (a different verb describing how the cars 'touched'), which was the independent variable. The mean speed estimates (the dependent variable) were compared *with each other*, rather than with a baseline (control) condition. This is perfectly legitimate; not all experiments have a (true) control condition, in the sense of a condition in which there is no manipulation of the IV. Can you think of what a control condition might have been?

3   Again, this was done to prevent *order effects* from contaminating the results. The critical 'broken glass' question needed to be no more or less 'conspicuous' than any of the non-critical questions, otherwise the 'yes' or 'no' response may have reflected the order of the questions as much as the influence of the verb used to describe the kind of contact between the cars. By randomly determining where the broken glass question appeared in the list, its position was prevented from becoming a confounding variable.

4   This is an easier question to ask than to answer. The meaning of words consists of both *connotation* (they evoke associations and feelings) and *denotation* (they *refer* to things). The 'touch'-related verbs used in the critical question evoke different associations and feelings so that, for example, 'contacted' connotes something quite gentle and non-violent compared with, say, 'smashed'. We are likely to hear reports of a 'car smash', but not a 'car contact', because it is only serious accidents that are reported in the first place. This demonstrates how we *learn* the connotations of words, which are often *implied* rather than made explicit. What words *denote* is more likely to be explicit than implicit, which is why it is easier to *define* some words than others.

5   In the *warnings technique*, participants are given false, misleading information, then warned that it is false and should be disregarded. This is essentially what happens when jurors hear the evidence of a witness who is later discredited, and are then instructed by the judge to disregard the testimony. In the *second-guess technique*, participants whose initial response is influenced by the misleading information are given a second opportunity to report what they saw. Both techniques are designed to challenge the substitution hypothesis, by showing that the original memory *can* be recovered (the coexistence hypothesis). However, the evidence for the latter is weak and the former is more likely to be correct (Cohen, 1993).

6   According to Pezdek and Roe (1996), the false memory was implanted by an older sibling, who, in principle, could have been there at the time, providing a plausible basis for Chris to assume Jim might remember, even if Chris did not at first. Also, getting lost in a shopping mall is not a remarkable event, and most children would probably have a pre-existing schema for a shopping mall, which could then be activated by the suggestion of a particular instance of getting lost. By contrast, 'It is hardly likely that most children would have a pre-existing schema for sexual abuse' (Pezdek and Roe, 1996). However, Freud made us aware of the possible universal existence of childhood fantasies of incest. Moreover, the incest *barrier* (taboo) is surely a very deep, pre-existing schema: 'It could also be argued that in some therapeutic, "recovery movement", and survivorship settings which are focused on abuse, the incoming participants do develop "pre-existing schemata of abuse prior to remembering abuse"' (Mollon, 1998; see Chapter 22).

CHAPTER 7: BARON-COHEN *ET AL.* (1997)

1   (a)   Smith *et al.* (1998) discuss a general methodological problem that arises whenever people with learning difficulties are tested, namely finding an appropriate *control group*. In the case of autistic children, it is usual to compare them with other children who have the same mental age (MA), but who are not autistic. However, if we compared a group of autistic children (MA 6) with a group of normal children (also with an MA of 6), while the latter's chronological age (CA) would be about 6, the former's might be, say, 12, representing a big difference in their experience. To overcome this, some researchers (as in the Baron-Cohen *et al.* study) use children with *other* learning difficulties, such as Down's syndrome, as a control group (in addition to normal children).

    (b)   Others (e.g. Leslie and Frith, 1988) used children with specific language impairments: since autism is often most conspicuous as a language and communication disorder, such children are a better match than children with Down's syndrome (Mitchell, 1997).

2   To the extent that the adults were *selected* because they had either high-functioning autism or Asperger's syndrome, or were normal or had Tourette's syndrome, the design was *independent groups/samples*. (They could not be randomly allocated to different conditions, and so the method was a *quasi-experiment*.) In that each participant was tested on the eyes task, the strange stories task and the control tasks, the design was (also) *repeated measures*. So, this was a 'mixed design'. (See Chapter 1.)

3   According to Baron-Cohen *et al.*, there are several similarities between the two syndromes:
   ● both groups had intelligence in the normal range;
   ● they had all suffered from a developmental disorder since childhood;
   ● these disorders all cause disruptions to both normal schooling and peer relationships;
   ● these disorders are also thought to involve frontal lobe abnormalities;
   ● both are thought to involve a substantial genetic component;
   ● they both affect males more than females.
   While there are also important differences between them, the similarities serve to control for an organic, childhood-onset psychiatric disorder.

4   A 'ceiling effect' refers to a task which is relatively easy, so that most people obtain a high score (they cannot do much better). The opposite is the 'floor effect', which is relatively difficult, such that most people will perform poorly (they will obtain a low score).

5   (a)   Ekman *et al.* (1972)/Ekman and Friesen (1975) identified six primary emotions: surprise, fear, disgust, anger, happiness and sadness.

    (b)   Some are basic in Ekman's sense (e.g. 1, 3, 7, 8, 9, 14, 16, 22), while others are more 'complex' (such as 5, 11, 12, 13, 18, 23, 25).

6   The two tasks are *positively correlated*.

7   Sometimes 'translated' as 'informal' or 'everyday' psychology, that is, the layperson's understanding of themselves and other people.

8   ● As Bryant (1998) observes (see **Theoretical issues**), Piaget's concept of egocentrism represents a domain-*general* approach, while ToM is domain-*specific*. For Piaget, the general lack of reversibility in children below seven years accounts for their egocentrism, which is also often discussed in terms of *centration* (or a *failure* to de-centre: the child can only focus on one aspect of an object or situation at a time, in this case, its own particular viewpoint, to the exclusion of other possible viewpoints). By contrast, underlying ToM is an independent mental module (ToMM), which is *specialized* for representing *mental* representations (Leslie 1987, 1994; Leslie and Roth, 1993).

   ● While ToM deficiency implies egocentrism, egocentrism does *not* imply ToM deficiency. It is 'normal' for children under the age of seven to be egocentric, but autistic children (if, indeed, their underlying cognitive deficiency is lack of ToM) will *remain* 'egocentric'.

   ● The critical age in normal children for the appearance of ToM is four years (see **Theoretical issues**), while, according to Piaget, egocentrism continues up to the age of seven. This alone suggests that they are not the same thing.

   ● Baron-Cohen *et al.* distinguish between *conceptual* and *perceptual* perspective taking. The former is what is being tested by their false belief task, while the latter is tested by the three mountains task (Piaget and

Inhelder, 1956). The three mountains task (best known as a test of *egocentrism*) is a test of perceptual perspective taking (visuo-spatial skills/seeing things from another's perspective), while the false belief task tests conceptual perspective taking (attributing beliefs to others, which may sometimes differ from our own). Evidence that autistic children succeed on perceptual but not on conceptual perspective-taking tasks indicates very clearly that they are testing quite different skills/abilities.

CHAPTER 8: TREFFERT AND CHRISTENSEN (2005)

1 • KP has been studied over an extensive period of time. He was first given psychological tests (including IQ tests) and MRI scans in 1988 (at the age of 37) and has been studied (and continues to be) since that time (in 2007 he was 56). The same researchers have been involved, so there has been continuity.

• The use of MRI scans makes the overall data more objective (and allows hypotheses to be formulated as to the relationship between brain abnormalities and savant skills). Although PK's skills are right-sided, his brain abnormalities are not the usual left-sided ones commonly found in savants. This makes PK's case of special interest within this particular research area.

• Through his influence on the writing of the screenplay for *Rain Man* (and through TV documentaries about him and his public speaking), KP has helped to make the public aware of autism (and, to a lesser extent, savant syndrome).

2 (a) Too many cooks spoil the broth. You can take a horse to water, but you cannot make it drink.

  (b) This is likely to involve a *literal* interpretation, such as, 'If there are too many people in the kitchen at the same time, they will get in each other's way and spoil the food.' 'Horses are very stubborn animals and if they are not thirsty they will not drink.'

  (c) Children under 11 years (in Piaget's pre-operational/concrete operational stages: see Chapter 25) will be unable to appreciate the *metaphorical* meaning of proverbs, and instead will interpret them literally.

3 This is one for class discussion or debate; there are no rights or wrongs here and the ethical issues are quite subtle. One issue relates to the case study as a method – most arise in the context of someone needing professional help (from a psychiatrist, etc.). But KP is being studied because his story is of great scientific and human *interest*.

CHAPTER 9: FESTINGER AND CARLSMITH (1959)

1 Independent groups (or independent samples).

2 The independent variable was the offer of either a $1 or $20 reward for telling another participant that the tasks were really interesting and enjoyable. The dependent variable was how participants rated the tasks when the experiment was supposedly over (their 'real' opinion of the tasks).

3 (a) The sample was biased, as it consisted of male psychology students, who have to spend a certain number of hours as participants in experiments as a course requirement. So it was *gender-biased* as well as *age-biased* (as well as all the other respects in which students as a group are unrepresentative of 'people in general').

  (b) Given the all-male sample, might there have been an interaction effect between (i) the size of the reward and (ii) the gender of the stooge? Perhaps lying to a female is seen (or was in 1957) as more acceptable (by males) than lying to another male: but much less so for $1 than for $20. Holding gender constant, would lying to an *attractive* female be more dissonant than lying to an unattractive one, and how would this interact with size of reward?

4 It removes *experimenter bias*, so that the interviewer could not be influenced by knowledge of how the participant was *expected* to rate the task. Since the participant was also ignorant as to the true purpose of the experiment, this represents a *double-blind technique*.

5 When participants believed the pill would relax them, the dissonance arising from the high-choice condition was still sufficient to produce attitude change (and it was contrary to what they expected to feel, so the 'discomfort/tension' must be due to the counter-attitudinal behaviour). When given no information, the situation was no different from Festinger and Carlsmith's $1 condition. But when told the pill would make

them feel tense, the tension was attributed to the pill rather than the counter-attitudinal behaviour – and so the question of high-/low-choice became irrelevant.

6 One possibility is that someone other than the experimenter asks the participant to 'tell the lie'; another is that the 'favour' is asked in a non-face-to-face way (e.g. in writing). You may be able to think of some other possibilities.

7 The obvious one is *deception*, probably the most common problem involved in experiments generally (see Chapter 10). But unlike most experiments, not only were Festinger and Carlsmith's participants deceived about the true purpose of the experiment, but they were being 'asked' to deceive another supposed participant about the tasks. As we have seen, there were powerful situational pressures that made it difficult for participants to refuse, so this represents a third 'layer' of ethical shortcomings.

CHAPTER 10: MILGRAM (1963)

1 Milgram identifies nine factors that could help explain the unexpectedly high obedience rate:
- The experiment took place at Yale University, one of the most prestigious in the USA (equivalent to Oxford/Cambridge). It would have been reasonable to see the staff as competent and reputable.
- The experiment was (supposedly) pursuing a worthy aim, namely to advance our knowledge of the role of punishment in learning and memory.
- Mr Wallace volunteered for the experiment; the fact that he happened to be allocated to the learner role does not change his obligation to the experimenter.
- They both had an equal chance of being allocated to the learner role, so Mr Wallace cannot complain.
- Like Mr Wallace, he answered the advertisement of his own free will and has the same obligation to the experimenter as Mr Wallace.
- This sense of obligation may have been strengthened by receiving payment. Although participants were paid on arrival, they were told it was just for attending – regardless of what happened from then on, 'the money is yours'.
- It is not clear just what psychologists can reasonably require participants to do before overstepping the mark; this is a novel situation for most participants.
- Participants are assured that the shocks are 'painful but not dangerous'.
- The learner continues to provide answers right up to 300 volts, suggesting that he is still willing to 'play the game'.

2 They were volunteers, answering advertisements in a local newspaper and by direct mail. So, they were a *self-selecting (volunteer) sample*. Although by definition not a random sample, can they be considered *representative*? Although they were male-only, Milgram claims that they represented a wide range of occupations (postal clerks, high-school teachers, salesmen, engineers and labourers); they also had a wide range of educational experience. However, what was different about these volunteers, compared with others who read the same newspaper and received the same direct mail, but did *not* volunteer? According to Rosenthal and Rosnow (1966), and others, people who volunteer for experiments are considerably less authoritarian than those who do not.

3 (a) Conformity = pressure exerted by one's peers (equals), while obedience = complying with the demands made by an authority figure (someone with greater power/higher status). Another difference is that in conformity group pressure is *implicit* (no overt demands are made by the group), whereas in obedience the authority figure *orders* the person to behave in a particular way (so the influence is overt and explicit).

(b) Conformity and obedience are both forms of *social influence*, in which there is an 'abdication of individual initiative in the face of some external social pressure' (Milgram, 1992): people deny the responsibility for their own behaviour which they usually accept.

CHAPTER 11: PILIAVIN *ET AL.* (1969)

1 (a) Costs for helping the drunk are higher (e.g. greater disgust, risk of violence, being vomited on, etc.) and costs for not helping are lower (less self-blame and censure because he is partly responsible for his plight).

(b) Costs for women of helping are higher (mainly effort) and costs of not helping are lower (less censure from others; it is not their role).

(c) Costs of not helping different-race victim are lower (generally less censure from others) and costs of helping different-race drunk are higher (greater fear of drunks and opposite race).

(d) Costs of not helping cane victim are high (more self-blame because of possible seriousness of problem), while costs of helping are generally low. *Seeing* the victim makes it impossible to justify non-intervention by hoping/believing that someone else has already intervened. As Piliavin *et al.* suggest, it is possible that the second/third/subsequent helpers were primarily going to the aid of the first helper rather than that of the victim.

(e) (i) A late model will elicit less helping because other people will already have reduced their arousal in some other way; (ii) unless arousal is reduced by other means, people will leave more over time because arousal is still increasing; (iii) discussing the incident helps to reduce self-blame by finding justifications for not helping.

2

	Advantages	Disadvantages
Field experiments	1. Results can be generalized much more easily (high *ecological validity*). 2. Participants not usually aware of participating, so *demand characteristics* not a problem.	1. Much more difficult to control extraneous variables. 2. Much more difficult to replicate. 3. More time-consuming and expensive.
Laboratory experiments	1. Much greater control over extraneous variables. 2. Much easier to replicate. 3. Less time-consuming and expensive.	1. Problems in generalizing to real-life situations, because of artificiality (low *ecological validity*). 2. Participants more likely to be influenced by *demand characteristics*.

3 In its most general sense, a *heuristic* is a strategy for solving problems which helps to select actions most likely to lead to a solution, but which (unlike an *algorithm*) cannot guarantee one. In the context of 'a model of response to emergency situations', it refers to a set of theoretical assumptions about the kinds of variables likely to determine the probability of a bystander going to the assistance of a victim.

4 On each trial, a team of four student confederates boarded the train. The females sat outside the critical area and recorded data as unobtrusively as possible during the journey. Like the male model and victim, the females were just 'other passengers' as far as the real passengers were concerned.

5 (a) *Prosocial behaviour* is a label for a wide variety of actions 'defined by society as generally beneficial to other people and to the ongoing political system' (Piliavin *et al.*, 1981).

(b) *Helping* behaviour refers to 'an action that has the consequences of providing some benefit or improving the well-being of another person' (Schroeder *et al.*, 1995).

(b) *Altruism* is 'behaviour intended to help another without regard for benefit to oneself' (Moghaddam, 1998).

CHAPTER 12: TAJFEL (1970)

1 *Prejudice* is an attitude; *discrimination* is a form of behaviour. Prejudiced attitudes are not a very reliable predictor of discriminatory behaviour, largely because the latter is more directly a function of the objective social situation than of individual attitudes.

2 (a) How obvious it is how one can benefit a member of the in-group relative to an out-group member.

(b) *Fairness/even-handedness*: awarding an equal number of points to any two individuals, regardless of the groups they belong to; *maximum joint profit* (*MJP*)/*maximum generosity* (*MG*): largest possible joint award to both people, but favouring the in-group; *maximum in-group profit* (*MIP*): largest possible award to an in-group member; *maximum difference* (*MD*): largest possible difference in gain between in-group and out-group member, favouring the former.

(c) Fairness: 7/8, 8/7 (A), 17/17 (B); MJP: 14/1 (A), 29/11 (B); MIP: 14/1 (A), 29/11 (B); MD: 14/11 (A), 29/11 (B).

3 *Intra*group choices involve two members of the *same* group (*intra* = 'within'), either two members of the in-group or two members of the out-group. *Inter*group choices involve one member of the in-group and one member of the out-group (*inter* = 'between'). Generally, when making intragroup choices, fairness prevailed. When choosing between two in-group members, participants tended to favour the largest total sums (MJP); when choosing between two out-group members, they tended to prefer smaller total sums (thereby indirectly conferring a relative advantage on the in-group). But when making intergroup choices, significantly more points were awarded to in-group members.

4 (a) This was done to control the variables of transparency and nature of choice (i.e. in-group/out-group, in-group/in-group, out-group/out-group), to ensure that there was no interaction effect. For example, if all or most of the in-group/out-group choices had involved very transparent matrices, this may have biased the results in the direction of in-group favouritism (making it a *confounding variable*). Tajfel was only interested in group membership as an influence on points allocation (this was the manipulated independent variable), so all other variables likely to affect the outcome had to be kept constant.

(b) Counterbalancing.

CHAPTER 13: HANEY *ET AL.* (1973)

1 ● Prisoners remained in the prison 24 hours per day.
   ● They wore a uniform (loose-fitting smock, etc.), with an ID number front and back.
   ● They were allowed no personal belongings and were issued only the minimum necessities for personal hygiene (toothbrush, etc.).
   ● They were stripped, sprayed, given uniforms, had 'mugshot' taken, etc., on arrival.
   ● There was a clear power difference between prisoners and guards, and 'social distance' was maximized.

2 The fundamental attribution error (FAE).

3 It is not possible to separate the effects of the prison environment from those of the prisoner and guard characteristics when trying to explain their behaviour. The two sets of factors get 'mixed up' and only an experimental study is capable of 'pulling them apart'/separating them.

4 Video/audio recordings can be analysed after the study is completed, without the pressure of needing to move quickly on to the next period of observation (as in direct observation); there is no danger of any relevant behaviour being 'missed' while earlier behaviour is being recorded/analysed.

5 (a) Any prior familiarity with other participants would mean that interactions were not determined exclusively by the *roles* to which they were assigned; (b) the experience of participating in the study with a friend/acquaintance could have adversely affected the relationship (especially if allocated to different roles).

6 You may wish to debate this in class or prepare a seminar paper. According to Reicher (in Brockes, 2001), while the participants knew they were on television, they could only self-monitor for so long: they cannot consistently behave for the camera. Also, volunteers were selected who understood that it was a serious piece of research – the group was the focus of interest, *not* personalities, as in *Big Brother*. Against this, Zimbardo (in Swain, 2005) criticizes the study because of the involvement of television. He argued that the visible cameras and microphones, and the participants' awareness that their actions would be screened nationwide, probably altered their behaviour.

CHAPTER 14: NISBETT *ET AL.* (1973)

1 'Organized whole', 'pattern' or 'configuration'; Wertheimer, Kohler and Koffka.

2 (a) The *independent variable* is the person whose behaviour was being explained (a paragraph on why my best

friend chose his college major, etc.); the *dependent variable* is the actual attributions made (entity versus disposition).

    (b)   Repeated measures.

    (c)   Essentially by a form of *content analysis*. The paragraphs were scored using a coding system, which identified each reason as either a pure entity or as invoking some dispositional property of the actor.

    (d)   If a reason referred in any way to the person doing the choosing (e.g. 'I need someone I can relax with'), and included any reasons which could be described as entity x disposition interaction (e.g. 'We can relax together').

3 (a)   *Parallel* forms.

    (b)   Reliability (specifically, *internal consistency*).

    (c)   The other major measure of internal consistency is the *split-half* method. *Test–retest reliability* is a measure of consistency over time.

4 (a)   Counterbalancing.

    (b)   To ensure that the order in which participants completed the questionnaires did not influence the tendency to attribute more traits to others than to self.

5 Participants were equally consistent in their tendency to attribute more traits to others, regardless of which trait dimensions were involved and which stimulus persons were being assessed.

6 It could be argued that seeing ourselves as acting in accordance with 'the demands and opportunities of each new situation as it occurs' involves an *illusion of freedom*. (See Chapter 9.) If our traits and dispositions are the exclusive 'causes' of our behaviour, then to this extent we are not free either: we cannot help acting in a particular way because 'that's the kind of person we are'.

CHAPTER 15: HAZAN AND SHAVER (1987)

1 (a)   Sample one is a *self-selected (volunteer) sample*; sample two is an *opportunity sample*.

    (b)   A self-selected sample, by definition, does not have to be recruited – it recruits (selects) itself. This means that the researchers do not have to spend time or effort finding participants. But if not every reader of the newspaper responded to the love quiz, there must have been something different about those who did. This means that they were not even representative of the population of 'readers of this local newspaper'. Even if every reader of the paper had responded, they still would not have constituted a representative sample – most people do not read that paper. An opportunity sample is 'on tap', already available; so it is cheap, convenient and quick. But it is unlikely to be representative – here, they were undergraduate students (although we are not told their subjects), and so were not even representative of the population of '18-year-olds'.

    (c)   In both samples there was a *gender bias*: there were twice as many women as men. This does not always or necessarily matter, because gender may not be a relevant variable to the behaviour or characteristic under investigation. But it would be surprising if gender were not an influence on attachment style and mental models of self and relationships. This makes the samples gender-biased. Also, sample one was described as 'primarily heterosexual'. Again, it would be very surprising if sexual orientation did not influence mental models. Also, we cannot just assume that attachment styles derived from the study of children apply equally to homosexuals as to heterosexuals. Really, the study needs to be repeated using homosexual (and bisexual) samples, and results may be different for gays and lesbians.

2 Anxious-ambivalent individuals worry that their partner does not really love them or will not want to stay with them. This may have the effect of actually producing what they most fear – a self-fulfilling prophecy (they are too 'needy'). Also, they 'want to merge completely with another person, and this desire sometimes scares people away' (they are too demanding and 'smothering'). They fall in love easily, but rarely find 'true love'. Their greater self-doubt may be difficult for potential partners to deal with.

CHAPTER 16: OLDS AND MILNER (1954)

1 (a) This is a polite way of saying the rats were killed. Their brains were frozen, sectioned, stained and examined microscopically to determine which structure had been stimulated.

(b) This is probably something that can best be discussed in a seminar or class debate. In truth, these kinds of animal experiments are rarely, if ever, conducted any more in psychology, and the animal rights debate is focused on *medical* research. However, many of the issues that arise in one area apply to the other, one of these being *speciesism* (Ryder, 1990: see Gross, 2005).

2 This was designed to allow the rats to get used to the apparatus.

3 Olds and Milner scored rats on the percentage of time they spent lever pressing during acquisition. In order to find out how much time the rat would spend in the *absence* of positive reinforcement, a similar score was calculated for extinction periods. This extinction score provided a *baseline*: a way of defining (operationalizing) positive reinforcement is when the acquisition score is greater than the extinction score. When the extinction score exceeds the acquisition score, we have punishment.

4 Eventually, food or water lose their reinforcing properties; so, for example, rats will stop pressing the lever.

5 (a) In *partial reinforcement*, reinforcers are only presented intermittently or unpredictably: in *interval* schedules (fixed or variable), reinforcers are given according to how much time has elapsed since the last reinforcement; in *ratio* schedules (fixed or variable), reinforcers are given according to the number of responses that have occurred since the last reinforcement.

(b) In *continuous reinforcement*, every single response is reinforced.

CHAPTER 17: DEMENT AND KLEITMAN (1957)

1 Although there is no particular reason for thinking that there are sex differences regarding REM/NREM sleep, it is always desirable to have roughly equal numbers of males and females. Perhaps more important is the very small sample; individual differences were found in relation to the ability to recall dreams, for example, so much larger samples (or replications) are needed before any generalizations can be made.

2 These drugs are known to affect normal sleep activity (e.g. alcohol suppresses REM sleep without affecting NREM sleep).

3 This information may have influenced their dream reports: if (through *demand characteristics*) they believed that they were 'meant' to report 'proper dreams' after REM sleep, they may not have given honest and 'objective' accounts of their dreams. (But see question 4.)

4 This was a way of ensuring that the differential dream reports for REM/NREM sleep were not 'contaminated' by the sequence of awakening. If a common pattern emerged even when, for example, one participant had been told s/he had only been woken from REM sleep, this would be a better test of the genuine difference between the two kinds of sleep.

CHAPTER 18: SCHACHTER AND SINGER (1962)

1 If participants in the Epi Inf condition became introspective, perhaps slightly troubled, then any differences between them and those in the Epi Ign condition on the dependent variable could be due to those factors rather than to differences in appropriateness (Schachter and Singer, 1962).

2 Perhaps being told about side effects (albeit the wrong ones) produced a higher level of arousal in the Epi Mis group, making them more sensitive to environmental cues about the meaning of their arousal. This interpretation is quite consistent with the hypothesis.

3 (a) Variables which would need to be taken into account include general susceptibility to the influence of other people; and general sensitivity to drugs such as adrenaline.

(b) This might depend on the appropriateness of the stooge's behaviour in terms of gender role; also, the perceived attractiveness of the opposite-sex stooge could affect the participant's level of arousal (which might be misattributed to the injection).

4   As a general principle, deception is discouraged, but it was fundamental to this experiment, and debriefing was carried out as a matter of routine. What is perhaps more worrying is the (apparent) lack of any medical checks/precautions when an injection was being given. We are told that a doctor administered the adrenaline, but not that any medical screening was carried out.

5   This is something that could be discussed in a seminar. LeDoux describes introspection as a 'blurry window into the workings of the mind'. If there is one thing we do know from introspection, it is that we are often in the dark about why we feel as we do. There is considerable experimental evidence to show that much emotional processing occurs (or can occur) *unconsciously*. Also, people often find their emotions puzzling; he claims that 'Consciously accessible appraisal processes cannot be the way, or at least not the only way, the emotional brain works'.

CHAPTER 19: ORNE (1966)

1   Correlate.
2   They are used to assess the *reliability* of the scale ('alternative or parallel forms'), i.e. the *consistency* with which the test measures whatever it is measuring. There should be a significant positive correlation between scores on the different forms if the test is reliable.
3   (a)   As in any repeated measures design, participants are likely to learn something about the hypothesis/purpose of the experiment from being tested in both conditions.
    (b)   Counterbalancing can be used to reduce this (and other kinds of order effects: half the participants are tested 'hypnotized'/'non-hypnotized'; half are tested 'non-hypnotized'/'hypnotized'. However, the difference in conditions (especially the instructions given) are *so* different (it is, after all, the instructions that are the independent variable), that this 'precaution' may be insufficient to prevent the results from being confounded.
4   See Chapter 1, p. 6.
5   Some of the questions you may wish to consider are:
    ● Is the hypnotist/experimenter displaying gratuitous sadism (just to make people look foolish)?
    ● Does it serve a valid scientific purpose?
    ● Does it contribute to the clinical use of hypnosis?
    ● Are participants properly debriefed?
    Your answers may, of course, depend on which particular experiment(s) you are considering, as well as whether you favour a state or non-state view of hypnosis.

CHAPTER 20: SPERRY (1968)

1   The technical material is almost exclusively logical, but in folk tales/stories many things happen at once: the sense of a story emerges through a combination of style, plot and evoked images and feelings. So, language *in the form of stories* can stimulate the right hemisphere (Ornstein, 1986).
2   Mentally rotating the object in space: right hemisphere (spatial abilities). Counting the boxes: left hemisphere (numerical/mathematical/symbolic/analytic abilities).
3   Not only have they undergone a commissurotomy, but they have had intractable epilepsy, that is, epilepsy which less drastic treatment has failed to control, such as anti-epileptic medication, which they have usually been taking for several years.
4   Split-brain patients have not been randomly allocated to the 'commissurotomy condition': it is difficult to find volunteers for such experiments! Participants are chosen because they already have a split brain.
5   When studying split-brain patients, their two hemispheres are being compared with each other (through targeting information to each hemisphere separately). Participant variables (such as their history, temperament, intelligence) are held constant, since it is the *same* participant whose two hemispheres are being compared.

6   *Localization* refers to the fact that some specific functions and processes are controlled by relatively precise and circumscribed cortical regions. For example, language is controlled partly by Broca's area in the frontal lobe (damage to which causes difficulties in *producing* language) and partly by Wernicke's area in the temporal lobe (damage to which causes difficulty in *understanding* language). For most people, these cortical areas are found in *one or other* cerebral hemisphere (they are *lateralized* on the right or left). Broca's and Wernicke's areas are usually found in the *left* hemisphere. So, language is both localized *and* lateralized.

CHAPTER 21: BLACKMORE (1988)

1   (a)   Blackmore claims that if tunnels and OBEs are a return to birth, people born by Caesarean section (CS) should not have them (i.e. *none*). However, in the two groups (36 CS, 218 normal), the *same proportion* reported these experiences. She does not give precise figures, but if just *one* of the 36 born by CS had such experiences, this would appear to invalidate her argument (unless 'same proportion' means zero in both groups – but then no conclusion could be drawn either way).

    (b)   Usually, when we refer to memory (and especially when speaking of autobiographical memory/AM), we are concerned with conscious awareness of representations of past experience (*explicit memory*). But there are other forms of memory that are not conscious. For example, classical and operant conditioning (and other forms of learning) clearly take place from birth but do not require conscious awareness. Also, we often form representations of early traumatic experiences which are not available to conscious recall or expression in language, and which may be startlingly accurate. Both these examples illustrate *implicit memory* (or *behavioural/enactive memory*: Mollon 1998).

    (c)   In *The Primal Scream* (1973), Janov describes how birth represents the primary trauma in an individual's life from which all others stem, and which, therefore, is the source of all anxiety. The aim of *primal therapy* is to help people overcome the defences built up against the intolerable pain associated with birth by experiencing the pain while re-enacting the birth process. The body 'remembers' the trauma, such that adult medical problems (e.g. asthma) may reflect the adult's difficult birth (e.g. difficulty in breathing/lack of oxygen). This is another form of *implicit remembering*.

2   These are all hallucinogenic drugs (*hallucinogens*), which produce profound effects on consciousness (perception, thinking and emotion). For this reason, they are sometimes called *psychedelics* ('mind-expanding' or 'mind-manifesting'). *Mescaline* comes from the peyote cactus, while *psilocybin* is obtained from the mushroom *Psilocybe mexicana* ('magic mushroom'). *Lysergic acid diethylamide* (LSD) is chemically synthesized (i.e. manufactured).

3   According to the *top-down* (or *conceptually driven*) approach, we make *inferences* about what things are like, drawing on our knowledge and expectations of the world (based on past experience). An example is Gregory's theory of *indirect* perception ('things are often *not* what they seem').

    According to the *bottom-up* (or *data-driven*) approach, we perceive things *directly*, based on sensory information (sense-data) presented to us (*no* inferences are involved: 'things *are* what they seem'). An example is Gibson's theory of perception.

4   As we have seen, Blackmore recognizes both the universal nature of NDEs and their cultural variability. Cross-cultural variations suggest the possibility that there is some underlying 'core' experience (which is universal), while the form of that experience (messenger, Jesus, Gabriel, 'just a light') may be influenced by cultural, religious and individual factors. In other words, NDEs may be 'real' (the 'underlying' core experience may be explicable in neuropsychological terms), but the particular form of the experience is shaped by non-physiological factors. This suggests that there is *more* to NDEs than the neuropsychological processes/events that Blackmore proposes: they cannot be explained simply or completely in terms of such processes, which makes the attempt to do so *reductionist*.

    The wider issue of the 'truth' of different models of reality lends itself to a seminar discussion (see Gross *et al.*, 1997).

CHAPTER 22: FREUD (1909)

1. (a) In relation to dreams, *condensation* involves the *same* part of the manifest content (what happens in the dream) representing *different* parts of the latent content (the unconscious – mainly sexual – wishes). In Hans's case, a single (conscious) fear (of horses) came to represent or embody a number of separate (unconscious) fears. *Transformation* refers to how one thing is changed into something else. In a dream, this might take the form of *concrete representation*, where an abstract idea (e.g. authority/power) is expressed as something 'real' (e.g. a king).

   (b) Fear of castration by his father (Freud), fear of his mother's threats to castrate him (Fromm), fear of being abandoned by his mother (Bowlby), and fear of horses as a generalized conditioned response (Wolpe and Rachman) can *all* be seen as condensed into the single fear of being bitten by a horse. Freud's account is, arguably, the only one broad enough to explain how these different elements could all form part of the same specific fear.

2. *Idiographic* theories maintain that every individual is unique and should be studied as such. They are also concerned with the *whole* person. Examples include humanistic theories (like those of Maslow and Rogers) and Allport's trait theory. *Nomothetic* (law-like) theories *compare* individuals in order to discover the factors that constitute *personality in general*. They do this by measuring personality through the use of standardized scales (e.g. the Eysenck Personality Questionnaire/EPQ). (See Gross, 2003.)

3. The investigator has little or no control over variables (making it impossible to infer cause and effect); it cannot be replicated (unlike experimental studies); it involves an individual (or siblings or a family), making it very difficult to generalize the results to people in general; and the investigator cannot be objective due to his/her role as therapist/psychiatrist, etc., in a (primarily) helping role (as opposed to a scientific role).

4. The case study is really Freud's interpretation of Hans's father's interpretation of his son's phobia (not the most direct link between Freud and his patient, whom he only met on two occasions). But Freud and the father were of one mind anyway regarding the Oedipal theory, and so would have probably reached the same/similar interpretation; but the 'price' paid for this agreement is fitting Hans's behaviour, dreams, etc., *into* the ready-made theory.

5. This is one you might wish to debate in class, or present as a seminar paper. Remember, Bowlby's interpretation, like Freud's, is made from a particular theoretical perspective; although a psychoanalyst, Fromm's viewpoint is probably more objective than the other two. Also, what about Wolpe and Rachman's explanation of Hans's phobia – is this compatible with Freud's?

CHAPTER 23: WATSON AND RAYNER (1920)

1.
   - 'In the 1920s' should be '1920'.
   - 'J.B. Watson' should be 'J.B. Watson and Rosalie Rayner'.
   - 'did a series of experiments with children' should be 'initiated some laboratory experiments with an infant, Albert B.'
   - 'how emotional responses can be conditioned and reconditioned': no mention of 'reconditioning' in the original' (the emphasis was very much on conditioning).
   - 'an eight-month-old orphan, Albert B.' should be 'nine-month-old Albert B., whose mother was a wet nurse in a children's hospital'.
   - 'who happened to be fond of rabbits, rats, mice and other furry animals' should be 'none of these induced a fear response'.
   - 'toy rabbit' should be 'white rat' (a real one).
   - 'Then the rabbit was displayed to Albert, and, half a second or so later, Watson made a sudden loud noise' should be 'joint presentations (of the rat and hammer on steel bar)'.
   - 'crashing metal plates together' should be 'hammer on steel bar'.
   - 'it spread to other stimuli...such as a glove, a towel, a man's beard, a toy, and a ball of wool' should be 'rabbit, dog, fur coat, cotton wool, Watson's hair, and a Santa Claus mask'.
   (You can work out the rest for yourself.)

2 It can be thought of as a whole series of *repeated measures*, and any one measure may depend, in subtle or complex ways, on the measures previously taken. If we know that the successive scores obtained from participants are independent of each other, then there is no *statistical* objection to single-participant designs (Robson, 1973). Single-subject designs have a long history in psychology, probably the most famous example being Ebbinghaus's pioneering study of memory. (See Chapter 5 and Gross, 2005.)

3 Stimulus generalization.

4 Discrimination.

5 Extinction; spontaneous recovery.

CHAPTER 24: BANDURA *ET AL.* (1961)

1 The earlier studies did not test *generalization* of imitative responses to new settings in which the model is absent. Bandura *et al.* considered this to be a more crucial test of imitative learning.

2 If a child has been reinforced in the past for imitating male or female models, it will be more likely to imitate such a model in the future.

3 (a) Matched pairs (or participants).
  (b) It controlled for the crucial participant variable of the child's 'natural' level of aggression.
  (c) Independent groups (or samples).

4 To ensure that they were 'under some degree of instigation to aggression', since (i) observation of other people's aggression tends to reduce aggression in the observer, and (ii) if participants in the non-aggressive condition expressed little aggression in the face of appropriate instigation, this would indicate the presence of an inhibitory process.

5 It seems that mere observation may be sufficient for *learning* of the model's behaviour, but for *reproduction* of that behaviour to occur (actual imitation), reinforcement of the observer's behaviour (or of the model's) may be necessary.

6 Deliberately exposing children to aggressive behaviour could be objected to on the grounds that they are learning how to act in a socially undesirable way. Equally, subjecting the children (in all three groups) to 'mild aggression arousal' (see question 4) by deliberately frustrating them is objectionable by its very nature. However, the study as whole could be defended if it is seen as contributing to our knowledge of the harmful effects of the media: it is a case of balancing the need to protect individual participants against the need to carry out socially beneficial research. (See Gross, 2005.)

CHAPTER 25: SAMUEL AND BRYANT (1984)

1 *Compensation* refers to the understanding that the attributes/dimensions of objects can 'cancel each other out'. For example, in the beakers of liquid task, the concrete operational child understands that the taller beaker is also thinner/narrower: if its contents are poured back into the original shorter (and wider) beaker, both the shorter beakers will (still) have the same amount of liquid. *Reversibility* refers to the ability to perform this pouring back into the original beaker *mentally*. More generally, it means understanding that things can be changed back to how they were originally. Together, these two operations enable the child to grasp that things can *look* different without having actually changed.

2 As Samuel and Bryant saw it, the fixed-array condition was used to check that children who answered the post-transformation question correctly in the other two conditions, did so by bringing over information from the pre-transformation display. It therefore served as a *control* condition. The finding that the one-question condition was easier than the fixed-array condition justifies its use.

3 (a) Counterbalanced.
  (b) To reduce the impact of order effects (e.g. practice or fatigue as a result of doing one task before another). This is an inherent problem in a repeated measures design.
  (c) Using the initial letter of each material (M = mass, N = number, V = volume), the following could have been used: MNV, NVM, VNM, such that one-third of the children within each age-group, and within each condition, were tested in each of these three, predetermined orders.

4   *Vertical décalage* refers to inconsistencies *between* different abilities or operations. For example, a child may have mastered all kinds of classification, but not all kinds of conservation.

CHAPTER 26: WERNER (1989)

1   (a)   Literally, 'looking backwards'; this examines events and development that have already taken place.
    (b)   'Prospective' (literally, 'looking forwards').
    (c)   The researchers can observe events and development as they unfold, rather than having to rely on people's memories. This can make it easier to identify cause and effect (although this is never as reliable as in a controlled experiment). However, following people's development as it happens, by definition, takes time, effort and money. Keeping the research team together is often difficult, which may reduce the continuity of the research.

2   The children themselves could not, of course, give their consent; it was their parents who did so, and this is considered perfectly ethical. By the time they were 18, they might have been able to withdraw from the study, if they had wished to (depending on the age of consent in Hawaii). But, psychologically, it is much more difficult to withdraw after having been a participant for so long. Parents also gave their permission for public health, educational and social services records to be accessed by the researchers.

3   If attrition of the sample is sufficiently great, the surviving participants may no longer constitute a representative sample (i.e. representative of the original sample). The 'survival' rates ranged from 96 per cent for the 2-year follow-up to 80 per cent for the final follow-up at 31/32 years. Also, 86 per cent of the resilient children were followed up at age 31/32. This constitutes acceptably low attrition.

CHAPTER 27: HODGES AND TIZARD (1989)

1

	Cross-sectional	Longitudinal
Advantages	1. Relatively simple and quick: it is a short-term study, so is relatively inexpensive. 2. Requires no continuity of the research team. 3. Data do not need to be 'frozen' over a long time period until participants have completed their development. 4. Provides age-related norms.	1. No cohort problem (same participants are being compared with themselves). 2. Smaller number of participants required. 3. Sensitive to changes in behaviour which occur quickly (assuming the intervals between successive observations are fairly short). 4. Provides individual growth curves (as well as age-related norms).
Disadvantages	1. *Cohort effect*: if widely different age groups/cohorts are compared, any differences could be due *either* to actual change in the variable under investigation, *or* the fact that the two groups represent different generations. 2. Participants need to be matched on relevant variables, which is time-consuming and expensive. 3. Larger number of participants required. 4. Can *describe* behaviour change over time, but cannot *explain* it.	1. Time-consuming and expensive. 2. Requires continuity of research team. 3. Participants who 'survive' may be affected in some way by repeated testing over the years: this may make them a less representative sample than they were originally.

2 A natural experiment takes place in the normal course of events, and is not due to any kind of interference on the psychologist's part: the changes which occur would have occurred anyway. Because the psychologist is not randomly allocating participants to the experimental/control conditions, there is no control over participant variables (and so the experiment is not a true experiment, but a quasi-experiment).

3 (a) The original 30 working-class children from London no longer seemed appropriate for the mainly middle-class adopted group, or the restored group who lived for the most part in disadvantaged homes.

(b) A comparison 16-year-old was found for each of the ex-institution adolescents, matched on gender, one- or two-parent family, socio-economic status, and position in the family. A second comparison group was formed, comprising same-gender classmate, closest in age (for assessing school-related data).

4 Without it, it would be impossible to know if it was the experience of growing up in an institution which accounted for the adolescents' relationships ('they might have turned out like that anyway'). This is the basic principle of *all* control (comparison) groups.

CHAPTER 28: DIAMOND AND SIGMUNDSON (1997)

1 *Hermaphrodites* (from the mythical Greek god/goddess Hermaphrodite, who had attributes of both sexes) have functioning organs of both sexes – either simultaneously or sequentially. Cases are very rare, and their external organs are often a mixture of male and female structures. Most cases studied by Money, on which biosocial theory is based, involve *pseudo-hermaphrodites*. This includes infants with AIS and AGS (see text), as well as those with chromosomal abnormalities (such as XO and XXY: see Gross, 2005).

2 The original criticism of how the first postulate (and biosocial theory as a whole) was derived (i.e. data based on studies of hermaphrodites and pseudo-hermaphrodites) would no longer be valid, as intersex individuals would be perfectly valid. However, to study such individuals exclusively means that unambiguous males and females are being omitted (i.e. the first postulate is based on a very unrepresentative sample of human beings). Not only are they in a tiny minority, but the very fact that efforts are made to 'normalize' them by making them male or female makes the resulting data more difficult to interpret.

3 The answer to this is really contained in the question: anecdotes are not *scientific*. Why not? By definition, they are examples given by individuals from their own personal experiences, which cannot be reproduced to allow others to inspect and examine them. Science is based on the principle that others should be able to check your data for themselves; this cannot be done with anecdotal evidence. It is the equivalent of 'hearsay' in a legal context – this is not admissible as evidence in a court of law.

4 (a) Bodies (female and male) which do not conform to the 'ideal' size, shape, etc. A flat-chested woman, or a man with 'boobs', are good examples.

(b) Much cosmetic surgery is aimed at 'feminizing' or 'masculinizing' the body. Specific examples include breast augmentation (enlargement) or reduction, or breast reconstruction (following mastectomy), elective female genital surgery ('designer angioplasty'). (Cosmetic surgery is also designed to keep people looking 'young' as opposed to 'old' – another influential dichotomy in Western culture.)

CHAPTER 29: BLAKEMORE AND CHOUDHURY (2006)

1 The dip in performance is linked to the growth (proliferation) of synapses that occurs at the onset of puberty. Until pruning occurs after puberty, synaptic connections in the prefrontal cortex produce a 'weak signal': the excess of synapses makes cognitive performance less efficient. Only after puberty are the excess synapses pruned into specialized, efficient networks; this may explain the improved performance post-puberty.

2 (a) The age of the participants – adolescents or adults.

(b) The use of black-and-white photographs could represent a confounding variable: adult participants may be more used to black-and-white photographs than the adolescents, thus making the task more 'familiar'. Also, the photographs showed the faces of middle-aged people; the adult participants could more easily relate to the facial expressions for this reason.

(c)   Baird (in Dobbs, 2005) repeated the experiment, but used colour photographs of adolescent faces. Under these conditions, there was little difference between the adult and adolescent scores. The more contemporary colour photographs are more 'engaging' for the adolescent participants.

3   This is an issue which could be the subject of a seminar, class discussion or debate.

CHAPTER 30: EYSENCK (1952)

1   The baseline represents the rate of spontaneous remission/recovery (recovery without any treatment); if psychotherapy works, it must aid recovery *beyond* the baseline.

2   Dream interpretation; free association; transference.

3   ● Systematic desensitization/SD involves step-by-step exposure to the phobic object (usually by imagining it), while simultaneously relaxing.
   ● Implosion involves exposing the patient to what, in SD, would be at the top of the hierarchy (a list of least to most feared contact with the phobic object) – without any relaxation.
   ● Flooding is exposure which takes place *in vivo* (e.g. with an actual spider, rather than imagining it), but is otherwise more like implosion than SD.

4   This refers to the replacement of a removed symptom (e.g. a phobia) by another symptom (e.g. a different phobia). It is what psychoanalytic theorists believe happens when only the behaviour itself (the fear), and not the underlying conflict, is dealt with (as in behaviour therapy).

5   *Psychodynamic* is a more general term than *psychoanalytic*. 'Psychodynamic' implies the *active* forces within the personality, the inner causes of behaviour (such as feelings, conflicts, drives and, especially, a variety of *unconscious* motivational factors). Freud's psychoanalytic theory was the first such theory, and all *depth psychology* stems, more or less directly, from psychoanalytic principles. The theories (and therapies) of Jung and Adler are psychodynamic, but *not* psychoanalytic.

6   (a)   The placebo effect refers to the patient's *expectation* of success or improvement. When we call a change a placebo effect, we usually mean that it was brought about by some means other than that intended in a particular treatment.

   (b)   In drug trials, a placebo denotes an inactive/inert substance (usually a sugar pill), which takes account of the psychological (as opposed to pharmacological) influences on physiological change. So, in drug trials, the placebo condition is the *control* condition.

   (c)   It is quite appropriate in drug trials to use an *intentional placebo* (as opposed to an inadvertent one), that is, a treatment *designed* to have no effect, in itself, on a particular disorder. However, their use in psychotherapy research is a misapplication of drug trial methods: in psychotherapy, the expectation is part of the treatment (Mair, 1992). This makes 'placebo' an unfortunate term, since it clearly does not denote something inactive/inert. Even non-placebo controls (such as delayed-treatment or no-treatment conditions) will produce expectations specific to that particular condition (e.g. disappointment and rejection, respectively) (Barkham and Shapiro, 1992).

CHAPTER 31: THIGPEN AND CLECKLEY (1954)

1   and 2   Questions (1) and (2) could both be debated (perhaps together) in a seminar or in your psychology class.

3   ● They have no particular (theoretical) axe to grind, so there is much less chance of bias in their interpretations.
   ● They asked independent experts to administer a variety of tests: psychological and neurophysiological, objective and projective.
   ● Thigpen and Cleckley could reach a diagnosis and interpretation together, while Freud had no co-worker with whom he could discuss his patients. (A noteworthy exception, of course, was Little Hans's father, but he was a 'Freudian' already, so was just as biased as Freud.)
   ● Eve's relatives were asked to help verify certain of her memories (and those of the alters) and to add information, and in this way to throw light on the case. (By contrast, Hans's father was also his major therapist.)

4

Dissociative identity disorder	Schizophrenia
1. Hearing voices is the only kind of hallucination, and is not a major symptom.	1. Auditory hallucinations are not the only kind, and are usually a major symptom.
2. Involves *amnesia* and *fugue* ('flight'), a kind of extension of amnesia, in which patients flee from home and self by wandering off, not knowing how they got there and unable to recall their true identity.	2. Does not involve amnesia or fugue.
3. Is a form of dissociative disorder (traditionally a form of *neurosis*).	3. Traditionally, a major (functional) *psychosis*.
4. Usually treated *psychologically* (psychotherapy).	4. Usually treated *physically* (major tranquillizers/antipsychotic drugs).
5. The different personalities/states are 'self-contained', although some are very specific/superficial. Each represents a 'part of the whole'.	5. The personality as a whole is split. For example, there is a breakdown between self and reality, self and other, emotion and cognition. (See Gross, 2005.)

5 (a) A 'blind tester' is someone who assesses performance on a test without knowing whose scores they are assessing (in Thigpen and Cleckley's study, the blind tester did not know the identity of the personality: Eve White, Eve Black or Jane).

   (b) The main advantage is that the tester will not be (unwittingly) influenced when assessing test performance by knowledge of whose performance is being assessed (i.e. there will be no *experimenter bias* – no chance of his/her expectations unconsciously biasing how the test is scored).

6 The *semantic differential* is a scale that comprises at least nine pairs of *bipolar adjectives*, for each of which there is a seven-point scale. The scale as a whole involves three factors: *evaluative* (e.g. good–bad), *potency* (e.g. strong–weak) and *activity* (e.g. active–passive). The attitude object is usually denoted by a single word (e.g. mother/husband), rather than a statement, and the factors are really tapping into the *emotional connotation/meaning* of the object.

CHAPTER 32: REES (1971)

1 Rees decided that if participants *rationalized* their experience (e.g. 'I saw him in my mind's eye') or expressed any doubt about the reality of the experience, then it did not count as a hallucination. Also, any experiences in bed at night counted as dreams *unless* they happened immediately after getting into bed.

2 If standardized questions had all been asked in the same order for all participants, with concentration on hallucinations, they might have talked much less freely about the deceased and their feelings, and may have been much more inhibited about 'admitting' to having hallucinations. This would have been self-defeating in this particular study.

3 (a) Ability to speak Welsh, sectarian allegiance with Christian faith, regularity of church attendance, Wales outside Llanidloes area, and outside Wales (by which he seems to mean England).

   (b) This is a very narrow and specific definition of 'cultural background'. Unless Llanidloes is taken to be representative of Wales as a whole, and Wales is taken to be representative of the UK as a whole, then very few generalizations can be made from these data. Rees does, in fact, offer some figures suggesting that his data tally with those for Wales as a whole and for England. But the numbers are very small and the 'culture' of the UK is hardly representative of 'human beings'.

4 No, because widows outnumber widowers by 4:1 in the general population. Although the participants were not selected on the basis of gender, they constitute an 'unintentional' *quota* sample.

CHAPTER 33: ROSENHAN (1973)

1   In order to be able to generalize the results: the hospitals should be representative of US psychiatric hospitals as a whole. They were in different states, on both coasts, both old or shabby and new; research-orientated and not; well and poorly staffed; mostly state, federal- and university-funded.

2   (a)   It is possible that genuine psychiatric patients (people with actual mental disorders) may be judged to be 'impostors' (pseudo-patients).

   (b)   In trying to avoid a type-two error (diagnosing a pseudo-patient as schizophrenic), the staff tended to make more type-one errors (identifying real patients as impostors).

   (c)   As members of a research and teaching hospital, the staff would pride themselves (prestige) on their ability to spot impostors posing as psychiatric patients (diagnostic acumen).

3   Where information about the person's psychiatric status was withheld, ratings should not differ according to whether the person was actually a psychiatric patient or not (especially as the tapes were carefully collected so as not to contain certain overt symptoms). For the other two groups, ratings should be more abnormal for those identified as schizophrenic, *regardless* of whether this attribution was correct.

4   ● Pseudo-patients trying to gain admission, but *without* complaining of hearing voices, or with different symptoms.

   ● Telling staff the results of experiment 1, but not telling them to expect any pseudo-patients.

5   However distasteful such concealment is, it was a necessary first step: 'Without concealment, there would have been no way to know how valid these experiences were; nor was there any way of knowing whether whatever detections occurred were a tribute to the diagnostic acumen of the staff or to the hospital's rumour network … I have respected their [individual staff and hospitals] amonymity, and have eliminated clues that might lead to their identification' (Rosenhan, 1973: Notes).

CHAPTER 34: BOUCHARD AND MCGUE (1981)

1   (a)   Figure 34.1 shows that the closer the genetic relationship between two individuals, the stronger the correlation between their IQ scores. At first sight, these data suggest that heredity is a major influence on IQ test performance. But as the genetic similarity increases, so does the similarity of the environment (i.e. family resemblance studies *confound* genetic and environmental influences).

   (b)   One way of overcoming the problem is to compare the IQs of MZ twins reared together with the IQs of MZ twins reared apart. This is a way of trying to *separate/disentangle* the effects of genetics and environmental factors.

2   The view that many pairs of genes are involved in the inheritance of intelligence (not just a single pair, as in eye colour, for example).

3   Some genes are more powerful than others. For example, the brown-eye gene is dominant over the blue-eye gene: if someone inherits one of each (the genotype), s/he will actually have brown eyes (the phenotype).

4   The tendency for organisms (including human beings) to select as mates/sexual partners those with characteristics similar to their own.

5   If a range of values includes some scores which are extreme in one direction only, then the mean will be distorted and the median will be a more 'typical' score.

6

Individual tests (e.g. Stanford-Binet; Wechsler intelligence scale for children/WISC)	Group tests (e.g. Raven's progressive matrices; British ability scales)
1. Used primarily as diagnostic tools in a clinical setting (e.g. disruptive behaviour at school).	1. Used primarily for purposes of selection (e.g. the 11-plus examination in England and Wales) and research.
2. Involves a one-to-one situation between the psychologist administering the test and the person being tested.	2. As many people are tested at one time as is practical (e.g. the number of tables and chairs in the room).
3. A face-to-face situation, in which it is important to put the testee at ease before testing proper begins.	3. Presented in the form of written questions (like an examination).
4. No standardized instructions as such.	4. Standardized instructions are used.
5. May/may not be timed.	5. Always timed.
6. Usually involves some *performance* items (e.g. jigsaw puzzle-type tasks).	6. No performance items.
7. Some scope for interpretation of the testee's answers by the psychologist.	7. No scope for interpretation. They are *objective* tests (only one answer can be accepted as correct), usually marked by computer.

CHAPTER 35: GOULD (1982)

1   Yerkes was one of the pioneers of modern primatology (the study of primates: see Chapter 3).

2   *Aptitude* tests are intended to measure someone's *capacity/potential* for achieving in a particular skill, occupation or academic subject; they claim to reduce to a minimum the effects of specific learning and experience. *Attainment* (or *achievement*) tests measure how much a person knows about a specific subject, or the person's current level of performance (e.g. reading ability). IQ tests have always claimed to be aptitude tests. However:
   ● they rely on reading/arithmetic or other acquired skills to assess capacity/potential;
   ● they can only measure capacity/potential by assuming cultural fairness;
   ● capacity/potential does not exist separately from some actual performance or behaviour.

3   A eugenicist believes that people with socially undesirable characteristics (such as low intelligence or criminal tendencies) should be prevented from producing offspring, in order to prevent the spread of these characteristics. (This is part of a broader belief in the need to *breed* human beings in order to achieve a 'better' society, based, of course, on the assumption that socially important abilities and behaviours are largely genetically determined.) In practice, this would be done through sterilization and/or institutionalizing certain individuals.

4   This clearly lends itself to a class debate/seminar discussion. It centres round the fundamental ethical conflict between the rights of the individual versus the rights of others ('society'), a conflict which has surfaced in relation to AIDS and 'safe sex', and the banning of smoking from public places.

5   Recent immigration had drawn the dregs of Europe, namely lower-class Latin and Slavic people (of naturally inferior intelligence). Those immigrants of longer residence belonged predominantly to superior (of naturally higher intelligence) northern stock. In other words, the positive correlation between years spent in the USA and IQ score was attributable to 'genetic stock', *not* to increased absorption of American culture. Ironically, this demonstrates the principle of not inferring cause from correlation. Although years spent in the USA undoubtedly *did* increase IQ scores (i.e. there was a cause-and-effect relationship), this antihereditarian argument was shown to be invalid by the further argument that the two variables (length of residence/IQ score) both stemmed from a *third* variable (genetic stock). Yerkes, therefore, used a valid form of reasoning to reach what is, almost certainly, an invalid conclusion.

6 According to Frijda and Jahoda (1966), *culture-free* tests actually measure some inherent quality of human capacity equally well in all cultures. Clearly, no such test is possible. By contrast, a *culture-fair* test could be a set of items which are equally unfamiliar to all possible persons in all possible cultures, so that everyone would have the same chance of passing/failing (this is a virtual impossibility); and it could comprise multiple sets of items, modified for use in each culture to ensure that each version of the test would contain the same degree of familiarity. This would give members of each culture about the same chance of being successful with their respective version. This is possible in theory, but very difficult to construct in practice (Segall *et al.*, 1999).

CHAPTER 36: RAINE *ET AL.* (1997)

1 A major reason is to do with the nature of the study: as with all quasi-experiments, because the IV is not manipulated by the investigator, we cannot be sure that it is the cause of the DV. Essentially, Raine *et al.* have found that certain brain abnormalities are *correlated* with certain types of violent behaviour. It is possible that developing violent tendencies actually changes the function of certain brain areas, rather than vice versa. Similarly, both the brain abnormalities and the violent behaviour could be the result of one or more social, psychological, cultural or situational factors to which Raine *et al.* refer. They claim that abnormal brain processes may *predispose* to violence. This implies that other factors (social, psychological, etc.) are necessary for the behaviour to actually occur. (See **Theoretical issues**.)

2 The sample was the largest sample of seriously violent offenders ever involved in a brain imaging study up to 1997. But murderers pleading NGRI cannot be taken as representative of all murderers, let alone all violent offenders. Raine *et al.* controlled for schizophrenia – the mental disorder most commonly associated with violent behaviour – but the control group was composed of non-violent non-offenders. A control group of (non-violent) offenders should also be used. It is also possible that murderers (and others who commit violent crimes) who are caught and brought to justice differ in certain important ways from those who escape justice. (See **Subsequent research**.) Since murderers are overwhelmingly male (as are their victims), the gender composition of Raine *et al.*'s sample is perfectly acceptable.

3 This is best considered as a seminar topic or in a class debate.

4 Ethologists consider aggression to be instinctive in all species and important in the evolutionary development of the species, allowing individuals to adapt to their environment. However, as applied to humans, there are different types of aggression (some positive, such as self-defence, some negative/destructive); violence is a term that would only be applied to an extreme form of human aggression in which a deliberate attempt is made to inflict serious physical injury on another person.

5 According to the *diathesis–stress model* (e.g. Zubin and Spring, 1977), schizophrenics inherit a predisposition (diathesis) towards developing schizophrenic symptoms. Whether or not they do so depends on environmental stressors (which may be biological, social or familial).

6 If research shows that violent behaviour is largely determined by biological factors, and if violent crime statistics reveal that black people and other minority groups are over-represented (which they are), then it could be concluded that black people have a biological predisposition towards violence. Unless the reasons for their being over-represented are explored in terms of social and cultural factors, the role of biological factors will appear to be all-important.

CHAPTER 37: BASSETT (2002)

1 She might mean that people who come into contact with the psychiatric services (especially those run by the NHS, rather than privately), whether as inpatients or in the community, are already disadvantaged (they are more likely to come from poorer and/or broken homes, mental illness is stigmatized much more than (most) physical illnesses, and so on). Alternatively, she might mean that provision for people with mental illness is inferior to that made for (most) physical illnesses and that they are treated as 'second-class citizens' within the NHS. In England, women are about 40 per cent more likely to be admitted to a psychiatric hospital than men, and two to three times more likely to be diagnosed with unipolar depression than men (Williams and Hargreaves, 1995).

2 'Making people have control' seems contradictory, because 'making people' and 'being in control' are *opposites*. Perhaps this is better described as a *paradox* rather than a contradiction: a statement that *appears* illogical but isn't – like 'helping people to help themselves'. Perhaps Cathy means that what psychiatric treatment should involve is showing patients (*not* forcing/coercing them) how to take control of and responsibility for their lives.

3 Based on experiments with dogs, Seligman proposed that animals acquire a sense of helplessness when confronted with uncontrollable aversive stimulation (electric shocks from which they could not escape): they finally gave up trying to escape. When later able to escape, they made no attempt to: they seemed to lose the ability and motivation to respond effectively to painful stimulation.

4 *Genuineness* (*authenticity* or *congruence*) refers to the person showing him/herself to be a real person, with feelings which should be expressed where appropriate. The patient needs to feel that the nurse is emotionally involved, and not hiding behind a façade of professional impersonality: the nurse must be 'transparent'.

5 Smith and Osborn (2003) state that IPA studies are conducted using small samples. The detailed, case-by-case analysis of individual transcripts is time-consuming, and the aim is to say something in detail about the perceptions/understandings of this particular group, rather than prematurely making more general claims. IPA studies have been published with samples of 1, 4, 9 and 15, so Bassett's is very 'respectable'. IPA researchers usually try to find a fairly *homogeneous* sample (i.e. participants should be quite similar). Smith and Osborn use the term *purposive sampling*, through which IPA finds a more closely defined group for whom the research question will be significant. Nurses were the target population in Bassett's study; he does not say how he came to select his sample, but as a nurse lecturer, they most likely came from among his colleagues and students (and so constitute an opportunity sample).

CHAPTER 38: AMETTLER *ET AL.* (2005)

1 If AN typically begins in mid adolescence – mean age of onset 17 years – then adult samples may be unrepresentative of AN patients as a whole. As in the Rieger *et al.* study, the adult sample may have been atypical. Amettler *et al.*'s sample had been diagnosed for only 18 months on average. Their BMI varied from 13.9 (underweight = less than 18.5) to 21.5 (normal = 18.5–24.9).

2 With an adolescent sample, dropout depends on the decision of parents, rather than of the adolescents themselves; that is, parents *withdraw* their adolescent children, while with adult samples it is the patients themselves who decide to withdraw. (Indeed, it is often a family member or individual other than the patient who initiates referral in the first place: Roth and Fonagy, 2005.) So dropout cannot be a reliable measure of a patient's adherence. In the case of weight recovery, this can be achieved by hospital admission without a patient's willing collaboration. Note that in their Discussion the authors state that taking hospital admission to measure motivation to change is 'The most important limitation of the present study'!

3 Amettler *et al.* give the following reason: 'in order to include patients in different situations, such as different BMI or treatment modality'. But doesn't this leave the question unanswered? In other words, what we want to know is *why* they should want to include patients in different situations. The answer should be something along the lines of: wanting to study a cross section of (adolescent) patients, in order to be able to generalize the findings. If they had all (or mostly) been inpatients, for example, the results could not necessarily have been generalized to outpatients.

4 *Interoceptive awareness* refers to the 'internal environment', that is, feelings and sensations that arise within the body. One example would be sensations of hunger. *Asceticism* refers to self-denial, in particular, going without material/physical pleasures (such as food).

CHAPTER 39: FERGUSSON *ET AL.* (2006)

1 ● Ethnic/cultural background: attitudes towards and 'traditions' regarding premarital sex and pregnancy, and abortion, are likely to differ between members of different ethnic and cultural groups.
  ● Religious background: beliefs regarding premarital sex and abortion are among the most easily identifiable features of many world religions.

● Whether or not the pregnancy was planned/wanted: although most abortions are likely to be associated with an unplanned pregnancy, this is not always the case. For example, the pregnancy might have been planned, but fears about the baby's abnormality (such as Down's syndrome and other genetic disorders) may lead the mother to seek a termination (and very young mothers – like much older ones – are more likely to produce babies with such abnormalities). Related to this are:

● The extent of family and partner (if there is one) support for seeking or not seeking an abortion.

● The woman's experiences in seeking and obtaining an abortion.

2   It is possible that the apparent associations between abortion and mental health may not reflect the traumatic effects of abortion itself, but other factors which are linked to the process of seeking and obtaining an abortion. For example, the results could reflect the effects of unwanted pregnancy on mental health rather than the effects of the actual abortion.

3   This is something you could discuss in a seminar or debate. But the implication seems to be that people are not ready to discuss such sensitive issues when they are younger, and/or that their memories may not be so accurate/reliable. There may also be legal and ethical issues involved.

4   (a)   *Disordered* implies undisciplined, unpredictable and impulsive. *Oppositional* implies acting in the opposite way to how others (especially those in authority) expect you to behave ('bloody-mindedness').

    (b)   It is very difficult for us to be objective about ourselves, including remembering past events. Also, we usually try to convey a favourable impression of ourselves, so the participants were likely to *under*estimate the degree to which they displayed conduct problems.

5   Again, an excellent topic for a seminar or debate. The issues here are at least as much ethical as they are psychological. An important distinction is that between 'required' and 'available'.

CHAPTER 40: HRABA AND GRANT (1970)

1   Race of interviewer was controlled in order to rule it out as a possible influence on the child's behaviour. For example, black children interviewed by a white interviewer might have felt obliged to express a preference for white dolls: they may have believed that, in some way, this was the 'right' choice to make.

2   'Baseline' or control (comparison) group. Without knowing white children's preference, black children's preference could not be meaningfully assessed. For example, if white children had preferred black dolls (for whatever reason), this would give a very different meaning to black children's preference for white dolls.

3   'A view of things in which one's own group is the centre of everything, and all others are scaled and rated with reference to it … Each group … boasts itself superior … and looks with contempt on outsiders. Each group thinks its own folkways the only right one' (Sumner, 1906). (See Gross, 2005.)

4   Because children's ethnic awareness and ethnic identity become more sophisticated as they get older. (See **Background and context**.)

5   As children get *older*, they are *less* likely to misidentify dolls' racial identity; or *younger* children are *more* likely to misidentify dolls' racial identity compared with older children.

6   The independent variable was the child's ethnic group membership, so the dolls must embody this characteristic (skin colour, as opposed to, say, size) and no other. If only skin colour differed, there could be a 'contradiction' between this and other racial/ethnic characteristics. For example, the black doll might have 'white hair and features' and the white doll 'black hair and features'. This makes interpretation of the results potentially more difficult.

CHAPTER 41: BEM (1974)

1   The criterion for selecting an item was that it should be judged independently, by males and females, to be significantly more desirable for men or for women. The implication is that males and females will have different ideas about what is desirable for the same and the opposite sex, so that only where they agree could an item reliably be considered sex-typed (and hence included). While the number of male and female judges did not have to be exactly equal, they needed to be *more or less* equal.

2 It is a measure of the test's *reliability*. Each item should be measuring the same variable and to the same extent (i.e. all items should contribute equally to the overall score). A common method for assessing internal consistency is the *split-half method*.

3 If they had remembered their original answers, it would not have been a measure of the test's reliability (as was intended), but of the participants' *memory* (which was not intended).

4 (a)   Concurrent.
   (b)   Face; predictive; construct.

5 Eysenck personality questionnaire (EPQ): the social desirability scale is known as the Lie scale (see Gross, 2005).

6 A test must be properly *standardized*, that is, tried out on a large, representative sample of the population for which it is intended; it establishes a set of norms for that population, so that any individual's score can be compared against those norms. Without the norms, an individual's score is meaningless. (In the case of *physical* characteristics, such as weight or height, an individual's score is meaningful, but we usually want to know how s/he compares with others of the same age (age norms) or ethnic group (ethnic group norms). But with *psychological* characteristics, the norms actually tell us what an individual's score *means*: it only tells us something useful if we know what *comparable others* are like with regard to that characteristic.

REFERENCES

Aboud, F. (1988) *Children and Prejudice*. Oxford: Blackwell Publishing.

Abramson, L.Y. and Martin, D.J. (1981) Depression and the causal inference process. In J.H. Harvey, W.J. Ickes and R.F. Kidd (eds) *New Directions in Attitude Research*, vol. 3. Hillsdale, NJ: Lawrence Erlbaum.

Adorno, T.W., Frenkel-Brunswick, E., Levinson, D.J. and Sanford, R.N. (1950) *The Authoritarian Personality*. New York: Harper & Row.

Ainsworth, M.D.S. (1989) Attachments beyond infancy. *American Psychologist, 44*(4): 709–16.

Ainsworth, M.D.S., Blehar, M.C., Waters, E. and Wall, S. (1978) *Patterns of Attachment: A Psychological Study of the Strange Situation*. Hillsdale, NJ: Lawrence Erlbaum.

Aitchison, J. (1998) *The Articulate Mammal*, 4th edn. London: Routledge.

Alba, J.W. and Hasher, L. (1983) Is memory schematic? *Psychological Bulletin, 93*: 2013–231.

Aldridge-Morris, R. (1989) *Multiple Personality: An Exercise in Deception*. Hove and London: Lawrence Erlbaum.

Allport, G.W. (1954) *The Nature of Prejudice*. Reading, MA: Addison-Wesley.

Allport, G.W. (1955) *Becoming: Basic Considerations for a Psychology of Personality*. New Haven, CT: Yale University Press.

Allport, G.W. and Pettigrew, T.F. (1957) Cultural influences on the perception of movement: The trapezoid illusion among Zulus. *Journal of Abnormal and Social Psychology, 55*, 104–13.

Altrocchi, J. (1980) *Abnormal Behaviour*. New York: Harcourt Brace Jovanovich.

American Psychiatric Association (1980) *Diagnostic and Statistical Manual of Mental Disorders*, 3rd edn. Washington, DC: American Psychiatric Association.

American Psychiatric Association (1987) *Diagnostic and Statistical Manual of Mental Disorders*, 3rd edn, rev. Washington, DC: American Psychiatric Association.

American Psychiatric Association (1994) *Diagnostic and Statistical Manual of Mental Disorders*, 4th edn. Washington, DC: American Psychiatric Association.

American Psychiatric Association (2000) *Diagnostic and Statistical Manual of Mental Disorders*, 4th edn, rev. Washington, DC: American Psychiatric Association.

Apter, A. (1991) The problem of who: Multiple personality, personal identity and the double brain. *Philosophical Psychology, 4*(2): 219–48.

Archer, J. (1999) *The Nature of Grief: The Evolution and Psychology of Reactions to Loss*. London: Routledge.

Archer, J. and Lloyd, B. (1985) *Sex and Gender*. Cambridge: Cambridge University Press.

Arendt, H. (1963) *Eichmann in Jerusalem: A Report on the Banality of Evil*. New York: Viking Press.

Arnold, M.B. (1960) *Emotion and Personality*. New York: Columbia University Press.

Arnold, M.B. and Gasson, J.A. (1954) Feelings and emotions as dynamic factors in personality integration. In M.B. Arnold and S.J. Gasson (eds) *The Human Person*. New York: Ronald.

Aronfreed, J.M., Messick, S.A. and Diggory, J.C. (1953) Re-examining emotionality and perceptual defence. *Journal of Personality, 21*: 517.

Aronson, E. (1988) *The Social Animal*, 5th edn. New York: W.H. Freeman & Co.

Aronson, E. (1992) *The Social Animal*, 6th edn. New York: W.H. Freeman & Co.

Aronson, E. and Carlsmith, J.M. (1963) Effect of the severity of threat on the devaluation of forbidden behaviour. *Journal of Abnormal and Social Psychology, 6*: 584–8.

Aserinsky, E. and Kleitman, N. (1955) A motility cycle in sleeping infants as manifested by ocular and gross bodily motility. *Journal of Applied Physiology, 8*: 11–18.

Asperger, H. (1944) Die 'Autistischen Psychopathe' in Kindesalter. *Archiv fur Psychiatrie und Nervenkrankheiten, 117*: 76–136.

Atkinson, R.C. and Shiffrin, R.M. (1968) Human memory: A proposed system and its control processes. In K.W. Spence and J.T. Spence (eds) *The Psychology of Learning and Motivation*, vol. 2. London: Academic Press.

Atkinson, R.C. and Shiffrin, R.M. (1971) The control of short-term memory. *Scientific American, 224*: 82–90.

Baddeley, A. (1966) The influence of acoustic and semantic similarity on long-term memory for word sequences. *Quarterly Journal of Experimental Psychology, 18*: 302–9.

Baddeley, A. (1970) Estimating the short-term component in free recall. *British Journal of Psychology, 61*: 13–15.

Baddeley, A. (1995) Memory. In C.C. French and A.M. Colman (eds) *Cognitive Psychology*. London: Longman.

Baddeley, A. (1997) *Human Memory: Theory and Practice*, rev. edn. Hove: Psychology Press.

Baddeley, A. (1999) *Essentials of Human Memory*. Hove: Psychology Press.

Bailey, C.L. (1979) Mental illness – A logical misrepresentation? *Nursing Times*, May: 761–2.

Bandura, A. (1965) Influence of model's reinforcement contingencies on the acquisition of imitative responses. *Journal of Personality and Social Psychology, 1*: 589–95.

Bandura, A. (1973) *Aggression: A Social Learning Analysis*. Englewood Cliffs, NJ: Prentice-Hall.

Bandura, A. (1977) *Social Learning Theory*. Englewood Cliffs, NJ: Prentice-Hall.

Bandura, A. (1986) *Social Foundations of Thought and Action*. Englewood Cliffs, NJ: Prentice-Hall.

Bandura, A. (1989) Social cognitive theory. In R. Vasta (ed.) *Six Theories of Child Development*. Greenwich, CT: JAI Press.

Bandura, A. and Huston, A.C. (1961) Identification as a process of incidental learning. *Journal of Abnormal and Social Psychology, 63*: 311–18.

Bandura, A., Ross, D. and Ross, S.A. (1963a) Imitation of film-mediated aggressive models. *Journal of Abnormal and Social Psychology, 66*: 3–11.

Bandura, A., Ross, D. and Ross, S.A. (1963b) Vicarious reinforcement and imitative learning. *Journal of Abnormal and Social Psychology, 67*: 601–7.

Bandura, A., Blanchard, E.B. and Ritter, B. (1969) Relative efficacy of desensitization and modelling approaches for inducing behavioural, affective and attitudinal changes. *Journal of Personality and Social Psychology, 13*: 173–99.

Banuazzi, A. and Mohavedi, S. (1975) Interpersonal dynamics in a simulated prison: A methodological analysis. *American Psychologist, 30*: 152–60.

Barber, T.X. (1969) *Hypnosis: A Scientific Approach*. New York: Van Nostrand.

Barber, T.X., Spanos, N.P. and Chaves, J.F. (1974) *Hypnotism: Imagination and Human Potentialities*. New York: Pergamon.

Barkham, M. and Shapiro, D. (1992) Response to Paul Kline. In W. Dryden and C. Feltham (eds) *Psychotherapy and its Discontents*. Buckingham: Open University Press.

Barnes, R.D., Ickes, W.J. and Kidd, R. (1979) Effects of perceived internationality and stability of another's dependency on helping behaviour. *Personality and Social Psychology Bulletin, 5*: 367–72.

Baron, R.A. (1977) *Human Aggression*. New York: Plenum.

Baron-Cohen, S. (1987) Autism and symbolic play. *British Journal of Developmental Psychology, 5*: 139–48.

Baron-Cohen (1988) Social and pragmatic deficits in autism: Cognitive or affective? *Journal of Autism and Developmental Disorders, 18*: 379–402.

Baron-Cohen, S. (1989) The autistic child's theory of mind: A case of specific developmental delay. *Journal of Child Psychology and Psychiatry, 30*: 285–97.

Baron-Cohen, S. (1990) Autism: A specific cognitive disorder of 'mind-blindness'. *International Review of Psychiatry, 2*: 79–88.

Baron-Cohen, S. (1993) From attention-goal psychology to belief-desire psychology: The development of a theory of mind and its dysfunction. In S. Baron-Cohen, H. Tager-Flusberg and D.J. Cohen (eds) *Understanding Other Minds: Perspectives from Autism*. Oxford: Oxford University Press.

Baron-Cohen, S. (1995) Infantile Autism. In A.A. Lazarus and A.M. Colman (eds) *Abnormal Psychology*. London: Longman.

Baron-Cohen, S., Leslie, A.M. and Frith, U. (1985) Does the autistic child have a 'theory of mind'? *Cognition, 21*: 37–46.

Baron-Cohen, S., Wheelwright, S., Hill, J., Raste, Y. and Plumb, I. (2001) The 'Reading the Mind in the Eyes' test revised version: A study with normal adults, and adults with Asperger syndrome of high-functioning autism. *Journal of Child Psychology and Psychiatry, 42*(2): 241–51.

Baron-Cohen, S., Golan, O., Wheelwright, S. and Hill, J.J. (2004) *Mind Reading: The Interactive Guide to Emotions*. London: Jessica Kingsley.

Baron-Cohen, S., Golan, O., Chapman, E. and Granader, Y. (2007) Transported to a world of emotion. *The Psychologist, 20*(2): 76–7.

Barry, H., Bacon, M.K. and Child, I.L. (1957) A cross-cultural survey of some sex differences in socialization. *Journal of Abnormal and Social Psychology, 55*: 327–32.

Bartholomew, K. (1993) From childhood to adult relationships: Attachment theory and research. In S. Duck (ed.) *Learning About Relationships*. Newbury Park, CA: Sage Publications.

Bartlett, F.C. (1932) *Remembering*. Cambridge: Cambridge University Press.

Bartsch, K. and Wellman, H.M. (1995) *Children Talk About the Mind*. Oxford: Oxford University Press.

Batson, C.D. (1991) *The Altruism Question: Toward A Social Psychological Answer*. Hillsdale, NJ: Lawrence Erlbaum.

Batson, C.D. (1995) Prosocial motivation: Why do we help others? In A. Tesser (ed.) *Advanced Social Psychology*. Boston, MA: McGraw-Hill.

Batson, C.D. (2000) Altruism: Why do we help others? *Psychology Review*, 7(1): 2–5.

Baumrind, D. (1964) Some thoughts on ethics of research: After reading Milgram's behavioural study of obedience. *American Psychologist*, 19, 421–3.

Bean, P. (1979) Psychiatrists' assessments of mental illness. *British Journal of Psychiatry*, 135: 122–8.

Beaumont, J.G. (1988) *Understanding Neuropsychology*. Oxford: Blackwell Publishing.

Beck, A.T., Ward, C.H., Mendelson, M., Mock, J. and Erbaugh, J. (1961) An inventory for measuring depression. *Archives of General Psychiatry*, 4: 561–71.

Beck, A.T., Steer, R.A. and Brown, G.K. (1996) *Beck Depression Inventory – Second Edition Manual*. Sydney, Australia: The Psychological Corporation.

Bee, H. (1994) *Lifespan Development*. New York: HarperCollins.

Bee, H. (2000) *The Developing Child*, 9th edn. Boston, MA: Allyn & Bacon.

Belli, R.F. (1989) Influences of misleading post-event information: Information interference and acceptance. *Journal of Experimental Psychology: General*, 118: 72–85.

Bem, D.J. (1967) Self-perception: An alternative interpretation of cognitive dissonance phenomena. *Psychological Review*, 74: 183–200.

Bem, D.J. (1972) Self-perception theory. In L. Berkowitz (ed.) *Advances in Experimental Social Psychology*, vol. 6. New York: Academic Press.

Bem, S.L. (1975) Sex role adaptability: One consequence of psychological androgyny. *Journal of Personality and Social Psychology*, 31: 634–43.

Bem, S.L. (1977) On the utility of alternative procedures for assessing psychological androgyny. *Journal of Consulting and Clinical Psychology*, 45: 196–205.

Bem, S.L. (1979) Theory and measurement of androgyny: A reply to the Pedhazur-Tetenbaum and Locksley-Cotton critiques. *Journal of Personality and Social Psychology*, 37: 1047–54.

Bem, S.L. (1984) Androgyny and gender schema theory: A conceptual and empirical integration. In R.A. Dienstbier (ed.) *Nebraska Symposium on Motivation*. Lincoln: University of Nebraska Press.

Bem, S.L. (1987) Gender schema theory and the Romantic Tradition. In P. Shaver and C. Hendrick (eds) *Sex and Gender*. Newbury Park, CA: Sage Publications.

Bem, S.L. and Lenney, E. (1976) Sex-typing and the avoidance of cross-sex behaviour. *Journal of Personality and Social Psychology*, 33: 48–54.

Bennett, M., Dewberry, C. and Yeeles, C. (1991) A reassessment of the role of ethnicity in children's social perception. *Journal of Child Psychology and Psychiatry*, 32(6): 969–82.

Bennett, P. (2006) *Abnormal and Clinical Psychology*, 2nd edn. Maidenhead: Open University Press.

Bennett-Levy, J. and Marteau, T. (1984) Fear of animals: What is prepared? *British Journal of Psychology*, 75: 37–42.

Bergin, A.E. (1971) The evaluation of therapeutic outcomes. In A.E. Bergin and S.L. Garfield (eds) *Handbook of Psychotherapy and Behaviour Change: An Empirical Analysis*. New York: John Wiley & Sons.

Bergin, A.E. and Lambert, M.J. (1978) The evaluation of therapeutic outcomes. In A.E. Bergin and S.L. Garfield (eds) *Handbook of Psychotherapy and Behaviour Change: An Empirical Analysis*, 2nd edn. New York: John Wiley & Sons.

Berkowitz, L. (1969) Resistance to improper dependency relationships. *Journal of Experimental Social Psychology*, 5: 283–94.

Berkowitz, L. (1993) *Aggression: Its Causes, Consequences and Control*. New York: McGraw-Hill.

Berry, J.W. (1969) On cross-cultural comparability. *International Journal of Psychology*, 4: 119–28.

Berry, J.W., Poortinga, Y.H., Segall, M.H. and Dasen, P.R. (1992) *Cross-Cultural Psychology: Research and Applications*. New York: Cambridge University Press.

Best, D.L. and Thomas, J.J. (2004) Cultural diversity and cross-cultural perspectives. In A.H. Eagly, A.E. Beall and R.J. Sternberg (eds) *The Psychology of Gender*. New York: Guilford Press.

Bettelheim, B. (1960) *The Informed Heart*. New York: Free Press.

Beutler, L.E. (1997) The psychotherapist as a neglected variable in psychotherapy: An illustration by reference to the role of therapist experience and training. *Clinical Psychology: Science and Practice*, 4: 44–52.

References

Bickman, L. (1974) The social power of a uniform. *Journal of Applied Social Psychology, 1*: 47–61.

Billig, M. and Tajfel, H. (1973) Social categorization and similarity in intergroup behaviour. *European Journal of Social Psychology, 3*: 27-52.

Bitterman, M.E. and Kniffin, C.W. (1953) Manifest anxiety and perceptual defence. *Journal of Abnormal and Social Psychology, 49*: 178–82.

Blackman, D.E. (1980) Images of man in contemporary behaviourism. In A.J. Chapman and D.M. Jones (eds) *Models of Man*. Leicester: British Psychological Society.

Blackmore, S. (1993) *Dying to Live: Science and the Near-Death Experience*. London: Grafton.

Blackmore, S. (1995) Parapsychology. In A.M. Colman (ed.) *Controversies in Psychology*. London: Longman.

Blackmore, S. (2003) *Consciousness: An Introduction*. London: Hodder Arnold.

Blackmore, S. (2005) Near-death experiences. In J. Henry (ed.) *Parapsychology: Research on Exceptional Experiences*. Hove: Routledge.

Blass, T. (1992) The social psychology of Stanley Milgram. In M.P. Zanna (ed.) *Advances in Experimental Social Psychology*, vol. 25. New York: Academic Press.

Bogen, J.E. (1969) The other side of the brain. In R. Ornstein (1986) *The Psychology of Consciousness*, 2nd edn, rev. Harmondsworth: Penguin.

Boring, E.G. (1923) Intelligence as the tests test it. *New Republic*, 6 June: 35–7.

Botwinick, J. (1984) *Ageing and Behaviour*, 3rd edn. New York: Springer.

Bouchard, T.J., Lykken, D.T., McGue, M., Segal, N.L. and Tellegen, A. (1990) Sources of human psychological differences: The Minnesota study of twins reared apart. *Science, 250*: 223–8.

Bower, G.H. and Miller, N.E. (1958) Rewarding and punishing effects from stimulating the same place in the rat's brain. *Journal of Comparative and Physiological Psychology, 51*: 669–74.

Bowers, K.S. (1983) *Hypnosis for the Seriously Curious*. New York: Norton.

Bowlby, J. (1951) *Maternal Care and Mental Health*. Geneva: World Health Organization.

Bowlby, J. (1969) *Attachment and Loss, vol. 1: Attachment*. Harmondsworth: Penguin.

Bowlby, J. (1973) *Attachment and Loss, vol. 2: Separation – Anxiety and Anger*. Harmondsworth: Penguin.

Bowlby, J. (1977) The making and breaking of affectional bonds: 1. Aetiology and psychopathology in the light of attachment theory. *British Journal of Psychiatry, 130*: 201–10.

Bowlby, J. (1980) *Attachment and Loss, vol. 3: Loss, Sadness and Depression*. London: Hogarth Press.

Bowler, D.M. (1992) 'Theory of mind' in Asperger's syndrome. *Journal of Child Psychology and Psychiatry, 33*: 877–93.

Boyd, R. and Richardson, J. (1985) *Culture and the Evolution Process*. Chicago, IL: University of Chicago Press.

Bradbury, T.N. and Fincham, F.D. (1990) Attributions in marriage: Review and critique. *Psychological Bulletin, 107*: 3–33.

Bradding, A. (1995) Questions of identity in adolescents of mixed parentage. *Psychology Teaching*, New Series (4): 53–66.

Bradley, B.P. and Baddeley, A.D. (1990) Emotional factors in forgetting. *Psychological Medicine, 20*: 351–5.

Bradley, J.M. and Cafferty, T.P. (2001) Attachment among older adults: Current issues and directions for future research. *Attachment and Human Development, 3*(2): 200–21.

Brand, C. (1996) *The g Factor: General Intelligence and its Implications*. Chichester: John Wiley & Sons.

Bransford, J.D., Franks, J.J., Morris, C.D. and Stein, B.S. (1979) Some general constraints on learning and memory research. In L.S. Cermak and F.I.M. Craik (eds) *Levels of Processing in Human Memory*. Hillsdale, NJ: Lawrence Erlbaum.

Brehm, J.W. (1966) *A Theory of Psychological Reactance*. New York: Academic Press.

Brewer, M.B. (1999) The psychology of prejudice: Ingroup love or outgroup hate? *Journal of Social Issues, 55*: 429–44.

Broadbent, D. (1958) *Perception and Communication*. Oxford: Pergamon.

Brockes, E. (2001) The experiment. *The Guardian*, G2, 16 October: 2–3.

Bromley, D.B. (1988) *Human Ageing – An Introduction to Gerontology*, 3rd edn. Harmondsworth: Penguin.

Bronfenbrenner, U. (1979) *The Ecology of Human Development: Experiments by Nature and Design*. Cambridge, MA: Harvard University Press.

Brosnan, M.J. (1998) The implications for academic attainment of perceived gender-appropriateness upon spatial task performance. *British Journal of Educational Psychology, 68*: 203–15.

Broverman, I.K., Vogel, S.R., Broverman, D.M., Clarkson, F.E. and Rosenkrantz, P.S. (1972) Sex-role stereotypes: A current appraisal. *Journal of Social Issues, 28*: 59–78.

Brown, H. (1985) *People, Groups and Society*. Milton Keynes: Open University Press.

Brown, R. (1965) *Social Psychology*. New York: Free Press.

Brown, R. (1973) *A First Language*. London: Allen & Unwin.

Brown, R. (1986) *Social Psychology*, 2nd edn. New York: Free Press.

Brown, R. (1988) *Group Processes*. Oxford: Blackwell Publishing.

Brown, R. (1996) Intergroup relations. In M. Hewstone, W. Stroebe and G.M. Stephenson (eds) *Introduction to Social Psychology*, 2nd edn. Oxford: Blackwell Publishing.

Bryant, P. (1998) Cognitive development. In M. Eysenck (ed.) *Psychology: An Integrated Approach*. Essex: Addison Wesley Longman Ltd.

Burks, B.S. (1928) The relative influence of nature and nurture upon mental development: A comparative study of foster parent–foster child resemblance and true parent–true child resemblance. *Yearbook of the National Society for the Study of Education*, 27: 219–316.

Burley, P.M. and McGuiness, J. (1977) Effects of social intelligence on the Milgram paradigm. *Psychological Reports*, 40: 767–70.

Burr, V. (2002) *The Person in Social Psychology*. Hove: Psychology Press.

Buss, A.H. (1971) Aggression pays. In J.L. Singer (ed.) *The Control of Aggression and Violence*. New York: Academic Press.

Butler, R.A. (1954) Curiosity in monkeys. *Scientific American*, February: 70–5.

Cahill, L. (2005) His Brain, Her Brain. *Scientific American*, 292(5): 22–9.

Caine, T.M. and Hope, K. (1967) *Manual of the Hysteroid–Obsessoid Questionnaire*. London: University of London Press.

Campbell, H.J. (1973) *The Pleasure Areas*. London: Eyre Methuen.

Cannon, W.B. (1927) The James-Lange theory of emotions: A critical examination and an alternative theory. *American Journal of Psychology*, 39: 106–24.

Cannon, W.B. (1929) *Bodily Changes in Pain, Hunger, Fear and Rage*. New York: Appleton.

Cardwell, M. (2005) Dehumanization. *Psychology Review*, 12(2): 2–4.

Carlsmith, J.M., Collins, B.E. and Helmreich, R.L. (1966) Studies in forced compliance: 1. The effect of pressure for compliance on attitude change produced by face-to-face role-playing and anonymous essay-writing. *Journal of Personality and Social Psychology*, 4: 1–13.

Carlson, N.R. (1992) *Foundations of Physiological Psychology*, 2nd edn. Needham Heights, MA: Allyn and Bacon.

Carlson, N.R. and Buskist, W. (1997) *Psychology: The Science of Behaviour*, 5th edn. Needham Heights, MA: Allyn & Bacon.

Carroll, D.W. (1986) *Psychology of Language*. Monterey, CA: Brooks/Cole Publishing Company.

Carson, J., Fagin, L., Brown, D., Leary, J. and Bartlett, H. (1997) Self-esteem and stress in mental health nurses. *Nursing Times*, 93(44): 55–8.

Ceci, S.J. and Williams, W.M. (eds) (1999) *The Nature–Nurture Debate: The Essential Readings*. Oxford: Blackwell Publishing.

Chen, H., Yates, B.T. and McGinnies, E. (1988) Effects of involvement on observers' estimates of consensus, distinctiveness and consistency. *Personality and Social Psychology Bulletin*, 14: 468–78.

Chisolm, K., Carter, M.C., Ames, E.M. and Morison, S.J. (1995) Attachment security and indiscriminately friendly behaviour in children adopted from Romanian orphanages. *Development and Psychopathology*, 7: 283–94.

Chomsky, N. (1957) *Syntactic Structures*. The Hague: Mouton.

Chomsky, N. (1965) *Aspects of the Theory of Syntax*. Cambridge, MA: MIT Press.

Chomsky, N. (1980) *Rules and Representations*. Oxford: Blackwell Publishing.

Choudhury, S., Blakemore, S.J. and Cahrman, T. (2005) *Development of Perspective-Taking During Adolescence*. Poster presented at Cognitive Neuroscience Society meeting, New York, April.

Christensen, A. and Jacobson, N.S. (1994) Who (or what) can do psychotherapy: The status and challenge of non-professional therapies. *Psychological Science*, 5: 8–14.

Clamp, A. and Russell, J. (1998) *Comparative Psychology*. London: Hodder & Stoughton.

Claridge, G. and Davis, C. (2003) *Personality and Psychological Disorders*. London: Hodder Arnold.

Clark, K. and Clark, M. (1939) The development of consciousness of self in the emergence of racial identification in Negro pre-school children. *Journal of Social Psychology*, 10: 591–7.

Clark, K. and Clark, M. (1947) Racial identification and preference in Negro children. In T. Newcomb and E. Hartley (eds) *Readings in Social Psychology*. New York: Holt, Rinehart & Winston.

Clark, M.L. (1992) Racial group concept and self-esteem in black children. In A.K.H. Burlew, W.C. Banks, H.P. McAdoo and D.A.Y. Azibo (eds) *African American Psychology: Theory, Research and Practice*. Newbury Park, CA: Sage Publications.

Clarke, A.D.B. (1972) Comment on Oklahoma's 'Severe deprivation in twins: a case study'. *Journal of Child Psychology and Psychiatry, 13*: 103–6.

Clarke, A.M. and Clarke, A.D.B. (1976) *Early Experience: Myth and Evidence*. London: Open Books.

Clarke, A.M. and Clarke, A.D.B. (2000) *Early Experience and the Life Path*. London: Jessica Kingsley.

Cohen, D. (1995) Now we are one, or two, or three … *New Scientist, 146*, 14–15 June: 17.

Cohen, G. (1975) Cerebral apartheid: A fanciful notion? *New Behaviour, 18* (September): 458–61.

Cohen, G. (1993) Everyday memory and memory systems: The experimental approach. In G. Cohen, G. Kiss and M. Levoi, *Memory: Current Issues*, 2nd edn. Milton Keynes: Open University Press.

Cohen, S. and Taylor, L. (1972) *Psychological Survival: The Experience of Long-Term Imprisonment*. Harmondsworth: Penguin.

Colapinto, J. (2000) *As Nature Made Him: The Boy Who was Raised as a Girl*. New York: HarperCollins.

Coleman, J.C. and Hendry, L. (1990) *The Nature of Adolescence*, 2nd edn. London: Routledge.

Collins, N.L. and Read, S.J. (1990) Adult attachment, working models and relationship quality in dating couples. *Journal of Personality and Social Psychology, 58*: 644–63.

Colman, A.M. (1987) Introduction. In A.M. Colman (ed.) *Facts, Fallacies and Frauds in Psychology*. London: Unwin Hyman.

Colvin, M.K. and Gazzaniga, M.S. (2007) Split-brain cases. In M. Velmans and S. Schneider (eds) *The Blackwell Companion to Consciousness*. Malden, MA: Blackwell Publishing.

Concar, D. (1998) You are feeling very, very sleepy. *New Scientist, 159*(2141): 26–31.

Connor, S. (2006) The teenage brain: A scientific analysis. *The Independent*, 5 November. (http://news.independent.co.uk/uk/this_britain/article1949463.ece)

Conrad, R. (1964) Acoustic confusion in immediate memory. *British Journal of Psychology, 55*: 75–84.

Coolican, H. (2004) *Research Methods and Statistics in Psychology*, 4th edn. London: Hodder & Stoughton.

Cooper, J. and Axsom, D. (1982) Effort justification in psychotherapy. In G. Weary and H.K. Mirels (eds) *Integrations of Clinical and Social Psychology*. New York: Oxford University Press.

Cooper, J. and Fazio, R.H. (1984) A new look at dissonance theory. In L. Berkowitz (ed.) *Advances in Experimental Social Psychology*, vol. 15. New York: Academic Press.

Cooper, J., Kelly, K.A. and Weaver, K. (2004) Attitudes, norms and social groups. In M.B. Brewer and M. Hewstone (eds) *Social Cognition*. Oxford: Blackwell Publishing.

Cooper, J.E. (1983) Diagnosis and the diagnostic process. In M. Shepherd and O.L. Zangwill (eds) *Handbook of Psychiatry: 1. General Psychopathology*. Cambridge: Cambridge University Press.

Cooper, J.E., Kendell, R.E., Gurland, B.J., Sharpe, L., Copeland, J.R.M. and Simon, R. (1972) *Psychiatric Diagnosis in New York and London*. Oxford: Oxford University Press.

Corbett, L. (1996) *The Religious Function of the Psyche*. London: Routledge.

Coren, S. (1992) *Left Hander*. London: John Murray.

Cornwell, D. and Hobbs, S. (1976) The strange saga of Little Albert. *New Society*, March: 602–4.

Craik, F.I.M. (1972) A 'levels of analysis' view of memory. Paper presented at the 2nd Erindale Symposium on Communication and Affect, March.

Craik, F.I.M. and Masani, P.A. (1969) Age and intelligence differences in coding and retrieval of word lists. *British Journal of Psychology, 60*: 315–19.

Craik, F.I.M. and Levy, B.A. (1970) Semantic and acoustic information in primary memory. *Journal of Experimental Psychology, 86*: 77–82.

Craik, F.I.M. and Tulving, E. (1975) Depth of processing and the retention of words in episodic memory. *Journal of Experimental Psychology: General, 104*: 268–94.

Crews, F. (1997) *The Memory Wars: Freud's Legacy in Dispute*. London: Granta.

Crick, F. and Mitchison, G. (1983) The function of dream sleep. *Nature, 304*: 111–14.

Crick, F. and Mitchison, G. (1986) REM sleep and neural nets. *Journal of Mind and Behaviour, 7*: 229–49.

Crocker, J. and Major, B. (1989) Social stigma and self-esteem: The self-protecting properties of stigma. *Psychological Review, 96*: 608–30.

Croyle, R.T. and Cooper, J. (1983) Dissonance arousal: Physiological evidence. *Journal of Personality and Social Psychology, 45*: 782–91.

Cumberbatch, G. (1995) *Media Violence: Research Evidence and Policy Implications – Report prepared for the Council of Europe Directorate of Human Rights*. Strasbourg: The Council of Europe.

Curtiss, S. (1977) *Genie: A Psycholinguistic Study of a Modern-day 'Wild Child'*. London: Academic Press.

Dalgleish, T. (1998) Emotion. In M. Eysenck (ed.) *Psychology: An Integrated Approach.* Harlow: Addison Wesley Longman Ltd.

Damasio, A.R. (2000) A neural basis for sociopathy. *Archives of General Psychiatry, 57*(2). (http://archpsyc.ama-assn.org/cgi/content/extract/57/2/128)

Dasen, P.R. (1994) Culture and cognitive development from Piagetian perspective. In W.J. Lonner and R.S. Malpass (eds) *Psychology and Culture.* Boston: Allyn & Bacon.

Davey, A.G. and Mullin, P.N. (1982) Inter-ethnic friendship in British primary schools. *Educational Research, 24*: 83–92.

Davis, K. (1940) Extreme social isolation of a child. *American Journal of Sociology, 45*: 554–65.

Davis, K. (1947) Final note on a case of extreme isolation. *American Journal of Sociology, 52*: 432–7.

Davison, G.C. and Neale, J.M. (1994) *Abnormal Psychology,* 6th edn. New York: John Wiley & Sons.

Davison, G.C. and Neale, J.M. (2001) *Abnormal Psychology,* 8th edn. New York: John Wiley & Sons.

Davison, G.C., Neale, J.M. and Kring, A.M. (2004) *Abnormal Psychology,* 9th edn. New York: John Wiley & Sons.

Dawes, R.M. (1994) *House of Cards.* New York: Free Press.

Deese, J. (1972) *Psychology as Art and Science.* New York: Harcourt Brace Jovanovich.

Dement, W.C. (1955) Dream recall and eye movements during sleep in schizophrenics and normals. *Journal of Nervous and Mental Diseases, 122*: 263–9.

Dement, W.C. (1960) The effect of dream deprivation. *Science, 131*: 1705–7.

Dement, W.C. (1994) History of sleep physiology and medicine. In M.H. Kryger, T. Roth and W.C. Dement (eds) *Principles and Practice of Sleep Medicine.* Philadelphia, PA: Saunders.

Dement, W.C. and Kleitman, N. (1955) Incidence of eye motility during sleep in relation to varying EEG pattern. *Federal Proceedings, 14*: 216.

Denker, R. (1946) Results of treatment of psychoneuroses by the general practitioner: A follow-up study of 500 cases. *New York State Journal of Medicine, 46*: 2164–6.

Deregowski, J.B. (1968) Pictorial recognition in subjects from a relatively pictureless environment. *African Social Research, 5*: 356–64.

Deregowski, J.B. (1969) Preference for chain-type drawings in Zambian domestic servants and primary school children. *Psychologica Africana, 82*: 9–13.

Deregowski, J.B. (1970) A note on the possible determinants of split representations as an artistic style. *International Journal of Psychology, 5*: 21–6.

Deregowski, J.B., Muldrow, E.S. and Muldrow, W.F. (1972) Pictorial recognition in a remote Ethiopian population. *Perception 1,* 417–25.

Dixon, N.F. (1971) *Subliminal Perception: The Nature of the Controversy.* London: McGraw-Hill.

Dixon, N.F. (1981) *Preconscious Processing.* Chichester: John Wiley & Sons.

Dobbs, D. (2005) Fact or phrenology? *Scientific American Mind, 16*(1): 24–31.

Dobbs, D. (2006) A revealing reflection. *Scientific American Mind, 17*(2): 22–7.

Dollard, J. and Miller, N.E. (1950) *Personality and Psychotherapy.* New York: McGraw-Hill.

Dollard, J., Doob, L.W., Mowrer, O.H. and Sears, R.R. (1939) *Frustration and Aggression.* New Haven, CT: Harvard University Press.

Donaldson, M. (1978) *Children's Minds.* London: Fontana.

Dovidio, J.F., Piliavin, J.A., Gaertner, S.L., Schroeder, D.A. and Clark, R.D. (1991) The arousal: Cost-reward model and the process of intervention. In M.S. Clark (ed.) *Prosocial Behaviour: Review of Personality and Social Psychology,* vol. 12. Newbury Park, CA: Sage Publications.

Doyle, J. and Paludi, M. (1991) *Sex and Gender: The Human Experience.* Dubuque, IA: William C. Brown.

Duncan, H.F., Gourlay, N. and Hudson, W. (1973) *A Study of Pictorial Perception Among Bantu and White Primary School Children in South Africa.* Johannesburg: Witwatersrand University Press.

Duyme, M. and Capron, C. (1992) Socioeconomic status and IQ: What is the meaning of the French adoption studies? *European Bulletin of Cognitive Psychology, 12*: 588–604.

Eagly, A.H. (1987) *Sex Differences in Social Behaviour: A Social-Role Interpretation.* London: Lawrence Erlbaum.

Eagly, A.H. and Chaiken, S. (1993) *The Psychology of Attitudes.* Fort Worth, TX: Harcourt Brace Jovanovich.

Ebbinghaus, H. (1885) *Über das Gedächtnis.* Leipzig: H. Ruyer and C.E. Bussenius. (Published in translation (1913) as *Memory.* New York: Teachers' College Press.)

Edley, N. and Wetherell, M. (1995) *Men in Perspective: Practice, Power and Identity.* Hemel Hempstead: Prentice-Hall/Harvester Wheatsheaf.

Eiser, J.R. and van der Pligt, J. (1988) *Attitudes and Decisions.* London: Routledge.

Ekman, P. (1992) An argument for basic emotions. *Cognition and Emotion, 6*: 169–200.

Ekman, P. and Friesen, W. (1971) Constants across cultures in the face and emotion. *Journal of Personality and Social Psychology, 17*: 124–9.

Empson, J. (1989) *Sleep and Dreaming.* London: Faber and Faber.

Empson, J. (1993) *Sleep and Dreaming,* 2nd rev. edn. Hemel Hempstead: Harvester Wheatsheaf.

Endicott, J. and Spitzer, R.L. (1978) A diagnostic interview: The schedule for affective disorders and schizophrenia. *Archives of General Psychiatry, 35*: 837–44.

Engel, G.L. (1977) The need for a new medical model: A challenge for bio-medicine. *Science, 196*: 129–35.

Engel, G.L. (1980) The clinical application of the biopsychosocial model. *American Journal of Psychiatry, 137*: 535–44.

Erdelyi, M.H. (1974) A new look at the new look: Perceptual defence and vigilance. *Psychological Review, 81*: 1–24.

Erikson, E.H. (1950) *Childhood and Society.* New York: Norton.

Erikson, E.H. (1963) *Childhood and Society,* 2nd edn. New York: Norton.

Erlenmeyer-Kimling, L. and Jarvik, L.F. (1963) Genetics and intelligence: A review. *Science, 142*: 1477–9.

Esterson, A. (1998) Jeffrey Masson and Freud's seduction theory: A new fable based on old myths. *History of the Human Sciences, 11*(1): 1–21.

Esterson, A. (2001) The mythologizing of psychoanalytic history: deception and self-deception in Freud's accounts of the seduction episode. *History of Psychiatry, xii,* 329–352.

Evans, D. and Allen, H. (2002) Emotional intelligence: Its role in training. *Nursing Times, 98*(27): 41–2.

Evans, F.J. and Orne, M.T. (1965) Motivation, performance and hypnosis. *International Journal of Clinical Experimental Hypnosis, 13*: 103–16.

Evans-Bush, N. and Greyson, B. (1996) Distressing near-death experiences. In L.W. Bailey and J. Yates (eds) *The Near-Death Experience: A Reader.* New York: Villard.

Eysenck, H.J. (1960) (ed.) *Behaviour Therapy and the Neuroses.* Oxford: Pergamon.

Eysenck, H.J. (1973) *The Inequality of Man.* London: Temple-Smith.

Eysenck, H.J. (1976) The learning theory model of neurosis – A new approach. *Behaviour Research and Therapy, 14*: 251–67.

Eysenck, H.J. (1985) *Decline and Fall of the Freudian Empire.* London: Viking Press.

Eysenck, H.J. (1992) The outcome problem in psychotherapy. In W. Dryden and C. Feltham (eds) *Psychotherapy and Its Discontents.* Buckingham: Open University Press.

Eysenck, H.J. and Rachman, S. (1965) *The Causes and Cure of Neurosis.* London: Routledge and Kegan Paul.

Eysenck, H.J. and Wilson, G.D. (eds) (1973) *The Experimental Study of Freudian Theories.* London: Methuen.

Eysenck, M.W. (1984) *A Handbook of Cognitive Psychology.* London: Lawrence Erlbaum.

Eysenck, M.W. (1986) Working memory. In G. Cohen, M.W. Eysenck and M.E. Le Voi, *Memory: A Cognitive Approach.* Milton Keynes: Open University Press.

Eysenck, M.W. and Keane, M.T. (1995) *Cognitive Psychology: A Student's Handbook,* 3rd edn. Hove: Lawrence Erlbaum.

Eysenck, M.W. and Keane, M.T. (2000) *Cognitive Psychology: A Student's Handbook,* 4th edn. Hove: Psychology Press.

Fahy, T.A. (1988) The diagnosis of multiple personality disorder: A critical review. *British Journal of Psychiatry, 153*: 597–606.

Farah, M.J. and Aguirre, G.K. (1999) Imaging visual recognition: PET and fMRI studies of the functional anatomy of human visual recognition. *Trends in Cognitive Sciences, 3*: 179–86.

Federoff, I.C. and McFarlane, T. (1998) Cultural aspects of eating disorders. In S.S. Kazarian and D.R. Evans (eds) *Cultural Clinical Psychology: Theory, Research, and Practice.* New York: Oxford University Press.

Feeney, J. (1999) Adult romantic attachment and couple relationships. In J. Cassidy and P.R. Shaver (eds) *Handbook of Attachment: Theory, Research and Clinical Applications.* New York: Guilford Press.

Feeney, J. and Noller, P. (1996) *Adult Attachment.* Thousand Oaks, CA: Sage Publications.

Feighner, J.P., Robins, E., Guze, S.B., Woodruff, R.A., Winokur, G. and Munoz, R. (1972) Diagnostic criteria for use in psychiatric research. *Archives of General Psychiatry, 26*: 57–63.

Fenwick, P. (1997) Is the near-death experience only N-methyl-D-aspartate blocking? *Journal of Near-Death Studies, 16*: 464–79.

Fernald, D. (1997) *Psychology.* Upper Saddle River, NJ: Prentice-Hall.

Fernando, S. (1991) *Mental Health, Race and Culture.* Basingstoke: Macmillan/Mind Publications.

Festinger, L. (1957) *A Theory of Cognitive Dissonance.* New York: Harper & Row.

Fillon, M. (2000) Their brains made them do it: Do abnormalities in grey matter cause violence? (http://www.webmd.com/news/20000710/their-brains-made-them-do-it)

Fishbein, M. and Ajzen, I. (1975) *Belief, Attitude, Intention, and Behaviour: An Introduction to Theory and Research.* Reading, MA: Addison-Wesley.

Fiske, A.P., Kitayama, S., Markus, H.R. and Nisbett, R.E. (1998) The cultural matrix of social psychology. In D.T. Gilbert, S.T. Fiske and G. Lindzey (eds) *Handbook of Social Psychology*, vol. 2, 4th edn. New York: McGraw-Hill.

Fiske, S. and Taylor, S. (1991) *Social Cognition*, 2nd edn. New York: McGraw-Hill.

Flanagan, C. (2005) Thirty years on: The Stanford prison experiment. (Interview with Philip Zimbardo). *Psychology Review, 1*(2): 14–16.

Fletcher, G. (2002) *The New Science of Intimate Relationships.* Oxford: Blackwell Publishing.

Fonagy, P., Steele, H., Steele, M. and Holder, J. (1997) Attachment and theory of mind: Overlapping constructs? In *Bondong and Attachment: Current Issues in Research and Practice*, Occasional Papers, No. 14. Association for Child Psychology and Psychiatry.

Foulkes, D. (1993) Data constraints on theorizing about dream function. In A. Moffitt, A. Kramer and R. Hoffmann (eds) *The Functions of Dreaming.* New York: State University of New York Press.

Freedman, J. (1963) Attitudinal effects of inadequate justification. *Journal of Personality, 31*: 371–85.

Freud, S. (1896) *The Aetiology of Hysteria: Standard Edition of Complete Works of Sigmund Freud, III.* London: Hogarth Press.

Freud, S. (1900/1976a) *The Interpretation of Dreams.* Pelican Freud Library, vol. 4. Harmondsworth: Penguin.

Freud, S. (1901/1976b) *The Psychopathology of Everyday Life.* Pelican Freud Library, vol. 5. Harmondsworth: Penguin.

Freud, S. (1905/1977) *Three Essays on the Theory of Sexuality.* Pelican Freud Library, vol. 7. Harmondsworth: Penguin.

Freud, S. (1913) *Totem and Taboo.* Standard Edition of the Complete Works of Sigmund Freud, vol. 13. London: Hogarth Press.

Freud, S. (1914) *Remembering, Repeating and Working Through.* Standard Edition of the Complete Psychological Works of Sigmund Freud, vol. 12. London: Hogarth Press.

Freud, S. (1915) *Repression.* Standard Edition of the Complete Psychological Works of Sigmund Freud, vol. 14. London: Hogarth Press.

Freud, S. (1920/1984) *Beyond the Pleasure Principle.* Pelican Freud Library, vol. 11. Harmondsworth: Penguin.

Freud, S. (1922) *Postscript (to the Case of Little Hans).* Pelican Freud Library, vol. 8. Harmondsworth: Penguin.

Frijda, N. (1988) The laws of emotion. *American Psychologist, 43*: 349–58.

Frijda, N. and Jahoda, G. (1966) On the scope and methods of cross-cultural psychology. *International Journal of Psychology, 1*: 109–27.

Frith, U. (1989) *Autism: Explaining the Enigma.* Oxford: Blackwell Publishing.

Frith, U. (1996) Cognitive explanations of autism. *Acta Paediatrics Supplement*, 416.

Frith, U. and Happé, F. (1994a) Autism: Beyond 'theory of mind'. *Cognition, 50*: 115–32.

Frith, U. and Happé, F. (1994b) Language and communication in the autistic disorders. *Philosophical Transactions of the Royal Society, Series B, 346*: 97–104.

Frith, U. and Frith, C.D. (2003) Development and neurophysiology of mentalizing. *Philosophical Transactions of the Royal Society of London, Series B, Biological Sciences, 358*: 459–73.

Fromm, E. (1970) *The Crisis of Psychoanalysis.* Harmondsworth: Penguin.

Fundudis, T. (1997) Young children's memory: How good is it? How much do we know about it? *Child Psychology and Psychiatry Review, 2*(4): 150–8.

Gabrielli, J.D.E. (1998) Cognitive neuroscience of human memory. *Annual Review of Psychology, 49*: 87–115.

Gallagher, S. (1998) The neuronal Platonist: Michael Gazzaniga in conversation with Shaun Gallagher. *Journal of Consciousness Studies, 5*(5–6): 706–17.

Gardner, B.T. and Gardner, R.A. (1971) Two-way communication with an infant chimpanzee. In A. Schrier and F. Stollnitz (eds) *Behaviour of Non-Human Primates*, vol. 4. New York: Academic Press.

Gardner, B.T. and Gardner, R.A. (1975) Evidence for sentence constituents in the early utterances of child and chimp. *Journal of Experimental Psychology: General, 104*: 244–67.

Gardner, B.T. and Gardner, R.A. (1980) Two comparative psychologists look at language acquisition. In K. Nelson (ed.) *Children's Language*, vol. 2. New York: Gardner Press.

Gardner, H. (1993) *Frames of Mind*, 2nd edn. London: Fontana.

Gardner, H., Kornhaber, M.L. and Wake, W.K. (1996) *Intelligence: Multiple Perspectives.* Orlando, FL: Harcourt Brace and Co.

Gardner, R.A. and Gardner, B.T. (1978) Comparative psychology and language acquisition. In K. Salzinger and F. Denmark (eds) *Psychology: The State of the Art, Annals of the New York Academy of Sciences, 309*: 37–76.

Garfield, S. (1992) Response to Hans Eysenck. In W. Dryden and C. Feltham (eds) *Psychotherapy and Its Discontents.* Buckingham: Open University Press.

Garmezy, N. and Rutter, M. (eds) (1983) *Stress, Coping, and Development in Children.* New York: McGraw-Hill.

Garner, D.M. (1991) *Eating Disorder Inventory-2: Professional Manual.* Odessa, FL: Psychological Assessment Resources.

Garry, M., Loftus, E.F. and Brown, S.W. (1994) Memory: A river flows through it. *Consciousness and Cognition, 3*: 438–51.

Gathercole, S.E. (1998) The development of memory. *Journal of Child Psychology and Psychiatry, 39*(1): 3–27.

Gay, P. (1988) *Freud: A Life for Our Time.* London: J.M. Dent & Sons Ltd.

Gaze, H. (1988) Stressed to the limit. *Nursing Times, 84*(36): 16–17.

Gazzaniga, M.S. (1998) *The Mind's Past.* Berkeley: University of California Press. (http://www.imprint.co.uk/gazza_iv.htm)

Gazzaniga, M.S. (2000) Cerebral specialization and interhemispheric communication: Does the corpus callosum enable the human condition? *Brain, 123*: 1293–326.

Geiselman, R.E., Fisher, R.P., MacKinnon, D.P. and Holland, H.L. (1985) Eyewitness testimony enhancement in the police interview: Cognitive retrieval mnemonics versus hypnosis. *Journal of Applied Psychology, 70*: 401–12.

Gelder, M., Mayou, R. and Geddes, J. (1999) *Psychiatry*, 2nd edn. Oxford: Oxford University Press.

Gibbs, W.W. (1995) Seeking the criminal element. *Scientific American, 272*(3): 76–83.

Gibson, J.J. (1950) *Perception of the Visual World.* Boston, MA: Houghton Mifflin.

Gill, O. and Jackson, B. (1983) *Adoption and Race: Black, Asian and Mixed Race Children in White Families.* London: Batsford.

Glanzer, M. (1972) Storage mechanisms in recall. In G.H. Bower (ed.) *The Psychology of Learning and Motivation: Advances in Research and Theory*, vol. 5. New York: Academic Press.

Glanzer, M. and Cunitz, A.R. (1966) Two storage mechanisms in free recall. *Journal of Verbal Learning and Verbal Behaviour, 5*: 928–35.

Goffman, E. (1968) *Asylum: Essays on the Social Situation of Mental Patients and Other Inmates.* Harmondsworth: Penguin.

Golan, O. and Baron-Cohen, S. (2006) Systemizing empathy: Teaching adults with Asperger syndrome or high functioning autism to recognize complex emotions using interactive multimedia. *Development and Psychopathology, 18*: 589–615.

Gold, K. (1995) Here be dragons and treasure too. *Times Higher Education Supplement*, 18 August: 18–19.

Gombrich, E.H. (1960) *Art and Illusion.* London: Phaidon.

Gopaul-McNichol, S.A. (1992) Racial identification and racial preference of black pre-school children in New York and Trinidad. *Journal of Black Psychology, 14*: 65–8.

Gould, S.J. (1981) *The Mismeasure of Man.* New York: Norton.

Gould, S.J. (1987) *An Urchin in the Storm.* Harmondsworth: Penguin.

Gould, S.J. (1996) *The Mismeasure of Man*, rev. and expanded edn. Harmondsworth: Penguin.

Grafton, S.T., Sinnott-Armstrong, W.P., Gazzaniga, S.I. and Gazzaniga, M.S. (2006/2007) Brain scans go legal. *Scientific American Mind, 17*(6): 30–7.

Green, S. (1980) Physiological studies I and II. In J. Radford and E. Govier (eds) *A Textbook of Psychology.* London: Sheldon Press.

Gregor, A.J. and McPherson, D. (1965) A study of susceptibility to geometric illusions among cultural out groups of Australian aborigines. *Psychologica Africana, 11*: 1–13.

Gregory, R.L. (1983) Visual illusions. In J. Miller (ed.) *States of Mind.* London: BBC Productions.

Greyson, B. (2000) Near-death experiences. In E. Cardena, S.J. Lynn and S. Krippner (eds) *Varieties of Anomalous Experience: Examining the Scientific Evidence.* Washington, DC: American Psychological Association.

Gross, R. (2003) *Themes, Issues and Debates*, 2nd edn. London: Hodder & Stoughton.

Gross, R. (2005) *Psychology: The Science of Mind and Behaviour*, 5th edn. London: Hodder Arnold.

Gross, R. and Kinnison, N. (2007) *Psychology for Nurses and Allied Health Professionals.* London: Hodder Arnold.

Gross, R., Humphreys, P. and Petkova, B. (1997) *Challenges in Psychology.* London: Hodder & Stoughton.

Gruzelier, J. (1998) A working model of the neurophysiology of hypnosis: A review of evidence. *Contemporary Hypnosis, 15*: 5.

Gruzelier, J. (2002) New insights into the nature of hypnotisability. In *Beyond and Behind the Brain*, 4th Bial Foundation Symposium, Fundação, Bial, 275–92.

Gubrium, J. (1973) *The Myth of the Golden Years: A Socio-Environmental Theory of Ageing.* Springfield, IL: Charles C. Thomas.

Gunter, B. and McAleer, J.L. (1990) *Children and Television: The One-Eyed Monster?* London: Routledge.

Gunter, B. and McAleer, J.L. (1997) *Children and Television,* 2nd edn. London: Routledge.

Hall, C.S. (1966) *The Meaning of Dreams.* New York: McGraw-Hill.

Hall, G.S. (1904) *Adolescence.* New York: Appleton & Co.

Happé, F. (1994a) *Autism: An Introduction to Psychological Theory.* London: UCL Press.

Happé, F. (1994b) An advanced test of theory of mind: Understanding of story characters' thoughts and feelings by able autistic, mentally handicapped, and normal children and adults. *Journal of Autism and Developmental Disorders, 24*: 129–54.

Hardy, C.S. and Legge, D. (1968) Cross-modal induction of changes in sensory thresholds. *Quarterly Journal of Experimental Psychology, 20*: 20–9.

Hare, R.D. (1991) *Manual for the Hare Psychopathy Checklist – Revised.* Toronto: Multi-Health Systems.

Hare-Mustin, R. and Maracek, J. (1988) The meaning of difference: Gender theory, postmodernism, and psychology. *American Psychologist, 43*: 455–64.

Hargreaves, D.J. (1986) Psychological theories of sex-role stereotyping. In D.J. Hargreaves and A.M. Colley (eds) *The Psychology of Sex Roles.* London: Harper & Row.

Harlow, H.F., Harlow, M.K. and Meyer, D.R. (1950) Learning motivated by a manipulative drive. *Journal of Experimental Psychology, 40*: 228–34.

Harris, B. (1997) Repoliticising the history of psychology. In D. Fox and I. Prilleltensky (eds) *Critical Psychology: An Introduction.* London: Sage Publications.

Harrower, J. (2001) *Psychology in Practice: Crime.* London: Hodder & Stoughton.

Haslam, S.A. and Reicher, S.D. (2005) The psychology of tyranny. *Scientific American Mind, 16*(3): 44–51.

Hayes, K.H. and Hayes, C. (1951) Intellectual development of a house-raised chimpanzee. *Proceedings of the American Philosophical Society, 95*: 105–9.

Hazan, C. and Shaver, P.R. (1990) Love and work: An attachment-theoretical perspective. *Journal of Personality and Social Psychology, 59*(2): 270–80.

Heather, N. (1976) *Radical Perspectives in Psychology.* London: Methuen.

Hebb, D.O. (1949) *The Organization of Behaviour.* New York: John Wiley & Sons.

Hebb, D.O. *et al.* (1952) The effects of isolation upon attitudes, motivation and thought. *Fourth Symposium, Military Medicine, 1.* Canada: Defence Research Board.

Heider, F. (1958) *The Psychology of Interpersonal Relations.* New York: John Wiley & Sons.

Heine, S.J. and Lehman, D.R. (1997) Culture, dissonance, and self-affirmation. *Personality and Social Psychology Bulletin, 23*: 389–400.

Hemingway, H. and Marmot, M. (1999) Psychosocial factors in the aetiology and prognosis of coronary heart disease: Systematic review of prospective cohort studies. *British Medical Journal, 318*: 160–7.

Hendricks, J.H. and Hendricks, C.D. (1977) *Ageing in Mass Society: Myths and Realities.* Cambridge, MA: Winthrop.

Hendry, L.B. (1999) Adolescents and society. In D. Messer and F. Jones (eds) *Psychology and Social Care.* London: Jessica Kingsley.

Herrnstein, R.J. and Murray, C. (1994) *The Bell Curve: Intelligence and Class Structure in American Life.* New York: Free Press.

Herrnstein, R.L. and Murray, C. (1996) *The Bell Curve: Intelligence and Class Structure in American Life* (with a new Afterword by Charles Murray). New York: Free Press.

Herskovits, M.J. (1948) *Man and His Works: The Science of Cultural Anthropology.* New York: Alfred A. Knopf.

Hewstone, M. and Antaki, C. (1988) Attribution theory and social explanations. In M. Hewstone, W. Stroebe, J.P. Codol and G.M. Stephenson (eds) *Introduction to Social Psychology.* Oxford: Blackwell Publishing.

Hewstone, M. and Fincham, F. (1996) Attribution theory and research: Basic issues and applications. In M. Hewstone, W. Stroebe and G.M. Stephenson (eds) *Introduction to Social Psychology,* 2nd edn. Oxford: Blackwell Publishing.

Hewstone, M., Fincham, F. and Jaspers, J. (1981) Social categorization and similarity in intergroup behaviour: A replication with penalties. *European Journal of Psychology, 11*: 101–7.

Hewstone, M., Manstead, M.S.R. and Stroebe, W. (1997) Emotion. In M. Hewstone, A.S.R. Manstead and W. Stroebe (eds) *The Blackwell Reader in Social Psychology.* Oxford: Blackwell Publishing.

Hewstone, M., Rubin, N. and Willis, H. (2002) Intergroup bias. *Annual Review of Psychology, 53*: 575–604.

Hilgard, E.R. (1974) Toward a neo-dissociationist theory: Multiple cognitive controls in human functioning. *Perspectives in Biology and Medicine, 17*: 301–16.

Hilgard, E.R. (1977) *Divided Consciousness: Multiple Controls in Human Thought and Action.* New York: John Wiley & Sons.

Hilgard, E.R. (1978) States of consciousness in hypnosis: Divisions or levels? In F.H. Frankel and H.S. Zamansky (eds) *Hypnosis at its Bicentennial: Selected Papers.* New York: Plenum.

Hilgard, E.R. (1979) Divided consciousness in hypnosis: The implications of the hidden observer. In E. Fromm and R.E. Shor (eds) *Hypnosis: Developments in Research and New Perspectives,* 2nd edn. New York: Aldine.

Hilgard, E.R. and Hilgard, J.R. (1984) *Hypnosis in the Relief of Pain.* New York: Kaufmann.

Hilgard, E.R., Atkinson, R.L. and Atkinson, R.C. (1979) *Introduction to Psychology,* 7th edn. New York: Harcourt Brace Jovanovich.

Hobson, J.A. (1988) *The Dreaming Brain.* New York: Basic Books.

Hobson, J.A. (1990) Activation, input source, and modulation: A neurocognitive model of the state of the brain-mind. In P.R. Bootzin, J.F. Kihlstrom and D.L. Schacter (eds) *Sleep and Cognition.* Washington, DC: American Psychological Association.

Hobson, J.A. (1999) Sleep and dreaming. In M.J. Zigmond, F.E. Bloom, S.C. Landis, J.L. Roberts and L.R. Squire (eds) *Fundamental Neuroscience.* San Diego, CA: Academic Press.

Hobson, J.A. (2002) *Dreaming: A Very Short Introduction.* Oxford: Oxford University Press.

Hobson, J.A. and McCarley, R.M. (1977) The brain as a dream state generator: An activation-synthesis hypothesis of the dream process. *American Journal of Psychiatry, 134*: 1335–48.

Hochschild, A.R. (1983) *The Managed Heart: Commercialization of Human Feeling.* Berkeley, CA: University of California Press.

Hockett, C.D. (1960) The origin of speech. *Scientific American, 203*: 88–96.

Hogg, M.A. and Vaughan, G.M. (1998) *Social Psychology,* 2nd edn. Hemel Hempstead: Prentice-Hall Europe.

Holahan, C.K. (1988) Relation of life goals at age 70 to activity participation and health and psychological well-being among Terman's gifted men and women. *Psychology and Ageing, 3*: 286–91.

Holmes, D.S. (1994) *Abnormal Psychology,* 2nd edn. New York: HarperCollins.

Holmes, T.H. and Rahe, R.H. (1967) The social readjustment rating scale. *Journal of Psychosomatic Research, 11*: 213–18.

Hooper, M. (2006) Teens: Old before their time. *The Independent,* 5 November. (http://news.independent.co.uk/uk/this_britain/article1949456.ece)

Horgan, J. (1993) Eugenics revisited. *Scientific American, 286*(6): 92–100.

Horn, J.M., Loehlon, J.L. and Willerman, L. (1979) Intellectual resemblance among adoptive and biological relatives: The Texas adoption project. *Behaviour Genetics, 9*: 177–207.

Horowitz, F.D. (1987) *Exploring Developmental Theories: Towards a Structural/Behavioural Model of Development.* Hillsdale, NJ: Lawrence Erlbaum.

Horowitz, F.D. (1990) Developmental models of individual differences. In J. Colombo and J. Fagan (eds) *Individual Differences in Infancy: Reliability, Stability, Predictability.* Hillsdale, NJ: Lawrence Erlbaum.

Howe, M.J.A. (1980) *The Psychology of Human Learning.* New York: Harper & Row.

Howe, M.J.A. (1997) *IQ in Question: The Truth about Intelligence.* London: Sage Publications.

Howe, M.J.A. (1998) Can IQ change? *The Psychologist, 11*(2): 69–71.

Howie, D. (1952) Perceptual defence. *Psychological Review, 59*: 308–15.

Howitt, D. and Owusu-Bempah, J. (1994) *The Racism of Psychology: Time for Change.* Hemel Hempstead: Harvester Wheatsheaf.

Hudson, W. (1960) Pictorial depth perception in sub-cultural groups in Africa. *Psychologica Africana, 52*: 183–208.

Hudson, W. (1962) Pictorial perception and educational adaptation in Africa. *Psychologica Africana, 9*: 226–39.

Hughes, S.J. (2003) The biopsychosocial aspects of unwanted teenage pregnancy. *Nursing Times, 99*(12): 32–3.

Hull, C. (1943) *Principles of Behaviour.* New York: D. Appleton-Century.

Hyde, J.S. and Phillips, D.E. (1979) Androgyny across the life span. *Developmental Psychology, 15*: 334–6.

Hyde, T.S. and Jenkins, J.J. (1969) Differential effects of incidental tasks on the organization of recall of a list of highly associated words. *Journal of Experimental Psychology, 83*: 472–81.

Hyde, T.S. and Jenkins, J.J. (1973) Recall for words as a function of semantic, graphic and syntactic orienting tasks. *Journal of Verbal Learning and Behaviour, 12*: 471–80.

Israels, H. and Schatzman, M. (1993) The seduction theory. *History of Psychiatry, 4*: 23–59.

Jacobs, M. (1984) Psychodynamic therapy: The Freudian approach. In W. Dryden (ed.) *Individual Therapy in Britain*. London: Harper & Row.

Jacobs, M. (1992) *Sigmund Freud*. London: Sage Publications.

Jahoda, G. (1966) Geometric illusions and environment: A study in Ghana. *British Journal of Psychology*, *57*: 193–9.

James, W. (1890) *Principles of Psychology*. New York: Holt, Rinehart & Winston.

Janis, I., Kaye, D. and Kirschner, P. (1965) Facilitating effects of 'eating-while-reading' on responsiveness to persuasive communication. *Journal of Personality and Social Psychology*, *1*: 181–6.

Janov, A. (1973) *The Primal Scream*. London: Sphere Books Ltd.

Jensen, A.R. (1969) How much can we boost IQ and scholastic achievement? *Harvard Educational Review*, *39*: 1–123.

Jensen, A.R. (1980) *Bias in Mental Testing*. London: Methuen.

Jewitt, J. (1998) Unpublished D. Clin. Psych. research thesis. University College London.

Joliffe, T. (1997) *Central Coherence in Adults with High-Functioning Autism or Asperger Syndrome*. Unpublished PhD thesis. University of Cambridge.

Jones, E.E. and Davis, K.E. (1965) From acts to dispositions: The attribution process in person perception. In L. Berkowitz (ed.) *Advances in Experimental Social Psychology*, vol. 2. New York: Academic Press.

Jones, E.E. and Nisbett, R.E. (1971) *The Actor and the Observer: Divergent Perceptions of the Causes of Behaviour*. Morristown, NJ: General Learning Press.

Jones, M.C. (1924) The elimination of children's fears. *Journal of Experimental Psychology*, *7*: 382–90.

Jones, M.C. (1974) Albert, Peter and J.B. Watson. *American Psychologist*, *29*: 581–3.

Joseph, J. (2003) *The Gene Illusion: Genetic Research in Psychiatry and Psychology under the Microscope*. Ross-on-Wye: PCCS Books.

Jouvet, M. (1967) Mechanisms of the states of sleep: A neuropharmacological approach. *Research Publications of the Association for the Research in Nervous and Mental Diseases*, *45*: 86–126.

Joynson, R.B. (1989) *The Burt Affair*. London: Routledge.

Juel-Nielson, N. (1965) Individual and environment: A psychiatric and psychological investigation of monozygous twins raised apart. *Acta Psychiatrica et Neurologica Scandanaviga*, Supplement 183.

Jung, C.G. (1967) *Memories, Dreams, Reflections*. London: Collins.

Kaland, N., Moller-Nielsen, A., Callesen, K., Mortensen, E.L. and Gottlieb, D. (2002) A new 'advanced' test of theory of mind: Evidence from children and adolescents with Asperger syndrome. *Journal of Child Psychology and Psychiatry*, *43*(4): 517–28.

Kamin, L.J. (1977) *The Science and Politics of IQ*. Harmondsworth: Penguin.

Kamin, L.J. (1995) Behind the curve. *Scientific American*, *272*(2): 82–6.

Kanner, L. (1943) Autistic disturbance of affective contact. *Nervous Child*, *2*: 217–50.

Kebbell, M.R. and Wagstaff, G.F. (1999) *Face Value? Factors that Influence Eyewitness Accuracy*. London: Police Research Group, Home Office.

Kebbell, M.R. and Gilchrist, E.L. (2004) Eliciting evidence from witnesses in court. In J.R. Adler (ed.) *Forensic Psychology: Concepts, Debates and Practice*. Cullompton: Willan Publishing.

Kelley, H.H. (1967) Attribution theory in social psychology. In D. Levine (ed.) *Nebraska Symposium on Motivation*, vol. 15. Lincoln: University of Nebraska Press.

Kelley, H.H. (1972) Causal schemata and the attribution process. In E.E. Jones, D.E. Kanouse, H.H. Kelley, R.E. Nisbett, S. Valins and B. Weiner (eds) *Attribution: Perceiving the Causes of Behaviour*. Morristown, NJ: General Learning Press.

Kelley, H.H. (1983) Perceived causal structures. In J.M.F. Jaspars, F.D. Fincham and M. Hewstone (eds) *Attribution Theory and Research: Conceptual, Developmental and Social Dimensions*. London: Academic Press.

Kellogg, W.N. and Kellogg, L.A. (1933) *The Ape and the Child*. New York: McGraw-Hill.

Kendell, R.E. (1983) The principles of classification in relation to mental disease. In M. Shepherd and O.L. Zangwill (eds) *Handbook of Psychiatry: 1, General Psychopathology*. Cambridge: Cambridge University Press.

Kendler, K.S., Neale, M.C., Kessler, R.C., Heath, A.C. and Eaves, L.J. (1993) A test of the equal-environment assumption in twin studies of psychiatric illness. *Behaviour Genetics*, *23*: 21–7.

Kent, G. (1991) Anxiety. In W. Dryden and R. Rantoul (eds) *Adult Clinical Problems*. London: Routledge.

Kihlstrom, J.F. (1980) Post-hypnotic amnesia for recently learned material: Interactions with 'episodic' and 'semantic' memory. *Cognitive Psychology*, *12*: 227–51.

Kilbride, P.L., Robbins, M.C. and Freeman, R.B. (1968) Pictorial depth perception and education among Baganda school children. *Perceptual and Motor Skills*, *26*: 1116–18.

Kilham, W. and Mann, L. (1974) Level of destructive obedience as a function of transmitter and executant roles in the Milgram obedience paradigm. *Journal of Personality and Social Psychology*, *29*: 696–702.

Kimura, D. (1992) Sex differences in the brain. *Scientific American*, Special Issue, September, 80–7.

Kimura, D. (1999) Sex differences in the brain. *Scientific American Presents*, *10*(2): 26–31.

Kintsch, W. (1970) Models for free recall and recognition. In D.A. Norman (ed.) *Models of Human Memory*. London: Academic Press.

Kintsch, W. and Buschke, H. (1969) Homophones and synonyms in short-term memory. *Journal of Experimental Psychology*, *80*: 403–7.

Kirkpatrick, L.A. (1992) An attachment-theory approach to the psychology of religion. *International Journal for the Psychology of Religion*, *2*(1): 3–28.

Kirkpatrick, L.A. (1994) The role of attachment in religious belief and behaviour. In K. Bartholomew and D. Perlman (eds) *Advances in Personal Relationships, Vol. 5: Attachment Processes in Adulthood*. London: Jessica Kingsley.

Kirkpatrick, L.A. (1999) Attachment and religious representations and behaviour. In J. Cassidy and P.R. Shaver (eds) *Handbook of Attachment: Theory, Research and Clinical Applications*. New York: Guilford Press.

Kitayama, S. and Markus, H.R. (1995) Culture and self: Implications for internationalizing psychology. In N.R. Goldberger and J.B. Veroff (eds) *The Culture and Psychology Reader*. New York: New York University Press.

Kitzinger, C. (2004) The myth of the two biological sexes. *The Psychologist*, *17*(8): 451–4.

Klosch, G. and Kraft, U. (2005) Sweet dreams are made of this. *Scientific American Mind*, *16*(2): 38–45.

Kluft, R.P. (1996) Treating the traumatic memories of patients with dissociative identity disorder. *American Journal of Psychiatry*, *153*: 103–10.

Koluchova, J. (1972) Severe deprivation in twins: A case-study. *Journal of Child Psychology and Psychiatry*, *13*: 107–14.

Koluchova, J. (1976) The further development of twins after severe and prolonged deprivation: A second report. *Journal of Child Psychology and Psychiatry*, *17*: 181–8.

Koluchova, J. (1991) Severely deprived twins after 22 years' observation. *Studia Psychologica*, *33*: 23–8.

Kosslyn, S.M., Gazzaniga, M.S., Galaburda, A.M. and Rabin, C. (1999) Hemispheric specialization. In M.J. Zigmond, F.E. Bloom, S.C. Landis, J.L. Roberts and L.R. Squire (eds) *Fundamental Neuroscience*. San Diego, CA: Academic Press.

Kraepelin, E. (1913) *Psychiatry*, 8th edn. Leipzig: Thieme.

Kraus, A.S. and Lilienfeld, A.M. (1959) Some epidemiological aspects of the high mortality rate in the young widowed group. *Journal of Chronic Diseases*, *10*: 207–17.

Krupat, E. and Garonzik, R. (1994) Subjects' expectations and the search for alternatives to deception in social psychology. *British Journal of Social Psychology*, *33*: 211–22.

Kübler-Ross, E. (1969) *On Death and Dying*. London: Tavistock Publications/Routledge.

Kübler-Ross, E. (1991) *On Life After Death*. Berkeley, CA: Celestial Arts.

Kupfer, D.J. (1976) REM latency: A psychobiologic marker for primary depressive disease. *Biological Psychiatry*, *11*: 159–74.

Lacy, D.W., Lewinger, N. and Adamson, J.F. (1953) Foreknowledge as a factor affecting perceptual defence and alertness. *Journal of Experimental Psychology*, *45*: 169.

Laing, R.D. (1967) *The Politics of Experience and the Bird of Paradise*. Harmondsworth: Penguin.

Lambert, M.J. and Bergin, A.E. (1994) The effectiveness of psychotherapy. In A.E. Bergin and S.L. Garfield (eds) *Handbook of Psychotherapy and Behaviour Change*, 4th edn. New York: John Wiley & Sons.

Landis, C. (1938) Statistical evaluation of psychotherapeutic methods. In S.E. Hinde (ed.) *Concepts and Problems of Psychotherapy*. London: Heinemann.

Latané, B. and Darley, J.M. (1968) Group inhibitions of bystander intervention in emergencies. *Journal of Personality and Social Psychology*, *10*: 215–21.

Latané, B. and Darley, J.M. (1970) *The Unresponsive Bystander: Why Does He Not Help?* New York: Appleton-Century-Croft.

Leahy, A.M. (1935) Nature-nurture and intelligence. *Genetic Psychology Monographs*, *17*: 235–308.

Leckman, J.F. and Mayes, L.C. (2007) Nurturing resilient children. *Journal of Child Psychology and Psychiatry*, *48*(3/4): 221–3.

LeDoux, J.E. (1989) Cognitive-emotional interactions in the brain. *Cognition and Emotion*, *3*: 267–89.

LeDoux, J.E. (1998) *The Emotional Brain*. New York: Simon & Schuster.

LeFrançois, G.R. (1983) *Psychology*. Belmont, CA: Wadsworth Publishing Co.

Leslie, A.M. (1987) Pretence and representation: The origins of 'theory of mind'. *Psychological Review*, *94*: 412–26.

Leslie, A.M. (1994) Pretending and believing: Issues in the theory of ToMM. *Cognition*, *50*: 211–38.

Leslie, A.M. and Frith, U. (1988) Autistic children's understanding of seeing, knowing, and believing. *British Journal of Developmental Psychology, 6*: 315–24.

Leslie, A.M. and Roth, D. (1993) What autism teaches us about metarepresentation. In S. Baron-Cohen, H. Tager-Flusberg and D.J. Cohen (eds) *Understanding Other Minds: Perspectives from Autism*. Oxford: Oxford University Press.

Levenson, R.W. (1994) The search for autonomic specificity. In P. Ekman and R.J. Davidson (eds) *The Nature of Emotion: Fundamental Questions*. New York: Oxford University Press.

Levenson, R.W., Ekman, P. and Friesen, W.V. (1990) Voluntary facial action generates emotion-specific autonomic nervous system activity. *Psychophysiology, 27*: 363–84.

Leventhal, H. (1980) Toward a comprehensive theory of emotion. *Advances in Experimental Social Psychology, 13*: 139–207.

Levi-Agresti, J. and Sperry, R.W. (1968) Differential perceptual capacities in major and minor hemispheres. *Proceedings of National Academy of Sciences, 61*: 1151.

Levinger, G. and Clark, J. (1961) Emotional factors in the forgetting of word associations. *Journal of Abnormal and Social Psychology, 62*: 99–105.

Levy, B.A. (1971) Role of articulation in auditory and visual short-term memory. *Journal of Verbal Learning and Verbal Behaviour, 10*: 123–32.

Leyens, J.P. and Codol, J.P. (1988) Social cognition. In M. Hewstone, W. Stroebe, J.P. Codol and G.M. Stephenson (eds) *Introduction to Social Psychology*. Oxford: Blackwell Publishing.

Liao, L.-M. and Boyle, M. (2004) Intersex. *The Psychologist, 17*(8): 446–7.

Light, P.H., Buckingham, N. and Robbins, A.H. (1979) The conservation task as an interactional setting. *British Journal of Educational Psychology, 49*: 304–10.

Lilienfeld, S.O. (1995) *Seeing Both Sides: Classic Controversies in Abnormal Psychology*. Pacific Grove, CA: Brooks/Cole Publishing Co.

Lilienfeld, S.O. (1998) *Looking into Abnormal Psychology: Contemporary Readings*. Pacific Grove, CA: Brooks/Cole Publishing Co.

Lilienfeld, S.O., Lynn, S.J., Kirsch, I., Chaves, J.F. *et al.* (1999) Dissociative identity disorder and the cacogenic model: Recalling lessons from the past. *Psychological Bulletin, 125*: 507–23.

Lindsay, W.R. (1982) The effects of labelling: Blind and non-blind ratings of social skills in schizophrenic and non-schizophrenic control subjects. *American Journal of Psychiatry, 139*: 216–19.

Lockhart, R.S. and Craik, F.I.M. (1990) Levels of processing: A retrospective commentary on a framework for memory research. *Canadian Journal of Psychology, 44*: 87–112.

Locksley, A., Ortiz, V. and Hepburn, C. (1980) Social categorization and discriminatory behaviour: Extinguishing the minimal intergroup discrimination effect. *Journal of Personality and Social Psychology, 39*: 773–83.

Loehlin, J.C. (1989) Partitioning environmental and genetic contributions to behavioural development. *American Psychologist, 44*: 1285.

Loftus, E.F. (1975) Leading questions and the eyewitness report. *Cognitive Psychology, 7*: 560–72.

Loftus, E.F. (1979) Reactions to blatantly contradictory information. *Memory and Cognition, 7*: 368–74.

Loftus, E.F. (1991) Made in memory: Distortions in recollection after misleading information. In G.H. Bower (ed.) *The Psychology of Learning and Motivation*. New York: Academic Press.

Loftus, E.F. (1997) Creating false memories. *Scientific American, 279*(3): 50–5.

Loftus, E.F. and Hoffman, H.G. (1989) Misinformation and memory: The creation of new memories. *Journal of Experimental Psychology: General, 118*: 100–4.

Loftus, E.F. and Zanni, G. (1975) Eye-witness testimony: The influence of the wording of a question. *Bulletin of the Psychonomic Society, 5*: 86–8.

London, P. and Fuhrer, M. (1961) Hypnosis, motivation and performance. *Journal of Personality, 29*: 321–33.

Lorenz, K.Z. (1966) *On Aggression*. London: Methuen.

Lubinski, D., Tellegen, A. and Butcher, J.N. (1981) The relationship between androgyny and subjective indicators of emotional well-being. *Journal of Personality and Social Psychology, 40*: 722–30.

Lubinski, D., Tellegen, A. and Butcher, J.N. (1983) Masculinity, femininity and androgyny. *Journal of Personality and Social Psychology, 44*: 428–39.

Luborsky, L., Singer, B. and Luborsky, L. (1975) Comparative study of psychotherapies: Is it time that 'everyone has won and all must have prizes'? *Archives of General Psychiatry, 32*: 995–1008.

Luria, A.R. (1966) *Higher Cortical Functions in Man*. Oxford: Basic Books Inc.

Luria, A.R. (1973) *The Working Brain: An Introduction to Neuropsychology*. Harmondsworth: Penguin.

MacKay, D. (1975) *Clinical Psychology: Theory and Therapy*. London: Methuen.

MacLeod, A. (1998) Therapeutic interventions. In M. Eysenck (ed.) *Psychology: An Integrated Approach*. Harlow: Addison Wesley Longman Ltd.

MacNamara, J. (1982) *Names for Things*. Cambridge, MA: Bradford MIT Press.

Maes, S. and van Elderen, T. (1998) Health psychology and stress. In M.W. Eysenck (ed.) *Psychology: An Integrated Approach*. London: Longman.

Maher, B.A. (1966) *Principles of Psychopathology: An Experimental Approach*. New York: McGraw-Hill.

Main, M. and Weston, D.R. (1981) The quality of the toddler's relationship to other and to father: Related to conflict behaviour and the readiness to establish new relationships. *Child Development, 52*: 932–40.

Main, M., Kaplan, N. and Cassidy (1985) Security in infancy, childhood and adulthood: A move to the level of representation. In I. Brotherhood and E. Waters (eds) *Growing Points of Attachment: Theory and Research*. Chicago, IL: University of Chicago Press.

Mair, K. (1992) The myth of therapist expertise. In W. Dryden and C. Feltham (eds) *Psychotherapy and its Discontents*. Buckingham: Open University Press.

Mair, K. (1999) Multiple personality and child abuse. *The Psychologist, 12*(2): 76–80.

Mamalek, A. and Hobson, A. (1989) Dream bizarreness as the cognitive correlate of altered neuronal behaviour in REM sleep. *Journal of Cognitive Neuroscience, 1*: 201–22.

Mantell, D.M. (1971) The potential for violence in Germany. *Journal of Social Issues, 27*: 101–12.

Maracek, J. (1978) Psychological disorders in women: Indices of role strain. In I. Frieze, J. Parsons, P. Johnson, D. Ruble and G. Zellman (eds) *Women and Sex Roles: A Social Psychological Perspective*. New York: Norton.

Marcel, T. and Patterson, K. (1978) Word recognition and production. In J. Requin (ed.) *Attention and Performance, 7*. Hillsdale, NJ: Lawrence Erlbaum.

Marris, P. (1958) *Widows and their Families*. London: Routledge and Kegan Paul.

Marshall, G.D. and Zimbardo, P.G. (1979) Affective consequences of inadequately explained physiological arousal. *Journal of Personality and Social Psychology, 37*: 970–88.

Marzillier, J. (2004) The myth of evidence-based psychotherapy. *The Psychologist, 17*(7): 392–5.

Maslach, C. (1979) Negative emotional biasing of unexplained arousal. *Journal of Personality and Social Psychology, 37*: 953–69.

Mason, M.K. (1942) Learning to speak after six and one half years of silence. *Journal of Speech and Hearing Disorders, 7*: 295–304.

Masson, G.E. (1992) *The Assault on Truth: Freud and Child Sexual Abuse*. London: Fontana.

Matt, G.E. (1993) Comparing classes of psychotherapeutic interventions: A review and analysis of English- and German-language meta-analyses. *Journal of Cross-Cultural Psychology, 24*(1): 5–25.

Mazhindu, D. (1998) Emotional healing. *Nursing Times, 94*(6): 26–8.

McCarley, R.W. (1983) REM dreams, REM sleep and their isomorphism. In M.H. Chase and E.D. Weitzman (eds) *Sleep Disorders: Basic and Clinical Research*, vol. 8. New York: Spectrum.

McCarley, R.W. (1995) Sleep, dreams and states of consciousness. In P.M. Conn (ed.) *Neuroscience in Medicine*. Philadelphia, PA: J.B. Lippincott.

McDermott, M. (1993) On cruelty, ethics and experimentation: Profile of Philip G. Zimbardo. *The Psychologist, 6*(10): 456–9.

McGarrigle, J. and Donaldson, M. (1974) Conservation accidents. *Cognition, 3*: 341–50.

McGhee, P. (2001) *Thinking Psychologically*. Basingstoke: Palgrave.

Meadows, S. (1995) Cognitive development. In P.E. Bryant and A.M. Colman (eds) *Developmental Psychology*. London: Longman.

Meeus, W.H.J. and Raaijmakers, Q.A.W. (1986) Administrative obedience: Carrying out orders to use psychological-administrative violence. *European Journal of Social Psychology, 16*: 311–24.

Melton, A.W. (1963) Implications of short-term memory for a general theory of memory. *Journal of Verbal Learning and Verbal Behaviour, 2*: 1–21.

Memon, A. (1998) Telling it all: The cognitive interview. In A. Memon, A. Vrij and R. Bull (eds) *Psychology and Law: Truthfulness, Accuracy and Credibility*. Maidenhead: McGraw-Hill.

Memon, A., Gabbert, F. and Hope, L. (2004) The ageing eyewitness. In J.R. Adler (ed.) *Forensic Psychology: Concepts, Debates and Practice*. Cullompton: Willan Publishing.

Milgram, S. (1970) The experience of living in cities, *Science, 167*: 1461–8. Reprinted in S. Milgram (1992) *The Individual in a Social World*, 2nd edn. New York: McGraw-Hill.

Milgram, S. (1972) Interpreting obedience: Error and evidence. In A.G. Miller (ed.) *The Social Psychology of*

Psychological Research. New York: Free Press. Reprinted in S. Milgram (1992) *The Individual in a Social World*, 2nd edn. New York: McGraw-Hill.

Milgram, S. (1974) *Obedience to Authority*. New York: Harper Torchbooks.

Milgram, S. (1977) Subject reaction: The neglected factor in the ethics of experimentation. *The Hastings Centre Report*, 19–23 October. Reprinted in S. Milgram (1992) *The Individual in a Social World*, 2nd edn. New York: McGraw-Hill.

Milgram, S. (1992) *The Individual in a Social World*, 2nd edn. New York: McGraw-Hill.

Milgram, S. and Hollander, P. (1964) The murder they heard. *The Nation*, *198*(25): 602–4. Reprinted as 'The Urban Bystander' in S. Milgram (1992) *The Individual in a Social World*, 2nd edn. New York: McGraw-Hill.

Miller, A. (1986) *Thou Shalt Not Be Aware: Society's Betrayal of the Child*. London: Virago.

Miller, D.T. and Ross, M. (1975) Self-serving biases in the attribution of causality: Fact or fiction? *Psychological Bulletin*, *82*: 213–25.

Miller, E. and Morley, S. (1986) *Investigating Abnormal Behaviour*. London: Lawrence Erlbaum.

Miller, G.A. (1956) The magical number seven, plus or minus two: Some limits on our capacity for processing information. *Psychological Review*, *63*: 81–97.

Miller, J. (1997) Theoretical issues in cultural psychology. In J.W. Berry, Y.H. Porting and J. Pandey (eds) *Handbook of Cross-Cultural Research, Vol. 1: Theory and Method*. Boston, MA: Allyn & Bacon.

Miller, N.E. (1948) Theory and experiment relating psychoanalytic displacement to stimulus-response generalization. *Journal of Abnormal and Social Psychology*, *43*: 155–78.

Milner, D. (1975) *Children and Race*. Harmondsworth: Penguin.

Milner, D. (1981) Racial prejudice and social psychology. In J. Turner and H. Giles (eds) *Intergroup Behaviour*. Oxford: Blackwell Publishing.

Milner, D. (1983) *Children and Race: Ten Years On*. London: Ward Lock Educational.

Mischel, W. (1986) *Introduction to Personality: A New Look*, 4th edn. New York: CBS Publishing.

Mitchell, D. and Blair, J. (2000) Psychopathy. *The Psychologist*, *13*(7): 356–60.

Mitchell, J. and McCarthy, H. (2000) Eating disorders. In L. Champion and M. Power (eds) *Adult Psychological Problems: An Introduction*, 2nd edn. Hove: Psychology Press.

Mitchell, P. (1997) *Introduction to Theory of Mind: Children, Autism and Apes*. London: Hodder Arnold.

Moghaddam, F.M. (1998) *Social Psychology: Exploring Universals Across Cultures*. New York: W.H. Freeman & Co.

Moghaddam, F.M. (2005) *Great Ideas in Psychology*. Oxford: Oneworld Publications.

Moghaddam, F.M., Taylor, D.M. and Wright, S.C. (1993) *Social Psychology in Cross-Cultural Perspective*. New York: W.H. Freeman & Co.

Mollon, P. (1998) *Remembering Trauma: A Psychotherapist's Guide to Memory and Illusions*. Chichester: John Wiley & Sons.

Money, J. and Ehrhardt, A.A. (1972) *Man and Woman, Boy and Girl*. Baltimore, MD: Johns Hopkins University Press.

Money, J. and Tucker, P. (1975) *Sexual Signatures: On Being a Man or Woman*. Boston, MA: Little, Brown & Co.

Moody, F.R. (1975) *Life After Life*. Covinda, GA: Mockingbird.

Moorcroft, W.H. (ed.) (1993) *Sleep, Dreaming and Sleep Disorders*. Lanham, MD: University Press of America Inc.

Moore, C. and Frye, D. (1986) The effect of the experimenter's intentions on the child's understanding of conservation. *Cognition*, *22*(3): 283–98.

Moray, N. (1959) Attention in dichotic listening: Affective cues and the influence of instructions. *Quarterly Journal of Experimental Psychology*, *11*: 56–60.

Morris, C.D., Bransford, J.D. and Franks, J.J. (1977) Levels of processing versus transfer appropriate processing. *Journal of Verbal Learning and Verbal Behaviour*, *16*: 519–33.

Morton, J. (1970) A functional model of memory. In D.A. Norman (ed.) *Models of Human Memory*. New York: Academic Press.

Moruzzi, G. (1996) The functional significance of sleep with particular regard to the brain mechanisms underlying consciousness. In J.C. Eccles (ed.) *Brain and Conscious Experience*. Berlin: Springer-Verlag.

Mowrer, O.H. (1950) *Learning Theory and Personality Dynamics*. New York: Ronald Press.

Mueller, A. and Roberts, R. (2001) Dreams. In R. Roberts and D. Groome (eds) *Parapsychology: The Science of Unusual Experience*. London: Hodder Arnold.

Mummendey, A., Simon, B., Dietze, C., Grunwert, M., Haeger, G., Kessler, S., Lettgen, S. and Schaferhoff, S. (1993) Categorization is not enough: Intergroup discrimination in negative outcome allocations. *Journal of Experimental Social Psychology*, *28*: 125–44.

Mundy-Castle, A.C. and Nelson, G.K. (1962) A neuropsychological study of the Knysma forest workers. *Psychologica Africana, 9*: 240–72.

Murphy, J. (1976) Psychiatric labelling in cross-cultural perspective. *Science, 191*: 1019–28.

Murphy, J., John, M. and Brown, H. (1984) *Dialogues and Debates in Social Psychology*. London: Lawrence Erlbaum/Open University Press.

Nagayama Hall, G.C. and Barongan, C. (2002) *Multicultural Psychology*. Upper Saddle River, NJ: Prentice Hall.

Nash, M.R. (2001) The truth and the hype of hypnosis. *Scientific American, 285*(1): 36–43.

Nash, M.R. and Benham, G. (2005) The truth and the hype of hypnosis. *Scientific American Mind, 16*(2): 46–53.

Neisser, U. (1964) Visual search. *Scientific American, 210*: 94–102.

Neisser, U. (1967) *Cognitive Psychology*. New York: Appleton-Century-Crofts.

Neisser, U. (1973) Reversibility of psychiatric diagnoses. *Science, 180*: 1116.

Nestler, E.J. and Malenka, R.C. (2004) The addicted brain. *Scientific American, 290*(3): 50–7.

Newell, R. and Dryden, W. (1991) Clinical problems: An introduction to the cognitive behavioural approach. In W. Dryden and R. Rantoul (eds) *Adult Clinical Problems*. London: Routledge.

Newman, H.H., Freeman, F.N. and Holzinger, K.J. (1937) *Twins: A Study of Heredity and Environment*. Chicago, IL: University of Chicago Press.

Nichols, K. (2005) Why is psychology still failing the average patient? *The Psychologist, 18*(1): 26–7.

Nicolson, P. (2000) Gender, power and the health care professions. In L. Sher and J.S. St. Lawrence (eds) *Women, Health and The Mind*. Chichester: John Wiley & Sons.

Nisbett, R.E. and Valins, S. (1972) Perceiving the causes of one's own behaviour. In E.F. Jones, D.E. Kanouse, H.H. Kelley, R.E. Nisbett, S. Valins and B. Weiner (eds) *Attribution: Perceiving the Causes of Behaviour*. Morristown, NJ: General Learning Press.

Nisbett, R.E. and Cohen, D. (1999) Men, honour and murder. *Scientific American Presents, 10*(2): 16–19.

Norman, D.A. (1969) Memory while shadowing. *Quarterly Journal of Experimental Psychology, 21*: 85–93.

Oatley, K. (1984) *Selves in Relation: An Introduction to Psychotherapy and Groups*. London: Methuen.

Oatley, K. and Johnson-Laird, P.N. (1996) The communicative theory of emotions: Empirical tests, mental models, and implications for social interaction. In L.L. Martin and A. Tesser (eds) *Striving and Feeling: Interactions Among Goals, Affect and Self-Regulation*. Mahwah, NJ: Lawrence Erlbaum.

Oberman, L.M., Hubbard, E.H., McCleery, J.P., Altschuler, E.L., Pineda, J.A. and Ramachandran, V.S. (2005) EEG evidence for mirror neuron dysfunction in autism spectrum disorders. *Cognitive Brain Research, 24*: 190–8.

Ochsner, K.N. (2004) Current directions in social cognitive neuroscience. *Current Opinions in Neurobiology, 14*: 254–8.

O'Connor, T.G. and Rutter, M. (2000) Attachment disorder behaviour following early severe deprivation: Extension and longitudinal follow-up. English and Romanian Adoptees Study Team. *Journal of the American Academy of Child and Adolescent Psychiatry, 39*: 703–12.

Ogden, J. (2004) *Health Psychology: A Textbook*, 3rd edn. Maidenhead: Open University Press/McGraw-Hill Education.

O'Grady, M. (1977) Effects of subliminal pictorial stimulation on skin resistance. *Perceptual and Motor Skills, 44*: 1051–6.

Olds, J. (1956) Pleasure centres in the brain. *Scientific American*, October: 105–16.

Olds, J. (1958) Self-stimulation of the brain. *Science, 127*: 315–23.

Olds, J. (1962) Hypothalamic substrates of reward. *Psychological Review, 42*: 554–604.

Olds, J. and Sinclair, J. (1957) Self-stimulation in the obstruction box. *American Psychologist, 12*: 464.

Orbach, A. (1999) *Life, Psychotherapy and Death*. London: Jessica Kingsley.

Orne, M.T. (1959) The nature of hypnosis: Artifact and essence. *Journal of Abnormal and Social Psychology, 58*: 277–99.

Orne, M.T. (1962) On the social psychology of the psychological experiment: With particular reference to demand characteristics and their implications. *American Psychologist, 17*: 776–83.

Orne, M.T. (1979) On the simulating subject as a quasi-control group in hypnosis research: What, why and how? In E. Fromm and R.E. Shor (eds) *Hypnosis: Research Developments and Perspectives*, 2nd edn. New York: Aldine.

Orne, M.T. and Evans, F.J. (1965) Social control in the psychological experiment: Antisocial behaviour and hypnosis. *Journal of Personality and Social Psychology, 1*: 189–200.

Orne, M.T. and Holland, C.C. (1968) On the ecological validity of laboratory deceptions. *International Journal of Psychiatry, 6*(4): 282–93.

Orne, M.T., Dinges, D.F. and Orne, E.C. (1984) On the differential diagnosis of multiple personality in the forensic context. *International Journal of Clinical and Experimental Hypnosis, 32*: 118–69.

Ornstein, R. (1986) *The Psychology of Consciousness*, 2nd rev. edn. Harmondsworth: Penguin.

Osgood, C.E. (1952) The nature and measurement of meaning. *Psychological Bulletin, 49*: 192–237.

Osgood, C.E. and Tannenbaum, P.H. (1955) The principle of congruity in the prediction of attitude change. *Psychological Review, 62*: 42–55.

Osgood, C.E., Suci, G.J. and Tannenbaum, P.H. (1957) *The Measurement of Meaning*. Urbana: University of Illinois Press.

O'Toole, K. (1997) The Stanford prison experiment: Still powerful after all these years. (http://www.stanford.edu/dept/news/pr/97/970108prisonexp.html)

Owusu-Bempah, K. and Howitt, D. (2000) *Psychology Beyond Western Perspectives*. Leicester: British Psychological Society.

Ozonoff, S., Pennington, B.F. and Rogers, S.J. (1991) Executive function deficits in high-functioning autistic individuals: Relationship to theory of mind. *Journal of Child Psychology and Psychiatry, 32*(7): 1081–105.

Packard, V. (1957) *The Hidden Persuaders*. New York: McKay.

Paludi, M.A. (1992) *The Psychology of Women*. Dubuque, IA: William C. Brown.

Panksepp, J. (1998) *Affective Neuroscience*. New York: Oxford University Press.

Parkes, C.M. (1970) The first year of bereavement: A longitudinal study of the reaction of London widows to the death of their husbands. *Psychiatry, 33*: 444–67.

Parkes, C.M. (1972) *Bereavement: Studies of Grief in Adult Life*. London: Tavistock Publications.

Parkes, C.M. (1986) *Bereavement: Studies of Grief in Adult Life*, 2nd edn. Harmondsworth: Penguin.

Parkes, C.M. (2006) *Love and Loss: The Roots of Grief and its Complications*. Hove: Routledge.

Parkes, C.M. and Weiss, R.S. (1983) *Recovery from Bereavement*. New York: Basic Books.

Parkin, A.J. (1993) *Memory: Phenomena, Experiment and Theory*. Oxford: Blackwell Publishing.

Parkin, A.J. (1998) Memory. In P. Scott and C. Spencer (eds) *Psychology: A Contemporary Introduction*. Oxford: Blackwell Publishing.

Parkin, A.J. (2000) *Essential Cognitive Psychology*. Hove: Psychology Press.

Parkin, A.J., Lewinson, J. and Folkard, S. (1982) The influence of emotion on immediate and delayed retention: Levinger and Clark reconsidered. *British Journal of Psychology, 73*: 389–93.

Parkinson, B. (1987) Emotion – cognitive approaches. In H. Beloff and A.M. Colman (eds) *Psychology Survey*, 6. Leicester: British Psychological Society.

Parsons, T. and Bales, R.F. (1955) *Family, Socialization and Interaction Process*. Glencoe, IL: Free Press.

Patterson, F.G. (1978) The gestures of a gorilla: Language acquisition in another pongid. *Brain and Language, 5*: 72–97.

Patterson, F.G. (1980) Innovative uses of language by a gorilla: A case study. In K. Nelson (ed.) *Children's Language*, vol. 2. New York: Gardner Press.

Paul, G.L. (1966) *Insight Versus Desensitization in Psychotherapy: An Experiment in Anxiety Reduction*. Stanford, CA: Stanford University Press.

Pennington, D.C., Gillen, K. and Hill, P. (1999) *Social Psychology*. London: Hodder Arnold.

Perner, J. and Wimmer, H. (1985) 'John thinks that Mary thinks that': Attribution of second-order beliefs by 5–10-year-old children. *Journal of Experimental Child Psychology, 39*: 437–71.

Pezdek, K. and Roe, C. (1996) Memory for childhood events: How suggestible is it? In K. Pezdek and W.P. Banks (eds) *The Recovered Memory/False Memory Debate*. London: Academic Press.

Phillips, W.A. and Baddeley, A. (1971) Reaction time and short-term memory. *Psychonomic Science, 22*: 73–4.

Phinney, J.S. (1990) Ethnic identity in adolescents and adults: Review of research. *Psychological Bulletin, 108*: 499–514.

Piaget, J. (1950) *The Psychology of Intelligence*. London: Routledge and Kegan Paul.

Piaget, J. and Inhelder, B. (1956) *The Child's Conception of Space*. London: Routledge and Kegan Paul.

Piliavin, I.M., Piliavin, J.A. and Rodin, S. (1975) Costs, diffusion and the stigmatized victim. *Journal of Personality and Social Psychology, 32*: 429–38.

Piliavin, J.A. and Piliavin, I.M. (1972) Effects of blood on reactions to a victim. *Journal of Personality and Social Psychology, 23*: 353–62.

Piliavin, J.A., Dovidio, J.F., Gaertner, S.L. and Clark, R.D. (1981) *Emergency Intervention*. New York: Academic Press.

Pinel, J.P.J. (1993) *Biopsychology*, 2nd edn. Boston: Allyn & Bacon.

Plomin, R. (1996) Nature and nurture. In M.R. Merrens and G.C. Brannigan (eds) *The Developmental Psychologists: Research Adventures Across the Life Span.* New York: McGraw-Hill.

Plomin, R. and Thompson, R. (1987) Life-span developmental behavioural genetics. In P.B. Baltes, D.L. Featherman and R.M. Lerner (eds) *Life-Span Development and Behaviour,* vol. 8. Hillsdale, NJ: Lawrence Erlbaum.

Plomin, R. and Loehlin, J.C. (1989) Direct and indirect IQ habitability estimates: A puzzle. *Behavioural Genetics, 19:* 331–42.

Plomin, R., DeFries, J.C. and Loehlin, J.C. (1977) Genotype-environment interaction and correlation in the analysis of human behaviour. *Psychological Bulletin, 84:* 309–22.

Poole, D.A. and Lindsay, D.S. (1995) Interviewing preschoolers: Effects of nonsuggestive techniques, parental coaching, and leading questions on reports of nonexperienced events. *Journal of Experimental Child Psychology, 60*(1): 129–54.

Porpodas, C.D. (1987) The one-question conservation experiment reconsidered. *Journal of Child Psychology and Psychiatry, 28*(2): 343–9.

Postman, L., Bruner, J.S. and McGinnies, E. (1948) Personal values as selective factors in perception. *Journal of Abnormal and Social Psychology, 43:* 142–54.

Postman, L., Bronson, W.C. and Gropper, G.L. (1953) Is there a mechanism of perceptual defence? *Journal of Abnormal and Social Psychology, 48:* 215.

Potter, M.C. (1966) On perceptual recognition. In J.S. Bruner, R.C. Olver and P.M. Greenfield (eds) *Studies in Cognitive Growth.* New York: John Wiley & Sons.

Powell-Hopson, D. (1985) The effects of modelling, reinforcement, and colour meaning word associations on doll colour preference of black preschool children and white preschool children. Unpublished doctoral dissertation. Hofstra University.

Powell-Hopson, D. and Hopson, D.S. (1988) Implications of doll-colour preference among black preschool children and white preschool children. *Journal of Black Psychology, 14:* 57–63.

Power, M.J. and Dalgleish, T. (1997) *Cognition and Emotion: From Order to Disorder.* Hove: Lawrence Erlbaum.

Premack, D. (1971) On the assessment of language competence in the chimpanzee. In A.M. Schrier and F. Stollnitz (eds) *Behaviour of Non-Human Primates,* vol. 4. New York: Academic Press.

Premack, D. and Woodruff, G. (1978) Does the chimpanzee have a 'theory of mind'? *Behavioural and Brain Sciences, 4:* 515–26.

Price-Williams, D. (1966) Cross-cultural studies. In B.M. Foss (ed.) *New Horizons in Psychology,* vol. 1. Harmondsworth: Penguin.

Prince, M. (1906) *The Dissociation of a Personality.* New York: Longmans, Green & Co.

Prochaska, J.O. and DiClemente, C.C. (1982) Trans-theoretical therapy: Toward a more integrative model of change. *Psychotherapy: Theory, Research, and Practice, 19:* 276–88.

Psychologist, The (2006) Physical therapists providing psychological support. *The Psychologist, 19*(3): 134.

Quinton, D. and Rutter, M. (1988) *Parental Breakdown: The Making and Breaking of Intergenerational Links.* London: Gower.

Rachman, S. (1977) The conditioning theory of fear-acquisition: A critical examination. *Behaviour Research and Therapy, 15:* 375–87.

Rachman, S. and Wilson, G. (1980) *The Effects of Psychological Therapy.* Oxford: Pergamon.

Raichle, M.E. (1998) Behind the scenes of functional brain imaging: A historical and physiological perspective. *Proceedings of the National Academy of Sciences, 95*(3): 765–72.

Raine, A. (1993) *The Psychopathology of Crime: Criminal Behaviour as a Clinical Disorder.* San Diego, CA: Academic Press.

Raine, A., Lencz, T., Bihrle, S., La Casse, L. and Colletti, P. (2000) Reduced prefrontal grey matter violence and reduced autonomic activity in antisocial personality disorder. *Archives of General Psychiatry, 57*(2): 119–27.

Raine, I., Ishikawa, S.S., Arce, E., Lencz, T., Knuth, K.H., Bihrle, S., LaCasse, L. and Colletti, P. (2004) Hippocampal structural asymmetry in unsuccessful psychopaths. *Biological Psychiatry, 55*(2): 185–91.

Ramachandran, V.S. and Oberman, L.M. (2006) Broken mirrors: A theory of autism. *Scientific American, 295*(5): 38–45.

Raphael, B. (1984) *The Anatomy of Bereavement.* London: Hutchinson.

Reicher, S. (1999) Differences, self-image and the individual. *The Psychologist, 12*(3): 131–3.

Reicher, S. and Haslam, S.A. (2006) Tyranny revisited. *The Psychologist, 19*(3): 146–50.

Riegler, E., Touyz, S. and Beumont, P. (2002) The Anorexia Nervosa Stages of Change Questionnaire (ANSOCQ): Information regarding its psychometric properties. *International Journal of Eating Disorders, 32:* 24–38.

Riegler, E., Touyz, S., Schotte, D., Beumont, P., Russell, J., Clarke, S., Kohn, M. and Griffiths, R. (2000) Development of an instrument to assess readiness to recover in anorexia nervosa. *International Journal of Eating Disorders, 28*: 387–96.

Ring, K. (1980) *Life After Death: A Scientific Investigation of the Near-Death Experience.* New York: Coward, McCann & Geoghegan.

Rivers, W.H.R. (1901) Visual spatial perception. In A.C. Haddon (ed.) *Reports of the Cambridge Anthropological Expedition to the Torres Straits*, vol. 2(1). Cambridge: Cambridge University Press.

Rizzolatti, G., Forgassi, L. and Gallese, V. (2006) Mirrors in the mind. *Scientific American, 295*(5): 30–7.

Roberts, G. and Owen, J. (1988) The near-death experience. *British Journal of Psychiatry, 153*: 607–17.

Robson, C. (1973) *Experiment, Design and Statistics.* Harmondsworth: Penguin.

Roe, C.A. (2001) Near-death experience. In R. Roberts and D. Groome (eds) *Parapsychology: The Science of Unusual Experience.* London: Hodder Arnold.

Roediger, H.L., Rushton, J.P., Capaldi, E.D. and Paris, S.G. (1984) *Psychology.* Boston, MA: Little, Brown & Co.

Rose, S. (1976) *The Conscious Brain.* Harmondsworth: Penguin.

Rose, S., Lewontin, R.C. and Kamin, L.J. (1984) *Not in Our Genes: Biology, Ideology and Human Nature.* Harmondsworth: Penguin.

Rose, S.A. and Blank, M. (1974) The potency of context in children's cognition: An illustration through conservation. *Child Development, 45*: 499–502.

Rosenhan, D. (1969) Some origins of concern for others. In P. Mussen, J. Langer and M. Covington (eds) *Trends and Issues in Developmental Psychology.* New York: Holt, Rinehart & Winston.

Rosenthal, R. and Rosnow, R.L. (1966) Volunteer subjects and the results of opinion change studies. *Psychological Reports, 19*: 1183.

Ross, C.A. (1997) *Dissociative Identity Disorder: Diagnosis, Clinical Features and Treatment of Multiple Personality.* New York: John Wiley & Sons.

Ross, L. (1977) The intuitive psychologist and his shortcomings. In L. Berkowitz (ed.) *Advances in Experimental Social Psychology*, vol. 10. New York: Academic Press.

Ross, L. and Nisbett, R.E. (1991) *The Person and the Situation: Perspectives of Social Psychology.* New York: McGraw-Hill.

Roth, A. and Fonagy, P. (2005) *What Works for Whom? A Critical Review of Psychotherapy Research*, 2nd edn. New York: Guilford Press.

Routtenberg, A. and Lindy, J. (1965) Effects of the availability of rewarding septal and hypothalamic stimulation on bar-pressing for food under conditions of deprivation. *Journal of Comparative and Physiological Psychology, 60*: 158–61.

Rumbaugh, D.M. (ed.) (1977) *Language Learning by a Chimpanzee: The LANA Project.* New York: Academic Press.

Rumbaugh, D.M. and Savage-Rumbaugh, S. (1994) Language and apes. *APA Psychology Teacher Network*, 2–9 January.

Rumelhart, D.E. and Norman, D.A. (1983) Representation in memory. In R.C. Atkinson, R.J. Herrnstein, B. Lindzey and R.D. Luce (eds) *Handbook of Experimental Psychology.* Chichester: John Wiley & Sons.

Rushton, A. and Minnis, H. (1997) Transracial family placements. *Journal of Child Psychology and Psychiatry, 38*(2): 147–59.

Rushton, J.P. (1991) Is altruism innate? *Psychological Inquiry, 2*: 141–3.

Rushton, J.P. (1995) *Race, Evolution and Behaviour.* New Brunswick, NJ: Transaction Publishers.

Rutherford, A. (2005) Long-term memory: Encoding to retrieval. In N. Braisby and A. Gellatly (eds) *Cognitive Psychology.* Oxford: Oxford University Press in association with the Open University.

Rutter, M. (1981) *Maternal Deprivation Reassessed*, 2nd edn. Harmondsworth: Penguin.

Rutter, M. (1987) Continuities and discontinuities from infancy. In J. Osofsky (ed.) *Handbook of Infant Development*, 2nd edn. New York: John Wiley & Sons.

Rutter, M. (1989) Pathways from childhood to adult life. *Journal of Child Psychology and Psychiatry, 30*(1): 25–31.

Rutter, M. (2006) The psychological effects of institutional rearing. In P. Marshall and N. Fox (eds) *The Development of Social Engagement: Neurobiological Perspectives.* New York: Oxford University Press.

Rutter, M. and Rutter, M. (1992) *Developing Minds: Challenge and Continuity Across the Life Span.* Harmondsworth: Penguin.

Rutter, M. and the English and Romanian Adoptees (ERA) study team (1998) Developmental catch-up, and deficit, following adoption after severe global early privation. *Journal of Child Psychology and Psychiatry, 39*(4): 465–76.

Rutter, M. and the English and Romanian Adoptees (ERA) study team (2004) Are there biological programming effects for psychological development? Findings from a study of Romanian adoptees. *Developmental Psychology, 40*: 81–94.

Rutter, M., Colvert, E., Kreppner, J., Beckett, C., Castle, J., Groothues, C., Hawkins, A., O'Connor, T.G., Stevens, S.E. and Sonuga-Barke, E.J.S. (2007) Early adolescent outcomes for institutionally-deprived and non-deprived adoptees. 1: Disinhibited attachment. *Journal of Child Psychology and Psychiatry, 48*(1): 17–30.

Ryan, J. (1972) IQ – The illusion of objectivity. In K. Richardson and D. Spears (eds) *Race, Culture and Intelligence*. Harmondsworth: Penguin.

Sabbatini, R.M.F. (1997) The PET scan: A new window into the brain. *Brain & Mind*, March/May. (http://www.cerebromente.org.br/n01/pet/pet.htm)

Sabom, M.B. (1982) *Recollections of Death*. London: Corgi.

Saks, E.R. (1997) *Jekyll on Trial: Multiple Personality Disorder and Criminal Law*. New York: New York University Press.

Sarbin, T.R. and Mancuso, J.C. (1980) *Schizophrenia: Medical Diagnosis or Moral Verdict?* New York: Pergamon.

Savage-Rumbaugh, E.S., Rumbaugh, D.M. and Boysen, S.L. (1980) Do apes use language? *American Scientist, 68*: 49–61.

Savage-Rumbaugh, E.S., Murphy, J., Seveik, R.A., Williams, S., Brakke, K. and Rumbaugh, D.M. (1993) Language comprehension in ape and child. *Monographs of the Society for Research in Child Development, 58*: 3–4.

Savin, H.B. (1973) Professors and psychological researchers: Conflicting values in conflicting roles. *Cognition, 21*: 147–9.

Scarr, S. (1968) Environmental bias in twin studies. *Eugenics Quarterly, 15*: 34–40.

Scarr, S. (1992) Developmental theories for the 1990s: Development and individual differences. *Child Development, 63*: 1–19.

Scarr, S. (1993) Biological and cultural diversity: The legacy of Darwin for development. *Child Development, 64*: 1333–53.

Scarr, S. (1997) Behaviour-genetic and socialization theories of intelligence: Truth and reconciliation. In R.J. Sternberg and E. Grigorenko (eds) *Intelligence, Heredity and Environment*. New York: Cambridge University Press.

Scarr, S. and Weinberg, R.A. (1977) Intellectual similarities within families of both adopted and biological children. *Intelligence, 1*: 170–91.

Scarr, S. and Weinberg, R.A. (1983) The Minnesota Adoption Studies: Genetic differences and malleability. *Child Development, 54*: 260–7.

Scarr-Salapatek, S. (1976) An evolutionary perspective on infant intelligence: Species patterns and individual variations. In M. Lewis (ed.) *Origins of Intelligence*. New York: Plenum.

Schachter, S. (1964) The interaction of cognitive and physiological determinants of emotional state. *Advances in Experimental Social Psychology, 1*: 49–80.

Schaffer, H.R. (1996) *Social Development*. Oxford: Blackwell Publishing.

Schaffer, H.R. (1998) Deprivation and its effects on children. *Psychology Review, 5*(2): 2–5.

Schaffer, H.R. (2004) *Introducing Child Psychology*. Oxford: Blackwell Publishing.

Scheff, T.J. (1966) *Being Mentally Ill: A Sociological Theory*. Chicago, IL: Aldine.

Scherer, K. (1997) Profiles of emotion-antecedent appraisal: Testing theoretical predictions across cultures. *Cognition and Emotion, 11*: 113–50.

Schiffman, R. and Wicklund, R.A. (1992) The minimal group paradigm and its minimal psychology. *Theory and Psychology, 2*(1): 29–50.

Schreiber, F.R. (1973) *Sybil*. Harmondsworth: Penguin.

Schroeder, D.A., Penner, L.A., Dovidio, J.F. and Piliavin, J.A. (1995) *The Psychology of Helping and Altruism: Problems and Puzzles*. New York: McGraw-Hill.

Schulman, H.G. (1970) Encoding and retention of semantic and phonemic information in short-term memory. *Journal of Verbal Learning and Verbal Behaviour, 9*: 499–508.

Schulman, H.G. (1972) Semantic confusion errors in short-term memory. *Journal of Verbal Learning and Verbal Behaviour, 11*: 221–7.

Segall, M.H., Campbell, D.T. and Herskovits, M.J. (1963) Cultural differences in the perception of geometrical illusions. *Science, 139*: 769–71.

Segall, M.H., Dasen, P.R., Berry, J.W. and Poortinga, Y.H. (1990) *Human Behaviour in Global Perspective: An Introduction to Cross-Cultural Psychology*. New York: Pergamon.

Segall, M.H., Dasen, P.R., Berry, J.W. and Poortinga, Y.H. (1999) *Human Behaviour in Global Perspective: An Introduction to Cross-Cultural Psychology*, 2nd edn. Needham Heights, MA: Allyn & Bacon.

Selfridge, O.G. and Neisser, U. (1960) Pattern recognition by machine. *Scientific American, 203*: 60–8.

Seligman, M.E.P. (1970) On the generality of the laws of learning. *Psychological Review, 77*: 406–18.

Seligman, M.E.P. (1974) Depression and learned helplessness. In R.J. Friedman and M.M. Katz (eds) *The Psychology of Depression: Contemporary Theory and Research.* Washington, DC: Winston-Wiley.

Seligman, M.E.P. (1975) *Helplessness: On Depression, Development and Death.* San Francisco, CA: W.H. Freeman & Co.

Seligman, M.E.P. (1996) The effectiveness of psychotherapy: The Consumer Reports study. *American Psychologist, 50*(12): 965–74.

Serpell, R.S. (1976) *Culture's Influence on Behaviour.* London: Methuen.

Serpell, R.S. and Deregowski, J.B. (1980) The skill of pictorial perception: An interpretation of cross-cultural evidence. *International Journal of Psychology, 15*: 145–80.

Shaffer, D.R. (1985) *Developmental Psychology: Theory, Research and Applications.* Monterey, CA: Brooks/Cole Publishing Co.

Shallice, T. (1982) Specific impairments of planning. *Philosophical Transactions of the Royal Society of London, Series B, Biological Sciences, 298*: 199–209.

Shallice, T. and Warrington, E.K. (1970) Independent functioning of the verbal memory stores: A neuropsychological study. *Quarterly Journal of Experimental Psychology, 22*: 261–73.

Shanab, M.E. and Yahya, K.A. (1978) A cross-cultural study of obedience. *Bulletin of the Psychonomic Society, 11*: 267–9.

Shapiro, D.A. and Shapiro, D. (1982) Meta-analysis of comparative therapeutic outcomes: A replication and refinement. *Psychological Bulletin, 92*: 581–604.

Shaver, K.G. (1987) *Principles of Social Psychology*, 3rd edn. Hillsdale, NJ: Lawrence Erlbaum.

Shaver, P.R., Collins, N. and Clark, C.L. (1996) Attachment styles and internal working models of self and relationship patterns. In G.J.O. Fletcher and J. Fitness (eds) *Knowledge Structures in Close Relationships: A Social Psychological Approach.* Mahwah, NJ: Lawrence Erlbaum.

Sheridan, C.L. and King, R.G. (1972) Obedience to authority with an authentic victim. *Proceedings, Eightieth Annual Convention, American Psychological Association.* Washington, DC: American Psychological Association.

Sherif, M. (1966) *Group Conflict and Co-operation: Their Social Psychology.* London: Routledge and Kegan Paul.

Sherif, M. and Sherif, C.W. (1953) *Groups in Harmony and Tension.* New York: Harper Brothers.

Sherif, M., White, B.J. and Harvey, O.J. (1955) *Experimental Study of Positive and Negative Intergroup Attitudes Between Experimentally Produced Groups: Robbers Cave Study.* Norman: University of Oklahoma.

Sherif, M., Harvey, O.J., White, B.J., Hood, W.R. and Sherif, C. (1961) *Intergroup Co-operation and Competition: The Robbers Cave Experiment.* Norman: University of Oklahoma.

Shields, J. (1954) Personality differences and neurotic traits in normal twin schoolchildren. *Eugenics Review, 45*: 213–46.

Shields, J. (1962) *Monozygotic Twins Brought Up Apart and Brought Up Together.* London: Oxford University Press.

Simpson, J.C. (2000) It's All in the Upbringing. *Johns Hopkins Magazine*, April. (http://www.jhu.edu/~jhumag/0400web/35.html)

Singer, P. (1993) The rights of ape. *BBC Wildlife Magazine, 11*(6): 28–32.

Sinha, D. (1997) Indigenizing psychology. In J.W. Berry, Y.H. Porting and J. Pandey (eds) *Handbook of Cross-Cultural Psychology*, vol. 1, 2nd edn. Boston, MA: Allyn & Bacon.

Sinnott, J.D. (1982) Correlates of sex roles of older adults. *Journal of Gerontology, 37*: 587–94.

Sizemore, C.C. and Pittillo, E.S. (1977) *I'm Eve.* Garden City, NY: Doubleday.

Skinner, B.F. (1938) *The Behaviour of Organisms.* New York: Appleton-Century-Crofts.

Skinner, B.F. (1987) Skinner on behaviourism. In R.L. Gregory (ed.) *The Oxford Companion to the Mind.* Oxford: Oxford University Press.

Skuse, D. (1984) Extreme deprivation in early childhood – II. Theoretical issues and a comparative review. *Journal of Child Psychology and Psychiatry, 25*(4): 543–72.

Small, E. (1995) Valuing the unseen emotional labour of nursing. *Nursing Times, 91*(26): 40–1.

Smith, J.A. (2003) Introduction. In J.A. Smith (ed.) *Qualitative Psychology: A Practical Guide to Research Methods.* London: Sage Publications.

Smith, J.A. and Osborn, M. (2003) Interpretative phenomenological analysis. In J.A. Smith (ed.) *Qualitative Psychology: A Practical Guide to Research Methods.* London: Sage Publications.

Smith, J.R., Brooks-Gunn, J. and Klebanov, P.K. (1997) Consequences of living in poverty for young children's cognitive and verbal ability and early school achievement. In G.J. Duncan and J. Brooks-Gunn (eds) *Consequences of Growing Up Poor.* New York: Russell Sage Foundation.

Smith, M.L. and Glass, G.V. (1977) Meta-analysis of psychotherapeutic outcome studies. *American Psychologist, 32*: 752–60.

Smith, M.L., Glass, G.V. and Miller, R.L. (1980) *The Benefits of Psychotherapy*. Baltimore, MD: Johns Hopkins University Press.

Smith, P.B. and Bond, M.H. (1998) *Social Psychology Across Cultures*, 2nd edn. Hemel Hempstead: Prentice Hall Europe.

Smith, P.K. and Cowie, H. (1991) *Understanding Children's Development*, 2nd edn. Oxford: Blackwell Publishing.

Smith, P.K., Cowie, H. and Blades, M. (1998) *Understanding Children's Development*, 3rd edn. Oxford: Blackwell Publishing.

Smith, R.E., Sarason, I.G. and Sarason, B.R. (1986) *Psychology: The Frontiers of Behaviour*, 3rd edn. New York: Harper & Row.

Solso, R.J. and Johnson, H.H. (1989) *Introduction to Experimental Design in Psychology*, 4th edn. New York: Harper & Row.

Sonderegger, T.B. (1970) Intracranial stimulation and maternal behaviour. *American Psychological Association Convention Proceedings, 78th Meeting*: 245–6.

Spanos, N.P. (1982) A social psychological approach to hypnotic behaviour. In G. Weary and H.L. Mirels (eds) *Integrations of Clinical and Social Psychology*. New York: Oxford University Press.

Spanos, N.P. (1991) A sociocognitive approach to hypnosis. In S.J. Lynn and J.W. Rhue (eds) *Theories of Hypnosis: Current Models and Perspectives*. New York: Guilford Press.

Spanos, N.P. (1994) Multiple identity enactments and multiple personality disorder: A sociocognitive perspective. *Journal of Abnormal Psychology, 94*: 362–76.

Spanos, N.P., Weekes, J.R., Menary, E. and Bertrand, L.D. (1986) Hypnotic interview and age regression procedures in the elicitation of multiple personality symptoms: A simulation study. *Psychiatry, 49*: 298–311.

Spence, J.T. (1983) Comment on Lubinski, Tellegen and Butcher's 'Masculinity, femininity and androgyny viewed and assessed as distinct concepts'. *Journal of Personality and Social Psychology, 44*: 440–6.

Spence, J.T., Helmreich, R.L. and Stapp, J. (1975) Ratings of self and peers on sex role attributes and their relation to self-esteem and concepts of masculinity and femininity. *Journal of Personality and Social Psychology, 32*: 29–39.

Spender, D. (1980) *Man-Made Language*. London: Routledge and Kegan Paul.

Sperry, R.W. (1974) Lateral specialization in the surgically separated hemispheres. In F.O. Schmitt and F.G. Worden (eds) *The Neurosciences Third Study Program*. Cambridge, MA: MIT Press.

Spies, G. (1965) Food versus intracranial self-stimulation reinforcement in food-deprived rats. *Journal of Comparative and Physiological Psychology, 60*: 153–7.

Spitzer, R.L. (1976) More on pseudoscience in science and the case for psychiatric diagnosis. *Archives of General Psychiatry, 33*: 459–70.

Spitzer, R.L., Endicott, J. and Robins, E. (1978) Research diagnostic criteria: Rationale and reliability. *Archives of General Psychiatry, 35*: 773–82.

Stephens, G.L. and Graham, G. (2007) Philosophical psychopathology and self-consciousness. In M. Velmans and S. Schneider (eds) *The Blackwell Companion to Consciousness*. Oxford: Blackwell Publishing.

Stephenson, G.M. (1996) Applied social psychology. In M. Hewstone, W. Stroebe, J.P. Codol and G.M. Stephenson (eds) *Introduction to Social Psychology*, 2nd edn. Oxford: Blackwell Publishing.

Stern, W. (1912) *Die Psychologische Methoden der Intelligenzprufung*. Leipzig: Barth.

Sternberg, R.J. and Grigorenko, E. (1997) Preface. In R.J. Sternberg and E. Grigorenko (eds) *Intelligence, Heredity and Environment*. New York: Cambridge University Press.

Stevens, R. (1998) Neuroscience. In P. Scott and C. Spencer (eds) *Psychology: A Contemporary Introduction*. Oxford: Blackwell Publishing.

Storms, M.D. (1973) Videotape and the attribution process: Reversing actors' and observers' points of view. *Journal of Personality and Social Psychology, 27*(2): 165–75.

Storr, A. (1966) The concept of cure. In C. Rycroft (ed.) *Psychoanalysis Observed*. London: Constable.

Storr, A. (1987) Why psychoanalysis is not a science. In C. Blakemore and S. Greenfield (eds) *Mindwaves*. Oxford: Blackwell Publishing.

Stroebe, W. (2000) *Social Psychology and Health*, 2nd edn. Buckingham: Open University Press.

Stroebe, W. and Jonas, K. (1996) Principles of attitude formation and strategies of change. In M. Hewstone, W. Stroebe and G.M. Stephenson (eds) *Introduction to Social Psychology*, 2nd edn. Oxford: Blackwell Publishing.

Strueber, D., Lueck, M. and Roth, G. (2006/2007) The violent brain. *Scientific American Mind, 17*(6): 20–9.

Strupp, H.H. (1996) The tripartite model and the Consumer Reports study. *American Psychologist, 51*(10): 1017–24.

Sumner, W.G. (1906) *Folkways*. Boston: Ginn.

Szasz, T. (1972) *The Myth of Mental Illness*. London: Paladin.

Swain, H. (2005) The changing of the guard. *The Times Higher Education Supplement*, 7 October: 23.

Tajfel, H. (1969) Social and cultural factors in perception. In G. Lindzey and E. Aronson (eds) *Handbook of Social Psychology*, vol. 3. Reading, MA: Addison-Wesley.

Tajfel, H. (ed.) (1978) *Differentiation between Social Groups: Studies in the Social Psychology of Intergroup Relations*. London: Academic Press.

Tajfel, H. and Turner, J.C. (1979) An integrative theory of intergroup conflict. In G.W. Austin and S. Worchel (eds) *The Social Psychology of Intergroup Relations*. Chicago, IL: Nelson-Hall.

Tajfel, H. and Turner, J.C. (1986) The social identity theory of intergroup behaviour. In S. Worchel and W.G. Austin (eds) *Psychology of Intergroup Relations*, 2nd edn. Monterey, CA: Brooks/Cole.

Tajfel, H., Billig, M.G., Bundy, R.P. and Flament, C. (1971) Social categorization and intergroup behaviour. *European Journal of Social Psychology*, *1*: 149–78.

Taylor, A. (1986) Sex roles and ageing. In D.J. Hargreaves and A.M. Colley (eds) *The Psychology of Sex Roles*. London: Harper & Row.

Taylor, J. (2007) Has dignity gone out of care? *Nursing Times*, *103*(4): 18–20.

Taylor, M.C. and Hall, J.A. (1982) Psychological androgyny: Theories, methods and conclusions. *Psychological Bulletin*, *92*: 347–66.

Terman, L. (1925) *Mental and Physical Traits of a Thousand Gifted Children, Vol. 1. Genetic Studies of Genius*. Stanford, CA: Stanford University Press.

Terrace, H.S. (1979a) *Nim*. New York: Knopf.

Terrace, H.S. (1979b) How Nim Chimpsky changed my mind. *Psychology Today*, November: 65–76.

Terrace, H.S. (1987) Thoughts without words. In C. Blakemore and S. Greenfield (eds) *Mindwaves*. Oxford: Blackwell Publishing.

Teyber, E. and McClure, E. (2000) Therapist variables. In C.R. Snyder and R.E. Ingram (eds) *Handbook of Psychological Change: Psychotherapy Processes and Practices for the 21st Century*. New York: John Wiley & Sons.

Thigpen, C.H. and Cleckley, H. (1957) *The Three Faces of Eve*. New York: McGraw-Hill.

Thigpen, C.H. and Cleckley, H. (1984) On the incidence of multiple personality disorder. *International Journal of Clinical and Experimental Hypnosis*, *32*: 63–6.

Tizard, B. (1977) *Adoption: A Second Chance*. London: Open Books.

Tizard, B. and Rees, J. (1974) A comparison of the effects of adoption, restoration to the natural mother and continued institutionalization on the cognitive development of four-year-old children. *Child Development*, *45*: 92–9.

Tizard, B. and Hodges, J. (1978) The effects of early institutional rearing on the development of eight-year-old children. *Journal of Child Psychology and Psychiatry*, *19*: 99–118.

Tizard, B. and Phoenix, A. (1993) *Black, White or Mixed Race?* London: Routledge.

Tizard, J. and Tizard, B. (1971) The social development of two-year-old children in residential nurseries. In H.R. Schaffer (ed.) *The Origins of Human Social Relations*. London: Academic Press.

Toates, F. (2001) *Biological Psychology: An Integrative Approach*. Harlow: Pearson Education Ltd.

Totman, R. (1976) Cognitive dissonance and the placebo response. *European Journal of Social Psychology*, *5*: 119–25.

Treffert, D.A. (2006) Savant syndrome: An extraordinary condition. Madison: Wisconsin Medical Society. (http://www.wisconsinmedicalsociety.org/savant/synopsis_article.cfm)

Treffert, D.A. and Wallace, G.L. (2004) Islands of genius. *Scientific American Mind*, *14*(1): 14–23.

Treisman, A.M. (1964) Verbal cues, language, and meaning in selective attention. *American Journal of Psychology*, *77*: 206–19.

Tulving, E. (1966) Subjective organization and the effects of repetition in multitrial free recall verbal learning. *Journal of Verbal Learning and Verbal Behaviour*, *5*: 193–7.

Tulving, E. (1972) Episodic and semantic memory. In E. Tulving and W. Donaldson (eds) *Organization of Memory*. London: Academic Press.

Tulving, E. and Madigan, S.A. (1970) Memory and verbal learning. *Annual Review of Psychology*, *21*: 437–84.

Turner, J.C. (1985) Social categorization and the self-concept: A social-cognitive theory of group behaviour. In E.J. Lawler (ed.) *Advances in Group Processes: Theory and Research*. Greenwich, CT: JAI Press.

Turner, J.C., Hogg, M.A., Oakes, P.J., Reicher, S.D. and Wetherell, M.S. (1987) *Rediscovering the Social Group: A Self-Categorization Theory*. Oxford: Blackwell Publishing.

Turpin, G. and Slade, P. (1998) Clinical and health psychology. In P. Scott and C. Spencer (eds) *Psychology: A Contemporary Introduction*. Oxford: Blackwell Publishing.

Tyerman, A. and Spencer, C. (1983) A critical test of the Sherifs' Robbers Cave experiment: Intergroup competition and cooperation between groups of well-acquainted individuals. *Small Group Behaviour, 14*(4): 515–31.

Tyrer, P., Lewis, P. and Lee, I. (1978) Effects of subliminal and supraliminal stress on symptoms of anxiety. *Journal of Nervous and Mental Disorders, 166*: 611–22.

Unger, R. (1979) *Female and Male*. London: Harper & Row.

Valentine, E.R. (1992) *Conceptual Issues in Psychology*, 2nd edn. London: Routledge.

Valins, S. (1966) Cognitive effects of false heart-rate feedback. *Journal of Personality and Social Psychology, 4*: 400–8.

Valins, S. and Nisbett, R.E. (1972) Attribution processes in the development and treatment of emotional disorders. In E.E. Jones, D.E. Kanouse, R.E. Kelley, R.E. Nisbet, S. Valins and B. Weiner (eds) *Attribution: Perceiving the Causes of Behaviour*. Morristown, NJ: General Learning Press.

Van Langenhove, L. (1995) The theoretical foundations of experimental psychology and its alternatives. In J.A. Smith, R. Harre and L. Van Langenhove (eds) *Rethinking Psychology*. London: Sage Publications.

Vivian, J. and Brown, R. (1995) Prejudice and intergroup conflict. In M. Argyle and A.M. Colman (eds) *Social Psychology*. London: Longman.

Vogel, G.W., Vogel, F., McAbee, R.S. and Thurmond, A. (1980) Improvement of depression by REM sleep deprivation. *Archives of General Psychiatry, 37*: 247–53.

Vygotsky, L.S. (1962) *Thought and Language*. Cambridge, MA: MIT Press. (Originally published in 1934.)

Wagstaff, G.F. (1981) *Hypnosis, Compliance and Belief*. Brighton: Harvester.

Wagstaff, G.F. (1987) Hypnosis. In H. Beloff and A.M. Colman (eds) *Psychology Survey*, 6. Leicester: British Psychological Society.

Wagstaff, G.F. (1991) Compliance, belief and semantics in hypnosis: A non-state sociocognitive perspective. In S.J. Lynn and J.W. Rhue (eds) *Theories of Hypnosis: Current Models and Perspectives*. New York: Guilford Press.

Wagstaff, G.F. (1995) Hypnosis. In A.M. Colman (ed.) *Controversies in Psychology*. London: Longman.

Wagstaff, G.F. (2002) Eyewitness testimony. *Psychology Review, 8*(4): 28–31.

Wahlsten, D. and Gottlieb, G. (1997) The invalid separation of effects of nature and nurture: Lessons from animal experimentation. In R.J. Sternberg and E. Grigorenko (eds) *Intelligence, Heredity, and Environment*. New York: Cambridge University Press.

Walker, S. (1984) *Learning Theory and Behaviour Modification*. London: Methuen.

Ward, I. (2001) *Phobia*. Cambridge: Icon Books.

Waterhouse, R. and Mayes, T. (2000) Unhealthy obsession. *Sunday Times*, 25 June: 16.

Watson, J.B. (1913) Psychology as the behaviourist views it. *Psychological Review, 20*: 158–77.

Watson, J.B. (1924) *Behaviourism*. New York: Norton.

Watson, J.B. (1931) *Behaviourism*, 2nd edn. London: Kegan Paul, Trench, Trubner & Co.

Watt, C. (2001) Paranormal cognition. In R. Roberts and D. Groome (eds) *Parapsychology: The Science of Unusual Experience*. London: Hodder Arnold.

Waugh, N.C. and Norman, D. (1965) Primary memory. *Psychological Review, 72*: 89–104.

Webb, W.B. and Bonnett, M.H. (1979) Sleep and dreams. In M.E. Meyer (ed.) *Foundations of Contemporary Psychology*. New York: Oxford University Press.

Weiner, B. (1979) A theory of motivation for some classroom experiences. *Journal of Educational Psychology, 71*: 3–25.

Weiner, B. (1985) An attribution theory of achievement motivation and emotion. *Psychological Review, 92*: 548–73.

Weiner, B. (1992) *Human Motivation*. Newbury Park, CA: Sage Publications.

Weiss, R.S. (1991) The attachment bond in childhood and adulthood. In C.M. Parkes, J. Stevenson-Hinde and P. Marris (eds) *Attachment Across the Life Cycle*. London: Routledge.

Weitzenhoffer, A.M. and Hilgard, E.R. (1962) *Stanford Hypnotic Susceptibility Scale, Form C*. Palo Alto, CA: Consulting Psychologists Press.

Werner, E.E. (1989) High-risk children in young adulthood: A longitudinal study from birth to 32 years. *American Journal of Orthopsychiatry, 59*: 72–81.

Westen, D. and Morrison, K. (2001) A multi-dimensional meta-analysis of treatments for depression, panic, and generalized anxiety disorder: An empirical examination of the status of empirically supported therapies. *Journal of Consulting and Clinical Psychology, 69*: 875–99.

Wetherell, M. (1997) Linguistic repertoires and literary criticism: New directions for a social psychology of gender. In M.M. Gergen and S.N. Davis (eds) *Toward a New Psychology of Gender: A Reader*. New York: Routledge.

Williams, B. (1999) Unpublished D. Clin. Psych. research thesis. South Thames (Salomons) University.

Williams, J.M.G. and Hargreaves, I.R. (1995) Neuroses: Depressive and anxiety disorders. In A.A. Lazarus and A.M. Colman (eds) *Abnormal Psychology*. London: Longman.

Wilson, A.N. (1978) *The Developmental Psychology of Black Children*. New York: United Brothers Communications System.

Wilson, J.E. and Barkham, M. (1994) A practitioner-scientist approach to psychotherapy process and outcome research. In P. Clarkson and M. Pokorny (eds) *The Handbook of Psychotherapy*. London: Routledge.

Wing, J.K., Cooper, J.E. and Sartorius, N. (1974) *Measurement and Classification of Psychiatric Symptoms*. Cambridge: Cambridge University Press.

Winner, E. (1998) Uncommon talents: Gifted children, prodigies and talents. *Scientific American Presents, 9*(4): 32–7.

Winson, J. (1997) The meaning of dreams. *Scientific American Mysteries of the Mind*, Special Issue, 7(1): 58–67. (Originally published in November 1990.)

Wittmann, W.W. and Matt, G.E. (1986) Meta-analysis as a method for integrating psychotherapeutic studies in German-speaking countries. *Psychologische Rundschau, 37*: 20–40.

Wohlwill, J.F. (1965) Texture of the stimulus field and age as variables in the perception of relative distance. *Journal of Experimental Child Psychology, 2*: 163–77.

Wolpe, J. (1958) *Psychotherapy by Reciprocal Inhibition*. Stanford, CA: Stanford University Press.

Wolpe, J. and Rachman, S. (1960) Psychoanalytic evidence: A critique based on Freud's case of Little Hans. *Journal of Nervous and Mental Diseases, 131*: 135–45.

Woodworth, R.S. (1918) *Dynamic Psychology*. New York: Columbia University Press.

World Health Organization (1973) *Report of the International Pilot Study of Schizophrenia*, vol. 1. Geneva: WHO.

World Health Organization (1992) *The ICD-10 Classification of Mental and Behavioural Disorders: Clinical Descriptions and Diagnostic Guidelines*. Geneva: WHO.

Zaitchik, D. (1990) When representations conflict with reality: The preschooler's problem with false belief and 'false' photographs. *Cognition, 7*: 333–62.

Zajonc, R.B. (1980) Feeling and thinking: Preferences need no inferences. *American Psychologist, 35*: 151–75.

Zanna, M.P. and Cooper, J. (1974) Dissonance and the pill: An attributional approach to studying the arousal properties of dissonance. *Journal of Personality and Social Psychology, 29*: 703–9.

Zeifman, D. and Hazan, C. (2000) A process model of adult attachment formation. In W. Ickes and S. Duck (eds) *The Social Psychology of Personal Relationships*. Chichester: John Wiley & Sons.

Zillmann, D. (1978) *Hostility and Aggression*. Hillsdale, NJ: Lawrence Erlbaum.

Zimbardo, P.G. (1973) On the ethics of intervention in human psychological research, with special reference to the 'Stanford prison experiment'. *Cognition, 2*(2): 243–55.

Zimbardo, P.G. (1975) Pathology of imprisonment. *American Psychologist*, October. Reprinted in D. Krebs (ed.) *Readings in Social Psychology: Contemporary Perspectives*. New York: Harper & Row.

Zimbardo, P.G. (1992) *Psychology and Life*, 13th edn. New York: HarperCollins.

Zimbardo, P.G. and Leippe, R. (1991) *The Psychology of Attitude Change and Social Influence*. New York: McGraw-Hill.

Zubin, J. and Spring, B. (1977) Vulnerability – A new view of schizophrenia. *Journal of Abnormal Psychology, 86*: 103–26.

Author Index

Abound, F. 440, 446
Abramson, L.Y. 161
Adorno, T.W. 125
Aguirre, G.K. 405
Ainsworth, M.D.S. 15, 164, 165, 166, 168, 169
Aitchison, J. 27, 28, 34–5
Alba, J.W. 66
Aldridge–Morris, R. 348
Allen, H. 419
Allport, G.W. 18, 135, 441
Altrocchi, J. 347, 349, 351
American Psychiatric Association 306
Amettler, L. 424–9
Antaki, C. 153, 158
Apter, A. 226, 347
Archer, J. 359, 360, 459
Arendt, H. 111
Arnold, M.B. 202
Aronfreed, J.M. 22
Aronson, E. 96, 107–8
Aserinsky, E. 183
Asperger, H. 70
Atkinson, R.C. 49
Axsom, D. 99

Baddeley, A. 24, 51, 52, 60, 66
Bailey, C.L. 369
Bales, R.F. 450
Bandura, A. 145, 261, 266–70, 271, 272, 273, 274, 275–6
Banks, C. 138–44, 145–7, 149–50
Banuazzi, A. 146
Barber, T.X. 209
Barkham, M. 337
Barnes, R.D. 120
Baron, R.A. 271, 273
Baron–Cohen, S. 13, 16, 71–7, 78–9, 80, 81
Barongan, C. 99, 162
Barry, H. 450
Bartholomew, K. 165, 170
Bartlett, F.C. 61
Bartsch, K. 78
Bassett, C. 16, 413–18, 419, 419–20, 421
Batson, C.D. 123
Baumrind, D. 110
Bean, P. 370
Beaumont, J.G. 179, 187, 222
Beck, A.T. 425
Bee, H. 172, 272, 283, 288, 294, 353
Belli, R.F. 67
Bem, D.J. 96–7

Bem, S.L. 11, 451–4, 455, 456–7, 457–8
Benham, G. 204, 212, 213
Bennett–Levy, J. 262
Bennett, M. 447
Bennett, P. 341
Bentall, R.P. 360
Bergin, A.E. 334, 336
Berkowitz, L. 120, 274, 275
Berry, J.W. 39, 45, 47
Best, D.L. 457
Bettelheim, B. 144, 145
Beutler, L.E. 334
Billig, M. 133
Binet, A. 388
Bitterman, M.E. 22
Blackman, D.E. 2
Blackmore, S. 229–32, 233, 234, 234–5, 237
Blair, J. 409
Blakemore, S.-J. 5, 236–7, 320–4
Blank, M. 278, 284
Blass, T. 111
Bogen, J.E. 215, 222
Bond, M.H. 110, 162
Bonnett, M.H. 188
Boring, E.G. 389, 393
Borrill, C.S. 418
Botwinick, J. 353
Bouchard, T.J. 5, 376–80, 382, 384, 385
Bower, G.H. 180, 205
Bowers, K.S. 204, 210
Bowlby, J. 165, 166, 171, 246–7, 297, 298, 360
Bowler, D.M. 72
Boyd, R. 386
Bradbury, T.N. 161
Bradley, B.P. 24
Bradley, J.M. 173
Brand, C. 399
Brennan 436
Brewer, M.B. 136
Brigham, C. 394, 395
British Psychological Society 351
Broadbent, D. 49, 50, 51
Brockes, E. 147
Bromley, D.B. 361
Brosnan, M.J. 225
Broverman, I.K. 456
Brown, H. 125, 138, 146
Brown, R. 28, 33, 126, 127, 128, 129, 134, 135, 136, 160, 450, 454, 459
Bryant, P. 4, 9, 78, 278–82
Buchsbaum, M. 403–5
Burks, B.S. 383
Burley, P.M. 110
Burr, V. 136

Subject Index

Page numbers in *italics* indicate figures and diagrams.

Subject Index

control
  autonomous   115
  emotional   407, 408
  of experiments   8–9
  in multiple personality   340, 341, 343–4, 345–6
  in prison simulation experiments   143, 148
  in total institutions   144–5
control conditions   6
controlled observation   15
coordinality assumption   57
copycat violence   275
corpus callosum   85, 322, 402, 404
  see also split-brain
correlation, in hypothesis testing   16
correlational studies   5, 13–14, 16
  brain dysfunction in murderers   404–6
costs and rewards, helping behaviour   120
crime
  juvenile   327
  murderer's study   403–10
criminal responsibility
  age in children   327
  and brain damage   410
  in multiple personality disorder   351
critical periods, in development   304
cross-cultural studies   38
  bereavement   359
  conservation tasks   285
  and dissonance   99
  mental disorder   372
  obedience to authority   110
  pictorial perception   39–47
  sampling   12
cultural difference
  and attribution   162
  and conservation tasks   285
  effect on experiments and results   11–12
  and helping behaviour   123
  and intelligence   400
  and NDEs   234
  and views of mental illness   370, 371, 372
  and violence   409–10
  see also collectivist cultures; Western culture
cultural psychology perspective   400
culture, definition   38
cumulative deficit   288

death
  and NDEs   232–3
  of spouse   353–61
debriefing, of volunteers   95, 119, 149
de-individuation   144–5
  see also control
demand characteristics   6, 109
dependent variables   3
  bystander intervention   114
  childhood experiences   299
  racial preference   442
  sanity/insanity experiment   364, 365

depression   161, 192
deprivation *see* maternal deprivation; privation;
  separation anxiety
depth perception   41, *41*, 44–5
depth of processing, memory   53, 56–7, 58, 59
desolation, in widowhood   361
diagnostic labelling, effects of   366–7, 369, 373
Diagnostic and Statistical Manual of Mental Disorders (DSM)
  363–4, 371–2
diary studies   253–60
differentiation, in sign language   32
diffusion of responsibility   117
direct reinforcement   272
directional hypotheses   16
discipline, in families   302
discontinuity theory of language   27–8
discrimination
  intergroup   125–36
  see also racial discrimination
disinhibited attachment   306–7
disinhibition   275
dismissive avoidant pattern   170, 171
dispositional attributions   139, 153, 155–7, 158, 160, 162
dispositional hypothesis   139, 140, 162
dissociation   347
dissociative identity disorder (multiple personality)
  340–52
distress-maintaining relationship pattern   161
dizygotic twins   377–9, *378*
dopamine   179, 181
dreaming   183–92, 225
drive   174
drive reduction theory   174, 178
drug use
  hypnotherapy for   213
  long-term effects   181
dual inheritance theory   386
dual memory theory   49, 50–2

early experiences *see* childhood experiences
eating disorders   423–30
Eating Disorders Inventory–2   425
eclectic psychotherapy   331–2, 334
ecological (external) validity   8, 334
egocentrism   78
Eichmann, Albert   111
elaboration coding   53
electrical self-stimulation of the brain   175–81
elevation, in pictorial perception   45
emotional connotation study   3, 18–26
emotional control, and prefrontal cortex   407, 408
emotional experience studies   3, 195–202
emotional intelligence (EI)   419
emotional labour   418–19
emotional well-being, and sex roles   457–8
emotions   194
  and conditioning   253–60, 261–2
  theories   200, 202
  understanding   323, 325

523